The Structure of a Moral Code

The Structure of a Moral Code

THE SON OF MANY BEADS: BIDAGA

The Structure of
a Moral Code

A PHILOSOPHICAL ANALYSIS OF ETHICAL DISCOURSE

APPLIED TO THE ETHICS OF THE NAVAHO INDIANS

JOHN LADD

Associate Professor of Philosophy
Brown University

HARVARD UNIVERSITY PRESS

Cambridge, Massachusetts

1957

Distributed in Great Britain by
GEOFFREY CUMBERLEGE
Oxford University Press, London

Library of Congress Catalog Card Number: 56–13287
Printed in the United States of America

Preface

It is inevitable that anyone who has reflected on the principles of rightness and wrongness will have wondered at some time whether those principles which he finds himself unable to doubt are just the products of his own cultural heritage or whether they are accepted by mankind at large. Philosophers have differed among themselves over the extent of similarity and dissimilarity of the moral thinking of people of entirely different societies; and they have differed just as much over the relevance of such facts for their own philosophical thinking. Nevertheless, these are questions which must have fascinated every one of us, regardless of the type of philosophy we are ready to profess. It was this general sort of curiosity which originally led me to wish to investigate for myself the ethics of a non-literate society.

I was fortunate to become associated with the Comparative Study of Values in Five Cultures Project of the Laboratory of Social Relations of Harvard University, whose funds come from the Rockefeller Foundation. Under the auspices of this project, I made a field trip to the American Southwest and studied the ethics of the Navaho Indians at first hand. The Project was most generous in paying the expenses of my trip, and providing me with much invaluable advice and assistance without which I, as a philosopher untrained in anthropology, would have been entirely lost.

The administration of Brown University was so kind as to allow me to absent myself from my classes to make the field trip. The Committee on Scholarly Publications of Brown University and the Department of Philosophy of Harvard University have generously provided financial assistance for the publication of this book.

I am deeply grateful to Professor Clyde Kluckhohn, without whose help this book could never have been written. He has continually given me encouragement, and has been most generous in the time he has spent in reading drafts of the manuscript and offering suggestions. I am also especially indebted to Professor Evon Z. Vogt, who was the first to initiate me into the mysteries of anthropological field work and whose advice was indispensable. Professor Vogt and Professor Ethel Albert have made many valuable comments on an early draft of this book.

Professor Henry D. Aiken has also kindly read the manuscript; and I have gained many an insight into the problems discussed here in conversation with him. Among others from whose suggestions and criticisms I have profited are the following:

Professor Richard Brandt, Professor A. E. Duncan-Jones, Professor Abraham Edel and his wife Dr. May Edel, Father Berard Haile, Professor William Lambert, Professor John M. Roberts, and my colleagues at Brown University, Professors Roderick M. Chisholm, C. J. Ducasse, John W. Lenz, Richard Taylor and Vincent Tomas. I should like to thank Mrs. William Rankin and Miss Rosalind Ekman for their help.

I am grateful to my wife, who has worked hard in preparing the manuscript, and to my aunt who patiently nourished me during the tedious months of authorship.

Above all I am indebted to my Navaho informants and particularly to Bidaga, whose ideas provided the basic materials of this study, and who has taught me much moral wisdom which I shall always value deeply.

J.L.

Contents

CONTENTS

CONTENTS

Foreword

Much of recent American philosophy has appeared to intellectuals in other fields as somewhat remote, alike from empirical data and from the central issues of contemporary thought. Philosophers have seemed to be writing almost exclusively for each other, preoccupied with fine points of the history of philosophy or with terminological quarrels among themselves. Behavioral scientists have been stimulated by the bold theories of Northrop, by the empirical research of Morris in the psychological-anthropological area, by an occasional book or article by such philosophers as Vivas and Geiger which has dealt with problems of central relevance to the social sciences. Natural scientists, humanists, and behavioral scientists have all sensed that the logicians and the "linguistic" philosophers were opening up questions pertinent to every branch of organized knowledge, but few have been able to struggle through the morass of technicalities. Bergson, Whitehead, and Dewey were perhaps the last philosophers to rouse widespread and generalized excitement. Philosophy, or at any rate American philosophy, seems to have moved off the center of the intellectual stage. Philosophy has largely abdicated its role as the general critic of abstractions and its function as the integrator of systematic information. Finally, in the perspective of the mid-twentieth century, Western philosophy — in spite of some valiant and significant efforts to consider thinkers of India and China — has appeared increasingly culture-bound.

This picture may not fairly represent the views of non-philosophers in the United States. Or, it may simply be that philosophy, like other disciplines, has necessarily become more and more specialized, and hence it will take a generation or more for the technical philosophy that is currently being produced to reach other fields in an effective manner. In any case, however, one "outsider" finds immensely refreshing and inspiriting a small counter-trend that has developed in recent years. The first feature of this "new" trend is the disposition to return — but without loss of philosophical rigor — to problems that are broadly human as opposed to those that engage the philosophical craft in a somewhat narrow sense. The second feature — and one especially welcome to the anthropologist — is the eagerness to treat seriously and with sophistication the discourse, the artistic productions, the ideas, and thought-processes of non-Western and non-literate peoples. Within the past decade, Vivas, MacBeath, Morris, Edel, Brandt, Albert, and others have made distinguished contributions to this end.

Professor Ladd's book is a particularly notable manifestation of this "trend." Like Morris and Brandt, he did not stop with careful study of the literature. He went into the field. I can testify from personal observation that he flouted the stereotype of the philosopher as a withdrawn, bookish person whose human warmth is exhibited only to his family and to a few close friends who probably also delight in high abstractions. John Ladd won — more rapidly than the modal anthropologist — the respect, confidence, and affection of his Navaho informants. And the significance of his field work by no means rests solely on the fact that he thus gained a first-hand acquaintance with the phenomena. He has added to ethnographical as well as to philosophical knowledge. Moreover, his professional training as a philosopher enabled him to elicit from the Navaho satisfying answers to queries that had puzzled anthropologists for many years. Indeed, his friend Bidaga read me a long lecture which culminated with the sentence: "I have been trying to explain these things to you for thirty years, but you never asked me the right questions."

Professor Ladd has clarified many points and systematized fragmentary facts that were well-known. With his characterizations of Navaho ethics as "materialistic prudentialism" and as "atomic egoism," the available data fit very nicely. There are other less central issues on which I confess myself less fully convinced. However, Dr. Ladd repeatedly makes explicit the tentativeness of many of his reconstructions and interpretations. As he indicates, much more empirical work remains to be done. His method, which is scientific in intent and in execution within the limits imposed by the incompleteness of information owing to time and the hazards of working through an interpreter, should be suggestive to behavioral scientists as well as to philosophers. It strikes an anthropologist as a more refined and systematic version of the approach which Ruth Benedict used, though, to my knowledge, she never troubled to specify her method in print. In fact, however, she also worked with reconstructions which were then tested against new data.

On the more strictly philosophical aspects of this book, I am not properly qualified to comment. But, even where I was not entirely persuaded, I found the argument of unusual clarity and elegance. And, whether the philosophers agree in detail or not, it is illuminating to an anthropologist to have Navaho ethics described as "Hobbesian," "modified by an Epicurean psychology and a Spinozistic sociology." Such comparisons are difficult and are almost inevitably arguable. Yet, in my opinion, they must be attempted. For both a universal anthropology and a universal philosophy require not only a depiction of the differences between peoples in their primitive categories and existential and evaluative premises, but equally of the similarities: those that are the products of historical contact or of adaptation to likenesses in environmental pressure; those that may be shown to be derived from "raw human nature" and from the samenesses in the human situation the world over.

In method, in analysis, and in content, Professor Ladd has taken some firm steps into a territory which philosophy and anthropology have perenially gazed upon, but which remains unmastered. The project for A Comparative Study of Values in Five Cultures of the Laboratory of Social Relations of Harvard University is proud to have had a part in Dr. Ladd's exciting explorations.

CLYDE KLUCKHOHN

Harvard University
September 15, 1956

The Structure of a Moral Code

The Structure of a Moral Code

Introduction

The object of *The Structure of a Moral Code* is to explore the problems involved in describing the ethics of societies other than our own. I shall call the investigation of the moral code and accompanying ethical conceptions of a person or group *descriptive ethics*. The kind of description sought would be a part of the more general description of the culture to which the people in question belong, and so descriptive ethics is a branch of cultural anthropology. Accordingly, it is a social science and should aim at conforming as closely as possible to the canons of the empirical sciences. In this book I shall develop a general theory of descriptive ethics, which will show how to formulate rigorously testable hypotheses about a people's ethics, and in this sense I hope to demonstrate that a scientific descriptive ethics is possible. In order to illustrate how this general theory can be used in actual anthropological research, I shall offer a detailed application of it to the ethics of the Navaho Indians.

At the outset, it is important to note the differences between descriptive ethics and what philosophers have called "normative ethics." These two disciplines are distinguished from each other in two respects, namely, in the kind of questions which they ask and in the subject matter with which they are concerned. Normative ethics asks such questions as: What ought I to do? What kinds of action are right or wrong? What is the good life? The answers to these questions are intended to provide guidance for conduct and for the evaluation of it. The act of accepting them ipso facto involves a commitment to living in accordance with them, and to counseling others to do so as well. In this sense, normative ethics has traditionally been understood by philosophers to be practical. Descriptive ethics, on the other hand, asks for a description of someone's answers to these questions. Thus, although its findings may be relevant to practice, its goal is theoretical in that it is possible to accept these findings without committing oneself to any kind of action. It follows that the subject matter of these two disciplines is entirely different; descriptive ethics is about someone's opinions while normative ethics is about conduct itself. Accordingly, the former might be said to be at a second-level or twice-removed from the actual actions of men. Indeed, the normative ethical activities of any person might well constitute the subject matter for an inquiry in descriptive ethics.

I do not wish to deny that there is any relation between descriptive and normative ethics. Obviously, the procedures and findings of the one may have relevance for those of the other; although the other parts of anthropology and the social sciences are probably more important than descriptive ethics for normative ethics. What I wish to deny is that the answers to the questions of descriptive ethics are also answers to those of normative ethics, and conversely. To assume that they are is either to commit a logical fallacy or to introduce a questionable premise. Thus, for instance, a fact about the ethical opinions of a people has no consequences with respect to the rightness or wrongness of their conduct, unless an additional premise in normative ethics is granted, namely, that the moral quality of actions is determined by people's opinions about it. This doubtful premise could be established only by arguments within normative ethics, and so cannot be derived from descriptive ethics alone. Conversely, the inferring of facts about people's opinions from the rightness or wrongness of their actions is also obviously a fallacy; unless, again, it is assumed that if an action is right people will think it is right. This, in turn, is an assumption which belongs to descriptive ethics and would in principle be capable of empirical confirmation or disconfirmation. In sum, the failure to distinguish between these two fields of inquiry has wrought confusion in both; and the result has been much inconsequential reasoning about what is right and wrong as well as about people's opinions about what is right and wrong. Unfortunately, it is an error which has not infrequently been committed by philosophers and anthropologists alike — a fact which readily becomes apparent if their arguments are subjected to rigorous logical analysis.

Although we cannot deduce our own ethical theories from the fact of agreement or disagreement with the majority of man's cultures, the study of descriptive ethics may make some contribution to the advancement of normative ethics. Philosophers usually suppose that non-literate peoples have little to offer in the way of insight into moral problems. But this view is a survival of an already outdated anthropological view which held such people to be 'primitive' and to have an undeveloped 'primitive mentality.' From my own experience in talking to a Navaho moralist, I am convinced that his ideas are as rationally coherent and systematic as any of those to be found in the moral codes of our own culture, although before I visited the Southwest I had no preconceptions one way or the other. The evidence seems to confirm the Greek conception of man as a rational animal — whether he can write or not, and whether he believes in witches or angels.

The study of other moral codes may suggest various new ways of approaching and solving moral problems, and call our attention to some modes of ethical reasoning which have not been 'dreamed of in our philosophy.' It may also help us to become aware of our own presuppositions about ethics, and thus make us more critical of our own approach to ethical problems. Finally, although information about the ethical ideas of other cultures cannot be used to prove or disprove the universal validity of our own principles, it may entail certain consequences with respect to their universal applicability, and as such may indirectly affect the tenability of a proposed ethical theory.

Many contemporary philosophers have been concerned not so much with normative ethics as with what may be called "theoretical" or "analytical" ethics, that is, a kind of second level analysis of moral judgments and ethical discourse. However, they have limited their discussion to those moral judgments which are accepted in our society and to which they themselves are committed. Perhaps an acquaintance with moral codes outside the Greek and Judaic-Christian tradition will help them to gain some perspective on their own theories and thus have a broadening effect on these analytical inquiries.

In sum, descriptive ethics should be carefully distinguished from philosophical ethics, whether it be normative or theoretical ethics, since its subject matter is cross-cultural, its aim is descriptive and its method is scientific.

Descriptive ethics must also be distinguished from other types of anthropological inquiry. Its subject matter does not include the more general range of cultural and social phenomena to which anthropologists have generally devoted their attention, but only the informant's ethical ideas as a system of ideas. The wider ramifications of ethics for social and personality systems are, of course, legitimate and important fields of inquiry; but there is more reason to hope for success in descriptive ethics if we approach the subject matter directly, and formulate its methods and findings in such a way that they are not logically dependent on these other inquiries.

Despite the fact that interest in the ethical opinions of other peoples goes back at least as far as Herodotus, there seems to have been little effort made to render the descriptions of these opinions scientific. A generation ago some writers concerned themselves with what was then called "comparative ethics," another name for descriptive ethics. However, the perfunctory character of their methods and data, as well as subsequent developments in the social sciences and philosophy have rendered their theories almost completely obsolete. In recent years, anthropologists and philosophers have paid relatively little attention to descriptive ethics.

Most of the available accounts of the ethics of non-literate societies seem to me to lack the precision and subtlety that are required to make them scientifically reliable and philosophically interesting. These inadequacies are due in part to the absence of any detailed analysis of basic concepts. Terms like "moral judgment," "moral sentiment," "obligations," "sanctions," "moral standards," and "ethics" are used with great abandon and little explication. There is rarely any awareness of what type of evidence would be relevant to the proof or disproof of the theories offered, and often no clear-cut distinction has been made between the evidence for a people's ethics and the evidence for other cultural and social phenomena. Indeed, it is possible to find descriptions of a people's ethics where no evidence whatsoever is offered, and we are supposed to accept them on the basis of the investigator's intuitions.

The methods that have been employed hitherto in descriptive ethics have resulted in conclusions about moral codes that seem to me to be inadequate not only for the reasons just stated, but also because they are apt to distort the views of the informant to fit a preconceived theory. Anthropologists have been prone to ignore the arguments and accompanying beliefs which the informant would give to support his moral convictions, although it should be evident that in ignoring them one is omitting an essential part of the ethical system. Philosophers who have engaged in descriptive ethics have often used anthropological data merely to buttress up their own philosophical theories instead of letting these theories follow from the facts. (This is especially evident in the writings of Westermarck and Hobhouse.)

It seems obvious, therefore, that before we can undertake to give a scientific description of a moral code, we must first enter into an extended philosophical discussion of methodological issues. Accordingly, our first task will be to develop a method for descriptive ethics which will enable us to obtain a coherent systematic account of the ethical opinions in question from the point of view of the informant; and such that it will guard us against ascribing to him views which he does not hold. Furthermore, we must formulate our hypotheses so that they can be tested in terms of evidence which is accessible to other investigators; in other words, our theories must be testable and the evidence for them must be made available. These are the minimum requirements which must be fulfilled to make descriptive ethics scientific.

In solving these problems some suggestions may be taken from the discipline of philosophy. The type of analysis suitable for descriptive ethics may be compared to that offered by historians of philosophy when they undertake to systematically reconstruct and expound the views of some great philosopher of the past. Here hypotheses are constructed which in turn are carefully checked with the texts and other relevant data. Part III of this book could in this sense be considered to be a sort of philosophical commentary on the statements of Navaho informants. The classifications and distinctions employed by teachers of philosophy in presenting the various types of ethical theory to their students may also be useful in developing the kinds of questions to be asked.

In addition to these techniques, the so-called "new approach" in philosophy has made possible an even more exact formulation of theories in descriptive ethics. This new approach has concentrated on the study of language and discourse as a means to understanding thought. Recent analyses of ethical ideas in terms of the meaning and use of moral judgments, as well as of the nature of ethical reasoning, provide us with a powerful tool for analyzing the ethical ideas of non-literate peoples. Much of the present study is based on these recent developments in philosophy.*

The new approach in moral philosophy with its emphasis on language and discourse coincides significantly with current trends in anthropology, such as the increasing stress put on obtaining an exact record of the informant's statements. A similar trend is exemplified in the development of descriptive linguistics. Therefore it is natural to attempt to combine contemporary philosophical and anthropological methods in descriptive ethics. In this spirit, I shall treat moral codes and the ethical ideas as-sociated with them entirely in terms of an analysis of discourse, that is, the explicit statements of the informant.

The book is divided into three parts.

Part I is devoted to a general analysis of the aims and methods of descriptive ethics. Here we shall be concerned with such questions as: What are we investigating when we are investigating a person's ethical ideas? What would constitute a scientific description of them? What is the best procedure for establishing such a description? What are the distinctive characteristics of ethical ideas which differentiate them from other ideas?

In order to answer these questions, it is necessary to examine the various theories offered by anthropologists and philosophers, as well as the implicit assumptions upon which actual research has been carried out. I shall give an explication of "ethics" in terms of ethical discourse, and shall propose the method of hypothetical reconstruction as a method for formulating and test-ing hypotheses.

In Part II, I shall examine the structure of ethical discourse; this includes those features of a collection of ethical statements in virtue of which they may be said to constitute a system. The questions to be answered are: What is an ethical system? What are the different elements of ethical discourse which differentiate one type of ethical system from another?

I assume that an ethical system is a logical system in the broad sense. Consequently, in order to answer our questions, we must examine the formal aspects of an informant's arguments, including the logical interrelations between ethical statements and the pragmatic conditions of ethical argu-mentation.

* For those unfamiliar with these developments, I recommend Aiken, 1955, which contains a relatively untechnical but thoroughly sound discussion of the new approach. Other accounts of recent developments may be found in Rice, 1955 and Frankena, 1951. See also Nowell-Smith, 1954.

Although this part is quite technical, I hope that it will be obvious that an analysis of this sort is necessary if we wish to formulate hypotheses in descriptive ethics in terms that are precise and unambiguous, so that we can dispense with vague metaphorical expressions like "pattern." Throughout my philosophical discussion I have explained the technical terms I have used in more detail than would be necessary if I were writing only for philosophers.

Part III consists of an application of the general theory of descriptive ethics to the ethical discourse of the Navaho Indians. Its main purpose is to illustrate the use of the method of hypothetical reconstruction in cultural anthropology. (Most of the materials which I have used were obtained during my visit to the Navahos.) My hypothesis is that the Navaho moral code is a form of materialistic prudentialism. The code as I have reconstructed it is an ethical system which is philosophically interesting in itself; and I hope that philosophers will be able to gain a deeper understanding of ethics, as I have, by examining this coherent rationalistic system which differs so markedly from those familiar to us.

The whole book should be regarded as a prolegomenon to the study of descriptive ethics. I do not pretend to offer any more than a survey of the relevant problems, and do not wish to claim to have conclusively established my theory. Actually such a theory could not be fully developed until further anthropological data are available and philosophical analysis of key concepts and logical structures has advanced beyond its present state. Particularly, I wish to emphasize that the part on Navaho ethics must be taken as a hypothesis illustrating the general theory, rather than as a definitive account.

PART I

THE AIMS AND METHODS

OF DESCRIPTIVE ETHICS

SOCRATES: Excellent. And do you accept my description of the process of thinking?

THEAETETUS: How do you describe it?

SOCRATES: As a discourse that the mind carries on with itself about any subject it is considering. You must take this explanation as coming from an ignoramus; but I have a notion that, when the mind is thinking, it is simply talking to itself, asking questions and answering them, and saying Yes or No. When it reaches a decision — which may come slowly or in a sudden rush — when doubt is over and the two voices affirm the same thing, then we call that its 'judgment.' So I should describe thinking as discourse, and judgment as a statement pronounced, not aloud to someone else, but silently to oneself.

— Plato, *Theaetetus*, 190

Taken objectively, morality is in itself practical, being the totality of unconditionally mandatory laws according to which we ought to act.

— Kant, *Perpetual Peace*, Appendix I

I

Ideology and Discourse

I. THE IDEOLOGICAL CHARACTER OF A MORAL CODE

A moral code is a collection of moral rules and principles relating to what ought or ought not to be done — what is right or wrong. An ethics includes both the moral code and all the ethical conceptions and argumentation which are associated with it. It is with these meanings that the terms "moral code" and "ethics" are ordinarily used, and they correspond not only to the primary senses of the words listed in the dictionary but to traditional philosophical usage as well. It follows from the very meaning of the terms that both the moral code and the ethics of a particular person or group are part of their ideology.

The word "ethics," however, has been used by many writers on the ethics of non-literate societies to include also actual conduct. Admittedly there is a way in which the English word "ethics" is popularly employed as a synonym for "morals," in the sense in which "morals" refers to an agent's actual conduct rather than to the principles he espouses. For instance: we sometimes hear people speak of someone's "unethical" behavior. (It should be noted that this meaning of the word does not appear in the *Oxford English Dictionary*.) But even admitting the possibility of this use of "ethics," such use is clearly derivative, since in order to determine whether someone's behavior is unethical we not only have to know the facts about his behavior but must also have a body of ethical ideals by which to evaluate them. Thus, all uses of "ethics" presuppose the meaning in which it refers to a body of ideas or principles.

The ethics of a particular person or group is distinguishable from other systems of ideas, such as beliefs about natural events, in that it is primarily concerned with what *ought* to be done, rather than with what is done, has been done, or will be done. In this sense, it is a system of ideals or norms. It is obvious that people do not always do what they think they ought to do; therefore, moral ideal and practice cannot be expected always to coincide. It has frequently been pointed out that one of the striking differences between moral laws and scientific laws is that the former can be violated, while the latter cannot be, except in the Pickwickian sense in which a statistical law allows for the possibility of negative instances. Hence, the fact of violability, or the logical possibility of nonconforming behavior, is an essential element in the conception of a moral code. It is this fact that makes possible the use of such terms as "transgression," "crime," "sin," "doing wrong," "temptation," or "remorse."

It would hardly appear necessary to point out that some distinction must be made between moral theory and moral practice if we do not wish to abandon the ordinary meaning of the terms "moral code" and "ethics." Even a cursory reading of anthropological writings on non-literate moral codes, however, reveals some confusion on this point. It is necessary, therefore, to explore the methodological implications of this distinction and to point out the consequences of ignoring it.

Assuming that there is a distinction between moral theory and practice, and also a distinction between a moral ideal which has been accepted and one that has not, it follows that a particular moral ideal may be related to the action which it calls for in three logically possible ways. First, the accepted ideal may be fulfilled when actual behavior conforms to it. Second, the accepted ideal may be violated when actions are not in conformity with it. Third, a given action may neither fulfill nor violate any ideal accepted by the agent, because he has accepted no ideal referring to that particular kind of action. These three situations may be illustrated as follows: a Mormon may abstain from drinking coffee, and thus conform to his ideal; he may drink coffee and thereby violate it; and finally, a non-Mormon may drink or abstain without either fulfilling or violating any of his own moral principles.

Since a person's overt actions might belong to any one of these three categories, it follows that observation of actions alone would never be sufficient to establish the fact that someone had accepted a specific moral principle. Thus, we should not be warranted in assuming that a man who does not drink coffee has accepted the Mormon theory that it is wrong to do so; nor are we entitled to infer that because he does drink coffee, he does not accept the Mormon ideal. It is clear that neither the performance nor the nonperformance of an act can be taken to prove either the acceptance or nonacceptance of a corresponding moral ideal. For this we must have other evidence than behavior. Furthermore, the use of overt actions even as indirect evidence for such conclusions must be regarded with suspicion unless the acceptance of the principle has already been fairly well established from non-behavioral evidence.

Nevertheless, the extensive use of behavioral evidence in anthropological accounts of the ethics of non-literate societies indicates either that these methodological consequences of the ordinary meaning of "ethics" have been ignored, or else that such words as "ethics" and "moral code" are being used in some esoteric sense departing quite radically from ordinary usage.

For instance: under the topic "Moral Standards and Social Organization" one writer begins by giving an account of the actions of his subject, and concludes therefrom that the man in question recognizes the principle of reciprocity as a moral standard.[1] The reader is not informed, however, whether this conclusion is based on any evidence other than the writer's observation of his subject's behavior for no other evidence is mentioned. Consequently, we are left in doubt whether the actions reported properly belong in the first category discussed here or in one of the other categories. There is no indication that the subject himself had thought of the principle of reciprocity, much less that he had accepted it as a moral standard as opposed to a principle of expediency, a rule of etiquette, or a matter of what might be called "natural friendliness."

If the use of behavioral evidence is justified on the grounds that such terms as "ethics," "moral code" or "moral standards" are intended in a technical sense which is not identical with the one I have been assuming, it is necessary to inform the reader of the special meaning assigned to these expressions. The failure to do so not only will mislead him, but also often allows the author himself to shift back and forth between different meanings with the result that irrelevant facts are not carefully sifted from those which are relevant and the reasoning is likely to become circular.

Thus, in some accounts of non-literate ethics where behavioral evidence is adduced, I suspect that the writers may be employing their own ethical principles as the standard of reference, and that their reports are often descriptions of the degree to which the conduct of non-literate peoples conforms or does not conform to these principles. This reflects a use of the term "ethics" which is perfectly legitimate. But from this use it follows that there is just one ethical system for all of mankind, and that the actions of all individuals must be evaluated by these universal standards.[2] It is misleading, however, to claim that by using such a definition of "ethics," we can provide an account of a people's moral code. In actuality it is an account of their moral practice based on standards of which the people in question may not be aware.[3]

Still other writers have explicitly identified the ethics of a person with his overt conduct or some aspect of it. If this identification is regarded as a stipulative definition, there can be no objection to it on theoretical grounds. If such a stipulation is made, however, it must be expressly stated so that the usual connotations of the term "ethics" will not be assumed by the reader, and the investigator himself must scrupulously adhere to the stipulated meaning and avoid using "ethics" in the ordinary sense. If he fails to do so, his argument is bound to be based upon an equivocation. Nevertheless, we find examples of such illegitimate argumentation in anthropological literature. For example, one writer contends that in a certain non-literate society theory and practice do not diverge as greatly as they do in American society, and there are insinuations that Americans are more hypocritical than simpler folk. But, as soon as we note that the "ethics" of the non-literate society is defined at least partially in behavioral terms, the statement about the non-literate society becomes true by definition and has no scientific value. And, since the statement about Americans is based on the usual meaning of "ethics," the two sets of facts are not comparable because they employ different definitions of "ethics."

The use of stipulative definitions of "ethics" in terms of behavior or some aspect of it has certain methodological consequences of its own. By employing such definitions the investigator automatically deprives himself of the opportunity both to investigate the extent to which people conform to their standards and to inquire into the functional relationships between moral codes and social organization or social mechanisms, for any inference made about the efficacy or function of a moral standard would be circular, and true by definition. Thus, if a behavioral definition of "ethics" is adopted, it would follow that every ethics has objective consequences, to the extent to which the actions of individuals have such consequences. Hence, any investigation of the function of moral codes, in this sense, would be of no empirical value because "moral code" has been so defined as to exclude any parts of it which could be nonfunctional as a result of having no objectively observable consequences.

It should be noted that in maintaining that a moral code is part of an ideology, and that it is to be distinguished from actual observable behavior, I do not wish to deny that there is any relation between them, such as a mutual causal dependence of the one on the other. Not only is a moral code supposed to influence conduct, it obviously often does influence it; conversely, the elements and general character of a moral code are dependent on situational factors and social functions. But if these dependencies are made true by definition, as the denial of the distinction would entail, an empirical investigation of them would become impossible.[4]

In sum, there are two reasons for regarding a moral code (or an ethics) as part of an ideology, and, thus, as distinct from practice or observed behavior. First, this is an obvious consequence of the meaning of the term "moral code" as ordinarily understood; and if we depart from this usage we can no longer claim to be discussing a people's moral code in the usual sense. Second, by adopting a definition which will in some way enable us to distinguish between a people's moral code and their overt conduct or some aspect or pattern of their behavior, we will make a noncircular investigation of the causal dependencies between them logically possible. The rest of Part I will be devoted to the problem of formulating a definition which will fulfill these two requirements, and which will make a scientific description of a moral code feasible.

If we assume that a moral code is part of an ideology, a moral principle is comparable to such other ideological entities as beliefs. Immediately, this presents the problem of how it is possible to investigate the parts of a person's ideology scientifically. In this and the following chapter we shall consider this wider problem of investigating ideologies in general. The principal thesis for which I shall argue is that ideologies can be investigated only through the explicit discourse of an informant.

2. THE BEHAVIORISTIC APPROACH

In the preceding section, I have presented arguments against the use of conduct as evidence of the nature of a person's moral theory. The views which I rejected maintained that the relation between ideal and practice was a direct one, and they were not based on more general philosophical theories about the nature of beliefs and thoughts. In this section, I propose to examine the theory that all thinking, and consequently an entire ideology, must be defined in behavioristic terms. This theory does not postulate the simple identification of moral practice and theory mentioned previously, but does entail that a moral theory would have to be defined or at least investigated in terms of some actual or possible mode of behavior. If all the contentions of the preceding section were accepted, it would follow that such a definition of "ethics" would be an extremely indirect one, resting on an analysis of psychological dispositions rather than on actually observed behavior. I should be willing to grant that if the wider category of belief could be defined in this fashion, there would be no reason for denying that ethical opinions could also be so defined. I shall therefore examine this view as it relates to beliefs in general.

The appeal of a behavioristic approach to thinking in general originates in the supposition that if such an approach is rejected, the results of the investigation will not be scientifically valid, since in order to be scientific an investigation must use evidence which is public and accessible to any investigator. Furthermore, it is thought that by using behavioristic methods some sort of operational definition of the key terms used in formulating the hypotheses can be provided. These purposes are, in my opinion, admirable, and I shall show later how they can be realized. But I shall now try to show that the view that these objectives can be achieved only through the employment of behavioristic analyses is untenable.

There are some general philosophical problems which arise from the attempt to define beliefs or opinions behavioristically. Many philosophers have tried to formulate a behavioristic definition of "belief." One rather common definition is that belief is a certain kind of readiness to act. To illustrate this definition, consider the belief that Route 1 is the shortest road to Boston. This would be defined as the tendency of a person to take that route if he wanted to go to Boston. Such a definition would be unsatisfactory, however, for it would be necessary to add: provided that there is another belief, namely, that the route he was taking was Route 1. Otherwise, the first belief might result in his taking Route 3 under the misapprehension that it was Route 1. It appears that in whatever fashion the definition is formulated the term "belief" or some equivalent must be reintroduced among the defining terms in order to provide an adequate translation. Therefore, it would seem that the more promising way to discover whether a person thought that Route 1 was the shortest road to Boston would be to ask him and that solely to observe his behavior might be totally misleading.[5]

Whether or not it is possible to define "belief" in behavioral terms, no satisfactory definition has been offered to date. Until it is available, the most reliable means of knowing about the nature of a person's beliefs is his own statements expressing them. A fortiori we shall have to accept the position that ethical opinions, as a species of belief or at least as analogous to them, can most profitably be investigated by means of obtaining statements from the informant.

The evidence that someone has a certain belief must therefore necessarily include some statements of his. But although such evidence is necessary, it may not be sufficient, because it is obvious that if a person never acts in a way appropriate to his beliefs or his admitted moral principles, we should be inclined to doubt the veracity of his statements. Thus, in the example given before, if the person continued to affirm that Route 1 was the shortest route to Boston, but persistently took Route 3 whenever he wanted to get there most expeditiously, we should finally conclude that he had been lying about his belief (or about his desire). Similarly, a person who states that stealing is wrong, but who steals whenever the occasion arises would justifiably be regarded as a hypocrite.

I shall call the effectiveness of any belief or opinion in determining a person's conduct its *operational efficacy*. The conception of "operational efficacy" (particularly of a moral principle) will be found to be of great importance in determining the interrelations between ideological and various other psychological and social factors. The operational efficacy of a belief obviously varies with its strength or psychological certainty, but it is also dependent on extraneous determinants such as emotional states and the situation in which the person finds himself.

A certain minimum operational efficacy is required before we are justified in asserting that a person holds the belief in question. In matters involving moral judgments, as contrasted with nonethical beliefs, the required operational efficacy is somewhat different.

In summary, it is clear that our primary evidence for determining a person's ideas, whether they be ethical or nonethical, must be that person's statements. Such statements are a *sine qua non* and, as such, the obvious starting points for an investigation of his beliefs. This follows from the philosophical consideration that a belief cannot be defined in terms of readiness to act or some kind of operational efficacy. However, after we have ascertained from the statements of an informant what his beliefs most probably are, we can then proceed to check his statements against his actual behavior in order to determine his veracity, and their strength, that is, their operational efficacy.

3. INFERRED BELIEFS

Frequently, the explicit statements of an informant are not available to us, and we must infer his beliefs from the limited evidence that we do have. Accordingly, it might be contended that we are forced to base our account of a person's beliefs on other kinds of evidence than his explicit discourse.

An inferred belief is one which we, as investigators, attribute to a person on the basis of any indirect evidence. However, it is important to recognize that there are many different kinds of inferred beliefs, and I suspect that the failure to make distinctions among them has resulted in some confusion in the descriptions of ideologies. I shall briefly call attention to four distinct types.

The simplest type of inferred belief is that held by the informant who is able to state his belief, but for some reason or other is unwilling to do so; this may be called a *concealed belief*. This situation arose sometimes while I was doing field work because my informant was anxious not to talk about a subject (for instance, ghosts). It is clear that he could have talked about it, and would have if the circumstances had been more propitious. The kind of inference which we must employ in such situations is logically identical with other inferences we make about objects which are practically inaccessible to us because of the accident of circumstances. For example: a detective infers that Jones committed the murder from evidence about Jones's gun provided by a ballistic expert. If the detective had been at the scene of action, he could have observed the murder himself. Thus, both the murder and the concealed belief are facts that only the particular circumstances prevented the inquirer from observing firsthand. Although such inferences from indirect evidence may be logically valid, during my investigation of Navaho ethics I was generally rather cautious about making such inferences about concealed beliefs.

A second type of inferred belief is one that the informant himself cannot at the time formulate to himself. We frequently encounter this circumstance in an argument with a friend: for example, "You really believe that Smith is a liar, don't you?" — "Yes, I think you are right, but I never thought of it that way." Such beliefs may be called *unformulated beliefs,* but they are not necessarily beliefs that cannot be formulated if sufficient effort is made. The essential characteristic of such beliefs is that generally they can be elicited by an interrogator who suggests alternative formulations until the appropriate one is discovered. In such cases the informant would be the judge of the correctness of the statement embodying his belief.[6]

There is a latent danger in trying to elicit an unformulated belief from an informant, since we may be forcing him to view things in a way foreign to him. In my field work I attempted to avoid doing this. As a matter of fact, the conception of a "moral code" which I shall propose does not rely upon the elicitation of such unformulated beliefs. I shall contend that an informant's ethical thinking is always formulated explicitly in a language that is intelligible to others. This characteristic, as I shall explain later, follows from the claim to legitimacy which characterizes moral and ethical statements.

A third type of inferred belief is that held by an informant whose actual statements are logically dependent upon some set of presuppositions, although he may not explicitly recognize such presuppositions or even be willing to consciously acknowledge them. Such inferred beliefs I shall call *reconstructed beliefs.* Philosophers are all familiar with such reconstructions. The various attempts to formulate precisely the presuppositions of the scientific method which the scientist in his laboratory unconsciously assumes illustrate this type of reconstructed belief.

It should be noted that such reconstructions are made by the investigator, and are the investigator's hypotheses about the explicit statements of the informant. The latter may not be aware of them at all. Furthermore, the sole evidence which is allowed for such reconstructions consists of the informant's explicit statements. The method of reconstructing beliefs will be discussed in greater detail in the next chapter.

Finally, there is another kind of inferred belief which is sometimes referred to as an *imputed belief* or an *implicit belief.* An oversimple example may illustrate what I have in mind. If we have observed a dog walking over to the food dish we can sometimes say, "he believed that there was food there." Our basis for saying this is his overt behavior, including such reactions as his manifest disappointment at not finding food there. Similarly, we may ascribe many sorts of 'implicit thoughts,' including 'implicit values,' to human beings.

This notion of "implicit" beliefs and conceptions is extremely useful in systematizing and classifying anthropological data which include both statements and observed behavior. It has been used with great success in the Harvard Values Project.[7] Philosophers who may be doubtful of the ontological status of such implicit conceptions should at least recognize their usefulness in furthering anthropological inquiry.

Perhaps ultimately the type of inferred belief which I have called a "reconstructed belief" may be assimilated into this broader category of implicit belief. The essential difference between the two types is that the evidence for a reconstructed belief is confined to the informant's explicit statements, whereas the evidence for an implicit belief may be taken from other sources besides explicit verbal statements.

Descriptive ethics, according to my conception of it, is restricted to reconstructions of the type mentioned, and in the present study I have employed inferred beliefs only insofar as they can be reconstructed from explicit statements. The first two types of inferred belief, that is, concealed beliefs and unformulated beliefs, were avoided whenever possible in my field work for obvious reasons. And, following the principle of "divide and conquer," I have also not employed the notion of implicit beliefs.

4. THE MENTALISTIC APPROACH

Another method which has been frequently employed for discovering a person's beliefs may be called the *mentalistic* or *phenomenological method*. In essence, this method relies upon the informant's reports about his beliefs, and thus ultimately rests on the subject's introspection. When the reports of the informant are not available, this method utilizes an indirect kind of evidence achieved through the sympathetic insight (*Einfühlung, Verstehen*) of the investigator himself.

The mentalist assumes a dichotomy between thought and discourse, from which it follows that the only direct way of knowing thoughts is by introspection. Furthermore, since introspective observation is private and not publicly accessible, the investigator must rely upon the subject's report of his self-observations and cannot directly verify any conclusions about these thoughts. Thus, he must distinguish between the ideas as thought by the informant and his report of them to the interrogator.

This method has great disadvantages. First, if one distinguishes between the thoughts and the verbal formulation of them, the thoughts themselves become elusive. Second, the inevitably subjective nature of the method makes the results less easy to check. For both reasons, therefore, this particular method of investigating thoughts is extremely unreliable. In addition, a mentalistic account is peculiarly unsatisfactory in anthropological studies of 'primitive' thought because many non-literate people are not used to describing their feelings in terms and categories which are familiar to us. The inadequacies of this method are well illustrated by the results obtained by earlier workers in the field of comparative ethics. For instance, Westermarck's conception of a "moral sentiment," which presumably can only be recognized introspectively, gives a certain doubtful character to his purported findings. Similarly, Hobhouse's use of the obscure expression "ethical consciousness," even if we overlook his outmoded view of the progressive development of mankind, makes his descriptions of ethical ideas quite unreliable.

In recent years, both social scientists and philosophers have shied away from the mentalistic approach and have turned to verbal utterances and the use of language as direct evidence of thought, and hence as providing a more reliable method of describing it. The main trend of contemporary analytical philosophy has been in the direction of studies of language. One of the most prominent schools of philosophy today is the so-called "ordinary language" group at Oxford, but philosophers of other persuasions have also changed to what Suzanne Langer calls a "new key." [8]

Although the claims of the ordinary-language philosophers are undoubtedly exaggerated, there is no doubt that they have discovered one rather fruitful way of describing ordinary thought processes. Hence, for our purposes there are many clues to be taken from their writings.

Despite the fact that there still are many mysterious aspects of the relation of thought and language, there are some points on which there should by now be a certain amount of agreement. In the first place, the processes of thinking and talking cannot always be considered separate and distinct activities. The older mentalistic view that a person's ideas were the cause of his making certain kinds of statements seems to be false. Talking intelligently is a kind of thinking aloud, and conversely certain kinds of thinking are a kind of talking to oneself. As one distinguished philosopher, H. H. Price, has written recently:

> It is true that symbols are used in two ways, for thinking on the one hand, for communicating on the other. But these two ways do not exclude each other. We may use symbols for thinking without at the same time using them for communication. But ordinarily *we think in the act of communicating;* and the very same symbols (words, gestures, diagrams, ritual actions, and in telepathy mental images) are used in both ways at the same time. We may think aloud without communicating, as has been shown. But ordinarily when we communicate by word of mouth we are also thinking aloud; and the same applies, *mutatis mutandis,* to other forms of communication. We may think publicly without communicating; but ordinarily, when we communicate we are also thinking publicly.[9]

In other words, talking (or communicating) is a kind of thinking. It follows that a person's statements, if we understand them correctly, are as reliable an indication of what he is thinking as his introspective accounts of it — perhaps more so. Therefore, we should rest assured that when we use a person's statements as evidence for his thoughts we have as good evidence as is available, and not a secondhand kind of evidence. This fact is incorporated into our ordinary use of language, for if we wish to find out whether or not a person believes something to be the case, we ask him directly whether it is the case. For example, if I wish to know whether Jones thinks that it is going to rain tomorrow, I would usually ask: "Is it going to rain?" rather than "Do you believe it is going to rain?" or "What are your beliefs about the prospects of rain?" The latter method of discovering Jones's beliefs would in all probability tend to upset the beliefs which he had already held by making him introspect.

The objection may be raised, however, that although a person's statements are his thinking, the converse — that thinking is talking to oneself — does not hold. One reason for maintaining this view is that there are thoughts which cannot be put into language and communicated. Price calls these "unformulated thoughts." If we assume that there are such thoughts, it would be impossible to reduce entirely all types of thinking to vocal or subvocal verbal activity. Not all thinking would be talking to oneself, and so, in principle, capable of being communicated to others.

If we grant that any formulated belief or thought can in principle be communicated and that the thinking of it is identical with the speaking of it, then the only question we need ask is whether the ethical ideas of an informant are formulated or unformulated thoughts. The question would amount to asking whether or not a person could think a certain action wrong without being able to say that it was wrong.

The theory of ethics which I wish to advance would deny that this was possible. Ethical ideas and thoughts are always in principle communicable because they are formulated in the language of the society concerned. In this sense, therefore, ethical ideas are of a very high order of thinking; they belong to the most sophisticated and explicit thoughts we can think. It seems to me that ethical thinking is always verbal thinking, whether aloud or to oneself.

If this contention is denied, and certainly it would be by some philosophers, I see no way of proving it. My view would be rejected by those who define ethical ideas in terms of emotional reactions such as guilt feelings and resentment, since such reactions are usually not susceptible of verbal description. Against such views it may be argued that the denial of the possibility of verbal formulation conflicts with the traditional assumption of most moral philosophers who have emphasized the 'reasonableness' of morality, which

entails that questions of right and wrong are capable of rational formulation
and perhaps solution. Moreover, if a moral philosopher maintains that in
the ultimate analysis ethical thoughts cannot be formulated and therefore
adequately communicated, he would have to admit that much, if not all,
public deliberation and discussion of moral questions will inevitably be futile,
since the disputants would be unable to explain what they mean. Therefore,
those moral philosophers who deny that ethical ideas are susceptible of
formulation and communication will have to take the consequences of denying the reasonableness and interpersonal character of moral disputation.

My conclusion is that ethical thinking may best be considered to be
ethical talking — whether to others or to oneself. The argument has tried to
show that making an ethical statement is commonly identical with thinking
an ethical thought (given the condition of veracity), and that ethical
thoughts are such that the thinking of them could always occur in the making of an ethical statement.

It should be noted that the approach suggested here differs from the
mentalistic method in that it treats the informant's statements as immediate
rather than indirect evidence of his thoughts. According to the mentalistic
method, the informant is required to report his thoughts, and it is assumed
that the thought exists independently of the statement. If the informant is to
follow this method he must himself introspect in order to discover his
thoughts. In contrast, it is proposed here that we consider the statements
themselves to be identical with the thinking of the thoughts, and consequently
we not only have direct evidence of what a person is thinking, but we also
avoid the pitfalls due to inaccurate reporting.

5. THE USE OF "STATEMENT" AND OTHER TERMS

Hitherto, I have been using such expressions as "statements" and "beliefs" in a way that may have raised some questions in the mind of the
reader. I shall now explain in more detail how I intend to use the following
words, "utterance," "sentence," "statement," "proposition," "prescription,"
"belief," "opinion," and "judgment."

To begin with, I should like to call attention to the difference between
an *utterance* and a *sentence*. Many words other than those normally con-
stituting a sentence can be uttered: for instance, "Hello!" More important,
however, is the distinction between the utterance of a sentence and the sentence itself. The essential difference is that between a single occurrence of
the sentence and the repeatable occurrence of the utterance-type. Thus, the
same sentence may be uttered many times and in different situations, but it
is still the same sentence although every utterance of it is different. If you
should say, "It's raining" twice, there would be two utterances but only one

sentence. The distinction which I have in mind here is a species of the token-type distinction first propounded by C. S. Peirce. In the present discussion an utterance would be a token and the sentence would be the type.[10]

The second distinction is that between a sentence and a *statement*. There are two differences to be noted here. First, various sentences may state the same thing. However, not only can we make the same statement using different words and word orders in the same language, but the same statement may be made in different languages. For instance, the two sentences, "Das Haus ist weiss" and "La maison est blanche," are different sentences which make the same statement. A characteristic of statements is that they can be translated into the indirect mode of speech. For example, a report of two persons uttering the sentences just mentioned could say: "They both stated *that* the house is white." Consequently, when I use the term "statement" I do not have to specify what words are employed to communicate it, nor do I even have to tell you what language it is in. This particular characteristic of statements in contrast to sentences is especially valuable in reporting my interviews with a Navaho informant, because, since I did not understand the Navaho language, I could not know what sentences were used by him, although I can know with some reliability what statements he made as a result of what my interpreter said.

A second important characteristic of statements which distinguishes them from sentences is that the word "to state" conveys an element of assertion. Ordinarily, if a person makes a statement, we can infer that he accepts it himself and wishes his hearer to accept it also. It conveys the speaker's endorsement, so to speak. Grammatically, this difference is often, although not always, expressed by putting the sentence employed in the indicative mood. Thus, when Jones says, "Smith is an American," we can assume that he is making a statement and that he believes that Smith is an American and wishes the hearer to do so as well.

Again, this second connotation of "statement" is useful for our purposes in descriptive ethics, because it is important to distinguish between the mere supposing or questioning of an ethical idea and the acceptance of it. We need some word to convey the fact that an informant does not merely utter an ethical sentence, but that he accepts it and wishes others to do so as well. I shall therefore use the term "ethical statement" in order to express both the fact that there was an act of stating at a particular time and place, and that this act expressed acceptance.

A statement thus consists of two elements, the act of stating (or asserting) and the content of the statement (or what is asserted). For example, when I say, "Jones stated that Smith is an American," the act is represented by "Jones stated" and the content by the words following "that." The content of a statement has often been called by philosophers a *proposition,* and accordingly it could be said: "Jones asserted the proposition that Smith is an American." Sometimes the assertion of a proposition is called a "judgment." However, I prefer the term "statement" because it suggests a social rather than a purely mental activity.

For reasons already given, I have departed from the usage of some contemporary writers on ethics by extending the use of the term "statement" to include moral and ethical statements. Many writers today scrupulously avoid using this term in connection with moral judgments for fear that they will bias the question whether such judgments are true or false. Accordingly, they use the term "ethical sentences" in preference to "ethical statements."

In order to accommodate possible objections to my use of "statement" in connection with "ethical statements," I shall assume that the content or 'object' of an ethical statement need not be a proposition, but may be a prescription or an evaluation. (There may be other types of content.) Thus, a moralist may make a moral statement to the effect that you ought to tell the truth, and this would be equivalent to his stating the prescription: "You ought to tell the truth" (or, simply, "Tell the truth!"). When we distinguish thus between at least two kinds of content of statements, that is, propositions and prescriptions, we do not have to commit ourselves on the question whether those statements stating prescriptions are either true or false. As I shall show later, whether or not prescriptions are propositions, we must at least recognize that they have certain peculiar characteristics of their own which differentiate them from many kinds of propositions.

If we accept this distinction between statement and content, and the difference between the kind of content which is a proposition and that which is a prescription, we may by derivation call the resulting two types of statement respectively *propositional statements* and *prescriptive statements*.[11]

I shall now turn briefly to a consideration of "belief" and related terms. I have already suggested some of the problems which must be considered when defining "belief." "Having a belief" and "making a statement" (even to oneself) may differ in that the belief lasts over a longer period of time and is there even though we are not thinking about it. This fact suggests that a belief is a disposition, a tendency or readiness to perform certain activities. One of the activities to which a belief disposes one is the making of statements, either to oneself or to others, which, I have already argued, is the same as thinking certain thoughts. In this sense, we can speak of a statement as reflecting a belief, or expressing a belief. It appears that a belief may be a disposition to do other things than make statements; perhaps a readiness to act. But inasmuch as the making of a statement conveys an endorsement or a stamp of approval and thereby makes the speaker responsible for it, I suspect that all the operational characteristics of beliefs can be reduced to characteristics of statements.

Again, in order to avoid having to identify the acceptance of a moral prescription with belief, I shall employ the word "conviction" to designate the corresponding disposition which is reflected in the making of a prescriptive or an evaluative statement.

To sum up the present discussion, I shall consider "statement" to be the generic term standing for the explicit acceptance of either a proposition or a prescription. A belief is a more or less stable disposition to make propositional statements, and an (ethical) conviction is the disposition to make and accept prescriptive or evaluative statements. (We shall see later that the acceptance of a prescription involves somewhat more than just the making of statements.)

Finally, the word *discourse* will be used to refer to a string of statements regardless of what type these statements may be. An argument is an example of discourse.

The term "judgment," and especially "moral judgment," will be avoided as much as possible for the sake of precision and clarity. Whenever it is employed I shall use it as a generic term standing for statements, beliefs and convictions.

6. OBJECTIONS

At this point, I shall consider several of the objections which have been raised against the selection of ethical statements and discourse as the subject matter of descriptive ethics. A frequent criticism of the approach proposed here is that it is too abstract and artificial since it wrests ethics from the normal context in which it functions in social action. In other words, it is thought that the analysis of ethics in terms of ethical discourse alone is unnecessarily superficial on the grounds that it excludes the more significant and deeper psychological and social significance ethics has for human life.

In answer, I should like to reiterate my earlier statement that descriptive ethics is concerned with the informant's theory of moral conduct, not with the operational efficacy of that theory nor even with what someone may say when he is involved in actual live disputes. In my view, the subject matter of descriptive ethics is much more limited than it is often conceived to be. By thus limiting the subject matter of descriptive ethics I hope to gain more precision and accuracy, but it will necessarily be at the cost of a certain richness of analysis that may be thought by some to be more desirable.

There are some more specific difficulties which arise when we employ discourse alone as the subject matter of descriptive ethics. These exist because there is the possibility that what the informant says may not always reflect his real convictions. There are several circumstances in which this can happen: when he is lying; when his views are improperly formulated;

and when the statements express only a transitory thought rather than a stable or permanent belief or conviction.

What if the informant should be lying? In ordinary life we have developed common-sense methods of determining the veracity of a statement. In the interview situation I have assumed that the informant generally had no motive to lie and that his statements represented his own thinking in this sense, and, except in some special circumstances, I see no reason to doubt his veracity. Since one's ethical opinions about general lines of conduct are relatively impersonal, it is unlikely that an informant would distort them, as he might if one were to pose questions about his private affairs. Furthermore, even if the informant should be lying about his own personal conduct, this does not mean that we cannot know from his statements what he thinks he ought to have done. Indeed, the picture he presents of himself may be more revealing than the actual truth about his conduct.

A more serious instance in which a person's statements do not reflect his actual opinions occurs when the informant confuses what he really believes with what he thinks he believes. I suggest that the disparity in such cases may arise from the fact that the beliefs are not clearly formulated in the informant's own mind. Clearly, there are degrees of accuracy and exactitude in the formulation of beliefs and opinions, and they vary from person to person, and from subject matter to subject matter for a single person. A more mature person who has had to give moral counsel to others and who has reflected on moral questions obviously will have more precisely formulated opinions on these matters. The ability to formulate and state ideas is what differentiates a thinker from a man of action — to use Radin's useful distinction.[12] It should be obvious, therefore, that we will encounter a more sophisticated explicit body of ethical opinions among the intellectual leaders of the community, and that others will more or less blindly accept their teachings. The relation of the ethics of the thinker to that of his society will be discussed later in connection with the Navahos.[13] In the meantime I should like to suggest that differences in degree of formulation of ethical opinions, if they are nothing but that, reflect merely a wealth or a paucity of ethical ideas, and do not prove that the proposed definition of descriptive ethics in terms of ethical discourse is inadequate.

A third difficulty which is encountered in considering the explicit utterances of the informant as representative of his ethical convictions comes from the fact that although he may say (or think) that he accepts a certain view, while being interviewed, in other situations he does not appear to do so. In other words, he may be just giving lip service to his moral thoughts. The extreme example of such a person is called a "Pharisee." (A Pharisee should be distinguished from a liar because he is not intentionally dishonest.) It might be contended that in order to determine whether a person really accepted the opinions he states, we should have to observe him in other contexts besides that of an interview; for instance, in his actual informal talk with others, and preferably in the context of action.[14] In accordance with the terminology proposed in the last section, we might have to distinguish between the uttered sentences of an informant and his statements, since the latter entail that the person making them accepts them. In other words, in order to determine whether a person really believes what he says the objector might contend that we must also observe whether he acts in accordance with his beliefs.

If this contention were correct, it would be necessary to employ its operational efficacy as a criterion of the acceptance of a statement or opinion. However, as was suggested earlier, while a minimum of operational efficacy is requisite before a mere thought can be considered a stable belief or conviction, a 100 per cent operational efficacy of moral judgments cannot be expected since every one of us at some time or other does or says something that he generally thinks is wrong. Hence, the insistence on handling ethical statements in their operational context may be as misleading as it may be helpful. It would seem that one can gain a better conception of an informant's theory when he states it in the "cool, calm hour of reflection" — the interview situation!

7. DESCRIPTIVE ETHICS AND DESCRIPTIVE LINGUISTICS

Descriptive linguistics has frequently been said to be one of the branches of social science that has been most successful in achieving scientifically reliable results. It may be helpful to point out some of the resemblances as well as differences between the proposed approach to descriptive ethics and the approach which has been so successful in descriptive linguistics. I do not intend to suggest thereby that descriptive ethics is any further along in development than descriptive linguistics was several centuries ago, but perhaps we can learn from it which paths to avoid.

It may first be pointed out that both descriptive ethics and descriptive linguistics are concerned with the overt culture of the informant. The 'patterns' they seek to establish are not general 'themes' or 'configurations,' but rather are related to specific 'culture content.'[15] Furthermore, they are both concerned primarily with verbal behavior and not with nonverbal behavior. Finally, as I shall argue later, both types of inquiry use special techniques and procedures of their own, rather than some of the approved methods used in other parts of anthropological research.[16] In addition to these general considerations, I should like to call attention to several other points of comparison.

We may perhaps sum up some of the principal characteristics of descriptive linguistics as follows.[17] First, it is concerned with describing how people actually talk, rather than with setting up norms or prescriptions for the way they ought to talk. In other words, it is a descriptive rather than a normative discipline. Descriptive ethics is analogous in this respect, since it is concerned with describing people's ethical opinions as they are reflected in ethical discourse, not with laying down norms or prescriptions either for that discourse or for conduct.

Second, "the linguist limits his field of inquiry by refusing to be concerned, except in a rather indirect way, with the content of the communication, that is, "what is being talked about." [18] In other words, the linguist is concerned with what I have earlier called utterances and sentences. Descriptive ethics obviously differs from linguistics on this point, for it is concerned with statements, which includes their content. It is conceivable, however, that if linguistics were to develop to include larger units of discourse than sentences (or syntax), it would come much closer to the type of analysis I recommend. An attempt in this direction has been made by Z. Harris in his articles on "Discourse Analysis." [19] If such discourse analysis could be conducted at a higher level so that it would not be limited by being dependent on a particular language, linguistics would come very close to the formal analysis offered in the present type of inquiry. The problem then would be that of differentiating between various types of discourse and the proper selection of those units of discourse which can be taken to reflect the informant's ethical views.[20] But, as yet, discourse analysis has not been able to dispense entirely with intuitive criteria concerning the content. Perhaps eventually descriptive ethics may become a part of descriptive linguistics.

Third, "the linguist limits his field by refusing to inquire into the mechanisms, psychological or otherwise, whereby human beings are able to use linguistic symbols." [21] Accordingly, the linguist considers his subject matter in isolation from its functional interdependence on motivation, situations, social functions, and so on. However, he does not deny that the relations of linguistics to psychology, sociology, and anthropology are legitimate topics for inquiry. Such studies of the relation of language to cultural systems or behavior patterns have been called "meta-linguistics" or "exo-linguistics." [22]

The reason for the impressive success of contemporary linguistics is that it has tried to keep to a minimum its dependence on the more general data investigated by the other social sciences. It is clear that this is a programmatic ideal which cannot be completely carried out in practice.

Similarly, I suggest that descriptive ethics may hope to be more successful than it has been hitherto, if it also tries to confine itself to actual ethical discourse as much as is possible. Again, this is only a program, and cannot be followed completely in the course of actual investigations. However, just as the development of descriptive linguistics has been at times retarded by rather vague and untestable psychological theories, which attempt to explain the origin of language in general and even the selection of particular sounds and words within a language on sociological or psychological grounds, so descriptive ethics may have been retarded by the temptation to do everything at once. More hope of success may come if we ignore the wider functional relations of the data of descriptive ethics, and concentrate on investigating the morphology of ethical discourse by itself.

If we do so, I see no reason why descriptive ethics cannot be treated as a more or less autonomous science, and some of the dead ends which it has hitherto pursued indicate that it may perhaps be more fruitful if it is considered as such — at least, for the time being. Thereupon, sufficient advance in descriptive ethics would warrant studies that might be called *exo-ethics* in analogy to exo-linguistics. Up to the present, it has seemed to me that most investigations of the ethical opinions of people, especially non-literate people, belong to exo-ethics, rather than to descriptive ethics proper.

It may not be amiss to call attention to some ramifications of descriptive ethics which would be analogous to the various branches of linguistics. For example, further inquiry should lead to the establishment of ethical typology as well as comparative and historical descriptive ethics. It seems scandalous that practically no work has been done in these fields.

One lesson that we can learn from descriptive linguistics is the importance of looking at things from the informant's point of view. The great impetus to the development of descriptive linguistics has been the use of the distinction between allophone and phoneme, the actual sounds uttered and the way in which they are discriminated by the hearer. Similarly, descriptive ethics should attempt to treat ethical terms and ideas as they are conceived by the informant. It is important to discover how the informant interprets a moral situation, and how he understands the various moral directives. The significance of this will become apparent when the various ways of classifying prescriptions is discussed in Chapter VII. It is quite clear, for instance, that the Navaho classifies types of actions differently from the ways we do.[23] Accordingly, we should beware of considering our own ethical categories to be as universal as the earlier linguists thought Western phonetic and grammatical categories to be. I hope that the method proposed for descriptive ethics will avoid this pitfall.

Before leaving this subject, I should like to point out that language studies may eventually throw as much light on the particular content and structure of a moral system as sociology. Already there have been significant articles on the relation of language and culture, and many of these suggestions can be applied to the ethical ideas of the culture.[24]

The Method of Hypothetical Reconstruction

In the last chapter, I repeatedly warned against formulating theories about ideologies, ethics in particular, which are not based on the evidence of the actual statements of the informant. It might be thought that the limitation of an inquiry such as descriptive ethics to the informant's ethical discourse would render the formulation of any theories about it impossible. Therefore, it is necessary to explain what kind of theories about ethical discourse can be formulated. This chapter will be devoted to expounding a method of hypothesis construction to be used in descriptive ethics. Since the methods proposed here may be applied to beliefs in an informant's ideology other than his ethical convictions, I shall discuss this topic before considering the differentiae of ethical discourse itself.

I. META-THEORIES

a. Levels of discourse

There are certain types of inquiry whose subject matter is discourse of one kind or another. These types of inquiry are discourse about discourse; that is, they may be said to be in discourse at a second level. Similarly, the statements made in such inquiries are also statements about statements, and so are second-level statements.

Philosophers of language have distinguished between these two levels of statements, calling that of the second level a *meta-statement* and that of the first level an *object-statement*. In like manner they have distinguished between meta-discourse and object-discourse, meta-languages and object-languages, meta-theories and object-theories.[1]

In discoursing about discourse confusions will arise if we are not careful to distinguish the discourse about which we are talking from the discourse in which we are talking. In order to differentiate between these two levels, philosophers speak of the *mention* as opposed to the *use* of a linguistic term. The second-level discourse mentions the linguistic entities of the object-language but uses those of the meta-language. To illustrate, suppose that we have a book in English on German grammar: in that case the book would have English for its meta-language and would *use* English, but it would mention German words and German would be the object-language. (For example, the German word "das Haus" refers to the object house and not to a linguistic entity.)

The device which is generally adopted to inform the reader whether the terms in question are being used or mentioned is to put all those which are being mentioned in double quotation marks.[2] Accordingly, our hypothetical grammar book should read: *"das Haus" is a neuter noun standing for house.* Some care must be taken when writing about languages to use the quotation marks correctly. Thus, the following statement would be false: *Paris is a five-letter word;* while the next one would be true: *"Paris" is a five-letter word.* This procedure will be followed in this book.

Since I have already proposed earlier that various mentalistic terms such as "thought," "conception," "judgment," may be regarded as discursive entities in disguise, I shall extend the use of quotation marks to such quasi-linguistic entities when they are being mentioned.

A rigorous use of quotation marks is absolutely imperative in an inquiry such as descriptive ethics, since it is most important to differentiate between those statements made by the informant and those made by the investigator about those of the informant. Our theory is a meta-theory, while that of the informant is an object-theory, for it is not about statements but about objects, such as right and wrong actions.

b. Kinds of meta-discourse

It should be obvious that there are many possible types of meta-discourse and meta-inquiry, for we can use different kinds of discourse to discourse about (that is, mention) many different kinds of discourse in turn. For our purposes we may ignore those varieties of meta-discourse arising from the multiplicity of natural languages known to mankind, and concentrate on those types of discourse which are differentiated by their objectives (purposes) and methods — scientific, ethical, or poetic discourse would be examples of types of discourse in this sense.

For instance, we can discourse poetically about science; then our meta-language would be poetic, and our object-language scientific. Conversely, we can speak scientifically about poetry; then our meta-language would be scientific, and our object-language would be poetic. Since there are many types of discourse, which are differentiated by their objectives and methods, there are even more types of meta-discourse, for by combination and permutation various types of meta-language can be constructed out of different kinds of discourse about different kinds of discourse.

In order to distinctively characterize the type of meta-discourse or inquiry in question, it is necessary to specify both the object-language and the meta-language, that is, the kind of discourse which is the subject matter of our inquiry, and the kind of inquiry we are making with regard to it. Thus, "descriptive ethics" may be defined as a *scientific meta-theoretical inquiry into the ethical discourse of a specified informant or group*. Its meta-language is therefore the language of science, while the object-language is the language of ethics.

Some further discussion of the various types of meta-theory may be appropriate here. The basic types may be classified according to the distinction between prescriptive discourse and descriptive discourse. These terms will be explained later, but we may understand that prescriptive discourse is aimed primarily at laying down prescriptions, norms, or rules of one sort or another, and that descriptive discourse is merely scientifically describing the objects referred to by it.[3]

Meta-discourse may be either prescriptive or descriptive. If it is prescriptive it sets norms or prescriptions for the language it is about, whereas if it is descriptive it describes it. This distinction may be illustrated by comparing two different kinds of grammar books. Many old-fashioned grammars tell us how we ought to talk; they prescribe correct usage. (An example is Fowler's *Modern English Usage*.) On the other hand, there are many descriptive grammars, which do not prescribe but merely describe how a certain language is actually spoken. It should be noted that we have meta-discourse in both cases since the subject matter is discourse itself. The difference, in effect, is that prescriptive meta-discourse dictates the character of its subject matter, whereas descriptive meta-discourse does not.

Another illustration of prescriptive meta-discourse is the discipline called "meta-logic" or "meta-mathematics." Logical statements such as "$(x)Px$" are in the object-language, whereas meta-logical statements are statements about logical statements. The rules of inference are often considered to be meta-logical prescriptions for transforming statements into other statements. In addition, meta-logic may lay down the general conditions under which certain statements are to be regarded as logically true. Quine, for instance, has effected an enormous simplification of symbolic logic by handling through meta-logic a large part of what was formerly treated under logic. Thus, meta-theorems are "principles describing general circumstances under which statements are theorems," (or logically true).[4]

On the other hand, philosophers have also presented meta-theories which are primarily descriptive. The chief example of such inquiry is what is generally called *meta-ethics,* which professes to be an empirical study of how ordinary people use ethical expressions. This type of study is not concerned with telling people how they ought to form and use their moral judgments, but limits itself rather to "an analytical or meta-ethical inquiry into the meaning or function of utterances."[5] In contrast to meta-ethics, which is descriptive, we might have a normative meta-theory about ethics which would prescribe the proper use of ethical terms and lay down rules for ethical discourse in general. I shall call this type of theory *reflective ethics*. A large part of Dewey's writings on ethics could be construed to be reflective ethics.

One of the contentions of those who are engaged in meta-ethics is that it is neutral with respect to its subject matter, normative ethics. Accordingly, meta-ethics purports to give a scientific description of moral utterances, rather than prescriptions for conduct or an assessment of the validity of those utterances. In Stevenson's words, it is a "metanormative inquiry being itself nonnormative." [6]

Those philosophers who have devoted themselves to meta-ethics, however, in my opinion, have not been clear about the methods which they employ, or about how they have selected their data. The presumption is that the appropriate method for meta-ethics is an empirical one, that is, that it would employ the scientific method. But in that case one should expect to find a more careful formulation and testing of hypotheses. Furthermore, if the results desired are to be anything more than trivial it would seem that meta-ethicists ought not to confine their investigation to 'ordinary English' or even Western culture, but should seek to test their theories with the comparative data available in anthropology. The study of descriptive ethics would be relevant here. Finally, the criterion by which meta-ethicists decide whether an utterance is ethical rather than nonethical is never made clear. It may be that meta-ethicists are concerned only with those judgments which they themselves accept or which they might accept. Perhaps the investigator cannot be neutral in his selection of the data (that is, of utterances to be examined). If this were the case, we can see why meta-ethicists do not include an examination of cross-cultural data.[7] Thus, meta-ethics may be construed either as an empirical study of ethical utterances in general, and so should include other languages than English, or else as a study concerned only with ethical utterances in English, and employing an intuitive criterion for labeling them "ethical."

"Meta-ethics" is thus a term which is in need of considerable clarification, for its proponents do not specify either what meta-language they are using, or how the subject matter is selected. And we have seen that every meta-theoretical inquiry must make these two points plain.

Because of the ambiguities inherent in the expression "meta-ethics," I have chosen to call the present study "descriptive ethics." "Descriptive ethics" is defined as an empirical scientific meta-inquiry. Since it is empirical and governed by the scientific method, it is ethically neutral with respect to its subject matter; in other words, it is non-normative. The object-language which is the subject matter of descriptive ethics is the ethical discourse of an informant or group of informants; hence for them it is normative. We may at present understand "ethical discourse" to mean any discourse containing moral prescriptions for conduct and the accompanying ethical conceptions. The specific differentiae of ethical discourse will be discussed in the following chapters.

2. HYPOTHESES IN DESCRIPTIVE ETHICS

a. Criteria of a good hypothesis

Having characterized descriptive ethics as a certain kind of meta-theoretical inquiry, we are now in a position to describe in greater detail what kind of theory is possible in descriptive ethics. I shall assume that it must be an empirical scientific theory, which means that it is capable of explaining the phenomena already observed and of predicting unobserved phenomena, and that it must have 'potential predictive force.' [8]

The essence of the experimental scientific method is the devising of hypotheses from which predictions can be made. These predictions are in turn used to confirm or disconfirm the hypothesis. If the predictions are not borne out by subsequent observations, then we have prima facie evidence that the hypothesis is untenable. On the other hand, if the predictions are verified we have some evidence that it is tenable.

Since descriptive ethics is meta-theoretical, it seeks to explain ethical statements and to predict future statements. Therefore, if we have an hypothesis that the informant Jones will make the statement that all X's are wrong, and he actually does make that statement, our hypothesis has been verified. If he asserts that A, which is an X, is not wrong, then our hypothesis has been disproved. More complications can be introduced into this example. If we find that Jones says that A, B, and C, which he also says are X's, are wrong, then our hypothesis has been confirmed to a certain degree. An analogous case can be made for its being disconfirmed if Jones states that A, B, or C, are not wrong.

Following this simple schema, we can formulate hypotheses of much greater complexity. We must be able to derive predictions from all of them about the informant's statements which can be compared to his actual statements. The results of this experimentation confirm or disconfirm the hypothesis.

As already mentioned, the ultimate test of an hypothesis consists in comparing the predictions derived from it with the actual phenomena as they occur. Of course, if in verifying an hypothesis one selects only a narrow range of the predictions which can be derived, the confirmation is weaker than if one had chosen a much greater variety of derived predictions. The more varied the tests, the greater is the probability of our hypothesis being true.

Hence, any scientist avoids repeating the same kind of tests but seeks instead to vary them as much as possible. The failure to do so has been called the "fallacy of selectivity." Furthermore, he is careful to look for disconfirming evidence, and avoids merely piling up evidence in favor of his hypothesis. This is the conception behind Mill's method of difference. In this spirit, Popper has contended that the basic maxim of the scientific method is to try as diligently as possible to *falsify* one's hypotheses, and according to his contention, science progresses through the continuous falsification of hypotheses.[9]

It follows from this maxim that hypotheses must be so formulated as to make them falsifiable in principle. This means that we must be able to derive from them consequences that *could* be refuted by actual observations. If it is impossible to derive such consequences, then the hypothesis in question would be unfalsifiable in principle. Many pseudo-hypotheses are so formulated that no evidence one way or the other could possibly falsify them; among these pseudo-hypotheses are those that are true by definition. The classic example is the statement that opium puts people to sleep because of its soporific qualities. No contrary evidence is logically possible here; hence the statement is unfalsifiable and not a genuine hypothesis. The indiscriminate use of *ad hoc* hypotheses also has the effect of making the original hypothesis unfalsifiable.

In descriptive ethics, if we wish to adhere to the scientific method, we must show how our hypotheses could be falsified as well as verified. By using predictions of the informant's statements, we have a readily available means of falsification as well as verification; for it is at least possible for our predictions to turn out to be false. In my interviews with Navaho informants I tried as often as possible to derive from my hypothesis predictions of statements which could be falsified either by the informant's explicit rejection of them or by his making other statements incompatible with them.

The criteria of a good hypothesis in descriptive ethics, as in all the sciences, must therefore include its testability and falsifiability. In this sense, the method I propose may be considered to be operational. An additional criterion is the fruitfulness of the hypothesis in generating consequences of many different sorts. In other words, not only should the hypothesis be so formulated as to account for those statements already available to us from our experience, but it should also enable us to make predictions covering a much wider range of ethical statements. Finally, a good hypothesis will have heuristic value; it will direct our attention to other areas than those which we had hitherto considered. Thus, for example, a certain hypothesis constructed to explain moral judgments about murder might lead us to consider an entirely different field of moral judgments which we had so far ignored, such as the ethical significance of belief in ghosts.

In summary, I have tried to show that by regarding the hypotheses of descriptive ethics as predictive of informant statements we are able to satisfy the requirements of a good scientific hypothesis: testability (falsifiability); fruitfulness; and heuristic value for directing inquiry.[10]

b. The method of reconstruction

The next question before us is how to formulate an hypothesis which will have the properties just mentioned.

The method of hypothesis construction which I propose is based on the supposition that the informant's statements fit into a systematic pattern of logical relationships. In the hypothesis it is assumed that the informant makes his statements *as if* he had thought them out reasonably. This does not, of course, imply that the informant is at all aware of the systematic elements in his discourse; on the contrary, hypothetical systems are the invention of the investigator to be used in predicting the informant's statements. Strictly speaking, the hypothetical system is in the meta-language of descriptive ethics, rather than in the object-language of the informant.

The formulation of an hypothesis therefore consists in a systematic reconstruction of the informant's discourse such that if he accepted this system he would make the statements already available as well as additional statements which we have not yet encountered. Of course, we assume in using this method of reconstruction that the informant's statements are coherent and systematic — even though he may not know this himself. The only way that they can be proven to be so is by showing the particular system from which his statements can be derived.

An ethical system, of course, includes not only statements of moral prescriptions (or moral judgments about what is right or wrong) but also all the arguments advanced in justification of them. Therefore, our reconstruction must pay special attention to the argumentation appearing in the informant's actual discourse. The method of hypothetical reconstruction will consist largely of a reconstruction of the arguments (or principles) of the ethical discourse in question.

Actual ethical discourse, like any other reasonable discourse, develops arguments in enthymemes, that is, by omitting certain premises and sometimes the conclusion. Thus, if someone says, "Your train is leaving in ten minutes," we can reconstruct an argument from the context as follows: "You ought to leave in time to catch your train. Ten minutes is just time to catch a train. Your train is leaving at. . . . Therefore, you ought to leave now!"

Anyone who understands the original statement can supply the missing premises and conclusion if he should want to.

Many parts of an argument are suppressed to save time and to avoid stating the obvious. Sometimes we have to fumble a little to discover the suppressed premise. Often this is easy. The conclusion is usually quite clearly known even when it is omitted. In ethical discourse the familiar query, "So what?" is usually easy to answer, for there is hardly ever any doubt about what the moralist thinks should be done.

Some premises, however, are so obscure that the speaker himself may be unable to state them. Such "hidden" premises are usually what is meant when we speak of a person's unconscious assumptions or presuppositions. If we assume that the argument is valid, then a modicum of logical training will enable one to supply a missing premise which will do the job, although it might be one which the speaker does not himself admit to be a presupposition.

In investigating the arguments presented in ordinary ethical discourse we must therefore discover the following missing parts: first, the conclusion which is fairly easy to discover if we are in a position to ask the informant directly; second, the various premises; and third, the mode of inference from the premises to the conclusion.

Thus, ethical reconstruction is a kind of jigsaw puzzle. Usually we have the conclusion and some premises. The task is to reconstruct the missing premises and mode of inference. But this is not an intellectual exercise which ends when we have found a system of statements whose implications are valid. In order to find out whether it represents the structure of the inform-ant's thinking we must go on to check our results. This can be done by deriving other conclusions and varying the premises. We can construct in this way many different sets of conclusions using different premises, and if we find these conclusions unacceptable by the speaker, our reconstruction has been incorrect. Therefore, *the ethical reconstruction can and must be empirically confirmed or disconfirmed, by the statements the informant makes.*

It may be thought that this procedure is artificial as well as intellectualis-tic in that it attributes to an informant more coherent thinking than is plausible. However, the method has worked out very successfully in predict-ing the ethical statements of Navaho informants. And, if it is successful in the one case, it may be so in others as well.

Perhaps the ordinary nonethical discourse of an informant will not be as consistent as his ethical discourse, because of the way I shall define his "ethical discourse." It might also be contended that the discourse of a moral-ist in a non-literate society, learned as it is by oral tradition over many generations, may acquire a certain consistency that cannot be expected in our own society. In addition, the peculiarly rationalistic character of Navaho ethical discourse, which will be discussed later, may possibly have rendered this technique peculiarly successful for this culture while it might not have been for other non-literate cultures.

If it should be proved that this method of reconstruction will work only for the ethical discourse of the Navahos, some other method will have to be devised. However, before doubting its universal applicability a priori, it should be tried with other cultures. Although it may not work for a Western society, such as American society, because we have many different moral codes which may be incompatible with each other, I strongly suspect that there are many cultures other than that of the Navahos to which this method can be applied.

The models which I have used in reconstructive hypotheses will be discussed in more detail in Section 4. Before turning to this subject, I should like to digress briefly to compare natural and artificial ethical systems with each other.

3. NATURAL AND ARTIFICIAL ETHICAL SYSTEMS

At this point, perhaps some justification is required for treating the ethical systems accepted by philosophically untrained moralists in non-literate as well as in literate societies at large as fundamentally similar to those propounded by philosophers with their special theoretical interests.

I shall use the term *natural ethics* to mean an ethical system which has been developed by peoples and cultures rather than by philosophers. It contains those moral and ethical statements which are actually accepted and for the most part actually adhered to by the man on the street. Such a code is often filled with inconsistencies of one sort or another and, of course, its presuppositions are not clearly formulated. These natural codes are the subject of anthropological investigation. Examples of natural moralities are those of non-literate societies, Christian morality, Hebraic morality, and possibly such codes as Stoicism or Epicureanism.

Artificial ethics is the invention of the philosopher. The moral philosopher is usually more interested in investigating abstract issues involving epistemology and psychology, than in giving concrete directives for conduct. On the whole, philosophical ethics tends to be consistent at the sacrifice of a certain richness which natural ethical systems possess.

Historically, the interrelations of artificial and natural ethics are complicated, especially in Western culture. The ideas of the philosophers have filtered down to the masses, and conversely the prejudices of the masses have penetrated the ivory tower of the philosopher.

In this connection, the attitudes of ethical philosophers fall into two general groups; some are revisionists, whereas others are conservatives. The revisionist always incurs the danger of being completely out of touch with the opinions of the masses, and consequently his ethics often falls flat. The conservative, on the other hand, does not question the correctness of popular moral judgments; his aim is to justify them and to analyze them in terms of epistemological, psychological, and linguistic conceptions. Most of the great moral philosophers of the eighteenth century were conservatives by explicit intent.[11]

The main concern of the conservative moral philosophers has been to understand popular morality. The first step in their inquiry, therefore, generally is to attempt a codification of popular morality by trying to reduce the multiplicity of moral principles to some sort of order, or else to indicate why such an order is impossible. Consequently, they investigate in some detail the various questions with which we shall be concerned.

The subject matter of conservative ethics is, of course, the ethical convictions of the philosopher's own society. The eighteenth-century moralists entirely ignored moralities which were different from their own. Actually, they tacitly and sometimes explicitly assumed that all reasonable men would agree to their own moral principles. Their provincialism, however, did not prevent them from making many valuable contributions which can be utilized in describing the moralities of other societies. In fact, the conservatives are the only moral philosophers who have made a detailed analysis of the type being undertaken here. Hence, their findings can be ignored by anthropologists and sociologists only at their own peril.

In addition to technical philosophical inquiries into morality, history provides us with many attempted codifications of moral principles. Most of these were revisionist, but their reforms were later accepted by the masses. The best examples of such codifications are the numerous ones made by priests and prophets among the ancient Hebrews. Thus the 613 ritualistic and ethical prescriptions were reduced to the two: loving God and loving your neighbor.

There is much to be learned from these sources about formulating hypothetical systems with which to reconstruct an informant's ethical discourse.

4. THEORETICAL MODELS

a. Artificial ethical systems as models

In reconstructing the ethical discourse of an informant, descriptive ethics is not interested in hypotheses explaining only particular arguments and segments of that discourse; its goal is to construct an hypothesis which will explain the discourse in its entirety and show its systematic character.

The formulation of a systematic reconstruction is possible only if we have some conception of what makes ethical discourse into a system instead of a heterogeneous conjunction of statements. Furthermore, we must have some ideas about what the various possible types of ethical systems are.

In arriving at such a concept, we may receive some help from an examination of the various artificial ethical systems developed by Western philosophers who have written on ethics, as well as from some of the great codified ethical systems, such as that of Judaism.

It seems natural to begin by asking ourselves whether the ethical discourse of an informant represents the system of utilitarianism, of egoistic hedonism, of self-realizationism, of a Kantian ethics, of a theological ethics, or of some other ethical system. Each of these systems will provide us with an hypothesis to be tested by the informant's statements.

The more the variety among possible hypothetical systems which we can apply to the data-statements the greater will be the probability of success in finding the best hypothesis; for it is only by falsifying a great many of them that we approach to the truth. Furthermore, even those hypothetical systems which do not appear to completely fit our data may help us to determine more precisely some of the component elements of the system.

By combining and permuting the various elements in the different models we have available, we can then proceed to construct new systems until we have reached a model which seems to serve our purpose more adequately than any other. A detailed analysis of the various elements which go to make up an ethical system will be presented in Part II.

b. Theoretical status of these models

The full-blown model ethical system which will enable us to predict the informant's ethical statements will include references to premises, rules of ethical reasoning, ethical conceptions and other factors which are themselves not part of the explicit ethical discourse being studied. We may therefore ask, what is the theoretical status of these reconstructed premises and other components of the system?

Since these terms occur only in the meta-language of descriptive ethics, and not in the informant's language, they must be considered as designating unobservable entities or constructs. I shall employ MacQuordale's and Meehl's useful distinction between hypothetical constructs and intervening variables to elucidate this conception. These authors use the term "hypothetical construct" to designate an unobserved entity whose existence is hypothesized to explain the phenomena which are observed. Intervening variables, in contrast, do not postulate the existence of an unobserved entity:

Such a variable will then be simply a quantity obtained by specified manipulation of the values of empirical variables; it will involve no hypothesis as to existence of nonobserved entities which are not definable either explicitly or by reduction sentences in terms of the empirical variables; and the validity of empirical laws involving only observables will constitute both the necessary and sufficient conditions for the validity of the laws involving these intervening variables.[12]

The terms which we shall employ in our hypothetical reconstructions must be considered intervening variables, as opposed to hypothetical constructs, if we understand the explicit statements of the informant to be 'observed entities' or 'empirical variables.' The use of terms like "premises" or "modes of reasoning" in these reconstructed systems does not presuppose the existence of any such entities in the informant's mind, and furthermore, they can be defined either explicitly or by reduction sentences in terms of explicit statements.

The reduction of a statement in the language of hypothetical reconstruction to that mentioning only the informant's statements can be illustrated by this example. If we reconstruct a certain set of ethical statements in such a way that we can say that the informant accepts a hedonistic utilitarian ethics, the reduction would be carried out in some such fashion as this:

By definition, $$Un = (a)(Rna \equiv Hna),$$

where n designates an informant, a designates an action, Un means "n accepts the premises of utilitarian ethics," Rna means "n states a to be right," and Hna means "n states that a will lead to the greatest happiness."

This formula can be put in words somewhat as follows: "To say that an informant accepts the principle of hedonistic utilitarianism is by definition equivalent to saying that if he calls an action right, then he believes that it will lead to the greatest happiness, and if he believes that an action will lead to the greatest happiness, then he calls it right." [13]

As the statements of the meta-inquiry become more complicated, the reduction also is more complex. But this simple paradigm shows how all the intervening variables involved in reconstruction can be entirely eliminated without changing the truth value of the analysis.

What useful purpose do such intervening variables serve in descriptive ethics? The answer is that they not only make the organization of materials easier, but they also direct our attention to certain aspects of the informant's discourse which we should not otherwise have noticed.

The fact that the system of reconstruction can in theory be eliminated by reduction to the observable statements in question shows that the hypotheses are thoroughly empirical and testable in the sense explained earlier. It should also warn us against supposing that somehow there lurks in the informant's mind an unconscious mind which does all his ethical thinking for him or that a tiny philosopher lies hidden inside to prompt him! No such hypothetical entities are necessary for the present theory.

5. THE METHOD OF VERSTEHEN

Because of the great importance that has been ascribed by philosophers and social scientists to the operation called *Verstehen* as a means of investigating such elements of a culture as its ethics, it may be appropriate to add a few comments on it here.

The conception of *Verstehen* originated among those philosophers who were interested in elucidating the distinction between the methods of the moral or human sciences (*Geisteswissenschaften*) and those of the natural sciences (*Naturwissenschaften*).[14] In essence, the purpose of the method of *Verstehen* is to look at human actions from the 'inside' rather than from the 'outside' (in R. G. Collingwood's terms). The outside view is characteristic of the natural sciences, which seek to explain and analyze phenomena through general laws. In contrast, the moral sciences, such as history, seek to understand human actions from the inside, as it were. The difference between these two methods has often been stated by means of the distinction between 'explaining' and 'understanding.'[15]

I have already stressed many times the importance of looking at the ethical ideas of an informant from the inside, that is from his point of view, rather than from the outside view of the observer. This would seem to imply that descriptive ethics must employ something like the method of *Verstehen*.

However, the notion of *Verstehen* is not sufficiently exact to help us. The German word cannot be translated simply by the English word "understanding," since the latter means something much more general. For our purposes, it may be rendered as sympathetic understanding or sympathetic insight.[16] This should be contrasted with another meaning of "understanding" which is conveyed by the German word "Begreifen," which means to grasp the meaning of something (for example, a statement).

The differences between these two senses of "understanding," *Verstehen* and *Begreifen,* is evident when we consider respectively the differences between understanding a person (or his actions and feelings), and understanding an idea, a theory, or a statement.[17]

It is clear that in descriptive ethics we must admit a special method over and above that of the natural sciences, namely, understanding in the sense of grasping the meaning of a statement (*Begreifen*), since the whole theory depends on an analysis of statements rather than of vocal utterances or other kinds of overt behavior. If we could not understand the informant's discourse, we could not investigate it.

In order to understand what an informant says with any degree of accuracy, one must be familiar with the language in which he is speaking. Because of the intimate relation of language and thought, it is probably impossible to understand the more subtle aspects of his ideas without a knowledge of his language. Those anthropologists who have studied the native language have a tremendous advantage in this respect over someone who has to rely upon an interpreter, for it gives them an understanding or grasp of the ideas which can not be achieved at second hand.

Nevertheless, understanding in the *Begreifen* sense should not be confused with *Verstehen*, which supposes a more intimate sympathetic or empathetic awareness of a person's feelings and motives which goes far beyond grasping his statements. Although understanding as it occurs in communication (*Begreifen*) is a mysterious process which has not been explained by either philosophers or social scientists, it does have a kind of public or interpersonal character which lends it a greater degree of objective validity than the more subjective process of *Verstehen*.

The proponents of the method of *Verstehen* are by no means agreed on how it is to be used. The more extreme view maintains that it can be used to verify judgments in the moral sciences, and therefore might be used in anthropology. Others who are more cautious say that it should be tempered by subjecting it to more objective tests of one sort or another.[18] But its use as any more than a problematical test of conclusions in descriptive ethics is dangerous, because it is likely that non-literate peoples differ more deeply from us in their ethical outlook than we are aware.

Nevertheless, sometimes the anthropologist has to employ this method in lieu of more concrete evidence for the simple reason that he has insufficient data at hand. But such use is foolhardy for anyone except a person who has a very intimate and profound acquaintance with the people whose views he is investigating. Needless to say, I do not put myself in that category.

It is obvious that the method of *Verstehen* can be used without any such qualms if it serves merely to provide hunches or guesses for new hypotheses and new approaches to the subject matter under investigation. Any device that will stimulate the investigator's imagination to explore new fields should be welcome.

With this last proviso we may conclude, therefore, that the method of *Verstehen,* as contrasted with that of understanding statements (*Begreifen*), may be dispensed with in descriptive ethics. Instead, we have seen that the meta-theoretical methods propounded earlier in this chapter provide us with a more reliable technique for testing and formulating its hypotheses than *Verstehen* can offer.

Scrutiny of Definitions of "Ethics," I

I. THE PROBLEM

Before it is possible to investigate the ethical discourse of an informant, it is obvious that we must decide upon some reasonably exact criterion of what is to be taken as ethical. In anthropological literature, discussions of the ethics of non-literate peoples are usually extremely vague, and anthropologists are sometimes confused about what they consider belongs under the category of ethics. It is probably no coincidence that many of the best books on non-literate cultures refrain from using the word at all, while those that do employ entirely different criteria according to the school to which they belong. The situation is no less discouraging in philosophical literature, for here we find little help in distinguishing at a pre-analytic level the data of ethics from that of other inquiries — although, of course, there is no dearth of theories offered to justify and explain these data.

In an anthropological inquiry into the ethics or moral code of another society, inevitably the conclusions arrived at will differ radically according to the way in which the anthropologist distinguishes 'moral facts' from other kinds of information available. Quite properly, most anthropologists are concerned with the wider ramifications of these facts and with their bearing upon general social structures and motivations. But, for our purposes, if we wish to study the ethical system as such, we must adopt some clear-cut differentia of ethical and moral data.

I have already presented arguments for my view that the most propitious method of investigating an informant's theory is through the examination of his explicit discourse, and I shall henceforth assume that we shall be concerned only with what the informant says, and not what he does. We must now find some way of differentiating ethical or moral discourse from other types of discourse.

If we wish to describe the statements of an informant which are peculiarly ethical, we are obliged to look at morality from his point of view rather than from ours. This excludes from our descriptions not only our own ethical evaluation of his opinions, but also our own sociological and psychological interpretations of these opinions based upon evidence other than his *ipsissima verba*. Therefore, a psychoanalytical or a functionalist explanation of the moral facts of the Navahos must come only after those facts have been isolated and identified, and in descriptive ethics they cannot be used to serve as a criterion of differentiation. I shall contend that, instead of employing an extrinsic criterion, we can best hope to reproduce the informant's point of view by using a definition of "moral statement" in terms of the uses and logic of discourse itself. Indeed, the same kind of arguments advanced earlier in favor of investigating ideologies through discourse, apply to the differentiation of ethical from nonethical discourse.

I think there will be general agreement that moral statements enunciate norms, in some sense or other of this meretricious word. But granting this, the field covered by norms is commonly acknowledged to be much wider than that of moral norms in particular. Norms are sometimes identified with values, but there are aesthetic, economic, and cognitive values which are not moral values. In another sense, norms include such things as rules of conduct — but again moral rules of conduct must be differentiated from the rules of etiquette or other parts of the mores. Thus, among the Navahos there is a culturally accepted set of rules to be followed by men and women when they commit adultery, but they are certainly not moral rules! In every culture there are rules governing actions which are not considered moral and may be considered immoral.

In this chapter and the next I shall examine some of the ways in which "moral obligation" has been analyzed by social scientists and philosophers. These two chapters will be largely exploratory and critical. My purpose in following this procedure is not only to call the reader's attention to the problems involved, but also to show him how the empirical materials presented in Part III will require different interpretations according to the criterion of "ethics" which is selected. Furthermore, some of the criteria discussed may serve as indirect clues to be used in handling the data obtained in fieldwork.

I shall begin by discussing in more detail the requirements of the kind of definition of "ethical discourse" which would be adequate for descriptive ethics. The ensuing critical examination of definitions that have been proposed and used will be organized around a discussion of Durkheim's analysis of "moral facts," [1] for I believe that he is very close to the truth in his essay, and the various elements to which he calls attention have been employed as criteria by others who have been interested in descriptive ethics. (Although, needless to say, in most cases they have not been influenced by his writings on the subject.)

The two basic elements of Durkheim's analysis are the conceptions of "obligation" and of "desirability." Accordingly, the theories to be examined fall into two broad groups: those which emphasize the regulative and constraining aspect of moral principles; and those which stress the value or desirable elements in moral conduct. The former tend to employ sanctions, in one or other sense of this ambiguous word, as a criterion of moral facts, while the latter tend to regard moral judgments from the point of view of the spectator. Although the distinction between these two groups cannot be followed rigorously, for convenience of exposition I shall consider the first group in this chapter, and the second group in Chapter IV. My own positive proposal will then follow in Chapter V. There I shall argue that the key concept of ethical discourse is that of *moral obligation* to do or not to do something. It will be suggested that "obligation in general" may best be analyzed in terms of a prescription or rule of action. But the concept of "obligation" by itself is not sufficient to identify a moral principle since there are many types of obligation which are not moral (such as those of etiquette, technology, or law.)[2] I shall contend that the distinctive characteristic of moral obligations is their 'special authority,' which will be analyzed in terms of their superiority and legitimacy.

2. REQUIREMENTS OF A SATISFACTORY DEFINITION

a. Explication

The type of definition which is sought here has come to be known among philosophers of science as an *explication*. In order to explain this notion I cannot do better than to quote from the writings of C. G. Hempel:

> Explication is concerned with expressions whose meaning in conversational language or even in scientific discourse is more or less vague (such as 'truth', 'probability', 'number', 'cause', 'law', 'explanation' — to mention some typical objects of explicatory study) and aims at giving those expressions a new and precisely determined meaning, so as to render them more suitable for clear and rigorous discourse on the subject matter at hand.[3]

Hempel then proceeds to list two major requirements of an adequate explication: first, "it must permit us to reformulate — at least a large part of what is customarily expressed by means of the terms under consideration"; and second, "it should be possible to develop, in terms of the reconstructed concepts, a comprehensive, rigorous, and sound theoretical system."[4]

I shall assume that we are in search of an explicative definition of "moral (and ethical) statements" which will fulfill these two requirements. Here again I may point out that a discursive differentia of "ethical" is more likely to satisfy these two requirements — since it probably will accord with customary usage while at the same time allowing for exactness and testability.

The second requirement is a demand for an explication (or definition) which promises to be pragmatically useful in prosecuting an inquiry in descriptive ethics. It must not only be unambiguous, but it must also be clear and precise enough to enable us to distinguish unequivocally between ethical and nonethical statements. I suspect that psychoanalytic criteria, for instance, do not satisfy this demand.

To these two requirements, I wish to add another; namely, that the definition be general enough to be applicable to the ethics of other cultures besides our own. That is, the definition must not be ethnocentric, for otherwise we shall surely obtain a distorted view of the informant's ideology. In order to achieve a presumption of such generality, I have tested the explications to be considered not only by comparing them with a variety of ethical systems of Western culture, but also with that of the Navahos. It might be contended that this testing in terms of Navaho ethical discourse makes my procedure circular — since I later accept or reject as ethical various statements by Navaho informants on this basis. But if it is a circle, it is a very large one for it includes many considerations other than those involving the Navahos.

In this connection, it might be pointed out that the explication to be offered is in a sense empirical — for like most definitions it is based on the supposition of the truth of various empirical propositions about different cultures.[5] Indeed, the definition I shall propose may be interpreted as an empirical generalization, that is, as an empirical anthropological hypothesis to the effect that all cultures contain as one of their elements an ethical system (or systems) in the sense defined. Whether or not the presence of such ethical systems is universal is a question which can only be settled through painstaking inquiry by anthropologists. Certainly if it were proved not to be universal, I should admit that the proposed definition ought in all probability to be revised, or that some further explanation of the absence of ethical systems in certain cultures should be forthcoming.

Thus the requirement of general applicability of any adequate explication of the concept of an "ethical system" or "moral code" to all cultures will provide one test of the adequacy of the definitions which I shall examine in this and the following chapters as well as of the one I shall advocate in Chapter V.

We may therefore summarize the requirements of a definition of "moral" and "ethical" adequate for the purposes of descriptive ethics as follows: first, conformity to ordinary usage of the terms; second, unambiguous, clear and precise meanings sufficient to enable us to identify the data involved; and third, a presumption of generality, in the sense that it is cross-cultural.

b. Justification and explanation

One of the dangers to which those engaged in descriptive ethics are prone is the confusion of the moral and ethical data to be analyzed with nonethical explanations of them. William James has called an analogous confusion in psychology the *psychologist's fallacy*. He writes:

> The great snare of the psychologist is the confusion of his own standpoint with that of the mental fact about which he is making his report. . . . The psychologist . . . stands outside of the mental state he speaks of. Both itself and its object are objects for him. Now when it is a cognitive state (percept, thought, concept, etc.), he ordinarily has no other way of naming it than as the thought, percept, etc., of that object. He himself, meanwhile, knowing the self-same object in his way, gets easily led to suppose that the thought, which is of it, knows it in the same way in which he knows it, although this is often very far from being the case. . . . Another variety of the psychologist's fallacy is the assumption that the mental state studied must be conscious of itself as the psychologist is conscious of it. The mental state is aware of itself only from within; it grasps what we call its own content, and nothing more. The psychologist, on the contrary, is aware of it from without, and knows its relations with all sorts of other things.[6]

Accordingly, it is our task to isolate and identify those thoughts (or statements) which are peculiarly moral or ethical, and not to confuse them with any explanations which we may have of them. This is another argument for my earlier contention that the definition of "moral fact" must be made independently of psychoanalytical or sociological explanations of these facts.[7] If this procedure is not followed, then such explanations would be circular since they would select the data to be explained which by definition will verify the explanation. For this reason I have contended that an independent criterion of "the moral" is a prerequisite for an inquiry into the psychological orgins or social functions of any ethical system as well as for descriptive ethics.

In descriptive ethics the situation is complicated by the fact that ethical discourse includes the arguments and reasons adduced by the moralist to justify a moral judgment. The moralist's reasoning which aims at inducing the listener to accept moral statements I shall call *justification*. In contrast to justification there is another type of reason which the investigator may give as the cause or function of the moral statement (or conviction). This process, to be distinguished from justification, will be called *explanation*.

An example will illustrate this distinction between justification and explanation. Suppose someone were to ask: "Why do the Navahos think it wrong for a son-in-law to look at his mother-in-law?" The question is ambiguous. It may be asking either for the reasons given by the Navahos for avoiding mothers-in-law, or for the cause of the mother-in-law taboo and the functions it performs in Navaho society. If the question is construed in the first way, it is about the informant's justification of the prohibition, and if construed in the second way, it is a request for an explanation by an anthropologist. The answers to these two questions would be entirely different. The Navaho justification of this taboo is that a violator will go blind, whereas a plausible anthropological explanation of it is that in a matrilocal society there must be a precaution against the danger of the mother-in-law stealing her daughter's husband.[8]

Philosophers who read anthropological literature on the ethics of non-literate societies are frequently misled by the failure of the authors in question to be clear when giving the reasons for certain moral rules about whether they are reporting the informant's justifying arguments or the authors' own explanatory interpretation of these rules. The same arguments advanced earlier about the use of actual statements of informants apply to giving reasons for a moral principle.[9] Since many of the most eminent anthropologists fail to include the informant's justification but instead supply us with their own explanations, much of the anthropological literature on the "ethics" of non-literate peoples is almost entirely worthless for the purposes of descriptive ethics.[10]

Justification, as investigated in descriptive ethics, occurs in the informant's discourse or in reconstructions verified by it alone. Explanation, on the other hand, goes beyond his discourse to non-discursive facts and seeks to account for the moral statements by employing wider psychological and sociological categories. As such, explanation may be etiologically more important and more profound, but it does not *describe* the informant's ethical ideology. The tendency to do descriptive ethics by introducing explanatory categories into the picture of the informant's ideology is therefore just another version of James's psychologist's fallacy.

In contrast to explanation, which is introduced illegitimately into descriptive ethics, the informant's justification is an intrinsic component of his ethical system. In fact, it is the justification itself which is often used to differentiate moral from nonmoral rules of conduct. The mode of justification not only serves to distinguish the moral from the nonmoral, but also gives us insight into the character of the ethical system before us. For instance, in a theological ethics, a moral rule is one which is justified by its purported origin in God's will, while nonmoral rules are considered to be those originated by man. For a Benthamite utilitarian a moral rule is one justified on the grounds that it promotes the greatest happiness of the greatest number, and those rules that do not are not moral.

It follows from this discussion that in our search for the differentiae of moral and ethical statements we may well look to their justification, but should carefully avoid employing our own explanatory categories in the definition.

c. Justification by explanation

There is a curious tendency among Western moralists, and I include here many social scientists who are covertly moralists, to convert an explanation into a justification. After having derived a plausible explanation of some moral phenomenon in terms of a specific causal factor or function, they thereupon employ this factor or function normatively to formulate and justify rules for action in the future. In such cases, the scientist has become a moralist.

There are two ways in which this conversion of explanation into justification has proceeded in Western thought. Since we should be careful to avoid this snare I believe it to be worth while to mention them here.[11]

One basic type of explanation is historical explanation. This seeks to explain a phenomenon in terms of its origin. Western thought has been much addicted to the use of *justification by origin,* which is merely a special case of justification by explanation. The appeal to authority, whether it be God or Society or History, is nothing more than the identification of an historical explanation (or one presumed to be so) with a justification. It is assumed that if one can give an historical account of the origin of a moral rule or a legal right, then this account may serve as a justification. (This assumes, of course, that the origin itself is authoritative.)

It is not unusual for some who profess to be social scientists to introduce a moral lesson from such accounts of origins. If the origin is not used to justify a moral statement, sometimes it is used to unjustify it, in the sense of rendering it unacceptable. The most notorious example of the latter is to be found among the Freudian moralists who impugn conventional morality by tracing its origin back to the incestuous Oedipus relationship. Nietzsche's *Genealogy of Morals* provides another illustration.

But the illegitimate transition from an explanation to a justification is not confined to justification by origin. It is possible to find social scientists turned moralists who, after having 'explained' moral judgments in terms of their function in sustaining society and various group relationships, then go on to suggest that moral standards derive their justification from this function and accordingly ought to be adopted with that end in view. This will be called *justification by function.*

Philosophers, having observed the more blatant examples of this illegitimate moralizing, are prone to suspect that perhaps moral prejudices (like those in favor of social stability and welfare) may sometimes unconsciously affect the objectivity of some of the accounts in anthropological literature which describe moral codes and offer explanations of them.

At any rate, it is important to be on our guard in pursuing the present type of inquiry, for it seems obvious to me that non-literate ethical systems are sufficiently different from our own to make somewhat questionable an interpretation of the underlying factors explaining them in terms miraculously corresponding to our own ethical ideals. This is merely a *caveat* at this point, and I shall return to a discussion of the relevance of descriptive ethics and related subjects to normative ethics in the final chapter of this book.

3. DURKHEIM ON THE AUTHORITY OF MORALITY

In his interesting essay entitled "The Determination of Moral Facts,"[12] Durkheim distinguishes between three different questions to be answered. First, what are the distinctive characteristics of moral facts? Second, what is the explanation of them? Third, how are they to be evaluated? The last two questions are beyond the scope of the present study, but the first question is precisely the one with which we are now concerned. Let us examine his answer in more detail.

Since Durkheim's analysis is a subtle one, it may be best first to list some of the points which he makes:

"All morality appears to us as a system of rules of conduct" (p. 35).

". . . moral rules are invested with a special authority by virtue of which they are obeyed simply because they command" (pp. 35-6). This gives rise to the characteristic of obligation.

The specific character of moral rules is evident when they are violated, for violation entails (synthetically) a sanction (blame, punishment) (pp. 42-3).

Morality is not only obligatory, "but also desirable and desired" (p. 45).

Morality presents certain analogies to the sacred, for it is not only an object of fear and respect, but also of love and aspiration (p. 48).

The two basic elements in Durkheim's analysis are the obligatory character of morality and its desirability. At present we shall only be concerned with the key concept of "obligation."

It should be noted that Durkheim considers moral facts to be essentially *rules of conduct*.[13] And he says: "To explain the characteristic of obligation in rules it is sufficient to establish the notion of moral authority" (p. 47). I shall begin by examining Durkheim's notions of "moral authority" and "sanctions," since these form the backbone of his conception of the differentiae of morality.

Durkheim is careful to differentiate sanctions from other unpleasant consequences of an act. Thus, if I violate a rule of hygiene, I may become sick — but this consequence is not a sanction. "A sanction is the consequence of an act that does not result from the content of that act, but from the violation by that act of a pre-established rule" (p. 43). In other words, a sanction is an unpleasant consequence of violating the command of the authority, that is, of defying the authority. It is clear therefore that the notion of "sanction" can only be understood if we already know what a moral rule is and what the authority is. We cannot even determine whether a particular unpleasant consequence is a sanction or not until we know whether a moral rule has been violated, although it is clear that blame and punishment may have some evidential value — not completely reliable — in indicating to us that there may be a moral rule which has been violated.

It is evident that the key concept in Durkheim's discussion of morality is that of a moral rule as a command of a special authority, which must be obeyed simply "because it commands." Durkheim thus follows in the tradition of many Western philosophers from Hobbes to Kant, who maintain that moral prescriptions are commands of a certain sort. Now, commands are proven to be moral in virtue of the moral authority of the commander, that is, in virtue of their origination (although Durkheim mollifies his account by introducing the notion of desirability).[14]

In the final analysis it is clear that Durkheim bases his notion of morality on justification by origin.[15] The validity of an authoritarian interpretation of morality depends upon two considerations: first, whether the commands can be proven to come from the moral authority (thus, in a theological ethics one of the problems is to prove the authenticity of a command as coming from God); second, whether the presumed originator of the commands is acceptable as a moral authority.[16] The acceptability of an authoritarian ethics of this type therefore depends on the credentials of the authority and the authentication of his commands. Durkheim admits that the only two types of authority which have the credentials necessary in order for them to be able to issue commands which are moral are God and society. "Between God and society lies the choice" (p. 52).

Whether Durkheim's theory of the moral authority of society can be philosophically justified or not is a question which cannot be discussed here. Since our present interest is in descriptive ethics we must look at his discussion from the point of view of someone who wishes merely to describe ethical systems.

It may be admitted that Durkheim's characterization of moral rules as the commands of a moral authority with the accompanying sanctions accurately describes many of the natural and artificial moral codes of our Western culture. Much of the Judaic-Christian tradition illustrates theological authoritarianism, and we could probably find many who, perhaps largely unconsciously, adhere to social authoritarianism. Furthermore, we may quite legitimately extend Durkheim's differentia somewhat, since there have been other kinds of authorities besides God and society which have been regarded as the source of moral precepts. Stoicism, for instance, derives moral laws from the authority of Nature, while Historicism as expounded by Hegel and some Marxists recognizes the authority of History. Finally, Kant's philosophy and those which may be described as Conscience theories are in certain respects authoritarian, since they are couched in the language of a command or imperativist ethics.

The authoritarian criterion, however, which includes the notion of commands and sanctions as elements, fails to apply to many other moral systems. For instance, I think it fails to do justice to Aristotle's ethics and with it the natural morality of the Greeks as it appears in their literature. Nor does it fit Epicureanism.

Moreover, the authoritarian approach is essentially alien to Navaho thought patterns — whether they be concerned with conduct or not. It would follow that were we to adopt Durkheim's characterization, we should have to deny that the Navahos, and possibly the Greeks, had any moral code whatsoever. I suspect that there are many other non-Western cultures which do not have an authoritarian ethics of Durkheim's type.

These considerations force us to conclude that Durkheim's descriptive criterion of "moral fact" in terms of a moral authority works well for certain ethical systems, but is not general enough. In this respect it is ethnocentric, and hence must be rejected in our present study. However, I believe that there is an important element of truth in Durkheim's analysis which needs only to be made more general, and this will be explained in Chapter V.

Durkheim's three differentiae, moral authority, obligation (constraint, sanctions), and desirability will serve as guides in the ensuing discussion of other criteria of the moral. The rest of this chapter will be devoted to an examination of those theories which stress constraint, and the next chapter will be concerned with those emphasizing the desirable element in morality. In Chapter V, I shall offer an explication of the "authority of morality" which will exclude the authoritarian element.

Many philosophers and anthropologists have agreed with Durkheim that one of the distinctive characteristics which differentiates moral rules (prescriptions) from mores and customs in general is that they constrain; that is, they frequently conflict with the private wishes and desires of the person concerned. This characteristic of constraint is accepted by such diverse thinkers as Hobbes, Locke, Kant, Malinowski, and the Freudians. But there are many differing opinions as to the source of constraint which characterizes morality. Most frequently the source of constraint is attributed to sanctions of one sort or another. I shall now subject this notion or, rather, these notions of "sanction," to scrutiny. I find that most of them are extra-discursive, and thus given from the point of view of the observer rather than from that of the participant — and this violates the methodological principle laid down earlier.

4. SANCTIONS AS A CRITERION OF MORAL FACTS

a. The ethical meaning of "sanction"

It is quite common for philosophers and social scientists to hold that the distinguishing characteristic of moral obligation or moral rules is derivative from the sanctions behind them. It is assumed that only thus is it possible to explain the constraining power of morality. This is a view which was well known to the British moral philosophers of the eighteenth century for it had been advanced by Hobbes and was accepted by others such as Gay and Bentham. It has now come to be accepted by many social scientists who discuss moral codes. For instance, Radcliffe-Brown defines "moral obligations" as rules of conduct the violation of which brings about a "moral or ethical sanction" which "may be defined as a reaction of reprobation by the community toward a person whose conduct is disapproved." [17] Because the notion of "sanction" has played such an important part in discussions of moral rules and has so frequently been used to define them, I shall devote the next few sections to a critical examination of its claim to be a differentia of morality.

The word "sanction" is used with great abandon in anthropological as well as philosophical writings. It has been used in an extremely broad sense to mean: "the underlying drives, motivations, 'unconscious system of meanings' that govern the reactions of a people." [18] It has also been used to designate unconscious psychoanalytical mechanisms as well as conscious organized applications of force. Bentham uses it very broadly to stand for any "source of pleasure or pain . . . capable of giving a binding force to any law or rule of conduct." [19] Many different kinds of sanctions have been mentioned in writings on ethics and the social sciences: physical sanctions, political sanctions, social sanctions, religious sanctions, internal sanctions such as guilt and shame, and so on. If we include such distinctions as those between diffuse and organized or conscious and unconscious sanctions, the list may be multiplied indefinitely. I believe that a careful scrutiny of this list will reveal that the word "sanction" is used equivocally, since it is impossible to group all of these under one genus.

We can best gain an insight into the notion of "sanction" if we consider it in its most specific and precise meaning. Like many words used in ethical discourse, this one has been stretched far beyond its narrow core meaning to cover other groups of phenomena by analogy, but still is almost always used with a savor of its original ethical meaning.[20] In other words, many of the definitions of "sanction" are used as persuasive definitions.[21]

The core meaning of "sanction" is that of a punishment due the violator of a law and administered by the authority originating the law. (In order to avoid repetition I shall consider only negative sanctions. There are, of course, rewards for those who obey the law.)

Thus the precise use of "sanction" in connection with ethics presupposes an authoritarian conception of morality as discussed in the preceding section. The authority not only commands the performance or nonperformance of certain actions, but attaches certain penalties for violation of these commands. Furthermore, just as the rightfulness of the act commanded originates in the authority, so also does the rightfulness of the punishment for violations. The notion of "sanction" (or "punishment") thus implies two sets of obligations: (*a*) that the agent *ought* or *ought not* to do something; and (*b*) that if he does not fulfill *a* then the law giver *ought* to punish him (or at least has the right to punish him); that is, the violator is deserving of punishment.[22] Thus the application of punishment involves the ethical notion of "desert"; punishment is an unpleasant consequence of one's acts which is deserved. There is hidden in the very meaning of "sanction" the connotation of propriety or fittingness.

In its strict sense, therefore, "sanction" is an ethical term involving the conception of the violation of a moral rule and the morally justifiable consequences which violation entails. Since the notion of "sanction" in this sense already includes moral conceptions, it cannot be used as a differentia of the moral without making our definition circular.

This, of course, does not mean that the notion of "sanction" in the sense of a penalty for violating a moral rule would be entirely useless, for it might be used as a kind of sign by which we could recognize a moral rule to be such. Thus, although it cannot be used to define a "moral rule," the seriousness with which breaches of those rules are regarded and treated might help us to recognize certain rules as moral.[23] However, there are two more serious disadvantages to using this differentia in addition to its circularity.

First, as already pointed out the presupposition of an authoritarian ethics makes it ethnocentric and hence does not fulfill the requirement of generality as set forth earlier. Second, it should be pointed out that sanctions in the strict sense are identifiable with punishments and rewards, and this supposes that every ethical system includes the idea of punishment and rewards. But I shall argue later that the Navahos have no conception of punishment similar to ours — at least in the retributive sense which involves the notion of desert. Punishment and blame are frowned upon by the Navaho moralist as forms of aggression, although he admits that they have to be taken into account as inevitable (though perhaps unjustifiable) consequences of one's crimes. Sanctions, as morally approved aggression, are not condoned in the Navaho culture.

b. Other meanings

In addition to meaning deliberately imposed and deserved punishment and reward, there are many other senses in which the word "sanction" has been used.[24]

First, there is, of course, the ordinary English verb "to sanction" which means to authorize. There is no significant usage of a corresponding noun which would interest us. But this sense of "authorization" is contained in the second sense of "sanction." Second, the "sanction" of a moral rule sometimes refers to the ground of its moral obligations, or the moral authority for the rule. In other words, a sanction in this sense is the rationale behind a moral prescription, or what is thought to make it moral. This meaning of "sanction" makes it an ethical term and leads us back to our original problem. (This particular conception will be discussed in Chapter V, sections 3 and 4.) It is important, however, to recognize the fact that "sanction" is often used in this sense, and we should beware of confusing this kind of sanction with others which have a more explicit psychological or sociological definition.[25]

Finally, "sanction" has come to stand for a large class of social and psychological conditions which tend to induce an individual to conform to some social usage or other, or some rule of conduct. To this group belongs Margaret Mead's definition of "sanction" as "the term . . . used to denote the mechanisms by which conformity is obtained, by which desired behavior is induced and undesired behavior prevented." [26]

It is customary to divide sanctions in this sense into internal and external sanctions, but this division has been criticized recently on the grounds that one kind of sanction, namely, shame, sometimes must be put into one group and sometimes into the other.[27]

I suggest that when sanctions are regarded as inducements to conform they may be better divided into two general groups: those inducements operating through the conscious anticipation of the agent; and those mechanisms of social and psychological control operating to produce conformity as observed by the anthropologist (but not always excluding those in the first group).

c. Consequences anticipated by the agent

In all ethical discourse, indeed in all practical discourse, the future consequences of a present choice are taken into account. This is as true of deliberation in private, as it is of public discussion of what course to pursue. Certainly the anticipation of unpleasant or pleasant consequences will at least sometimes and in some degree modify the agent's choices and behavior.

Accordingly, many writers, especially philosophers, have defined "sanc-

tions" as those conscious anticipations of pleasant or unpleasant consequences which are motivationally effective in inducing conduct in conformity
with certain rules. As such they are part of the agent's conscious beliefs,
and can be investigated in terms of his explicit discourse (as I proposed
earlier in Chapter I). They can, therefore, be discovered in the ordinary
course of interviewing an informant. Such motivationally effective anticipations might be called "internal sanctions," and they could be construed as
such if we understand by the term the mere fact that they are 'internalized'
to the extent of being effective in themselves (automatically). In that case,
it would be difficult to say what an external sanction could be.[28]

If, however, we consider sanction in the sense under discussion from the
point of view of the agent, we can see that he could divide the anticipated
unpleasant consequences into those coming from outside him and those
coming from within. This is the traditional philosophical distinction between
external and internal sanction. For example, it is the distinction made by
J. S. Mill. Thus, 'pangs of conscience' are conceived to be internal sanctions,
whereas among external sanctions would be included all those which appear
to the agent to come from external sources such as nature, society, or supernatural beings. Under external sanctions of this kind we should subsume
Bentham's four sources of pain and pleasure: physical, political, moral
(social), and religious sanctions.[29]

If sanctions are divided in the way just mentioned, what is called the
"sanction of shame" should often be classified as an external sanction, since
the unpleasant consequence of 'being shamed before others' is expected to
come from the outside in exactly the same sense as other unfavorable reactions of the community or of supernatural beings. Perhaps the anticipated
damage is psychological rather than physical — but this distinction would
depend upon some mind-body dualism, which is rejected by at least one non-
literate culture, namely, the Navaho. Again, in order to decide whether
shame is internal or external, we must appeal to the statements of the informant.

A totally different distinction between internal and external sanctions can
be made while still employing "sanctions" in the same sense discussed here,
namely, as pains or pleasures anticipated by the agent. In this new distinction, "internal sanction" is used to refer to an anticipated consequence which
does not correspond to any actual consequence known to the anthropologist.
Thus it is one which is effective, but merely because of some misinformation
on the part of the agent. So-called "supernatural sanctions," such as envisaged punishments by ghosts, would be internal sanctions. In contrast, an
external sanction would be an anticipated pain or pleasure which comes
from a force which does actually exist in reality. To this group we could
count the so-called "social sanctions"; that is, the unfavorable reaction of

the community to a violation of a standard of conduct, provided, of course, that such reaction really takes place. Thus an external sanction would be one observed by both the agent and the anthropologist, and the conception is based on the fact that even human beings in non-literate societies are frequently able to judge correctly of the consequences of their actions.[30]

If we employ the last distinction, the sanction of shame may be either an internal (imaginary) sanction or an external (real) sanction, depending upon the particular circumstances. Where the agent correctly anticipates being shamed before his fellows, it is obviously external but where, on the other hand, he may be "ashamed before the earth or sun," etc.,[31] — we must call it an "internal sanction."

Both these types of sanction, external and internal, appear equally real to the agent, but the latter is unreal to the anthropologist. Hence, this is primarily an anthropologist's rather than an informant's distinction. Consequently, for descriptive ethics it is irrelevant.

To return to the notion of "sanction" in the general sense under discussion we may ask whether any useful purpose is served by calling such conscious anticipations of unpleasant consequences, "sanctions." They might better be called *grounds* or *reasons* for doing or avoiding certain actions, for this in effect is what they are. The only possible reason for using the term "sanction" is that we suggest thereby that they operate to secure conformity to a rule or prescription. But we must distinguish between those rules which are adopted in order to enable us to avoid certain unpleasant consequences, and those for which the unpleasant consequences act as incentives to conformity. In other words, we may ask: which comes first in the mind of the informant — the unpleasant consequences or the rule? Do the consequences beget the rule, or does the rule beget the consequences? It would seem that only in the latter case could we properly use the term "sanction," since its meaning seems to depend on a rule or precept which is prior to it.[32]

These considerations suggest that the term "sanction" is employed with the tacit assumption that rules (precepts or social usages), must have sanctions to enforce them. But to assume that the informant looks at the rules and unpleasant consequences in this order of logical priority is gratuitous. It may quite likely be the case that he thinks of moral rules as similar to a doctor's prescriptions. We obey the doctor's counsels to avoid being sick, but the prospect of getting sick could hardly be spoken of as a sanction enforcing conformity to the doctor's prescriptions. To do so would be to construe his prescriptions as commands of an authority with penalties attached for disobedience. The term "sanction" ordinarily presupposes an authoritarian and command interpretation of moral prescriptions.

In view of these ambiguities, I suggest that we avoid using the term "sanction" except in connection with authoritarian ethical systems, and that instead we use the expressions "grounds or reasons for performing or not performing an action."

d. Mechanisms of control known mostly to the observer

From the point of view of social science, perhaps the most useful meaning of "sanction" is that in which it stands for the various mechanisms promoting conformity to social custom as they are observed by the social scientist, regardless of whether the agent himself is aware of them. Under sanctions, in this sense, we should have to include some of the agent's conscious anticipations, which were construed as sanctions in the previous subsection, since the agent is often aware of these mechanisms. On the other hand, there are some mechanisms, such as unconscious ones, of which the agent may be entirely unaware or, at least, only dimly aware.

Here the notion of "sanction" refers primarily to the efficacy with which various culturally learned mechanisms secure social conformity. This emphasis on efficacy suggests that at least some of the sanctions in the sense of anticipations should not be included in this category, since there are some beliefs which may seem important to the informant but which may not have any important effect on social behavior in general.

When the term "sanction" is used in the sense of mechanism inducing conformity, it refers to a much wider range of phenomena than it does when it is used in any of the other senses discussed previously. Thus it applies to almost all the types of sanctions mentioned in the various lists. For example, it would include 'social sanctions' construed both as the anticipatory beliefs of the agent and as the actual reactions of the community which are observed by the anthropologist. Similarly, it would include shame and guilt as consciously anticipated consequences and as unconscious psychoanalytic mechanisms.

Since this conception of "sanction" is so general, it serves the theoretically useful function of providing a scheme for uniting the various dynamic elements in a culture. But, although its generality may make the conception useful for social anthropology, this generality destroys its usefulness as a criterion of the moral to be employed in descriptive ethics.

There are two types of sanction belonging perhaps almost exclusively to this category on which I should like to comment, namely, the psychological sanctions of guilt and shame and the anthropological sanction of reciprocity. Both of these groups have been used to define the "ethics" of an individual or group. There is some excuse for employing these notions in the definition since such sanctions usually accompany, in our society at least, the violation of those rules we consider to be moral.

Let us first consider guilt and shame, in the sense of psychoanalytical mechanisms rather than of anticipated unpleasant consequences.[33] (In yet another sense these have been called "internal sanctions.")

First, we may subject these criteria to the test of the requirement of generality.[34] Here there seems to be some dispute about the universality of guilt, although perhaps the question cannot be settled until more satisfactory criteria of 'guilt' cultures are devised. At present the presumption that certain cultures, such as that of the Navahos, do not foster guilt reactions to any important extent, if at all, indicates that guilt sanctions should be rejected as a criterion of the moral. The criterion of guilt is too narrow for our purposes.

When we turn to the internal sanction of shame, psychoanalytically conceived, the opposite holds; that is, it is too broad. This is apparent in our own culture, where shame appears as a reaction to activities that are by no means thought to be moral or immoral. For instance, I may be ashamed of my bridge playing or of some social faux pas, but these are not thought to be morally wrong. I have no moral obligation to play bridge well or to dress elegantly, even though the failure to do so may cause me immense shame.

Both of these psychological criteria fail to account for the assumption made by most Western moralists that the having of guilt (or shame) feelings should be governed by moral considerations, rather than the other way around. Our moral principles frequently tell us that such feelings are attached to the wrong object. For example, one often hears the statement, "You ought not to feel guilty about that because you did exactly as you ought to have done." Such statements as these would be absurd if "obligations" were defined in terms of those feelings.[35]

One reason for the exaggeration of the importance of guilt feelings in defining the "moral" is, I believe, an overnarrow use of the word "moral" to stand for Victorian moral teachings about sex. Thus Freudians are prone to attack 'morality' (in the Victorian sense) while at the same time they are obviously preaching their own 'new morality.' This is evident in the following statement by Flugel: "It is easy to see what an immense improvement in human relations would be brought about by the more general adoption of such an attitude, in which we substitute a cognitive and psychological approach for an emotional and moral one." [36]

Is it possible to consider this anything but itself an ethical injunction? But if it is, then we shall have to find some criterion other than the one which Flugel uses and by implication rejects.

Let us now turn to the principle of reciprocity as a criterion of a moral rule. Reciprocity describes the 'mutual obligations' of members of a society to one another, which are based upon a "well-assessed give-and-take, always mentally ticked off and in the long run balanced." [37] It is a kind of positive sanction which operates so that if repayment, in one form or another, is forthcoming, the individual will be favored with further benefits.

Although the principle of reciprocity has been used at times to define "moral rules," as well as to describe them, I believe that it cannot always be so used without giving a distorted picture of the ethical systems involved. This may be easily illustrated in our own culture, where we usually find it advisable to reciprocate the favors of others and perhaps etiquette demands it, but there is not always a *moral obligation* to do so. In fact, gangsters may observe the practice of mutuality in their relations with one another — and the principle of reciprocity may serve thus to back rules governing immoral as well as moral activities.

There is no doubt that Malinowski's conception of reciprocity throws much light on the dynamics of social relations in all their different manifestations. However, it is much too general to be employed as a distinctive characteristic of moral rules, for if it were we should have to label as moral almost any rules governing the behavior of one person towards another.

Another reason for rejecting this principle as a criterion of the moral is that there are many ethical systems which would deny the moral obligatoriness of such a principle. Some types of Christian ethics, for example, would deny that the source of one's obligations to his neighbor lies in what he and others will do in return.

In concluding this subsection, I should like to point out that the definition of "moral fact" in terms of sanctions, conceived either as psychoanalytic or as social mechanisms, violates two principles set forth in section 2. First, neither of these types of sanctions are always an obviously recognizable element in the informant's discourse. That is, the criterion is not a discursive one — as required. Second, they both employ explanatory categories rather than justificatory categories in identifying moral facts. In doing so, they may give a perfectly satisfactory account of why people behave in accordance with moral rules, but they have not shown why these rules are thought to be moral nor what it means to be thought to be moral.

e. Arguments against using sanctions as a criterion

We have found that the word "sanction" is extremely ambiguous, and consequently we had to discuss each of its various senses in turn. Behind all of them lies the covert assumption that they are factors enforcing conformity to rules of one kind or another. This, in turn, suggests that the rules are logically prior to the sanctions, and that "sanctions" in the final analysis can only be explicated in terms of the rule to which they secure conformity. Finally, behind the whole conception we discerned a proclivity to the authoritarian interpretation of moral rules as commands with punishments attached for disobedience and rewards for conformity. Therefore, if the notion of a moral prescription is prior to that of "sanction," we must look elsewhere for a definition of moral judgment and ethical discourse in general.

Scrutiny of Definitions of "Ethics," II

In the last chapter we examined various definitions of "ethics" all of which shared the assumption that moral facts are rules of conduct (or prescriptions). We shall now turn to a consideration of those definitions which revolve around the notion of "moral values."

Although I shall argue in this chapter that the approach to ethics through judgments of moral value is not as fundamental as that through prescriptions, we shall find in the various theories discussed here some clues to specific differentiae which will enable us to distinguish moral from nonmoral prescriptions. Very roughly, the definitions discussed in Chapter III may be regarded as indicating to us the *genus* of moral statements (that is, statements of prescriptions), while those to be discussed in this chapter will provide suggestions for identifying their *differentiae,* which I take to be their imputed superiority and legitimacy. However, it should be noted that this is only a crude outline of the general argument.

Again, I repeat that the purpose of this critical exploration is not only to show the deficiencies of some of the approaches that have been used in descriptive ethics and to discover clues to a more satisfactory definition, but also to convince the reader that many of the divergencies in findings about the ethics of non-literate peoples stem from the use of totally different criteria of "ethics."

I shall begin by considering the relation of obligatory actions to values in general. Then I shall turn to the so-called "spectator approach" to ethics, that is, the view that conceives of moral judgments as evaluative of actions. I shall examine under this heading those definitions of "ethics" which are given in terms of approval or disapproval of bystanders, such as the disinterested spectator. Finally, in order to insure a modicum of completeness, I shall discuss briefly some of the ways that other philosophers and anthropologists have handled the problem of determining moral facts.

I. MORAL FACTS VS. VALUES IN GENERAL

Hitherto we have neglected the obvious intimate relation which morality has to values in general. (This is one of the distinctive characteristics of moral facts, which was called its "desirability" by Durkheim.) Our conception of moral and ethical discourse will acquire more richness if we consider the possibility that moral statements enunciate moral values in some sense or other.

For the present purpose, we may interpret the term "value" in an all-inclusive sense, for I should like to avoid entering into the complexities of a general theory of value or into the many controversies connected with it. In order not to prejudice the issue of the ontological status of values, it will be best to consider values in terms of value judgments or valuations, since in the present study we are interested only in the opinions of an informant — his statements or judgments — rather than in what kinds of things have value or what it means to say that they have. The discursive approach through judgments should be acceptable even to those who deny that values are constituted by value judgments.

Accordingly, the question to be considered may be expressed thus: what are the similarities and differences between a person's judgments of value in general and his moral judgments, or between his value statements and his moral (or ethical) statements?

Let us assume that objects valued are ipso facto objects which are cathected, in that they are objects of affective-conative attitudes or interests. Moreover, we may grant that cognitive elements are involved in the process of valuation — if only in the conceiving of the object valued.[1]

In addition to recognizing the objects of value judgments as objects of interest (in Perry's sense), we may suppose that valued objects are differentiated from mere objects of interest by some distinction between the desired and the desirable. Let us grant for the nonce that when an object is valued it is not merely the object of a personal passing preference but in some sense is less arbitrary or more 'objective.' Accordingly, values or the desirable have been conceived of as being the object of a certain kind of interest, for example, an interest which is "wider and more perduring," "being compatible with the personality as a system or with society or culture as systems," or "intelligent." [2]

The question of the relation between moral judgments and valuations may be briefly considered in terms of these characteristics of objects of value judgments. Whether or not moral judgments are to be conceived of as a species of value judgments, it seems to me indisputable that their objects, namely, right and wrong acts, partake of all these characteristics; they are cathected, and they are thought to be 'objective' in a sense that connotes that they are not objects of arbitrary and fleeting preferences. Indeed, I suspect that with respect to this latter quality, moral judgments are even more 'objective' and 'impersonal' than value judgments. This characteristic I shall later call the "legitimacy" of moral prescriptions, and we may postpone a discussion of it until the next chapter.

Nevertheless, there are certain distinctive characteristics which differentiate moral judgments from value judgments in general — or moral values from values in general.

To begin with, it must be admitted that there are many things which are thought to be desirable which are not regarded as moral, but rather as non-moral or immoral. For instance, cognitive and aesthetic values are not the same as moral values. Such valued objects as good weather or absence of earthquakes, which are beyond human control, are not the subjects of moral judgments. There are at least two characteristics which distinguish moral values from other kinds of values. I believe that moral philosophers of every persuasion would accept both, although some would make the distinction even stronger. However, since we are interested in a theory of maximum generality, it is sufficient to call attention to these two.

First, objects of moral judgments (or moral values) are distinguished from other types of valued objects by their being intimately connected with human conduct, where it involves voluntary actions. This does not mean that all morally valued objects are necessarily only actions, but rather that they have some reference to actions. Moralists think of moral values as attaching to such objects as goals, ideals, motives, or character, and all of these are related in one way or another to voluntary action or choice. Actions themselves may be either prescribed or evaluated by a moral code. Thus, the Ten Commandments prescribe certain actions or non-actions, while other moral principles tell us when we should evaluate a third person's actions as praiseworthy or blameworthy.

Many other values, in contrast to moral values, have nothing to do with voluntary actions since they are not susceptible of human control. Thus, the first distinctive characteristic differentiating moral from other values is its relation to conduct. Later I shall argue that moral judgments are essentially prescriptive and that the peculiar relation of moral values to conduct is due to their being objects of prescriptions. For the time being it is sufficient that we recognize the intimate relation of moral values and moral judgments to possible voluntary actions.

This relation to possible actions, however, is not a sufficient condition of conferring the property of being moral on other kinds of value. There may be things which are themselves valued, but which are not acceptable as goals of action — or as such even become disvalues. For instance, a certain person's death might be considered extremely desirable, but the committing of a murder to achieve it would be thought morally undesirable.

No one would admit that an action acquires moral value simply by virtue of its producing an object of value, that is, that any instrumentally valuable act is ipso facto morally valuable. This would reduce morality to what Kant called "hypothetical imperatives," and would obliterate the distinction between moral values and technological, economic, aesthetic, and cognitive values.

Even utilitarians could not accept this unscrupulous application of the principle that any end justifies the means. They would insist that the costs should be weighed against the values expected, and moral value attaches only to those voluntary actions which will produce the greatest amount of value in general. Thus the utilitarian sets up a supreme principle of morality (utility) and in this sense recognizes a kind of *superiority* and ultimacy of moral values with respect to other types of value. The principle of utility could be said to possess a special "authoritativeness" for the utilitarian.

At the opposite end of the spectrum from utilitarianism, we find those philosophies which deny that the moral principles governing conduct are concerned with producing values at all. For these the right is entirely irreducible to the good, although they admit that certain actions may be morally good as well as right. This view has been called "deontological" ethics, or "formalism." [3]

Thus both extremes, utilitarian and deontological, admit that moral values are distinguished from values in general not only in that they have an intimate relation to voluntary actions, but also because they possess a certain kind of superiority with respect to them. Therefore, even if a moral judgment is a species of value judgment, it is more highly selective and exclusive than other value judgments. In this rather hasty examination of the relation of values and morality, I hope to have brought out two essential characteristics of moral judgments: their legitimacy and their superiority. My own explication of these notions will be given in Chapter V.

2. APPROBATION AS A CRITERION OF MORAL FACTS

The conception of moral judgments as a species of value judgments and of the corresponding moral actions as a species of values has lent considerable plausibility to the approach to ethics through the moral evaluation of actions. This approach considers actions apart from their character as what might be called "actions-in-view"; that is, the moral evaluation of actions does not always aim at directing and guiding conduct itself. For instance: we can morally evaluate actions committed in the past or by people other than ourselves. Moral evaluations are, therefore, often said to be from the point of view of the "spectator" of conduct rather than from that of the "agent" performing the actions. The spectator approach to ethical discourse is widely accepted by many philosophers and is frequently employed by anthropologists.

All those theories which discuss moral judgments in terms of approval or disapproval of cèrtain lines of conduct by others or by the community at large exemplify this approach. For instance, in discussing what he calls "moral standards" Firth frequently refers to approval or disapproval, moral condemnation, or the evaluation of types of action, and thereby commits himself to the spectator theory of morality.[4] Any writer who bases his account of a moral code on such items ipso facto has adopted the spectator approach. Among older writers, Westermarck is the most important exponent of this view of moral judgments, since he derives all moral judgments from the emotions of approval or disapproval.[5]

The use of moral evaluation of actions, that is, of an informant's approbations and disapprobations, as a method of understanding ethical systems appears to have many advantages. It has much greater breadth than if we consider moral judgments only as rules of conduct, for, in contrast to the latter, which are directly concerned only with actions themselves, moral evaluations can have as their objects men's characters, their motives, their intentions and wishes, and from these we can infer the moral ideal of the good man.

Because of the extensive use as well as the intrinsic plausibility of the spectator approach to morality, we must examine it at greater length. I shall argue that at many points it is unnecessarily obscure, and also that it distorts the picture of certain moral codes. I think it can be shown that the apparent advantages that it has over the prescriptive approach are not as great as might be supposed, if we have a sufficiently sophisticated conception of the latter.

I shall begin by discussing the notions of "moral approval and disapproval."

a. Moral approval and disapproval

It is clear that to say of an action that it is approved or disapproved is not exactly the same as saying that it is liked or disliked, although if it is approved (or disapproved) we can probably conclude that it is also liked (or disliked). "Approval" and "disapproval" are stronger terms than "liking" and "disliking"; they connote some sort of impersonality and objectivity. Indeed, this consideration has led more rationalistically inclined philosophers to hold that moral approval and disapproval are analyzable only as judgments of value which are either true or false, and that they thus partake of the same type of objectivity possessed by other kinds of cognitive judgments. It is unnecessary for our purposes to go to this extreme, as long as we recognize that approvals and disapprovals cannot be identified with the more personal preferences of the person who has them. The distinction between these two kinds of reaction may be expressed in terms of the contrast between the desirable and the desired, or between values and objects of desire.

The distinction between moral approval (or disapproval) and personal preference has frequently been formulated by stipulating the conditions under which the favorable (or unfavorable) reaction takes place. There are two general types of theory which are relevant to descriptive ethics; the first identifies moral approval with the reaction of a disinterested or impartial spectator; the second identifies it with the reaction of the community at large.

Adherents of the disinterested spectator doctrine usually specify other conditions in addition to disinterestedness which must be fulfilled by the spectator before his reactions qualify as moral approvals; for instance, the spectator must be normal, calm, and must have knowledge of the relevant circumstances. One version of this view requires that the spectator be 'ideal,' and accordingly that he must be omniscient and omnipercipient. Among those who have employed the notion of "disinterestedness" in descriptive ethics are Brandt and Westermarck.

Westermarck defines "moral emotions" in terms of their disinterestedness.

When pronouncing an act good or bad, I mean that it is so quite independently of any reference it might have to me personally. [That is, they are] moral emotions if they are assumed by those who feel them to be uninfluenced by the particular relationship in which they stand both to those who are immediately affected by the acts in question and to those who perform the acts.[6]

In older philosophical versions of the disinterested spectator doctrine, such as those of Adam Smith and Hume, it was assumed uncritically that there would be universal agreement among impartial spectators of quite different cultures about the worth of an action. More recently, however, advances in cultural anthropology have shown that approval and disapproval are to a large extent culturally conditioned (though perhaps not entirely so). In contemporary thought, therefore, a certain type of ethical relativism has been the logical outcome of this approach. This is illustrated by Westermarck's theory, which he calls "ethical relativity."

The anthropologist, when he applies the criterion of approval or disapproval, is faced with practical as well as theoretical difficulties in determining who should be considered a disinterested spectator. It is obvious that a definition of "disinterestedness" requiring the spectator to be free from the prejudices of his society would be unsatisfactory from the point of view of the anthropologist, since he is interested in studying moral reactions within the context of culture. Furthermore, it is difficult to see how an abstract definition of "disinterestedness" could be applied with any logical rigor to the concrete data collected by anthropologists. Perhaps we could assume that a practical criterion of "disinterestedness" is employed when one elicits the informant's opinions of actions which he does not think of as immediately affecting his own personal welfare. But even this may be impossible — for in a comparatively small society like that of the Navahos every crime is deemed to affect the personal welfare of all. Therefore, it is clear that disinterestedness, as a criterion distinguishing moral approvals and disapprovals from personal preferences, is a difficult if not an impossible criterion to apply in anthropology despite Westermarck's facile use of it. (There are philosophical problems relating to the definition of "disinterestedness" which it is unnecessary to discuss here.)[7]

Accordingly, some writers have substituted for the disinterested spectator or judge the approval or disapproval of the community at large. However, the attempt to distinctively characterize moral facts in these terms has certain weaknesses which even the disinterested spectator view does not share. Among these is the fact that people often think that the favorable or unfavorable reactions of the community may be morally wrong. Reformers, prophets, and individualistic rebels against society have played an important role in the evolution of Western moral ideas, and this definition would automatically exclude their exhortations as irrelevant to ethics. Even so-called "primitive" man has been known to criticize modes of action which his society has approved.[8] If the "moral rightness" or "wrongness" of acts were defined in terms of such public reactions, it would be logically impossible for an individualist or a reformer to criticize public opinion on moral grounds. The speciousness of this notion is illustrated by the absurd consequence that if a certain community condoned lynching an innocent man, that action would *by definition* be right! [9]

Finally, the approbationistic criterion of the moral is open to some of the objections presented earlier to the identification of moral values with values in general, for it fails to distinguish the peculiarly moral character of virtuous actions and tends to reduce them to a species of aesthetic value. Thus, the morally good action becomes indistinguishable from the beautiful action, and a morally good person would be no different from a person with an aesthetically pleasing character. This reduction of moral value to a species of aesthetic value is a consequence of the fact that impartiality seems to amount to what in aesthetics is called "aesthetic distance" or "aesthetic disinterestedness." I believe that the view that moral values are aesthetic values does a grave injustice to both.[10]

These considerations suggest that "moral facts" can be defined in terms of moral approval or disapproval only if a more satisfactory explication of the difference between moral and other kinds of reaction is forthcoming.

b. Prescriptive and evaluative aspects of moral judgments

It seems self-evident that a moral code which does not include directives for conduct is no moral code at all. One absolutely essential element in any moral or ethical system consists of its answers to the question: What ought one to do? Such answers may be called "prescriptions," "rules of action," "moral counsels," "guides," or "moral precepts," but by whatever name they are called, one of their characteristic functions is to direct conduct. Linguistically, such prescriptions are usually expressed in statements using words like "ought," "duty," "right," or "wrong."

Moral evaluations, on the other hand, consist in assessing the worthiness or unworthiness of an action often without any reference to guiding possible actions in accordance with them. This type of judgment employs a different set of terms from prescriptive judgments; namely, "good," "evil," "virtuous," "morally desirable," "praiseworthy," and "blameworthy." Prescriptions are concerned with the *right*, whereas evaluations are concerned with the *good*.

Approbationists maintain that judgments about the rightness and wrongness of actions (or moral prescriptions) can be derived from judgments about the goodness or evilness of actions and people (or moral evaluations). There are several difficulties which will be encountered by anyone attempting such a derivation, and I shall now examine some of these. I shall begin by mentioning two philosophical objections to approbationist ethics, and shall then give a reason for believing that it is not the most promising approach for anthropological inquiries into ethical systems.

First, we must recognize that the objects of a moral evaluation are frequently not the same as those of a moral prescription, nor are the criteria of a good or evil (praiseworthy or blameworthy) action the same as those of a right or wrong act.

The difference between these two kinds of judgment may be illustrated by our own Western moral conceptions. Most Western moralists would agree that in the moral evaluation of an action we should take into account not only its rightness or wrongness, but also the motives of the agent, the state of his knowledge, and the conditions under which he acted. A right action performed in the face of great obstacles or temptations is usually thought to have more moral value than one done where the circumstances made it easy. The commission of a wrong action may be forgiven if it is done by reason of ignorance. Also, we ordinarily place a higher value on an action done from a worthy motive than on one done from an unworthy one, even though the former be wrong and the latter right. On the other hand, when we are talking to someone about how he ought to act, the question of his motives and extenuating circumstances are irrelevant. We say: "You ought to keep your promises," but not: "You ought to seek obstacles and temptations to overcome in keeping them." The act is right or wrong independently of whether or not one is tempted to do the contrary. Furthermore, there is good reason to think that it is absurd to say that one ought to do a certain act from one motive rather than another. The moral prescription tells us to keep our promises, but *not* to keep our promises from a sense of duty rather than, say, for prudential motives.[11] Although these specific differences may not occur in all ethical systems, they are quite apparent in our own culture.[12]

But other distinctions between prescriptions and evaluations of actions may occur in non-Western cultures. For instance, as I shall explain later, the Navaho also uses distinct criteria for judging whether an act is right and whether it is good in the sense of being praiseworthy. The rightness of an act depends only upon the envisaged consequences to the agent, whereas its praiseworthiness is based on its consequences for the community.

The second philosophical objection to the derivation of moral prescriptions from the evaluations of actions is that there is some difficulty in explaining how an evaluation, as such, can entail a prescription. How can we deduce the conclusion that "X ought to be done," from the statement that "X is a good action" (in the sense that it is worthy of reward or praise)? It appears that this can only be done if we add the premise that "one ought to do those actions that are good" (worthy of reward or praise). Without this addition we must interpret the evaluative statement as also being prescriptive. Accordingly, one would have to say that the statement, "lying is evil," contains the implicit prescription: "Do not lie." Somewhere along the line the prescriptive element must be introduced whether it be in the evaluative statement itself or in a moral prescription later on. In any event, it seems to be the case that a mere evaluation in itself is not sufficient to tell the agent what to do.

This difficulty is particularly evident where the moral evaluation of actions is identified with social approval or disapproval or even with that of a disinterested spectator. The fact of approval or disapproval, whether it consists in the statement of it or in the expression of it, cannot of itself tell anyone what to do. We can derive a prescription from it only by adding a prescription to the effect that one ought to do those acts which are approved. If this is true, it would be easier to start with prescriptions as primary, and to consider evaluations of conduct only insofar as they are relevant to determining which actions are prescribed and to justifying prescriptions.

Finally, I should like to mention a methodological objection to the use of approvals and disapprovals as differentiae of moral facts. In trying to delimit the field of moral facts it seems to me that one should select those data which are most readily and precisely identifiable. Approaching a study of an ethical system through its prescriptions for conduct seems more promising in this respect than an approach through its evaluations of conduct, because the standards of right and wrong action are usually much more explicitly formulated and 'objective' than those by which people evaluate actions. In ordinary discourse, the statement, "That is the right (or wrong) thing for one to do," is much stronger and less open to disagreement than the evaluative statement, "That was a good (or bad) thing for him to have done." Many of our evaluations, in other words, are nonmoral, and we are confronted with the difficulty of providing some criterion by which to distinguish moral from nonmoral evaluations. I suggest that this is actually more difficult for evaluations than for moral prescriptions, since the considerations upon which they are based are more complicated and subtle. Moreover, evaluations are generally *post factum,* and it does not make as much difference how we evaluate as it does how we prescribe for future behavior. For practical reasons people tend to be more careful when telling someone what to do than when they are merely voicing their approval or disapproval afterwards.

It is also my impression, based on field experience, that a native informant is much more clearly aware of the rules for action to which he subscribes than of the vaguer and less exactly formulated evaluations of actions and personalities. Prescriptions by their very nature tend to be definite and precise, whereas evaluations are subtle and indefinite — and probably more subjective.

c. Spectator and agent ethics

The two approaches to moral judgments which we have been examining are sometimes called "spectator" and "agent" ethics respectively. A great many modern moral philosophers have followed the spectator interpretation of morality, although most of ancient ethics treated it from the point of view of the agent. (The agent approach is obvious in the ethics of Aristotle, the Stoics, and the Epicureans.) It has recently been contended that ethical writers should abandon the spectator approach and devote their attention to the agent's problems and that modern moral philosophy should return to the ancient tradition of agent ethics.[13] I agree with this contention, and should add that it appears to me that the spectator approach is ethnocentric, for not only is it not to be found among the Greeks but I find nothing resembling it in Navaho culture.

The attractiveness of spectator ethics can be attributed to the assumption that moral judgments made by a spectator rather than by the agent are more likely to achieve 'objectivity.' That is: if the judge of the actions is himself not involved in the violent confusion of the choice situation, it is supposed that his judgment is more apt to be considered reasonable and impersonal. In other words, it is assumed that there is more control if the spectator rather than the agent (or his adviser) makes the judgment.

This supposition may be justified within our Western cultural traditions, since we are brought up not only to respect certain norms of conduct, but also to follow certain norms of approval or disapproval. We are told that we ought to like certain kinds of things and not others. We are taught that we should judge actions to be worthy of commendation in some circumstances and in others to be worthy of blame. There are standards of moral evaluation as well as standards of conduct. In the same spirit, our ethical discourse makes frequent reference to what is deserved.

These facts have led some philosophers to extend the prescriptive approach in ethics to evaluations themselves, thus turning the tables on spectator ethics. Accordingly, a good or virtuous action is said to be one that "ought to be praised," and an evil action one that "ought to be censured." [14]

The prevalence of spectator ethics in Western thought may be explained in the following way. In practical life we compare the spectator who evaluates actions with the judge who renders his judgment. It is no accident that the terms "impartial spectator" and "impartial judge" are often used interchangeably by adherents of this type of approbationism. A judge when rendering his decision presumably is disinterested personally, and his judgment is influenced by legal norms of one sort or another. There is a kind of objectivity demanded in legal justice (which may, however, be peculiar to our own culture). Furthermore, the judge's decision resembles moral evaluations in that the considerations which are relevant, such as the accused's intentions, are *post factum* and only indirectly related to any prospective actions. Although the verdict has the consequence of bringing pain of some sort, it is based only on those actions which have already taken place, unless the accused is acquitted. Therefore the judge is ordinarily more interested in finding out what reaction is deserved than he is in guiding action itself. [15]

This conception of "legal justice" is alien to the Navaho mind. The function of what might be called a judge is not to make awards on the basis of desert, but rather to conciliate the parties in controversy and to restore social harmony. In other words, these quasi-judicial offices are viewed in the context of the facing of choices by the agent, rather than in the context of the making of disinterested decisions by a judicial spectator. [16]

Spectator ethics is therefore perhaps more properly called *judicial* ethics. In those societies where there is no institution which exactly reproduces our form of judicial justice, we should hardly expect to find the type of judicial ethics with which we are familiar. [17]

One further reason for the plausibility of the view which stresses the disinterestedness of the judge is that in our own ethical discourse we frequently do appeal to disinterestedness. For instance, we use such admonitions as: "Look at it from the other fellow's point of view," or "Look at this matter impartially." Such arguments may be interpreted as implicit references to the impartial spectator or judicial criterion of morality. This kind of argument never occurs in Navaho discourse as far as I can ascertain, and I do not remember it occurring in Greek moral discourse. I take this as one more reason for regarding the spectator approach as ethnocentric.

In conclusion, I should like to make it clear that I do not wish to underestimate the importance and frequency of evaluations of other people's conduct in terms of some sort of approval or disapproval. I do not deny that moral evaluations of conduct and personality perform a crucial role in many ethical systems by supplying the grounds and content of moral prescriptions. Some moral codes employ the conception of the Ideal Man, or of praiseworthy actions, to define the goal of moral conduct, as, for example, the ethics of Aristotle. Other codes introduce the proposition that certain actions will be approved or disapproved by others in arguments supporting moral prescriptions — the ethics of the Navahos. In this connection all I contend is that we should start with the prescriptions and work back to their justifying grounds, and that we may find moral systems in which either these evaluations themselves or the fact of other people's evaluations are considered completely irrelevant. In other words, evaluations may be important in some moral systems and unimportant in others.

Furthermore, I have tried to point out that the notion of an impartial spectator or judge is theoretically obscure and difficult to apply in anthropology, and that it is most probably an ethnocentric conception. Common sense alone would tell us that we ordinarily approve and disapprove of actions and people according to the way they treat us and according to the effect of their conduct on the common welfare. In other words, we should naturally expect evaluations of conduct to be from the point of view of the *patient* — the person who is actually or may be affected — rather than from the point of view of a disinterested spectator. (This is actually the type of evaluation which I find in Navaho society.)[18]

In passing, I might remark that some of the explanations of the content of moral judgments offered by adherents of the spectator doctrine may still be applied to what might be called "patient reactions." Thus the importance in such evaluations of considerations of public utility, emphasized by Hume and Adam Smith, occurs also in the patient evaluations of the Navahos. Furthermore, Westermarck's analysis of "moral emotions" as basically retributive, as either resentments or retributive kindly feelings, could also be applied to patient evaluations. A person to whom a favor has been done is likely to approve of the giver, and a person who has been injured is likely to feel resentment against the injurer — and these reactions will be expressed as approvals or disapprovals. Nevertheless, I would not agree that either Adam Smith's or Westermarck's theory of disinterestedness is the correct analysis of moral judgments either in the sense of prescriptions or of evaluations as they occur in all cultures.

3. OTHER CRITERIA

In addition to the two main groups of criteria of "moral fact" which I have already discussed, sanctions and approbation, there are some other criteria which have been either explicitly proposed or else actually used without explication by philosophers and anthropologists. I shall now examine a few of these.

Since a great deal of contemporary philosophic writing has been devoted to ethics, either in the form of ethical theory offering an explanation of legitimate ethical judgments, or in the form of meta-ethics offering a linguistic analysis of ethical sentences, we should expect to find some attempt by philosophers to state in precise terms how we are to recognize an ethical judgment or sentence. However, so-called "ethical data," which are the presumed data of ethical theory and meta-ethics, are rarely characterized in such a fashion as to enable us to distinguish them from nonethical data — or, indeed, to help us to discover what the data of the inquiry are at all. As far as I know, the only philosopher who has explicitly attempted to give us a pre-analytical criterion of "ethical statements" or "moral judgments" is Duncan-Jones. I shall discuss his views at the end of the present section.

a. The intuitive approach

Philosophers and anthropologists are prone to use what might be called the "intuitive" approach to ethics, with respect to both the meaning of ethical terms and the content of moral judgments. Most philosophers openly espouse this method, whereas anthropologists have tended to be unaware that they have used it (especially in their assumptions about the proper content of moral rules). I shall maintain that the intuitive approach in all its various versions is methodologically unsatisfactory for descriptive ethics, especially because it may lead the investigator to a completely distorted view of the ethical system under study. We require an objective rather than a subjective standard of comparison if we wish to study systems of thought that we do not accept, in other words, those which do not accord with our own intuitions.

Almost the only method of identifying moral and ethical data which has been employed in Western philosophical literature on ethics is an intuitive one. It is assumed that everyone knows what a moral judgment is, and that consequently there is no need for a criterion by which to decide whether a judgment is ethical or not. This assumption may take either of two forms. Its weak form is that everyone understands the meanings of such terms as "duty," "ought," "right," and "wrong," although he does not always know which particular acts are right or wrong. Its strong form is that all men know both the meanings of these terms and their application, that is, what actions are right or wrong. In the eighteenth century many moral philosophers even believed that such moral knowledge is absolutely certain.

In its weak form, the intuitive approach assumes that we can always recognize ethical discourse from the meaning of the expressions which it employs. Thus it involves the linguistic vehicles which are used in ethical discourse. The linguistic approach will be discussed later, when I shall try to show that it tends to share in common with the other types of intuitive approach the assumption that no criterion of differentiation can be given. In other words, we must rely on our intuitions to recognize it.

The strong supposition that we actually do have ethical or moral knowledge, whether it be with absolute certainty or with some degree of reliability, is usually thought by its supporters to provide us with a criterion by which we could determine whether a judgment is ethical or not. If a judgment agrees with those ethical judgments which we believe to be true, it would ipso facto be ethical, whereas if it does not it would be nonethical. For instance, granted that stealing is wrong, any judgment which permitted stealing would be nonethical. Thus, to determine whether a judgment is ethical or nonethical it would be sufficient to compare it with those ethical judgments which we accept as being true. Of course, this would entail that the Navahos and people of other cultures have no ethics at all, or at best a very incomplete ethics.

This procedure is not as absurd as it sounds if we compare it with a frequent use of the word "scientific." The popular criterion for whether an opinion is scientific is its accordance with those judgments which have been established and accepted by scientists. Any belief which is incompatible with science as it is known by us would be called "unscientific." It follows that so-called "primitive peoples" have very few if any scientific opinions. For instance, the belief that certain kinds of sickness are caused by witchcraft is not scientific — whatever else it may be.

"Science" in this narrow sense refers to a body of true and established beliefs, and hence includes only those truths which have been achieved, and not the pious hope of achieving such knowledge or the methods applied in seeking it. This is certainly a familiar use of the word "science," and it gives rise to the question whether certain disciplines are sciences even though they have not achieved results comparable to those of the natural sciences. That is why many people deny that the social sciences are sciences at all, for certainly it must be admitted that social theories do not have the degree of finality possessed by those of the more exact sciences. Such a conception of "science" is based on achieved results rather than intent or methods or subject matter.

Similarly, if it is assumed that certain ethical judgments have as high a degree of warrantedness as those of the exact sciences, we can conceive of "ethics" as the body of true and established beliefs about the rightness and wrongness of acts.

According to this procedure, "ethical," like "scientific," applies only to what we know or to what is valid, and not to what we merely believe. Consequently, there could be no such thing as a false science or a false ethics, although there might be opinions masquerading as scientific or ethical which could be called "quasi-scientific" or "quasi-ethical."

Just as we can say that non-literate peoples have beliefs about nature and causal processes, but have no science, we could also say that they have convictions about conduct, but no ethics. Instead of science, they have quasi-scientific beliefs, and instead of ethics, quasi-ethical convictions.

But even granting that we do have such scientific and ethical knowledge, it is apparent that this way of defining "science" or "ethics" does not help us in an anthropological investigation, because it gets rid of these words altogether only by introducing the new ones: "quasi-science" and "quasi-ethics," which in turn require definition. Attempts are often made to solve this problem by using as a criterion of quasi-scientific or quasi-ethical statements those statements with roughly the same subject matter as is found in the statements of genuine science or ethics. Let us briefly examine some theories of this type.

b. The identification of ethical discourses in terms of content

Quite frequently it has been taken for granted that, although the scientific and ethical opinions of non-literate peoples do not agree with our own, nevertheless we may expect them to be concerned with fundamentally the same problems and therefore the same subject matter.

Now, "scientific" (or "quasi-scientific") beliefs may be defined with partial adequacy in terms of their subject matter when they are about causal uniformities of natural processes. Even this is not entirely satisfactory, however, since the 'primitive' person's conception of the difference between the natural and the supernatural is not the same as our own. The division of 'primitive' beliefs into those about natural and those about non-natural things probably reflects our own bias more than it does native opinion. According to the Navaho conception, witchcraft and the actions of the Holy

People are in one sense no less natural than, say, the way plants grow, and though unobserved they would be considered by them to be just as natural as we should consider radio phenomena which we also cannot see. There is a pressing need for a study of the basic categories of belief among non-literate peoples, but it cannot be undertaken here. At any rate, "quasi-science" could be considered a kind of belief and we could investigate it under the general category of belief.

Similarly, we might be tempted to define "ethical" (or "quasi-ethical") convictions in terms of subject matter. This is a criterion which is frequently used in describing the ethics of non-literate peoples. It consists merely of reporting the informant's reactions towards those actions which are the objects of our own moral judgments, such as actions involving sex, homicide, veracity, promise-keeping, destruction of property, and robbery. But this method distorts our picture of the moral code in question even more than it does the beliefs about natural phenomena — perhaps because the subject matter of ethics is not as readily determinable as that of science.

To assume that certain specific lines of conduct are objects of moral judgments is already to beg the question in favor of a certain type of ethical system; and any other facts ascertainable from informants would be irrelevant. Thus it would be question-begging to assume that ethical judgments are only those which apply to such things as sex or homicide, for this would automatically exclude certain acts which might be considered morally right or wrong by the informant although not by us.[19]

The same approach through the content of moral judgments often leads the anthropological investigator to draw the line between moral rules and nonmoral rules, like those of etiquette, ethnocentrically. This is evident in many writings which list moral principles on one page and rules of etiquette on another. But until we have a criterion which is unbiased with respect to the content of a moral code, it is impossible to be sure that these lists accurately reflect the informant's moral code.

A somewhat more subtle form of the use of content to identify moral principles is found among those writers who assume without question that ethics is always and exclusively concerned with those actions which are conducive to social order or disorder. For example, it is frequently supposed that we should regard as ethically relevant only those rules involving lines of conduct which serve a social function. The bias in favor of social welfare is characteristic of Western morality, but it is too much to assume that native informants regard their own moral code as similarly oriented.[20]

I suggest that the intuitive approach lies at the bottom of the use of the content of our own moral principles as a criterion of what is to be taken as ethical, for it is based on the assumption (intuition) of the adequacy of our own ethical convictions, and uses them indirectly as a measuring rod to determine whether or not a judgment is ethical in much the same way as the assumptions of the more naive intuitionists discussed above might be used. All these approaches refuse to study an informant's ethics as he conceives it, but instead try to fit it to the Procrustean bed of Western moral systems.

c. The linguistic approach

Another approach which is highly favored among philosophers may be called the "linguistic approach." The linguistic approach, however, tends to become intuitive in the weak sense mentioned above.

Those philosophers who have devoted themselves to meta-ethical inquiries have regarded as ethical those statements (or sentences) which use so-called "ethical expressions," namely, words like "duty," "ought," or "good." Since these are English words, the inquiry must obviously limit itself to ethical discourse in ordinary English. Clearly, this will not help us to investigate the ethical discourse of a non-English speaking people, like the Navahos. The meta-ethicists might reply: "Make up a list of ethical expressions in Navaho, and then you may proceed as we do with ordinary English." But how are we to make up such a list? It cannot be done without relying upon someone's intuition of synonymy with certain English expressions. Again, such a procedure is fraught with the danger of reading our own intuitions, or those of our interpreter, into our translations.

Despite the fact that they achieve some objectivity in identifying their data by means of a list of ethical expressions, the meta-ethicists frequently have to add that they are discussing words like "good" in *their ethical sense* — and this has to be determined intuitively. The linguistic approach is thus inadequate even for discussions of ethical statements in ordinary English, since it must rely upon intuition to discover the ethical sense. In addition we must recognize the obvious fact that a great many ethical discussions are held, even in English, without using so-called "ethical expressions" at all.

The linguistic definition of "ethical statements" must therefore also be rejected since ultimately it relies upon intuition, and more obviously, for our purposes, because it is impossible to apply vigorously to the comparative study of the ethical systems of peoples using different languages.

Although for these reasons we cannot accept the linguistic expressions which the informant uses as criteria to decide whether he is discoursing ethically, nevertheless, they provide one among many clues which can be of practical use in field work. However, we must be careful to check his statements in terms of other more reliable criteria, since the words used are neither a necessary nor a sufficient characteristic of ethical statements.

A broader approach, and one more easily applicable to a foreign culture, is one which proceeds not through particular words, or through intuitions, but through the implicit presuppositions upon which these particular methods are based — through the way statements are used. In practice, even the meta-ethicist employs this criterion in deciding whether "good" is being used in its ethical or its nonethical sense. By studying the context in which statements occur, we shall avoid slavish adherence to the details of a particular language, such as 'ordinary English,' and at the same time, we gain a standard by which we can compare the ethical statements of peoples of different languages and cultures. This approach will be discussed in Chapter V, section 2(c).

d. The criteria offered by Duncan-Jones

A rare attempt by a philosopher to give us some common and peculiar characteristic by which to mark off moral from nonmoral judgments has recently been undertaken by A. E. Duncan-Jones. He points out that ethical theories, both naturalistic and nonnaturalistic, seem to presuppose some criterion, and one "might expect to find the answer to these questions in the first chapter of any ethical treatise. But most moral philosophers do not seem to have attempted an answer." [21]

He then proceeds to set out "what seem to be necessary conditions of its being true, of any person, that he makes a moral judgment." His purpose is to give us a pre-analytical account which would be acceptable to ethical theorists of all schools, and which would be neutral towards the controversies between them. This, of course, is the type of criterion which we are at present seeking. As this is the most clear-cut discussion of the question, I shall summarize Duncan-Jones's account of the three conditions which are thought to be required for the making of a peculiarly moral judgment.

The first condition is that the person making the judgment must stand in the relation "of being, in some way, favourably, or unfavourably, disposed towards that action, or class of actions, or end." The maker of the judgment must have an attitude of some kind towards the object of his judgment. This condition was accepted in section 1 of this chapter.

"Secondly, a man cannot be said to make a moral judgment unless the attitude we have spoken of remains unchanged in direction, and more or less unchanged in strength, whoever may be supposed to do the action, or pursue the end, which forms the goal of the attitude." In other words, his attitude must be 'universalizable.' His attitude must be "free from partiality for particular places, ages, and social groups, and from self-partiality," or at least "*relatively* free from those partialities."

The criterion of "universalizability" raises some problems for the anthropologist who is seeking an intercultural definition of "ethics" or "moral judgment." It seems to be a fact that at least some non-literate people consider their moral code to be restricted to members of their own group. Thus deceiving a fellow tribesman may be wrong, but not a stranger. However, the issue is complex. We should be careful to differentiate between universalizing from the point of view of the agent, from that of the patient, and from that of the spectator.

The universal aspect of our own code which we generally emphasize refers to the patient, as when we say: "Treat all men as equal!" It seems to be an axiom of Western Christian morality that we should consider the claims of all men as equal in some sense, or perhaps more exactly that we should recognize that every man has at least some moral claim, however slight, upon each of us. But where to draw the line is not always certain: should we include idiots, animals, and flowers? Many cultures, such as Hinduism, extend the application of morality beyond humanity, while others restrict it to some section of humanity. Since the extension of the patients of a moral act varies so greatly and would require considerable preliminary definition, it does not seem to offer us a very reliable criterion of moral judgment.

"Universalizability" may also be applied to agents of the moral action, in the sense that under the same circumstances everyone ought to do so and so. The moral law is usually thought to be a law binding upon all men, irrespective of race and culture — whether or not they recognize it to be binding. Thus the judgment that it is wrong to commit incest seems to mean that it is wrong for anyone to commit it, even though certain circumstances, such as ignorance, may excuse the person who does. Again, the extension of the agents of morality is more complex than it appears at first glance. We Westerners do not judge it wrong for animals to break moral rules, and usually we do not think that idiots or babies have duties. Some cultures do not conceive of "right" or "wrong" as applying to the acts of children or slaves. Such agents are "beyond the pale of morality." I suggest that perhaps non-literate tribal morality looks upon the actions of members of another tribe as we do those of animals, babies, and idiots. Morality is simply not applicable. (I shall discuss this issue under the heading of ethical competence in Chapter IX, section 4.)

Again, moral judgments may be universalizable from the point of view of the spectator who judges the actions of others completely free from any partiality on his part. Duncan-Jones, with many other moral philosophers, has a tendency to espouse a spectator ethics, and his treatment reflects this bias. I have already commented in detail on this type of ethics in an earlier section of this chapter. Duncan-Jones seems at times to treat moral judgments as if they were essentially an evaluation of the act by a third and impartial spectator.

Duncan-Jones's criterion of "universalizability" seems to me, for the reasons outlined, unsatisfactory for an inquiry in descriptive ethics. The main difficulty is in defining with any precision how universal the judgment must be, or perhaps we should say how general it should be. I think that there is no doubt that moralists in most cultures make moral judgments that are impersonal in the sense that they are not thought merely to reflect the bias of the individual making the judgment. Such generality applies to the patients of the act, to the agents, and to those who evaluate it disinterestedly. I should therefore be inclined to substitute for Duncan-Jones's term "universalizability" the term "generalizability" or "impersonality."

The third condition offered by Duncan-Jones is that the man "cannot be said to make a moral judgment unless his attitude remains unchanged in direction, and relatively unchanged in strength, towards his own conduct, even when it conflicts with his inclinations, or with prudent pursuit of his own interests." Unless prudence is understood in an extremely narrow sense, the moral judgments of some ethical systems like those of the Greeks (Aristotle and Epicurus) as well as that of the Navahos, would automatically be eliminated. I think Duncan-Jones's point may be stated more satisfactorily as the requirement that the person making the judgment be able to apply it without essential change to his own actions as well as those of others. With certain provisions, I believe he is right in maintaining that the moral judgment must be as binding on the person making the judgment as on others. (I shall try to show why this is so in Chapter V, section 2.)

The three criteria given us by Duncan-Jones appear to be rather general and vague. It seems to me that he has omitted two important criteria from which all of the above follow: first, that moral judgments prescribe for conduct, and second, that they claim some superiority and legitimacy which is binding upon people in general, and not just upon the person making the judgment. These characteristics will be explained in the next chapter.

A view which much more closely approximates the definition proposed in the next chapter is to be found in an article by William Kneale,[22] where it is suggested that to say of an action that it is right is to say that it is "in accordance with the moral law." "The moral law is supposed to be something more fundamental or natural than the law of the land."[23] This in turn is analyzed in terms that account rather generally for its superiority and legitimacy. Unfortunately, like Duncan-Jones, Kneale ultimately concludes that these properties can be explicated only by means of the conception of the "impartial spectator." Although we are in agreement on many essential points, I find Kneale's analysis not as precise or detailed as is desirable for the development of descriptive ethics.

4. THEORETICAL UNSATISFACTORINESS OF ALL THESE CRITERIA

The discussion of the last two chapters may be summarized at this point. All the criteria of "moral facts" which have been explicitly formulated and those which have been ordinarily used in anthropological investigation fail to meet the requirements laid down in Chapter III, section 2, namely, conformity to the customary meaning of "moral" in such a way as to distinguish it from the "nonmoral" or "extra-moral"; a formulation that is sufficiently precise to enable us to apply it to the data available in anthropological field work; and sufficient generality to enable us to apply the criterion to other moral systems than our own.

I believe that I have discussed most of the criteria ordinarily recognized. Many are inadequate because they are too general in that they would commit us to extending the conception of a moral code to include many other species of values or of social usages, while others are too narrow and appear to be the result of an ethnocentric view of morality. One rather common failing is the tendency to neglect the point of view of the people who participate in the moral system in favor of the explanatory categories of anthropology.

Despite these shortcomings, I believe that we have uncovered many of the essential ingredients of a moral system upon which the theory of the next chapter will be based. Furthermore, even though none of the criteria discussed can be taken as an infallible mark of a moral fact, nevertheless, they may often serve as valuable clues — either in identifying those facts or in directing our attention towards those areas in which such facts may be expected to occur.

V

The Definition in Terms
of Moral Prescriptions

I. MORAL DISCOURSE IN GENERAL

In the two preceding chapters we examined some of the definitions of "ethics" which have been adopted by philosophers and anthropologists in their various inquiries. All of them were found to be unsatisfactory for the purposes of descriptive ethics, mainly because they do not give us an adequate explication of the notion of "moral obligation" [1] and because they fail to approach ethics from the point of view of the informant. In this chapter I shall offer an analysis of "ethical discourse" which seems to me to be more satisfactory for descriptive ethics than any of those that have been considered.

We shall begin by examining the kinds of discourse which we ordinarily consider to be typical of a moralist.[2] There are two principal questions which a moralist is expected to answer: first, *"What* ought I to do?" second, *"Why* ought I to do what you say I ought to do?" that is, what are the grounds for accepting an answer to the first question. The answers to the first question will be called "moral statements," and the answers to the second, "ethical statements" (although this latter term will also be taken as a generic term standing for both kinds of statements).

Let us consider these two questions in more detail. The first question is a request for moral advice and direction. When he answers it, the moralist counsels, admonishes, and also, perhaps, preaches. The answer may be expressed in imperative form, "Do so and so!" or in more polite language, "You ought to do so and so", or, "I think so and so is the best thing to do." In any case, the answer is itself a directive for action, which may be either a specific plan of action or a rule covering certain types of action. The generic term which I shall use to stand for such directives is *prescription*. The usual expression of a prescription is an ought-statement.

Often, of course, the answer is not forthcoming immediately. But in all public discussions as well as in private deliberations in which the various alternatives are considered and assessed, the outcome sought is always a common or private acceptance of a prescription or decision to act in a certain way. Deliberate decisions will be considered as self-imposed prescriptions, and so may be treated along with prescriptions in general.

In the second place, a proposed prescription (or decision) may always be questioned: "Why should we act thus?" One possible answer is: "Because the acts named are morally obligatory or morally wrong." In other words, because the prescription is a moral prescription. A large part of ethical discourse consists of trying to find out whether the acts in question are the objects of moral prescriptions, and of establishing their claim to be such. I shall call discourse purporting to establish such claims the *ethical justification* of a prescription.

As has been pointed out, not every prescription or decision is a moral one. There may be practical decisions which do not involve moral considerations at all: for instance, whether we should go to the movies or to a play. There are also rules of action which are not moral: for example, rules of games (chess, tennis); rules of etiquette; technological prescriptions; or a doctor's prescription.

There may even be prescriptions which are considered immoral. Machiavelli's prescriptions for becoming a successful prince might fit into this category, or Fagin's instructions to his apprentice pickpockets, or the Navahos' rules to be followed when committing adultery. It is hardly necessary to point out that a prescription which is deemed moral in one society may be thought to be immoral or nonmoral in another, or perhaps no such prescription is recognized at all. It is our task, therefore, to identify that distinctive characteristic in virtue of which we can determine whether the prescription is regarded as moral or not by the person whose ethics is under investigation.

We already have a clue to this distinctive character of moral facts in our earlier discussion of Durkheim's analysis — that "moral rules are invested with a special authority." To be more specific, we should amend this and say: "Are *thought* to be invested with special authority." [3]

The peculiar authority of moral prescriptions has also been recognized by philosophers. I may cite Bishop Butler who states this unequivocally:

Somewhat further must be brought in to give us an adequate notion of it [i.e. man's nature]; namely, that one of those *principles* of action, conscience or reflection, compared with the rest as they all stand together in the nature of man, plainly bears upon it *marks of authority* over all the rest, and *claims the absolute direction* of them all, to allow or to forbid their gratification — a disapprobation of reflection being in itself a principle manifestly *superior* to a mere propension . . . And this conclusion is abundantly confirmed from hence, that one may determine what course of action the economy of man's nature requires, without so much as knowing in what degrees of *strength* the several principles prevail or which of them have actually the greatest influence.[4]

Recent writers on ethical theory have also emphasized the public authority of morality, although frequently they have discussed it in terms of the analysis of language rather than of prescriptions.[5] These analyses, like Durkheim's, have usually been more concerned with *explaining* the peculiarities of moral judgments than with giving an *explication* of these peculiarities themselves. In other words, their point of view is more frequently that of the observer than that of the informant. Although this is an important undertaking, it is irrelevant to our present problem.

As I have already intimated, the term "authority" taken in the strict sense is misleading, since it entails a command ethics. Thus, Durkheim could write: "They are obeyed simply because they command." Insofar as an authoritarian characterization of moral prescriptions entails a command ethics it may be considered ethnocentric. We must therefore attempt to find an explanation of this notion of the "special authority of morality" in such a way as to exclude such authoritarian elements.[6]

It will be contended that the two distinctive elements of this special moral authority are its presumed superiority and legitimacy. This means that the moral obligatoriness of an act is thought to be a consideration which is more overwhelming and demanding upon us than, say, the intense distaste we may have for doing it. Moral considerations are in this sense superior to nonmoral ones. Moreover, the demands for superiority must be thought to be legitimate, for many sorts of actions make questionable demands of one sort or another upon us. In other words, these demands must be regarded as valid and binding. The conception of "legitimacy" introduces the elements of impersonality and objectivity mentioned in the last chapter.

The concepts of "superiority" and "legitimacy" will be explicated in later sections of this chapter. I believe that these concepts will account for all the essential characteristics connoted by the term "peculiar authority" when it is applied to moral judgments. Moreover, I hope that they will also clarify some of the other notions that have been acknowledged by previous writers, a few of which we have already encountered in the preceding chapters: namely, morality's acknowledged character of constraint; prerogativeness; unconditionality; stringency; desirability; impersonality; disinterestedness; generalizability; sociality; reasonableness; objectivity; and sacredness.

These two properties of superiority and legitimacy will provide us with an analysis of the distinctively moral character of moral obligation. "Obligation" itself will be explicated in terms of prescriptions for conduct. By means of the proposed conception of "prescription" I hope to account for the so-called "normativeness" and "ideality" of moral conceptions, as well as the directive function associated with obligations in general.

All the considerations mentioned here, as well as those presented in the preceding two chapters, lead me to propose the following key definitions of the main conceptions involved in the notion of "ethical discourse."

A *moral statement,* a statement of moral obligations, will be defined as "A statement expressing the acceptance of a prescription for conduct which claims superiority and which is regarded as legitimate." (In virtue of being a statement, it not only expresses the acceptance of a prescription, but it also is used to commend the acceptance to others, and to apply the prescription to acts of third parties.)[7]

An *ethical statement,* such as a statement about goals, means, or virtues, is either a moral statement or a statement made in connection with one; for example, in justification of it.

A *moral code* is a body of moral statements occurring in the discourse of some specified informant or group. An *explicit ethical system* is a body of ethical statements of the same. A *reconstructed ethical system* is a hypothetical reconstruction in descriptive ethics intended to explain and predict statements made in an explicit ethical system.

The rest of this chapter will be devoted to explaining the proposed definition of "moral statement." The wider question of the nature of an ethical system, which involves the elucidation of the conception of "ethical justification," will be the subject matter of Part II.

2. PRESCRIPTIONS

a. "Oughtness"

The satisfactory analysis of "ought-statements" has puzzled philosophers since the time of Plato, and consequently there is an extensive literature on the subject. I do not intend to try to solve here all the problems involved, but rather to elucidate some of the interrelations of a particular kind of ought with actions and discourse.

The ought has frequently been identified with value or norms in general. I regard this identification as objectionable for two reasons. First, the conception of value or norm is itself equally obscure. Indeed, sometimes "value" has been defined as "ought-to-be-ness" (W. H. Urban) or as a "fact that ought to be."[8] Secondly, it has often been contended, and in my opinion rightly, that strictly speaking the only appropriate subject of an ought-statement is a person or group of persons with respect to things directly or indirectly under their voluntary control.

This last point requires some explanation. It is indeed true that we use the word "ought" in connection with all sorts of things other than persons. We say, for example: "It ought to be a good day," or "There ought to be a cure for cancer." The first example illustrates the use of "ought" to indicate expectancy. Here it obviously means only that from all the evidence available we can predict with a certain probability that it will be a good day. This expectancy sense of "ought" is very frequent. The second example is probably a restatement of a value judgment, meaning only that it would be good if there were a cure for cancer. But it might also mean that people ought to try to discover the cure for cancer. Thus it is ambiguous. In addition to these two types of ought-statements which do not refer explicitly to persons, there are such statements as: "The cats ought to keep out of the cellar," where I believe we can say that there is a metaphorical extension of the use of "ought" from people to animals.

Nevertheless, if taken in the strict sense applicable in ethics, I shall assume that Ross is correct when he writes:

> 'Ought' properly asserts an obligation, and it would be absurd to assert of, say, a state of pleasure or a beautiful object that it is under an obligation to be, or of a state of pain or an ugly object that it is under obligation not to be. It is true that we sometimes *say* of such things that they ought or ought not to be, but it is always, if we use language with any approach to strictness, with the underlying thought that it is or was or will be some one's duty to bring them into being, or to prevent them from being.[9]

Accordingly, we shall restrict this discussion to "oughtness" and "obligation" in the sense in which they are applicable only to persons, and we shall disregard any sense in which they might be applied to states of affairs. Even if there are other senses of these terms in which they could be applied to states of affairs in their own right, we can safely ignore them since we are interested in descriptive ethics rather than in values in general. It should be noted that in this ordinary ethical use, "oughtness" and "obligation" are applied to persons with regard only to those actions which are susceptible of voluntary control; for we do not think it possible for a person to be obligated to do something outside his power, for example, to change the color of his eyes. This follows from the generally acknowledged principle that in some sense "ought" implies "can."

Assuming that ought-statements apply only to agents and their possible voluntary actions, we may ask: "What does an ought-statement say about them?" It seems difficult, if not impossible, to answer this question without using the word "ought" or some synonym over again. We could only answer that such a statement says that he ought to perform (or not perform) the act in question. This suggests that perhaps the term "ought" cannot be entirely eliminated in terms of other concepts not connoting it in some way or other. The question of the eliminability of the "ought" is still an open question, but it is one which does not concern us here. If the reader has doubts about its eliminability, he can regard the present analysis simply as an elucidation of some of the characteristics entailed by oughtness or obligatoriness.

Since at present we are interested in obligations in general, we may look for enlightenment about oughtness by directing our attention to one subspecies of ought-statements applying to actions; namely, those which say that a person ought to do a certain thing if he wishes to achieve an end-in-view. For example, a doctor might say: "If you want to get well, you ought to stay in bed." This type of obligation has usually been called a "hypothetical obligation." (I shall explain the difference between hypothetical and moral obligations later.)

Upon examination, hypothetical obligations appear to have these characteristics: they are *ideal* in the sense that they involve an imagined rather than an actual course of action. (This may be called "an-action-in-view.") They tend to be *constraining* — since they demand that contravening desires be suppressed. (Thus, the doctor's prescription conflicts with the wish to leave one's bed.) Finally, they are *directive* in the sense that they tell us which way to act, and to which factors in the situation we should pay attention.[10]

It is these characteristics which I wish to include when I call ought-statements, whether hypothetical or otherwise, *statements of prescriptions*. A prescription functions as an action-in-view which is constraining and directive.

If an ought-statement is made or assented to, either privately to oneself (as in deliberation) or publicly to others (as in exhortation), it involves all the characteristics which I have pointed out. In order to understand the use of ought-statements and the consequences which follow from them, I suggest that we consider them to be what I have called "prescriptive statements." The directive and guiding element in ought-statements is accounted for by the prescriptive content of these statements, that is, the prescription. A person who makes or assents to an ought-statement may be said to have "internalized" the ought in the sense mentioned. This "internalization" will be analyzed in terms of the acceptance of a prescription. Thus an ought-statement or a prescriptive statement indicates that the speaker has accepted the prescription and is ready to commend its acceptance to others.

It should be evident that the key concept in the present analysis is that of the "acceptance of prescriptions." The rest of this section will be devoted to an explication of this notion.

An obligation (or prescription) by its very nature can only operate through a person's 'will.' 'Will,' in the language which Aristotle uses to define "voluntary action," acts as "a moving principle in the agent himself of which he is aware."[11] Thus, actions which are invoked by prescriptions are more than habits of conduct since the agent is aware of their being prescribed, and they are not simple responses to the press of the environment, natural or social, because they must be mediated through the agent's 'will' (or 'intelligence'). In this sense prescriptions must be internalized.

It follows that in discourse with others the moralist commends a prescription and exhorts his hearers to adopt it, which is quite different from merely inciting him to the action prescribed. The latter may take place without the interposition of any voluntary element in the agent.

b. Explication of "prescription"

Prescriptions have been variously called "principles of action," "maxims," "rules," "precepts," "ends-in-view," or "plans of action." Since I wish to speak of guiding and constraining principles of action in the most generic sense, I prefer the expression "prescription." Prescriptions may be general or particular. Rules are a subspecies of prescription specifying general types of acts to be done or avoided. A specific plan of action, or end-in-view, might be considered to be a particular prescription. Prescriptions may also be positive or negative; that is, injunctions or prohibitions, and they may be moral or nonmoral. The expression "prescription" is selected on the grounds that as well as being relatively free from misleading connotations we can also form from it the adjective "prescriptive," and the noun "prescriptum" (the act which is positively or negatively prescribed).

It should be noted that a prescription is not to be identified with a command. Therefore, the conception of "prescription" does not require that we have a term for the person setting the prescription (a "prescriber") — since the person who first enunciates a prescription is not always to be regarded as its originating authority.

Now prescriptions may be originated in that they are first recognized and expressly formulated by individuals (including great moralists) or else through cultural traditions which hand them down from generation to generation. The historical origin of prescriptions, however, is irrelevant to the conception of "prescription" itself. Of course, this does not exclude the relevance of such origins for the justification of a prescription; but the grounds for accepting a prescription are not to be identified with part of the prescription *qua* prescription. If we think of the kind of prescription which a doctor gives, we shall come closer to the conception intended here, than if we consider prescriptions to be precepts laid down by an authority — an authoritative prescriber.

We might speak of a "prescriber," in another sense, namely, applying to a person who recommends a prescription to another. For example, a doctor could be called a "prescriber." However, I should like to exclude these special uses of "prescriber," since in my terms a moralist does not prescribe but rather commends prescriptions and exhorts the hearer to adopt them.

Since the prescription, if it is accepted, must operate through the agent's own volition (or voluntary actions), we might be entitled to say that the agent prescribes to himself in that he commands himself to perform the required act. In this sense, every moral agent would be a prescriber.

Accordingly, we may expect to gain a better insight into the nature of prescriptions if we examine the way they affect the agent who accepts them, rather than the aims of the person setting the prescriptions, since there need not be any such person. The conception of the "acceptance of prescriptions" involves various elements which must be analyzed separately. If we start with ought-statements as expressing the acceptance of prescriptions, we may distinguish the content of such statements (prescriptions) from the acceptance of them, and the acceptance from the fulfillment of a prescription; and all of these must be distinguished from the linguistic vehicles which are used to express and commend the acceptance of prescriptions. The following subsections will examine these conceptions in turn. I shall begin by examining ought-statements from the point of view of their content, that is, prescriptions.

Philosophers are likely to ask whether what I have called "ought-statements" are to be properly considered statements at all. I gave various reasons for using "statement" in my discussion of the term Chapter I, section 5. Here it is necessary only to mention that the making of a statement implies that the speaker endorses it, and hence the making of an ought-statement indicates that the ought has been accepted as binding by the speaker and that he is ready to commend it to others; in other words, that he has accepted the prescription. It will be remembered that I distinguished between prescriptive and propositional statements, and suggested that doubts about the legitimacy of using the word "statement" be translated into questions about the differences between prescriptions and propositions. We are now ready to examine some of these differences.

We may begin by asking whether or not prescriptions are propositions. This question is usually regarded as equivalent to asking whether prescriptions can be true or false. The answer depends, of course, upon a more detailed analysis of the question itself. However, I should like to mention a few points in connection with the relation of prescriptions to propositions.

Prescriptions are like propositions in that they are the content (or meaning) of a statement, for we have prescriptive statements as well as other kinds of statements. Just as other statements assert propositions, a prescriptive statement 'asserts' or connotes the acceptance of a prescription. There may also be unaccepted (unasserted) prescriptions. This has led some to contend that prescriptions are a species of propositions.[12] I do not wish to dispute this here, but even granting that they are I should like to point out how prescriptions differ from many other types of propositions.

In the first place, prescriptions have a direct relevance to action which propositions in general do not have. The acceptance of a prescription as contrasted with that of a non-prescriptional proposition creates a demand on the 'will' and may be taken to entail some slight degree of expectancy of conduct in conformity to it. In other words, prescriptions are practical in the traditional sense.[13]

In the second place, if it is assumed that prescriptions are to be construed as propositions they are a quite special kind of proposition in that they have two 'reference points'; for a prescription would have not only the reference point which would make it true (a 'moral fact'?) in virtue of being a proposition, but it would also have a reference point in the occurrence of the prescribed action which fulfills the prescription. I shall call the latter reference point its *objective*. There is no such corresponding category of objective (or fulfillment) for other types of propositions; for the occurrence which might be taken to fulfill a prediction is ordinarily considered to be identical with the fact verifying it.

Third, whenever prescriptions are exactly formulated they contain some such term as "ought" or a synonym, or they are expressed in a non-indicative grammatical mood such as the imperative or hortative. In contrast, other types of propositions can be formulated exactly without using any such terms or grammatical devices. Perhaps they can never be expressed in the imperative. This, of course, would only require that prescriptions be treated as a distinct subspecies of propositions. Insofar as the present investigation is concerned, it is more important to recognize the differentiae of prescriptions; the question of whether they belong to the genus of propositions, can be left open.

c. The acceptance of a prescription

When a prescription is stated, asserted, or willed by a person, I shall say that he has accepted it. Thus, if an informant makes a moral statement (without intending to deceive) we can infer that he has accepted it. But it should be noted that the acceptance of a prescription does not entail the fact of its fulfillment — the performance or nonperformance of the act prescribed — but only that the agent intends to fulfill it if the occasion arises.

When I speak of the acceptance of a prescription, I do not wish to suggest that there is a particular act of acceptance, a conscious choice of prescriptions, as it were. It merely implies that a person who has accepted a prescription is aware that he has accepted it, although he may not know exactly when and under what circumstances he began to accept it.[14]

Furthermore, the subject who has accepted a prescription is aware of its making a demand upon him. As such, under the appropriate circumstances it tends to influence his choices and his voluntary actions in general. In other words, it is a present although not always efficacious factor influencing his volitions.

The acceptance of a prescription consists of the acquisition of a certain type of psychological disposition, sometimes called a "motor-affective attitude." As a disposition it is present in the subject even when it is not being activated, in the same sense in which solubility is present in sugar even when it is not being dissolved. The dispositional quality of the acceptance of a prescription not only accounts for the fact that we can accept a prescription and not immediately act on it, but also for the fact that the performance of an act in accordance with the prescription is connected with the acceptance of it.

Dispositions in general have been analyzed in terms of contrary-to-fact conditionals of the sort that state: *"If* such and such is the case, *then* such and such will happen." Prescriptive dispositions can also be so formulated. For example, the acceptance of a medical prescription to take one pill before meals can be stated: "If the agent is about to eat a meal, then he will take a pill," and so on.

Every prescription, whether moral or nonmoral, presupposes some antecedent condition which is required to invoke the prescribed act. Thus, one cannot tell the truth unless one is speaking to someone under conditions that make it possible. It is these antecedent invoking circumstances of which the agent must be aware, which constitute the "if" component of a prescriptive disposition which activates it. (These antecedent conditions must be distinguished from the *grounds* which justify the prescription. For example, a Christian Scientist might accept the medical prescription as hypothetically valid, but would reject it on moral grounds. I shall discuss the grounds of prescriptions later.)

By analyzing the acceptance of a prescription in terms of the acquisition of a prescriptive disposition, we can explain its internalization and its continuance over a period of time as well as the need for the appropriate occasion before it is manifested in actual behavior.

A prescriptive disposition can be compared to a similar, if not identical, phenomenon we encounter in the process of 'making up our minds' to do something. A decision to do something tomorrow morning, is a kind of setting oneself now to act in a certain way later. This again, is a kind of disposition which is acquired now but is activated only when the time arrives. It is a kind of prescribing for oneself.[15]

As I have already pointed out, prescriptions may be of particular acts, or of a sequence of acts (plans of action), or of a class of acts (rules). Decisions can be of these types also. A person can decide to get up early tomorrow, he can decide to get a college education, or he can decide to go for a walk every day. The only important difference is that decisions are more frequently deliberate choices whereas many prescriptions are accepted without our being aware of explicitly choosing them. (Although, of course, we are aware that we have accepted them.)[16]

A psychological account of the nature of prescription, of its acceptance and of the conditions for its fulfillment might be possible. Presumably an ingenious psychologist could invent various tests to determine the existence of the disposition — as a determining tendency or a specific kind of learned habit.[17] Perhaps a more or less behavioral definition could be developed. But this is beyond the scope of the present study.

d. The acceptance vs. the fulfillment of a prescription

It is important to distinguish between the acceptance and the fulfillment (or nonviolation) of a prescription. To *fulfill* a prescription is to perform the act prescribed, or not to do the act which is prohibited. Thus, the fulfillment of the prescription is the objective of the prescription. For example, if there is a prescription that people should be buried in a certain way, the prescription has been fulfilled when a dead person is buried in this way. I shall call the nonfulfillment of a negative prescription (prohibition) a *violation* of the prescription.

On the other hand, to *accept* a prescription means to adopt it as a directive for action. In ordinary language, we say: "I have decided or made up my mind to do as you say I ought." In more technical language, to accept a prescription is to acquire a disposition to act in a certain way in the proper circumstances.

I shall restrict the term "fulfillment of a prescription" to those actions which are a consequence of the acceptance of a prescription. This eliminates those cases where an action, which is prescribed without being so recognized by the agent, is performed accidentally as it were and so happens to accord with the prescription. Thus, non-literate people may act conformably to certain of our prescriptions without having any corresponding prescriptions of their own; for example, they may tell the truth where there is no accepted prescription of veracity. In such cases, I shall not use the word "fulfill" to describe their actions. (This is purely a matter of terminology.)[18]

Although a prescription cannot be fulfilled or violated unless it is accepted, the converse is not true. In many cases, and perhaps in most, prescriptions are accepted without ever being fulfilled. There are many different conditions which may account for this. In the first place, the circumstances providing the appropriate occasion for the action prescribed may never occur. For instance, in the example given above, you may never be in a position to have to bury a dead person. You have accepted the prescription but may never have to fulfill it. Prescriptions about marital relations may be accepted by children under moral instruction, but if they never get married they will never have the opportunity to follow the prescribed conduct. Again, a person may intend always to pay his debts promptly, but if he never has contracted any debts the prescription is never fulfilled.

It is obvious that in every society, the average individual has accepted many more moral prescriptions than he will ever have occasion to fulfill. The moral instruction of children consists in cultivating in them prescriptive dispositions of such variety that they will be able to handle an extreme variety of situations — many of which they may never encounter.

There are other reasons for the nonfulfillment of an accepted prescription. We may be overwhelmed by temptations of strong passions or desires, or else we may simply forget. A person who is drunk usually does not fulfill the prescriptions he would if he were sober, and a person being tortured may against his will be forced to reveal some secret which he had agreed not to divulge.

Thus fulfillment is a function of the circumstances, external and internal, as well as of the prescriptive disposition.[19] All this follows from the usual conception of a "disposition": that it exists even when not being activated, and that it will be activated only when the conditions are appropriate.

We may well ask: "How do we know whether a person has accepted a prescription or not?" Common sense tells us that there are two sorts of evidence which we ordinarily use in determining the fact of acceptance: the words of the agent and his overt actions. Our previous experience with the individual concerned will tell us whether to believe him or not when he tells us that he intends to act according to a prescription. His subsequent conduct will verify our surmise. There is no certain proof upon which we can rely, for even conduct contrary to the prescription is not conclusive evidence that the agent does not have a disposition to act in accordance with it — although it is often a fairly reliable indication. It is interesting to note how frequently in the reports of Navaho moral instruction, the instructee says: "I am going to quit drinking," etc. (* 13). And according to the informant the individuals who had decided to do this actually did as they said they would.

e. Linguistic analyses

Until now I have only considered a possible psychological analysis of prescriptions. However, much has recently been written attempting to explicate "prescriptions" in terms of language. There are two general kinds of theories that have been developed: the first analyzes "prescriptions" syntactically as imperatives; the second employs as a differentia the uses of discourse. (I include the emotive theory among the latter.) Although there are deficiencies in both approaches, they do offer us some valuable suggestions about the characteristics of prescriptions.

Imperatives. There is an important school of thought which maintains that sentences concerning obligations (prescriptions) may best be distinguished from other types of sentences, such as those of science, by invoking the syntactical difference between sentences in the imperative and those in the indicative mood.[20]

This doctrine acquires some plausibility from the fact that many moral principles of Western civilization have been expressed imperatively: for example, the Ten Commandments. Furthermore, because prescriptions are directives for action, it must be conceded that it is possible to express any prescription in the imperative — if the situation is appropriate.

More significantly, the imperativist analysis of prescriptions calls our attention to one of the distinctive characteristics of prescriptions: their reference to a (usually unfulfilled) state of affairs demanding fulfillment. I have called this "an objective." It has been contended that imperatives are best understood in terms of their objectives (the situations demanded), whereas indicatives are understood in terms of their referents (the situations which make them true or false). For instance, "Close the door!" tells the listener to do something. Its meaning depends on the act envisaged, but it does not state that the action will or will not be done. An indicative statement, on the other hand, such as, "The door is closed," refers to a particular state of affairs and is either true or false with respect to it. It is generally thought that an imperative cannot be true or false. In other words, it cannot express a proposition. For this reason, those who have identified prescriptive judgments with imperatives in disguise, have concluded that prescriptive judgments, including moral judgments, are not true or false.

For our purposes, it is only necessary to recognize that prescriptive statements share in common with imperatives the peculiarity of having an objective which is distinct from a fact. This consideration makes the various types of logic of imperatives especially relevant later. But granting this, I think we must recognize certain limitations to the imperativist analysis.

In the first place, "imperative" is a grammatical rather than a philosophical category. Just as prescriptions stated in the indicative can be translated into imperatives, so imperative sentences in moral discourse can be translated into indicative sentences. The choice of language and mood is not essential in order to convey the meaning.

It is clear that prescriptions are often given in the indicative. In English we have many ways of doing this. The most frequent way is by employing the word "ought." When Jahweh said: "Thou shalt not make any graven images," he might equally well have said: "You ought not to make any graven images." In addition, we should consider the possibility of there being languages in which there is no imperative mood or which do not employ it in moral discourse. Father Berard Haile, when translating the Ten Commandments, used the impersonal third person form in Navaho, which has somewhat the effect of saying: "One does not make any graven images!" [21] This, rather than an imperative, is the grammatical form in which moral instructions are given by their leaders to the Navaho people.

It should also be noted that for moral discourse the indicative mood is often preferable to the imperative mood. Imperatives are the ordinary way of communicating commands of any sort, but a moral prescription cannot always be conceived of as a command, and whenever it is, it must come from some moral authority. When a mother tells her child: "It is wrong to lie," she is communicating something quite different from what she intends when she says: "Don't lie!" The child might be quite justified in inferring that the latter was merely an expression of his mother's personal wishes, but could not do so for the former. It is only when the origin of the command is in the will of a preeminent authority, such as God, that it assumes its moral character. (I shall comment on the interpretation of prescriptions as commands presently.) The difficulty with the imperative formulation is that it generally lacks the objective and impersonal character of a prescriptive statement.

Thus the reduction of prescriptions to imperatives of one sort or another must be rejected on two grounds: because the imperative is an accidental grammatical category, the use of which is not essential; and because an imperative lacks the impersonality of prescriptions which is communicated by putting them in the indicative.

Uses of language. Because of the over-narrow dependence of the imperativist analysis on the linguistic vehicles employed, many philosophers have adopted a broader approach which analyzes the various uses of language. This type of analysis (meta-analysis) may be illustrated by the example of a command. There are many different linguistic forms that can be used to communicate a simple command. Thus, instead of saying "Close the door!" we could say "I wish you would close the door!" or, "It would be nice of you to close the door," or, "It's getting cold here." All of these sentences are called "commands" because of the way they are used.

Accordingly, we may ask whether prescriptions cannot best be analyzed in terms of the use of prescriptive utterances, whether they be formulated in the imperative or in the indicative mood. So we should inquire into the uses of prescriptive utterances in general, or of moral judgments in particular.

Some philosophers have suggested that the distinctive use of moral judgments is to express certain attitudes, while others have maintained that their primary function is to persuade or incite the listener to act in a certain way or to adopt certain attitudes. I shall briefly examine each of these views.

First, we may consider the so-called "emotivist" contention that the principal use (or 'meaning') of moral judgments is the expression of the favor or disfavor of the speaker with respect to some object. Ayer, who is the most noted exponent of this view, writes:

> But in every case in which one would commonly be said to be making an ethical judgment, the function of the relevant ethical word is purely "emotive." It is used to express feeling about certain objects, but not to make any assertion about them.[22]

That moral statements express or reflect the speaker's attitudes is obviously true, but it is a trivial truth. I assume that an utterance may be taken to "express" a feeling of the utterer, if we can justifiably infer from it that he has the feeling in question (even though he does not state that he has it). But it is evident that every utterance may be taken to reflect some 'attitude' of the speaker — especially if we include so-called "epistemic" attitudes. Thus, if I say: "It is a nice day today," you can safely infer that I favor it, as well as that I believe that the sun is shining and so on. Even the utterances of a scientist made in disclosing a new discovery to his colleagues justify us in inferring that he is expressing his beliefs as well as perhaps his enthusiasm for them. I do not see how it is psychologically possible for people to speak at all without expressing something or other — whether it be beliefs, feelings, likes, good humor, or sadness. The expressivist contention is therefore trivial, and of no value in differentiating the peculiarly ethical quality of moral judgments.[23]

Second, it has also been maintained that the distinctive characteristic of moral judgments is that they are used to persuade or incite others either to actions or to attitudes. Let us consider each of these objects separately.

It might be thought that the immediate aim of moral discourse as prescriptive discourse, is to incite the listener to certain acts or forbearances. Linguistic utterances are frequently used to obtain an immediate behavioral reaction. For instance, if someone shouts "Look out!" he hopes to procure an action at once, with the least possible mediation of a conscious volition or decision on the part of the agent. Similarly, many commands partake of this character; they aim at an immediate behavioral response. (For example, the command, "Cease fire!") However, as I have already stated earlier, the peculiarity of prescriptive statements is that they do not aim to immediately affect conduct, but only mediately through the 'will' of the agent. Perhaps the ultimate goal of the speaker may be to have the agent do some act or other; nevertheless, the means which he employs is by inducing him to 'will' to do it himself. Discourse which does not aim at being thus mediated (or internalized) is not prescriptive discourse. This point is evident if we consider the absurdity of speaking of a person "being forced against his will to act on moral principles." Prescriptive discourse seeks to 'guide' rather than to 'goad.' [24]

Following the distinction made in the previous subsection, the agent cannot be persuaded to fulfill a prescription unless he has first accepted it. We shall have to conclude therefore that if prescriptive discourse is used persuasively, its primary aim is to procure the acceptance of a prescription rather than the performance of the prescribed acts. This may be described as the "inciting or evoking of an attitude." We shall now turn to an examination of this second version of the persuasive view of ethical discourse.

According to some philosophers the characteristic use of ethical discourse is to evoke or redirect attitudes.[25] Unquestionably, the commending of a prescription has such an end-in-view, for the acceptance of the prescription consists in the acquisition of some kind of attitude. However, this analysis is inadequate for our purposes because it is too broad in one sense and too narrow in another.

It is too broad because it fails to specify the kind of attitude which is involved. It has been pointed out that the term "attitude" may refer to any sort of belief, such as an epistemic attitude, as well as likes and dislikes of many heterogeneous varieties. It has frequently been used with the specific reaction of feelings and emotions in mind. However, the particular kind of attitude which is acquired in the acceptance of a prescription is a specific type of tendency to voluntary actions as opposed, on the one hand, to beliefs and feelings, and on the other hand, to miscellaneous nonvoluntary bodily activities. We can account for the guiding or directive character of prescriptions only if we differentiate the attitude involved in prescriptions from those other kinds of attitudes.[26]

Furthermore, even granting that this inciting of an attitude is the characteristic function of practical discourse in general, that is, of discourse commending prescriptions, this analysis still does not account for the peculiarity of ethical discourse as contrasted with other types of practical discourse. This I shall attempt to do in the next section.

In another sense, this characterization of ethical discourse is too narrow, for much of such discourse consists of questioning, doubting, inquiring, discussing, deliberating, and other sorts of 'mental' activities rather than in merely attempting to propagate the conclusions which one has reached. Public discussion and private deliberation seek to decide upon which prescription to accept and to propose to others, but although this is the ultimate goal of these inquiries it does not constitute the whole of ethical discourse.

Nevertheless, with certain qualifications, the view of ethical discourse which is concerned with the evoking of attitudes must be accepted. The qualifications which must be made are: that the specific type of attitude be identified as a prescriptive disposition; that we recognize that not in the whole of ethical discourse but only in its outcome does it aim at the acceptance of prescriptions; that other intermediate interests of such discourse be admitted (such as those occurring in deliberation); and that this be regarded as a characterization of practical (or prescriptive) discourse in general, rather than of specifically ethical discourse.

This characteristic use of ethical discourse will be found to be of considerable value for descriptive ethics when we have to distinguish the ethical from the nonethical statements in the discourse of an informant.[27]

f. Prescriptions vs. commands

Since so many moral philosophers as well as social scientists have identified prescriptions with commands, it seems desirable to examine briefly the differences between them.

A very clear definition of "command" is this one given by Hobbes:

Now counsel is a precept in which the reason of my obeying it, is taken from the thing itself which is advised; but command is a precept, in which the cause of my obedience depends on the will of the commander. For it is not properly said, thus I will and thus I command, except the will stand for a reason.[28]

If we interpret Hobbes to mean by "precept" what I have called "prescription," he has drawn our attention to the fact that there may be other kinds of prescriptions besides commands. The peculiarity of commands is that they originate in the commander's will and are grounded in it. If a command is questioned: "Why should I do that?" the only answer is: "Because I desire it." Once it is seen that the peculiarity of a command is the type of justification which it implies, we can understand why it is possible to express a command by indicative sentences as well as by imperatives. Examples were given at the beginning of the previous subsection.

The identification of prescriptions with commands entails that the only way in which a prescription can be justified is by appeal to the fact that its objective is willed (or desired) by someone. Other facts are irrelevant. But this requirement has often been confused with the contingent fact that the speaker in uttering the prescriptive statement also happens to desire the fulfillment of the objective. Thus, when a doctor gives a prescription we may assume that he wishes his patient to recover, but the grounds for accepting and acting on his advice are not any facts about his will. In Hobbes's terms, such a prescription would be a "counsel" rather than a "command."

It might be contended that although not every prescription is a command, all moral prescriptions are commands. But there are obvious difficulties in the simple identification of moral judgments as commands. If they are commands, they must originate in some will — but whose will? If it is a human will, or that of a group of human beings, we should have to admit that whenever the person(s) changes his mind, morality would change. And if he should die, morality would cease to be!

A command ethics is plausible only if a supernatural Will is involved or that of some fictitious entity which has the required degree of stability and persistence. The theological version is, of course, the most plausible type of command ethics because in God (or Jahweh), we have a Will which is unchanging but yet personal.

In order to save the command doctrine many varieties of fictitious Wills have been invented: Rousseau's General Will, Durkheim's Society, Hegel's *Weltgeist,* and Kant's Rational Will are examples. It is clear, however, that these "Wills" are purely metaphorical notions which do not correspond to wills in any ordinary sense of the term. It seems likely that they are proposed only in order to save the command element in ethics, and to find a plausible substitute for the God of theological ethics.

It follows from the analysis presented here that if we interpret any moral rule accepted by an informant as a moral command, we must be ready to name the commander acknowledged by him. When this is difficult, we should beware of fabricating fictitious entities to fulfill this function unless we have some evidence that the informant himself believes in them. In the absence of any clear conception of a commanding will, it is more likely to be the case that the ethical system in question is not a command ethics.[29]

For these reasons, I believe that prescriptions in general, including moral prescriptions, cannot always be considered to be commands, although they may often be expressed in the imperative mood.[30] To treat them as such is certain to distort the picture we obtain of any but a very specialized system of ethics, which is by no means generally accepted by all men.

g. Objections

At this point we may consider the most frequent objection raised against the analysis of "ought-statements" in terms of prescriptions; namely, that it fails to account for statements about what ought to have been done in the past, and about what people who are not in communication with us ought to do. For example, the proposed analysis would appear to be unable to explain how such statements as these would be possible: "Brutus ought not to have killed Caesar;" and "Eisenhower ought to do such and such." If ought-statements are basically prescriptive and directive, it would seem absurd to use them about actions which cannot be affected by them.

In answer, I should first point out that I do not identify prescriptions with prescriptive statements. The latter depend for their existence upon the conditions of utterance confronting the speaker. Generally, prescriptive discourse is directed at the commending of prescriptions, and, of course, it would be undertaken only if there were a possibility of their being accepted by the listener.

It should be recalled that the whole analysis of prescriptions offered here assumes that a prescription may be accepted and never fulfilled because the appropriate occasion has not arisen. Accordingly, discourse may be prescriptive even if the speaker is aware that there is little chance that the prescription accepted will be fulfilled. There is the additional possibility, of course, that although the listener who accepts a prescription never will fulfill it, he may pass it on to others in the form of moral advice or instruction. Thus there may be a whole host of prescriptions commended in prescriptive discourse without the speaker having to assume that the listener will be immediately affected by them. This fact accounts for many moral statements about situations in which the listener could not be directly involved.

Nevertheless, it is clear that a great deal of indirect ethical discourse, such as statements about the obligations of people geographically or temporally remote from us, must be analyzed somewhat differently. Although the corresponding prescriptions cannot be fulfilled, there is no reason for denying that actions beyond our immediate control, and those of the past, can be subjects of the prescriptions which we have accepted. If this is true, then when we say "Brutus ought not to have murdered Caesar," we are in effect saying that Brutus violated the moral prescription against murder. We must therefore be prepared to admit statements about violations and fulfillments of prescriptions, in addition to direct prescriptive statements, as such, and this accounts for a large class of ought-statements, which are not practical in intent.[31]

The translation of ought-statements into statements about prescriptions is not unusual. We often say, for instance, that it was wrong for a player to have moved the queen in chess, and all that is meant is that to have done so was a violation of the rules of chess. Or a fussy person might say, "Jones signed the document in the wrong place; he ought to have signed on the dotted line," meaning no more than that he violated the instructions (prescriptions). (I assume that no significant consequences will follow.)[32]

It is interesting to note that such indirect moral statements are more often informative than prescriptive. Thus in the last example, the statement informs the listener about what Jones failed to do, but does not prescribe any action. Most moral judgments about historical personages of the past tell us more about that person's actions than they do about morality.[33]

Statements about the obligations of people who cannot be affected by them may be given a similar analysis. Thus, if I should say "Eisenhower ought to do such and such," I cannot hope thereby to commend a prescription to him. I am merely calling to the listener's attention the fact that a certain course of action is the one in conformity with the prescriptions which are accepted by me.

It is clear that ethical discourse is extremely complicated in the various ways in which those statements expressing prescriptions and those about prescriptions can be interwoven. I have considered only a few simple interpretations, and there are many others. However, I suggest that all genuine ought-statements can be analyzed in one manner or another in terms of prescriptions.

In order to avoid misunderstanding, I should point out that the analysis just offered applies only to ought-statements such as statements about duties or about right and wrong acts, and not to evaluative statements about actions. That the two must be distinguished is evident from those cases in which they do not coincide. For instance, I might say that although it was wrong for Brutus to kill Caesar, it was still good — either because of its beneficial historical consequences or because it was a noble action.[34]

3. THE SUPERIORITY OF MORAL PRESCRIPTIONS

The last section was devoted to an explication of "obligation in general." In it the generic characteristics of prescriptions were stressed, without reference to whether they were considered to be moral, or nonmoral. I shall now set forth my proposals with regard to the differentiae by which moral are distinguished from nonmoral prescriptions.

The various types of prescriptions just mentioned may be differentiated by specifying the grounds or reasons for accepting and fulfilling them. For example, a technological prescription which says "You ought to have your car lubricated," is grounded on the end-in-view (or desire) of having the car operate without mishap. This is obvious if someone were to ask "Why?" with respect to this prescriptive statement. The answer would be: "Because the car will operate better, and I assume that you wish that." Similarly, a prescription of etiquette, such as, "You ought to wear evening clothes to that party," might be justified on the grounds that to do so is necessary in order to avoid social disapproval, or for some other similar reason.

These examples illustrate what I have called *hypothetical obligations* because their binding quality is recognized to be contingent upon a particular end-in-view, such as having a good car or being accepted into society. However, the moralist may ask of each one of these grounds whether they ought to be desired, or whether they ought to be accepted as ends-in-view.[35] In such cases the answer is no longer hypothetical. We may call it *categorical*. In this sense, moral considerations are superior to hypothetical obligations, and have a 'special authority' over them.

We must now explicate the "special authority" of moral prescriptions which sets them apart from and above nonmoral prescriptions. In order to avoid the dangers of interpreting moral judgments according to an authoritarian bias, we must look for the valuable elements in the conception of authority and discard those which are based on a command ethics. These elements will be considered in two groups: the superiority, and the legitimacy of moral prescriptions.

The presumed superiority of moral considerations is illustrated in the following dialogue:

Mother: "You ought to help your grandmother."
Child: "But I don't want to."
Mother: "It is your duty to."
Child: "But I still don't want to, I want to play with my friends."
Mother: "But doing your duty to your grandmother comes before what you would like to do yourself."

Although the example may appear trivial, it brings out the superior consideration which moral prescriptions demand. This is one of the most distinctive characteristics of morality.

The superiority of moral prescriptions must, however, be analyzed further. I submit that it consists of the autonomy of morality and its priority.

a. Autonomy

Moral prescriptions claim a certain kind of autonomy which makes them independent of other reasons for action. This independence is manifested in two ways.

First, morality is autonomous in the sense that once a moral prescription has been accepted, no further justification of it is considered necessary. Thus, the recognition that one is morally obligated to perform a certain act or to forbear is thought to provide a *sufficient* reason for doing or not doing it. It is theoretically superfluous to adduce other reasons in addition to the moral reasons already accepted. A moral demand, in theory at least, needs no outside help. It is sufficient of itself.

Second, morality is autonomous in the sense that it cannot be justified nonmorally. To insist upon an extra-moral reason for doing an act morally prescribed is in effect to deny that it is morally prescribed. The consequence of this is that any reasons which are adduced to justify a moral prescription ipso facto become moral reasons.

This is a point which has frequently been overlooked by moral philosophers. It has sometimes been asked: "Why should I be moral?" and ostensibly nonmoral reasons have been offered in reply. Thus, for instance, a theological moralist might say: "If you are not virtuous, God will punish you in the next life, but if you are, then he will reward you." But it seems evident that in giving such an answer, the moralist has abandoned his theological ethics for a prudentialist ethics, which states, in effect, that one's moral obligation is to avoid being punished and to seek being rewarded. All similar attempts to buttress up morality by appeal to other principles of conduct amount only to a substitution of a new basic moral principle for the old one.

I believe that this is one of the conceptions which Kant had in mind when he called the schematic form of moral principles the *Categorical Imperative*. Moral prescriptions are categorical in that they need not and cannot depend upon other prescriptions for their justification.

Two possible misunderstandings of this conception of the autonomy of moral prescriptions should be warned against. First, when we speak of a moral prescription as being categorical, we are not denying that it may require as a condition of fulfillment the occurrence of the appropriate occasion which invokes it. As stated earlier, every prescription must specify the circumstances under which it is to be fulfilled. The moral prescription of marital fidelity is not any less categorical for being dependent upon the circumstance of being married.

Second, the categorical character of moral prescriptions does not entail that they cannot be prescriptions with respect to an end or goal to be sought. In some ethical systems such prescriptions may define as the objects of moral obligation the pursuit of, say, the agent's own greatest happiness — and accordingly acts tending towards this end are morally prescribed and consequently require no outside justification.[36]

Both these possible misunderstandings will be avoided if we follow the account of prescriptions given in sections 2(c) and 2(d) of this chapter and the discussion to follow on the designation of prescribed acts in Chapter VII.

The autonomous character of moral prescriptions, therefore, may be summarized in terms of their sufficiency and ultimacy.

b. The priority of morality

The sufficiency and ultimacy of moral prescriptions does not exhaust their special claim over us, since it is possible that there may be other considerations which partake of this character. For instance, in some cases an innocent pleasure may be both sufficient and ultimate — for the enjoyment of it requires no justification beyond itself. However, it is not **always** a moral end because it may be overridden by moral considerations. This characteristic of morality, namely, the demand for precedence over other lines of conduct may be called its *priority*. In the little dialogue given previously, the mother expresses this when she says that duty comes 'before' pleasure. Similarly, all hypothetical obligations are subject to being out-weighed by moral considerations.

The priority of moral prescriptions over nonmoral ones appears in two different forms — a strong one and a weak one. I shall explain presently why there are these extremes.

In the strong form of priority, moral prescriptions always demand precedence over any conflicting lines of conduct. Thus if an act is thought to be morally wrong, this consideration should overrule all other considera-tions such as its pleasantness, utility, or social acceptability. In this sense, a moral prescription is mandatory. It is true, there may be situations in which moral rules themselves conflict, such as the rule against lying and the rule against hurting others, but if a moral prescription conflicts with a nonmoral one, the nonmoral prescription should give way.

It is clear, however, that although some moral prescriptions are manda-tory there are others which are not quite so exacting. These weaker moral prescriptions permit themselves to be overruled at times, although perhaps not always. For instance, I may have a duty to give to charity, but this cannot be taken to override the use of my money for other nonmoral purposes. This brings out the fact that there are *degrees of stringency* among moral prescriptions. Some make absolute demands upon us, whereas others merely claim some consideration. This variation in stringency of moral prescriptions has been grossly neglected in the literature of ethical theory, and I shall consider it in more detail later in Chapter VI.

The less stringent moral prescriptions may be said to demand priority in a weak sense. Although they may sometimes be neglected, and this permitted neglect varies considerably, every moral prescription (even the weakest) has the modicum of priority which stipulates that it should not always be neglected and that no justification is needed for preferring the morally prescribed line of conduct. That is, if I consider an act to be morally desirable, that consideration by itself is sufficient to justify me in ignoring other considerations, although it does not demand that I do so. For instance, if I think I ought to give some money to charity no one can argue with me cogently that I ought to spend it on a young lady. (Unless this in turn is taken to involve some moral element.)

In its weak form the priority of moral prescriptions means that they are unassailable; in its strong form it means that they are never to be neglected. I shall contend later that both types of moral prescriptions occur in any moral code. In any case, all moral prescriptions are distinctively char-acterized by one or other of these kinds of priority.

4. THE LEGITIMACY OF MORAL PRESCRIPTIONS

We have just seen that moral prescriptions make special demands for superior consideration. It is clear, however, that these demands must be thought to be legitimate, or in some sense valid, for life is beset with many demands, internal and external, which claim superiority but which do so unjustifiably. The claims of any particular moral prescription must be recognized as rightful claims before we are bound by them.

The legitimacy of a moral prescription is, in turn, a rather complicated notion. It entails that the claims are well-grounded. This again involves, generally, that some kind of proof or argument is available to justify these claims.

The first element in legitimacy is, therefore, the possibility of justification. Now this does not imply that argument from more basic premises is always possible, but only that if it is not possible, some reason for there being no such argument must be given. (Only if we admit this possibility can we account for some types of intuitionism and moral sense theories.)

A second element in legitimacy is the requirement of intersubjective validity; that is, *ceteris paribus* moral prescriptions must be considered equally binding upon oneself and others. In this sense, they may be said to be "impersonal" or "social." Thus a moralist when honestly commending a moral prescription must be able to assume that if he were in the same position as the listener he would try to fulfill it. As we have seen, ethical discourse is to be distinguished from a mere expression of the speaker's preferences or wishes, and this insistence on what has been called "intersubjective validity" accomplishes at least part of this differentiation. Moreover, it accounts for the obvious fact that in order to be successful a speaker commending moral prescriptions must be thought by the listener to accept them himself. A pseudo moralist who gives moral advice which he himself would not follow is regarded as a hypocrite, and his ethical discourse is as liable to the same failure as that which anyone faces when he tries to get the listener to believe something which he himself obviously does not believe.

It should be noted that this suggested intersubjective element in legitimacy is not nearly so strong a requirement as some of those discussed earlier. It assures us some sort of disinterestedness without involving the spectator approach to morality.[37] Again, it provides a kind of generalizability but does not insist on universalizability.[38] The conception of "intersubjective validity" is therefore neutral with respect to an ethics of disinterestedness, of egoism, of altruism, of social welfare, of universal laws, and so on, while at the same time it makes possible some type of genuine agreement or disagreement about moral prescriptions. If this element is denied, ethical disputes would be transformed into disputes about private tastes over which there can proverbially be no argument; hence, the element of intersubjective validity is a necessary condition of public ethical discussion as well as moral counseling. Again, the way in which it is assured varies with different ethical systems.

The third element in legitimacy is the requirement that moral prescriptions be in a sense founded on the nature of things. This requires that they be in some way derived from man's conception of human nature, or of the world, or of reality in general (including supernatural reality). This demand is satisfied in many different ways by various ethical systems. For example, ethical hedonism is founded on psychological hedonism, contemporary intuitionism assumes that ethical characteristics are properties of real things, and Stoicism is founded on the Logos of Nature. I suggest that every ethical system must have such a foundation, although, of course, moral prescriptions cannot strictly be deduced from it without committing the so-called "naturalistic fallacy" (the fallacy of deducing a prescriptive from a nonprescriptive statement).

This intimate relation with a fundamental part of reality is what lends to morality the quality of sacredness mentioned by Durkheim. In view of the numerous variations of doctrine, it is impossible to define "sacredness" any more specifically.

Legitimacy consists then of these three elements: justifiability, intersubjective validity, and a foundation in reality. It is clear that each of these involves the others, and it is difficult to distinguish one from another. Thus, for instance, the possibility of ethical argumentation already entails that it be communicable to others, and its realistic foundation gives it a kind of ground which is intersubjectively valid and justifies the moral prescription in question.

It is apparent that the whole conception of legitimacy revolves around the type of justification which is available for a proposed moral prescription. Hence we can expect to reach a better understanding of it after we have examined the various modes of justification that are employed by the different ethical systems. This will be undertaken in Chapter IX.

The requirement of legitimacy in these three aspects accords well with many of the traditional theories of ethics which consider morality as characteristically an object of reason, in the sense in which this notion is common to all the different types of ethical theory, such as intuitionism, hedonism, or eudaimonism. It is also perhaps what many have meant by the "objectivity of moral judgments."

Before leaving this topic, I should like to remind the reader that the entire discussion of superiority and legitimacy must be considered from the point of view of descriptive ethics; that is, I have been describing the characteristics that moral prescriptions are *thought* to have. Whether or not any specifically proposed moral prescription does have these characteristics is a question for normative and not descriptive ethics. In this study we are concerned merely with finding out how people think and talk about moral questions, and not with whether what they think or say is correct. Thus, a morality which supposes its legitimacy to be founded on a superstitious belief in animism, would still have all these three characteristics attributed to its moral prescriptions by the informant, although the whole system might appear absurd to us.

5. CLUES FOR THE IDENTIFICATION OF ETHICAL DISCOURSE

The analysis which has been presented explicates statements about moral obligation in terms of prescriptions for conduct which are superior in that they claim sufficiency, ultimacy, and priority, and are thought to be legitimate in that they are justifiable, intersubjectively valid, and founded in reality.

It may be thought that this characterization of moral prescriptions is much too general and vague to be applicable in specific investigations in descriptive ethics. I should be the first to admit its deficiencies. My proposals are admittedly tentative and are intended to be suggestive of the type of approach considered most promising. Further analysis is necessary both for theoretical philosophical reasons, and in order to produce an operationally more precise and usable definition of "ethical discourse." However, I hope that the analysis offered here may be of some help in showing us where to look for ethical data.

At this point, it may be worth while to note some clues following from the analysis which may be used in identifying ethical discourse. First, the emphasis throughout has been upon moral prescriptions as providing the core of any ethical system. This suggests that we should begin the investigation of an informant's ethics by attempting to discover what moral prescriptions are accepted by him. Since the acceptance of the moral prescriptions in question must be explicitly recognized by the informant himself, we can rely upon his statements with respect to them as direct evidence. To begin with, therefore, we must seek to obtain specific prescriptive statements from the informant.

There might be some doubt, however, as to whether the prescriptions expressed in these statements are moral or not. Here we must resort to more indirect means to determine this. We should try to discover whether he regards them as having the required superiority and legitimacy. This can be done in several different ways.

We may begin by finding out what prescriptions are proposed in certain situations in which we should normally expect ethical discourse to occur. It does not seem too arbitrary to assume that we may expect to encounter ethical discourse in the relatively formal discourses given by leaders to their people on the conduct expected of them. For instance, where the talks to children are conducted in a more serious atmosphere, we should expect the requirement of legitimacy to be fulfilled. The prescriptions commended can then be ranged in order of superiority by comparison with other prescriptive statements. Gradually, the moral prescriptions will become evident.

In addition to the instruction of children, there are other situations in which ethical discourse in a relatively pure form is likely to occur. Such contexts will appear quite clearly to the investigator after he starts his interviewing. For instance, among the Navahos we find a practice, which is probably typical of non-literate societies, of appealing to certain elderly wise men who are 'good talkers' to come in from the outside and to give moral talks and mediate disputes. These wise men give formal moral talks at important gatherings: at weddings, curing ceremonies, before and after a person's death, as well as during the airing of disputes. Such people I have called *moralists,* and it is clear that the whole community regards their discourse as worthy of respect.

From the definition of "ethical discourse" which I have offered, it follows that such discourse is peculiarly characteristic of the moralists, and may rarely be encountered in the common man, the man of action. Only the 'thinker' is able to discriminate clearly between moral and nonmoral prescriptions, and to recognize with some degree of exactitude and precision the prescriptions which he thinks should be advocated and followed.

Another important set of clues can be derived from the linguistic vehicles employed by the informant. Thus words like "duty," "right," "wrong," "obligation," as well as "good," "bad," "virtuous," and so on, serve conveniently to identify ethical as distinct from nonethical discourse. Grammatical structure may also serve as a clue. These are, of course, the easiest means available to the investigator, but must be used with care. All these English words can be used in nonethical contexts as well as ethically. In ordinary English, we distinguish between ethical and nonethical usages intuitively — this actually amounts to taking into account the way they are used as well as the context in which these expressions occur — we note who is doing the talking, his manner of talking, the listeners, and his purposes. All these considerations are covered by what has been already mentioned above, and I suggest that their relevance is entailed by the analysis of moral prescriptions and ethical discourse offered in this chapter.

PART II

THE STRUCTURE OF ETHICAL DISCOURSE

In Part I it was argued that the subject matter of descriptive ethics is ethical discourse and that the method it should employ is the method of hypothetical reconstruction. It will be recalled that this consists of discovering some ethical system which can serve as a model for explaining and predicting the statements of informants. Our task now is to determine the nature of ethical systems in general, for only when we have a clear conception of what we mean by an "ethical system" will we be able to formulate hypotheses in descriptive ethics. I shall approach the conception of "ethical system" by examining the various types of ethical reasoning. Since ethical reasoning is a complex process we must consider its various elements separately: the components of a prescriptive statement, the logic of ethical inference, and the pragmatic conditions of ethical argumentation.

VI

Components of a Prescription: Prescriptive Qualities

I. LOGICAL ANALYSIS OF PRESCRIPTIVE STATEMENTS

The logical structure of prescriptive statements is complex. Prescriptive statements may indicate either the acceptance or the rejection of a prescription. In this sense, they are like any other type of statement which affirms or denies a proposition. This aspect of prescriptive statements may be illustrated by the following pair of statements: "It is true that lying is always wrong" (affirmation); and "It is false that lying is always wrong" (denial). (Note that the latter does not say either that lying is sometimes right, or that it is indifferent. It is merely a denial of the first statement.)

The prescriptions themselves, whether accepted or rejected, also have a complex structure. Any prescription consists of two parts: the description of the act prescribed (for example, lying); and the quality of the prescription, which determines whether the act is enjoined, forbidden, or permitted,[1] (for example, its rightness or wrongness). These two components will be referred to respectively as the *prescriptum* and the *prescriptive quality*.

The completed action, which constitutes the fulfillment of the prescription as a whole, I have called its *objective*. Thus, when the objective is a fact, the prescription has been fulfilled. As I indicated earlier, I shall refer to the nonfulfillment of a negative prescription as a *violation*.[2]

To illustrate the use of these terms, let us consider the following example. If someone says, "It is wrong to shoot the tyrant," this prescription consists of the prescriptum, "shooting the tyrant," and of the prescriptive quality, "wrongness." The same prescriptum might serve as a component in the positive prescription, "It is obligatory to shoot the tyrant." Prescriptive qualities may be communicated by using the imperative (or prohibitive) mood, or by using words like "ought," "right," "duty," "desirable," "fitting," and their opposites. We may also include as a prescriptive quality, the quality of permittedness, which is often suggested by such terms as "all right" or "neither right nor wrong." (Strictly speaking, this must be analyzed in terms of the denial of a prescription.)

The objective of the prescription, "It is one's duty to shoot the tyrant" is the tyrant's being shot; whereas the objective of "It is wrong to shoot the tyrant" is his not being shot. If in the latter case, he actually is shot, the prescription has been violated.

a. Imperatives and prescriptions

The kind of distinctions mentioned above and their significant logical consequences have been brought out in contemporary discussions of the logic of imperatives.[3] The syntactical structure of imperatives reveals that some such distinction as I have made is necessary in order to understand the logical interrelationships of imperatives. Since their syntactical structure is the same, we may expect the logical interrelationships between prescriptions to be like those between imperatives.

There are two general lines of approach to the logic of imperatives. The first divides an imperative into an act and an imperative quality (deontic quality). This procedure results in a logical system analogous to modal logic. It is the one adopted by von Wright. The second method is to extract that element in an imperative which refers to the state of affairs enjoined or prohibited and to construct imperatives out of this. This element can be called an unasserted proposition. The advocates of this approach contend that we can construct positive and negative imperatives as well as assertions and denials out of the same proposition. For example, take the unasserted proposition, "shooting the tyrant," from which we can form the following combinations:

Assertion: (a) "shooting the tyrant" is false; "the tyrant was[4] not shot."
              (b) "shooting the tyrant" is true; "the tyrant was shot."
Imperative: (a) "shooting the tyrant" is obligatory; "someone ought to shoot the tyrant." (?)
              (b) "shooting the tyrant" is wrong; "no one ought to shoot the tyrant." (?)

Various names have been given to the unasserted propositional component and the imperative quality: *descriptor* and *dictor* (Duncan-Jones), *phrastic* and *neustic* (Hare), the *what* and *quality* of the imperative (Hall).

Both the modal and the propositional methods have advantages and disadvantages. One of the disadvantages of the propositional approach is that it appears to entail that we can construct imperatives out of any proposition. For example, we may not only assert or deny that the sun will rise tomorrow, but can command it to or not to. On the other hand, the propositional approach makes certain kinds of inference structurally more elegant.

Von Wright's modal approach is more useful for the analysis which I shall develop in the next few chapters, and the distinction which I have adopted of prescriptum and prescriptive quality is analogous to his, although not identical.

b. Kinds of negation

The complexity of prescriptive statements may best be elucidated by distinguishing between the three different senses in which they may be said to be affirmative or negative. These different senses constitute three antitheses and it is important not to confuse them.

The first is between the affirmation and the denial of a prescription. Thus, if you advance a prescription by saying, "You ought to give up smoking," or "Smoking is wrong," I can well counter by denying this prescription and say, "No, it is false that I ought to give up smoking," or "No, smoking is not wrong." It is noteworthy that the denial of a prescription, if the prescription is a prohibition, is equivalent to affirming the permissiveness of the act in question. In the examples just given, the denial of the prohibition against smoking is the same as saying, "It is all right to smoke." According to the views that I have presented earlier, this antithesis is embodied in the prescriptive statements themselves, which may either affirm or deny the prescription, that is, express acceptance or non-acceptance of the prescription.

The second antithesis we encounter in prescriptions is that between enjoining and forbidding an action. An injunction tells a person to do something, whereas a prohibition tells him not to do it. "Give up smoking!" expresses an injunction, while "Do not smoke!" expresses a prohibition. Injunctions may be expressed by positive imperatives or by such words as "ought," "duty," or "right," whereas prohibitions may be expressed by negative imperatives or by "ought not," or "wrong." According to my terminology, these are all expressions for prescriptive qualities — hence the second antithesis corresponds to the difference between positive and negative prescriptive qualities.

The third antithesis which may occur in a prescription is that between the performance and the nonperformance of an act, that is, the doing or the not doing of something. For example, I may say: "Giving up smoking is obligatory," or "Not giving up smoking is wrong," or "It is desirable to give Jones $5," or "It is desirable *not* to give him $5." Thus, in forming a prescription we must decide both whether the prescriptive quality is to be positive or negative, and whether the performance or the nonperformance of the act is in question. It is obvious that there are certain equivalences and even identical uses of expressions between the second and the third antithesis. For example, "You ought not to smoke," might express either the prohibition of smoking or the injunction of not-smoking. The relations will become clear presently.

Although the first two antitheses can be described by using the terms which I have introduced earlier, prescriptive statements and prescriptive qualities, it should be noted that my third technical term, prescriptum, does not apply in the third antithesis. This antithesis is between the performance and nonperformance of a certain act, but the term "prescriptum" refers to the act in question, irrespective of whether its performance or non-performance is required. In order to facilitate the following discussion, I shall coin a new set of terms to stand for these opposites: *positive prescript* and *negative prescript*. (I shall show later that these terms can be dispensed with.)

By combining these three antitheses, we can construct eight different complexes. These combinations, with examples, are listed in the following table. I have included the objective, the action which would fulfill or not violate the prescription, in order to bring out the equivalences.

(a) *Statement*	(b) *Prescriptive Quality*	(c) *Prescript*	(d) *Objective*
1. Affirmation (of)	Injunction	to commit an act (A)[a]	Performance of A Truth-telling
e.g. "It is obligatory to tell the truth"			
2. Affirmation (of)	Prohibition	to commit an act (B)	Nonperformance of B Not lying
e.g. "It is wrong to lie"			
3. Affirmation (of)	Injunction	to omit an act (B)	Nonperformance of B Not lying
e.g. "It is obligatory not to lie"			
4. Affirmation (of)	Prohibition	to omit an act (A)	Performance of A Truth-telling
e.g. "It is wrong not to tell the truth"			
5. Denial (of)	Prohibition	to commit an act (C)	No objective
e.g. "It is not wrong to smoke"			

(Other denials can be constructed on 1–4. None of them have an objective.)
Denial of an injunction will be called an *option:*[b] "It is not obligatory — "
Denial of a prohibition will be called a *permission:* "It is not wrong — "

Denial of both an injunction and prohibition with respect to same prescriptum is an affirmation of its *indifference:* "It is neither obligatory nor wrong to do — ."

a. It should be noted that the letters (*A*), (*B*), and (*C*) stand for prescripta.

b. There is no accepted expression for a statement that denies that an act is a positive duty without at the same time denying that it is wrong (that is, indifference). So I have used the word "optional" with this special meaning. Since the situation is rather rare, if it ever occurs, the distinction between option and permission is unimportant.

c. Immediate logical relations

An examination of the objective of the kinds of prescriptions reveals the essential equivalences and differences between these various combinations. It is clear that (1) and (4) are equivalent, and that (2) and (3) are also equivalent, and furthermore that all the denials of prescriptions are permissions, options, or statements of indifference.

These facts have suggested that there are actually only three basic types of prescriptive statements; namely, those stating injunctions, prohibitions, and permissions (to do and not to do). These three would be

A is obligatory

  (Performance enjoined)
  Objective: Performance of **A**

A is wrong

  (Performance forbidden)
  Objective: Nonperformance of **A**

CONTRARIES

SUBALTERNS

CONTRA- DICTORIES

CONTRA- DICTORIES

SUBALTERNS

SUB-CONTRARIES

A is not wrong

  (Performance permitted
    or not prohibited)
  No objective

A is not obligatory

  (Performance not enjoined)
  No objective

A is indifferent

  (Performance neither prohibited
    nor enjoined)
  No objective

(See page 116)

equivalent to another set; namely, prescriptions for the performance of an action, prescriptions for the nonperformance of an action, and denial of prescriptions.

If we assume this to be correct we may construct a square of opposition similar to that used for modal logic (p. 115). If we give the usual interpretation of such squares we arrive at the following: (1) for contraries, if one is affirmed the other must be denied, but both may be denied (for example, if A is obligatory it cannot be wrong, and if it is wrong it cannot be obligatory, but it may be neither obligatory nor wrong); (2) for contradictories, if one is affirmed the other must be denied, and if one is denied the other must be affirmed (for example, if A is obligatory then it is 'false' that A is optional, and conversely); (3) for subalterns, if the first is affirmed the second may be affirmed (for example, if A is obligatory then A is not wrong), but not conversely; (4) for subcontraries, both cannot be denied, but both may be affirmed (for example, A may be neither wrong nor obligatory, but it cannot be both wrong and obligatory).[5]

This square provides us with some obvious immediate inferences in dealing with prescriptions. For instance, the prescription that it is obligatory to shoot the tyrant cancels prescriptions forbidding the shooting or permission not to shoot him. Since these inferences are trivial I shall omit them in the following discussion.

These logical interrelationships have suggested to philosophers the project of defining some moral concepts by others. For example, von Wright defines "obligatory" and "wrong" in terms of "permittedness" and "nonperformance," as follows:

A is obligatory	$=$	Not permitted nonperformance of A,
A is wrong	$=$	Not permitted performance of A,
A is not wrong	$=$	Permitted performance of A,
A is indifferent	$=$	Permitted performance and nonperformance of A.

It should be noted that the denial of prescriptions generated three different kinds of permittedness: permittedness to do (not wrong), option not to do (not obligatory), and the combination of these (which is called indifference). (Von Wright uses "permittedness" only in the first sense, but defines "indifference" by the combination.)

It is obviously just as easy to define these concepts in terms of "wrong" and "nonperformance":

A is obligatory	$=$	Nonperformance of A is wrong,
A is permitted	$=$	Performance of A is not wrong,
A is optional	$=$	Nonperformance of A is not wrong,
A is indifferent	$=$	Nonperformance of A and performance of A are not wrong.

This part of the logical analysis of prescriptions (imperatives) is fairly clear and plausible. However, it is also evident that it is just as easy to define "permittedness" and "nonperformance" in terms of "obligatoriness" and "wrongness," since, in any case, the number of primitive terms remains the same. For various reasons, which I shall give presently, it seems desirable to eliminate the notion of "nonperformance," and with it the terms "positive" and "negative prescript." By so doing we can define all the relationships mentioned in this section in terms of positive and negative prescriptive statements, positive and negative prescriptive qualities, and a prescriptum (which is neutral).

The reductions given above do not seem to me to do full justice to the richness of the language of morality — or, more specifically, to the variety of types of prescriptions. The artificiality of these analyses will be criticized on two points: the error of reducing obligatoriness to wrongness; and the neglect of the varying types of stringency of moral prescriptions.

2. POSITIVE AND NEGATIVE PRESCRIPTIVE QUALITIES

a. The notion of nonperformance

As we have seen, some philosophers have contended that the prohibition of an act is equivalent to the injunction of the nonperformance of it. We may begin by examining this notion of nonperformance.

The nonperformance of A is not to be identified with the performance of non-A, that is, the performance of acts other than A. This is evident from the fact that the nonperformance of A does not entail the performance of non-A; nor does the performance of non-A entail the nonperformance of A. In other words, the performance or nonperformance of A is perfectly compatible with either the performance or nonperformance of non-A. For example, I can refrain from lying (A), and still do many other things, such as eat or sleep (non-A's); or I can refrain from doing these other things and still refrain from lying.

In contrast to the compatibility of the nonperformance of A with the performance or nonperformance of non-A, the performance and nonperformance of A are incompatible. If one is prescribed the other cannot be, and in this sense they may be said to be logically incompatible. In the terms introduced earlier, the objectives of an injunction of the performance of A and of the nonperformance of A are contradictory.

Thus far we have considered entailment and incompatibility only in the logical sense. We may however also introduce what might be called "etiological entailment" and "etiological incompatibility," which are the consequence of the causal dependencies of actions on other actions. Thus the act of sleeping is etiologically incompatible with the act of telling a lie; or, the act of sleeping etiologically entails that one is not lying. If these etiological categories are introduced, it is obvious that some of the statements made above will have to be modified. Thus, an injunction of the nonperformance of A might etiologically entail the performance of certain non-A's, and so on. For example, in order to obey the prescription against looking at one's mother-in-law (nonperformance of A), the performance of certain other acts, such as leaving the hogan or asking someone to tell her that one is in the hogan will be entailed.[6]

But since we are at present interested only in the purely logical aspects of prescriptive discourse, we may ignore these etiological relationships. The injunction not to perform A does not by itself logically entail the performance of any other act. Thus I can fulfill this injunction by doing anything else but A, or by doing nothing at all. In other words, it is evident that the injunction of the nonperformance of A is only about A and not about any other possible acts.

Now, if an injunction of the nonperformance A can be understood only in its reference to A and not to any other acts, we may ask: "What does it say about A?" What is meant by the terms "nonperformance of A"? I submit that the only way that these questions can be answered is by introducing the notion of "prohibition." In other words, if the nonperformance of A is enjoined, we mean nothing more than that it is prohibited or that it ought not to be done. Unless some further explication of "nonperformance" is offered, it would seem that there is no more reason to prefer it as a primitive term than terms standing for negative prescriptive qualities, such as "wrongness" or "ought-not-to-be-doneness."

So far I have argued that the notion of "nonperformance" does not advance our understanding of the conception of "prohibition." Therefore, there does not seem to be any good reason for translating "prohibitions" into "injunctions of nonperformances." I shall now try to show that such a translation is impossible because of certain basic dissimilarities between prohibitions and injunctions.

b. Differences between injunctions and prohibitions

There are certain logical differences between injunctions and prohibitions, and they awaken doubts about the equivalence of the prohibition of an act to the injunction of its nonperformance.

In order to bring out the contrast, let us assume hypothetically that there is only one act (or class of acts), A, which is prescribed. We can then compare the injunction of A with the prohibition of it. According to the view under scrutiny the prohibition of A would be the injunction of the nonperformance of A, and the injunction of the performance of A would be equivalent to the prohibition of the nonperformance of A. All non-A's would in the former case be permitted, and in the latter case optional (since by hypothesis there are no other prescriptions).

What do such prohibitory and injunctive statements maintain? The prohibition of A says in effect: "Whatever you do, it must not be A." Thus it circumscribes one's actions so as to exclude A. If the statement is a universal prescription, as many are, it excludes all A's; for example, "All lying is wrong." Such universal negative prescriptions have two distinctive characteristics: first, the line between prohibited acts (A's) and nonprohibited ones (non-A's) is sharply drawn; and second, the class of prohibited acts (A's) may be infinite in extent or at least there may be an indefinitely large number of possible A's; for example, many acts of lying.

An injunction, on the other hand, says in effect: "Whatever you do, it must include A(s)." It thus demands inclusion rather than exclusion of A in one's conduct. But does it enjoin the inclusion of all A's, or merely of some A's (that is, at least one)? Let us consider these alternative interpretations.

Suppose that we assume that an injunction of A demands that all possible A's be performed. If an injunction can be transformed into a prohibition of nonperformance, this would entail that every nonperformance of a possible A is wrong. But if the class of A's is infinitely large (as was assumed above), then it would be impossible not to violate the prohibition (or to fulfill the injunction) to do them for it would require performing an infinite number of acts. Thus, for instance, the injunction "always tell the truth" would entail that one ought to do all possible acts of truth-telling; and it is obvious that this is impossible even if one spent his whole life doing nothing but that! The injunction could never be fulfilled because the performance of an infinite number of possible acts is physically if not logically impossible. (Incidentally, the practical effect would be that the performance of any non-A would be wrong, since there would be no time left for anything except doing A's.)

In contrast, it is possible to conform to a prohibition, even though it may cover an infinite number of acts (A's). Therefore although the class of A's is infinite in extent, one difference between prohibitions and injunctions (according to this interpretation) is that it is possible to completely conform to the one, whereas it is impossible for the other.

This suggests that injunctions should be treated somewhat differently from prohibitions of nonperformances. Only if it be admitted that they are in a sense looser than prohibitions, is it possible to explain how they can be fulfilled. That they are less determinate and sharply drawn than prohibitions may be seen in the two prescriptions: "You ought not to commit adultery"; and "You ought to help your parents." The first is precise and definite, whereas the second is relatively indefinite, for it calls not for every possible act of help, but rather for an unspecified number of them.

This difference does not, however, mean that injunctions and prohibitions are not opposed to each other, for the opposition between an injunction and a prohibition of the same act (or class of acts) consists in the incompatibility of their objectives; that is, the act(s) which fulfill the injunction would violate the prohibition and *vice versa*. For example, if A is enjoined, the fulfillment of this injunction would consist in performing at least one A; whereas if it were prohibited, the fulfillment would consist in never performing any A's — and the performance of any single A would constitute a violation of the prohibition. Thus the objectives of an injunction and a prohibition are incompatible inasmuch as any single occurrence of A is incompatible with the nonoccurrence of all A's. In logical terms, the incompatibility of the objectives of an injunction and a prohibition of the same prescriptum is like the contradiction between a particular affirmative proposition and a universal negative proposition; it is the same kind of opposition which exists between "no lies are told" and "some (at least one) lies are told." Hence, the opposition between a negative and a positive prescription is based on the incompatibility of their objectives; but it is a weaker opposition than that which is assumed between all performances of A and all nonperformances of A.

This new interpretation accords more closely with our ordinary use of ethical terms like "ought," "duty," or "right," for these do not usually demand every conceivable act of the kind prescribed, but instead they require at least one. The contrast as well as the basic opposition between positive and negative prescriptions can be illustrated by the two following statements: "You ought to commit adultery"; and "You ought not to commit adultery." The first calls for at least one act of adultery, whereas the second excludes every possible act of adultery. Moreover, the first is indeterminate because it does not state when, where, and under what circumstances it should be done, but the second does, for it simply says never, nowhere, and under no circumstances.

That this contrast is not confined to the type of prescriptions just considered may be brought out by the example given earlier about shooting the tyrant. Compare the two prescriptive statements: "You ought to shoot the tyrant," and "You ought not to shoot the tyrant." The first of these offers some freedom of choice in carrying out the prescription. For instance, it does not specify when one should shoot, nor with what kind of gun, nor after what kind of preparations, and so on. These are all left up to the agent — and any one of the effective means which he selects will fulfill the injunction. On the other hand, in the case of prohibition there is no choice whatsoever of these particulars — it is wrong at all times and with all kinds of guns and with all possible types of preparation. In positive prescriptions, at least a few of the conditions of fulfillment are indeterminate, in the sense of being left to the choice of the agent, whereas for negative prescriptions the conditions of violation are determinate, and they are not up to the choice of the agent.[7] In the latter, the agent can choose to do or not to do, but not how not to do. Injunctions of this type demand only that *at least one* effective action be performed, whereas prohibitions demand that *all* effective actions be avoided.[8]

The point which I wish to make may be brought out if we fill in the prescription used as an example above. Suppose the example said: "You ought to shoot the tyrant, but decide for yourself when and how to do it!" The analogous negative prescription does not make sense: "Do not shoot the tyrant, but decide for yourself when and how to (or not to) do it!"[9]

There are many puzzles involved in analyzing the differences between positive and negative prescriptions, as there are in all philosophical problems connected with negation. It will be sufficient to recognize that positive prescriptions involve a greater latitude of choice than negative ones do (given the same prescriptum).

So far we have considered prescriptions, positive and negative, with unrestricted application, where the circumstances under which they are invoked are not specified. It must be admitted that although unrestricted positive prescriptions are less determinate than the prohibitions of the same prescriptum, nevertheless there are some positive prescriptions which are universal and determinate in the same way as negative prescriptions.

For example, although it would be absurd to construe "all truth-telling is obligatory" as the prohibition of any nonperformance of the act of truth-telling, if we add the restriction "while talking," it does not appear to be absurd. Thus the amended statement, "Whenever talking, truth-telling is obligatory" seems to be strictly equivalent to "It is wrong to lie." Where there is a limitation of the context of relevant actions, through a specification of the invoking circumstances (such as acts of talking), it would appear that a restricted positive injunction can be at once universal and convertible into a corresponding prohibition of nonperformance.

In many such cases there is such a strict equivalence, but I suggest that these ostensibly positive prescriptions are *prohibitions in disguise*. That they are merely disguised negative prescriptions can be proven as follows. In the pairs given above, "truth-telling" and "lying" can be defined as acts which are the negatives of each other. Thus, "lying" is synonymous with "not telling the truth," and "not lying" with "telling the truth." Let us call the one class of acts A and the other class of acts non-A. We can then form a new class which has as members all the acts which are A or non-A, and no members which are neither. Let us call this class B. Then any member of B

must be either an A or a non-A, and if it is A, it is not non-A, and, if it is non-A it is not A. (In logical terms, B is the logical sum of A and non-A; and the classes A and non-A exclude each other.)

In a restricted context, namely, one in which every act belongs to a class (B) of which every member is either A or non-A, but not both, the performance of A would entail the nonperformance of non-A, and the performance of non-A would entail the nonperformance of A. In other words, the nonperformance of A would be equivalent to the performance of non-A. Consequently, the injunction of A would be equivalent to the prohibition of non-A.

To illustrate: suppose that the only acts in question were acts of talking (B), then any one of such acts must be either an act of truth-telling (A), or an act of lying (non-A); but it cannot be both. It would follow that the injunction of truth-telling is strictly equivalent to the prohibition of lying. In this case, the injunction would be universal in the sense that it applies to all the acts of talking, that is, all of B; and thus its logical structure would be identical with that of a prohibition.

For these reasons, it should be apparent that an injunction cannot be translated into a prohibition except in cases in which the nonperformance of the prohibited act is equivalent to the performance of the enjoined act. We have seen that this condition only holds for limited contexts of a type where given a certain activity there are only two possibilities, and the doing of one excludes the doing of the other.[10]

If we exclude those injunctions which are prohibitions in disguise, we must conclude that injunctions cannot be reduced to prohibitions of nonperformances. It follows that we should adopt as primitive the opposites, positive and negative prescriptive qualities, as expressed in such terms as "ought" and "ought not," "obligatory" and "wrong," or "right" and "not right" (a weaker form of "wrong"). By doing so, we can dispense entirely with the notion of "nonperformance" in our analysis of prescriptions. The "nonperformance of A" can be defined as the "objective of a negative prescription."

Consequently, I conclude that we should regard every prescription as positive or negative, an injunction or a prohibition, by virtue of its prescriptive quality alone. All acts, prescripta, will be considered positive (or neutral), and when the act is performed it either fulfills an injunction or violates a prohibition.

The fact that we are unable to reduce or define positive prescriptive qualities in terms of negative ones is more of an advantage than a disadvantage, because it directs our attention to the characteristic differences between them. I shall now briefly examine some ways in which these contrasting properties of positive and negative prescriptions are exemplified in ethical discourse.

c. Directive and constraining qualities

We have seen that prescriptions with negative prescriptive qualities define their objectives, that is, their conditions of violation, more determinately and unambiguously than do positive prescriptions. Characteristically, negative prescriptions are determinate and allow no freedom of choice; whereas positive prescriptions are more vague and allow some latitude in fulfillment, if only as to time and place. The lines drawn by negative prescriptions tend to be sharp whereas those drawn by positive prescriptions are fuzzy. The example given above which compares the injunction and the prohibition of shooting the tyrant is a basic paradigm of every prescription, since, as I shall argue later, most if not all prescripta involve either the choice of at least one means or the avoidance of all conditions leading to a particular state of affairs.[11]

In consequence, we may expect to find that the logic of positive prescriptions differs from that of negative prescriptions. Thus, in the injunction, "help others," there is considerable latitude of choice in selecting those actions to fulfill it since there are many possible ways of helping others. In contrast, in a prohibition of marital infidelity, the unpermitted lines of conduct are unequivocal. (For further illustrations see Part III.)

These characteristics of positive and negative prescriptions bring out the basic differences between what may be called an *ethics of direction* and an *ethics of constraint*. If a moral code consists only of positive prescriptions, the directives are general and vague. Moreover, since no particular action is unequivocally demanded because there are alternative actions which will do just as well, there are no sharp lines between what is morally prescribed and what is not prescribed. A positive morality therefore has a tendency to spread over the whole of conduct, while at the same time it never applies to any one particular act with absolute stringency.

A moral code of negative prescriptions, on the other hand, does draw a sharp line between permitted and unpermitted (wrong) acts. Those acts which are thought to be wrong are unequivocally so, and there is complete unrestricted freedom to do anything one wishes outside the areas of conduct prohibited. So in a negative morality we may expect to find large segments of behavior which are not the subject of morality, as well as certain specific parts which are absolutely prohibited, whereas in a positive morality there may be no such clear-cut distinction between the moral and the nonmoral. A negative morality tends to limit the jurisdiction of morality, which in a positive morality is unlimited.

These distinctive characteristics of negative and positive moral codes may explain some of the differences between the codes of so-called "primitive" peoples and those of more advanced cultures. From the accounts which we do have of primitive moral codes, it would appear that they are characterized by the properties just mentioned.

The transformation from negative to positive prescriptions can be seen in the development of Hebraic ethics. Originally, we are told, all of the Ten Commandments were expressed as prohibitions. Of the 613 prescriptions of the Mosaic law, 365 are considered as prohibitions, and 248 are called "mandates". In all probability, most of the latter are disguised prohibitions.

When these prescriptions were subsumed under the two laws, love God and your neighbor, the ethics had been converted into a positive moral code. The typical difference between the legalistic approach of the priests and the more positive teaching of the prophets (and of Jesus), brings out the contrast between a negative and a positive moral code — an ethics of constraint and an ethics of direction. For example, in the incident reported in the Gospels in which the Pharisees criticize Jesus for healing a man on the Sabbath, we see at the same time the severity of the one and the greater flexibility of the other. It was right to heal someone, although surely Jesus would not have done wrong if he had not. His actions can only be interpreted positively.

The moralists who developed the legalistic system of Judaic ethics made the mistake, however, of extending the scope of morality to almost every detail of daily life. By doing so, they distorted the characteristic pattern of negative morality which leaves a large area of conduct completely free for the individual. In order to achieve a modicum of viability for their system, they had to admit degrees of stringency. (This will be discussed presently.) A better example of a moral code which is largely negative is that of the Navahos. There are probably many others which could be cited. Many so-called "primitive" ethical systems restrict the sphere of morality to definitely prohibited lines of conduct, and thus admit many indifferent actions.

The properties of an ethics of direction which are entailed by its use of positive prescriptions are illustrated by Greek ethics (for example, Aristotle), large parts of Christian ethics, and those of some contemporary naturalists (for example, Dewey). Among all these, we may observe the twofold pattern of extending the sphere of morality to cover almost all of a person's conduct, and the vagueness of their prescriptions. For instance, Aristotle proposes some general positive standards of conduct (listed as virtues), but the application of them ('choice') is to be determined by the agent: there are many ways of being courageous or temperate, and no single class of actions is determinately prescribed. We also find this characteristic 'fuzziness' in Dewey's ethics; not only does he equate ethics with practical reasoning in general (like Aristotle), thus covering almost the whole of conduct, but he also leaves the choice of how to carry out the basic principle of 'growth' (or whatever it may be) up to the discretion of the individual.

3. DEGREES OF STRINGENCY

a. Moral injunctions, counsels, prohibitions, and discounsels

Moral philosophers have tended to neglect one most significant aspect of moral prescriptions, namely, the fact that they vary in degree of stringency. By this I mean that certain prescriptions are regarded as more forceful and demanding than others. I shall assume that the degree of stringency of a prescription is contained in its prescriptive quality. Some further distinctive characteristics of positive prescriptions may be revealed in this variability of stringency.[12]

In all ethical discourse we find many different degrees of rightness and wrongness ascribed to actions. Certain obligations may not be as demanding as others: for example, an obligation to keep a promise may be more 'absolute' than one to give to charity. Some obligations require immediate and undeferable actions, whereas others merely demand occasional fulfillment. Often this difference is conveyed by the use of "obligatory" (or "duty") for the one, and of "right" (or "fit") for the other. On the side of negative prescriptions, there are similar distinctions between 'big' wrongs and 'little' wrongs: for example, mortal and venial sins. The lesser duties have sometimes been called "duties of supererogation."

I shall call those positive prescriptions with a high degree of stringency *moral injunctions* and those with a lesser degree of stringency, *moral counsels*. Similarly, I shall distinguish among negative prescriptions between *moral prohibitions* and *moral discounsels*.

The distinction I have in mind corresponds roughly to that made by some Christian moralists between "precepts" and "counsels of perfection": "The difference between a precept and a counsel is this, that the precept is a matter of necessity while the counsel is left to the free choice of the person to whom it is proposed." [13] The Biblical text usually cited is the story of the advice given by Jesus to the young man who asked him what he should do to have eternal life. Jesus first replied by citing the Ten Commandments (precepts), but when the young man said that he had always obeyed them, Jesus added: "If thou wilt be perfect, go and sell that thou hast and give to the poor," etc.[14] It is not necessary to be a saint, but the counsels of perfection tell us how to become one.

Similarly in the Rabbinic moral code with its numerous prescriptions, some distinction has to be made between those which are mandatory and those which are preferred. Sometimes this was done by distinguishing between the ethical and the ceremonial law. Certain rabbis even went so far as to say that only a certain proportion (50 per cent!) of these prescriptions must be fulfilled.

I suspect that every natural moral code must recognize some such variation in stringency, which I have expressed by distinguishing between injunctions and counsels, and prohibitions and discounsels. (I shall apply this distinction later to the prescriptions of the Navaho moral code.)

A few philosophers have also recognized this variation in prescriptive quality. The distinction has sometimes been made in terms of duties of justice and those of benevolence. Accordingly, acts of justice are duties which it is wrong not to do, whereas benevolent acts are not duties but "fit, right and meet to be done." [15]

Kant recognizes the distinction in a footnote in his most widely read work on ethics. It will be recalled that in his discussion and illustrations of the application of the categorical imperative he distinguished between *perfect* and *imperfect duties:* "by perfect duty I here understand a duty which permits no exception in the interest of inclination." [16] This seems to correspond to the distinction between injunctions and counsels for the former allow no exceptions whereas the latter do.

Kant later uses this distinction to divide duties into those of 'right' (justice) and those of virtue, the two being discussed in the parts of the *Metaphysik der Sitten* called respectively, "The Metaphysical Principles of Right" and "The Metaphysical Principles of Virtue." The former include promise-keeping and various acts coming under legal justice, while the latter involve cultivating one's talents and making others happy.

b. Philosophical analysis of these types

If we admit degrees of stringency as just outlined, the question immediately arises whether counsels and discounsels are rightly to be taken as moral prescriptions at all. If a counsel prescribes a certain act (or class of acts) and admits of exceptions, does this not abdicate its claim to priority — a claim which was earlier advanced as one of the distinctive marks of a moral prescription?

One way of assuring ourselves that counsels and discounsels are moral is to show that they can be derived from injunctions and prohibitions which are admitted to be such. By examining the interrelationship between these less stringent prescriptions and the more stringent ones, we may discover whether this is possible; at the same time we may uncover some additional properties of negative and positive prescriptive qualities which we have not yet considered. I shall begin by discussing the reduction to prohibitions.

It has sometimes been maintained that within a moral system every act is either obligatory, wrong, or indifferent. Thus, it would be held, for example, that my visiting my grandmother is either obligatory, wrong, or morally indifferent. Following Hall, I shall call this *the law of exhaustiveness*.[17] This law follows from the definitions of "obligatory" and "wrong" in terms of "permittedness" as given by von Wright (cited earlier). According to this analysis, the performance of any act is permitted, or its performance is wrong, or its nonperformance is wrong (obligatory).

On the basis of the characteristics of negative prescriptions already discussed, it is evident that if all moral prescriptions are negative (including disguised prohibitions), the law of exhaustiveness acquires some plausibility. However, if there are genuine positive prescriptions this law does not hold. Consider the following example: if you were collecting money for the Red Feather campaign, you could hardly claim that giving to the campaign was either obligatory, wrong, or indifferent. Obviously, it is somewhere in between being obligatory and indifferent. You might say that it was right, or fitting, or desirable, but it would be incorrect to say that it was either obligatory or indifferent, that is, if it is assumed that an act that is obligatory or a duty is one which it is wrong not to do. (I have commented upon this already.) But there are other acts which it is right to do, but not wrong not to do.

In a sophisticated version of the view discussed earlier, namely, that an obligatory act is one the nonperformance of which is wrong, there is a plausible analysis to account for the different degrees of stringency expressed by the prescriptive terms "obligatory" and "right" ("fitting"). If it is valid, it would save the law of exhaustiveness. Such an analysis might be given in the following manner.

An absolutely obligatory act would be one that it is wrong not to do. It will be recalled that this is a disguised prohibition, since we can only admit such obligatory acts if the context in which they are invoked is restricted so that the performance of any alternative would be wrong.[18]

A right act would be one which allows of alternatives. Suppose, for example, that there is an absolute obligation to give money to charity; then it would be right to give it to the Red Feather campaign, but it would be equally right to give it to the Salvation Army, the Home for Little Wanderers, and so on. Logically, then, "*A* is right" would be equivalent to: "There are other possible actions, *B*, *C*, *D*, etc., such that it is obligatory to do either *A* or *B* or *C*, etc., but (by itself) *A* is not obligatory, and *B* is not obligatory, etc." Then, in turn, by substituting "wrong not to do" for "obligatory" we can reduce this type of "right-statement" to a "wrong-statement".[19]

By following this procedure, it may be possible to reduce all prescriptions (including counsels) to prohibitions, and thus retain the law of exhaustiveness, namely, the principle that every action must be obligatory, wrong, or indifferent.[20] However, there are still some objections against this reduction.

In the first place, it would have the consequence of enormously complicating an analysis of the many varieties of positive prescriptions. To give a complete reduction would require that every alternative action in a certain context be listed, and furthermore that the context itself be rigorously defined. In practice, of course, this is impossible.

Second, even if such a reduction could be accomplished, it would hardly correspond to any natural way of thinking about positively prescribed acts. When, for example, I think that a certain act is right (or fitting), it never enters my mind that this means that it is a member of a class of alternative acts one of which is obligatory. I may never think of all the alternatives, and possibly of none of them. In other words, the reduction is artificial in the extreme.

Third, the most telling objection against this reduction is that it fails to account for one characteristic variety of positive prescriptions, namely, those in which an action is morally desirable, but never obligatory, and not even a member of a class of obligatory actions. Moreover, it also does not explain why it is morally desirable to do a greater number of right acts. For instance, granted that acts of charity are right, the analysis given above does not show why the more acts of charity one does, the better it is morally. In other words, it provides no standard of comparison between various right acts and quantities of right acts.[21]

These considerations suggest that we may do better to construe the degrees of stringency of prescriptions in terms of positive prescriptive qualities. If these are considered to be irreducible to negative qualities, we could assume that they contain within themselves a variability of stringency. Perhaps the fundamental positive prescriptive quality could be referred to as *moral preferableness*. This is, of course, a comparative term and we could accordingly interpret the statement that a certain act is "morally right" as equivalent to saying that it is "morally preferable" to alternative actions being considered. But it should be noted that this does not require a complete listing of alternatives because it is necessary to include comparison only to those actions envisaged. An obligatory act would be one with the highest moral preferability, and other degrees of rightness could be ranged along the scale until they shade off into complete indifference.

This interpretation of moral qualities has led some philosophers to contend that the primitive moral conception is that of moral "betterness." Accordingly, that act which is obligatory or right is the one which is morally better than others.

This reduction to positive prescriptive qualities, however, has disadvantages of its own. To begin with, just as the reduction of positive to negative prescriptions generated the problem of properly explicating positive qualities as well as degrees of stringency, so in turn, the present reduction encounters some difficulty in interpreting negative prescriptive qualities, such as wrongness. The usual procedure is to regard as wrong, any action which is less morally preferable than its alternatives. Thus Dewey writes:

> The better is the good; the best is not better than the good but is simply the discovered good. Comparative and superlative degrees are only paths to the positive degree of action. The worse or evil is the rejected good. In deliberation and before choice no evil presents itself as evil. Until it is rejected, it is a competing good. After rejection, it figures not as a lesser good, but as the bad of that situation.[22]

The net result of the view that a wrong action is one that is less morally preferable is the substitution of a law of the excluded middle for the law of exhaustiveness. According to this law, every action is either right or wrong, and there are no indifferent acts. This view might be called "ethical Puritanism."

It should be noted that moral preferableness is applied to compare the right act with any other act, including those which might otherwise be considered indifferent. For example, my giving money to the Red Feather campaign is morally preferable to spending it on theater tickets. According to the law of exhaustiveness the latter might be considered indifferent, but the introduction of a comparative prescriptive quality makes it no longer indifferent. Hence the law of the excluded middle is entailed by it.

The use of the notion of "moral preferability" and the consequent application of the law of the excluded middle can be illustrated by Bentham's utilitarianism. Bentham's system admits of no indifferent acts, for an action produces either a surplus of pleasure over pain, or a surplus of pain over pleasure. (The one exception would be the case in which it produced an equal quantity of both.) Indeed, according to G. E. Moore's even more rigoristic interpretation of utilitarianism, it holds that:

> . . . if we had to choose between two actions one of which would have intrinsically better total effects than the other, it always would be our duty to choose the former, and wrong to choose the latter; and that no action ever can be right *if* we could have done anything else instead which would have had intrinsically better total effects, nor wrong, *unless* we could have done something else which would have had intrinsically better total effects.[23]

According to this extreme interpretation, in most cases there would be only one right act, and every other act would be wrong! This contrasts with an ethics of constraint, that is, a negative morality, which assumes that there is a limited number of wrong actions, and all others are indifferent.

We have seen that by treating either positive or negative prescriptions as the basic type of prescription to which the other may be reduced, we are led to either of two extremes entailing the law of the excluded middle on the one hand, or the law of exhaustiveness on the other. In other words, if we wish to make such a reduction, we can choose only between holding that every action is either a duty or wrong, and holding that every action is either a duty, wrong, or indifferent. Neither of these extremes accords with common sense, which recognizes both positive and negative prescriptive qualities, and, in addition, degrees of both.

Counsels and discounsels have prescriptive qualities which place their objectives somewhere in between being completely indifferent and being morally preferable to all alternatives. By combining the notion of "indifference" in the sense of not being wrong to omit, and the notion of "moral preferability" in the sense of the act's being preferable (although not necessarily so) to some other acts, we can come closer to an understanding of their peculiar characteristics.

Although the negative and positive analyses just presented give us the two extremes to be avoided, they point out some minimum requirements. Thus the negative approach subsumes counseled acts under a class of alternative acts of which the nonperformance of at least one is wrong. We may state this as follows: if a person never did any 'fitting' acts (for instance, an act of charity) he would not be fulfilling his duty. We may picture the situation if we imagined a complete moral code consisting of all the possible moral counsels, that is, all those acts which are 'fit, right, and meet to be done' — then we should say that it is obligatory to do at least one of these. But the positive approach adds: the more the better.

Each of the various ethical systems has its own peculiar method or 'logic' by which such counsels are justified. One analysis, for instance, might run as follows: in the normal course of life there are certain actions which have a tendency to some effect; thus, an act of good will tends to promote the happiness of others, and the more of such acts performed the greater the tendency. Such acts, in other words, have a cumulative effect, although no single one is efficacious of itself nor is it necessary. They would be the objects of counsels although not of prescriptions. (I shall later analyze Navaho moral counsels and discounsels along these lines.)

4. IMMEDIATE INFERENCES

I have argued at some length against the reduction of positive prescriptions to negative prescriptions through the notion of "nonperformance," and the converse reduction of negative to positive prescriptions. The 'facts' of ethical discourse indicate that it is better to recognize two basic types of prescriptive qualities, and dispense with the notion of "nonperformance" altogether.

Given this irreducibility can anything more be said about the logical relationship of positive to negative prescriptions? I have suggested that the objective of the one is incompatible with that of the other, that is, that the one cannot be fulfilled without violating the other, and vice versa. This means, in simple language, that the same act(s) cannot be both obligatory (or right) and wrong, but not that it must be either obligatory, wrong, or even indifferent. (In other words, this interpretation entails neither the law of exhaustiveness nor the law of the excluded middle as far as prescriptive qualities are concerned.)

With the conception of "logical incompatibility" we can make certain immediate inferences. Most of these are trivial, and need not be discussed. However, if we admit the additional conception of "etiological incompatibility," we can derive some interesting consequences.[24]

Two of these consequences may be noted here. First, if an act A is etiologically incompatible with an objective which is enjoined, that act would be forbidden. For instance, if a certain act would inevitably make salvation impossible, and if the seeking of salvation were an enjoined objective, that act would be wrong. Second, if another act inevitably produces a situation incompatible with a prohibited objective, that act is enjoined (at least as a right act). Thus, for example, if one way to avoid committing adultery is to leave a tempting woman, then that action is right. (But, note that since there are other ways of avoiding the forbidden act, this action is not stringently obligatory.)

There are other immediate inferences of injunctions from prohibitions that can be drawn by combination and permutation of these principles. Some of these will be explored in Chapter IX, section 2(d). The derivation of counsels and discounsels will also be discussed at the same time.

This chapter has been devoted to the analysis of some of the logical characteristics of prescriptions which are entailed by their prescriptive qualities. It might well be asked what bearing this could have on descriptive ethics, that is, the study of natural moral codes. These, it would seem, do not exemplify the rigorous conceptions discussed here. That is true, and we must recognize the fact that perhaps no natural moral code is completely unambiguous or consistent in the way it conceives of the interrelations of various types of prescriptions. On the other hand, only if we are aware of some of the logical possibilities can we proceed with the type of logical analysis which has been proposed in the method of reconstruction. Thus, we have seen the consequences of a code of constraint as contrasted with those of a code of direction. This already provides some clues to the structure of the ethical system under investigation.

In concluding this chapter, I should like to repeat: that we shall gain a much deeper insight into the nature of a moral code if we start off by recognizing the distinctive characteristics of positive and negative prescriptions; if we give full consideration to the variations in stringency among them; and finally, if we seek to explicate the interrelations between all these different types of prescriptive qualities as they occur in the specific moral code under examination.

Components of a Prescription: Prescripta

If we wish to describe and classify the moral prescriptions of any code we must determine how the actions prescribed are designated. I have called this component of a prescription its "prescriptum." The action-designations may refer to one or more factors, and it is therefore necessary to examine these component factors and to discover how they are used in describing a prescriptum.

We may inquire of any prescription: who is to perform it? what is to be performed? to whom is it to be performed? where, when, and under what circumstances is it to be performed? These four factors will be called respectively the *agent,* the *act,* the *patient,* and the *circumstances.* The term "action" as contrasted with "act" will be used more generally to stand for the whole complex of these factors. Normally, a description of the action prescribed will contain a reference to at least one and probably several of these factors.

Some prescriptions may explicitly designate all four factors and others may omit one or more. Where no specific mention is made of one factor, it may be usually assumed that the prescription applies universally, to all agents, patients, or circumstances as the case may be.

These distinctions are illustrated by the following examples. Incest taboos forbid sexual intercourse (act) with one's mother (patient) under all circumstances. Western moral prohibitions against lying prohibit lying (act) to any person (patient). Prescriptions about the observance of the Sabbath prohibit certain actions on the Sabbath day (circumstances). Once I encountered the sign: "It is forbidden to spit in church" (circumstances). Children (agents) should take care of their aged parents (patients).

It is obvious that prescriptions may designate the actions they prescribe by specifying one instead of another of these factors. Often it is indifferent whether the patient or the circumstances are designated. Sometimes the same action can be described by mentioning different factors. Hence, the division of a prescribed action into the four elements is not clear cut, and one element may replace another in the description. For instance, the obligation to repay a loan may be described either as "You ought to give money to the person from whom you borrowed it" (patient-specification), or as "When you have borrowed money (circumstances), you ought to pay it back."

An examination of the various factors in a prescription will reveal that there can be varying degrees of generality involved for each factor. For instance, the prescription may forbid a certain act for all agents, or only for some; for all patients, or only for some; under all circumstances, or only under some.

a. Agents

Some moral prescriptions specify which agent is to perform the act. This is most frequently done by designating the agent by means of some role which he performs. Thus, there are special duties for parents, chiefs, priests, judges, U. S. citizens, and so on. Most of the actions prescribed by a moral code may, however, be defined without designating the agent. The reference to a specific agent may be replaced by a reference to a specific patient instead. For example: the duty of a child is equivalent to a duty to parents (patients); or, the duty of a judge is equivalent to a duty to administer justice impartially to those brought before one in court. Sometimes, the agent may be indirectly described by designating the circumstances; when acting as a judge, one ought to administer justice impartially.

Therefore, since specific reference to the agent may be made in terms of the other factors, I propose to regard all *moral prescriptions as anonymous with respect to the agent*. This is only another way of saying that moral prescriptions prescribe for all agents, or that they are impersonal. By adopting this approach it is possible to explain the impersonality of prescriptions (mentioned in Chapter V, sections 2 and 4). Furthermore, it enables us to make sense of the requirement that prescriptions be considered binding upon others besides the individual agent involved, thus satisfying the requirement of intersubjectivity. We shall see that this requirement appears to be necessary in the process of justification.

Since it is not essential to designate the agent directly in a prescription, I shall henceforth restrict the use of the term "prescriptum" to actions described by the other three factors — acts, patients, and circumstances. Hence a prescriptum is that action the performance of which fulfills or violates its prescription irrespective of the agent of the action.

There still are some restrictions upon agents, however, which result from the nature of prescriptions themselves. Prescriptions are binding only upon those who are capable of what I have elsewhere called "voluntary actions." [1] That is, since prescriptions require acceptance before they can be fulfilled or violated, the agent must be capable of accepting them. This capacity is usually attributed only to people who have reached a 'responsible age' or are 'moral beings,' and ordinarily animals, small children, and idiots, are excluded. Cultures vary considerably as to whom they admit as potential agents. But at any rate as far as I know, no one would extend the sphere of agents of prescriptions to cover everything in the universe!

Closely allied with this restriction of potential agents is an analogous conception to be discussed later which I shall call "ethical competence." This refers to the ability to follow and accept a line of ethical reasoning. If it is extended to include the understanding and acceptance of an authoritarian ethics, ethical competence is identical with potential agentship.[2]

b. Acts

Every prescription must specify the particular kind of act which is prescribed. The acts which are most frequently included among prescripta are such acts as: lying, murdering, stealing, sexual intercourse, and fighting. Some moral codes prohibit such acts only with respect to certain classes of patients, and others extend them to all patients. Similarly, under certain circumstances such acts may be permitted, or even enjoined. Where the patients and circumstances are omitted, we may assume that they apply to all patients in all circumstances. The specification provided by these last two factors will be discussed presently.

The definition of the term "act" is difficult, and it is unnecessary to give one here. Acts cannot be designated by referring to overt bodily movements alone. Usually they are described in terms of an external effect of such movement. Thus, Ross defines an "act" as the "production of a change in a state of affairs."[3] And we must add that in order to refer to an act, the change must be specified.

For example, to "hit" someone means that through an object brought into motion by your own body you cause some contact, generally injurious, to him. If there has been no contact, you have not hit him. To pay a debt is to act with the consequence that what is owed comes into possession of the person owed to. If the latter does not come into possession, he has not been paid. These examples make it plausible to suppose that in the final analysis we can refer to an act only by indicating some selected consequence of it.

Granted that the designation of a consequence is the basic core of a description of an act, there are many ways of classifying acts with reference to their consequences. There are intended acts, which are acts which normally could be expected to have the consequence of that type, but for some extraneous reason fail to do so. Thus, intended murder is an act which, except for such extraneous circumstances, would have resulted in the victim's death. An "act of anger" might be similarly defined as one which normally would result in injury to the object of anger.

Careful attention to the way in which the prescribed act is described will resolve one of the problems that has been discussed at length by moral philosophers, namely, the so-called problem of 'objective' and 'subjective' duties. The question is whether an act which is a duty is the act which actually has the objective consequences, or whether it is the act which the agent thinks will have those consequences. Is it one's duty to do what the actual situation calls for, or to do what the supposed situation calls for? It has been contended by some philosophers that all that is demanded by an ought-statement or prescription is what has been called the "setting oneself to do something." Prichard writes that "an obligation must be an obligation, not to *do* something, but to perform an activity of a totally different kind, that of setting or exerting ourselves to do something, i.e. to bring something about." [4]

The usual argument for this contention is roughly as follows. If I have a duty, I must know and be capable of performing the duty. This follows from the principle that "ought" implies "can." Since I can never be certain of the facts of the situation, if duty depended upon them, I could not know my duty, and so could not perform it. Hence, duty depends on my thoughts about the situation and it can only consist of setting myself to perform what the supposed situation calls for.[5] There are other versions of this argument, but they are much like this one.

It follows from the theory which I have presented in this book, that this "setting of oneself" in the sense in which it is involved in any conceivable obligation refers only to the act of acceptance of a prescription, rather than to part of the content of the prescription itself. According to my analysis, a prescription calls for a certain kind of act, and not merely the setting of oneself to perform the act, although in the act of agreeing that one ought to perform this act, one is actually setting oneself to perform it. If the analysis being examined were correct, it would entail that if a person had set himself to do an act, even if that act did not have the intended consequences, it would ipso facto be fulfilled. But it does seem absurd to say that a person has fulfilled his obligations by merely setting himself to fulfill them.[6]

Assuming that there is no a priori reason for maintaining that every prescription must be 'subjectively' defined in the sense that any prescriptum must be a 'setting of oneself,' it does not follow that in some other sense of 'setting oneself' there may be prescripta which are so defined. Thus, there might be prescriptions which demand that a person try to do something quite apart from whether he will succeed or not. Conceivably, the Biblical injunction, "Be ye therefore perfect even as your Father which is in heaven is perfect," [7] merely requires that we try to be perfect although we may never succeed. Other 'subjectively' defined prescripta would be such injunctions as "you ought to follow your conscience."

Whether the prescripta are subjectively or objectively defined depends upon what criteria of an act are used in the prescription; namely, whether the act is designated by actual objective consequences or whether it is designated by the agent's suppositions about these consequences. These are two different kinds of prescriptions referring to two different kinds of acts. To prove that the prescription against homicide has been violated there must be a *corpus delicti,* or else there is no violation of this prescription. To think one has murdered someone may be a violation of another prohibition against intending to murder. Either may be violated without violating the other; one may intend to murder and not succeed, or one may kill without intending to.

Different moral codes designate duties differently, either 'objectively' or 'subjectively' or sometimes both. Perhaps a good deal of our own Western morality involves subjectively defined duties. On the other hand, other moral codes emphasize the objective definition, as in the case of the Navahos. It seems natural to suppose that if moral prescriptions are to function sociologically to direct and constrain actual conduct, the actual rather than the supposed consequences should determine the acts prescribed.[8]

One source of the misunderstanding which gives rise to the insistence upon the 'subjectivity' of duties is the confusion of prescriptions for conduct with the evaluation of actions. The criteria which determine the fulfillment or violation of a prescription are quite different from those employed in assigning punishment or blame for the action. The latter is an evaluation *post factum* — by a judge, for example. It may be that a person has violated the prohibition against homicide by doing something that he could not know would result in the victim's death, and in consequence of his ignorance he should be excused. Or on the other hand, he may have intended murder without succeeding and ought to be punished. Such evaluations probably come under prescriptions for handling delinquents, and are not necessarily the basis for the prescriptions of the acts themselves.

c. Categorizing acts

There are a great many possible ways of classifying the acts which occur in prescriptions. Each moral code appears to have its distinctive method of describing these acts, and hence, in order to understand it, we must first determine how it categorizes the acts which it prescribes. Only a few of the more basic modes of categorization can be examined here.

One general method of categorizing acts may be called "teleological", that is, the prescribed act is specified as a means to some end or other. The end may be positive or negative, that is, a desirable or undesirable state of affairs. For a positive end the required acts are means of procuring it; whereas for a negative end they are means of averting it. For example, a prescription may call for acts which will procure happiness, or on the other hand, will avert unhappiness.

In connection with this kind of prescriptum, I should like to point out that "to prescribe an end" is equivalent to "prescribing those acts which are means to the end." Likewise, to choose an end is the same thing as choosing the means to the end, and should be sharply distinguished from merely desiring or wishing for an end, which, for various reasons we do not choose to pursue.[9] Thus if I choose to go to the doctor, I choose ipso facto the first act necessary to produce the end of getting there. Similarly, if happiness is the prescribed end, then those acts (or at least one act) which will produce happiness are prescribed also. On the other hand, there are many ends (or 'values') which cannot be prescribed because there are no acts which can produce them.

In this category of acts, it is the actually effective means which are prescribed, and not merely subjective intentions or vain attempts to do them. Thus, if I actually perform an act which I mistakenly suppose to be the means to the prescribed end, I have not fulfilled the prescription, because in this case the prescription requires those acts which succeed in achieving the end. In other words, prescriptions in this category refer to 'objective' rather than 'subjective' duties. There might be a different category of prescriptions referring to subjective means to the end. But I know of no ethical system which prescribes these. Generally such acts are actual means to a subjective end.

There are two types of means-end relationships which are involved in actions and which are frequently not distinguished. A means-act may be an intrinsic component of the end, that is, it may itself be part of the end sought; or, on the other hand, it may be entirely external to the end. The first I shall call an *intrinsic means,* and the second an *extrinsic means.* The conception of "intrinsic means," as a constituent of the end, may be illustrated by the following examples: a certain color may be a means to the entire painting (end); or obeying the rules of chess may be a means to playing chess. In either case, the means is part of the whole painting or of the activity of playing chess. Most activities which are ends-in-themselves contain such intrinsic means. Mountain climbing, playing music, and riding have as constituent means all the various particular acts involved in the whole activity. For both Aristotle and Dewey, as well as for others, moral acts are intrinsic means in this sense. (This explains Dewey's diatribe against the separation of means and ends in the moral life.)

Extrinsic means are mere means. In themselves they are indifferent or even undesirable. Earning a living belongs in this category for a great many people. Drudgery of all kinds is extrinsic. Utilitarianism employs this type of means to designate its prescripta.

It should be evident that completely different ethical systems can be

constructed out of these two kinds of means-acts. In general, those emphasizing intrinsic means tend to be more subjective and those emphasizing
extrinsic means more objective.

A completely different way in which acts may be designated is in terms
of a selected consequence, such as injury to someone, or deception of someone. Moral systems which consist of moral rules or laws generally employ
this way of describing the acts prescribed. A legalistic ethics such as that
propounded in the Decalogue (or the Torah) is a good example.

Sometimes the acts are designated as those which are intended to have
certain consequences instead of actually having those consequences. Perhaps
this is ultimately the scheme by which the British intuitionists (for example,
Prichard and Ross) designate the acts prescribed.

Another possible way of designating acts is by referring to the conditions
under which they normally arise; for example, acts of anger or of love, or
acts of sympathy. Acts thus described are characterized by their antecedents
rather than by their consequences. Of course, both methods may be combined; for example, acts of revenge are acts arising out of some previous
injury intending some injury as a consequence.

There is one more important category of acts to be mentioned, namely,
acts which are symbolic of an attitude or relationship. In our own culture,
such acts as shaking hands or kissing fall under this group. Perhaps in the
end, a large proportion of our social acts belong here. Thus, for instance,
Durkheim maintains that the punishment of criminals serves a symbolic
rather than a practical function in our society.[10] I believe that many of the
prescriptions advanced by moral philosophers can also be regarded as employing the symbolic character of the act to describe it. For instance, Kant's
categorical imperative may conceivably be interpreted as enjoining those acts
which are symbolic of respect, in the sense that they recognize the intrinsic
dignity of others as ends-in-themselves. According to this interpretation,
lying is wrong because it is symbolic of disrespect.

There may quite likely be other categories of acts which are significant
for formulating moral prescriptions. My examination of them has been cursory and impressionistic. A more detailed list will be given under the topic
of basic prescriptions in Chapter IX, section 2(b).

Before leaving this topic, I should like to stress its importance for descriptive ethics. There is no reason to believe that non-literate people classify
actions in the ways that we do. Certainly, the conception of an "act" itself
must vary with the structure of the language in which the prescriptive statements occur. Hence, if we wish to investigate this topic in more detail we
must consult the linguist.[11]

d. Patients

Almost all the prescriptions of a moral code are defined by an effect the act has on some other human being. This affected person has been called the "patient." Sometimes, of course, the patient may be the agent himself. If we wish we may even extend the use of "patient" to include nonhuman objects, such as animals and inanimate objects.

Moral philosophers have tended to overlook the fact that the majority of the moral prescriptions of a natural code involve specific classes of patients. Thus we have special obligations to our family, to the members of the various groups to which we belong, to our fellow countrymen, to friends, and if one is a theist, to a specific individual, God. Furthermore, we have obligations to particular people, as patients, by virtue of some previous act of our own or of theirs. For instance, I ought to give Brown $5 because I borrowed it from him, or because he was so kind to me when I was in need. This is entirely different from a prescription to give $5 to every or any patient whatsoever (which would be a general prescription). Even if the prescription were to state that one ought to return money which is borrowed to the lender, the prescription is not absolutely universal, in the sense of applying to every or any patient, but only to lenders.

Moral prescriptions generally restrict the patients of an action to some class defined by specific characteristics such as: blood ties, association, previous relationships, and so on. Prescriptions involving sexual relations provide an obvious illustration: the class of patients of a sexual prohibition always includes the agent's nuclear family and usually members of the same clan. In addition, it may include unmarried girls and women married to men other than the agent. Positive injunctions may exist requiring that the agent marry into a certain class of patients.

Many prescriptions define the relevant patient in terms of some previous relationship to the agent. Obligations of gratitude or even returning a loan may fit into this type. Any direct relation with another person usually involves a situational relationship of some kind, and puts that person in a special class of patients with respect to moral prescriptions. For example, the stranger who happens to be a guest, in virtue of this host-guest relationship, creates certain obligations on the part of the host which are binding even if the stranger is of a completely different tribe and has no other relationship to the host. In talking with the Navahos, I had the impression that moral prescriptions involved only those people with whom one has some such direct relationship, and it did not matter whether he was a Navaho or a white. For them, an obligation to someone they knew was more stringent than one to someone far distant. In Judaic-Christian morality, the original conception of "neighbor" likewise perhaps referred to the persons with whom you were thrown in direct contact.

The extent to which moral prescriptions of our Western world are universal with respect to patients is therefore probably highly exaggerated. In practice, we all recognize the particular obligations (positive and negative) we have to certain people as distinct from those we owe to someone merely by virtue of the fact that he is a member of the human race. We may well ask which of the prescriptions that we accept do demand this universality of application. Perhaps most of these prescriptions are negative ones, like the prohibition of murder or stealing.

Moral philosophers of the last few centuries have tended to ignore the special obligations which we have towards particular people. Hence, they fail to do justice in their analyses to the natural morality of Christianity which recognizes the peculiar obligations resulting from various associations, such as the family, the State, and the Church. Hegel is perhaps the only important modern philosopher who based his ethics on these associations. Other philosophers have concentrated on the universality of patients in formulating their moral prescriptions. Thus, Kant states that we must treat everyone as an end, never merely as a means, and Bentham says that every person should count for one.

The case of prescriptions involving nonhuman patients provides many interesting problems. Some moral codes contain prescriptions referring to animals. The Hindu code prohibits killing them. In comparison to such a code our own seems to be much more restricted and less general as far as patients are concerned. The Navahos also prescribe certain acts towards animals, and many other societies have taboos referring to animals or other natural objects. The theoretical grounds for such obligations probably rest on some doctrine of affinity to human beings or on some type of animism.

We find, therefore, that a prohibition against killing may designate as patients one's own intimate group, one's neighbors, one's nation, one's species, supernatural beings, or other living things. It is evident that a further understanding of the restrictions and extensions of patients involved in the various prescriptions must await an investigation of the grounds of the prescriptions themselves.

e. Circumstances

Many prescriptions require the acts prescribed to be performed only at certain times and places. Many religious prescriptions illustrate this: there are certain things one is forbidden to do in church, or during the mass. Among the Navahos, one is not supposed to leave the hogan at a certain time during a Sing.

The reference to the circumstances quite frequently is made indirectly by specifying the consequences of the act, since consequences follow only if the accompanying circumstances are appropriate. Thus if one is enjoined to pay a debt, the consequence of having the lender in possession of the money can be achieved only if the agent has the money to give him; in other words, he must be in the appropriate financial circumstances. The specification of the act presupposes the circumstances in this case.

It is a peculiar characteristic of many negative prescriptions that they forbid an act under *any* circumstances (except perhaps where there is a conflict of prescriptions). Some codes prohibit murder under any circumstances, and Kant went to the absurdity of stating that lying was wrong under any circumstances.[12] Certainly, incest taboos should also be included in this category. This characteristic of certain negative prescriptions follows from some of the considerations advanced about negative prescriptive qualities in the preceding chapter.

One school of contemporary moral philosophers has maintained that all prescripta are to be defined in terms of the situation. The situation includes, of course, the consequences. Prichard, for example, gives as a preliminary characterization of the form of a moral rule the following: "When the *situation* in which a man is contains a thing of the kind A capable of having a state of the kind X effected in it, and when also it is such that some state or combination of states Y which the man can bring about directly would, if brought about, cause a state of the kind X in A, the man ought to bring about that state or combination of states." [13]

According to this view, the act which is characterized by "oughtness" or "ought-notness" is designated by the situation rather than by any of the other factors we have examined. Such a procedure is perfectly correct since the other factors may be regarded as circumstantial factors in the situation itself. However, from our point of view, this procedure is undesirable because it unnecessarily complicates the classification and description of prescripta.

Prichard's reason for designating the acts situationally is that in his theory it is the accompanying circumstances that are the crucial consideration in determining one's duties, rather than the type of act by itself or the patient. He contends that it is *only* the situation (or one's view of it) which can serve as a reason or ground for an act's being right or wrong. The moral character of one's act is apprehended immediately and intuitively upon reflecting upon the situation. Accordingly, "the sense of obligation to do, or of the rightness of, an action of a particular kind is absolutely underivative or immediate." [14]

This intuitionistic form of what may be called "situationalism" belongs to the group of systems which I shall later refer to as "extreme particularism." Such systems maintain that there are no general principles from which duties can be derived, but rather that each situation, being unique, determines the relevant duty uniquely. It is contended that the reliance upon principles rather than the reflection upon each particular situation reflects human laziness rather than rationality.[15]

2. GENERAL AND PARTICULAR PRESCRIPTIONS

From the foregoing it is evident that the character of generality or particularity of prescriptions can be understood in terms of any of the four factors considered: they may be general or particular with reference to agents, acts, patients, or circumstances.

A simple illustration will show these differences. Compare the general prescription, "It is wrong to lie" with the particular prescription, "You ought not to lie to Jones about Elsie when he asks you next time you meet at the Club." In the latter, all four factors are designated specifically. Instead of the particulars we could generalize each of the factors and obtain different types of general prescriptions: for "you" we could substitute "one" or "everyone"; for "lying about Elsie" we could substitute "lying about anything"; instead of mentioning the particular place and time, we could generalize for "all times" or "all places."

At this point I should like to make some terminological distinctions in the use of "general," "particular," "universal," "individual," and "specific." *General* refers to a characteristic which is frequently repeated, while *specific* refers to one which recurs less frequently. "Lying is wrong" is relatively general while "lying about Elsie is wrong" is relatively specific.

Universality is distinguished from generality as meaning "all with no exceptions." The prescription, "All lying is wrong" is universal, whereas "Lying is usually wrong" is merely general. *Particular* can be contrasted with specific as referring to a situation hardly ever expected to recur: for example, "You ought to pay off that big debt" would be particular, whereas "You ought to pay any debts for more than $100" would be specific. An *individual* prescription is one which is absolutely unique in that it refers to some aspect of the action which in principle can never again be repeated: for example, "You ought to bury your dead father with jewelry." The distinguishing characteristic of an individual prescription is that it can be fulfilled or violated only once.

These distinctions allow us to introduce prescriptions which are universal, general, specific, particular, and individual with respect to agents, patients, acts, and circumstances. From these we can develop many alternative systems of classification of prescriptions. An examination of the types of prescriptions which are accepted in a moral code will reveal important elements in its structure.

There may be moral codes which claim that all prescriptions are particular or individual. This I have called "extreme particularism"; it is exemplified by the theories of Prichard and his followers. This system denies any universal moral prescriptions, and maintains that general prescriptions are only rather crude guides to the discovery of particular prescriptions.

There are other systems which accept one or more universal prescriptions from which the particular prescriptions are derived. Some systems admit both universal and general prescriptions. These will be discussed presently. The different ways in which prescriptions may be general will be relevant for the modes of derivation of one prescription from another.

3. MORAL RULES AND MORAL PRINCIPLES

General prescriptions are introduced into moral codes for two purposes: either as general rules to guide conduct or as principles from which particular prescriptions can be derived. These two uses can be illustrated by the example: "It is wrong to lie." This prescription may serve directly as a guide to conduct or it may serve to validate another prescription such as, "You ought not to lie to Jones." When used for the first purpose, general prescriptions will be called *moral rules,* and when used for the second, they will be called *moral principles.*

In some ethical systems the same general prescriptions function both as moral rules and moral principles. Where the rule against lying is at the same time used as a principle from which other prescriptions are derived we have an example of such a system.

In other ethical systems, moral rules are not used to justify actions of other prescriptions, but instead they serve as rules of thumb or recipes to be followed because they are usually successful in directing us in the proper course of conduct. Such rules are in part employed because they save time which would otherwise have to be spent in reflection, or else because they act as reminders. These rules are formed because they are useful, and their function is therefore instrumental. They derive what validity they have from their utility, rather than from their being constituents in the logical structure of the system. Furthermore, such rules are usually only general and not universal prescriptions; that is, they are binding only "for the most part" and should not always be followed blindly.

General prescriptions such as those against lying, murder, or stealing, function only as moral rules in Bentham's utilitarianism. In Dewey's system their role is similar, and we shall find that among the Navahos such prescriptions are rules rather than principles. Again, in the extreme particularistic system of Prichard and Carritt, general prescriptions are also only rules.

In all except the last system, we find that in addition to rules there are also underlying principles, which are universal prescriptions used to justify the particular prescriptions and the moral rules. Bentham's principle of utility is not a moral rule but a moral principle in this sense. Indeed, the principle is too general to be able to serve as a rule for conduct. All the systems we shall discuss except those similar to that of Prichard have at least one moral principle in their system. In a sense, Prichard's system itself may be said to have moral principles, for each particular prescription is such a principle.

It is interesting to note that those moral codes which are derived from a single supreme principle of morality quite frequently have only this moral principle and all the other general prescriptions are merely moral rules. Hence, the fact that such systems maintain that their moral rules are not always binding, or that such rules are not used to justify an action, does not entail that there is no underlying principle or universal prescription which has these characteristics.

VIII

The Logic of Ethical Discourse: Validation

I. VALIDATION IN GENERAL

Whenever a prescription is commended (or discussed) it is always legitimate to ask for a reason for fulfilling or not violating it. Why ought I to keep my promise? or Why ought I not to lie? are examples of such questions. Even the extreme particularists of the Prichard school feel constrained to offer some reason or other, if it be only that "it is your duty" or a reference to the "nature of the act." [1]

a. Validation and justification

Of any particular ethical argument two questions can be asked: does the conclusion follow from the reasons given? and will the reasons persuade the listener? (or ought they to persuade him?). The relation between reasons, or premises and conclusion, is generally referred to as logical entailment of one sort or another, and so the first question is: do the premises entail the conclusion? In every sphere of discourse arguments can be constructed in which the premises do logically entail the conclusion, but the argument is unacceptable because the premises are not accepted. Furthermore, the argument may not be accepted by the listener for such other reasons as the inability to follow the reasoning. So that even if the answer to the first question is affirmative, the answer to the second may be negative.

The inquiry into the logical relations of premises and conclusion is generally called *logic,* and I shall extend this term to cover the investigation of the formal relations between reasons and the derived prescription in ethical discourse. The reasons will be said to validate this prescription. Hence, the logic of ethical discourse is the inquiry into ethical validation.

The investigation of the conditions of persuasiveness of the argument as a whole I shall call by the ancient term of Aristotle: *rhetoric.* If the argument as a whole is acceptable, we may be said to have justified the prescription. Therefore, the rhetoric of ethical discourse is an investigation of ethical justification. (In science this is sometimes called "scientific methodology.") [2]

There are several important differences between validation and justification which must be noted.

First, validation is a relation between premises (or reasons) and a conclusion. In a valid argument the premises validate the conclusion. Justification, on the other hand, is a more complicated relation involving the speaker and listener as well. If the argument persuades a reasonable listener, then the speaker will be said to have justified the conclusion to the listener. In other words, premises validate whereas speakers justify.

Second, justification is stronger than mere persuasion, for it differs from the latter in being legitimate. One condition of such legitimacy is that the reasons offered validate the conclusion. Therefore, validation is a necessary condition of the process of justification.

Third, validation may be hypothetical, for the premises can validate a conclusion regardless of whether the premises are themselves accepted or not. In contrast, justification is categorical for it includes the unconditioned acceptance of the premises, and consequently of the whole argument.

From these considerations it is evident that "justification" is a much more inclusive concept than "validation," since it involves not only an acceptable validation, but also acceptable premises and other conditions of persuasiveness which will be mentioned later. Therefore, I shall examine the validation of prescriptions first.

In recent years it has become unfashionable to use the words "valid" and "validation" in connection with ethical discourse because they suggest a cognitivist approach to ethical problems. Furthermore, it is contended that these terms apply to propositions but not to prescriptions. I might have used Hall's term "legitimacy," but I prefer to reserve it for later use in connection with justification. In order to avoid excessive barbarisms in the ensuing discussion I shall use "validation," although it will become clear shortly that the way in which reasons validate prescriptions is somewhat different from purely logical validation.

b. Logical form of validation

A full inquiry into the nature of the logic of ethical thinking awaits the completion of an adequate logic of imperatives. The importance of the study of imperatives for the logic of prescriptions has already been noted. Unfortunately, most of the discussions of the logic of imperatives have been confined to the formulation of laws, which, for our purposes, are relatively trivial. Such laws involve connectives such as conjunction and disjunction, and various kinds of transposition.[3]

The laws which interest us are analogues of the rule of inference known as *modus ponens* and *modus tollens*.[4] These laws may be employed for prescriptions in the following way:

<table>
<tr><td align="center">*Modus ponens* (*A*)</td><td align="center">*Modus tollens* (*A*)</td></tr>
<tr><td>

(*a*) If you do *X*, then you must do *Y*;

(*b*) You ought to do *X*;

(*c*) Therefore you ought to do *Y*.

</td><td>

(*a*) If you do *X*, then you must do *Y*;

(*b*) You ought not to do *Y*;

(*c*) Therefore you ought not to do *X*.

</td></tr>
</table>

Modus ponens (*B*)

(*a*) If situation *X* exists, you ought to do *Y*;

(*b*) Situation *X* exists;

(*c*) Therefore you ought to do *Y*.

Modus ponens (*A*) is the usual form in which a prescription to do an action which is a means to a prescribed goal is validated. For example: if you are to win the war, you must have an army; you ought to win the war; therefore you ought to have an army.[5] *Modus tollens* (*A*) is the familiar form which negative prescriptions of avoidance take. For example: if you look at your mother-in-law then you will become blind; you ought not to become blind; therefore do not look at your mother-in-law (reconstructed Navaho taboo).

Modus ponens (*B*) could be illustrated by various prescriptions of the ethics of duty: if you have promised Smith, you ought to pay him; and you did promise him; therefore you ought to pay him. There is no *modus tollens* of this type. Such an argument might be an instance of the so-called "pathetic fallacy". For example: if he hurt you, you ought to be angry; you ought not to be angry; therefore he did not hurt you. This is obviously an invalid inference. It suggests that there may be a rule that if a prescription is contained (nonvacuously) in the premises then the conclusion must be prescriptive. (This also illustrates some of the logical difficulties involved in uncritical application of the rules of the logic of propositions to prescriptions.)[6]

A more lengthy discussion of the various rules and combinations of them which are possible will not be undertaken here. In accordance with what was said earlier about prescriptions, when we pursue a logic of this kind it must not be forgotten that the prescriptive statements can refer only to possible actions — and this limitation restricts some of the possible combinations. Thus it outlaws *modus tollens* (*B*).

The types of argument which are used in practice may throw further light on the nature of ethical validation. Let us consider the following examples:

Suppose someone uttered the moral statement: "You ought to help Smith!" If you asked the speaker: "Why?" some of the possible reasons which might be offered in justification of this prescription would be the following:

(1) "because (a) you have an obligation to support Smith,"
　　　　　(b) you ought to make others happy,"
　　　　　(c) it would be wrong to let him get into trouble."
　　　(This is an appeal to a moral principle.)

(2) "because (a) he needs help,"
　　　　　(b) he helped you when you were in need,"
　　　　　(c) he is your uncle."
　　　(This is an appeal to a nonprescriptive fact.)

(3) "because if you help him, (a) then he will be happy,"
　　　　　　　　　　　　　(b) he will repay you,"
　　　　　　　　　　　　　(c) everyone will feel better."
　　(This is an appeal to desirable consequences of the act.)

(4) "because if you do not, then (a) he will starve,"
　　　　　　　　　　　　　(b) he will dislike you,"
　　　　　　　　　　　　　(c) we shall all feel badly."
(This is an appeal to undesirable consequences of nonperformance.)

(5) "because *only* if you do (a) will he be happy,"
　　　　　　　　　　　　(b) will he repay you,"
　　　　　　　　　　　　(c) will everyone feel better."
　　(This points out that the act is necessary to the attainment of desirable consequences. Note that logically this is a transposition of (4).)

All these arguments are enthymemes, but it is fairly easy to supply the missing premises. Some of the suppressed premises are: (1a) "supporting Smith involves helping him"; (2a) "you ought to help those who need help"; (3a) "you ought to make him (or others) happy"; (4a) "you ought not to let him starve"; (5a) "you ought to do what is necessary to make him happy." (The statements could easily be formulated in more rigorous language.)

It will be noted that all of these arguments contain two different kinds of premises: prescriptions and nonprescriptive statements of fact. I suggest that all non-trivial ethical inferences when fully expanded must contain both kinds of premises if the conclusion is to be a prescription.

All the arguments except those under (3) can be formulated so that they are instances of the three rules of inference given above:

(2) may be *modus ponendo ponens* (*B*);
(4) is *modus tollendo tollens* (*A*);
(5) is *modus ponendo ponens* (*A*); also perhaps (1).

Arguments (3) and (1), if interpreted in one way, do not follow the rules given. As a matter of fact, they would be fallacious according to the invalid principle of affirming the consequent:

(*a*) If *p,* then *q;*	(3*a*) (*a*) If you help him, then you will make him happy;
(*b*) *q* is obligatory;	(*b*) You ought to make him happy;
(*c*) Therefore *p* is obligatory.	(*c*) Therefore you ought to help him.

The fallacy in the argument comes from the logical possibility that there may be other conditions which will make Smith happy, for it might also be true that if you got his children to help him you would also be making him happy. This reflects the principle that there are alternative means, any one of which may be sufficient to produce the end desired. (See footnote 5.)

c. Schematic ethical syllogism

In order to avoid certain logical complications, I shall use the old-fashioned Aristotelian logic of the syllogism to handle all the types of argument to be discussed except that involving *ponendo ponens* (*B*). The schema of these arguments given in quasi-syllogistic form therefore would be as follows:

(*a*) All actions of type *A* are obligatory (or right or wrong) — *Major prescriptive premise;*
(*b*) *X* is an action of type *A* — *Minor nonprescriptive* (factual) *premise;*
(*c*) Therefore *X* is obligatory (or right or wrong) — *Conclusion: a prescription.*

Examples are:

(*a*) All acts promoting happiness are obligatory (or right);	(*a*) All stealing is wrong;
(*b*) Helping Smith is an act promoting happiness;	(*b*) Taking that money is stealing;
(*c*) Therefore helping Smith is obligatory (or right).	(*c*) Therefore taking that money is wrong.

(a) Acts prohibited by Jahweh ought not to be committed;

(b) Murder is prohibited by Jahweh;

(c) Therefore murder ought not to be committed.

(a) Avoid all acts of excess!

(b) Becoming drunk is an act of excess;

(c) Therefore avoid becoming drunk!

The major premise is a prescription, either positive or negative. The acts prescribed may be designated in any one of the ways mentioned in Chapter VII, section 1. Thus they may be categorized as means to an end, means of avoidance, or symbolic actions. The minor premise subsumes the particular act or kind of act under this prescribed category. This premise is not a prescription, but a nonprescriptive statement, or what may be called a "factual premise," if the latter is understood broadly to include beliefs such as those derived from revelation, as well as empirical beliefs.[7]

The syllogistic formulation has certain advantages over the 'propositional' formulation. First, it restricts the 'what' of the prescriptions to actions; second, it enables us to explain the "if-then" relation more explicitly; third, it allows us to generalize the argument without having to resort to more complicated logical formulations; fourth, it shows how an argument of type (3) above is valid. These advantages outweigh the more intuitively obvious transitions of the arguments when they are formulated 'propositionally.'

By a slight extension of the syllogistic form we can make some of the distinctions that are required in various arguments that we shall encounter. For instance, in ordinary means-ends validation we meet three versions which correspond roughly to the prescribed action: one means among alternatives; a necessary means; and the only means in the situation at hand. Accordingly, we can define the class of prescribed actions under which the particular action is to be subsumed in three different ways:

(1) The class of actions which are *sufficient* to produce the goal desired (for example, sending a check would be one member of this class of actions resulting in the payment of a debt);

(2) The class of actions *necessary* to produce the goal desired (for example, eating would come under the class of actions necessary to survival);

(3) The *unique* class which consists of the only action which will produce the goal desired (for example, there is one action that will promote the greatest happiness in the existing situation).

All these various types of premises are susceptible of rigorous logical formulation, but I shall not give them here. Their application to provide degrees of stringency will be examined in Chapter IX, section 2(d).

The syllogistic formula corresponds to some interpretations of the classical **practical** syllogism.[8] The best historical exposition of an argument of this type was given by J. S. Mill. Mill distinguished between premises in the indicative and in the imperative mood. The former are derived from Science, the latter from Art. Art proposes the ends, while Science describes the means available. The conclusion from these premises of Art and Science combined is a rule or precept. According to Mill the major premise must always be supplied by Art and is imperative.[9] In other words, the major premise is prescriptive, and the minor premises are nonprescriptive or factual. This accords with the interpretation which I have given above.

It will become apparent very soon that the syllogistic formula is only a mere skeleton of the actual procedures used in validation. Ethical arguments are very complex, and generally involve whole series of premises — some prescriptive and some factual. The complex ways of constructing the syllogisms of the various ethical systems will be called *modes of validation*. The discussion of this topic should dispel the doubts of those who may think that the present discussion has distorted the nature of ethical argument unnecessarily in order to fit it into a traditional logical formulation.

d. The notion of "basic prescription"

In ethical argument, as in all other types of argument, the series of validating premises cannot regress to infinity. There must be some premises which themselves are not validated — and which presumably not only cannot be but also do not need to be validated. These are the 'axioms,' as it were, of a deductive system. Any ethical validation must therefore assume certain prescriptions which themselves cannot be validated. These primitive prescriptions I shall call *basic prescriptions*. A basic prescription is one which is used to validate other prescriptions but which is itself not validated within the system.

The problem of how these basic prescriptions are established, and the specific requirements for basic prescriptions will be discussed in the next chapter. At present we are only concerned with basic prescriptions as they are used to validate other prescriptions.

2. MODES OF VALIDATION

Although it may be assumed that all ethical systems employ the basic syllogistic formula propounded in the last section, there are many different ways in which it can be applied. It is important to recognize that ethical systems differ not only in the content of their basic prescriptions, but also in the procedures used to validate the derived particular prescriptions. Contemporary ethical theorists have called our attention to the semblance that ethical argumentation gives of using a "third mode of inference." [10] However, I suggest that these writers are really concerned not with the logical form of validation, which may be syllogistic, but rather with the procedures according to which this syllogistic form is to be applied, namely, the modes of validation. (Modes of validation may be considered as special rules of inference analogous to the special rules employed in inductive inference.)

The basic differences between various ethical systems may be accounted for in part by the differences between the modes of validation which they employ. Modes of validation may differ from one another in at least two respects. First, some systems assume only one basic prescription while others assume more than one (these may be called "monistic" and "pluralistic" systems respectively). Second, some systems deny that any validation from a superior moral principle is possible; others deny that such a principle is sufficient to validate any derived prescription, although they admit that it is necessary; and still others maintain that one or more basic prescriptions are sufficient as well as necessary to validate particular prescriptions. If the various differences are combined and permuted, several types of validation are possible.

As far as I can determine, however, there are four basic modes of validation into which can be grouped most of the ethical systems we know. I do not pretend that these four types exhaust the possibilities. There may be other types, and perhaps further philosophical analysis and anthropological inquiry will uncover them.

The four modes of validation are based on the following principles:

(1) Every particular prescription is self-validating (*mode of extreme particularism*);

(2) Every particular prescription is derived from one of a plurality of basic prescriptions, but there is no prescribed way of deciding which of these basic prescriptions applies in the case of conflict (*mode of selection*);

(3) Every particular prescription is validated by simple application of a single basic prescription (*mode of application*);

(4) Every particular prescription is validated by creative interpretation of a basic schematic prescription (*mode of interpretation*).

The first two modes are pluralistic, the one being underivative and the other derivative. The last two are monistic, the one postulating a determinate and sufficient basic prescription, and the other being based upon an indeterminate and vague basic prescription. The precise character of each will become evident when they are discussed in detail.

Ethical validation involves a peculiar problem that does not arise for validation in many other spheres of discourse; namely, that it must be able to produce as its conclusion a prescription which is directly applicable to concrete choices. This requires not only that it be concrete in the sense of being reasonably specific, but also that it be determinate and unequivocal.

The requirement of determinacy or unequivocalness is especially pressing in the case of negative prohibitions, because in order not to violate them we must know which particular acts are forbidden. Moreover, it generates an acute problem in pluralistic systems, since such systems accept several moral principles which may be incompatible in concrete instances: for example, there may be one prohibition against lying and another against making others unhappy, and at times it may be necessary to choose between these two prohibitions.

The various modes of validation are answers to this peculiar problem. They may be regarded as ways of applying the syllogistic schema so as to validate the determinate prescriptions and choices demanded by concrete situations. The theoretical problem posed by this requirement arises from the fact that any discursive mediating reasoning must use general concepts, while at the same time the conclusions must be applicable to a concrete unique case. Every ethical system should have an answer to this problem, for otherwise the moralist would be evading his task, namely, to answer the question: "What ought I to do and why?"

a. Extreme particularism

The first possible answer to this problem is to deny that it exists by affirming that all prescriptions are basic and underived. This is the view I have called "extreme particularism." Strictly speaking, it is not a mode of validation at all, since it denies that any moral prescription can be validated.

The only kind of reason that can be offered for a moral prescription in this type of system is evidence about the nature of the act involved — including some of its consequences or conditions. These are purely factual reasons. (The only argument that can be employed is of the *ponendo ponens* (B) type.) An action is prohibited because it is wrong, and it is wrong just because the situation is as it is; and similarly with obligatoriness.

Although this doctrine is usually associated with the intuitionism of Prichard and his followers, who hold that the particular moral judgments are self-evident, we can find examples of the same general position among empiricists. The various theories of conscience or moral sense usually belong in this category, as well as possibly Adam Smith's theory of the impartial spectator. This view may perhaps reflect the attitude of the man in the street in our own society more closely than any of the other more abstract formulations to be considered later. In everyday life, when pressed for a reason for saying that a particular action is wrong, the answer given by the average man is often: "I just feel that it is wrong" or "It just obviously is wrong."

Particularism, as I have described it, denies in essence that there is any system to be found among our (true) moral judgments. Each case must be judged on its own merits, and the attempt to systematize moral prescriptions by subsuming them under more general moral principles is thought to be fallacious. Hence, one corollary of the particularistic doctrine is the rejection of general moral rules as logically prior to particular prescriptions. In other words, general moral rules are never considered to be moral principles. General rules are thought to be derived from the particular instances, instead of conversely. Sometimes they are even said to be obtained 'inductively.' [11]

This is not the place to criticize such a theory, but I should like to urge the genuine possibility that some if not a great many natural moralities *may* exemplify this mode of validation. The only way that we can conclusively show that a natural moral code is not of this type is to prove that it belongs to one of the other ones.

On the other hand, from the point of view of descriptive ethics it might also be possible to reconstruct a system from which the explicit moral statements of a philosopher like Prichard could be derived. This system would be one that would be explicitly rejected on philosophical grounds by the informant (Prichard!) but would still represent the structure of the moral code implied by the particular prescriptions he accepts.

b. The mode of selection

The second mode by which particular prescriptions are validated is by subsuming them under any one of various general moral principles. An example of an argument in this mode would be the following: "You ought not to lie to Jones." "Why not?" "Because lying is wrong." [12] This mode accepts a plurality of basic moral principles: for example, the duty to produce good in others and ourselves, the duties of reparation and gratitude, of keeping promises, and so on. Every particular prescription must be validated by one of these principles.

I have called this the *mode of selection,* because it proceeds by selecting the specific principle to be used in validation of any particular prescription from a numerous set of accepted moral principles. Thus it concedes the need for validation from a higher principle, and shows how this is possible. However, it is obvious that since a plurality of moral principles is accepted there can be cases in which there is an apparent conflict between them. For example: it appears that an act could be validated as wrong because it is a lie; while at the same time also it could be validated as right because it is a beneficent act. This view characteristically generates the problem of the conflict of duties.

There are at least two general methods for resolving these conflicts. The first method, which may be called the method of "selective definition," assumes that there is only one principle which is relevant to the act in question, and that the other apparently relevant principles are not truly so. For instance, an act which appears simultaneously to be a lie (wrong) and a beneficent act (right) is thought to be necessarily either one or the other but not both. The problem then becomes one of correctly defining the act so that it comes under the principle proper to it.

The kind of argument using this method is well known to jurists. In lawsuits the issue often revolves around the question of whether the particular case is to be subsumed under one principle or another; for example, whether the theft of a stolen airplane should come under the law against stealing automobiles or some other law. The decision rendered by the judge is in effect a more precise definition of the act so as to make this subsumption plausible. (This is frequently done by pointing out analogies between the act in question and other acts admitted to be clear cut cases of the law used to validate the decision.) Political arguments often follow the same course: "That plan is illegal and dishonest," one politician might say, while the other counters: "No, it is for the protection of the nation against its enemies." In both situations, it is assumed that the subsumption of the act in question under one moral principle automatically excludes its subsumption under any conflicting one.

The second method of selection concedes that there may be many moral principles relevant to the determination of the rightness or wrongness of a particular act, and that at times these may conflict with each other. In one sense, therefore it is admitted that the same act can be both right and wrong. Ross calls acts which are right or wrong in this sense "prima facie duties." The act in question in the ultimate analysis must be either absolutely right or absolutely wrong, although prima facie it may be both. There is no overarching principle which can aid us in determining which group of prima facie duties the particular act comes under. In this sense, the selection of principle is arbitrary. As Ross says: "There is much truth in the description of the right act as a fortunate act." [13] Perhaps this second method could be called the method of "fortunate selection."

The generic characteristic of both methods of selection is their common assumption that a basic general prescription, or a moral principle, is a necessary condition of validation, but not sufficient for unique determination, since there is no unequivocal procedure by which it can be proven that a particular act comes under one rather than another of the plurality of principles.

It should be noted that the plurality of moral principles assumed by this mode need not necessarily be restricted to formalistic rules governing particular kinds of action as the examples given suggest. There may be a multiplicity of goods or goals which generate a plurality of basic moral principles, and the same considerations apply to principles of this type.

Again, this view partially reflects the reasons given by the average man in our society about what is right and wrong. A certain action is wrong because lying is wrong, and another is wrong because hurting others is wrong. These general principles are used to validate the particular prescriptions. They themselves appear to require no validation.

It is also typical of our own moral code that it often produces situations in which duties conflict; and it offers no prescribed method for solving such conflicts.

I have mentioned the obvious similarities between this mode and the law as administered by the law courts, which is faced by conflicts of applicable laws. However, the analogy is not quite correct, because every legal conflict must be resolved by the judge in court according to accepted procedures. There are therefore no ultimate legal conflicts as there are ostensible moral conflicts within a pluralistic system of this type.

c. Finding and making the law

The third and fourth modes of validation I have called the "mode of application" and the "mode of interpretation" respectively. Both, in contrast to the first two, are monistic. The distinction between these two modes may be made clearer by referring to the ancient controversy in jurisprudence over whether the judges find (and apply) or make the law. In the Middle Ages, it was maintained that the judge only applied the law to the individual case, and that his function was to find the law under which to subsume the particular situation. This attitude towards the judicial process is called "mechanical jurisprudence" by Roscoe Pound. In opposition to this, it has been held by the legal realists, that the judges actually make the law, in other words, that they legislate for the particular case before them.

In connection with this controversy in jurisprudence Kelsen has pointed out that it is impossible for the judges completely to make the law, although they may do so in part. He shows that in making the law the judge is in a way actually applying it. This is because a prior law sets up the judge and certain procedures, and these are necessary to validate the particular legal decision. Thus in rendering his decision according to accepted procedures, the judge is ipso facto applying the law. Furthermore, the law generally lays down certain general limits within which the judge may exercise his discretion.[14]

Kelsen goes on to show that there are two ways of validating a legal norm. These he calls *static* validation and *dynamic* validation. A static validation consists in the simple subsumption of a particular case under a general validating principle, and the particular prescriptions are "obtainable by means of an intellectual operation, viz., by inference from the general to the particular" (p. 112). In a dynamic system, on the other hand, the basic prescription (norm) establishes in individuals the authority to create prescriptions (norms). "The norms of a dynamic system have to be created through acts of will by those individuals who have been authorized to create norms by some higher norm . . . Its various norms cannot be obtained by any intellectual operation" (p. 113).

If we apply these distinctions to modes of validation in ethics, we find that among ethical systems there are also these two types of validation: static and dynamic. The static systems merely apply the basic prescription to particular actions, whereas the dynamic systems delegate the prescription-creating authority to the individual agent, who is to follow certain procedures. Furthermore, as I shall show, the dynamic systems generally accept some general indeterminate principle which limits the discretion of the individual agent (like the judge). The agent acts rather as a creative interpreter of the basic moral prescription than as a creator *ex nihilo!* The static and dynamic types correspond to the modes of application and interpretation respectively.

d. The mode of application

The mode of application exemplifies the ethical syllogism propounded in the last section in its simplest form. It consists of the simple subsumption of the particular prescription under a basic prescription. There is only one basic prescription, and all the other premises in the argument are non-prescriptive.

In Western moral philosophy the most obvious example of this mode is Bentham's utilitarianism:

> (*a*) The act promoting the greatest happiness is obligatory;
> (*b*) X is such an act;
> (*c*) Therefore X is obligatory.

Certain forms of theological ethics also fit into this category:

> (*a*) Actions forbidden by God are wrong;
> (*b*) Murder is forbidden by God;
> (*c*) Therefore murder is wrong.

Finally, we shall see later that there is good evidence that the Navaho ethical code also belongs to this category.[15]

Several comments should be made on this mode. First, as is evident from the theological example, the ethics need not be utilitarian. This mode can be employed for a great variety of basic prescriptions. Second, the minor subsuming premise need not be scientific or empirical in the ordinary sense. For example, the commands of God may be known by an "inner light," through oracular pronouncements, by various mechanical devices such as throwing dice or ordeals, and so on.

Third, the argument need not always carry certainty with it but may involve probabilities, for we may not be certain that a particular action comes under the class of actions prescribed by the basic prescription. The subsuming premise may easily be subject to error. Bentham takes this consideration into account by introducing the factors of certainty and uncertainty into the hedonic calculus. As we shall see, among the Navahos, certain actions have fairly predictable consequences and others are less predictable. Navaho ethics is always tentative. These differences of probability may be reflected in the relative stringency of various particular prescriptions.

Fourth, ethical disputation in the applicational mode is always about the minor subsuming premises. Consequently, it always concerns questions of fact (understood broadly). The single ethical premise is taken for granted, and hence the reasons given in an ethical argument are not moral principles nor do the statements usually contain ethical expressions. This characteristic is illustrated very clearly by the ethical teachings of the prophets in the Old Testament. Hardly ever do the prophets and the Pentateuchal casuists justify the prescriptions by deriving them from more general principles, but instead they cite as the main argument: "This is what the Lord says." The most frequent introduction to the sermons of the prophets is: "Thus saith the Lord," and the argument purports to be a report of what the Lord said; in other words, the argument does not employ prescriptive but rather factual premises. Similarly, among the Navahos we shall find that particular prescriptions are justified by appeal to facts rather than to other prescriptions.

e. The mode of interpretation[16]

In the fourth mode, the intermediate premises are not purely factual but are also partially prescriptive. Some of the intermediate subsuming premises are not *found* empirically or by testimony (oracles), but are in part *created* by the person performing the subsumption. In this procedure an ethical validation presupposes an ultimate but schematic basic prescription which is vague and indeterminate, and which needs to be given concrete content by intermediate premises obtained through creative interpretation. Thus it employs both an ultimate schematic basic prescription and procedural prescriptions in order to validate the particular prescription.

The two best philosophical examples of this mode are the ethics of Aristotle and of John Dewey. For Aristotle, there is a basic schematic principle prescribing action in accordance with the mean between excess and deficiency which is relative to us and is specifically determined by "that principle by which the man of practical wisdom would determine it." [17] In other words, the particular application of the principle of the mean is left up to the wise man (*spoudaios*).

Similarly, John Dewey explicitly denounces absolute ethical principles from which particular prescriptions can be determinately inferred, but prefers a looser system which allows for creative interpretation of the individual. Perhaps his ultimate schematic prescription would be something like: "Seek to grow or to develop." The particular interpretation of this general and vague principle is to be made by employing the 'scientific method.'[18]

In both philosophical systems we find two different kinds of ethical principles: first, a basic schema giving general directions about conduct (the mean, growth); and second, a principle of interpretation establishing how the process of interpretation is to be carried out (deliberation, scientific method).

In connection with the philosophy of law, these two types of principle have been called by Kelsen "adjectival," and "substantival" law. Adjectival law defines the authority who is to create the law and the procedure to be followed; substantival law defines the general limits within which the law-creator may exercise his discretion.[19]

A basic prescription of an interpretive system thus usually contains both a substantival element consisting of a vague general description of the acts prescribed, and an adjectival element consisting of a principle of interpretation. However, some interpretive systems assign a more important role to one of these elements than to the other. There are many different systems which give us adjectival or procedural principles and barely mention the substantival. For instance, impartial spectator ethics is primarily concerned with adjectival procedures. Similarly, the ethics of sympathy (for example, Schopenhauer's) also usually neglects the substantive content of morality. (However, even adherents of these procedural systems would probably reject as invalid a conclusion reached by an interpreter which, for instance, approved of inflicting wanton suffering. Such systems generally have an unclear and unformulated substantival principle in the background.)

According to some interpretations of Kant's categorical imperative, it would be an example of a purely substantival principle, since Kant gives no directions as to how to proceed in applying the principle. We also find examples of interpretive systems among natural moralities. The best example of this is the rather sentimental application of 'Christian love' in pacifism (such as is found in Tolstoy). The principle of "Love" as the basis of a moral code serves both the adjectival and substantival functions, since in order to know what to do we must assume the attitude of love for the procedure of interpretation; while, at the same time, love defines certain kinds of acts as right or wrong in very general and vague terms. Other natural and artificial ethical systems which are based upon some subjective attitude usually belong to the same group. The Golden Rule may also be included here.

Three comments should be made in connection with interpretive systems. First, the difference between adjectival and substantival principles is made clearer by considering their bearing on the process of invalidation. A conclusion arrived at according to an adjectival procedure which is contrary to that stipulated is merely *not valid*, whereas if it conflicts with the substantival principle it is *invalid*. This is evident because the adjectival principle only lays down a procedure to be followed in validating a conclusion, and if this procedure is not followed it can only be said that the prescription is *not* validated. On the other hand, if the prescription is contrary to the ultimate substantive principle it is invalid. In the first case, we have no right to affirm the prescription, whereas in the second we must deny it. This may be illustrated as follows:

If the scientific procedure which must be used to validate a prescription according to Dewey is not followed, or even some unscientific procedure is used, the conclusion is not valid. It would not necessarily be invalid, however, for it is conceivable that a correct answer could be derived with incorrect procedures. Dewey would be the last to maintain that all prescriptions not derived scientifically were invalid. On the other hand, if the prescription conflicts with the principle of 'growth' it is invalid. Similarly, for Aristotle, it is perfectly possible for an unwise man to accept a prescription which is not invalid, but which he was unable to validate. In contrast, if the prescription should call for an act of excess (for example, intoxication) it would be invalid, and so it ought to be rejected.

This also illustrates one of the shortcomings of a purely procedural ethics; namely, it cannot directly show that certain prescriptions are invalid but merely that they are not validated. (Of course, it could prove that it was invalid by showing its contradictory to be valid.) This peculiarity also provides us with a test by which we can determine whether a particular principle is adjectival or substantival. For example, it would elucidate the validational status of the principle of 'love.'

The second comment is that most interpretive systems emphasize positive prescriptions rather than negative ones. This is easy to understand if it is recalled that the former allow a latitude of choice in selecting the action to be performed, whereas the latter allow no such discretion. Hence, Aristotelians are fond of emphasizing that all moral principles permit what they call, "freedom of choice," or an "indifference" towards the means.[20]

The third point I wish to make is that in interpretive systems the intermediate interpretive premise always contains an element of prescriptiveness, and consequently it employs ethical expressions in its formulation. In other words, the intermediate premises are 'mixed premises,' since the interpreter is also creative in his validation. For instance, he may judge a certain act to be the *best* means to well-being, and hence obligatory. Thus, Aristotle's virtuous man, or Dewey's scientific moralist, subsumes the particular prescription under the ultimate basic one by using intermediate premises that such and such an action is virtuous or is desirable. It follows that the distinction between prescriptive and factual premises is never sharply drawn, since every premise is both at the same time. This is one ground for Dewey's contention that all judgments are practical.

Finally, it appears to be a characteristic of some interpretive systems that the description of the person who is the interpreter is given in ethical terms. Thus, for Aristotle, the right course of action is the one that the virtuous man would choose. In other words, a correct decision is defined in terms of the one which would be made by man who is "good," "wise," "intelligent," "sympathetic," or "impartial" — all of which are either overtly or covertly ethical expressions. A moral character appears to be a necessary condition of interpreting correctly.[21]

f. Identifying characteristics of the various modes

By way of a summary of this section on the modes of validation, it may be helpful to point out some of the identifying marks of these modes to be expected in the arguments occurring in actual ethical discourse.

First, if in ethical discourse no appeal is made to moral principles, we should suspect that the mode being employed is either the particularist or the applicational mode. This follows because in the former no principle other than a reiteration of the particular prescription itself is necessary, and in the latter the principle is always the same and understood to be so by the listeners.

Second, if there is consistent reference to various different moral principles we may suspect that the mode of selection is being used. However, we must be careful not to assume that it is without other evidence because such general prescriptions may be being used as 'rules of thumb' to direct our attention to certain general characteristics to be anticipated from the action contemplated.

Finally, if the moralist cites certain conditions, such as partiality, in the individual who is deliberating as favorable or unfavorable to a correct decision, we should surmise that the interpretive mode is involved. It is evident that the interpretive mode tends to assume that certain subjective psychological conditions (or ethical conditions) in addition to ordinary intellectual ability are necessary for the procedure to be considered valid.

The Rhetoric of Ethical Discourse:
Justification

I. ETHICAL ARGUMENTATION IN GENERAL

Having examined some of the constituent elements in the structure of ethical discourse, we can now turn to a consideration of ethical reasoning in general. Ethical discourse, as was contended earlier, is essentially a social process, for it consists of talking about moral obligation to others (or to oneself). Therefore, we can best investigate it in a context involving a speaker and a listener. (This is Aristotle's approach in the *Rhetoric*.)

From this point of view we may ask: What is the aim of the speaker? How does he seek to achieve it (or, what are his methods)? What are the conditions of success? That is, when and under what conditions may the speaker expect to convince the listener?

The ultimate aim of ethical discourse is to procure the acceptance of a moral prescription. (This, of course, includes intrapersonal discourse or deliberation.) In other words, the moralist-speaker's purpose is to secure moral conviction about some course of action in the listener. This has earlier been identified with the acquisition of a prescriptive disposition.

In order to achieve this goal, there are two distinct aspects of moral prescriptions which must be justified. First, the action or forbearance itself must be justified. This follows from the consideration that the acceptance of a prescription is a certain kind of disposition to act or forbear. Since the reasons for adopting a prescriptive disposition are the same as those for the actions or forbearances themselves, the speaker can achieve his purpose of inducing the disposition only by giving reasons for performing or not performing the act in question. Hence, the reasons offered in ethical discourse are *rationes agendi* or incentives, and as such are to be distinguished from the reasons given in other kinds of discourse.

The second requirement is that the speaker must convince the listener that the acts have a special authoritativeness; that is, that the prescriptions are to be accepted as superior and legitimate. He must not only offer *rationes agendi,* but also *rationes preferendi!*

The primary aim of most ethical argumentation is therefore to induce the listener to adopt an incentive for acting which is superior and legitimate.

This aim defines the means to be used in realizing it. The character of legitimacy requires that the prescriptions be capable of being legitimately established. Of course, the acceptance of moral prescriptions may be procured without going through this process of legitimation. Undoubtedly, many if not most of those moral prescriptions which are accepted have been acquired in other ways: perhaps by imitation or through suggestion. The important point is that the claim of a moral prescription to be legitimate entails that it be susceptible of being established as legitimate, although it need not always be so established. For the present purpose, however, we are interested only in that kind of ethical discourse which aims at showing certain prescriptions to be legitimate. I shall call this process "ethical justification."

Since ethical justification is the process of legitimating the moral claim of a prescribed act, it itself must be legitimate. Hence, it should not be confused with mere propaganda. If one wishes, it might be described as propaganda using legitimate methods (which is rhetoric in Aristotle's sense). The legitimacy of a moral prescription therefore depends upon their being an ethical justification of it available.

In part, ethical justification consists in deriving particular moral prescriptions from basic moral principles by one of the modes of validation outlined in the last chapter. A necessary condition of ethical justification is that it be valid. Validation (in one of its modes) is therefore an essential constituent in justification.

The use of validational procedures already confers upon the moral prescriptions so derived as well as upon the process of justification part of their legitimacy; for the mere employment of discursive argumentation gives the discourse a kind of intersubjective (or interpersonal) validity. However, the authoritativeness of moral prescriptions cannot be established through validation unless the basic prescription from which they are derived itself has this property. Therefore the most important aspect of ethical justification involves the conception of "basic prescription."

With respect to basic prescriptions the following must be established: that they are *rationes agendi* (incentives), that they are sufficient, ultimate and prior, and that they are legitimate. If any proposed basic prescription is accepted as possessing these characteristics, then those derivative prescriptions which follow from it in accordance with the rules of validation will also possess them. A large part of this chapter will be devoted to explaining how basic prescriptions can have these characteristics.

Finally, no argument in ethical discourse can hope to succeed in convincing a listener unless certain conditions are fulfilled. There are many such conditions. For instance: he must be able to understand and follow the steps of the argument; he must be in a frame of mind which is not unfavorable to accepting it if it is legitimate; and finally he must agree with the speaker on some fundamental presuppositions. These conditions will be referred to as the conditions of *ethical competence.*

2. DESCRIPTION OF BASIC PRESCRIPTIONS

The basic prescriptions of an ethical system are used to validate other prescriptions, but they cannot themselves be validated. In those systems in which no intermediate validational processes are admitted, such as extreme particularism, every moral prescription is basic. However, in every system there are primitive principles for which we cannot demand validation. Other indirect means of establishing them will be discussed later.

Since a basic prescription confers the quality of moral prescriptiveness on other derived prescriptions, we must be able to give an account of how it acquires this quality itself.

a. Ground-motives

A basic prescription in essence is a *ratio agendi:* namely, an incentive for acting or not acting. Therefore, if a prescription is accepted the agent has accepted a reason for acting in a certain way, and by our earlier analysis this means that he has acquired a prescriptive disposition to act.

A prescriptive disposition in turn may be analyzed in terms of a kind of motive. The word "motive" is highly ambiguous, but all that is intended here is that we understand by it some driving force or energy, which may be activated by the proper circumstances and directed into certain channels by the prescriptive disposition. The basic prescriptive disposition, which constitutes the acceptance of the basic prescription, is therefore identifiable with a certain basic kind of motive. I shall call this the *ground-motive* of the ethical system.

Since the basic moral prescription must have the authoritative characteristics earlier described in terms of sufficiency, ultimacy, and priority, the ground-motive in turn cannot be a simple motive but must have some properties which will account for these characteristics of the corresponding basic prescription. Thus the ground-motive is not a *primus inter pares,* but one which is preëminent among motives.

In a sense, the ground-motive and the basic prescription (if accepted) may be regarded as the obverse and the reverse of the same coin. The one accounts for the motivating energy behind morality, while the other explains its directiveness. It might be possible to eliminate the conception of basic prescription entirely and to handle the problems at issue in terms of the ground-motive. This would most likely be more adequate to describe the explicit moral convictions of the average person, who may not be aware of the basic prescriptions which he accepts but is morally motivated towards certain kinds of conduct. However, I prefer to retain the conception of basic prescription because it makes it possible to handle the validational aspect of ethical discourse with greater logical simplicity and elegance.[1]

It is beyond the scope of the present study to give an analysis of the conception of ground-motive. It is important to note that it is a psychological disposition, and in that sense it is not always operative. It may be characterized as a motor-affective disposition like Perry's interest, for it is manifested in action of one kind or another. It is also a stable continuously existent and more or less general disposition. Furthermore it contains conative, cathectic, and cognitive factors within it.

We must recognize that one element in the ground-motive is cognitive, for it involves 'existential' beliefs or assumptions about the world around us. These constitute what Perry calls "mediating judgments." I shall call this mediating cognitive element the *existential ground* of the ground-motive. An example of such a ground is given in Judaic ethics, namely, certain beliefs about God; that he is all good, merciful, and our Creator. It is grounds like these that give rise to the motive, and mediately through the motive are the foundation of the basic prescription.

Insufficient attention has been paid in recent ethics to this phenomenon of the existential ground of morality. This ground consists of significant beliefs about life in general (a *Weltanschauung*) — hence the term "existential."[2]

The preëminence of the ground-motive is usually dependent upon the existential grounds upon which it is based. The belief that the universe is put together in a certain way cannot fail to have an influence upon which motive is to be regarded as paramount. If there is a God, this is an important consideration. Likewise, the Stoics felt that the Logos of the World or Nature, was a ground from which their ethics inevitably flowed. The plausibility of the Marxist position for so many comes from the fact that it grounds its ethics in the dialectic of history.

Thus the existential ground serves to give special authority to the ground-motive, which in turn is the source of the basic prescription of a moral code. This is why moralists have so often sought to base their ethics upon metaphysics.

The ground-motive can be considered either phenomenologically or objectively: that is, from the way it appears to the subject or as it appears to an observer. Usually the phenomenological description of the ground-motive involves explicit reference to the ground and some evaluation of it. In the theological example given above, God is described as just and merciful, and these are evaluative as well as purely descriptive terms. If asked why one ought to obey God's commandments, the only possible answer would be to describe him in such 'existential' terms.

b. Classification of basic prescriptions and ground-motives

Some of the possible types of basic prescriptions and ground-motives are given in the accompanying table. The list does not pretend to be an exhaustive classification of possible basic prescriptions. However, it may serve as a guide in formulating hypotheses in anthropological inquiries in descriptive ethics. Such a list was used when investigating Navaho ethics to test the various possibilities.

Table of Basic Prescriptions

Group I. Actions which are extrinsic means to an end
    (1) Extrapersonal ends: e.g. utilitarianism (Bentham), agathistic utilitarianism (Moore)
    (2) Intrapersonal ends: (a) This-worldly—e.g. egoistic hedonism (Epicurus)
                                  (b) Other-worldly—e.g. egoistic hedonism (Paley)
    (3) Transpersonal ends: e.g. Nirvana (?), common good of group (T. H. Green)

Group II. Actions which are intrinsic means to an end
    (1) Intrapersonal ends: (a) Only this-worldly, e.g. happiness (Aristotle)
                                  (b) Also other-worldly, e.g. beatitude (Aquinas), sanctification (some versions of Judaism)
    (2) Transpersonal ends: e.g. self-realizationism (absolute idealism)

Group III. Actions specified by particular conditions and consequences
    (1) Pluralistic (Prichard, Ross, etc.)
    (2) Commands of an authority (other versions of Judaism)

Group IV. Actions which are symbols of an attitude
    (1) Various positive attitudes: love, respect, loyalty, piety

A few comments in elucidation of the table are necessary.

(1) Philosophers who teach ethics are accustomed to offer their students various classifications of ethical systems. The scheme I have adopted is rather conventional. It will be noted that Groups I and II belong to the type of ethics usually called "teleological" or "utilitarian," while Groups III and IV are usually called "formalistic" or "deontological."

(2) The distinction between Groups I and II is important and frequently neglected by theories that discuss the means-end relationship as the basis of prescriptions. I have already mentioned earlier the two types of means-end relationship. An extrinsic means is one which is itself not a constituent of the end, and its only value derives from the fact that it is a cause of the end's coming into being. For instance, for Bentham a prescribed action may be indifferent as far as its own pleasantness or unpleasantness is

concerned, but its value consists in its being a means to the end. Intrinsic means are, on the other hand, constitutive elements in the end. Thus, for Aristotle a virtuous action is a means to happiness because happiness is virtuous activity. Similarly, for Dewey moral activity is an end-in-itself as well as a means. The relation of intrinsic means to an end is sometimes described as that of a part to the whole.

(3) By the term "impersonal end" I mean an end that does not necessarily involve a state of affairs in the agent at all. Thus, for Bentham a person may be obliged to do an action which may give him as agent no pleasure at all, or, indeed, may give him only pain. There cannot be prescriptions of this type in Group II, because since actions are intrinsic means the ends must always be 'in the agent.'

The term "intrapersonal" end is intended to signify an end which is *only* within the agent. All forms of 'atomic' egoism belong to this group (for example, Navaho ethics). Finally, the term "transpersonal" end is used to designate those ends which include the agent but transcend him. Some of these systems maintain that the agent is absorbed into a higher good or state. Sometimes the relationship between the personal end and this transpersonal end is said to be that of intrinsic means. Many theories of the group-soul belong to this group; the ends of the individual are realized by the common good.

(4) In all teleological theories the end of moral conduct cannot be a simple "end-in-view" in Dewey's sense; that is, moral prescriptions never prescribe the means to a particular achievable state of affairs. If this were the case, then once the end had been achieved or lost forever, the prescription would be cancelled — and the agent would not have to worry about morality any more. Morality is not like winning a game, which when won allows the participants to retire in glory.

The end involved in basic moral prescriptions must therefore be a continuous end. This continuity is assured by the various species of teleological theories in different ways. In a theory like Bentham's, this character is accounted for by the fact that the greatest happiness is a continually shifting goal, which changes as the situation changes. This requirement illuminates some essential aspects of Navaho ethics, for the end of their moral prescriptions is in principle achievable, namely physical security: health, absence of poverty, and friends. However, the continuity is assured by the belief that even though these ends may be attained, the possession of them is always being challenged by unsympathetic forces from the outside.

(5) The basic prescriptions which come under Groups III and IV require no extensive comment. In connection with 'command-ethics,' it should be pointed out that it is not always easy to classify it under Group III, for

sometimes obedience to commands is a means to the end of, say, sanctification or other-worldly reward, and in this case it should come under Group I or II. Or else, the actions conforming to an authority's commands may be considered to be actions symbolic of piety or respect, and so should be placed in Group IV.

(6) This list of basic prescriptions suggests that there are two general types of ground-motives behind them. The first type of motive is the desire to bring into existence a certain state of affairs (for example, happiness). The teleological theories all presuppose some motive of this type, and most philosophical exponents of them introduce into their systems some fundamental desire for the end prescribed, such as the desire for pleasure (Epicurus) or for happiness (Aristotle). In such systems the ground-motive could be described in traditional terms as a desire. I shall call such ground-motives *aspirational*.[3]

The type of ground-motive involved in nonteleological systems is much more difficult to analyze. The notion of "respect" or "love," for instance, is not exhausted by describing them in terms of the production of a state of affairs. They may demand the promotion of states of affairs, but such ends-in-view are in a sense means to expressing the attitudes involved. Perhaps the simplest way to describe these difficult phenomena phenomenologically is to say that they seek to "objectify" or to "express" their feelings or attitudes toward some object. I shall call this type of ground-motive *attitudinal*.

c. Philosophical explanations of the ground-motives

Since the time of Plato, philosophers have sought to explain the priority of the ground-motive over all other motives. It is worth while to consider briefly some of these explanations. The traditional views fall into two broad groups, which I shall label the "split personality" theory and the "holistic" theory respectively.

The first of these theories maintains that the ground-motive is a motive distinct from other motives in the personality, which in many, if not all cases, opposes these other motives. Phenomenologically it appears almost as if it were "an external compulsion" or the "voice of God." This type of ground-motive is often called by its advocates "conscience" or "the sense of duty." Quite frequently the peculiar authoritativeness of this motive is ascribed to some special origin, for example, it is said to be "implanted in us by God." The Freudians employ the argument in reverse contending that the Super-Ego having originated in childhood conditions should *not* have the authority ascribed to it. It is important always to bear in mind that almost all the so-called "conscience" theories not only describe conscience or the moral sense as the faculty of apprehending moral truths, but also regard it as a motive to performing the actions whose moral quality is thus apprehended. In addition, its existence within us is usually attributed to God's providence, and thereby it is existentially grounded.

The holistic theories, on the other hand, contend that the ground-motive is a combination of all the other motives in the personality. Thus it is not a distinct motive, but rather is all of them put together. It represents the interests of the whole as opposed to each distinct interest which is only partial. Therefore, its authoritativeness is that of the whole over any of its parts (or perhaps of the majority of them over the others).

It is an essential principle of the holistic view that each separate interest is a constituent element in the whole, and must not be totally ignored. Every motive must at some time at least partially be satisfied, in order to keep harmony in the personality. An extreme form of this tolerance of every interest is exemplified in Perry's principle of inclusiveness, which requires that the claim of every interest must be respected. Aristotle's principle of the mean is also an expression of this view, for it states that a motive should not be pursued to excess and thus infringe upon others, but at the same time also not to deficiency so that it is never satisfied. Modern theories influenced by Freudian psychology also provide examples of this type of theory (for example, Fromm).[4]

The organization of motives which constitutes the whole is usually described in metaphorical terms such as "harmony," "integration," or "growth." It is obviously necessary to formulate the conception of "whole" of the interests so that it is not just a mere resultant of their various strengths, for if this whole is only a resultant the ground-motive would be a slave rather than a master of the situation, and it would lose all its effective preëminence. The office of integrating all the various motives is usually thought to be performed by reason or intelligence.

I submit that neither of these two kinds of theory provides an adequate account of the ground-motives of many natural moralities; the first is too narrow and second is too broad. Such moralities do not pretend that morality is designed to satisfy all the needs of man, but only the *basic* needs. The other needs can tag along provided that they do not get in the way. The priority assigned to the ground-motive is due to the assumption that it is a basic need, indeed, the most important need. This seems to be the case with the Hebrew prophets who regarded the need for sanctification as prior to all others. It also seems to be true of the Navahos, who regard material security as the most important need.

Only if we develop a theory along these lines will we be able to solve some of the crucial problems of morality. For instance, it may help to answer such questions as the following: why are there varying degrees of stringency attached to moral prescriptions as they are found in the difference between moral injunctions and moral counsels? How can we account for some of the differences between positive and negative prescriptions? A negative prescription calls for a negative ground-motive, an avoidance motive, which cannot be assimilated easily to the other positive motives. Some theory of the ordering of motives according to the priority assigned them will accomplish these tasks more readily than either the holistic or the split personality doctrines.

d. Derivation of prescriptions of varying stringency

In the earlier section on prescriptive qualities I suggested that philosophers have seriously neglected the problems arising out of the relationships between negative and positive prescriptions, and of the varying degrees of stringency of moral prescriptions. Having examined some of the basic prescriptions upon which an ethical system can be founded, we are now in a better position to inquire into the ways the different systems can account for these variations.

The most stringent positive prescriptions and negative prescriptions were referred to as "injunctions" and "prohibitions" respectively. The less stringent positive prescriptions were called "moral counsels," and for the correspondingly less stringent negative moral counsels I coined the term "moral discounsel."

On the whole, the teleological basic prescriptions present a different type of solution to these problems from that of the formalistic systems. I shall therefore consider them separately.

The prescripta of a basic teleological prescription are those actions promoting the basic end, which may be positive or negative. Thus, they are defined in terms of a *summum bonum* to be sought or a *summum malum* to be avoided. The ground-motive for a positive goal is some kind of desire, whereas for a negative goal it is an aversion. The problem is: How can positive injunctions be derived from negative goals, and negative prohibitions from positive goals?

With respect to any state of affairs (good or evil) there are actions which will promote it and actions which will avert it. Consequently, if the prescribed end is negative, those actions which promote the evil state of affairs are forbidden, and those averting it are enjoined. Similarly, if the end is positive, the actions promoting it are enjoined and those averting it are forbidden. Thus actions may be enjoined either because they promote a positive end, or avert a negative end; and they may be forbidden either because they promote a negative end, or avert a positive end.[5]

Actions which are enjoined because they are productive of a desirable state of affairs are commonly called "means" to the end. In the case of negative goals such positive actions may be considered as means to averting the evil. The means-ends relations involved in both positive and negative goals determine the variations in the stringency of the prescription they entail.

Unfortunately, in English there is no corresponding term for the opposite of "means," that is, an action which will produce an undesirable state of affairs. It is important to recognize those classes of actions which promote evil or avert good: for example, war is productive of unhappiness. Perhaps we might coin the word *dismeans* to stand for this kind of negative action. A dismeans should not be confused with a non-means, which is an action that does not promote the desired end. It is important to observe the distinction between an act that produces evil, and one that does not produce good.

Some means are *necessary* and other means are *optional*. For instance, it is necessary to eat and sleep to have pleasure; but it is optional whether I go to the movies or read books; either will do. Similarly, in order to avoid pain (a negative goal) one must also eat and sleep regularly; but the choice of foods is optional. The neglect of necessary means will result in the nonexistence of the end-state of affairs, whether it be a good or absence of an evil. Therefore, we should expect positive prescriptions about necessary means to be more stringent than those about optional means.

There is a similar distinction to be found among actions which are forbidden, whether as dismeans that promote an evil or that avert a good. Some actions are *sufficient* to promote the evil, and some are insufficient or merely *contributory*. Thus, supposing death to be the supreme evil (negative goal) suicide would be sufficient, whereas poverty would be merely contributory. Similarly, if happiness (in this life) were the supreme positive end, suicide would again be sufficient to avert this good by making it impossible, whereas hurting oneself would contribute to the nonattainment of this goal but would not make it impossible. Those forbidden actions, which are sufficient, make it impossible to avert an evil or to attain a goal, whereas those which are contributory do not make it impossible unless enough other contributory conditions are added. Again, we should expect those actions which are sufficient to produce the supreme evil or to avert forever the supreme good, to be more stringently prohibited than those which are merely contributory.

Furthermore, within these two less stringent categories of optional means and contributory negative conditions (dismeans) there are degrees of 'fecundity,' which result from the fact that they vary in the extent to which they contribute to the production of good or evil. One means may be more efficacious on the whole than another. For instance, in the long run I may get more pleasure from one course of action rather than another.

Or, again, one action may contribute more than another to bringing on the evil, or averting the good.

Another factor which should be mentioned is the degree of certainty with which the effect is supposed to follow from the action. It is likely that where there is a high degree of uncertainty, the stringency tends to be lowered. However, this is not always the case, because the seriousness of the effect may often offset some doubtfulness about the efficacy of the actions producing it. This is a problem which requires further investigation. The examination of the Navaho ethical code may throw some light on it.

All these considerations provide us with clues to explaining the relative stringency of the various kinds of moral prescriptions. The order of various degrees of stringency can be summed up in a table as follows:

I. *Negative Goal*

    (1) Prohibition of actions sufficient to produce it (= sufficient dismeans)
    (2) Injunction of acts necessary to avert it (= necessary means)
    (3) Discounsel of acts contributory to it (= contributory dismeans)
    (4) Counsel of acts contributory to averting it (= contributory means)

II. *Positive Goal*

    (1) Injunction of actions necessary to promote it (= necessary means)
    (2) Prohibition of actions sufficient to avert it (= sufficient dismeans)
    (3) Counsel of actions contributory to it (= contributory means)
    (4) Discounsel of actions contributory to averting it (= contributory dismeans)

(Counsels and discounsels may also be ordered in terms of their fecundity).

There are probably significant differences between an ethical system based upon negative goals and one based upon positive goals. I suggested earlier that the former tends to be an ethics of constraint and the latter an ethics of direction. Probably an ethics of negativity is in general more stringent than one of positivity. This depends on whether item (1) or item (2) is the more stringent in the system. Usually (2) is less stringent than (1) because there is less certainty about which acts belong in this group. It might be that where negative goals are involved the agent is advised not to take chances.[6]

The relation between negative and positive goals within any moral code raises interesting problems. There are three possible interpretations of this relationship: first, the goal of morality may be negative, and positive goals derived from it; second, the goal of morality may be positive, and negative goals derivative; and third, there may be two goals, one positive and one negative, and neither one is reducible to the other.

There are many systems where the goal appears to be almost purely negative. Perhaps we may consider Nirvana to be an instance of such a negative goal, since it seems to mean only the absence of all suffering. "The annihilation of desire, the annihilation of hatred, the annihilation of error — this, friend, is what is called Nirvana." [7] Probably Stoicism also reflects a similar negative ethics. Some hedonists (such as Epicurus) stress the end of avoiding pain more than that of seeking pleasure. I believe, as I shall argue later, that the Navaho moral system belongs to this group.

Moralists who assume that the prescribed end is both negative and positive are faced with a dilemma: either they must admit an irreducible dichotomy of ends and so must set up two inherently unconnected series of moral prescriptions, or else they must assimilate the positive ends to negative ones or vice versa.

Hedonism provides a good example of such attempted assimilation. Common experience shows us that there are two distinct kinds of affective sensations — pleasure and pain. Shall the hedonist prohibit pain-producing acts or enjoin pleasure producing ones? Hedonists tend to fall into two camps, the one stressing the former (Epicurus), the other the latter (Santayana). However, most of them feel uncomfortable about ignoring the other side, so they attempt an assimilation by tacitly assuming that there is a continuity between pleasure and pain. They suppose that absence of pain is pleasant, so that in promoting the absence of pain they are ipso facto producing pleasure. The negative prohibition, "Avoid pain," is assumed to be equivalent to the positive injunction, "Seek pleasure."

A similar situation is to be found in the various theories that use "harmony" as the end of life (for example, Aristotle and Plato). The absence of harmony is assumed to be disharmony, and the absence of disharmony is harmony. Therefore, "Avoid disharmony" is equivalent to "Seek harmony." Aristotle's maxim of the mean illustrates this because the actions it prescribes are the avoidance of excess and deficiency, and at the same time by implication the pursuit of the intermediate. However, I believe if we look more closely we can see that Aristotle's system is fundamentally positive rather than negative, for he allows for choice of the means — which is not normally admitted in negative systems. [8]

It seems plausible to suppose that all the ends involved in basic prescriptions of Group II, which prescribe actions that are intrinsic means to an end, are positive. It seems difficult to conceive of an action being an intrinsic means to a negative goal, although admittedly there are examples of particular actions which are parts of a negative goal; for example, a painful act might be such an intrinsic condition of the negative end, a painful state of affairs. In the examples given of this Group, I believe that the end is always positive. However, perhaps further investigation will reveal that there is no reason to restrict teleological ethics of constraint to Group I.

When we come to examine the problem of comparative stringency in formalistic systems the situation is much more complicated. I shall therefore only suggest a few points in connection with them.

In Group III, where principles and commands state the actions to be or not to be performed, the stringency is often conveyed by the statement itself. Moralists of the British intuitionistic school generally concede that obligations to keep promises are more stringent than those to beneficence. However, from the very nature of their theories, no further analysis of this is possible. In a command ethics, the stringency of the prescriptions is often determined by the harshness of the penalties for disobedience or the rewards for obedience. Presumably the nonfulfillment of some of the ceremonial injunctions of Jahweh is not thought to be punished as severely as a violation of one of the Ten Commandments.

The quality and stringency of the symbolic prescriptions of Group IV depend upon the attitude which they express. Some attitudes demand to be expressed by the nonperformance of certain actions. For instance, to act respectfully means (in part) to act with a certain restraint, and thus excludes things one might wish to do.[9] Other attitudes demand positive actions of one type or another, for example, 'love' may be taken to prescribe helping others. We may thus divide the ground-attitudes in Group IV into positive and negative attitudes. The positive attitudes generate injunctions and the negative ones generate prohibitions.

However, as was the case with negative and positive goals, moralists have often felt uncomfortable not to be able to assimilate the negative and the positive to each other. Thus, for instance, Kant describes 'respect' as a combination of 'fear' and 'love' — a negative and a positive attitude.

It appears to be a peculiarity of theories of Group IV that the injunction of one kind of act is equivalent to the prohibition of its absence. "Thou shalt love thy neighbor" means in effect the same as "Thou shalt not regard thy neighbor without love." [10]

This equivalence follows from the fact that in many cases the opposite of an attitude is merely its absence where it is to be expected. A disrespectful act is one lacking respect. However, it should be added that the absence of an attitude becomes its opposite *only in the situation* calling for the attitude itself. Thus a disrespectful act is an act which manifests absence of respect where respect is to be expected. Hence, the conception of a disrespectful act can be understood only in relation to the corresponding respectful one. This is why those who aspired to be Satanists at the end of the Middle Ages had to perform such impious acts as Black Masses, which were nothing but acts deliberately lacking piety where piety was enjoined.

Part of the context of such acts as those of love, respect, and piety include the deliberate intention of the agent; he must be aware of what he is doing and why. This explains why certain actions where respect is absent need not be considered disrespectful if one takes into account the agent's ignorance or his lack of deliberate intent. Ignorance or lack of deliberate purpose may excuse one in such ethical systems.

Therefore, for at least some systems in Group IV, there is a sort of law of the excluded middle; within a context an action is either obligatory or wrong, and if it is obligatory then its nonperformance is wrong, and so on. This, of course, does not entail that every action is either right or wrong, because there may be contextual conditions where actions are indifferent. But within the context it does hold. This characteristic makes it possible to derive negative prohibitions directly from positive injunctions, and vice versa.[11]

The problem of degrees of stringency has no such simple solution. Probably a good many systems of this group do not distinguish between such degrees; all prescriptions may be roughly of the same level. Other systems may find an order of stringency in the actual or presumed importance of the actions to the object of the attitude. Thus, acts prescribed by love may vary in their stringency according to the way they affect the person loved.

Obviously, none of the suggestions that I have made about the relation of negative to positive prescriptions, or about the problem of relative stringency constitutes an adequate analysis of the various systems discussed. Such a task is perhaps impossible because of the wealth of variations and subtleties. Nevertheless, some analysis along these lines is necessary for any adequate account of a moral code. The purpose of this section has been merely to call attention to some of the problems involved.

3. THE VINDICATION OF BASIC PRESCRIPTIONS

A basic prescription, by definition, cannot itself be validated, since there is no higher prescription from which it can be derived. In this sense, *de principiis non est disputandum.*

The indisputability of basic principles is not a unique characteristic of ethical discourse, but is to be found in every sphere of discourse, logic and science included. There is no sense in asking for a validation of, say, the law of contradiction in logic, or of the principle of induction in science, and similarly we cannot ask for a validation of basic ethical principles. But, on the other hand, their not being susceptible of validation does not entail that such basic principles are arbitrary. Although they cannot be validated, there are indirect means of defending them and of convincing the listener of such principles. The classic instance is Aristotle's defense of the law of contradiction by showing the absurdities which follow from its denial.

I shall use the term "vindication" for these indirect nonvalidational modes of proof of basic prescriptions.[12] I intend thereby exactly what Mill had in mind when he wrote:

Questions of ultimate ends are not amenable to direct proof . . . We are not, however, to infer that [their] acceptance or rejection must depend on blind impulse, or arbitrary choice. There is a larger meaning of the word proof, in which this question is as amenable to it as any other of the disputed questions of philosophy . . . Considerations may be presented capable of determining the intellect either to give or withhold its assent to the doctrine; and this is equivalent to proof.[13]

We may ask: What is the purpose of the vindication of a basic moral principle? Mill's answer is that it is "to make good its claim to be believed." Thus, in offering this kind of indirect proof we are not merely seeking to persuade others to adopt the principle in question as a principle of action, but we are also seeking to convince them that to do so is not arbitrary and unreasonable. It is obvious that we are not only interested in convincing others but ourselves as well.

There are many ways in which a moralist may approach the task of vindicating his basic moral prescriptions. In the first place, he may try to establish it by showing that their epistemological status is similar to that of other beliefs; thus he may appeal to self-evidence or inability to doubt. Second, he may appeal to the opinions of others in order to show that his own view is not a mere personal whim. Finally, he may offer considerations which appear to support the particular basic prescription in question. I shall now examine some of these procedures of vindication in more detail.

In the history of ethics one of the most common methods of vindication to be found is the claim of self-evidence for the basic prescriptions proposed. In making such a claim one is attributing to such prescriptious an epistemological status which is analogous to that of the basic principles of logic and the foundations of knowledge. However, the notion of "self-evidence" has come into considerable disrepute in recent years because many principles that were supposed to be self-evident have been proven to be false. It has been rejected by many, therefore, as a psychologistic criterion with dubious cognitive validity. But even granting that the appeal to self-evidence is not always unjustified, the notion of "self-evidence" seems to me to be peculiarly inapplicable to the basic principles of an ethical system. Ordinarily, self-evidence is supposed to involve a clear and distinct apprehension of the principle in question whereas, probably many, if not most, natural ethical systems are based on basic prescriptions which are *not* clearly and distinctly apprehended by their adherents. Indeed, in descriptive ethics, these basic prescriptions are reconstructions and as such are not explicitly enunciated and recognized by the informant at all.

That the basic ethical principles in natural moralities are rarely clear and distinct in the speaker's mind is confirmed by the fact that in almost all societies ethical argument is indirect. This is evident even in our own culture, for we hardly ever argue directly from basic principles but usually quite indirectly. Probably the fact that we are not completely clear about our assumptions makes ethical discussions feasible even with those who appear to disagree with us quite fundamentally. Most moral disputation is conducted on the intermediate level, and presupposes some basic principles which the average person would find difficult to formulate precisely.

Such considerations therefore suggest that self-evidence in the sense in which it involves a clear and distinct formulation of the principle apprehended is not a very common form of vindication of basic assumptions. Nevertheless, we must admit that some ethical systems do make frequent appeals to the self-evidence of specific moral principles, such as the wrongness of breaking promises. This kind of appeal is characteristic of the mode of selection.[14] Consequently, we may have to decide that the appeal to self-evidence can be introduced into some kinds of ethical system and not into others. But even those systems which assume a plurality of self-evident moral principles might in the end be found susceptible of a reconstructive analysis which uncovers a basic prescription from which they can be derived, and of which the adherents are not clearly and distinctly aware.

A much weaker form of vindication for basic principles uses as a criterion the person's "inability to doubt," which leaves open the possibility that he may be wrong. As Peirce says: "In point of fact, an inquiry, to have that completely satisfactory result called demonstration, has only to start with propositions perfectly free from all actual doubt. If the premises are not in fact doubted at all, they cannot be more satisfactory than they are."[15] This final standard which is advanced by Peirce as the basis of knowledge has been employed by philosophers in many different fields of knowledge, such as perception and logic. There are certain central beliefs which we should be extremely loath to relinquish, and these can serve as a firm foundation for our demonstrations. Among such beliefs some have included ethical convictions. Accordingly, the process of ethical vindication may take the form of rendering explicit these basic convictions.

A second broad category of modes of vindication appeals to the opinions of others. That this is a frequent way of establishing unprovable propositions is obvious if we consider how we settle disputes about colors with a color-blind man; certainly, in such cases the opinions of others has final authority.

Again in the history of Western moral philosophy we often encounter arguments citing the general agreement of mankind: This principle is accepted by men of all nations, so it should be accepted by us. Such an argument is generally called the *argumentum ex consensu gentium;* and although facts about universal agreement cannot be used to validate such principles, perhaps we shall have to admit that they may serve to vindicate them.[16] But we immediately encounter a difficulty in the fact, which had been overlooked in the eighteenth century, that there does not seem to be universal agreement among men about their ethical principles. Now, since the claim we are considering is only one of vindication, this fact cannot upset the principle in question, but it does render the argument worthless. Some attempt might be made to rescue it by introducing a category of what might be called "implicit" acceptance of moral principles, and it might be asserted that all men implicitly accept the principle in question. But, in that case, an elucidation of "implicit acceptance" is required.

The plausibility of the appeal to the agreement of everyone in order to vindicate a basic prescription seems to rest on an assumed analogy between moral qualities and sensory qualities like color. But there are philosophical reasons for rejecting this analogy.[17] If it is rejected, some reason must be offered for believing that the average normal man is capable of discovering and judging for himself the basic principles of ethics. For these reasons the appeal to the agreement of large numbers appears to be a rather doubtful type of vindication.

In addition, it must be noted that there have been many moral philosophers who would vociferously reject the opinions of the masses as definitive about ethical questions. Plato, Aristotle, and Nietzsche, for example, scorn the ethical convictions of the populace. Furthermore, ethnologists tell us that some tribes despise the opinions of other tribes. For such systems agreement proves nothing at all. For all of them, the only kind of agreement that counts is the agreement among those who are wise and know. In an aristocratic ethics a man consults only his peers, and in a tribal ethics he consults only his fellow tribesmen. The people who are worth listening to in an ethical dispute will be referred to as those who are *ethically competent.* Therefore, the argument from consensus carries conviction with it only if it is limited to the consensus of competent people. It follows that the appeal to the almost universal agreement of mankind can be used to vindicate basic moral prescriptions only if we have some reason for believing that the masses are ethically competent.[18]

Both of the two broad types of vindication which we have examined must resort ultimately to the use of the conception of "ethical competence" and "ethical incompetence"; for the only way in which we can handle a person who does not have self-evident intuitions, does not accept moral principles not doubted by us, or does not agree with the opinions of others, is to declare him incompetent.

The third type of vindication we shall consider is one which does not employ this conception but approaches the justification of basic ethical prescriptions more directly. While the other methods in the end may be said to aim at showing that we have good reasons for adopting our basic principles, the third method seeks to persuade the hearer to adopt the principle itself. There are several ways in which this may be done.

Quite frequently vindicative arguments take the form of convincing a person that he 'really' has already accepted the principle in question, even though he does not consciously acknowledge that he has done so. A paradigm of this type of argument is provided in the opening pages of Plato's *Republic* where Socrates convinces Cephalus that he 'really' does not believe that justice consists in paying one's debts because that would entail returning a weapon to a madman. Certainly, much of the argumentation which occurs in our own ethical disputes consists of showing the absurd consequences of one principle as well as showing that the particular moral judgments we make are consequences of some more general principle which we 'implicitly' accept.[19]

Finally, we come to perhaps the most fundamental type of vindication, namely, that which directly aims at convincing others to accept a basic prescription. This is the kind of vindication with which Mill was concerned in the passage quoted above. It consists of securing the acceptance of the basic prescription by eliciting the ground-motive which corresponds to it. The ground-motive in turn is elicited either by calling attention to the existential beliefs upon which it is founded, in cases where these beliefs had been ignored, or else by persuading the hearer to adopt them. The assumption on which this type of indirect proof is based is that if a person attends to the correct existential beliefs, he will automatically have the correct motor-affective attitude or ground-motive.

There are many illustrations of this type of argument. If one asks a theist: "Why should I obey God's commandments?" his answer would be: "Because He is your Creator, He is the Almighty," and so on. If one should ask an eudaimonist like Aristotle: "Why should I seek happiness?" he would answer: "Because all men naturally desire happiness." And if one should ask Mill: "Why is pleasure desirable?" the answer would be: "Because everyone desires pleasure."

None of these answers is intended to provide a validation of a basic prescription but only a vindication of it by offering a 'consideration to determine the intellect.' The frequent appeal by moralists to metaphysical principles are to be interpreted in this sense, and if they are not so interpreted their arguments become nonsense. Metaphysical or existential beliefs are grounds but not premises for an ethical system; and this is why they are relevant to ethics. This explains why the Stoics claim that their ethics is founded on the Logos of Nature; Plato and Aristotle refer to the structure of reality; Hobbes begins his Leviathan with the exposition of materialism; Bentham refers to psychological hedonism as a ground for his ethical hedonism; and some contemporary naturalists ground their ethics in basic human needs and drives. Even the rather thin theories of the British intuitionists state that somehow ethical qualities are qualities of real objective things.

But this use of existential statements is not just a peculiarity of the artificial moralities of the philosophers. Natural moralities also are based upon existential beliefs, perhaps even more obviously so than philosophical systems. Beliefs about God, the world and man form an integral part of such ethics, not only as factual premises in the process of validation, but also as existential grounds for their basic prescriptions.

The appeal to existential grounds is the ultimate method by which the basic prescriptions of a system can be vindicated, and, perhaps, in some instances repudiated. The attribution of certain qualities to a presumed divinity naturally is followed by the desire to follow his wishes, and the belief that there is no such being is also naturally followed by the repudiation of prescriptions based on this belief. In a similar fashion, a naturalistic world-view generally implies that the relevant grounds of morality are to be found in the nature of man.

Existential grounds confer superiority and legitimacy on the ground-motive and the corresponding basic prescription, and thereby show them not to be merely arbitrary but "based upon the nature of things," and in this sense authoritative.

On the basis of our examination of various modes of vindication it should be obvious that arguments of all types aim at showing that the basic prescription in question possesses those characteristics which define a "moral prescription," namely, legitimacy and superiority. Bearing in mind that "legitimacy" is a complex notion, we can see that the various modes are concerned with establishing different elements of legitimacy with respect to the basic moral prescription: sometimes its inherent reasonableness, sometimes its intersubjectivity, and sometimes its foundation in reality.[20]

4. ETHICAL COMPETENCE

a. Competence in general

Rational discourse in the sense of reasonable disputation and argument, is possible only between people who are reasonable. "To be reasonable"

in this sense, means at least to have the minimum of intelligence and training to be able to grasp the argument and to infer the necessary conclusions.
I shall refer to the conditions which must be presupposed of the participants
in reasonable discourse as the *conditions of competence*. If these conditions
are absent, then such discourse is futile.

It is evident that a modicum of competence is assumed to be necessary
in every sphere of reasonable discourse — in the sciences and in the arts
as well as in ethics. The type of competence required obviously varies
with the particular kind of discourse involved. Thus, a scientist can argue
scientifically only with a person who is qualified, that is, who has scientific
competence. No scientist would waste his time by arguing with fanatic
or superstitious opponents. He would simply reject their talk as that of
incompetents. Similarly, in ordinary life it is futile to argue about even
simple matters with an imbecile or a drunk. They are passed off as incompetent, either permanently or temporarily so.

Although this conception of rational competence has been seriously
neglected by philosophers, I suggest that some assumptions about the
requirements of competence are made whenever we reason with others, and
that an examination of these assumptions will throw a great deal of light
on the nature of the discourse itself.[21] For instance, it is obvious that the
basic requirement for scientific competence is the employment of the
scientific method.

The implicit and explicit requirements of competence vary not only with
the particular kind of discourse involved, such as science or ethics, but also
with the theoretical presuppositions of the specific system which the
speaker professes. The extreme requirement is complete agreement with the
statements of the speaker, who regards those who disagree with him as ipso
facto incompetent, stupid, or ignorant. Where the criteria of competence tend
to coincide with the acceptance of the discourse as presented, to invoke
incompetence is clearly a form of *petitio principii*.

This question-begging extreme is exemplified by all those systems which
rely upon self-evident principles, whether they be logical, metaphysical or
ethical. A person who does not 'see' their 'truth' is ipso facto 'blind.' In
practice, this criterion of competence is ordinarily presupposed in logic and
mathematics, as well as in intuitionistic ethics.

It is interesting to observe that where the criteria of competence approximate acceptance in the sense just mentioned, there are no other
explicitly required conditions of competence. This explains why people do
not write books on the methodology of logic or mathematics, and also why
the ethical intuitionists are unable to explain in detail the conditions under
which intuitions are to be achieved.

On the other hand, where the requirements of competence are more rigorously defined, there is much more freedom to disagree within these limits. Thus anyone who accepts the scientific method is free to disagree with even the most eminent scientist without incurring the risk of being considered incompetent. Hence, the scientific requirements of competence, being more rigorously defined, will involve a *petitio principii* only with respect to those who are unscientific and not to those who merely disagree.

Similar variations from the vague criteria, which tend to be question-begging, to more precise criteria, which are not, are to be found in the different kinds of ethical systems. I shall discuss them presently, but first I shall make a few remarks on the general conditions of competence.

There are certain general conditions of competence which are ordinarily required in every sphere of discourse. First, we must assume that the listener is able to understand the language in which the discourse is conducted. It is obviously futile to argue with a Hottentot who does not understand English. However, exactly the same situation obtains where technical terminology is employed, as in the sciences. It would be interesting to know how and to what extent the language barrier is used as a criterion of incompetence in ethical discourse. It may be that this is one reason why non-literate people do not seek to propagate their own moral ideas to other peoples: "they just won't understand, because they don't speak our language." The intimate relationship between moral discourse and language is widely recognized, but I suggest that further study might reveal significant facts about the relation of language to conceptions of intellectual and especially ethical competence.

Secondly, a modicum of intelligence is always necessary before the speaker can assume his listener to be competent. Hence, idiots and small children are ordinarily excluded, although there are tremendous variations in application. Such variations probably depend largely on the type of reasoning involved and the quantity of previous information presupposed. If the reasoning is intricate or a good deal of information is necessary, then children must be older before you can reason with them. In any case, it is clear that no one ever assumes that human beings are always rational, and that we can reason with anyone. Consequently some distinction between the competent and incompetent must be made in every system, ethical as well as scientific, although where the line is to be drawn varies with the subject matter, the type of argument involved, the information required, and the particular system in question.

Since it is beyond the scope of this study to examine competence in general more thoroughly, I shall now turn to its application in ethical discourse.

b. Ethical competence

Like other spheres of discourse, ethical discourse can be conducted only with people who are able to follow the arguments and capable of accepting the conclusions. Ethical systems vary considerably in the conditions of ethical competence which they suppose to be necessary within the listener in order to make ethical discourse feasible, and to avoid futile argument. In addition to the general requirements noted in the last subsection, there are special requirements which are common and peculiar to all ethical discourse.

Ethical reasoning of all types ultimately aims at the acceptance of prescriptions. Since such acceptance involves various motivational factors and dispositions, the listener must be at least potentially capable of being motivated to the actions prescribed. This involves not only being induced to act accordingly, but also willing or deciding to do so in the sense discussed earlier in Chapter V, section 2. This requirement automatically excludes such people as maniacs or unregenerate criminals as incompetent.

Furthermore, when arguments are offered the listener is assumed not only to be capable of making the intellectual transition from premises to conclusion, but also of transferring motivation from the basic prescription to the particular prescription accepted. In many cases this involves a certain flexibility of character as well as of intellect, for at least in some ethical systems rigid and inflexible habits of action and attitude may make ethical argument futile. (Perhaps these requirements amount to demanding that the listener have free will in some sense.)

Both of these considerations imply that all ethical discourse rests on the basic assumption of the dispositional presence of the ground-motive. This does not necessarily mean that the basic prescription itself must be accepted actually and explicitly, but only that there is a psychological possibility of its being operationally efficacious. I believe that this holds for every existing ethical system: for instance, it would be useless for a theist to attempt to justify a prescription on the grounds that it will bring sanctification to a listener who is incapable of being interested in sanctification; or for a moralist to appeal to a person's sense of duty if he has no such sense; or even for a hedonist to appeal to the pleasure principle if the agent does not want pleasure. Most frequently ethical systems suppose that *in principle* many people who are not aware of these basic motivations are in some sense capable of having them.

Another kind of competence which is involved in ethical discourse consists of being in the possession of certain kinds of information; in other words, one must accept certain factual beliefs. Since there are quite considerable differences between factual beliefs adduced in the ethical systems of different cultures, we may expect the conditions of competence relating to them to be multifarious. Thus, the factual opinions of doctors ordinarily must be accepted before moral prescriptions concerning sickness and health can be justified. In the eyes of many, but not all, in our own society, a person who rejects the opinions of medical experts is thought to be incompetent, and therefore unreasonable. A similar situation may be expected in other societies: for example, among the Navahos, the experts, the medicine men or Singers, are assumed to know what is to be done in certain situations to secure agreed-upon ends; and a person who ignores them is thought to be crazy. Theistic ethics also sets up criteria of factual competence: certain types of revelation are considered to be reliable and those who do not accept them to be incompetent.

The variations in these requirements explain at least in part some of the basic differences between different ethical systems. Since any segment of ethical discourse presupposes some competence on the part of the partici-pants, as a necessary condition of its success, I suggest that an examination of these criteria will throw considerable light on the course of reasoning involved in the various ethical systems.

Furthermore, I should like to stress the importance of the notion of *incompetence* not only because it throws light on the corresponding criteria of competence and ethical reasoning, but also because it will help us to understand some of the characteristic solutions to the problem of handling those who disagree incorrigibly and irretrievably with the moralist. Such incompetents may be said to be "beyond the pale of morality," for moral considerations have no influence upon them, and nondiscursive means must be employed to secure their conformity to the moral code. Every moral system must face the problem of how to deal not only with children and morons, but also with unregenerate criminals and 'lost souls' of various types. The questions involved here have traditionally been discussed under what has been called "moral psychology." It is clear that every ethical system must have a moral psychology which includes some doctrines about the nature of men's reasoning, motivations, and actual behavior.

c. Criteria of ethical competence

I have contended that whenever a moralist undertakes to talk about morals he assumes his listener to be ethically competent. We may therefore expect to gain some insight into the criteria of competence which he employs, if we ask: to what sort of person and under what conditions does the moralist address his ethical discourse? Or, conversely, with whom and in what situations is moral discourse thought to be inappropriate?

There is an extraordinary variety of answers to these questions, but only a few of them need be mentioned in order to bring out the importance of the notion of competence for understanding the differences between various ethical systems.

In the first place, in a large number of ethical systems ethical competence is limited to an elite which alone is qualified to reason ethically. Everyone outside this elite group is incompetent. Such ethical systems will be called *esoteric systems*. Most esoteric systems develop an exoteric code on authoritarian principles for the masses. (I shall discuss this in the next subsection).

Even within those systems which do not assume an ethical elite, there are also wide variations. All systems must treat children and idiots as relatively incompetent, but there are important differences as to where the line is to be drawn. Thus, it is my impression that moral teaching, as such, is given to the Navaho child much later than it is to children in our own culture; and if this is true, it suggests that greater maturity in thinking powers and information is required in Navaho moral discourse than in our own. We tell children that a story they have told is wrong "because lying is wrong," whereas the justification is more complicated in the Navaho ethical system.

Furthermore, even when the individual is mature and normally intelligent, all ethical systems suppose that certain psychological states of mind make him ethically incompetent. Thus, among the Navahos, drink is thought to make an individual incapable of listening to moral discourse. Perhaps in our society we feel that we can talk with drinkers more successfully than do the Navahos. This again may be due to the different structure of our ethical reasoning, which makes moral discourse with children as well as drinkers more feasible.

On the other hand, many Western ethical systems stress psychological conditions of competence which may not be found in other systems. For instance, some of our moralists have stressed the absence of extreme passions: to reason ethically one must reflect 'cooly' and 'calmly.' [22] Other moralists reject such calmness and believe that the favorable psychological condition for moral knowledge is the 'fervour of enthusiasm' caused by supernatural inspiration.

Other conditions which have been held to be necessary for ethical competence are disinterestedness and impartiality; in so far as a person is influenced in his thinking by his own personal interests, he is considered to be ethically incompetent, and he is thought to be incapable of following and accepting legitimate moral discourse. As I shall try to show later, this particular criterion of competence is rejected by the Navahos. It is, of course, incompatible with all forms of egoism.

Even more specialized psychological conditions of ethical competence are advocated by some moral philosophers. For instance, it has been maintained that a person must be capable of being influenced by sympathy, benevolence, altruistic sentiments, and so on, before it is possible to discourse morally with him.

All these various conditions are determined for each of the various ethical systems by the different factors which enter into their respective procedures of justification. Thus, the use of one mode of validation instead of another may make discourse with children or drinkers easier, and the use of a mode like the interpretive mode of validation may require additional criteria such as impartiality and sympathy to assure the feasibility of moral discourse.

Furthermore, some criteria of competence may be necessary to assure adherence to the basic prescription(s) of the system. Thus, an altruistic system must presuppose altruistic motives in a person before he is capable of accepting an ethical argument; or a theistic system must assume the presence of religious faith before its arguments will be acceptable.

The significance and complications of the conception of ethical competence were clearly recognized by Aristotle when he said that one of the conditions of practical wisdom and moral deliberation was the virtuous character of the individual involved. He maintained that a vicious man whose appetites are uncontrolled would not even be capable of knowing what he ought to do, much less of being able to do it.[23]

d. Authoritarianism

We have seen that in some ethical systems the conditions of competence are so difficult to fulfill that they cannot be achieved by a large proportion of the population. Such esoteric systems must therefore develop a sort of auxiliary exoteric ethical system for the masses of incompetents. Such secondary ethical systems are what I shall call *authoritarian systems*.

An authoritarian system implies the existence of an elite which is ethically competent and of subjects who are not so. The elite, acting as authority, lays down the moral prescriptions for the subjects in the form of commands. Consequently, the basic prescription of any authoritarian system is: to obey the commands of the authority is obligatory and to disobey them is wrong. Plato's *Republic* provides a classic illustration of an authoritarian system, since the guardians are the only ones competent to know the good, and the masses must blindly accept and follow the commands of the guardians because they themselves are incompetent.

There is a tremendous diversity of authorities which the various authoritarian systems recognize. The authority may be an ethical elite which is defined by special training, divine election, birth, social role, political or priestly office. It may consist of one individual or a group of individuals. The authority may not even be a human being, but may be a supernatural being or a quasi-human agency. In the latter case, the whole society of men to whom the authoritarian system applies are considered incompetent.

It should be noted that authoritarianism is a system designed for the ethically incompetent and that it does not apply to the authority itself. The failure to recognize that authoritarianism is not the ethics of the authority itself results in many paradoxes, which have been skillfully propounded in the debate between Socrates and Thrasymachus in the opening pages of Plato's *Republic*. The ethical system which is presumed valid for the ethically competent authority may belong to any one of the many possible types. For instance, the authority might espouse utilitarianism, or eudaimonism. Hence, authoritarianism can be used to support many different kinds of ethical systems, because it is defined without reference to the ethics of the competent and is primarily a system for the incompetent.

The credentials of the authority rest upon its presumed ethical competence, and the reason for our obeying it is because we are incompetent. The moral prescriptions of the authoritarian system, being commands, are justified by their origin, which is enough to make them binding upon us. Moreover, since we are completely incompetent we must blindly obey these commands; and of the subjects of the authoritarian ethics we could say: "Their's not to reason why, their's but to do and die." As a consequence the only virtue is obedience and the only vice disobedience.

Another characteristic of authoritarian systems is that they frequently employ sanctions in the form of threat of punishment or promise of reward for disobedience or obedience. Such sanctions are required to supply the motivation for conformity to the commands of the authority, since the ground-motive for the authority's own ethics would presumably be ineffective for those who are incompetent. The sanctions involved here are sanctions in the strict sense: namely, punishments and rewards which are imposed by the authority (or his agents) as a consequence of the actions or non-actions of the individual concerned. Furthermore, these punishments and rewards themselves require ethical justification, although this justification will be in terms of the authority's own ethical system, not the authoritarian system.[24]

Accordingly, the marks of an authoritarian system are as follows: the assumption that the majority of mankind are ethically incompetent and that there is an ethically competent authority; the formulation of moral prescriptions as commands which are justified by their origin; the emphasis on obedience for its own sake; and sometimes, but not always, the introduction of sanctions.

Ethical authoritarianism as it has been outlined here should not be confused with other senses in which the word "authoritarianism" has been used. In order to bring out its distinctive characteristics, ethical authoritarianism may be contrasted with certain other doctrines and procedures which are sometimes identified with it.

First, in ethical authoritarianism the appeal to authority applies to the basic moral prescriptions and not to incidental authoritative arguments involving subsidary premises. For instance, the opinions of a doctor or any specialist may be incidentally authoritative in this sense, but they do not provide the basic moral prescription itself.

Second, the use of a command (or imperative) in particular situations does not imply that the speaker is an authoritarian in ethics. Commands of one type or another are necessary in practical life, but it is only when these commands are moral prescriptions claiming to be legitimate and superior that they are constituent elements in an authoritarian system. Any such moral commands must be derived from basic prescriptions which themselves are commands. Hence they are commands not only by accident.

Third, punishments and rewards may be introduced as relevant considerations in moral discourse without implying an authoritarian ethics. To be authoritarian they must be related to the disobedience or obedience of the commands of the ethical authority, and must not be merely natural or social consequences of one's actions. An undesired consequence is a punishment only if it is the result of defying a command, and authoritarianism is involved only if this command is *eo ipso* a moral prescription.

Finally, ethical authoritarianism must not be confused with the rule of force. The fear of force can be introduced into ethical discourse legitimately, but only as a consideration which is relevant to the means and conditions of actions, that is, in the derivation of particular prescriptions from basic ones. Force, alone, cannot serve as the source of moral obligation. Before it can do so, it must have some ethical foundation. Thus, an ethical authority may use force, but it also claims to do so legitimately, because it has a right based on its ethical competence.[25]

A few examples of authoritarian ethical systems will illustrate these characteristics. The relation between child and parent (or elders) in the first few years in most societies is probably authoritarian in the sense proposed here. The child is presumed incompetent, the parent competent. His directives are issued as commands and justified by his authority, and they are backed by threats and promises. I have already cited the philosophical illustration provided by Plato's *Republic* where the guardians have authority grounded on their special talents and training, and the artisans are told the noble lie to get them to obey the guardians. Examples of other ethical systems which are based upon this duality of authority and masses probably would be found in societies where kings, priests, or the party have special ethical authority.

In addition to human authorities, there is an important group of theories which are founded on a superhuman authority. Two of these will be examined briefly: theism and conventionalism (relativism).

In theistic systems we often find a rather interesting version of authoritarianism, namely, the doctrine that God (or the gods) is the only person in the system who is ethically competent. Thus in some interpretations of Judaism, the commands of God must be obeyed because he is the only one who knows what is good for the people.[26] This system, instead of having a human authority, is founded upon a divine nonhuman authority, on the assumption that man is not competent to determine what is good for himself, and cannot see the reasons for doing the actions prescribed.[27]

Since so much of Western thought shows traces of the influence of authoritarianism, it may be worth while to point out the fundamentally authoritarian character of what has been called "conventionalism" (or "ethical relativism").

Conventionalism is the doctrine that identifies moral prescriptions with the mores of Society, and asserts that the only justification for these prescriptions is to be found in their origin, namely, society or culture. In this view we find all the elements listed above. First, the fundamental irrational character of moral judgments is emphasized to bring out man's own ethical incompetence. It is assumed that Society knows what is good for itself — an assumption made plausible by the accounts of social scientists of the extraordinary sociological mechanisms which function to preserve social equilibrium. Thus, the conventionalist imputes to Society the same ethical competence ascribed to God in the theistic systems mentioned above. Second, moral prescriptions are justified by their origin in the mores ('commands of Society'). Third, the rather indiscriminate use of the word "sanction" attests to a covert assumption that Society punishes those who disobey her "commands." (All these elements are to be found in Durkheim's theory discussed earlier in Chapter III, section 3).

It is evident that ethical authoritarianism is a hybrid doctrine, and that it frequently develops into some other type of ethical system. For instance, where the main emphasis is placed upon the sanctions enforcing the commands of the authority, the ethical system quickly transforms itself into a kind of hedonistic egoism. Thus theistic and conventionalistic authoritarianism may reduce the basic prescription of obeying the authority to a maxim of prudence which says that you had better obey in order to avoid punishment in the next life or to avoid social ostracism. On the other hand, other types of authoritarianism appear to derive their prescription of obedience from a higher prescription which is accepted both by the authority and the subjects of the authority alike. For example: according to some moralists the reason for obeying God is that he knows better than we do what are the best means to our becoming happy; similarly, a conventionalist might justify his prescription of obedience to the dictates of society on the grounds that in doing so the welfare of everyone will be promoted.

Authoritarianism in its pure form, however, states its basic prescription of obedience in such a way that there is no need for a higher validating principle. We must obey simply because we are commanded by the moral authority, and the only reason for obeying is that he is ethically competent. In effect, it seems to me, any moral code which, in the final analysis, can express its prescriptions only in the form of commands is authoritarian in this sense.

It remains an open question whether there are any authoritarian systems in the pure sense, since so many of the systems which appear authoritarian are actually 'parasitic' systems founded on other more basic ethical principles. In general, it is clear that authoritarianism, even if not entirely 'pure,' is a type of ethical system which rests on rather specialized assumptions, which are not only unacceptable to most Western moral philosophers but also are quite likely not accepted by non-Western societies. Nevertheless, in their descriptions of the moral codes of non-literate peoples, many investigators have employed authoritarian paradigms — especially of the theistic or conventionalistic variety. This has blinded them to some of the obvious differences between our own and other moral codes.

PART III

A SYSTEMATIC RECONSTRUCTION
OF NAVAHO ETHICS

X

The Application of the General Theory

It is obvious that any description of the ethics of a non-literate people will be determined in part by the methods employed by the investigator. Accordingly, my hypothetical conclusions about the Navaho moral code depend upon the approach which I have proposed in Parts I and II. I shall begin my discussion of the application of the theory by explaining what procedures I have adopted to solve three general problems: How are the specific hypotheses to be formulated and tested? How are ethical statements to be identified as such? and, How are such statements to be obtained?

1. THE FORMULATION OF HYPOTHESES

The method of hypothetical reconstruction consists in developing a systematic reconstruction of an informant's discourse by which his particular statements can be explained and predicted. In Part II, many of the component elements of an ethical system were pointed out and some of the possible variations among them were explored. The interrelations among these elements constitute the structure of the ethical system in question. When investigating an informant's ethical discourse we must try to isolate these various elements and establish the structural relations between them.

The order of exposition in Part II led from the more specific to the more general aspects of a moral code. In our formulation of hypotheses about any particular moral code, somewhat the reverse order of exposition will be followed. Therefore, we shall begin by establishing the rhetorical principles of the informant's ethical discourse and the kind of ethical justification which it employs, and then work back to the more concrete aspects of the system. While doing this, we can construct various more or less independently verifiable subsidiary hypotheses, each one of which can be tested by the ethical statements of the informant.

For convenience, we can divide the subsidiary hypotheses about an ethical system into two groups: those relating to the structure of the system; and those relating to its content. The content of an ethical system depends to a large extent upon the specific factual beliefs accepted by the informant and encompasses a great many detailed arguments. The structure, on the other hand, is more general and abstract. For this reason, the verification of the latter is more difficult and the evidence tends to be cumulative. However, these two aspects of a system cannot be entirely separated, and it will be evident later that the proof that the system has a particular content will also serve to confirm the hypothesis about its structure.

The procedure in determining which hypothetically reconstructed system can best explain the ethical discourse being investigated consists of finding out the answers to questions such as the following:

Structure:

(*a*) Is the system authoritarian? If so, what kind of authority is assumed, etc.?
(*b*) What are the conditions of ethical competence?
(*c*) What modes of validation does it employ?
(*d*) What type of basic prescription is it founded on (for example, negative, positive, teleological, formalistic, etc.)?
(*e*) What type of ground-motive is involved?

Content:

(*f*) What is the content of the basic prescription?
(*g*) How are prescripta designated?
(*h*) How do the prescriptions vary in stringency? Why do they do so?
(*i*) What are some of the specific factual beliefs which are important for the system?

This is only a brief summary of some of the questions which can be asked. There are many others which can be derived from the discussion in Part II. It is unnecessary to point out that a certain answer to one question automatically excludes as irrelevant other questions which could have been asked. The answers themselves are, of course, hypothetical reconstructions of one type or another, and as such must be subjected to testing procedures.

The testing of hypotheses is simple in principle. It consists in assuming an hypothetical system which enables us to derive from the data available certain new statements, which in turn can be verified or falsified by the informant's actual discourse. Thus, for instance, to check the adequacy of a specific hypothetical basic prescription we can, with the aid of factual beliefs known to be accepted, infer from it certain new prescriptive statements. These new statements will be essentially predictions of what the informant will say. If these predictions are fulfilled, then our hypothesis has to that extent been confirmed; if they are not fulfilled, we have some evidence that it is not the correct hypothesis. The procedures are more complicated than this as we shall see in Chapter XVI, section 1. The important point to keep in mind is that every subsidiary hypothesis, as well as the hypothesis as a whole, must be tested by actual statements by the informant. No hypothesis can be regarded as confirmed until it has been thoroughly tested — and, of course, this means not only that we have collected evidence in favor of it, but more important that we have sought out all the evidence that might be against it. By attempting to falsify the hypothesis we can avoid the 'fallacy of selection.'

When all the questions listed above have been answered to our satisfaction, and these answers have been adequately tested, we should have a fairly adequate picture of the reconstructed system. However, if none of the hypotheses we construct seem to be adequate to the data available, there are two possible explanations: either we have not exhausted all the possibilities, or the informant's ethical discourse is unsystematic. If his discourse is unsystematic, it may be so either because he accepts more than one system or because he accepts no system at all.

I know of no general method by which it can be proved or disproved that an informant's ethical discourse is coherent or systematic; it can be shown to be coherent or systematic only by establishing the reconstructed system which explains it. However, it should be recalled that many types of ethical discourse which are ordinarily regarded as unsystematic, would not be so according to the present theory (for example, extreme particularism).

2. THE THINKER AND THE MAN OF ACTION

Any anthropologist who intends to investigate the ethics of a non-literate society must at the outset decide whether he is interested in the ethical ideas current among the people at large, or whether he wishes to study the ideas of the experts or cultural leaders. There are individuals in every society who 'know more about' moral standards than the average person. Such people are generally looked up to by the layman, and it is to them that people turn when in need of advice or in times of crisis.

Paul Radin has made a useful distinction between a 'thinker' and a 'man of action' which is relevant here. It has been one of the main theses of his writings that among primitive people we find individuals who are temperamentally thinkers ('philosophers') in perhaps roughly the same proportion to the population as they occur in our own society.

The thinker is a man who is interested in general principles and explanations. He is not satisfied with taking things as they are, but rather demands some "logical coördination and integration of events." The man of action has not given much thought to such things, but "in the main, he unhesitatingly accepts the form which the thinker has given [them]. In all such matters he follows the lead of the thinker or, at least, repeats somewhat mechanically what the latter has said." [1]

For our purposes, it is not necessary to attribute originality and creativity to the ethical thinker, as long as we recognize that he differs radically from the man of action in his interests and in the point of view from which he approaches practical problems. The important point is that the man of action takes his ideas from the thinker without reflecting upon them. There is, of course, no sharp line between these two types, but they should be familiar to all of us; the peasant and the priest, to whom he goes for moral counsel, illustrate them and their relationship.

Now, it may be asked, in investigating the ethics of a non-literate people, should we be more concerned with the ideas which are unreflectingly accepted and repeated by the man of action, or should we go to his source, the thinker? The choice between these two approaches must obviously be determined by the particular theoretical interests of the investigator. It is clear that each of them will have a different outcome: in the case of the man of action, the ethical ideas will be poorly formulated, unsystematic and perhaps inconsistent; whereas in the case of the thinker they will be well integrated, and clearly and distinctly formulated. The man of action will have only a vague and hazy notion of what actions are right or wrong, and of the reasons for their being so. The thinker, on the other hand, will have a wealth of ethical ideas. The choice might be said to be between extensity and intensity of ethical opinions.

I have chosen to investigate the ethical ideas of the Navahos as they are known to the thinker rather than to the man of action. My reasons are twofold: a personal preference and a theoretical reason.

My first reason for preferring this approach is that as a professional philosopher I am more interested in the ideas of a person who thinks than in those of a person who merely acts. A philosopher could not but be as bored in investigating the thoughts of a man of action in a non-literate society as he would those of one in our own. On the other hand, he may find a conversation with a 'primitive philosopher' immensely rewarding.

In the second place, the use of a thinker's ethical discourse rather than that of a man of action seems entailed by the criterion of "ethical discourse" presented earlier. It is the thinker who discourses while the man of action acts.

Furthermore, it is an essential characteristic of ethical discourse that it be thought to be superior and legitimate, since it consists of deliberating about and commending moral prescriptions, which were defined earlier as prescriptions for conduct claiming superiority and legitimacy. Accordingly, moral talk is distinguished from other kinds of practical talk by its seriousness, its thoughtfulness, and its authoritativeness. An elderly man, who is considered wise (a thinker), would logically be the one we might expect to be able to give such moral talks. Hence, the very definition of "ethics" seems to imply that we should turn to the thinker in our investigation.[2]

Such wise and thinking men who are recognized to be exceptionally well-qualified to discourse about right and wrong conduct, will be called *moralists*. The moralist is the one who is generally acknowledged to 'know the answers'; to him the man of action turns when in need of advice; it is to him that people appeal to resolve disputes; and finally, he is the one whom people get to teach their children how to 'live straight.' Should we not expect to find more satisfactory answers to our questions if we also go to him?

3. FIELD WORK WITH THE NAVAHOS: DECEMBER–JANUARY 1951–52

The principal materials upon which this study is based were collected during a field trip to the Southwest in the winter of 1951–52. Although I spent only about five weeks in the field, because of the excellent conditions under which I worked (made possible through the Values Study Project), I was able to have a considerable number of interviews with Navaho informants. In addition, the fact that I went there in winter was advantageous both because the people did not have much to do, and because 'in the winter-time' the Navahos can tell some of their secrets!

a. The Navaho moralist: Bidaga

I was fortunate to be able to procure as an informant a man who fulfilled all the qualifications laid down in the preceding section. This Navaho moralist was the Son of Many Beads, more widely known as Bidaga — and in the anthropological literature as Mr. Moustache. Bidaga was an old man of about eighty-five years (although he told me that he was ninety-six!). He was one of the most respected men in the community, and for many years its leader. In addition, he was a medicine man or Singer (of Blessing Way). He was relatively unacculturated, and did not speak a word of English.[3]

Kroeber has made some most illuminating comments on Mr. Moustache as the exemplification of a personality type which can also be found in other Southwestern cultures. In him "there is a strong sense of teaching and following, of receiving basic wisdom and passing it on. . . . We may thus suspect that among non-literate tribal folk some normal elderly persons are likely to feel their life not as something interesting in its individuation and distinctiveness, but as an exemplification of socialization. Such a person is conscious of himself first of all as a preserver and transmitter of his culture."[4]

The appositeness of Kroeber's characterization should be evident in every page of the record of Bidaga's statements to me. The fact that he regarded himself as a transmitter of the old Navaho ways, made him especially valuable as an informant on Navaho ethics (although, of course, this fact does not entail that he *was* a transmitter). In addition, his place in the community was that of a practicing moralist, while his knowledge as a ceremonialist gave him a background in the deeper cosmological foundations of Navaho thought.

b. Other sources

Although most of my interviews were with Bidaga, when he disappeared for Sings I spent two days with another fairly unacculturated medicine man, John Hawk. In addition to these two Singers, my interpreters also served as informants.

Since it was not possible to cover the whole field of ethics in the short time available with Bidaga, and other informants, I have relied heavily on information obtained by other investigators, which was available either in published form or in the Values Project Files of the Harvard Department of Social Relations. Walter Dyk's autobiography, *Son of Old Man Hat,* is an especially rich source, since Old Man Hat himself was a moralist in much the same sense as Bidaga. From the point of view of descriptive ethics, the contrast between this book and the later *Navaho Autobiography,* in which ethical discourse hardly occurs, brings out the necessity of going to the moralist rather than to the layman for information about ethics.

4. NAVAHO ETHICS VS. THE ETHICS OF A NAVAHO

Since so much of this study is based upon interviews with one informant, Bidaga, it has been suggested that it would be better to call my reconstruction a description of the ethics of Bidaga rather than of the ethics of the Navaho people. I should like to give my reasons for not accepting this suggestion.

First, I have made considerable use of statements of other Navahos besides Bidaga. Therefore, strictly speaking, the theory presented could only be accurately described as the "ethics of Bidaga and some other Navahos." Although an objection might be raised against treating material from such diverse sources as essentially homogeneous, I am more concerned with establishing the general structure of Navaho ethical discourse than with describing the details of the moral prescriptions and arguments accepted by particular individuals. I strongly suspect that even where there are certain variations in specific content, the basic structure is the same for all the Navahos whose statements have been used.

Second, I repeat that the theory offered here is to be taken as a speculative hypothesis rather than as a well-established reconstruction. The evidence upon which it is based is sparse and not entirely reliable, and the hypothesis requires further testing. The theory would possess this hypothetical character even if it were limited to a reconstruction of the ethical views of Bidaga. Hence, I see no reason for preferring to consider it a 'little' hypothesis about one man, thus making it comparatively trivial, instead of considering it to be a general hypothesis about the ethical part of Navaho ideology.

Third, the question may be raised as to whether Bidaga's opinions are typical of Navahos in general. It is clear that they could not be held to be typical in some statistical sense, since we must not forget that the moralist-thinker's opinions will inevitably be more sophisticated than those of the man of action, or the average Navaho. They would be typical only in the sense in which the esoteric beliefs of the Singers are typical. Nevertheless, I suspect that some of the elements of the reconstructed moral code are shared by all unacculturated Navahos — especially the general 'materialistic' and 'prudentialist' approach. The Navaho layman may not know in detail the arguments and reasons for obeying certain prescriptions, but quite likely he at least believes that there are reasons, and that a man like Bidaga knows what they are. This surmise is something that could be verified statistically.

These considerations convince me that no useful purpose can be served by restricting my hypothesis to one man, Bidaga, for to do so might have the undesirable effect of seeming to claim more reliability and validity for the theory than it has.

5. SOME PRACTICAL DIFFICULTIES IN FIELD WORK

Since philosophers have often expressed disappointment at the inaccuracy and incompleteness of the answers which I obtained from my interviews, it may be worth while to point out some of the difficulties facing an investigator in the field. To begin with, all my interviewing had to be done through a native interpreter. Hence, some of the linguistic subtleties which are so important to an investigation of this sort were inevitably missed. The interpreters were remarkably satisfactory, but the situation can be compared to a conversation between two specialists in any field mediated by an ignorant and comparatively uneducated layman; it would be like trying to talk to Plato with an Attican peasant as interpreter! In my field notes I have written down verbatim what the interpreter said, but the gist of the informant's statements can sometimes only be surmised. Frequently, there was no connection between my question and the reply that 'came back' through the interpreter.

Like many other field workers I was sorely pressed for time, and so was unable to pursue many questions which I should have liked to explore in more detail. Inevitably a good deal of time had to be spent in arranging interviews and in bringing the informant and interpreter together at the same time. Both the informant and the interpreter often had more important business, and were not available for days at a time. Bidaga was constantly involved in Sings, either as a patient or as a Singer, and so the time left for interviewing was limited.

In addition, in field work one's rapport with an informant is likely to be tenuous. He may not like the questions asked, and disappear for good. The questioning has to be done diplomatically, and if the informant does not wish to answer it may be inadvisable to press him. For example, the Navahos have many secrets which cannot be revealed except under appropriate conditions; thus I felt that it would be prudent to drop the interesting subject of ghosts at one point during the interview. (* 109)

Finally, I cannot stress too emphatically the difficulty of posing questions in such a way that they can be understood by informant and interpreter. Abstract questions were impossible. For instance, it might seem obvious that the way to start off would be to have the informant give a list of things he considered right or wrong, good or bad. But this technique was a complete failure with Navaho informants. On the other hand, I found that problems referring to concrete and familiar contexts were readily and easily answered. As Father Berard Haile once said in conversation: "The Navahos do think abstractly, but their ways of abstracting are different from our own."

Navaho Ethics in General

1. NON-LITERATE RATIONALISM[1]

Any philosopher who visits the Navahos cannot fail to be impressed by the extent to which 'talking it over' and 'thinking hard' are prized and practiced by these people. Hasty and undeliberated actions are frowned upon. Every decision made must first be discussed by all who happen to be around, and it is thought desirable to consult everyone, especially the older and wiser members of the family, before any course of action is decided upon. Even the most trivial matters must be mulled over before acting. One does not have to visit the Navahos to become convinced of this fact, for the published autobiographies of Navahos give detailed descriptions of such 'talks.' Furthermore, it is evident that this emphasis on public discussion is a theme deeply rooted in Navaho culture, since their religious myths are full of accounts of family councils among the Holy People who "talked it over before doing anything about it." (* 98–100)

I submit that this emphasis on public deliberation embodies the essential core of ethical rationalism — the view which stresses the crucial and necessary function of reason in the moral life. Although Western philosophy has traditionally assumed that reasoning is an intrasubjective process, taking place privately within the mind of the thinker, I have suggested earlier that we may consider talking to be a form of thinking, and perhaps thinking in private to be a kind of 'talking to oneself.' Hence, public deliberation is not an accidental by-product of intrasubjective thought processes, but as natural a manifestation of thinking as private deliberation. Accordingly, an emphasis on talking may be regarded as an emphasis on thinking publicly.[2]

Reasoning, being a kind of discourse, is that kind of talking and thinking which is distinguished from unorganized and casual thought by conforming to the rules of argumentation and by being concerned more with the subject matter than with the expression of the speaker's feelings or with his desire to impress others.

Navaho 'talks' are reasonable in precisely this sense, for if the reports of these 'talks' are examined, it will be evident that they are not merely oratory or attempts to show off or to persuade — by any means, fair or foul; instead, they consist of carefully stated arguments for and against a particular course of action. In my opinion, many of these public deliberations come as near *in form* as is practically feasible to what could be called "reasonable discourse." One explanation for the 'cool reasonableness' of Navaho talk may be found in the strong cultural disapproval of 'trying to be better than the other fellow,' and this may possibly result in more attention to subject matter and logic than ordinarily occurs in similar situations in our society where our Egos often stand in the way of objectivity.

Therefore, when placing such stress upon 'talking it over,' the Navaho is assuming in his own way the crucial function of reason in practical discourse. This may be contrasted with ethical systems which rely upon ex cathedra utterances of an authority or which base moral choices on unquestionable intuition, for in such systems discursive thinking plays only a subsidiary role. Thus, the Navaho moralist is a rationalist par excellence. The fact that the Navahos have many beliefs which from our point of view are unscientific is beside the point. In calling the Navaho a "rationalist," I am referring to his use of reason in practical life, not to the content of his beliefs. Perhaps because of these false beliefs we might not wish to call his philosophy "rational," but to insist that others hold the same beliefs as are established by science in order to be called "rationalistic" as well as "rational" would entail that we withhold this label from all the great rationalistic philosophers of the past, as well as from the Navahos, for almost every great philosophical system contains some false beliefs.

In addition to the importance attached to talking and thinking in practice, Navaho ideology contains certain tenets about their causal efficacy which are characteristically rationalistic. In the first place, it is believed that 'talking it over' is the way to 'straighten out troubles' (disputes of one type or another). "Way back there, the Navaho people didn't have any kind of law. They used to just talking it together, and the things straightened up by talking together — maybe three or four people talking together." (* 125)

Second, the Navahos believe fundamentally, and this belief is reflected in their mythology as well as in their daily life, that talking is the most effective means of persuasion. The spoken word has a peculiar form of 'compulsiveness' for them. It is supposed that if you ask for something in the correct manner, for example, four times, the person asked finds it difficult to refuse you. This technique is the fundamental method of invoking the help of the Holy People, and is used towards animals and other natural forces as well.[3] Talk is the preferred means of dissuading a person from doing something wrong. (* 91) The Navahos dislike the use of force and are ever fearful of employing it.

A third aspect of Navaho rationalism is its adherence to the Socratic tenet that virtue is knowledge and vice ignorance. A good man is one who 'has sense,' 'thinks hard,' or has a 'good head,' whereas a bad man is one who has none of these. To live successfully, one must think well: "All depends how the people thinks that makes them happy." (* 30) This follows from the characteristic Navaho principle that knowledge is power[4] — specifically, the power to achieve happiness.

Similarly, vice is ignorance, and is attributed to not thinking. A boy who does bad things is "one who hasn't any sense at all." [5] A frequent characterization of a person who has committed some crime, is to say that he is 'crazy' or 'has lost his mind.' [6] One should therefore expect that going crazy would be one of the most feared evils among the Navahos, and it probably is.[7] Becoming drunk is also regarded as a kind of loss of sense: "If you drink looks like you lose your mind and you think of things you never thought of, and you get into trouble." (* 9) The liquor problem is very acute for the Navahos, and my informant continually returned to the topic. Drinking is especially wrong because it makes you lose your mind.

A corollary of 'talking things over,' is that one must also *listen*. (Perhaps one reason why practical discussions in our own society are so often unreasonable, is because we do not listen to what others say, but are more intent on what we ourselves are going to say and on its effect.) Since the Navahos are aware that listening is as important a constituent of talk as speaking, they stress 'listening' and 'minding each other' as essential to the full efficacy of talk, and they consider them as desirable for the same reason. "They must work together and listen to each other." (* 48)

Another reason for listening is that only by listening can one learn. We find constant reiteration of the value of learning. Children are told to listen to their elders and to learn from them what to do and how to think about something correctly. In other words, virtue can be learned by listening, and can be taught to any pupil with the necessary intelligence. That virtue can be taught is usually regarded as a corollary of the proposition that virtue is knowledge.

Thus, we find the Navahos constantly stressing 'talking,' 'listening,' 'learning,' and 'thinking hard' as both necessary and, ideally at least, sufficient for the good life. This is the essence of what I have called "rationalism." However, one element which is generally associated with philosophical rationalism as it appears in the systems of Plato or Descartes is missing, namely, the belief that knowledge is certain and adequate. Here the Navaho parts company with the so-called "rationalistic" philosophers. You can never be certain that things will go as you planned. Mistakes are inevitable. (* 100) Human knowledge is always partial and incomplete. Everyone is always learning and he can never rest assured that he knows enough. Moreover, the Navaho is very much of an empiricist or experimentalist in that he is always ready to try something new. He is also a pragmatic pluralist for he usually tries everything at once! This is well illustrated by the Navaho willingness to try out the white doctors as well as their own medicine men, and by the way they continually switch medicine men if one is not successful in curing the sickness. Thus, the Navaho combines ethical rationalism with experimental fallibilism in a fashion which is reminiscent of the philosophy of John Dewey.

Ultimately, the best evidence for the natural rationalism of Navaho thought is provided in the kind of ethical discourse which they conduct. Every prescription has a reason. Whatever one is told to do or not to do can be justified by some reason, and these reasons are generally mentioned in the course of the discussion. In my interviewing, I rarely had to ask the informant for a reason for some prescription he had mentioned — he gave it to me automatically. (This aspect of Navaho rationalism will be examined in more detail in Chapter XV.)

2. ESOTERIC KNOWLEDGE

A complete investigation of the ethical opinions of a non-literate people like the Navahos is frustrated at every turn because there are many things which the informant will not discuss, which may be essential elements in his whole scheme of thought. Some of these beliefs are common knowledge to the Navahos; for instance, beliefs about ghosts and witches are probably widely accepted, but are not immediately revealed to a white investigator, unless he knows the informant fairly intimately. In comparison to other non-literate groups they are communicative, but when compared to whites they are not. There are other beliefs that can be told only during the winter months, when there are no snakes and no danger from lightning. Finally, there is esoteric knowledge which is supposed generally not to be available to the average Navaho, but is guarded as the sacrosanct possession of the ceremonial Singers.[8] In order to obtain such knowledge, one must in theory be apprenticed to a Singer, or at least pay him something for it. One ancient practice was for an aged father to tell some of these secret stories and rites to his children just before he died. But again, the person who tells these things must always withhold some of it — for if he tells all, it is thought that he will lose his power.

In actuality, there is no rigid separation of esoteric and exoteric knowledge. Probably an intelligent layman among the Navahos picks up a good deal of esoteric knowledge during his lifetime. On the other hand, the fact that such knowledge is regarded as esoteric means that it is not cited in public moral discourses or in the teaching of children. The essential beliefs involved in ethical discourse are therefore entirely exoteric for the average

Navaho. Ethics can be talked about freely. "They can talk about good living and living a long life anytime." (* 116)

For this reason, the esoteric beliefs are not an essential component of the reconstructed Navaho moral code, although we shall find that they do throw light on certain aspects of Navaho argumentation which might otherwise be obscure.[9] However, a complete investigation of Navaho ethical opinions is still frustrated (at least, at the outset) by the Navahos' withholding of beliefs that they 'are afraid to talk about.' I believe it likely that a good deal more of their ethics is grounded upon these beliefs than would appear on the surface. For instance, it is possible that the prohibition against murder may involve reference to the victim's ghost.

For convenience, I shall refer to these two kinds of secret beliefs as *esoteric* and *concealed* beliefs. An esoteric belief is one that is not supposed to be known by the average Navaho, whereas a concealed belief is one that is known to all Navahos but which 'they don't like to talk about' — especially to strangers.

3. THE NAVAHO PHILOSOPHY OF LIFE[10]

a. General existential beliefs

The Navaho world view is essentially mechanistic and naturalistic. There is no final overarching purpose to life or the world in general. We just find ourselves in it and have to make the best of it that we can. There are forces which are hostile, and some which are friendly, and a great many which are innately indifferent and potentially either. Man's life ends with his death, or else what survives death, the ghost, is doomed to a pretty miserable afterlife. The divinities, or Holy People, are in general indifferent, except they may help out if appealed to in the correct manner. In general, the Navaho world view reminds one of Bertrand Russell's "Free Man's Worship," or perhaps of the naturalism of Epicurus. The world runs by inexorable laws — and all the various kinds of beings inhabiting it, Holy People and Earth Surface People, as well as animals, plants, and the weather are subject to them.

Although the Navaho conception of the world is not anthropocentric, it is anthropomorphic, that is, the various forces of nature are conceived of in quasi-human form. The weather, mountains, and animals are a kind of 'people.' The world is fraught with dangers, for any one of these quasi-human powers as well as the human beings one encounters may turn out to be hostile. In order to avoid these dangers the Navaho child is brought up to observe a large number of taboos, for instance, that one should not bother or kill snakes. These dangerous forces are liable to make one sick. Accordingly, sickness is generally attributed to having antagonized one of these forces. These beliefs and their implications for the Navaho ethical system will be discussed in Chapter XIII.

b. Practical concerns

The content of the Navaho moral code reflects a practical concern with practical problems. The foremost of these is the problem of getting enough food to survive and to support one's family. When my informant was young, the means of subsistence were largely sheep herding and farming. Hence, much of what a parent taught his children concerned the proper care of the sheep and other animals and how to grow corn successfully.[11]

In addition to this concern with subsistence, Navaho culture is pre-occupied with the problem of sickness, sometimes to the extent that the outsider receives the impression of the Navahos being hypochondriacs. The peculiarity of what has been called Navaho "religion" is that it is ostensibly devoted almost entirely to curing sickness — although the Navaho includes under the category of sickness many conditions which we do not. For instance, the having of bad dreams calls for a religious curing ceremony. A tremendous portion of the time and money of the typical Navaho household is spent on such curing ceremonies.[12]

A third sphere of problems which are dealt with by the Navaho moralist concerns social relations. This kind of problem is of course, universal, and there are some moral philosophers who hold that all moral problems are essentially social problems. However, I shall try to show later that these social problems must be interpreted as less important for the Navaho code as a whole than are those of subsistence and sickness, for there are very few stringent moral prescriptions regarding behavior towards other people that are not derivable from those involving either sickness or subsistence. Admittedly, there are many social regulations governing the behavior towards relatives and others, but these are generally not expressed as moral prescriptions in my sense of the term. On the whole, the prescriptions about conduct towards other people are less stringent than they are in our own society.

Nevertheless, as I shall explain, the Navaho code tends in the end to promote harmonious social relations and to provide some of the elements necessary for social equilibrium. Perhaps the fact that the Navahos live apart from each other and are spread out over the whole countryside in family groups, or 'outfits,' contributes to this looseness of their code. Within their own immediate circle or outfit mutual help seems so obviously necessary and desirable that regulations take the form of what Malinowski called 'customs' rather than 'laws.' On the other hand, people living at a distance can be ignored if need be, and hence the social conditions which probably give rise to more stringent social prescriptions are absent.[13]

In general, however, almost all the psychological and social problems with which the Navaho moral code deals belong to one or other of three groups: they reflect anxieties about subsistence, sickness, or social relations.[14]

c. Navaho materialism and individualism: The concept of property

Materialism and noncompetitive individualism are two related and quite evident general characteristics of Navaho practical life. Navaho culture places great emphasis upon property. The Navaho child is taught to work hard so he can have a "good hogan, lots of horses, lots of jewelry," etc. In *Son of Old Man Hat,* the theme of how to get rich is reiterated constantly, and the same interest is to be found in the other biographies.[15] According to Navaho opinion, the good man is a prosperous man, and the bad man a poor man. "He's no good. He's going to be hard up, wear poor clothes, poor shoes, he's going to be raggy." (* 47) There are certain provisos necessary, since it is undesirable to be thought too rich or stingy. But in the abstract, riches are considered the mark of a good man.

The emphasis on property starts early, for the old Navahos used to give sheep even to young children so that as children they would already possess the nucleus of a herd. Their ownership was respected by the parents, and it was up to the child to decide how to dispose of them; he could slaughter or sell the sheep and use the proceeds for his own use.[16]

Since the Navaho concept of property differs considerably from our own, it is worth while to point out some of these differences. Property includes certain intangible goods such as esoteric knowledge. Songs and medicines are the private property of the owner and must be paid for; indeed, if they are not paid for they will not be efficacious and something might happen to the owner. On the other hand, the Navahos do not think of a house as being owned by someone, and in general land is "owned only in the sense that it is used." [17] Furthermore, before they were influenced by the ideas of the whites, a man was never paid for helping with building a hogan or planting corn. In other words, labor was not a commodity. He was rewarded by being given lots to eat, but never paid outright. "Whatever the arrangements [for help] are they are informal and indefinite and always cast in the ideology of help, not of labor and wages." [18]

It is quite apparent that ownership in Navaho society does not imply sole and exclusive responsibility for one's possessions. The child herder is as responsible for the sheep of his parents and of others as he is for his own, and generally, sheep and other possessions will be cared for by others during long periods of absence of the owner. This suggests that the ancient Navaho concept of property emphasizes different aspects of ownership from those of our Western ideal.

The core of the Navaho idea of ownership is the "freedom to dispose" of the object as one sees fit;[19] others are not to interfere with the possessor's disposal of the object. I suggest that in theory this right is probably as absolute as any right among the Navahos. In *Son of Old Man Hat* and the *Autobiography* the reader is quite impressed by the remarkable reticence of even close relatives about a person's disposal of his property. The phrase "it's up to you" constantly recurs. This is one context where the rule "mind your own business" is almost unexceptional.

The respect for individual ownership takes such an extreme form among the Navahos that they feel constrained about even offering advice on disposal of one's property. When I asked my informant how he would advise me to dispose of an imaginary five hundred sheep, his reply was: "It's up to you." (* 31) If this analysis is correct we should expect to find *few if any moral prescriptions about the disposal of property*, except those involving payment for damages. And, as far as I can see, this is the case. The absolute freedom to dispose is not limited by any directives whatsoever. This, of course, is quite different from our own moral discourse, in which we are constantly being advised about how to spend and where to give our money.

A complete analysis of the Navaho concept of property along the lines I have suggested is impossible without further knowledge of the language. Perhaps such an analysis would provide the clue to the individualism which is so characteristic of Navaho culture and which is well illustrated by the tendency to say that "it's up to you"; the unwillingness to approve of taking a person's property without his consent even for good purposes, "I won't say for the man: Yes or No" (* 73); and the general absence of moral prescriptions in this realm.

I should warn the reader that this inviolacy of property is merely the moral ideal. In practice, there are on the one hand customary rules for giving gifts, and on the other not infrequent stealing and other violations of property rights. Furthermore, as I shall show later, the respect for property has a quite different ethical basis from our own.

d. Property and sex

Before leaving the subject of property, it may be pointed out that the conception of property is so central that the moral prescriptions which it involves are frequently extended to spheres which would hardly seem to us to come under property. The most noteworthy extension of this area occurs in sexual matters. An example of this is the application of property prohibitions to a person's sexual organs; "we have no business discussing it — it belongs to him and to none of us. So why do we talk about it?" [20]

There are many other ways in which sex is assimilated to property. Illicit sexual intercourse is "just like stealing." [21] There is an ancient practice of paying a woman with whom one has had sexual intercourse. Moreover, if a woman takes a piece of property she wants to be seduced, and if she has been seduced she appropriates a piece of the man's property.[22] There are numerous other practices which illustrate the same close relationship between sex and property; for example, the bride-price custom and the custom of paying women partners at squaw dances.[23]

4. AN HYPOTHESIS ABOUT NAVAHO ETHICS

The problem of formulating an hypothesis about the Navaho moral code falls roughly into two parts. We must first determine which of the prescriptions enunciated by the informants are moral and which are not. Then we must proceed to formulate a reconstructive hypothesis according to the scheme outlined in Chapter X. These two problems will be considered briefly here; the details and proof will be given in the later chapters of Part III.

a. The identification of moral prescriptions

One has the impression after reading many of the available descriptions of Navaho ethics that its investigators have arrived at contradictory conclusions. However, there is actually not so great a discrepancy among these conclusions as would appear on the surface, since there seems to be general agreement about the facts. The discrepancies can be traced to differing interpretations of the facts.

The most serious disagreements arise from the use of varied definitions of "ethics." Thus: an authoritarian definition results in a description of Navaho ethics which is authoritarian, either theistic or social;[24] the use of criteria based on our own ethical principles entails the conclusion that Navaho moral principles are quite similar to our own;[25] and, the use of approbationist, functionalist, or psychological definitions will result in still other completely dissimilar accounts of Navaho ethics.[25]

The purpose of the discussion in Part I was to develop a definition of "ethics" which would be neutral with respect to such differences. By adopting the proposed definition, questions about the character of the Navaho moral code become empirical and substantive, and none of the various alternatives are established or excluded on a priori grounds — by definition. Accordingly, we must examine the evidence for each of the possible interpretations of the code in turn. Here, I might point out three of the possibilities that are not thus precluded by definition, and which I shall contend actually are to be found in Navaho ethics: first, that the stereotyped rationale offered by the informant for his moral prescriptions are to be taken seriously;[27] second, that many of the norms regulating social conduct are not moral at all;[28] and third, that the basic prescription grounding all moral principles is egoistic and in that sense asocial.[29]

b. Contexts in which moral discourse is assumed to appear

Since any inquiry has to make some initial assumptions with regard to where its data are to be found, we shall have to assume some context in which moral discourse is likely to occur. If we bear in mind that the earlier definition of moral prescriptions includes legitimacy and superiority, we may expect such prescriptions to be enunciated in public discussions and in the teaching of children. Perhaps it is not too much to suppose that an old man, about to die, will tell his children to follow such directives; and perhaps in other 'extreme' situations moral statements will also occur.

In Navaho life there are several such contexts. First, we have many accounts of the teaching given children by aged parents which constantly emphasize the same prescriptions. Second, there are public occasions in which an older person preaches to the young; for instance, at weddings (* 115), or after a death, or during ceremonies. Third, there are public airings of disputes which give rise to such moral exhortations; for example, in marital disputes the pros and cons of continuing a marriage are discussed in such a way as to give us considerable insight into the Navaho moral code. Finally, there are particular occasions where the agent is advised against or reprimanded for committing some act; for instance, if he is caught stealing or being too familiar with a close relative of the opposite sex.

All these situations generally give rise to moral utterances of one sort or another. The prescriptions which arise from them will be described in detail in Chapters XIII and XIV. In addition to these 'natural' contexts, during the course of my inquiry I invented imaginary situations in order to test further some of the conclusions which I had arrived at. The tests will be discussed in chapters following Chapter XIV. A brief description of the moral teaching given to children will be included in this chapter.

c. Navaho prudentialism

When I first went out to visit the Navahos, I had no preconceptions about what kind of moral code they accepted, if any at all. But after a few interviews I realized that there was a clear and unmistakable pattern to my informant's ethical thinking. The hypothesis which I am offering occurred to me only after the interviewing had begun, and thus may be said to have "grown out of the facts." During the rest of my visit, the interviews were devoted to verifying and testing the hypothesis.

In general terms I shall contend that the Navaho moral code can be called "rationalistic," "prudentialistic," "egoistic," and "utilitarian by derivation." By using the term "rationalism" I intend to suggest that the Navahos stress the necessity and sufficiency of 'reasonable discourse' to establish their moral prescriptions. The process of justification is, for them, non-authoritative and consists in providing reasons for every prescription. By "prudentialism," I mean not only that their system is rationalistic but that it is oriented to the welfare of the individual agent. In other words, it is egoistic, although it differs from Western egoism in that the welfare of the agent is not subjectively defined in such terms as pleasure, self-assertion, self-realization, or sanctification. From the basic prudentialist prescription and by means of certain factual assumptions, the Navaho moralist derives particular moral prescriptions and rules which are, in effect, utilitarian, that is, they tend to promote the greatest good (happiness) of everyone.

A more precise formulation of my hypothesis can be given in terms of the concepts expounded in Chapter X and may be outlined as follows:

Rationalism:
(*a*) Criteria of ethical competence: nonauthoritarian;
(*b*) Mode of validation: applicational;

Prudentialism:
(*c*) Basic prescription: extrinsically teleological;
(*d*) Goal: 'egoistic' (intrapersonal), negative, materialistic;
(*e*) Ground motive: fear (?);
(*f*) Various factual premises involving beliefs about God, nature, supernatural beings, and the uniformity of natural laws;

Utilitarian:
(*g*) Various particular prescriptions derived from the above prescribing altruistic behavior.

5. SAMPLES OF ETHICAL DISCOURSE

a. Father's teaching

The talks given by fathers to children, and by the leaders at marriages, give a typical picture of some of the main tenets of the Navaho moral code. The core of a father's teaching may be summed up by the statement, "You must look ahead for yourself and your stock," [30] for a great deal of the child's early training is designed to make him a tough and hard worker, who knows how to handle his stock. A typical list of paternal teachings might run as follows:

(*a*) Get up early and run and roll in the snow (in the wintertime), so that you will be 'on the alert,' 'tough,' and 'lively.' [31]

(*b*) Care for your sheep, farming and horses. Learn about them. Don't be mean to them and learn songs to make them strong, "and you'll have lots to eat . . . That's the way to become a rich man."[32]

(c) A child is taught "not to lie or not to steal and not to tell stories about what he didn't see." Also, not to gamble because "they would lose and get nothing out of it." Also, of course, not to drink. (* 4)[33]

(d) He was also told to listen to his parents, and to help them, "for he wouldn't be able to get anything — not even his clothes — by sitting around." (* 6)

If the child does all these things he will become rich and live a long life: "If I was to live right way, I'll be living for years and years." (* 163)

b. Talks at weddings

The reports of talks at weddings stress roughly the same things as the teachings for children. The husband is told to build a good hogan, work hard, think hard, be honest, and not to get mad at anyone especially his wife and in-laws. In addition, he is told to help his father-in-law and to go to him for advice. The wife is told to take care of her home, clean the dishes, learn to weave, and so on. She should "tell the truth about everything that is going on." "Do right to your people." Don't be mean but rather kind to everyone. Teach your children properly. Husband and wife should listen to each other ('mind each other'). Then it is added: "In that way you can make your people get along with you. Now if you do that you're going to live a long time." (* 115)[34]

It is interesting to note that in all these talks the accent is placed upon taking care of one's possessions and becoming rich. In some accounts the prescriptions about social relations are entirely omitted; They appear to be secondary to the informant.

c. Descriptions of the good and bad man

This general account of the tone of Navaho ethics can be summarized by citing some of the characterizations of the good man and the happy man, and of their opposites.

"The good man is honest, and tell the truth to the people, and have lot of money and livestock. And he's helping some people, poor people — so he's good man." (* 164) He never makes any trouble. "My son is a good worker. He never goes out for nothing, and he doesn't know anything about gambling, and he never goes around to the singings. He only knows about the sheep, horses and cattle. And he takes good care of himself. He's not like these men, who don't know anything." [35] A good man 'everybody likes.' In general he is rich, honest, kind, generous, and 'cares for himself, for his livestock, and for others.'

A bad man 'nobody likes.' Everybody laughs at him, and he will be poor and have raggy clothes. (* 48) A bad man is one who 'puts you into troubles,' and, even worse, is a 'mean" man, who will 'hit you' or 'steal from you', and so on. (* 165) He is a person who doesn't do what is right. There are many different ways a man can be bad, varying from just making mistakes to being a witch.

XII

Beliefs About Man and the World

In the present and the next two chapters, I shall present the data upon which my final hypothesis rests and which it is intended to explain. It should be noted that many of these materials are based on statements made by other Navahos besides Bidaga. Hence, perhaps not all of them would be found to be accepted by any single informant. Since I am interested, however, in the general structure of Navaho thinking, and ethical thinking in particular, the *type* of reason given by some informant is of more significance than the specific reason given by him. Thus, it is more significant that an informant X justifies, say, a moral prescription Y by arguments of type Z, and that another informant Q justifies R by arguments of the same type Z, than that they both accept the same statement and offer the same reasons for it.[1]

In order to give the reader a better understanding of the types of argument to be examined later, I shall begin by briefly sketching Navaho beliefs about man and the world. We have already seen that their talks to children about how to herd sheep and how to farm involved teaching something about why things happen and how they may be predicted to behave in the future. In the same way, moral talks about other matters consist largely of telling the listener about the way things act and may be expected to act. I shall offer an explanation of this characteristic later.

I. EXOTERIC BELIEFS

These beliefs might be described as those which a relatively unac-culterated Navaho, such as either of my two informants, would expect every Navaho to know. As such they are exoteric, and not restricted to the professional Singers. However, some of them are concealed beliefs, according to my earlier definition. The following summary of these exoteric beliefs about the kinds of beings inhabiting the universe will be impressionistic, since that is all that is necessary for our purposes. More detailed expositions of these beliefs can easily be found in the anthropological literature on Navaho religion.

a. Friendly and unfriendly powers

The Navaho world is inhabited by various kinds of beings which can be differentiated by the amount of power they possess, and by their tendency to act favorably towards human beings. There are some beings who generally are kindly; there are others who generally are 'mean'; and there are a large number of beings who are potentially one or the other, depending largely on how they are treated by the person concerned. The prescribed behavior towards these beings is determined by the kind of power they possess and by the extent to which they are tractable. Thus, they fall roughly into the following classes: kindly disposed, persuadable, persuadable with difficulty, unpersuadable (essentially evil), and we may perhaps include 'unpredictable' beings.[2] The more power they possess, for good or evil, the more careful one must be in one's behavior towards them. The unpersuadable, 'mean' beings who are powerful should be avoided whenever possible.

b. Special kinds of beings

There are many kinds of beings occurring in Navaho thought. For our purposes, a list of them will suffice. They have been divided into certain groups, although it will be obvious that these groups do not reflect clear-cut distinctions.

Holy People — are the divinities, who are distinguished from ordinary human beings, the Earth Surface People, by possessing special supernatural powers and by being immortal. The Navaho word translated by "holy" defines "power which exceeds human effort," and in the term "Holy People" it stands for the concept of supernatural power and immunity, but does not connote moral sanctity. There is a tremendous number and variety of these beings; they are the subjects of the myths, which are mostly esoteric. Sometimes the Holy People are helpful, but often they are dangerous; they are invoked to help out the Earth Surface People in their ceremonials and sweat baths. Only two points need be mentioned. First, all these supernatural beings are subject to some extent to the laws of human behavior; that is, they react the way human beings do; they get angry, they like sex, they can be jealous. Second, the Navaho layman is not supposed to know too much about them; he is informed about them only in general terms and under suitable circumstances. Hence, except under these circumstances, the Holy People are not relevant to moral discourse.[3]

Natural forces — are conceived of as quasi-human beings, and belong properly among the Holy People. Some of them are peculiarly dangerous; for example, thunder, lightning, and whirlwinds. Others are generally favorably disposed towards human beings; for example, rains, mountains, and corn.

Animals — constitute another large group which is also a kind of divinity. They are referred to by the Navahos as the "non-speaking ones," although originally they were people and 'talked like people.' (* 98) The Navaho conception of animals is that all the individual animals of a species are the 'manifestation' of a Man, or 'inner form'; and, in a sense, the particular animals may be said to belong to him.[4] Thus, behind every coyote, there is the Coyote-Man, and behind every bear, the Bear-Man. The inner form or inner man must be taken into account when killing the particular animals that come under him. For example, in order not to antagonize him one should not slaughter too many of the species, one should thank him, and so on.

Ghosts — are the malignant parts of dead people and are a most feared group of beings. Everyone who dies, except those who die of old age or in infancy, continues a kind of shadowy existence. Ghosts are inevitably dangerous in that they are evil and powerful, and therefore, they must be assiduously avoided. It does not make any difference whether they were good people when alive. Navaho children are told about ghosts, and one may safely assume that there are many concealed beliefs about ghosts entering into Navaho ethical discourse. However, such beliefs are difficult for a stranger to investigate because the Navahos think it is dangerous even to talk about them.[5]

Human beings — are called "Earth Surface People," and are differentiated from the other kinds of beings mentioned by being mortal. Like the Holy People, they too can be classified as friendly or unfriendly. An ordinary human being may be good or bad, depending upon what type of person he is, and this depends in turn on the kind of 'wind' he has. The Navaho 'psychology' is complicated, but there is no doubt that it contains a strong element of predestination or fatalism. (* 99) Generally, one can expect one's own family to be kindly; but one cannot be sure about others.[6]

Witches — are human beings who are thought to possess supernatural powers, and are evil. There are many similarities between them and the Singers, or medicine men, who are human beings possessing supernatural powers which they use for good purposes. Witches are believed to be so powerful that they need not be afraid of ghosts or of breaking taboos which are extremely dangerous for an ordinary man to break. Thus, witchcraft activities generally include dealings with corpses and having incestuous relations with siblings. (The first witches, according to Navaho mythology, were the divinities First Man and First Woman, who were brother and sister as well as husband and wife.)[7] Fear of witches, as of ghosts, is deep-rooted in the Navaho mind. One must be constantly on one's guard not to antagonize them or allow them to get power over one. Ultimately, the only sure way to handle them it to kill them.[8]

(*White*) *government or law* — is another force which should perhaps be added to this list. It is probably conceived of as extremely powerful and, on the whole, kindly and generous; it may be the modern counterpart of the Holy People, who are invoked to settle those troubles which the Navaho people cannot solve and yet who must be treated circumspectly, so as not to arouse antagonism. (* 32, 35, 36)[9]

I believe that some information about all of these beings is available to the Navaho layman. Therefore we may consider the beliefs about them to be exoteric. However, the Navaho layman is not as consciously aware of the general laws of behavior which he attributes to these beings as he is of the particular behavior to be expected from them. In order to understand how these beliefs function in his ethical system, it is necessary to attempt a provisional reconstruction of those general laws which the beliefs about the behavior of these beings presuppose.[10]

2. RECONSTRUCTION OF NAVAHO CATEGORIES OF EXPLANATION

The beliefs summarized in the preceding section can safely be regarded as data since they have been well established by previous investigations, and can be verified by consulting the literature. This section is highly speculative, and I do not pretend that what I say here can be verified without a great deal more research. Many of my theses are not essential to the hypothesis about Navaho ethics. However, if true, they will shed some light on Navaho reasoning processes in general. The only point of which I am certain is that the Navaho modes of explanation differ from our own in many important respects. Hence, this section is designed to put the reader on his guard against attributing to the Navaho the lines of reasoning which we as educated people in an age of science normally follow.[11]

a. Mechanism

The Navaho is a mechanist par excellence in two senses: namely, in that he is a determinist, and in that he rejects final causes. He assumes that every event has a cause, even though an ordinary human being may not always be able to identify the cause of a certain event or predict the effects of an event. If one had enough information, the causes and effects could in principle be determined. Furthermore, given certain causes, other effects follow with ineluctable necessity.

Navaho thought supposes that there are some general laws which govern the whole of reality — and supernatural beings are as subject to them as are human beings. The main difference between the former and us is that they are more powerful, and hence can manipulate events to suit their own purposes by means that are not ordinarily available to human beings. But in the end, the divinities are liable to sickness and other misfortune, and must use the same kind of 'medicine' to cure them.

Moreover, these mechanical processes are conceived of nonteleologically. They are not only inevitable, they are also indifferent to human purposes; they may be favorable or unfavorable, but this is a matter of accident or manipulation on our part. Accordingly, there is a strong element of Stoicism in Navaho thinking, so that when things get out of control the Navaho is content to say, "Nothing can be done about it."

b. Temporal and spatial aspects of causality

In the history of Western philosophy it has usually been assumed that cause and effect must be contiguous in time and space. Action at a distance, either temporal or spatial, has been rejected, or at least it has been regarded as a perplexing problem.

It is generally agreed that the Navaho conception of time is quite different from our own.[12] The difference appears strikingly in their thinking about causality. A cause may be temporally quite remote from its effect. There are numerous examples of this principle of *temporally remote causal efficacy*. Sicknesses are frequently attributed to having done something or eaten something ten or twenty years ago. (* 76)[13] Furthermore, something that is done today may not bear fruit until a long time afterwards. (* 65) This willingness to accept as causes events which happened a long time ago, incidentally, is a way of reinforcing the general supposition of determinism; it is always possible to find some antecedent event in the past to explain the present one, especially if one looks back far enough. It also renders the diagnosis of sickness by specialists like handtremblers more plausible, since their patients are likely to remember violating a taboo long ago which could be considered the cause of their present sickness; even if they cannot remember any such act it is quite possible that it was committed some-time in the dim past.

Perhaps, from the Navaho point of view, this theory of causality is not so absurd; it takes time for crops to grow, for babies to be born, and for one's action to take effect in influencing others. (I do not wish to suggest that temporally discontinuous causation is a category of thought which is unique to the Navahos. However, it is interesting to reflect how many examples of apparently remote causation assume the existence of some continuous causal agent. For instance, when it is said that the sins of the fathers are visited on the children, it is assumed that there is some connecting link, namely, God's wrath.)

Although temporal propinquity is not demanded, I submit that the Navahos' conception of causality entails that spatial proximity is necessary, and, indeed, at times sufficient for causal efficacy. *Action at a distance is not possible.* The Holy People cannot help out at Sings unless they actually come to them. A witch cannot effect his malpractices unless he is physically in contact with the person's body or some part of him.[14] Telekinesis would appear impossible for a Navaho.

If this interpretation is correct, there are several conclusions that follow from it. First, power that is spatially remote, and which will remain so, is not regarded as a danger. Hence, the most effective way of avoiding such dangers is literally to run away. There are many illustrations of this tendency to run away to be found in accounts of Navaho behavior.

Second, causal power varies with the ability to travel. If a being is capable of getting somewhere in practically no time, he is extremely powerful. Hence, the emphasis on the capacity of the various divinities to travel back and forth at tremendous speeds. The potency of thunder, lightning, and whirlwinds may be explained on this principle. Ghosts and witches are thought to be capable of "roaming at great speed." [15] It would seem that ability to travel is a necessary adjunct of power, and consequently of dangerousness.

This principle of spatial proximity might appear to contradict some of the beliefs held about the efficacy of actions which are not directed towards an object itself, but towards something previously associated with it and now no longer in contact with it. For instance, witchcraft practices are supposed to make use of hair, articles of clothing, and other objects, taken from the victim surreptitiously. Similarly, lightning is supposed to continue to affect any object struck by it, even though it is no longer in the place where it was struck, and when there is no longer any lightning around. However, these apparent exceptions merely illustrate the principle cited by Kluckhohn; namely, that "the part stands for the whole." [16] The only requirement is that the part representing the whole have been in physical contact with the whole at some time. These examples may also exemplify the simultaneous application of both the principles of spatial proximity and temporal remoteness.

Third, a most interesting consequence of this category of physical propinquity, is that spatial proximity often seems to be considered sufficient as well as necessary for causal efficacy. Thus, for example, the places where a person has died (his hogan) and where he is buried are to be sedulously avoided because his ghost has power there. By the same reasoning, the place where lightning has struck must also be avoided. On the other hand, when the Holy People are invoked and 'come around,' as in Blessing Way, they bring favorable conditions to everything in the vicinity—to the hogan, the clothing, the sheep, all the people around, as well as to the patient seeking cure. (* 79)

The importance of the concept of place has been often pointed out by Father Berard Haile in his writings on the Navaho language. The language contains a kind of place-pronoun, *ho,* which is employed to refer to the general condition of the place. The word, hogan, is thus a "place-home but only for humans." Father Berard has shown that the elusive words, *hozhon* and *hochon,* are etymologically derived from conjunctions using this prefix. Thus, these two words may be translated "pleasant conditions (places)" and "ugly conditions (places)" respectively.[17]

There is no doubt of the importance of this place-condition concept in Navaho ceremonial thought. However, I suggest that its significance for the analysis of their ethical discourse has not been recognized. Thus, the Navaho tends to generalize both his prescriptions and the reasons for obeying them by referring them to general place conditions. The prescribed behavior towards ghosts takes this form. The all-important notion of "trouble" is also generalized in the same way. Trouble is a kind of condition which may be general to a certain place, such as a hogan, and in this respect is comparable to other conditions like happiness or well-being — or general ugliness or dangerousness.

The general importance of movements and place names is evident throughout Navaho culture.[18] In the language itself, Hoijer has shown that "in three broad speech patterns, illustrated by the conjugation of active verbs, the reporting of actions and events, and the framing of substantive concepts, Navaho emphasizes movement and specifies the nature, direction, and status of such movement in considerable detail. Even the neuter category is relatable to the dominant conception of a universe in motion . . ."[19]

c. *The principle of general effects*

Closely allied to this notion of spatial proximity is the Navaho tendency to think of causes as 'infectious,' in the sense of having ramified consequences. The effects of a particular action, such as the breach of a taboo, a quarrel, or a curing ceremony, are general rather than limited. Each of these actions affect the welfare not only of the agent but also of all those who surround him. Hence, although many actions have a presumed direct effect upon the agent, and consequently are of immediate interest to him, they also affect others, and so become matters of general interest. Thus, a breach of a taboo will bring trouble to the family as well as to the agent; holding a Blessing Way ceremony will bring blessings to everyone around; marital disputes will affect the whole community; and the prosperity of one person will bring prosperity to others in the group. Since these are all matters of general interest and not just the business of the person concerned, we can explain why there is strong social disapproval of doing things that are held to be wrong, and approval of doing what is considered right. (I shall comment upon this in more detail in Chapter XVII, section 2.)

The generality attributed to effects accounts for the fact that the consequences of an act are referred to in general terms, like sickness or trouble. For instance, diseases are generally classified in terms of their presumed causes such as ghosts, rather than in terms of their symptoms; and a sickness is diagnosed as a sickness resulting from this or that cause. 'Trouble' is also conceived of in general terms. Hence, as we shall see later, the fact that the particular sickness or trouble is not mentioned as a consequence of one's acts, does not entail that the Navaho is just repeating an empty formula, "sickness" or "trouble"; rather it reflects this tendency to generalize the effects. Whether this notion of general effects is derivable from that of spatial proximity need not be determined here.

d. The principle of many reasons

Another principle that appears to lie behind Navaho causal explanations might be called the principle of *multiple causation*. In diagnoses of sicknesses, it is not at all unusual to hear more than one cause cited as an explanation; for example, the same sickness may be said to be caused by having eaten a fish, killed a snake, and having sung too many Blessing Way ceremonies. (* 76)[20] An analogous principle is found in their ethical thinking, namely, *multiple justification*, which is illustrated by the tendency to give more than one reason for a prescription.[21] Actually, this is a corollary of the principle of general effects, as I shall show later.

All these principles of causation may amount to a rather complicated theory of probability which assumes that physical proximity will increase the probability of causal dependence, and that causal factors will probably have general effects. In general, I think that it is safe to say that the Navaho believes in the principle of sufficient reason 'with a vengeance.' Every event (and prescription, as we shall see) must have a reason (cause), and in most cases it has many reasons, causes, and effects.[22]

e. Some causal laws

In addition to the general categorial principles already discussed, the Navaho thinker appears to assume certain more specific causal laws governing human behavior. It has been widely acknowledged that the Navaho tends to accept the categorial principle that like produces like. The many applications of this principle in ordinary affairs and in mythology need not be discussed here.[23] However, there is one specific application of this principle which is extremely important for an understanding of Navaho ethics: namely, the 'law' that a certain kind of behavior towards others will produce on their part like behavior towards you — or, good produces good, and evil produces evil. For example, there seems to be a general belief that if you treat others kindly, they will treat you kindly in return, if you help others, they will help you 'back.' It should be noted that this is a matter of psychological not moral necessity; the doctrine, as I interpret it, is that the recipient of favors *will* reciprocate and not just that he *ought to* reciprocate. Conversely, if you treat someone 'roughly' he will be 'rough' to you. Hence, in *Son of Old Man Hat* the father advises 'not cussing' the animals; instead, "If you think kindly and talk in the kindest manner then they'll know you're a kind man, and then everything will go to you." [24]

Two other general principles of behavior which are relevant to the ethical prescriptions regarding the handling of disputes may be noted. First, there is a tendency to explain aggressive behavior in terms of sexual jealousy. This applies to the explanation of the undesirable conduct of supernatural beings as well as to that of ordinary human beings. Second, there seems to be a general presumption that people who have been provoked can be pacified by giving them something — 'making a payment.' This is the rationale behind the stereotyped mode of handling offenses such as murder, stealing, or adultery; in all of them the dispute is settled by making a payment to the injured party.

Both of these principles are closely bound up with each other by the intimate relationship between sexual and property concepts. As was noted above, adultery is spoken of as a 'kind of stealing,' and the antagonism which is aroused thereby is eliminated by 'paying' for it. In a sense, perhaps we could say that the Navaho thinks that most disputes arise from sexual jealousy and can be avoided by conforming to property prohibitions or can be settled when they occur by transfer of property. This is wild speculation, for clearly, further elaboration and testing would be required to establish it. [25]

There are a few other principles which I need only mention here. The Navaho 'economic theory' assumes that there is a potential abundance of goods, and that through coöperation the amount of goods will be increased for everyone; in other words, they would deny the basic assumption upon which much of our own economic theory depends, namely, the scarcity of goods. This economic principle is another consequence of the principle that good produces good, and of the principle of general effects. [26]

The efficacy of talk for manipulating others should also be included among the principles listed here. As I shall show later, talk is considered both necessary and sufficient to reform a wrong-doer and to settle disputes. [27]

The list of principles given here is not only incomplete, but is also admittedly quite impressionistic. Illustrations will be found in later chapters. Further investigation would undoubtedly uncover other more basic categories of Navaho thinking; and it would determine whether those which I have suggested are in fact to be found in Navaho etiological discourse in the form I have given them. Such an investigation should proceed by the method of hypothetical reconstruction; if it does so, we may eventually hope to arrive at a deeper as well as truer understanding of Navaho thought in general.

An investigation of their principles is far beyond the scope of the present inquiry. My purpose in mentioning them is merely to bring out the manifold ways in which Navaho reasoning about natural processes and human behavior differs from our own. Only if we take full cognizance of the fact that there are such differences will we be able to appreciate the arguments which are offered to support their ethical principles.

The Data: Negative Prescriptions

I. THE CLASSIFICATION OF PRESCRIPTIONS

In reports of anthropological investigations, it is always important to keep the data separate from the theoretical interpretation of them. Accordingly, this chapter and the next will contain a fairly complete list of statements of prescriptions and of the arguments offered in justification of them. These will be the primary data to be explained by my hypothesis, which will be expounded and tested in detail in the later chapters.

The various prescriptive statements can be divided into groups which correspond roughly to the general types of justifying reasons given for them by Navaho informants. For purposes of exposition, some classification must be adopted, and any classification is, in a sense, question-begging. Thus, a scheme of classification which reflects the categories of our own moral code would tend to assimilate the Navaho code to our own, and would, in my opinion, be entirely superficial if not misleading. Whether or not the classification I have employed accurately reflects the way a Navaho would group the various prescriptions in his code can be decided by the reader. There might be some question as to whether all, or merely some, or perhaps none of these prescriptions are moral. Again, pending later discussion, the reader must answer this question for himself.

If we adopt the principle of classification which I have suggested, ethical statements fall naturally into two groups, statements of negative prescriptions and of positive prescriptions, and within each of these groups there is an order of degrees of stringency.

a. Navaho ethical expressions[1]

A common and important word in Navaho ethical discourse is *bahadzid.* (Literally, this means "for it there is reverence or fear.") It is translated by the native interpreter as "It's dangerous" or "Something is going to hurt you," (* 169) and can be applied to anything that we ordinarily would call "dangerous" such as driving a car recklessly, lightning, fire, or war. *Bahadzid* is often used to keep children from hurting themselves. In some instances, it appears to bear with it the connotation of the numinous. (*169–172)

The word for "wrong" is *doo 'akotee da* (literally: "not right"). It is applied to actions and may be used in a technological sense; for example, when a mother teaches her child how to cook, she can say "That's not the right way to do it." Some actions are not right because they are *bahadzid*, and other actions may not be right for some other reason.

The general word for "good" is *ya' at' eeh*, and for "bad," *doo ya' at' eeh da* (literally: "not good"). *Ya' at' eeh* is used more broadly perhaps than our own word "good" and stands for anything that is fine, pleasant, works well, O.K., and so on. It may be applied to people, and is used in the expression translated as "good man." There are stronger words for "good" and "bad," but it is not necessary to mention them here. The interesting point to note is that the Navaho words for bad and wrong are negatives of "good" and "right." [2] (*173)

It should not be assumed that these linguistic expressions have only ethical uses or that ethical discourse cannot be conducted without them, any more than is the case with their English equivalents. I have already mentioned the impersonal third form which may be used to convey ethical exhortations. The context in which the statements are uttered is perhaps as important a means for identifying ethical statements as the linguistic vehicles employed.[3]

Perhaps more important for our purposes than any of the Navaho expressions I have mentioned are the English words which constantly recur in the interpreter's translations. As Kluckhohn has pointed out, the Navaho interpreter uses the same clichés over and over again, providing good examples of the patterning of linguistic expression. He writes:

> For example, when the sense is that a person ought to avoid persons, animals, or objects, the preferred English word is "bother." "Don't bother your wife" (usually with the meaning: don't have sexual intercourse with your wife). Similarly: "Young boys shouldn't bother the girls." When a helper in a chant was being sent out to gather materials used in the bath a part of the instructions given him was translated, "Then bring it right back to me — don't bother horses, sheep, or herders on the way." Now "avoid" is admittedly far too literary a word to expect as a translation of the Navaho verb in question, but "keep away from", "don't go near", "stay away from", and other words and circumlocutions would be distinctly congruent with the vocabulary of these interpreters. Indeed those I have mentioned are also heard but, in my experience, they are most significantly rarer than "bother." [4]

Other expressions in the interpreter's English translations which exemplify this kind of patterning are "making trouble," "straightening it out," "they won't like it," "treat pretty rough," and so on. I have tried to retain these expressions in my exposition so as to convey some of the naturalness of the interpreter's language.

b. Types of negative prescriptions

Negative prescriptions seem to fall into three natural groups according to the reasons offered for not violating them. An action may be said to be wrong because it is dangerous — *bahadzid;* because it will 'put you into trouble'; or because if you do that people will 'laugh' at you, or will 'talk' about you. I shall label these three types of negative prescriptions: *taboos, social prohibitions,* and *social interdictions*[5] respectively. In general, any action that is dangerous will get you into trouble, and any action that causes trouble will make people talk about you. In other words, the taboos are also social prohibitions, and social prohibitions are also social interdictions. The converse, however, does not hold, for there are actions which people talk about which are not trouble producing, and there are trouble-producing actions which are not dangerous. The explanation of this fact has been suggested already, and I shall discuss it at greater length in Chapter XVII, section 2.

I shall consider first those actions which are prohibited on the grounds that they are *bahadzid.* This group may be subdivided again into: (*a*) those actions which are 'naturally' dangerous, in that they are part of the natural order of things — and all beings (supernatural as well as human) are subject to them; (*b*) those actions which 'bother' or antagonize some superhuman being and which are dangerous because they provoke him; (*c*) those actions which 'bother' or antagonize human beings, and which may provoke them to drastic physical aggression in retaliation. However, for convenience, I shall discuss the prescriptions of subgroups *a* and *b* under the *bahadzid* or taboo group, and purely humanly caused dangers (those in group *c*), under social prohibitions. Since this classification is merely for descriptive purposes, it does not matter greatly where these prescriptions are placed, and different informants will probably stress different aspects of particular prescriptions.

2. TABOOS: "THAT'S BAHADZID"

a. Taboos in general

There are a great many prohibitions in Navaho society whose principal justification consists in the assertion that the actions are *bahadzid,* or dangerous to do. This means that violations are supposed to bring bodily harm to the person himself. This harm is generally referred to as "sickness" of one sort or another. As suggested at present, I shall not consider bodily injury inflicted by an ordinary human being, and so with this proviso I shall define a *taboo* as a prescription, which cites some sickness or injury as the likely effect of violation. Of course, this definition would include injuries resulting from such accidents as burning oneself in the fire or breaking one's leg, but this inclusiveness merely illuminates the concept of "taboo," for essentially it includes any prohibitions intended to preclude such injuries.[6]

The notion of taboo, involving as it does the idea of sickness, is closely bound up with the Navaho theory of curing. Quite frequently the sickness resulting from a violation of a taboo is thought to be curable either by a layman's medicine or by the Singers in the curing ceremonies. However, according to Navaho beliefs, even if a correct diagnosis has been made a cure is not always possible either because it has been started too late or because it is an incurable disease.[7] The whole conception of cure, which is a kind of restoration or straightening things out, will be considered in its ethical aspects under positive prescriptions.

The Navaho believes that the more powerful a being is the more immune he will be to the sicknesses resulting from the violation of taboos. If a being possesses supernatual power then he can 'get away with it,' and in this sense he is not bound by these prescriptions. Hence, the Holy People and witches can do things that an ordinary human being would be afraid to do. Nevertheless, the Holy People themselves have often gotten into trouble and consequently have had to resort to curing ceremonies. The techniques of curing originally used by the Holy People were given to the Earth Surface People to help them out. The accounts of this are the subject of the esoteric myths belonging to each curing ceremony.

The concept of "taboo" may be summarized by quoting Father Berard Haile's statement that "to disregard anything to be feared or tabooed (bahadzid) is to expose one's self deliberately either to danger or death, or to be branded as a witch." [8]

For the following taboos listed, I believe that there would be general agreement among those who accept them that some sickness or other will result from their violation. However, sometimes the informant will offer an explanation of why and how the sickness comes. To a certain extent such explanations are esoteric, and although I shall mention some of them, it is not necessary to think of them as essential parts of the exoteric ethical discourse of the people, any more than the technical knowledge of experts is necessary to understand the practical implications of other ethical systems.

b. Specific taboos

Dangers due to the order of nature. We may begin our detailed examination of prescriptions with those which are grounded on dangers arising from the general order of nature rather than from the power of some particular being. In other words, the violation of these taboos brings sickness to every type of being in the universe, including supernatural beings.

(1) "A man must not look at his mother-in-law and she must not look at him." The usual reasons offered are that you "will go blind" (* 117, 153), and that "You will not be very strong and your body will be weak all over."

This taboo is still observed by many Navahos despite the influence of white teaching to the contrary.[9] The practical difficulties arising from the custom of having the son-in-law live with his wife's family can easily be imagined. The field notes of every anthropologist who has visited Navaho families attest to this fact. Quite likely many young men avoid their mother-in-law in order to appease her, or the community at large. The practice is to be found among many non-literate societies, but perhaps not the same rationale.[10]

Certain exceptions are allowed. For example: if the son-in-law is a Singer and has sung over his mother-in-law in a ceremony, she automatically becomes a relative, and the taboo is voided. (* 151) If a man has married the mother first, and the daughter later, the taboo does not hold.[11]

It should be noted that this prohibition is stated in rather general terms. It forbids any kind of contact, touching, speaking, and even seeing. In practice the mere seeing of the other is not as dangerous as more intimate contact.[12]

I was told by one informant that there is no cure for the resulting blindness (* 153), and according to another informant, this taboo applies to the Holy People as well as to ordinary human beings; First Woman had to hide under the earth to avoid her son-in-law, the Sun.[13]

(2) "You ought not to 'bother' your close relatives." This is the prohibition against incest, which applies to siblings, parent-child relationships, and to members of the same clan. The reason is that "If you do you will go crazy and jump like a moth into the fire." (* 152, 156) The sickness consequent upon violation, however, can be cured by the ceremony called Moth Way.[14] (* 156) One of my informants suggested that the symptoms of incest sickness might be observed among white people. (* 152)

This prescription covers a variety of acts of familarity besides sexual intercourse. A brother is not supposed to use obscene language in front of his sister.[15] If a sister "asks for a shoe or a plate he can't hand it to her. He puts it on the ground first. Then she takes it."[16] Dancing with kinswomen is likewise forbidden. Here we have another illustration of the tendency to generalize the prescriptum in terms of the source of the danger rather than in terms of a description of a particular act as we are accustomed to in our prescriptions. Moreover, the principle of general effects mentioned earlier, also appears here, because the incestuous act is thought to affect the children as well as the couple involved (* 156), and is thought to be likely to have undesirable consequences for other people associated with them.

Incestuous relations are attributed to witches, since they are powerful enough to 'get away with it.' However, even the originator of incest among the divinities, Coyote, had to be given medical treatment by the Holy People. (* 157)

(3) There is a group of prescriptions associated with menstruation. "Do not beat your wife while she is menstruating." (* 172) "One should carefully avoid menstrual blood." [17] Menstrual blood is *bahadzid*, because "it will break your back." [18] (* 172) A menstruating woman is herself subject to a number of restrictions; for example, she may not attend ceremonials, she should not walk through corn fields, and so on, because her doing so will affect them adversely. A woman cannot become a Singer until after the menopause.

These prescriptions are further evidence of the Navaho tendency to generalize prescripta in terms of the source of the danger. Blood has power — particularly menstrual blood. This power may be evil, but also in some contexts may be good. Thus, there is a belief that intercourse with a menstruating woman will surely produce a baby; men are not generally willing to take the risk.[19] (* 172)

Menstruating and having children are intimately associated in the Navaho mind. (* 172) An instance of this is the belief that the first woman to menstruate was the powerful divinity, Changing Woman, because menstruation was necessary before she could have children. The female puberty rites are held to have begun at that time.[20]

(4) There are many prohibitions with regard to eating birds, fishes, and various kinds of animals. Some of these taboos, and possibly all of them, do not properly belong under the kind of taboo being discussed here, but we may conveniently consider them all together at this point. The most widespread of these food taboos is probably that applying to fish. "Never eat fish" because "anyone who ate them would fill up with water (dropsy) and die." [21] My principal informant attributed his sickness to having eaten a "great big fish." (* 76)

Other foods that have been reported dangerous to eat are turkey, pig, dogs, wolves, coyotes, foxes, rats, snakes, lizards, horntoads, ants, birds, etc.[22] Perhaps the danger is explained by the fact that eating these animals violates the taboo against killing them. (Discussed below.) The resulting sickness is often described as the acquisition of undesirable characteristics of the animals eaten.

Dangers from supernatural beings. There is another large group of taboos threatening sickness which is explained by one's having 'bothered' or antagonized some specific being which has supernatural power. The layman probably does not know how to explain the particular workings of this being — but he is aware that certain prohibited acts are associated with it.

(5) Taboos associated with lightning, thunder, and whirlwinds. "One ought not to look at an animal struck dead by lightning." [23] "Don't touch or use objects struck by lightning" (animals, wood, etc.). "Never talk or laugh loudly during a thunderstorm," for it might be taken to be mocking the thunder bird, and "Any person who incurred his anger would be in danger of being killed by lightning." [24]

There are many other acts which may result in being struck by lightning. The anthropologist is frequently frustrated in his investigations because it is believed that telling certain stories or talking about esoteric matters will have this effect. In the winter months, there is no lightning, so it is all right to tell them. (Perhaps this is another example of the causal principle of spatial propinquity.) Similarly, certain games, such as the moccasin game, should only be played in winter.

Objects resembling lightning are also dangerous. Thus there are many taboos connected with arrows, knives, and so on.[25]

Father Berard Haile has given us an account of the explanation offered for these taboos. In Navaho thought, thunder is identified with lightning, and it is the thunder rather than the lightning which strikes. The retaliatory acts of thunder in connection with handling thunderstruck objects is explained in one esoteric myth in terms of jealousy. "The interpretation which at present is given of his (sex) jealousy is, that thunder will give evidence of his (sex) jealousy, whenever a patient deliberately shows disrespect to lightning-struck objects." [26]

It should be noted that some of the acts which are forbidden because of their connection with lightning are also associated with snakes, and other dangerous beings — an example of multiple causation.

(6) Next we consider taboos associated with animals. There are a great many animals which should not be killed. "Don't kill a snake or you will get sick of acute indigestion." (* 76) "Never kill a lizard . . . If a person kills a lizard, breaks its back, or harms it in anyway, that person will be punished by spinal trouble." [27]

In general, the Navahos think it is wrong to kill birds, snakes, reptiles, spiders, bears, and other creatures, although some rationalization is offered where such killing seems to be necessary. Thus, one informant says that it is all right to kill coyotes that are nearby and causing trouble, and another says that it is all right to kill a bear if you "tell him you're sorry." [28] It is bad to kill a coyote (one reason being that he brings rain). (* 154) "If a coyote crosses in front of you, you should turn back." (* 154) This is a fairly widespread taboo.[29]

Children are forbidden to play with string in the summertime, because it will make the Spider mad.[30] It is interesting to note that the Navaho layman has only a hazy idea of these explanations of sickness: in *Son of Old Man Hat,* an encounter with a snake is attributed to making string figures in the summertime.[31]

The general rationale behind all these taboos is the belief that violation of them will bring down the wrath of the Man-animal behind each of these species. Thus, one ought not to kill too many animals of a single species lest one antagonize the Man-owner of them. The same reasoning lies behind the numerous taboos involved in hunting.[32]

(7) There are taboos associated with the danger of antagonizing ghosts. Many precautions must be taken when someone dies. "The hogan in which a person has died must be burned (or abandoned)." (* 158) The corpse must be buried with jewelry and other belongings, including sometimes a good horse. "If this is not done, he comes back for his belongings, they say." [33] Not to bury a person properly is *bahadzid.* (* 169) Moreover, taking the belongings of a dead man is extremely dangerous — only witches do that. Since there are so many detailed reports of mortuary prescriptions, it is not necessary to describe them more fully.[34]

The important role of belief in ghosts in Navaho ethical discourse should not be underestimated. Since no Navaho likes to talk about them, they are often concealed premises, which must be uncovered, if possible, by the investigator. Some prescriptions associated with ghosts are the following: "Never whistle at night" because "ghosts whistle at night"; "Do not comb your hair at night" because "Ghosts comb their hair at night"; and so on.[35]

(7a) There are apparently certain prescriptions against crying too much, either before or after a person dies. My interpreter, Bill Begay, said it is thought that if you cry too much for the deceased his ghost will come back and get you. I did not succeed in verifying this statement when I asked my principal informant, Bidaga, about it. Bidaga's statements were rather obscure — possibly because of his distaste for discussing ghosts.[36]

(8) There are taboos arising from danger of witchcraft, for the average Navaho is very much afraid of witches. Prescriptions regarding this danger may be divided into three groups: the avoidance of dangers of exposure to witchery; the danger of provoking a person who might be a witch; and the fear of being thought to be a witch. Since the last two types of prescription are essentially the same prescriptions as those applied to ordinary human beings, excepting that they have a higher sense of urgency, I shall defer the discussion of them to the section in this chapter on Social Prohibitions.

The prescriptions belonging to the group considered here are "burn or bury hair and finger-nail parings," [37] being careful about disposing of faeces, and defecating in private. "Hair, clothes, nail parings, faeces and saliva are taken by witches. They take these to a place where someone has been buried and then pray over them. Then they leave them there. The man to whom these belong will die as the witch prays. He may die easily or with great suffering." [38] Taboos of this group may be summed up thus: "Don't let a witch get something on you."

(9) There is another group of taboos that might be called "modesty" taboos, which I did not have time to investigate fully. (Modesty in defecating has already been mentioned.) They are rather generally observed among the less acculterated Navahos. Parents and other older relatives continually insist on little girls keeping their dresses down and so on.

Some of the reasons that have been offered for modesty are "A man who looks upon the sex organs of a woman will be struck by lightning," and "If anyone sees up your legs they will go blind." [39]

"When you have to urinate, you want to do it by yourself. You don't want your grandfather or your brother to see you. If you do this before people, you'll burn yourself, they say." [40]

(10) There are many taboos resulting from special states or activities, which need only be mentioned.

> (a) Pregnancy and birth taboos — for example, expectant parents should not see certain dead animals.[41] (* 96) Violations might affect the baby, and the parents as well, unless some cure is undertaken.
>
> (b) Technological taboos — connected with such activities as farming, herding, hunting, basket-making, weaving, pottery-making, and tanning. Most of these are justified not only in terms of their effect on the success of the undertaking, but also in their effect upon the health of the persons involved.[42]
>
> (c) Ceremonial taboos — these are prescriptions relating to a ceremony or Sing. The Singer must always be paid; (* 147) he is "not supposed to sing to too many persons a month." The consequences of violation are sickness for the Singer. (* 77) People who attend a ceremony are told not to leave the hogan at certain times. (* 82) To do so is *bahadzid*. (* 169) During the Sing, a patient is not supposed to "talk bad words to his wife, children, sheep," etc. and "he is not supposed to sleep with his wife." "That's bad. Not for me [that is, the Singer] but for them. They going to get sick. It hurts them — not me." (* 80) It's *bahadzid* for them.[43] (* 169)

c. The theoretical significance of taboos

I have dealt with various taboos extensively in order to call attention to the tremendous number and variety of prescriptions for conduct which are justified on the grounds that violation will bring on sickness caused either naturally or supernaturally. It should be noted that many prescriptions which concern the social interactions of human beings are included in this group. Indeed, there is an unmistakable tendency in Navaho moral discourse to justify the most stringent prescriptions of the system on the grounds that the acts in question are *bahadzid*. This is in marked contrast to our own moral discourse, which hardly ever justifies moral prescriptions by referring to physical dangers for the agent, although it includes some prescriptions which are similar in content to those described here; for example, no Westerner would justify modesty prohibitions or duties to animals in terms of dangers to the agent. Unless we clearly recognize these striking differences between our own approach and that of the Navahos to morality, we are likely to obtain a distorted picture of their code.

The appeal to the physically dangerous character of certain actions should not be dismissed lightly, for, as I have pointed out earlier, it is founded on beliefs which occur not only in Navaho ethical discourse, but also in their religious theory and practice. If we dismiss these justifications as 'mere talk,' we face the dilemma of having either to deny that the actual explicit statements of the informant should be taken seriously (including his statements about curing), or of having to admit that such prohibitions as those involving incest and modesty are of no ethical significance. It has been my thesis throughout this book, that an ethical system is part of a person's ideology, and it follows from this that his ethical convictions will be closely related to his other ideological beliefs.

If the justifications quoted above are to be taken at their face value, it would seem that we have a new motive for abandoning the concept of morality professed by many who maintain that morality is essentially social. For, although many of these prohibitions are social in content, ideologically they are stated in terms of their consequences to the individual agent. Hence, if the social definition of morality is accepted, one would have to ignore these justifications.

There are a few insights into Navaho moral thinking to be gained from the study of their taboos. In the first place, we can see that the Navaho moralist tends to generalize in various ways that may seem foreign to us.

Thus, the consequences of violation of a taboo are referred to in rather general terms such as "sickness," and if a particular kind of sickness is not mentioned, we just hear that "It will make you sick." As I have already remarked, this may sound like an empty formula, but, for our purposes, it might be worth while to take the Navaho at his word and consider this general reference to sickness to be indicative of his attitude towards disease rather than of his attitude towards giving reasons.

We encountered the Navahos' tendency to generalize also in the formulation of prescriptions themselves. There is a general category of acts which are referred to by such terms as "bothering" or "looking at," and under which more specific acts can be subsumed with varying degrees of stringency. For instance, these general terms are employed in prescriptions which thereby forbid eating, sexual intercourse, touching, approaching, or speaking to and even seeing the object — but the dangers involved vary according to the closeness of contact with the object. Explicit prescriptive statements of informants may cite different specific acts included under these general pre-scripta. Such formulations are exemplified by the prescriptions involving mothers-in-law, incest, death hogans, lightning-struck objects, and animals. The extremes for these taboo statements are on the one hand, the highly stringent prohibition of sexual intercourse or eating, and on the other hand, the less stringent discounsel against seeing the object. (Contrast this with the very specific prohibitions of our own sexual code.)

Second, the arguments for the taboos illustrate the Navaho tendency to cite more than one reason for not doing something, or for the occurrence of something; in other words, they exemplify the principle of many reasons. "That's for two reasons you mustn't look at your mother-in-law." (* 117, 168) As we shall see later, Navaho moral discourse frequently 'piles on' reasons of various sorts to justify a prescription. Anyone tempted to deny the cogency of these reasons on the grounds that so many are offered should bear in mind that the same type of reasoning occurs in the diagnosis of sick-nesses.[44]

It is interesting to speculate on the question why it seems necessary to justify so many prescriptions by a plurality of reasons. In the present in-quiry, a sociological explanation, such as a theory that these are 'rationaliza-tions' for prescriptions serving some latent function, would be irrelevant. The kind of question to ask here concerns the manifest function of this 'piling on' of reasons: or, what does this kind of reasoning contribute to the ethical system as a whole? I suspect that the answer is to be found only in the categories of explanation alluded to earlier.

Third, the taboos contribute to an understanding of Navaho ethical dis-course by providing us with some clues about their theory of human be-havior, since the supernatural beings are conceived anthropomorphically and are thought to act, for the most part, like ordinary mortals. The extent to which the kinds of behavior attributed to these supernatural beings reflect those attributed to ordinary human beings will become clearer as we pro-gress, so I shall call attention here only to a few points of similarity. It is evident that supernaturals must be approached carefully, and that they are liable to cause trouble if one is not circumspect. The same is true of human beings. The underlying principle is: Be careful not to antagonize people! As with human beings, one of the chief ways to antagonize the supernaturals is to appropriate their belongings which, under the Navaho concept of property, includes sex and ceremonial knowledge. Moreover, the conception of property is not a moralistic one, in the sense that a person has an inherent right to his belongings, but seems rather to refer to the kind of things that "people get mad about." [45]

3. SOCIAL PROHIBITIONS: "THAT WILL PUT YOU INTO TROUBLE"

a. Social prohibitions in general

A second main division of negative prescriptions contains those prohibitions which are justified on the grounds that if you "do that you will get into trouble" with other people. (It should be noted that the Navaho interpreter uses the word "trouble" inclusively to stand for sickness as well as social friction. I am here restricting the meaning to social troubles.) I have called these prescriptions social prohibitions because they involve social relations of one sort or another. I do not mean to suggest that they are such because they are justified by the authority of society, or by social practice. I believe the essence of the Navaho concept of "trouble" is that one normally gets into trouble by doing something which will provoke retaliation on the part of the victim or his friends, or else public disapproval. There are distinct analogies between this kind of trouble and sickness. Both may be thought of as states of 'disharmony' or 'disorder,' and both require 'straightening out.' [46]

The frequency with which a Navaho informant cites "trouble" as the consequence of certain actions is well attested. A glance at the Field Notes in the Appendix will verify this. One quotation will suffice: "The main thing he used to talk was about his people not to get into trouble — not stealing things from neighbors . . . So he said all he was trying to do was to make people good neighbors." (* 10) The trouble generally referred to may extend all the way from being hurt or killed, to having people speak badly of one. Thus there are varying degrees of seriousness of trouble.

Prohibitions which rest on the avoidance of trouble also vary in stringency according to the chances of "getting away with it." "If he lets you go, then it will be fine," [47] and ". . . as long as they don't get caught, they're all right." (* 20) Statements to the effect that an act is "all right" if "you don't get caught" or "if you don't get into trouble" are to be found in all the reports of field work among the Navahos, and will appear frequently throughout my discussion of social prohibitions. If you are sure to be caught, and if the trouble will be serious personal injury, then the act may be said to be wrong because it's *bahadzid*. But whether it is *bahadzid* or not depends on the particular circumstances.

Two comments upon the general character of Navaho prescriptive statements of this division are necessary before proceeding. First, as is probably true of all moral teaching, the Navaho moralist in his talks to people does not stress the matters that are obvious. The trouble incurred by murder and adultery, for instance, are so immediately apparent that they need not be mentioned as often as other prohibited actions. His sermons are concerned only with the things that the listener is likely or tempted to do. Hence, we find no mention of these extreme actions in the teachings in *Son of Old Man Hat* or in the early interviews with my own informant. Usually, moral talks in ordinary life stress "not to lie, not to steal and not to tell stories about what he didn't see." [48] (* 3) However, when the situation arises, or when questioned by the anthropologist, Navahos appear to have no doubts as to why these more serious acts are wrong.

The second comment I wish to make is that the categories of actions which we employ in our own prohibitions (like the Ten Commandments) are probably not quite the same for the Navaho. In general, I think it is true to say that the various prohibitions mentioned below are not distinct from each other, but rather they tend to fall into a general group of "trouble-making" actions. Thus, instead of saying "Thou shalt not murder," "Thou shalt not commit adultery," and so on, the Navaho would tend to say: "Thou shalt not make trouble." Consequently, the separation of prohibitions into groups in this chapter is more or less an artificial device.

All prohibited actions listed in this section are said to be wrong because they make trouble; but they may make more trouble for other people than for the agent himself. Therefore, there appear to be two kinds of reasons for such acts being wrong: first, they bring trouble to the agent; and second, they bring trouble to others. Many of the arguments used give the appearance of being utilitarian in the sense that they seem to argue that an action is wrong because it promotes trouble for everyone. I believe they are utilitarian in this sense. Nevertheless, even when the immediate welfare of the agent is not affected by his trouble-producing acts, it usually will bring mild trouble to him in the form of social disapproval — "people won't like it." Hence, avoidance of public disapproval is always at least one reason for not committing these acts. Since this reason is cited so frequently, I shall omit it from my discussion of particular prescriptions except where it appears essential. The significance of 'public opinion' in the Navaho ethical system will be treated later under Social Interdictions.

In reports of actual statements of informants containing the social prohibitions which follow, four different kinds of statements occur. Since it is important to summarize the data as they appear in verbatim reports, it is worth while to call attention to these four ways of expressing these prescriptions.

(*a*) Quite frequently we encounter a simple statement of the prescription: for example, "Don't lie."

(*b*) At times, the statement will say: "Don't do so and so, because it will get you into trouble." In other words, it cites the trouble anticipated for the agent.

(*c*) At other times, the moralist refers to the general trouble that an action will make: "Don't do so and so, because it will make trouble." Such statements appear prima facie at least, to adduce the consequences for the group rather than for the individual agent in justifying the prescription. (* 10, 16)

(*d*) Finally, there are statements that one ought not to do so and so, because 'people' or some particular person "won't like it." Thus, we hear: "Don't lie" because "your father and mother won't like it," (* 47) or because "your father-in-law and mother-in-law won't like it," (* 115) as well as those statements referring to "people" in general. (* 47) One rather common version takes the form: "I don't want to hear people say that you're doing so and so." (* 58)

If any single one of these four formulations is regarded as primary, it might be taken as prima facie evidence of the acceptance by the Navahos of any one of four different types of ethical system: (*a*) statements which could be taken to indicate a formalistic ethics; (*b*) statements which would be evidence for prudentialism (egoism); (*c*) statements which appear to be utilitarian; and (*d*) statements which seem to imply an approbationist ethical system.[49]

I shall not attempt to prejudice the issue while I am reporting the data. However, it is relevant to point out that we can find all four of these formulations for each of the following social prohibitions, and this fact might be taken as evidence that they are regarded by the Navaho as essentially equivalent. Also, one should not forget the principle of general effects mentioned earlier, according to which every wrong action affects everyone in the community; in other words, what has evil consequences for one is thought to have evil consequences for everyone.

b. Specific social prohibitions[50]

(1) "Don't drink," because "that's just for put himself in trouble." (* 40) This is a general prohibition which perhaps should come under the group of personal prohibitions to be given later. However, there is no doubt that excessive drinking does get the average Navaho into trouble, because when drunk he is likely to violate the other prohibitions of the code. Incidentally, this prohibition is found only in accounts of Navaho moral prob-

lems which arise after the advent of the whites. It appears to be absent in reports of Navaho moral discourses prior to that time, for example, in *Son of Old Man Hat*. Nevertheless, it seems to be uppermost in the mind of my principal informant, because it was a theme to which he continually re-turned.[51]

(2) "Don't kill anyone." (* 73, 76, 108, 109) "Killing is bad — something might happen. He might have some other help which the people don't know." (* 73) There is frequent reference in justification that the family and friends of the victim might take vengeance. "You's going to get into trouble." (* 91)

My field notes suggest, however, that this prohibition does not rest solely on the expectation of retaliation, but upon something that seems to be even more stringent and absolute. I suspect that part of this horror of killing human beings is due to concealed beliefs about the person's ghost. "Yes, the ghost will come back on these people who kill." (* 109) Because of my informant's reluctance to talk about ghosts, it was impossible for me to pursue the subject any further. Possibly my conjecture about the relevance of ghosts receives some confirmation from the supposed need of exorcizing the ghosts of people who have been killed; for example, it was thought desirable to hold Enemy Way chants over Navaho veterans returning from the war to protect them from the ghosts of dead Germans.[52] Nevertheless, the precise rationale behind the prohibition against homicide is not entirely clear.[53]

One exception to the prohibition of murder exists where witches are involved — because this is the only sure way of getting rid of them. Furthermore, killing in revenge is not entirely wrong, for if a person kills your children, then "I think it all right to kill that man." (* 75)

(3) "Don't fight," "Don't beat up anyone," and "Don't quarrel." (* 4) It is bad to have beaten up others because "If they had, if they'd beaten her, they'd have started trouble, and we'd have trouble now."[54] If a person 'whips' one man, then one can expect this man to collect his friends and 'whip' him back. (* 38) However, the whipping of one's wife, a frequent occurrence, is not as serious as whipping another man — it is only wrong, not *bahadzid.* (* 172)

Under this prohibition against quarreling, we should include 'cussing others' and calling them names. My informants agreed that it was dangerous to call someone an evil man, *hastiin doo ya'at'eeh da,* to his face: "But I won't say in front of man, he might get me." (* 173) [55]

The seriousness of the resulting trouble appears to determine the degree of stringency of this prohibition. In general, it receives the same kind of justification as that against homicide, and in everyday life, a sober Navaho usually avoids becoming involved in a quarrel.

(4) "Don't bother other men's wives." Adultery is frequently held to be *bahadzid*, because the "Man might shoot you." (* 171) It is commonly supposed that the husband will want to kill both his wife and the man involved.[56] "So it's bad for you. Soon you'll be in trouble." [57]

Adultery is all right, however, if you don't get caught. "Those kind of fellows — as long as they don't get caught — they're all right." (* 20) The trouble comes if they are caught. The reasoning is based on the almost stereotyped expectation of anger on the part of the wronged spouse. When the wronged person does not retaliate, everyone is surprised and pleased.[58] Of course, he is not supposed to avenge himself because of the prohibitions against homicide and injury, but it is thought that he would take drastic action.

Usually, the outraged husband is advised to accept the situation stoically, because "We're all doing just the same to one another . . . I know everyone of you has been around with another man's wife. Nothing can be done about it. It's always that way, with no end to it. And so I think there's no use talking about it." [59]

Sometimes the disapproval of people in general is cited against adultery. Such disapproval can be explained by the fact that a person who is a successful adulterer might be successful with one's own wife, or that a wife who commits adultery might seduce one's own husband. Or, at least, people will always suspect the worst.[60] There is likely to be plenty of gossip about these matters.

Nevertheless, the situation is complicated by the rather flexible marriage arrangements among the Navahos. Adultery may be the prelude to a new marriage, since there is almost complete freedom, theoretical at least, to separate and marry as one pleases.[61]

It is evident that the prohibition of adultery is binding only under certain circumstances. In general, it is considered wrong because it bodes trouble not only to the participants but to others as well. As I have indicated earlier, adultery is thought of as a kind of 'stealing.' [62]

(5) "Don't steal." (* 4, 10, 138) The main reason given for obeying this prohibition is that you might get caught, and so get into trouble. Stealing is *bahadzid* only because you might be put in jail. (* 171) "No chance of getting away with it nowadays." (* 7) Otherwise, the argument against stealing is that one would be shamed if one were caught.[63] In the old days, "no dishonor was attached to a thief as long as he was not actually caught. The dishonor consisted in getting caught red-handed." [64] If a thief "didn't get caught, he just keeps it." (* 7)

In general, stealing is disapproved because it causes trouble (* 16), and makes people mad. (* 10, 72–3) One tells a child that people won't like it. "Father and mother won't like it." (* 47)

(6) "Don't lie." (* 4, 46, 138, 160) Veracity is not prized for its own sake, but rather for the trouble that lying may cause. Therefore, small lies don't matter. It may be significant that in *Son of Old Man Hat* (pp. 15–16), the child is not scolded after the parents have discovered that he has told a deliberate lie. When I proposed to my informant the problematic situation made famous by Kant's denial of the "supposed right to tell a lie from altruistic motives," there was no question in his mind that he should tell an untruth.[65] (* 91)

The device commonly used to evade answering questions or to refuse requests is to say: "I don't know" or "I don't have it." Such little lies may be the Navaho equivalent of a "white lie," except that the motive is somewhat different.

The seriousness of lying depends upon the situation in which it occurs. One kind of lie that does have serious consequences is slanderous gossip. This is *bahadzid*. The victim "might get mad because that fellow's making up stories about him." (* 172, 135–6) Malicious gossip just makes trouble among the people. (* 136) The report is bound to get back to the man talked about. (This also is related to witchcraft — see below.)

The Navahos regard breaking a promise as a kind of lying. If you promise a person something it is as good as having given it to him — according to one dialogue in *Son of Old Man Hat* (pp. 214–215). To fail to repay a loan is a kind of lying. (* 88) The repayment of loans and keeping promises of gifts involve the same considerations as stealing. To someone who fails to repay a loan, one can say: "If you don't pay back, you don't get any more money." (* 89) It should be noted that my aged informant did not like to lend money because he was unable to go around and collect it. Instead he made outright gifts. By implication he all but said that it was foolish to lend money, especially to those who were known to be untrustworthy and if you cannot bring pressure on the debtor. The main argument for repaying is so that you can get another loan.

Another reason given for not lying is that "If you telling lie . . . we're not going to help you . . . If you want to keep yourself like the way you are now, we won't be with you." (* 160) In other words, people like and are willing to help an honest man, but they will not if he is dishonest.

Perhaps the most significant argument against lying is the same as the general one against stealing, namely, that if you are caught you will feel ashamed before people. In the case of breaking a promise, the circumstances are normally such that you will inevitably be caught. Hence, there seems to be a sort of sense of honor about keeping promises except that it involves what people will say and is not internalized. This is illustrated by the dilemma of a medicine man who has to break his promise to come and sing:

"Lot of people will say that I was a big liar . . . [But others] they pretty near all know that's not lying the people." [66] (* 144)

This worry about what people will say is also well exemplified by Slim Jim's statement in *Son of Old Man Hat:* "And I'm so ashamed of myself for the people with whom I made a promise. We promised to have a wedding, and you both have spoiled the whole thing. That's what makes me so ashamed. I don't know *what the people will say* to me about it." [67]

Another rather extraordinary account of this notion of shame is given by Matthews:

> Why should I lie to you? I am ashamed before the earth; I am ashamed before the heavens; I am ashamed before the blue sky; I am ashamed before the darkness; I am ashamed before the sun; I am ashamed before that standing within me which speaks with me. Some of these things are always looking at me. I am never out of sight. Therefore I must tell the truth. That is why I always tell the truth. I hold my word tight to my breast.[68]

It should be remembered that Matthews' informant was a highly sophisticated Singer, and as such was acquainted with and probably accepted esoteric beliefs concerning the anthropomorphic character of these natural phenomena. I believe that we must take his words literally, not metaphorically — the supernatural people in the universe are looking on and will talk about him. I do not believe that the Navaho layman would ever utter such a speech, but it does show in an extreme form the anticipation of public disfavor which makes truth-telling binding.

Prescriptions which are based upon what people will say have been labeled "social interdictions" and I shall postpone further comments on these until later.

(7) "Don't run around and sleep with different women (or men)." This is the prohibition against indiscriminate promiscuity. Navaho marriages are often informal, both in the way they begin and the way they end.[69] The main thing is that one settle down with one woman or man. Hence this prohibition is directed at "running around" or "getting different men and changing around." (* 58)

There are several arguments offered against sexual promiscuity. First there is a danger of veneral disease; therefore it is *bahadzid.* (* 120, 169) Second, it was customary in the old days to pay the mother something for sleeping with her daughter; (* 119) and the family would usually put pressure on the boy to marry the girl. Nowadays, one may get into trouble with the authorities and even have to go to prison. So again it's *bahadzid.* (* 171)

Besides these, the main reason for avoiding promiscuity is that one will get a bad reputation. People will say that you're a bad woman or man. "I don't like to hear you're still bad woman yet." (* 58) In the old days there appears to have been some apprehension of being ashamed about people knowing of one's sexual escapades.[70] Nevertheless, there is no odium attached to having fatherless babies — a frequent occurrence even today. (* 124) Since Navaho society is matrilineal, the baby will always have a family, and children are considered a welcome addition to any family.[71]

Talks about 'quitting running around' are generally coupled with positive arguments about the desirability of settling down and having a regular husband (or wife), (* 58) so that you can have a "good home" and do "good work."

To sum up: there are many people who consider promiscuity *bahadzid;* but there are others who just consider it wrong. (* 171) If it is not *bahadzid,* it is wrong because people will talk about it unfavorably, and because the right thing to do is to settle down.[72]

(8) There are many social prohibitions connected with *witchcraft,* which stem from the necessity (*a*) of avoiding suspicion of being a witch, and (*b*) of not antagonizing witches.

(*a*) Since the customary treatment accorded witches is to kill them, one's life is in danger if one is thought to be a witch. The chief way to incur suspicion of being a witch is to violate the taboos listed earlier. Even if one has his doubts about the truth of the beliefs on which the taboos are founded, it is usually a good idea to observe them. Moreover, there are special kinds of actions ascribed to witches which one ought not to do: "no one must step over another person at any time . . . This would bewitch the person stepped over." [73]

Another prohibition probably associated in the same way with witchcraft is that of not addressing a person by his name. The Navahos usually have several names, of which the secret or ceremonial names are 'powerful' and should not be used unadvisedly. " 'What does he want to do with it . . . that he inquires about our baby's name?' So at once they would become suspicious." [74] The use of a person's name in his presence is thought to be done "with intent either to dishonor or insult," and generally it is "very impolite to use someone's name in his presence." [75] Perhaps the connection with witchcraft is not always consciously realized, so that this prescription tends to become a social interdiction. (See below.)

The sudden acquisition of wealth may also arouse suspicions — witches rob graves. "He's a witch. That's why he has lots of sheep, horses and cattle, and beads of all kinds, and all kinds of skins." [76] Not only may a rich man be suspected of being a witch, but he is also considered the favorite object of witches' attacks. Therefore, there are two good reasons for not becoming overrich: "You'll die for no sickness — that richness going to kill you. So better not to — not too rich. Not too much." [77] (* 112)

(*b*) Except that they are more stringent, the same social prohibitions and injunctions applying to others hold for conduct towards people who may be witches. Thus, one must be particularly respectful towards older people "because otherwise the old would witch them." [78] Singers and rich people must be especially carefully treated.[79] Becoming a leader is undesirable, because in fulfilling this role one inevitably must antagonize people, and some of these may be witches, so "they kind of afraid of being leader." (* 139)

4. SOCIAL INTERDICTIONS: "PEOPLE WILL TALK ABOUT YOU AND LAUGH AT YOU"

a. Social interdictions in general

A social interdiction is a negative prescription which is justified by adducing what "people will say" of the actions concerned. I have already pointed out the frequency with which arguments for social prohibitions assert that "people won't like that" or "people will say you are a bad person," or that if you are caught you will be "ashamed" before people.[80] Since this is often the only plausible basis for the prohibition, it suggests that we may distinguish prohibitions so grounded from those which cite some particular trouble for the miscreant as their basis. As examples, we may take any of the prohibitions listed above provided that they do not rest upon the anticipation of immediate trouble for the agent.[81]

Four comments on interdictions in general may clarify this notion. First, it should be noted that the people who are mentioned in these statements are not some fictitious person or group; they are the people whom one knows and must associate with daily. Instead of using the general term "people," the speaker might as easily have listed the names of all the people who would talk. Sometimes this is done, for example, when it is said that "Father and mother won't like that," etc. I suggest that whether or not specific people are mentioned, the reason is of fundamentally the same type.

In the second place, it is important to recognize that the reaction is not disapproval in the sense in which it is sometimes used, namely, to refer to a moral judgment. The wrongdoer is not judged, nor are his actions judged. The reaction is a more immediate psychological reaction or attitude; that is, people just won't like it! Moreover, it is usually easy to explain why people won't like the action, for it will bring trouble to them, or is likely to do so. Therefore, even though breaking a promise, for instance, will not have any immediate evil consequences for the promiser, it does for the promisees — and so they won't like it. Similarly, a woman who wanders around from man to man may not herself be immediately injured thereby, but she upsets normal family relations — and so people won't like it.

These explanations, which may usually be found in actual statements of Navaho informants, reflect the general underlying explanatory principle of general effects introduced earlier. Anything that upsets the harmony of social life will be disliked by people, and so they may be expected to talk about it unfavorably.

There are, however, some social interdictions which are not so easily explained. For instance, there is no reason to believe that the unsophisticated Navaho is able to relate the ridicule that he expects from wearing raggy clothes to any trouble-making. He only knows that he can expect people to talk unfavorably about it. Thus, there are undoubtedly some interdictions which can be related to the welfare of the people who are doing the talking only by a sophisticated moralist, and perhaps even he cannot always do this. This suggests an analogy with taboos, for there we saw that the layman expects some sickness or other from violating the taboo, but he is not always able to explain it etiologically. Similarly, with social interdictions, the layman can expect ridicule but may not be able to connect it with other etiological factors relating to general welfare.

Third, the reasoning involved in social interdictions does not imply a utilitarian ideal of trying for its own sake to make other people happy, nor an ideal of social conformity as an end in itself, but rather it is of personal interest to the agent that those around him like him and are friendly to him. The motive for pleasing others is to have them be kind to you. This is shown in some of the statements referred to earlier.[82] (* 160) In the type of society in which they live, getting on with others is absolutely essential for one's own well-being. Thus, being in disfavor is truly being in trouble, although it may be milder than some other kinds of trouble. Similarly, if you are being laughed at, people will not take your needs seriously.

Finally, we should note that social interdictions vary in intensity, just as disliking does. There are some actions which people merely do not like, some they positively dislike, and others which they dislike to the extent of being willing to do something about it. In addition, there is a category of actions which provoke ridicule — and so "People will laugh at you," or "make fun of you." But being laughed at may be serious or not. On the one hand, people may laugh and add: "If you want to do that again, we might just as well shoot you"; (* 103) on the other hand, laughter may be simple joshing. It is interesting that the joshing which is traditional between joking relatives often takes the form of accusing the other person of having violated some moral prescription; for example, the object of the joshing may be accused of illicit sexual relations or of laziness.[83] In any case, whether serious or in jest, the victim of the laughter may be 'embarrassed' or 'ashamed.'

Probably the only way to gauge the seriousness of the talk or laughter is in terms of the trouble that occasions and explains it, and the consequences to be expected. If the trouble is grave, one had better take the talk seriously.

b. Specific social interdictions

We need consider here only those prescriptive statements which refer specifically to 'what people will say' and which do not refer to other evil consequences for the agent. They fall into two groups. The first consists of prohibitions of actions for which there is a simple explanation of why people would disapprove — or, actions which the Navaho layman can see will obviously make trouble for somebody. These prohibitions include all those listed previously where the circumstances are such that the agent himself will not immediately get into trouble. Thus, lying, stealing, sexual promiscuity, as well as breaking taboos, are all thought to affect the interests of the community and so can be expected to provoke public disapproval. It is not necessary to discuss this group of interdictions any further.

The second group of interdictions is concerned with those actions which every Navaho knows will cause people to laugh at him, although he may not be able to explain how such actions will immediately affect the interests of those who laugh. In this group could be included any one of the taboos or social prohibitions which it is beyond the capacity of the agent to justify by relating it to sickness or serious trouble. It is quite possible that all the interdictions of this type are logically related to the more stringent prescriptions of the Navaho code, although they are generally not known to be so related.

(1) "One ought not to be seen unclothed, especially in such a way as to expose one's sex organs." There is such frequent reference in the literature on Navaho ways to the rather extreme requirements of modesty that I shall not go into detail.[84] I do not know to what extent this prescription is based in the average Navaho mind upon the anticipation of sickness, but it certainly causes embarrassment or shame when it is not observed.[85] The rationale behind this may be that it exposes the onlookers to danger.

(2) "One ought not to use a person's name in his presence." This again is a prohibition which has been mentioned earlier in its relation to witchcraft. It is possible that many Navahos are not aware of its connection, but accept the prescription because not to do so would cause them shame. In addition to this, there are many different ways in which the use of names may bring ridicule. In general there are three kinds of names, secret or war names, nicknames, and English (or Spanish) names. The use of secret names was formerly thought to be dangerous. Since nicknames may be 'funny' or 'insulting,' it may be advisable not to use them before the person to whom they refer.[86] In my own experience, at least one relatively unacculturated informant refused to tell me his Spanish name — a case of generalizing the prescription to cases not covered by the reasons given above. On the other

hand, the influence of white ways has tended to break down the observance of this restriction.[87]

(3) "Don't go to Sings dressed in raggy clothes." "Without good clothes you couldn't go anywhere where there were lots of people. Might get ashamed where they had good times." [88] This prescription reflects the general belief that a good man is well off, and a poor man is 'no good.' To appear in 'raggy clothes' would be a public admission that one has been lazy and has not properly cared for his sheep and other belongings.

(4) "Don't be stingy." "A rich man never helps his people with what he has. Nobody likes him." (* 114) This prescription is connected with prohibitions involving witchcraft on the one hand,[89] and on the other it refers to a positive moral counsel to help and be generous to others, which will be discussed later.

c. The relationship of social interdictions to other moral prescriptions

Social interdictions are so intimately bound up with other prescriptions, positive and negative, that it is not necessary to go into more detail. It is true to say, I believe, that every negative prescription can be considered a social interdiction, and that the nonperformance of any positive prescription may also be a social interdiction.

This suggests that public approval and disapproval are quite basic to the Navaho moral system. Whether this is correct or not will be investigated later. It is clear, however, that the content of social interdictions is usually derived from other prescriptions, like social prohibitions.

A social interdiction holds up the consequence of being 'shamed before others' if one is caught violating it. In this it resembles a 'rule of etiquette' in our own culture, since the main reason for not putting food into one's mouth with a knife in our society is that it would bring shame to us and our family. This presents us with a dilemma: are we to regard social interdictions merely as rules of etiquette? or are they rules of morality? That this issue has not been faced squarely is to be seen by the rather arbitrary way in which most of these prescriptions are reported in the literature on the Navahos — sometimes one prescription is referred to as a rule of etiquette and another prescription which has the same basis is classed as a moral rule. Perhaps the term "restriction" is the term which is least question-begging, although it does not explain what kind of a "restriction" it is.

XIV

The Data: Positive Prescriptions

I. RECTIFICATION: "STRAIGHTENING THINGS OUT"

a. Restoration and the theory of curing

An important and perhaps the most interesting part of Navaho moral discourse concerns the rectification of wrongs or evils, which the Navaho interpreter calls "straightening it out." These words are applied alike to sickness and troubles arising out of disputes. This fact suggests that there are analogies between sickness and disputes, and that the procedures for getting rid of them are analogous. Actually, if we examine the 'theory' of curing disease, we shall see that some of the main elements to be found in it, also appear in the 'theory' of settling disputes.

There are two basic principles underlying the curing ceremonies. First, a cure is conceived of as a restoration to normality. Thus, a Blessing Way Sing is held over a patient in order to "bring him back to where he was before. Get his mind and talking strong like he was before." (* 43) [1] (This explains why the expression "straightening out" is used.) Second, the method which is employed to effect this restoration is to determine the 'etiological factor' responsible for the sickness, or, the supernatural being causing it, and "the most efficacious remedy is to be sought in a demand upon the etiological factor himself to right the disturbed physical condition of a human." [2] For instance, if White Thunder is the cause of the sickness, his aid is sought in restoring the patient.

Similarly, the Navaho appears to regard the rectification of social troubles as a kind of restoration. The aim is "to try to get straightened up . . . so there won't be no hard feeling against one another," or to "make the other people feel better about him then." (* 92) Furthermore, it is generally assumed that the fault lies with one particular person, and he (or she) as the 'etiological factor' must be the one to restore good feeling by compensating for the injury and by assuring the victim that there will be no further attack.

Characteristically, these social disputes are settled by prolonged talks between the principals involved, the agent and the victim, and their respective families. Generally, two or three older ones "that leads a good life" are invited to help out. (* 12, 13) "Way back there, the Navaho people didn't have any kind of law. They used to just talking about it together, and the things straightened up by talking together — maybe three or four people talking together." (* 125)

It is thought that, in order to restore good feeling, the agent must make a 'payment' to the victim or his family. In addition, the injured party must be convinced that the agent will not make any more trouble in the future. Hence, one of the chief purposes of 'talking it over' is to persuade the agent to mend his ways by showing him that "he will only make trouble for himself" if he continues, and pointing out that he has much to gain by behaving himself. The arguments are essentially the same as those for the corresponding prohibitions given earlier. The miscreant is always given another chance to reform. (* 26, 160) Finally, he is *persuaded rather than forced* to make up. If he doesn't want to pay, "I don't know what would happen." (* 74) Since a man's family and relatives are more interested in keeping peace, they will 'put pressure' on him to 'fix it up.' Thus, the role of the older and wiser members of the family is paramount in these talks.

b. Specific accounts of "straightening out troubles"

The sicknesses that result from violation of taboos are cured by Singers in the various curing ceremonies. There is no need to discuss this kind of 'straightening out', since it is covered in the anthropological studies of Navaho ceremonial practice.

(1) *Murder*. "In the old days, if this man killed somebody, he was bad already — but they don't kill him right away. They've got to talk it over first. They have to fix it up so this man won't be killed," because his family might cause further trouble. The customary way to fix it up was to pay the family something.[3] (* 75)

(2) *Fights*. The main purpose is to avoid further bloodshed. This is done by 'talking it over' and 'not getting mad.' The chief talker, who is generally an older relative, points out that only more trouble can come from fighting (* 91): "You don't want to make more trouble for yourselves."[4] If there has been some injury, "They make this [guilty] man pay the medicine man for the man he shot." (* 74)

(3) *Injury*. A person who is responsible for an injury must pay something so there "won't be no hard feeling . . . The man can pay for his trouble." Even if the injured person does not need the money, the payment must be made to "straighten up on both sides."[5] (* 92)

(4) *Stealing*. The goods or their equivalent must be returned, and that

"Man can pay . . . [the victim] . . . just a little to make [him] feel good about it." (* 150)

(5) *Sexual intercourse with an unmarried girl.* If a boy has seduced a girl, and a marriage is not desired by either of the families, the boy or his family must pay the girl's mother. "They talk over that case and they'll say they'll pay for it, and tell the girl and boy not to do that any more." (* 119) Although it is generally supposed that the woman is not unwilling and is often herself the seducer, this payment has to be made on the boy's part. "That payment will make the father and mother feel good about it." (* 119) This prescription is probably only a special case of the practice of paying a woman for sleeping with her.[6]

The troubles which have been listed so far are interfamilial, and here the normal way to restore good feeling is by means of payment. When there is trouble within a family, this payment is sometimes impossible because there is no one to pay. If someone is killed by a member of the same clan, "There would be no one to pay and no one to punish."[7] In these cases, the main object is to conciliate the parties, and reform the wrongdoer.

(6) *Marital disputes and separation.* Because of the rather informal marriage arrangements already mentioned, a spouse who is treated badly or discontented is likely to get up and leave. Such informal separation is generally the occasion for the respective families and neighbors to get the couple together and talk it over, to straighten it up. There is a certain ambivalence among these interested parties about restoring the marriage: on the one hand, it is usually to their general interest to have the marriage continue; on the other, they do not want to 'force' things which will make even more trouble. It should be noted that these motives explain their concern, but *the general interest is never cited in the arguments presented to the man and woman involved.*

The main argument for continuing a marriage are "They were making a good living" (* 13), and that the woman "couldn't find no other man like this fellow they're trying to move off" (* 17), etc. In other words, the appeal is always to the personal interest of the couple involved.

Marital disputes appear generally to rise from two different causes. First, they may be the result of quarrelling, or of one mate speaking 'roughly' to the other, or of the husband 'whipping' his wife. In many cases, this occurs when the man is drunk, and he recognizes his foolishness when he sobers up.[8] (* 12–13) The argument consists of pointing out that this is "just a little thing that happens," and getting the guilty one to promise to reform. "Anything like that can be talked over and settled down." (* 13, 19)

A second and more serious cause of marital trouble is the infidelity of one of the spouses. This can sometimes be patched up, if there is evidence that the guilty one intends to reform.[9] (* 18, 19) In talking to an unfaithful wife, it is pointed out that she has a 'good,' prosperous husband, the implication being that it is to her advantage to stop going around with other men. "Some of them do get better and they live right [after these talks]. Others they just separate from each other." [10] (* 21)

Adultery is also 'straightened out' characteristically by the making of payments. "If a woman catches her husband having intercourse with a woman, both the woman and the husband are expected to pay the wife. However, if the husband apprehends his wife, only the guilty man is required to pay the husband. If payment is to be obtained, the council is informed and the payment is made before the entire assembly." [11]

2. PERSONAL PRESCRIPTIONS: "CARE FOR YOURSELF"

By "personal prescription," I mean a prescription which is concerned with what will be to the personal advantage or disadvantage of the agent himself without reference to the welfare of others. The immediate objects of such prescriptions are those actions which will affect the health or possessions of the agent. They may be summed up in the injunction, "Take care of yourself and of your possessions." [12]

Although the prohibitions included in this section might more properly belong under negative prescriptions, it will be evident, I think, that they are closely related to the positive injunctions to be examined here. As I shall try to show later, every prescription in the Navaho moral code is personal, in that it receives its ultimate justification by reference to the welfare of the agent. However, in order to present the data without prejudice for or against my hypothesis, we must regard these prescriptions provisionally as merely another group instead of the basic type from which the others are derived.

a. Specific personal prohibitions

(1) "Don't drink." At the top of the list we should repeat the prohibition against getting drunk, since being drunk affects the agent's welfare in every spere of activity — his social relations and his life and health. If drunk, one might wander off the road and freeze to death in the winter. (* 172, 19)

(2) "Don't gamble." The reason is "They start betting . . . they would lose and get nothing out of it." [13] (* 4) This prohibition is based on the moralist's teaching that if you gamble you will lose.

(3) "Don't be lazy." This is equivalent to the positive injunction, "work hard."

(4) All the taboos could also be included here since they refer to actions which affect the health or possessions of the agent.

b. Specific personal injunctions[14]

(1) "You must be lively all the time." [15] There are prescriptions to act
to keep the body in good physical 'trim.' These include running in the early
morning, and rolling in the snow in the winter. (* 2) It is explicitly stated
that the purpose of such activities is to make young men brave.

(2) "Take care of your possessions." There is great emphasis on
such prescriptions as "Work hard, don't be lazy," "Take care of the sheep,"
and other possessions, especially those which are productive of wealth. The
Navahos teach that if you work hard, you will have "lots of sheep and
horses," because each sheep or horse "has hundreds" of others within her.[16]
I have already mentioned the categorial basis for the Navaho economic
'theory' that there is a potential abundance of goods. From this 'theory' it
follows that there is no scarcity which cannot be overcome by intelligent individual effort. Moreover, since this economic 'theory' rejects the idea of
scarcity, no man is thought to be in competition with his fellow. Rather, it is
assumed that a neighbor's success will contribute to one's own welfare.[17]
Thus, the doctrine says that if you work hard and intelligently you will be
successful and wealthy; "It all depends on you." Conversely, if you are lazy
you will lose everything you have. In other words, hard work is not only
sufficient for becoming wealthy, but also is thought to be necessary.[18]

The argument for all these injunctions, therefore, is that the prescribed
actions are necessary in order to become rich. I shall defer an examination
of this materialistic goal until Chapter XVII, section 1. Although this list
of personal injunctions is short, the few prescriptions in it are of paramount
importance in the Navaho moral code, for a large part of their prescriptive
discourse is devoted either directly or indirectly to them. It should be
pointed out that many actions are prohibited because they are incompatible
with these basic injunctions. For instance, a young man is advised not to
go to too many Sings because this will interfere with his work. (* 118) A
similar argument is employed against separations of husband and wife.[19]

We need not discuss further the details of sheep herding and farming
which should also be included under these injunctions. (* 112)

3. SOCIAL INJUNCTIONS: "TAKE CARE OF OTHERS"

Under the term "social injunction" are included all the positive prescriptions demanding actions which will promote the welfare of other people.
They may be summed up by the injunction, "Take care of others and help
them wherever possible." As far as I know, there are no positive prescriptions
involving relations to others that cannot be included under this prescription
(except, of course, rectifications).

Before examining the specific prescriptions which come under this heading, I shall make two general comments. First, the Navaho ideal is that one ought always to help other people and be generous to them. The usual argument is that if you help others they will help you back. *In theory*, the prescription applies to anyone whomsoever — whether ·he is related to you or not. *In practice*, there are customary preferences in helping and in asking for help. The latter will be discussed later in this chapter under the heading, "Traditional Practices."

Tacitly, at least, there appear to be degrees of stringency among the obligations to help, and in accordance with the terminological distinctions made earlier, the more stringent prescriptions will be called "injunctions," the less stringent ones, "counsels." Injunctions of care and help have stronger reasons than do counsels and apply to people in special relationship to the agent.

Second, it should be pointed out that help, whether it be in the form of labor or gifts, is thought to be "free" in that it does not have to be paid for. Gifts or help are offered to create general good will, and ostensibly without the thought or expectation of reciprocation; and the reciprocation, when it does come, is not considered a return but a new act of good will.[20] Accordingly, there is no conception of a moral obligation to reciprocate, as is the case in our own moral system, which often conceives of gratitude as a kind of indebtedness. We might say: "Many thanks, I am most obliged." In contrast, it is my impression that the Navaho word for "thanks" (*'ax'he*) carries only the connotation of good will, and that when a Navaho says: "Thanks," he is likely to have in mind more things to come, rather than that he owes something in return.[21]

a. Specific social injunctions

(1) "You ought to take good care of your children." (* 126) The usual reason offered for this is that if you treat your children well, they will remember you in your old age and take good care of you then. (* 23, 67) Of course, in most cases natural affection makes such an admonishment unnecessary.[22]

(2) "Children should take care of their parents." Since their parents have taken good care of them, a child should "help his mother and father backward." (* 6, 23) If the children did not love their father, they could let him go. (* 25)

This type of argument which refers to the past help that someone has given to persuade others to help him "backward" occurs several times.[23] (*6, 23, 101) For instance, we find the following argument for helping an old man: "He used to be a good man when he was young and always helped people." (* 56) The reasoning appears prima facie to be incompatible with my hypothesis of prudentialism, and seems to assume some kind of reciprocal obligation. (Whether this is so or not will be discussed later in Chapter XVI, section 3(e).) At any rate, if the man had *not* helped when he was young, then you can "Let that man go." (* 57)

(3) In general, people ought to help the aged. It has been suggested that the obligation to treat old people well is peculiarly stringent because if they have reached an old age they may be assumed to have special powers, and may even be witches.[24] Since my principal informant, Bidaga, was himself very old, it is understandable that he did not mention this reason.

(4) "One ought to help a person who is in dire need." Although this prescription was never stated explicitly in this form by any of my informants, they did state that you ought to give food to a poor man who would otherwise die of starvation. (* 69, 71) I suspect that the reason for this is a concealed fear of being pursued by the dead man's ghost if he were refused. This case will also be considered later.

(5) There are other people whom it is particularly important to help — for rather obvious reasons: one's wife, and her family. (* 115)

(6) In general, "You ought to help anybody who needs it or requests it." A person who is too lazy to help, can be told that "Whenever he needs help they won't help him." (* 56) A good man helps poor people (* 164), and people like him (* 114), whereas a person who does not help is not liked.

Thus, the arguments tend to stress the advantages to be gained by helping others, either in help later on or in being favorably spoken of. Finally, to repeat a statement made earlier, one should help *anybody* — "no matter whether a man or woman is not related to you."[25] (* 115, 55)

b. Moral counsels

It will be recalled that a moral counsel is a positive moral prescription which "allows of exceptions"; it states that an action is 'fitting' or right, but not obligatory. This distinction between "right" and "obligatory" appears in my material, and might be described as the difference between a preferred and a mandatory ideal of behavior.

A little act of help seems to be good to do, but if a person does not do it, "There isn't anything that's going to happen to him." (* 65) But a man who "looks ahead" will always help a person. Similarly, helping someone 'back' for earlier favors is desirable, but if "he didn't help still it's all right . . . that won't hurt anything." (* 62)

If we take these clues seriously, we may distinguish a separate category of prescriptions which prescribe actions because they are 'good to do' but are still not 'bad not to do,' namely, in cases where the omission does not have very serious consequences. It will be recalled that one distinguishing mark of such counsels is that they may be ignored sometimes but not in every case.[26]

c. Explanation of the varying stringency of prescriptions

In the theoretical Part II of this study, I suggested that positive prescriptions offer considerably more latitude of choice than do negative ones. One reason for this is that negative prescriptions usually define and delimit those actions which are prohibited, whereas positive prescriptions, referring as they do to a wide sphere of possible actions, are much less determinate.[27] This analysis is confirmed by the data which has been presented in these two chapters, for if we compare the two lists of negative and positive prescriptions, we can see that the first group is detailed and comparatively precise, whereas the second group is vague, general, and allows great freedom of choice in performance.

The point may be illustrated thus: any particular act of help (for example, building a hogan) can be justified on the general ground that "people will help you back." However, the same prescription could call for many other different kinds of help — there are so many possible ways of helping people that a person would never have time to do his own business if he were always to fulfill this prescription. The line must be drawn somewhere — although it is generally not a very sharp line.

We have seen that the moral prescription itself says to help *anyone,* but because some selection is necessary, there are *patterns of selection,* or preference, which are adopted in actual practice. These patterns give precedence to helping one's relatives, and certain others under special circumstances. Thus any particular act of help fulfills the general moral injunction, but the selection itself is morally indifferent. Therefore, in addition to the prescriptions that have been examined, we must also recognize certain modal patterns of behavior which might be called "quasi-prescriptions" or "traditional practices."

4. TRADITIONAL PRACTICES: "THAT'S JUST THE WAY THEY DO THAT"

The prescriptions listed above all share two characteristics: first, they are all explicitly stated and recognized as binding by the Navaho moralist, and are to be found in his moral discourses; and second, they are generally given a justification in terms of the consequences of the action prescribed. Even if such a justification is not always explicitly included, we have seen that in the enormous majority of cases there is one.

Anthropological studies of the various aspects of Navaho culture have called attention to many rules or norms of behavior which do not fit into the above list. Thus, the various complicated patterns of 'clan obligation' do not appear among the moral prescriptions as I have given them.

Kluckhohn has shown the importance of distinguishing within the overt culture of a society the ideal pattern of conduct enjoined by the culture and the modalities of behavior which are nothing but "a stylized set of behaviors observed as one modal way of meeting a specified situation." [28]

The prescriptions given above are to be considered the ideal pattern of conduct. For our purposes, we may divide the modalities of behavior into two groups: (*a*) Modalities which are recognized by the Navahos to be styles of conduct, and referred to in conversation (I shall call these *traditional practices*); (*b*) Action patterns which are evident only to the outsider (among these we should include Navaho motor habits).[29] This last group need not be considered here.

There are certain practices which my informant referred to as "how they do things." "I don't know why they did that, but they used to do that." (* 61). Such practices are distinguished by the absence of any reason other than "that's the way it was done" offered in justification.

An important characteristic of traditional practices is that they usually give rise to expectations on the part of others, so there may be a hidden though not openly admitted motive for conforming to them, namely, not to disappoint others (and so incur disapproval). These practices therefore are much more likely to be observed than the more abstract rules of morality, since they have a kind of 'social sanction' behind them; and I think that the average Navaho does respect them more than he does the prescriptions of morality.

Traditional practices must be divided into three kinds: they may be styles of behavior which indicate the expected ways of carrying out moral prescriptions; they may be morally indifferent; or they may even conflict with morally prescribed conduct. Perhaps these practices have the same relation to moral principles as do the rules of etiquette in our own society; many of them are stylized modes of fulfilling our moral obligations to our neighbors, some of them are morally indifferent, and perhaps others are incompatible with our accepted moral principles. If one asks: Why should I do it in that particular way? the only answer is: That is the way it is done. Furthermore, our rules of etiquette create expectations, and are probably observed more diligently than are our accepted moral principles. There are, of course, great differences between our own code of etiquette and Navaho practices; the former is much more formalized than the latter. Perhaps a better illustration of a quasi-prescription, or practice, in our own society would be the kind of rules for 'dating' adopted by our young people. In any case, it is such social practices which serve, as it were, as the grease which keeps the social machine operating smoothly.

Because my knowledge of this aspect of Navaho culture is imperfect,

I can give only a tentative and impressionistic account of these traditional practices, the main purpose of which is to bring out by contrast the difference between them and genuine moral prescriptions. I shall begin with those traditional practices which are selective applications of social injunctions and counsels.

(1) There are many styles of present-giving. In the old days, a guest was given presents upon leaving.[30] (* 60) At the Sings, various people are expected to give gifts at certain times.[31]

(2) Relatives are expected to help whenever the occasion arises. For instance, they are responsible for helping with Sings, and they generally give their kin a piece of land with corn on it, etc.[32] However, these practices are not couched in prescriptive terms. Clan 'obligations,' therefore, probably should be considered traditional practices rather than moral prescriptions.

(3) Procedures for dividing up the property of a deceased relative probably also belong to this group.[33] (* 50–53)   .

(4) It is most likely that the various arrangements about marriages should also be counted as traditional practices rather than as prescriptions. (* 127–128)

All these four groups of traditional practices, and probably many more, are patterned *applications* of moral principles which we have already encountered; for example, applications of the injunctions to help, to talk it over, or not to cause trouble. As such they might be compared to our rules of driving on the right hand side of the road; some rule is required, but whether it be one rather than another is indifferent, and once the rule has been selected, we should abide by it because the actions of others are based upon the expectation that we will follow it. I do not intend to suggest that the Navaho moralist reasons exactly in this fashion, but I do think that he may cite the same grounds as are given for the general prescriptions in order to persuade others to conform to them. Thus, we tell a person to drive on the right side in order to avoid an accident; similarly, a Navaho might urge a man to help his cousins so that he will be helped back. The specification is conventional, the general principle is not.

There are many nonmoral practices which are not derived in this loose sense from moral prescriptions. I suspect that the complicated rules for addressing and behaving towards various classes of relatives may belong to this group; for example, the rules about joking with relatives.[34]

Finally, there are some traditional practices which appear at times to conflict directly with various prohibitions mentioned earlier. For instance, the "carrying out of adulterous acts is most distinctly patterned in ways of which Navaho are rather explicitly aware."[35]

5. GENERAL REMARKS ON THE DATA

a. Prescriptions and actual behavior

Before concluding this chapter, it is necessary to point out the rather obvious fact that among the Navahos actual behavior diverges quite considerably from the ideal of the prescriptions presented. This should not be surprising, since there may never have been a time or society where people did what they were supposed to do. I believe that it would not be too difficult to give an example of an actual violation of every single prohibition listed. In *Son of Old Man Hat* and a *Navaho Autobiography* (Dyk, 1947) numerous instances may be found (although we should be careful not to exaggerate the importance of various sexual exploits, since prohibitions involving these are of less stringency than other kinds). The process of acculturation has probably increased the extent of violation of these prohibitions. There have been several significant studies of this process. I have only a few suggestions to make.

In the first place, the neglect by a Navaho of these moral prescriptions may take place under two different conditions: first, when the agent accepts the prescriptions but succumbs to temptations to violate them; and second, when the agent no longer accepts them. The nonacceptance of a specific prescription may be explained at least in part by the implausibility of the arguments for it. Thus, the argument for the mother-in-law taboo, which predicts blindness for the violator, is probably seriously doubted by those who have been told by whites that it will not happen. Similarly, a good many other taboos will be rejected because of a rejection of the beliefs upon which they are founded.

It is interesting to note, however, that as a matter of fact some of the taboos seem to be held to more persistently than other prescriptions. The social prohibitions, especially those whose basis is mostly that of a social interdiction, seem to be the ones most frequently ignored. This suggests that the changing conditions of life brought about by the influx of white ways may make the individual much less dependent upon people living around him — and after all, the essential ground of the plausibility of social interdictions is the belief that everyone is dependent upon his neighbors for help of all kinds.

On the other hand, perhaps the appeal to "what people will say" may be a rather flimsy basis on which to build up an ethics. The plausibility of this kind of argument obviously varies with the living conditions of the listener. Furthermore, such arguments will be persuasive only as long as people's talk has not changed — it is certain that if people tend to gossip about everybody then the miscreant will not be the exception held up as an example, but instead he would be following the normal pattern of behavior.

There are several questions for investigation which suggested themselves in this connection. It would be interesting, for instance, to find out which prescriptions are violated most frequently, and to what extent these areas of deviance correlate with degrees of acculturation. (I shall explore these questions in more detail in Chapter XVIII, section 2(a).)

My aged informant ascribed the 'breakdown' of Navaho morality to excessive drinking on the part of the young. There is no doubt that drinking presents a twofold problem for the Navaho moralist: first, the type of argument advanced in his moral discourse will have no appeal to a person even slightly inebriated — after a few drinks you don't care what people will think; second, a person who has been drinking is considered to "have lost his mind" and according to the Navaho 'theory,' he cannot even be expected to know what is wrong. This contrasts with our own Western opinions, according to which we assume that a drunk knows what he ought to do but just does not have enough 'will-power' to make himself do it. Thus, the Navaho moral code has eliminated itself on the basis of its own presuppositions from having anything to say to people who are intoxicated! No wonder that my informant could think that the only possible cure was to call in the white authorities to handle this problem. (* 36–7)

b. Summary of ethical statements

All the prescriptions given above can be summarized, without eliminating any important ones, in the following two principles which are to be found in these two statements: "Take care of yourself and take care of others," [36] and, "Don't hurt yourself and don't hurt anybody." (* 165)

It is quite apparent that the Navaho moralist is prepared to give reasons for the various prescriptions he commends. Sometimes, of course, the reasons are not mentioned, but can be discovered either in other discourses on the same subject by the same informant, or in those given by other informants. Without attempting to beg the question about the type of ethical system to which these prescriptions belong, I shall add a list of the kinds of reasons which appear to me to exhaust those given in the preceding sections:

(a) Don't do that because it's *bahadzid* (dangerous).

(b) Don't do that because it will put you in trouble, *or* do do that because it will get you out of trouble ("straighten things out for you").

(c) Don't do that because no one will help you *or* do do that because then others will help you.

(d) Don't do that because people will not like it *or* do do that because people will like it.

c. *Two methodological problems*

I have already indicated that there are two methodological problems which arise directly from the data presented. First, there is the problem of whether the data are reliable, and whether the reasons given should be taken seriously. If the reasons are not to be taken seriously, then my whole hypothesis collapses. Hence, it will be necessary to discuss this question in more detail later.[37]

The second problem is to decide which of the prescriptions listed are moral and which are nonmoral. Any one of the groups given could be considered moral, and the others nonmoral. A Western moralist would be tempted to dismiss taboos as superstitions and to take the quasi-prescriptive traditional practices as the essence of morality. The expressions used by some anthropologists suggest this kind of presupposition about the moral. But if the traditional practices are considered moral prescriptions, we should have to admit not only clan 'obligations' but also the rules observed in committing adultery as part of the moral code; and within our own culture we should be required to include all of etiquette and the rules for 'dating' as moral prescriptions!

On the other hand, if we are to adhere to the conclusions of Parts I and II, it would seem that taboos are the most stringent and hence the most undoubtedly moral of all the prescriptions. For our purposes, the best procedure is to accept all the groups of prescriptions presented, but not the quasi-prescriptions. The different kinds of prescription may vary in degrees of stringency, but they all appear to have the properties presented earlier as criteria of a moral prescription; namely, superiority and legitimacy.[38]

XV

The Structure of the Reconstructed Code

I. OUTLINE OF PROCEDURE

Having reviewed the data upon which any hypothesis concerning Navaho ethics must be founded, we are now ready to examine specific reconstructive hypotheses. The procedure I shall follow was outlined in Chapter X, section 1, and the hypothesis I wish to defend was summarized in Chapter XI, section 4(c). The present chapter will discuss the structure of the code — its logic and rhetoric; the next chapter will discuss the content of the code — its basic prescription. It should be noted that the evidence for the logical and rhetorical principles of the reconstructed code must be extremely general, and that in the final analysis it is cumulative. From the nature of the hypothesis itself, it follows that my conclusions concerning the content of the code can be true only if my analysis of its rhetoric and logic is correct. Consequently, in establishing its content we are *eo ipso* proving contentions about its structure. The reverse — that the structure hypothesized implies that a certain basic prescription has been accepted — does not hold; it is entirely possible to have many other different kinds of ethical systems which have the same rhetoric and logic. For this reason, it seems advisable to begin with the more general aspects of the systems reconstructed, and then turn to its more specific characteristics.

The fundamental approach expounded in Parts I and II will be followed as rigorously as possible here. It will be recalled that an hypothesis in descriptive ethics is to be regarded as a theoretical scheme which is used to explain and predict the ethical statements of informants. In accordance with this methodology, the sole evidence admissible for the hypothesis will be the verbatim statements of the informant; all other evidence (such as actual behavior) will be considered irrelevant. Furthermore, all elements of the hypothesis must be subjected to tests of one sort or another. Ideally, such 'experimental' tests consist of deriving predicted statements from the hypothetical reconstruction and then observing whether or not they correspond to actual statements made by the informant. (Specific examples will be given in Chapter XVI.)

If this methodology is followed, the conclusiveness of the results obtained will depend upon the variety of possible hypotheses which were tested as well as upon the outcome of the tests themselves. In order to avoid the fallacy of selection, we should constantly keep in mind the importance of trying to falsify any proposed hypothesis. Consequently, we must pay particular attention to any negative evidence, and assiduously avoid allowing our intuitions to determine our conclusions.

2. TAKING THE INFORMANT'S REASONS SERIOUSLY

Many accounts of Navaho ethics, like other studies available in descriptive ethics, have failed to define with any precision the criterion of "ethics" they employ. I have argued at some length in Part I for the criterion which I am using. Later, I shall show that the use of other definitions will produce quite a different picture of Navaho ethics.[1]

The use of criteria of "ethics" other than the one employed here, as well as the preoccupation with other aspects of Navaho culture, has encouraged anthropologists to neglect the pattern of arguments which, in the informant's mind, justify the moral prescriptions in his code. It should be clear on the basis of the analysis I have presented that the 'rationale' behind these prescriptions is an essential part of the ethical system as a whole. Of course, if certain definitions of "ethics" are used, it would follow a priori that the informant's arguments are irrelevant. For example, if a person's ethics is taken to consist of those principles of behavior which promote social stability, it would follow that what the informant says in addition to admitting such principles would have nothing essential to do with his ethics. Similarly, if ethics is considered to be a certain pattern of affective attitudes, such as respect or love, it would follow that his actual arguments should be disregarded.

Since these a priori arguments have already been considered I shall examine here only more specific arguments for not taking seriously the reasons given by Navaho informants. There are two such arguments.

The first is based on the fact that the reasons given appear stereotyped, and that quite frequently there are several reasons presented. Since rejecting the arguments of the Navaho informants on this count has already been discussed, I shall merely reiterate what I have said before; namely, that the kind of reasoning which occurs in their ethical discourse is exactly like that which occurs in other parts of the Navaho ideology.[2] The arguments merely exemplify the principles of general effects and of many reasons.[3] It seems to me that the only reason for rejecting the arguments offered is that they do not appear *to us* to be genuine, because our own etiological thinking is different. Moreover, if we deny that the factual premises introduced into ethical arguments reflect genuinely held beliefs, then we would be unable to explain why there are curing ceremonies designed to cure the sicknesses resulting from the violation of taboos. For example, if we were to discount the argument that incest is wrong because "it will drive you crazy," then how are we to account for the existence of the Moth Way chant for curing incest sickness?

Second, it might be held that the reasons offered by the informant are not grounds of the rightness or wrongness of prescribed acts, but rather are merely persuasive devices to secure conformity to the rules of morality. In other words, they might only be 'reinforcing' reasons which are offered as incentives to either act or forbear, instead of themselves being the reasons for the act's being right or wrong. This distinction is recognized in our own moral discourse. Thus, we might attempt to dissuade someone from committing murder by pointing out that murderers are given capital punishment; the fact that we offer this as an incentive cannot be taken to prove that we think that murder is wrong only because of the punishment. How are we to determine, therefore, whether a reason given for an action is just a reinforcing reason or incentive, or whether it is regarded as the actual ground of the act's rightness or wrongness?

In the example just mentioned, there are three conditions which we should accept as evidence that the threat of punishment is not the real moral reason in the informant's mind for not murdering someone. First, if the act were thought to be wrong even though no such punishment were anticipated. Second, if there are acts which would be considered right even though they are punished. (For example, if it were right to resist a tyrant's unjust commands at the risk of being punished.) Third, if there are other reasons given for not committing murder in addition to the threat of punishment. We could proceed likewise to test the genuine moral quality of any of the reasons given by Navaho informants.

Theoretically, it would be desirable to check each reason given by investigating these possibilities. However, there are practical difficulties in the way when interviewing an informant who is unfamiliar with our Western ways of abstracting. For instance, while investigating whether an act is wrong even though it had no particular consequence, I found that it was usually futile to get the informant to imagine a situation which had what would seem to him unnatural consequences. Thus, I could not obtain more than an artificial answer if I were to ask whether a tabooed act would still be wrong even if the doer did not become sick. The answer was usually, "But one would get sick." [4] There are, however, some situations for which it is perfectly easy for an informant to conceive of 'getting away' with it; for instance, adultery is such an act, and here the anticipated consequence seems a necessary condition of its being thought wrong.

The second method, which proceeds by inquiring whether there are actions which are all right given evil consequences, was employed. Examples of this will be given later.

The heart of the problem of whether the reasons given are merely reinforcing reasons seems to me to depend at least in part on *whether there are any other reasons* given. I have attempted to inquire into this possibility throughout my investigation.

To dismiss every reason offered as merely a reinforcing reason seems to me to be a way of begging the question in favor of a formalistic interpretation of the ethical system. Since, as I believe, the posing of situations which are difficult for the informant to imagine is an unsound procedure, the evidence for and against the formalistic character of the system must be sought in the actual prescriptions accepted. This means that we must ask whether there are prescriptions for which justifying arguments are not available. This question will be investigated in the next chapter.

Furthermore, it seems to me that if the informant's reasons are dismissed, no matter on what grounds, some plausible explanation of why he gives such reasons ought to be supplied. In the absence of such an explanation, it is absurd to deny that the reasons which he gives are genuine evidence for hypotheses concerning his moral code.

3. NONAUTHORITARIANISM

Following the procedure outlined earlier, we must first ask whether the ethical discourse being investigated can be interpreted as an authoritarian system. By this I mean a system which cites the commands of a moral authority as the reason for doing a prescribed act. (I have argued at some length that not every ethical system is authoritarian in this sense, as many have held.)[5]

The types of authoritarianism best known to us are those which identify the moral authority issuing the prescriptions (commands) either with a supernatural being or with society. Accordingly, they base their ethics on religious beliefs or on the traditions of the social group. I have called these two types of authoritarianism, "theistic" and "conventionalistic." [6]

As a result of the popularity of these two forms of authoritarianism, we find among some investigators a predisposition to look for the foundations of Navaho ethics either in their religious doctrines or in the various group relationships and group 'sanctions.' [7]

I have called attention previously to the distinction between the order of explanation and the order of justification.[8] A peculiarity of much Western thought is that it identifies the cause of something's coming into existence with the justification for it. This confusion is peculiarly tempting in sociological analyses where teleological explanations are employed. However, I should like to reiterate that it is important to separate our own explanation of the group behavior and prescriptions of the Navahos from the justifications which they themselves give for them. At present, I am interested solely in the latter.

It is quite conceivable that the Navaho mind is entirely unaware of the possibility of justification by appeal to origin. Although the Navahos are extremely interested in the origins of things, their accounts of these origins appear to be purely historical explanations which, as such, are not intended to justify any values or norms. This neutral attitude towards origins is illustrated by numerous mythical stories of the origin of evil, which presumably are intended only to explain how evil began. See (* 97, 99, 157).[9]

Nevertheless, Navaho discourse does make references both to what the Holy People said and to what the Navaho people "used to say in the old days way back," and so it is incumbent on us to investigate whether the Navaho code may be interpreted as a theistic or conventionalistic authoritarian system. If it *is* authoritarian then it will be difficult if not impossible to find a single basic prescription from which all the particular prescriptions can be derived. This difficulty is evident in the case of Judaism, where there is a multiplicity of 'laws,' which can only be reduced to one principle at the expense of formulating it in such vague language as to make it incapable of concrete application; for example, the law of loving God and one's neighbor.

As evidence of authoritarianism we must look for the following: (*a*) some notion of moral prescriptions which emanate as commands from a legitimate authority, and which are justified solely by their origination in that authority; (*b*) a belief that violation of these commands will have unpleasant consequences due to the fact of violation and imposed by the authority or his delegate; in other words, it must include a conception of "sanctions"; (*c*) obedience for its own sake must be demanded by the moral code itself, and the defiance of authority must be regarded as morally wrong.

a. The relation of the Holy People to morality

I have already called attention to the distinction made by the Navahos between esoteric and exoteric knowledge. Accordingly, my informant distinguished ceremonies and stories from the ways of living.[10] I assume that the latter includes ethics.

Ethical discourse must necessarily be exoteric insofar as it consists of commending moral prescriptions to the people. But even though moral teaching is exoteric, the justification for the prescriptions may rest either on exoteric or esoteric beliefs. If the reasons for the prescriptions are intrinsically esoteric, the system will be authoritarian in my sense of the term. The question before us is, therefore: Are the Navaho moral prescriptions justified by reference to esoteric beliefs about the divinities?

The passages in the Field Notes where I have investigated this question are not completely clear and unequivocal; some of the statements appear to contradict each other. Furthermore, the issues are too subtle to discuss adequately without a more complete knowledge of Navaho language and of the ceremonies and myths. However, I suggest that an explanation for the obscurity of the answers to my questions could be that the conception of "authority" as it is familiar to us was completely strange to them. For instance, my question as to whether the Holy People originated the prescriptions about right and wrong conduct was understood to be a question about the origin of good and evil (the actualities, not the prescriptions). (* 97–9)

The absence of any notion that the Holy People are thought of as moral authorities or moral legislators may best be shown by a summary of some of the statements about their presumed relations to human beings.

The Holy People "didn't teach the people anything except about the Sings . . . They just go where there's a Sing." (* 85) The 'theory' is that the Holy People originally developed the curing ceremonies (Sings) to cure themselves, and then gave them to the Earth Surface People with instructions on how to do them. This is well attested in all the published records of the various myths 'explaining' how the ceremonies were acquired.[11]

The implied justification appears to be that since these cures worked for the Holy People they will work for the Earth Surface People also. But one must be careful to follow all the instructions precisely. If the Sing is done wrongly, there will be evil consequences. (* 87) It is not clear that these consequences should be interpreted as punishments for disobeying the instructions of the Holy People. I suspect that they are either predictions made by the Holy People of what will happen if one does not abide by the prescriptions, (* 87) or else that since the Holy People are thought to attend and to help out in each performance of a Sing, the failure to abide by the 'rules' will result in doing something to antagonize them. (* 146)[12]

During the performance of a ceremony the prohibitions against adultery, quarrelling, and so on, are more stringent than at other times. This increased stringency certainly involves the participants' relationship to the Holy People — and this may conceivably be an authoritarian one. However, the social prohibitions binding in situations other than Sings appear to have no such basis. (* 97)

There are two other considerations which militate against an authoritarian interpretation of Navaho morality:

The Holy People, or divinities, are thought to have been the original causes of the existence of evils as well as of goods. Thus, the Holy Man who puts the 'wind' into a person's body when he is born, decides whether this 'wind-soul' is to be "good," "happy," "mean," or "bad." (* 161) The Holy People also decided to let the Monsters stay alive (that is, Sleep, Hunger, Old Age, Poverty, and Death). (* 99ff.) The first person to steal and commit incest was the divinity Coyote. (* 97, 157) And witchcraft originated with First Man and First Woman.[13]

Moreover, there appears to be no compunction against criticizing or even defying the Holy People, if one can get away with it. People criticize the Holy People for letting the Monsters live. (* 99) The pattern of all the myths is the story of the young hero who successfully defies the commands of the Holy People and "gets away with it," by making them cure him of all the evil effects of the punishments they have inflicted upon him for disobedience.[14] Contrast this with the attitude in the Old Testament towards Jahweh, whom no one could defy without in the end coming to his doom. In the one case, defiance appears possible (at least to one possessing superhuman powers) and ultimately beneficial for Earth Surface People, whereas in the more familiar instance defiance is sinful and impossible — even for the superhuman Satan. Nor is their attitude towards the divinities like that of the Greeks, for whom defiance may not be sinful but is inevitably unsuccessful (for example, Prometheus).

The main argument in support of the thesis that Navaho moral prescriptions are not based upon supernatural authority, is the complete absence of any arguments which could be construed as appeals to such an authority, with the exception of prescriptions pertaining to Sings. Hence, I think we can safely assume that the moral code is not based on the commands of the Holy People. This conclusion is confirmed by Father Berard Haile, who writes: "In the Navaho system, too, there is no supreme law giver or pantheon of lawgivers concerned with the morals of humans and supernaturals." [15]

b. The appeal to tradition

It has been frequently maintained that for 'primitive' people the principal justification for their moral principles is an appeal to tradition. "The 'right' way is the way which the ancestors used and which has been handed down. The tradition is its own warrant." [16] We should therefore inquire whether the moral code we are investigating is justified on the grounds that it is "the way the old people used to do it."

There is no doubt that my informant, Bidaga, had great respect for the 'old ways' and for what he had been taught by his parents. Thus, in describing his moral instructions he said that he had started "with the old ways of living . . . his grandfather had taught him." (* 6) And he often said: "My father said not to lie," etc., and "I know now that my father was right," and "I still believe in the old ways." (* 1, 94) Similarly, the teachings of the father in *Son of Old Man Hat* obviously made a great impression on his children. On the other hand, some of the other autobiographies hardly mention the father, and they contain no passages in which the father passes on his moral wisdom to his children. This fact suggests that the personality of the father may be a crucial factor in determining the occurrence of such reminiscences.[17]

Furthermore, one often has the impression of a nostalgic feeling for the 'old days' in the comments of my aged informant. "Seems like pretty nice among Navahos the way they used to live those days." (* 34) There seems to be some evidence that the Navaho doctrine is that the world is getting progressively worse, rather than better — with the Golden Age in the dim past (as with the Greeks). The advent of the white man, coupled with wars, droughts and drunkenness, provide good proof of this for an Indian. (* 87)

Nevertheless, the mere fact of agreement with the old people or approval of the 'old ways' cannot be taken as proof that these moral teachings derive their warrant from tradition, since it is perfectly possible to regard the 'old ways' as the best ways without having to assume that they are the best ways *because* they are the 'old ways.' If the arguments presented by Bidaga are examined carefully, it will be evident that the authority of tradition is never employed as a *ground* for a moral prescription. Although he regarded the ways of the old people as better and wiser, he usually provided reasons to show why they were better and wiser. The references to the old days may be made merely to show that the prescriptions worked well then, and hence may be inferred to work now also. If we grant the fundamentally pragmatic character of Navaho moral thinking, this would appear to be more of a pragmatic argument than an authoritarian one.

If moral precepts are not ultimately justified by appeal to tradition, it follows that when the old ways are no longer satisfactory, they should be abandoned. There is some evidence that this is Bidaga's view, since he felt no compunction in occasionally criticizing the old way of doing things. For example, he mentioned that the old ways are unable to cope with present-day conditions arising from the introduction of liquor (* 44), and he stated that the 'white ways' of handling illegitimate babies are superior to the old Navaho ways. (* 125)

These considerations indicate with some conclusiveness that Navaho *moral prescriptions* do not cite the 'old ways' as grounds for performing the acts prescribed. However, this type of justification may be used for what I have called "traditional practices," and I suspect that the plausibility of a conventionalistic authoritarian interpretation of Navaho ethics is due to the acceptance of traditional practices as the paradigm of moral prescriptions.[18] In contrast to moral prescriptions, Bidaga could say of traditional practices: "He didn't know why they do that, but they say they used to do that." (* 73)

There seems to be no good reason for believing that the Navaho moral code derives its justification from either the divinities or tradition. Indeed, it is doubtful that the Navaho moralist would employ the argument from origin. Hence, we may conclude that his moral code is nonauthoritarian. This conclusion will be confirmed progressively by the evidence for the other parts of the hypothesis.[19]

4. ETHICAL COMPETENCE AND NAVAHO MORAL PSYCHOLOGY

"Ethical competence" was defined earlier as the capacity of a listener to follow and accept an ethical argument. Whenever a moral discussion takes place there is always a presumption on the part of the speaker that the listener is ethically competent. (Otherwise, it would be like talking to a stone wall.)[20] The types and degrees of competence which are presupposed vary with different ethical systems. It will be recalled that an authoritarian system is based on the presumption that most if not all of the population is ethically incompetent, and thus rests on a qualitative dualism with respect to ethical competence.

In the preceding section I have tried to show that the Navaho ethical system is not authoritarian, and hence not dualistic; that is, it does not assume qualitative differences of competence between classes of individuals. The following discussion will provide more evidence for this conclusion.

Even though an ethical system does not admit a qualitative diversity in ethical competence, inevitably, it must recognize that there are degrees of competence. Among the Navahos such degrees depend upon the individual's experience, age, and wisdom in dealing with human affairs. There are the people who "talk pretty good," and to whom one should "listen" (moralists). But, as I shall try to show, the average adult generally is assumed to be competent to understand and follow the 'talker's' arguments.

The principles considered in this section are closely interwoven with the questions of the relation of knowledge, will, action, and character, which have been traditionally treated under the heading, "moral psychology."

a. The distribution and conditions of ethical competence

The Navaho moralist assumes that every adult individual is competent to understand and accept ethical arguments. In this sense, his moral code is an example of extreme democratic egalitarianism. The evidence for this is derived from the fact that he believes that moral matters can be "talked over and settled down." (* 13) The emphasis on the importance and efficacy of talk already cited could be considered as additional proof.[21] The principal classes of people to whom one cannot talk are children and drunks. We shall gain some understanding of the structure of the Navaho moral code if we examine the reasons for their being considered incompetent.

It is my impression that the instruction of children is divided into two phases, although the division is not sharp. In the early years the child is told what to do and what not to do by his parents with little or no argument. The main form in which these commands are expressed are: "I want you to do so and so." [22] The violation of these rather specific directives is punished by 'whipping.' Sometimes the child is told that doing something is *bahadzid,* for example, playing with knives. (* 170) The main misdemeanors for which a child is punished are such things as losing sheep, or throwing rocks at other children. (* 45) It may be doubted that moral prescriptions in the full sense are taught at this stage.

When the child has reached the age of discretion, the whip is abandoned and a new method is introduced — to give him a 'good talking.' At this time, one can speak about what is right or wrong. Before this, "a child wouldn't understand" the word "wrong," because you have to tell him *why* it is wrong (* 171), and he would not understand. In other words, a child is considered ethically incompetent because he cannot understand the reasons for an action's being wrong. We may conclude from this that a condition of ethical competence is the ability to follow a certain kind of reasoning.[23]

If there is any truth in this "two-stage" idea, it suggests a contrast with our Western notions of moral training, where we start teaching about right and wrong as soon as the child learns to talk, or even before. It also suggests a slightly different conception of ethical competence.

Ethical incompetency arises also from drinking. When he has been drinking a person "don't know what he's doing," whereas a sober person "knows what he is doing." (* 40) It appears that not only is a drunken man incompetent, but even the desire to drink makes him unable to 'listen' to moral talk. (* 6, 126) One easily observable consequence of Navahos drinking is that they get into fights and beat up their wives. In contrast, a sober man has "no hard feeling against anyone." (* 40)

I suspect that the idea underlying both these types of incompetence is that competence involves a person's ability to keep the consequences of his actions before his mind. Children and drunks are not able to 'know' what is wrong because they can be aware only of the immediate effects of their acts and are unable to keep in mind their more remote and pernicious consequences.

The full significance of the Navaho conception of ethical competence is brought out by contrasting it with some of the conceptions prevalent in both Western philosophy and Western thought in general. None of the special conditions of ethical competence mentioned in Chapter IX is to be found in Navaho ethical discourse. Thus there is no insistence on impartiality, sympathy, benevolence, religious faith, and so on. One characteristic form of argument occurring in our own ethical discourse is completely absent, namely, the appeal to the listener to be disinterested or sympathetic: "If you were in his place, how would you like it?" or "Look at it from the other's point of view!"[24]

From these considerations it is evident that the Navaho conception of ethical competence amounts essentially to the same kind of ability to listen and understand as would be involved in any ordinary affairs of life, for instance, in practical matters such as sheep raising or farming. There are no special conditions of ethical competence.

b. Virtue is knowledge

It is a peculiarity of Western thought that we ordinarily do not believe that ethical 'knowledge' is a sufficient condition of action. In other words, we assume that it is quite possible for a person to know what is right, and yet not do it. Indeed, it is often supposed that wrong acts are always committed with the full knowledge that they are wrong, because of, say, succumbing to temptation. The theoretical basis of this view rests on the distinction between the "Will" and "Reason" — a distinction which gives rise to the problem of the "Freedom of the Will." Thus, we frequently say that "his Reason told him what was right, but his Will was too weak to obey it."

Such a conception appears to be alien to Navaho thought. The commission of a wrong act is attributed to a person's not knowing what he is doing. (* 40) To do something especially wrong is evidence that one 'has lost his mind,' or has 'gone crazy.'[25] On the other hand, acting rightly most of the time shows that one has a "good head," "thinks hard," "has good idea."[26] It all depends on how a "person thinks." (* 30)

The consequence of this identification of ethical knowledge with moral conduct, and the implied omission of the concept of "will" from Navaho moral psychology is that there is no place left for anything resembling our Western notion of "sin."[27] It is therefore no mere coincidence that the Navaho interpreter speaks of wrong actions as *mistakes,* rather than as "sin," "crime," "guilt." Thus, although psychological explanations of the absence among the Navahos of a sense of sin in such terms as "guilt" may be perfectly true, it should also be recognized that the conception of "sin" is also incompatible with their 'theory.'

If we conjoin the doctrine of almost universal ethical competence with the belief that ethical knowledge is sufficient to effect right action, it follows that in principle *coercion is never necessary.* Every dispute can be settled amicably by 'talking it over.' The exception to this principle occurs only when a person is incompetent. In this way we can provide a justification for using force and punishment against people who drink. (* 35, 125–6) Of course, children fall into the same category.[28] Therefore, except for these cases, persuasion rather than threat of force is thought to be the most efficacious means of affecting another person's conduct.

It is obvious that all these doctrines will have significant implications for a theory of punishment. In the first place, they suggest that punishment ideally is unnecessary and to be resorted to only on utilitarian grounds of prevention or deterrence of incompetents. In the second place, since there is no conception of sin we should expect that the whole rationale of guilt and responsibility would be different. I shall now turn to a brief examination of the latter.

c. Character and responsibility

The Navaho theory of the 'soul' is complicated and elusive. In bare outline it holds that there is a "wind soul, which enters the body at birth, controls every action and movement of the human being, and leaves the body again at death." [29] There is a divinity who acts as the dispatcher of 'winds,' and who decides how long the wind is to stay, or how long the individual is to live, and what kind of wind the body is to have. (* 95, 158, 161) Informant John Hawk told me that there were four kinds of winds which result in four different kinds of people: good, happy, bad (makes mistakes), and mean. (* 161) Hence, it is maintained that a person's character is fixed at birth by the dispatcher, and so it "would be pretty hard to change it." If he is happy, he cannot make himself unhappy, and if he is unhappy he cannot become happy. (* 29) Similarly, a person may be born mean and nothing can be done about him.[30]

There are several consequences which follow from this doctrine of what might be called "predestination." First, one cannot hope to change a person's ways if he has that kind of wind. Not only will persuasion be ineffective, but threats of punishment will be just as futile. This is another reason why coercion is frowned upon — because it is doomed to fail. You cannot change a person's inborn 'wind.' Moreover, the only attitude that can be taken towards the pernicious behavior of others is a fatalistic one. You have to "just let this thing go." [31]

A second consequence is that the misbehavior of a person is attributed to his 'wind,' rather than directly to him as an individual. Father Berard Haile suggests that the 'wind-souls' "appear to absolve the individual person from responsibility in their earthly career." [32] The conception of personal responsibility seems to vanish, since the 'wind-soul' can be blamed.

The consequence of this belief is that a crime or transgression is just 'taking chances' — since the individual feels no responsibility for his misdemeanors — they 'fall to the side' of the 'wind-soul' within him. 'Getting caught' is too bad, but that is the chance one takes.

The saving factor in this fatalistic doctrine is that no one can know what kind of 'wind' a particular individual has. His family naturally thinks that it is good; his enemies may think that it is mean. So there is no use disputing over such matters, although they may be subjects for speculation. This accords with the characteristic emphasis on particular concrete actions, "events, not actors or qualities, are primary." [33] The main interest is in 'straightening things out' by rectifying the trouble, and not by trying to change the criminal's personality or to save his soul.

I believe that Father Berard Haile has done a great service by calling to our attention the significance of the theory of the 'wind-soul.' As he points out, the details are matters of esoteric belief, but the general conception is probably understood and accepted by the Navaho layman. It is introduced in various ways into the Navaho language so that even our Western conceptions of "crime" suffer a distortion in meaning when translated into Navaho.

I conclude this section with a summary of the main conceptions of Navaho moral psychology. The ethics is individualistic and egalitarian, in the sense that it can be understood and learned by almost everyone; thinking and doing are inextricably interwoven, and there is no conception of an intervening 'will'; a person's character is determined by a supernatural dispatcher of 'winds'; persuasion is the accepted means of influencing others, and coercion is neither necessary where the subject can be influenced successfully (when he is not incompetent) nor is it sufficient if he is incorrigible; finally, there is a strong 'fatalistic' element in the theory of human behavior, which is reflected in the practical attitude towards others.

5. MODE OF VALIDATION: APPLICATION[34]

The general procedure underlying the employment of the logic of ethical argument was designated earlier as a mode of validation. This section will be concerned with a preliminary characterization of the mode of validation which is implicit in the moral discourse of my informants; but, again, full confirmation of the theses advanced here is cumulative and additional evidence for them will be found in the next chapter.

The outstanding characteristic of the informants' arguments is that they do not appeal to moral principles as such. For instance, it is never argued that X's telling a lie is wrong because lying is wrong, or that one ought not to steal because stealing is wrong. Moral principles are not cited in moral discourse. Instead, the reasons are always nonprescriptive or factual; for example, that will get him into trouble, or that's *bahadzid*. The argument consists in pointing out the conditions and consequences of the act, rather than in subsuming the case under a general moral principle.

Thus, explicit moral discourse is composed exclusively of factual premises and prescriptive conclusions. Of course, frequently the conclusions are stated without citing the premises; for example, "don't lie, don't steal, etc." [35]

This suggests that the mode of validation is not what I have called the "selective mode," which justifies a prescription by subsuming it under one of several possible moral principles (although, I do not think that we should rule out this mode as a theoretical possibility, since we might be able to reconstruct such validating principles). Ordinarily we should expect the citing of moral principles if this mode were used, and this does not occur in Navaho ethical discourse.

Nor do the arguments given seem to exemplify the mode of interpretation, for there are no references to procedural conditions in the individual judge, and there is no evidence that there is any discretion in the interpretation of a basic schematic prescription. A system utilizing the interpretive mode would say characteristically, "It's up to you to do what you think right." It is true that we encounter, "It's up to you" in Navaho discourse but it occurs practically never, if at all, in connection with any of the prescriptions given in the preceding chapters. As I have suggested earlier, it seems to be the correct answer when one is asked about the disposal of one's property.[36] It suggests a principle of noninterference, rather than the assumption that a moral decision is left up to the discretionary judgment of the individual concerned. Moreover, any limitation of the conditions of ethical competence, which is typical of the mode of interpretation, is absent in Navaho ethical discourse, and this also indicates that they do not employ this mode.

Finally, we must explore the possibility that the Navaho code is an example of extreme particularism, that is, the theory that the obligation in any individual situation is immediate and underivative. The lack of appeal to moral principles, and the reference to the factual characteristics of the situation are both properties of this mode. However, there is one point at which the Navaho system diverges from the views of the exponents of this mode, namely, in their justification of general moral rules.

It will be recalled that for a particularist system a general moral rule is a general prescription which serves as a guide to action, but is not a validating principle. General prescriptions like "not to steal, not to lie," which are frequently commended in Navaho moral discourse are general rules in this sense and are not used to validate particular prescriptions. The particularist (Prichard) would agree that such general prescriptions are only rules.

However, the Navaho informant departs from the particularist in his conception of how these general rules are themselves justified. It will be recalled that rules for the particularist are inductively derived from the particular moral judgements that are ultimate; that is, they are validated by these particular judgments.

In contrast, in Navaho moral discourse, these rules are established *in the same way* as are any particular moral prescriptions. A glance at the transcript of arguments presented by the informants will show that *exactly the same arguments* are used for general prescriptions (rules) as for particular prescriptions. (* 6, 56, 70)

If this is a correct description of the data, then it would appear probable that both general and particular prescriptions are derived from a more ultimate general basic prescription or prescriptions, and the system would not be particularistic.

The precise identification of the mode of validation for any ethical system is difficult and always open to doubt. One reason for this is that the analysis presented in Chapter VIII is admittedly incomplete, for not only was I unable to give very precise and unambiguous differentiating characteristics but also it is quite probable that all the possible modes were not exhausted in the four types which I listed. A more detailed analysis of the Navaho code might reveal that it employs yet another fifth mode. In the meantime, I believe that it is worth while to explore the possibility that it uses the simple applicational mode, in accordance with which particular prescriptions are validated by simple application of a single basic prescription. In the next chapter, I shall try to argue this in more detail.

In conclusion, I should like once more to stress the significance of the subjects discussed. I have advanced three basic theses: that the moral code is nonauthoritarian; that ethical competence is assumed to be found in almost all adult human beings; and that the mode of validation is the mode of application. If any one of these theses is proven to be false, the rest of the reconstruction to be expounded in the next chapter will be invalid, although some modification might be possible to save it. Finally, I shall reiterate that since these three theses are more general than the rest, they cannot be tested as conclusively, as the later ones can be.[37]

The Content of the Reconstructed Code

I. HYPOTHETICAL RECONSTRUCTION OF THE BASIC PRESCRIPTION

a. Division into two theses

I shall now turn to a discussion of the reconstructed basic prescription from which, according to my hypothesis, the particular prescriptive statements and practical rules of morality of the Navaho code are derivable. For convenience of exposition this part of the hypothetical reconstruction may be divided into two principal theses.

The first is that the basic prescription is extrinsically teleological in that it enjoins and forbids actions in terms of their promoting or averting an end-state of affairs. The reader may be reminded that such a basic prescription can generate various types of prescriptions: prohibitions, injunctions, counsels, or discounsels.[1]

The second thesis is that the end in terms of which the actions are prescribed is egoistic. In other words, the goal of moral action is the personal welfare of the agent. In addition, it is an intrapersonal goal which is a state of affairs that resides only within the agent himself and of which the welfare of others is not an intrinsic or constitutive element. (This will be called "atomic egoism.") In this sense, Navaho morality will be held to reject any purely altruistic ends, the common good, and the greatest happiness of the greatest number, as ultimate goals of moral life, since all of these include the welfare of others besides the agent as intrinsic components of the agent's moral goals.

In addition to the egoistic thesis, there are some subtheses by which I shall attempt to define the intrapersonal end of moral action more precisely. These are: that the end-state of affairs is naturalistic and this-worldly; that it is conceived of in concrete rather than subjectivistic terms; and that it is negative. (Incidentally, I think that it follows from these that the ground-motive is the continuous fear of specific dangers in the world and society.)

The meaning of these theses and subtheses will be made more precise later. The order of exposition will be as follows: first, I shall show the positive evidence for these theses which is provided by the data already presented; second, I shall examine and test the teleological thesis in more detail; third, I shall do the same for the egoistic thesis; finally, in the next chapter, I shall discuss the subthesis about the goal of moral life. Until I come to this topic I shall refer to this intrapersonal end indifferently as either the positive goal of the agent's welfare or the negative goal of his misfortune. I have chosen these words to avoid more heavily loaded words such as "happiness," "well-being," "good," and "evil."

b. Derivation of ethical statements given as data

The task of reconstructing an ethical system consists in finding the premises missing in the arguments presented by the informant, from which in conjunction with his own stated reasons we can derive his conclusions according to a logical scheme (which in this case is the mode of application). Since the data provide us with a good many minor factual premise statements, I shall first concentrate on the basic prescriptive premise from which the conclusions can be derived. Accordingly, in the preliminary analysis of the code's content *the only item which will be reconstructed is the basic prescription.*

It is possible to state the basic prescription in terms either of a positive or a negative end. In either case, all the prescriptions, whether positive or negative, can be derived from the basic prescription conceived of as enjoining necessary means to the positive goal of the agent's welfare, or as prohibiting actions sufficient to produce the negative goal of his misfortune. By suitable transformations we can derive the prohibition of actions preventing the positive goal or the injunction of means to averting the negative goal. These transformations have been given in Chapter IX, section 2(d), and so it is unnecessary to repeat them in detail here.

Accordingly, the alternative formulations would be as follows.

(1) Positive formulation — Positive goal, agent's welfare. Basic positive prescription: Do all those actions necessary to promote your own welfare! Immediately derived prohibition: Do not do any action sufficient to prevent or jeopardize your welfare!

(2) Negative formulation — Negative goal, agent's misfortune. Basic negative prescription: Do not do any action leading to your own misfortune! Immediately derived injunction: Do all those actions necessary to avert your misfortune!

Although either the positive or negative formulation of the basic prescription is possible, I shall give the derivations in terms of a negative goal, misfortune. My reason for preferring this is that it makes the derivations slightly simpler to grasp, and may correspond more closely to the natural thinking of the informant. I shall try to justify my choice later in Chapter XVII, section 1. In the meantime it should be noted that a positive formulation is equally possible, and that I am presenting only the negative formulation to avoid excessive duplication.

Let us first see how this basic prescription can be applied to give the negative prescriptions already presented. The arguments for the three groups of negative prescriptions given in Chapter XIII suggest premises to the effect that, first, one ought not to do anything that will make oneself sick (taboos); second, one ought not to do anything that will get one into trouble (social prohibitions); and third, one ought not to do anything that will cause people to laugh at one, and so on (interdictions). Although it is possible that not every negative prescription reported earlier is justified in terms of one or more of these three general principles, at least one of them is presupposed in *most* of the informant's arguments.

There appear therefore to be three kinds of evils: sickness, being in trouble, and being talked about adversely. Using the term "misfortune" as a collective term for these evils, we can reduce them to the basic prescription: "One ought not to do anything that will produce misfortune for himself," *or* "Do not do anything that will bring misfortune to you!"

Examples: (1) (a) All actions producing misfortune for you are wrong;
          (b) 'Bothering your sister' will produce misfortune for you (incest sickness);
          (c) Therefore, 'bothering your sister' is wrong.
      (2) (a) Don't do anything that will produce misfortune;
          (b) Stealing (and getting caught) will produce misfortune (trouble);
          (c) Therefore, don't steal!

The account given in Chapter XIII of the specific arguments for negative prescriptions will show that they usually consist in factual statements, which I interpret to function logically as minor premises subsuming the specific action under the basic egoistic prescription.

Positive prescriptions are derived from a basic prohibition as injunctions to do acts which are necessary to avert the evil. Thus, we may state a general positive prescription as follows: "Do those actions which are necessary to avert your own misfortune." Such actions may be divided into two groups, those actions which aim at getting rid of misfortune and those which are designed to insure against misfortune. These two ways of averting correspond to the two groups of positive prescriptions, rectification and injunctions proper.[2]

Again, we can offer a validation of the positive prescriptions in such terms as these:

(1) For rectification:
  (a) Do those actions necessary to get rid of your misfortune,
  (b) Payment for injury is necessary to get rid of misfortune ('to straighten it out');
  (c) Therefore, make payments, etc.
(2) For social injunctions:
  (a) Do those actions necessary to insure against your misfortune;
  (b) Helping others will insure against misfortune (because only if you help others will they help you back);
  (c) Therefore, help others!

It should be noted that these arguments for positive injunctions are formulated less precisely than were those for negative prescriptions. The reason for this is that they are based on an intermediate premise, often stated overtly by informants, that the good will of family and neighbors is the best insurance for times of need. In this sense, most of the straightening out of actions is intended to promote this good will; it is to be done so there will be 'no hard feeling' or so that people will 'feel good' about it. Therefore, these arguments might be amended by inserting a premise such as this:

(b') Actions producing good feeling towards oneself are necessary to avert misfortune.

Then, the other actions involving social relations can also be subsumed under the same premise.

One comment on social interdictions may be included here. It is quite likely that the reason why it is considered so important for the agent that people speak well of him is that it indicates that he is 'well-insured' in the above sense. Thus, if people are inclined to laugh at a person or to dislike him, this means that they are unlikely to help him when he needs it. If this suggestion is correct we should reformulate the argument for social interdictions that appeal *only* to popular favor or disfavor. Such a reformulation would be as follows:

  (a) Do those actions necessary to insure against misfortune;
  (b) Actions producing good feeling towards oneself are necessary to insure against misfortune;
  (c) Doing X (for instance, sexual promiscuity) is sufficient to prevent good feeling;
  (d) Therefore, do not do X!

I think that it will be seen that the common pattern reflected in the prescriptions given in Chapters XIII and XIV can be given a rigorous formulation in terms of derivations from the one single basic prescription. I have indicated schematically how this can be done. A more rigorous formulation and application in detail are unnecessary here.

In giving the formulas of the various arguments I have tried to assume only one premise which is not explicitly stated by the informant; namely, the basic prescription. I believe that all the other minor premises which would be filled in when applying the formulas to specific prescriptive statements actually are asserted by the informant, although perhaps in slightly different words. It is essential to the undertaking of a hypothetical reconstruction of an ethical system that one limit the reconstruction to as few premises as possible, and preferably to the basic prescription alone. Otherwise the hypothesis is liable to become completely untestable.

The reader should be warned against too hasty an acceptance of the hypothetical reconstruction offered here. I should call his attention to the fact that there are several lacunae in my argument. In the first place, the evidence that the arguments reported are always used, or are always available upon request to the listener, is incomplete. The actual arguments are scantier than one might wish. In the second place, there are some prescriptions which do not fit as easily into this scheme as most. The chief of these are what I shall call "reciprocal obligations." These difficulties will be explored later in this chapter.

The procedure which I shall adopt here, and which I also adopted in my field work, will be to assume this reconstruction as a working hypothesis, and to test it by deriving new prescriptions and new arguments in addition to the ones upon which the original hypothesis was based. In that way we can hope to subject the hypothesis to more rigorous examination and criticism.

c. Methods of testing hypothesis

Following Popper's maxim that the essence of the scientific method consists in the persistent attempt to *falsify* the hypothesis, we must be able, in principle at least, to falsify this one. I believe that it is possible to formulate tests which, if they were positive, would require the rejection of the hypothesis.

Thus, if we can discover prescriptions or arguments that are neither teleological nor egoistic, or even some that are incompatible with these theses, the hypothesis must be rejected. The specific procedure to be used in an investigation in descriptive ethics consists in predicting the occurrence of other statements by means of derivations from the hypothetical basic prescription according to the methods outlined in Part II.

Since there are two kinds of data-statements available to us, prescriptive statements and justifying factual statements, there are two directions in which we can proceed in testing the hypothetical basic prescription: we can start either from given prescriptive statements or from given factual statements. The first method of testing is to derive a new prescription from the hypothetical basic prescription by using a factual statement which is available as datum from interviews with informants. We can then check this predicted prescriptive statement with the informant. If he accepts it, we have some confirmation of the hypothesis, and if he rejects it we have some disconfirmation.

The second method is to predict the acceptance of some factual belief as accounting for the derivation of a known prescription from the hypothetical basic prescription. We can thereupon ascertain whether such a predicted factual belief is accepted or not, and accordingly our hypothesis will be partially confirmed or disconfirmed.

Thus, in principle, since we have two kinds of data-statements, we have two ways of testing the hypothesis. In application the procedure is more complicated, because we must have exhausted all the alternative factual beliefs which may conceivably be relevant to the reconstructed argument.

Unfortunately, there are many practical difficulties lying in the way of using this ideal method. In the short time available in the field, I was able to employ it only in a few instances. Hence, the following discussion must be taken primarily as an elucidation of the procedures to be followed under ideal conditions, and the results which I have obtained must be accepted provisionally. More conclusive results must await future 'experimentation.'

2. THE TELEOLOGICAL THESIS

a. Evidence which would falsify this thesis

The teleological thesis states that the sufficient and necessary condition of an action's being either right or wrong is its tendency to promote or avert an end-state of affairs. Therefore, if we discovered an accepted prescriptive statement which is not or cannot be validated by reference to the promotion or averting of the end, we should be required to reject this thesis.

There is a certain danger in a direct approach to this thesis; namely, the deriving of prescriptions which seem to us, the investigators, either to depend upon or to be independent of their being means to an end. The content of the end itself may be conceived differently from the way to which we are accustomed. For instance, a Western philosopher is naturally inclined to think of hedonistic utilitarianism as the prime example of a teleological ethical system. However, the proof that a certain system is not utilitarian, cannot be taken to prove that it is not teleological. There are many other versions of teleologism besides hedonistic utilitarianism. Hence, we must beware of limiting the alternatives to some oversimplified dichotomy such as utilitarianism vs. formalism. Teleologism does not necessarily entail that the end is hedonistic, a common good, a positive end, or any other specified end, but merely that the consequences of one's action alone are morally relevant. Furthermore, not only may the end be conceived of differently, but also the factual beliefs involved in the argument may be entirely different from what we should expect. For instance, the Navaho conception of causality may imply somewhat different expectations for the consequences of actions, and their beliefs in such things as ghosts or witches will also lead to different conclusions. All these considerations suggest that we must be extremely careful not to conclude that the Navaho moral code is either teleological or non-teleological before we have carefully examined all of the relevant evidence.

How can we establish that an ethical argument is teleological or non-teleological in the sense intended here? From the general characterization given at the beginning of this section follow certain characteristics which suggest three possible methods for deciding.

Since the teleological moral prescriptions are justified on the grounds that the actions will promote or avert an end, *all factual references must be prospective,* in the sense that they must refer either explicitly or implicitly to future consequences of an action. Of course, the speaker may refer back to past events such as someone's past conduct, but such references can be used only to establish certain expectations about the future; for example, that the person may be expected to do the same later on.

Therefore, the use of a purely retrospective argument would be evidence that the speaker does not accept a teleological code. A purely retrospective argument would be one in which past events are not appealed to for predictive purposes. An example will illustrate this. According to our ordinary Western principles of justice, we think it wrong to punish an innocent man. Proven guilt is assumed to be necessary to permit punishment, although it may not be sufficient to require it. Therefore, a necessary component of any discussion of whether or not to punish must consist of a purely retrospective reference to the past deed; the accused must be proven to have done it. The establishment of guilt, per se, has nothing to do with any predictions about the culprit's future behavior or that of any other person — for utilitarian arguments about prevention, deterrence, or reformation, are all considered irrelevant if the man is not guilty.

The first method of trying to falsify the teleological thesis is therefore to look for evidence of purely retrospective arguments; that is, arguments in which past events are cited apart from their bearing on future events.

Second, teleologism would also be disconfirmed if we could discover positive evidence that a moral prescription was based on some principle ('law') rather than on the consequences. An ethical system of this type is generally called "formalistic." As we have seen, the Navaho informant never appealed directly to moral principles in justifying arguments, but we should investigate the possibility that there is an implicit appeal to a 'covert' principle which would entail that the Navaho is covertly formalistic.

In order to establish the fact that a moral code is formalistic, it is necessary to show that there are moral prescriptions which are not justified by reference to certain consequences. In other words, formalism is proven only by showing the absence of teleological justification.

Accordingly, the first method of falsification is to show the *presence* of nonteleologism, whereas the second method is to show the *absence* of teleological arguments in crucial cases. To throw doubt upon the hypothesis it is sufficient to find one or more reliable instances of either.

A third method of testing consists in seeking positive evidence for the acceptance of the teleological thesis. This is done by deriving prescriptions in accordance with a teleological premise and then checking them with the informant. If the results agree with the predictions then the thesis has to that extent been confirmed. However, if they do not agree, we should not be too hasty in rejecting our thesis, because it may be that we have overlooked some crucial and relevant belief that may even be concealed deliberately.

In employing these three methods it is difficult to keep them entirely separate. Therefore, in the following discussion I shall not attempt to do so. I shall begin by considering some of the moral principles which are usually advanced by formalistic moralists as ultimate moral 'laws.' [3]

b. Probing with Western formalistic principles

The remarkable similarity between many Navaho moral rules and those accepted in Western society lends plausibility to the hypothesis that they may be formalistic like many of our moral laws are held to be. The obvious candidates for such investigation are the prohibitions against lying and stealing, the injunctions to keep promises, and those connected with the conception of justice. Although I was not able to test these principles exhaustively, some of the relevant findings may be mentioned here. The reader may be reminded that earlier I have given instances of statements in which each of these prescriptions was explicitly justified in teleological terms,[4] and hence our tests are aimed primarily at falsifying the teleological thesis.

(1) *Lying.* For this I tried two different tests. (*a*) If we assume that a person ought to do those actions which will keep him out of trouble, it appears that he should lie if this will keep him out of trouble. Accordingly, I asked my informant whether an unfaithful husband should lie to his wife in order to avoid trouble. The answer was that she'll find it out anyway, "Indian women they sure smart." [5] (* 90)

This example teaches us several things. It is clear that the situation was 'defined' quite differently by the informant from the way the questioner conceived it. First, that lying would be unsuccessful. Second, that the trouble consequent upon being caught lying is considered more serious than the trouble which could be avoided by not doing so. It is important to note the moralist's strong conviction that one cannot get away with it. However, the fact that the lying is believed to be doomed to failure merely serves to confirm the teleological thesis, at least this instance cannot be regarded as negative evidence.

(b) Just after the informant appears to have stated that lying under any circumstances was wrong (* 89), I proposed Kant's famous problem about lying from altruistic motives, and asked him what he would do. The account which followed included telling the would-be-murderer an untruth. By implication, therefore, under some circumstances it *is* all right to tell a lie; namely, where the consequences of not doing so would be trouble! (* 91)

This example illustrates the futility of asking abstract questions such as is it always wrong to lie? Furthermore, it may indicate that the term "lie" is used emotively, in the sense that it refers to a deception which is wrong, rather than descriptively to a certain kind of objectively defined action. (In the same way as the word "murder" is distinguished from "homicide"; "murder" refers to homicide that is wrong.)

(2) *Keeping promises*. Borrowing a suggestion from the work of Richard Brandt, I asked whether one ought to keep a promise to use his money in a certain way made in private to a man who died shortly thereafter. (* 168) Should a person keep the promise although no one knew about the promise and there were better ways of using the money? Yes, it was a promise, it would be a kind of stealing, and so on. But I soon discovered that a concealed belief in ghosts lay behind the answer. The ghost "comes back for his belongings" [6] and only witches dare rob the dead. Therefore, breaking a promise involving money to a dead man is worse than promises to the living, for it is *bahadzid*, whereas in the case of the living it is not — only witches do that.

Again, this provides only positive confirmation of the teleological thesis. However, it does suggest two points for consideration. First, it emphasizes the danger of overlooking concealed beliefs, for if it had not occurred to me to ask about the ghost, I should have assumed that the promise was binding upon purely formalistic principles. Second, it shows us the much greater importance attached to the pernicious consequences of an act than to any positive good that may come of it. This indicates that, in the future, tests of the teleological thesis should be made in terms of negative rather than positive effects of the proposed action.

(3) *Obeying established authority*. Perhaps the most remarkable instance which gives the appearance of a formalistic principle is that one ought not to leave prison if put there by the white authorities. This example was taken

from Socrates's discourse in the *Crito,* and interestingly enough, my informant's answer was *in effect* the same as that of Socrates: Stay until they let you go. (* 15) Why? Because "they put him in jail"!

Surely, this resembles a formalistic principle of obedience to the established authority. But I do not believe that there is anyone who knows anything about the Navahos who would accept this explanation. For one thing, it is quite evident that the average unacculturated Navaho, and especially the informant's grandfather, would have no understanding of the meaning of "legitimate political authority." It is most likely that the rationale behind this decision to stay was the fear of provoking further wrath of the powerful whites, who, since they were so bewilderingly different, might cause trouble that was even worse than being in prison.

The only kind of principle which could plausibly be involved in this example might be called the "Principle of Stoical Resignation" to things that come "like that to them." (* 15) Given a teleological ethics and the inability to do anything without making things worse, what other action besides resignation would be possible? This example should serve as a warning against too glib an ascription of formalism to Navaho moral prescriptions.

Unfortunately, I do not have any more tests to describe. The ones which were undertaken did not shake the teleological thesis. However, they do reveal an important characteristic of Navaho moral discourse, namely, that it always advises against taking chances. This distinguishes the ideal talk of the moralist sharply from the actual behavior of the people for whom it is designed. *The moralist says: "Don't take chances,"* whereas the average Navaho does take chances all the time, and furthermore the conduct of the divinities in Navaho mythology provides him with many good precedents for taking chances.[7]

c. Justice

The principles of justice are those which are most frequently cited by Western moral philosophers as involving nonutilitarian moral laws. Is there a natural justice recognized by the Navaho moralist?

It is inevitable that Navaho ideas about justice would differ in some essential respects from our own because of the intimate relation between justice and the State in Western thought. At the time when the Navaho moral code grew up, the Navaho lived in a state of nature, in the sense that there was no political authority. (This is what Hobbes and Locke meant by a "state of nature.") There was no law and no judicial apparatus to administer justice. Hence, we shall have to limit our questions about justice to the kind of justice conceivable in a state of nature — sometimes called "natural" as opposed to "legal" justice.

Furthermore, the Navaho conception of justice may be expected to differ from our own because of their disapproval of coercion. Many of our own ideas about justice are concerned with the just use of coercion, but since coercion is ordinarily regarded as neither necessary nor sufficient to secure the ends of society, the content of the Navaho prescriptions about justice can in this respect be expected to be quite different from that of our own.

Since the time of Aristotle, Western thought has distinguished between two kinds of justice: corrective justice and distributive justice. The former is concerned with the just handling of offenses (for example, criminal justice), whereas the latter involves the just distribution of benefits and burdens (for example, the distribution of wealth or of taxation).[8]

Corrective justice. Here I shall discuss the question of assignment of punishment and fines to correct some wrong done. For convenience, the subject may be divided according to the following topics: (*a*) the purposes of corrective justice, (*b*) the methods used (for instance, punishment), (*c*) the conditions (for instance, guilt).

(*a*) Many Western thinkers have maintained the doctrine of *lex talionis,* that is, the opinion that it is obligatory that every crime be punished, "an eye for an eye, a tooth for a tooth." This is sometimes called the "retributive" theory of punishment. Hegel even went so far as to maintain that a criminal had a right to be punished! [9] For this view, the purpose of corrective justice is to rectify the criminal, and punishing the guilty may be considered an 'end-in-itself.'

It is evident that there is no such doctrine among the Navahos. The main consideration is a utilitarian one; namely, to prevent a recurrence and to rectify the situation rather than the agent. If the criminal promises to reform "so we just let him go. So they won't punish him." (* 166) Punishment is only the last resort.

It might be thought that the injunction to make payment for injuries is justified by the 'ends of justice.' However, my informants explicitly stated that the purpose is "so there'll be no hard feeling." [10] (* 92)

(*b*) The methods of correction follow from these purposes: making payments to the injured party; and the use of 'talk' to prevent recurrence. Where the person continues his malpractices, then he can be punished "and by punish he might stop that." The distaste for coercion is an important factor here.

(*c*) By the term "conditions" of punishability, I mean those conditions which make it morally permissible to punish a person. In our culture, we consider it necessary that the person be guilty, and accordingly hold the punishment of an innocent man to be reprehensible. One test that I used with the Navahos showed that it was thought that a good man ought not to be given up to a hostile tribe to prevent their ravaging the countryside. (* 106) This answer may reflect the reluctance to give up any fellow Navaho especially one that is liked.[11]

It appears that punishment in the form of coercion ought not to be inflicted upon a good man, even though guilty, but a bad man may be punished. It is admitted that under present conditions brought on by drinking: "People needs some punishment . . . That's the reason we have a lot of bad people." (* 36)

Questions involving the inflicting of punishment are bound up with the Navaho attitudes towards white law-enforcing authorities, whose actions are held to be inevitable and inscrutable. The combination of their view of white criminal procedures and the absence of any conception of "retributive punishment" is illustrated by another example. A good man, convicted of murder by the white authorities, will have his fines paid by his friends. A bad man can just stay in jail. "It all depends on what kind of person he is." (* 14, 25–6)

The first condition of punishability therefore appears to be that the person be bad and be a troublemaker. It is possible that this presupposes a theory of personal merit or demerit instead of a theory of innocence and guilt as the necessary condition to permit punishment. However, the situation is not clear and requires further investigation. Certainly one important consideration is the utilitarian one; namely, the prevention and deterrence of further crime. It is possible that behind these statements there is a sense of reciprocal obligation to a good person, and lack of it to a bad one. This residual category will be discussed presently.

Another condition which is referred to in procedures relating to corrective justice involves the question of who is at fault. This consideration is important in the process of rectification of injuries, or 'straightening out.' I have already commented on this in Chapter XIV, section 1. There seems to be a latent principle to the effect that the faulty party must make compensation to the injured party. In practice, the burden of making the payment falls upon the family and clan rather than exclusively on the guilty individual. Further investigation of the question of exactly *who* should pay, and of who *may* pay, might throw more light on the conception of "fault." I suspect that the issue hinges upon what will be considered to be the most efficacious remedy of the 'trouble,' rather than whether or not the guilty one is the person to pay. If this surmise be correct, then it is merely a utilitarian consideration that is involved here.

Perhaps a more important purpose involved in the ascription of fault to an individual is to 'secure immunity against further attack.' Apparently, it is assumed that a person who injures someone once, may be likely to do so again. This must be prevented. Therefore, the relevance of the question who is at fault is again purely utilitarian, for it aims at preventing recurrences of the injurious act.

This brief examination of possible formalistic principles of corrective justice indicates that there is a likelihood that they will be proven to be teleological, in that they are the means to the promotion of an end or the prevention of evils. The possible exception is the differential treatment to be accorded a good man, but even this may be justified on utilitarian grounds, for a good man is more likely to benefit others than a bad man. However, I do not wish to be dogmatic in the rejection of the possibility of formalism. A conclusive answer to the question connected with corrective justice requires a great deal more data than I have available. Direct questions involving the punishment of an innocent person are not very successful because of the repudiation of physical coercion as a means, and, in addition, the responsibility of innocent fellow-clansmen to pay for injuries merely reflects the desire to keep trouble away. With sufficient ingenuity these extraneous factors might be eliminated, and questions devised which would provide an adequate test of whether punishment (or fines) should be contingent upon the guilt of the person concerned.

Distributive justice. Under this heading I propose to discuss the principles of allotting those surplus benefits and burdens for which no particular person has a prior claim or responsibility.

Aristotle conceived of distributive justice in connection with the assignment of rewards and honors by the State. We may also include Bentham's dictum that "each person should count as one" in the distribution of pleasures and pains. Similarly, I should like to put into this category the moral problems involved in contemporary issues such as assignment of tax burdens and support by public welfare agencies. There has been no general agreement among Western moralists about the principles of distributive justice; some have maintained that distribution should be according to merit, others have thought that need (or ability to pay) was more relevant, and still others have insisted upon the principle of equality.

In principle, it may be impossible to formulate the notion of distributive justice without referring to communal organizations of some sort or other, (the State, for example); and these were absent in Navaho society in the old days. Furthermore, our inquiry into this subject is complicated by the fact that Navaho property concepts differ from ours. Thus, one instance which would ordinarily provide a good example for testing the principles of just distribution is the allotment of land for farming or grazing, but, since in the old days land was not thought of as owned in the Western sense, the problem is more confusing than it would seem at first glance.

(1) *The distribution of goods.* I asked my informant how he would distribute a gift of five hundred sheep. (* 66–69) He would give it to his

family. How should *I* distribute them? That's up to you. An anonymous rich man would be advised to give it to the 'better' people. Why? "So they don't waste it."

This gives the semblance of being a principle of distribution according to merit (like Aristotle). However, it is also evident that it is future expected merit that counts, not past virtue. "For unto every one that hath shall be given, and he shall have abundance." [12] The good man is the proper recipient not because he should be rewarded, but because he can be depended upon to take care of the goods given. Possibly this reflects the same principle noted earlier under corrective justice, that a good man should be treated more considerately than a bad one.

In the case of a poor man in dire need, one should give him some money or otherwise he might die! (* 69) Here, the principle of distribution seems to be entirely utilitarian, for it is directed at averting the evil of someone's dying.

It is not too difficult to subsume these statements under a utilitarian theory of distribution: Distribute so that good will be increased and evil decreased. However, again the evidence is meager.

(2) *Distribution of burdens.* I presented to my informant the problem of how to collect tribute to pay to an enemy tribe. (* 72) The answer was characteristic of Navaho procedure: Call a meeting and talk it over. The burden would be met only by voluntary contributions. There should be absolutely no coercion to dispossess someone of his property. (Would the Navaho moralist, therefore, in theory have to disapprove of taxation?)

Whether there are any assumed principles of equitable distribution of burdens requires further evidence and testing by formulating questions which do not involve coercion or the inviolacy of property. In both kinds of distribution there are practical factors operating to secure some equity. For instance, no one would 'keep everything to himself' or fail to contribute voluntarily for the public good, for fear of being thought 'stingy.' Probably many of the rules relating to distribution which are moral prescriptions in our society, are merely traditional practices among the Navahos.

d. Residual categories: possible nonteleological principles

It is not too much to assume that Navaho moralist does not accept, even covertly, exactly the same moral principles as are accepted in our own society. I suspect that further inquiry will establish this conclusion better than does the incomplete evidence offered here. However, it is quite conceivable that Navaho moral discourse may presuppose some formalistic principles other than the ones just examined. There is one such principle, the principle of reciprocity, which obviously must be considered seriously; and there may be others.

The principle of reciprocity.[13] The most difficult cases to account for on my hypothesis are those prescriptions which call for "helping a person backward," where there is no chance of reciprocation by the person helped. The obvious example of a problematic situation where the principle of reciprocity might be invoked is in getting children to help their aged and helpless parents, since we may assume that these recipients of help cannot return the help in the future. The argument for helping in such cases merely rests on statements like: "Their mother had given them milk," etc.[14] (* 23)

The arguments for the injunction to help 'backwards' are prima facie purely retrospective, for they appear to limit themselves to statements about the past help that the agent has received. Therefore, the common sense assumption that aged people will not be able to proffer help but only to receive it, coupled with the fact that the explicit reasons offered in justification of the prescription are purely retrospective, provide some evidence that the Navaho moralist presupposes a nonteleological moral principle, the principle of reciprocity.

It is impossible at this juncture to say whether this phenomenon requires that the hypothesis be rejected, and if so, which part is incorrect. This problem will be discussed later. In the meantime, it is worth while to consider possible explanations of this divergence from the suggested pattern of Navaho moral discourse.

First, there is always the possibility that some concealed belief is involved. It has been suggested that the aged are thought by the Navahos to possess extraordinary powers as evidenced by the fact that they have lived so long. It does not, however, seem probable that a moralist would cite the possibility that one's parents might be witches in order to induce the child to help them. (Possibly the fear of ghosts is also relevant.)

Second, there are certainly other arguments that could be offered. Such an argument might appeal to "what people will say," for it is inevitable that neglect of one's parents would cause an unfavorable reaction among the neighbors. However, this argument was not used in any of the statements available to me.

Third, there seems to be some reason to believe that the Navahos accept a fiction that even an infirm aged parent can always do something for his children. The arguments offered tend to assimilate this hard case to the usual argument, that one should help his parents so they will help him back: "No use trying not to do anything for the family and won't get no help" back. (* 6)[15]

Finally, if none of these explanations are accepted, and, of course, they could be tested, the only possible explanation left is a complicated one involving Navaho psychological doctrines. Most Navaho beliefs about people helping each other appear to employ the categorical principle of "like causing like," which implies that if you help someone then this will generally have the reciprocal effect of making him help you back. This reciprocal effect is considered a matter of fact. This is well attested to by the other arguments for helping people mentioned earlier.[16] Hence, given the existence of this belief, it is likely that there is a high expectancy that a child will help his parent back, because, after all, he has received more help from his father or mother than from any one else. The neglect of one's parents is therefore perhaps inconceivable according to Navaho psychological principles.

Consequently, it is possible that a prescription to care for one's parents might be an entirely unnecessary part of the moral code, and in this sense would be similar to a prescription that one ought to sleep with one's wife, or that one ought to eat and sleep. It is not too absurd to assume that prescriptions exist only where there is a presumed likelihood of nonperformance.

However, it is obvious that, at least under contemporary conditions, children do neglect their parents. Perhaps this was not the case when the Navaho moral code was first developed.[17] If the analysis suggested were correct, then in this particular instance, the code is presented with a problem for which it has no answer. It would follow that this prescription "to care for one's parents" is a residual category not only for my hypothesis, but also for the moral code itself! Accordingly, we might have to say that the principle of reciprocity either is not a moral prescription at all, or else that this is one case in which the informant was inconsistent.

3. THE EGOISTIC THESIS

a. Definition of "atomic egoism"

The second main thesis I wish to defend states that all moral prescriptions are ultimately justified by appeal to the personal welfare of the agent. I have called this the "egoistic" thesis. Again, there seems to be a considerable amount of positive evidence in favor of this thesis; namely, the use of such arguments as the following: If you violate that prohibition you will get sick, get into trouble, or people won't like you; whereas if you do what is right you will get rich, people will like you, and you will live a long time.

In order to determine what kind of positive evidence would falsify the egoistic thesis we should first be clear as to what is meant by "egoism." Egoism asserts that the rightness or wrongness of any action depends exclusively upon its effect on the welfare or misfortune of the agent. Therefore, any reference to the well-being of others implies that their well-being will affect that of the agent. (It should be noted that I am employing "egoism" in the technical philosophical sense, and that it has no connotation associated with such notions as the Ego-Ideal. The latter might be called "Egotism.")

Perhaps the most extreme antithesis to egoism is found in the Kantian principle that one should "treat others as ends-in-themselves." This might be labelled "pure altruism." Ethical systems based upon sympathy generally assume some such principle, and it is noteworthy that there is never any appeal to sympathy in Navaho moral discourse. Egoism denies that other people are moral ends-in-themselves.

Another group of ethical systems which I also take to be incompatible with egoism, are those systems which are based upon the conception of a "common good." There are many versions of the doctrine of common good, but they all share the view that the good of the group is an end-in-itself, and in addition they usually maintain that the individual does or should accept the common good as one of his ends. For want of a better name, I shall call these theories *societarian*. Examples are to be found in the ethics of Aristotle, Aquinas, and absolute idealists like Hegel and Green.[18] Many if not most of these theories are egoistic in a broad sense, since they hold that the individual realizes his ends in the common good. In contrast to this societarian type of egoism, the kind of egoism I have in mind might be called "atomic egoism." For convenience I shall use the simple term "egoism" with this restricted meaning.

The full meaning of "atomic egoism" can be understood only after the personal goal of welfare, or misfortune, has been delimited more precisely. Those moralists who espouse this type of theory usually describe their goal in rather concrete terms (for example, hedonistically or materialistically), and it is evident that such states of affairs cannot be shared in any but a metaphorical sense. Only where the goal is described in more 'ideological' terms such as the "common good," can it be shared in the sense that the goals of several agents can be said to be identical or common. Hence, the final clarification of my notion of "egoism" must wait until the goals of morality are examined in the next chapter.

It is characteristic of societarian theories to maintain that the common good has priority over purely personal goods conceived concretely. Therefore, in case of conflicts, the common good ought to be preferred. Furthermore, in justification, an appeal to the common good, irrespective of the individual good, is regarded as sufficient validation of a prescription. This provides us with a possible clue for discovering the acceptance of a societarian system, namely, the prescription of the sacrifice of personal to group interest.

The tests of the egoistic thesis fall into three groups. First, we may try to falsify the egoistic system by looking for positive evidence of the acceptance of a *nonegoistic system;* such evidence might be the existence of prescriptions justified by appeal to the welfare of others which is indifferent or even injurious to that of the agent. Second, the *nonacceptance* of an egoistic system might be shown by the absence of reference, either explicit or concealed, to the agent's welfare, especially in cases in which the agent could not be affected. Finally, the derivation from the egoistic premise of additional prescriptions which are confirmed by the informant will provide some positive evidence for the thesis, although this method is not as reliable as the first two methods, since it cannot be used to falsify the thesis.

A general warning may be given before we proceed. In a natural egoistic morality one should not expect to find explicit mention of the agent him-self in every statement. The enthymemic character of actual discourse implies that where the relevance to the agent's own welfare is obvious it need not be stated. An example will show that this is true even in our own conversa-tion. A doctor who tells you that a certain medicine will cure a sickness, which you happen to have, does not have to say, therefore, that you, the patient, ought to take the medicine. That is understood. All that is neces-sary is to inform you of the general effects of the action on people in general, and you will automatically apply it to your particular case. Hence, the absence of reference to the agent in many items of moral discourse cannot be taken per se to prove the nonacceptance of egoism, for it is quite possible that a reference to the general trouble that a certain action makes may involve the agent as well as others, although this is not explicitly stated and the reference to the agent's welfare is taken for granted.

Two consequences of egoism which are often ignored by ethical theorists may also be pointed out. First, in Western thought the exclusive devotion to promoting one's own welfare is often thought to be incompatible with the welfare of others. It is assumed that the egos are in competition with one another. This belief is, of course, quite foreign to Navaho thought. Conse-quently, there is nothing anomalous in a speaker employing arguments appealing to the self-interest of the listener to induce him to do something which he himself is also obviously interested in. The moralist does not cite his own interest in justification of the prescription, but only that of the agent. The moralist's interest per se is irrelevant to the cogency of the argument.

A second and similar consequence relates to the evaluation of actions, which may be identified with the approval or disapproval of persons other than the agent. Evaluation is also egoistic, since the basis of approval or disapproval is the effect of the action on the welfare of the evaluator. In egoistic systems one cannot be expected to approve of another person's actions on the grounds that they promote that person's interests, but rather on the grounds that the same actions serve one's own interests as well. Prescriptive and evaluative discourse thus have different points of reference, since the prescription and the evaluation of the same action are justified in terms of its consequences for the agent and for the evaluator respectively. However, it follows from Navaho beliefs about the consequences of men's actions, that the same action will be prescribed and valued because it will have good consequences for both parties, or evil consequences for both.[19]

b. Specific tests of this thesis

Several different problematic situations involving self-sacrifice were propounded to the informant in order to ferret out any possible positive evidence of nonegoistic principles.

(1) *Sacrifice in war.* Was it right to run away when in peril? No. Why not? Because the others would get mad and might shoot you. If they were killed and you returned home people wouldn't like it, and they would make fun of you, etc. (* 103) The results of this test provide unambiguous confirmation of the egoistic thesis. Incidentally, the informant included a giveaway statement when he said: "I be glad to shoot some of the enemies as long as they don't shoot me." (* 103)

(2) *Self-sacrifice to save others.* The problem was presented through the story of a South Pole explorer who sacrificed his life in order that the others might have enough to survive (* 108) It is evident from the text that the informant did not clearly grasp the question. Phrases such as the following recur: "I don't think there is anything else a man could do to save himself," and "I don't want to harm myself," and so on. I suggest that his floundering around in answering may be explained by the assumption that self-sacrifice in this sense just didn't make any sense to him. (Incidentally, the example of a South Pole explorer was deliberately chosen because the physical situation would be so entirely different from anything known to the informant, that he would be unable to avoid the problem by thinking of some way of getting around it. Nevertheless, this, in effect, is what he did do.)

(3) *Killing others to save oneself.* Normally, under our conception of "egoism," we should expect that it would justify killing others to save one's own life. The informant thought this was wrong. (* 108–9) His argument is not clear. One statement was to the effect that killing others wouldn't save oneself anyway. I strongly suspected that a concealed belief in ghosts was relevant here, but the informant was reluctant to discuss this aspect. It is notable that this is the only occasion in which ghosts were mentioned during my interviews with him, and he tried to change the subject at once. (He appears to have confirmed my surmise however, although the statements on this are confused.) If this guess is incorrect, we may have to assume a residual principle of "not abandoning others."

(4) *Sharing one's food at the risk of starving.* "Even if I have very little food — not enough to get home with, I give it to the man." (* 71) This statement is prima facie a complete denial of egoism, for one of the conditions was that the agent would probably die. If so it could be another

example of a residual principle of "not abandoning others." However, again the ghost of the unsuccessful supplicant might be a relevant concealed belief. We must not overlook this possibility, which had not occurred to me at the time of questioning. My other informant said that he would keep the food. (* 155) In both accounts, it is interesting to note the attempts to evade the question by telling about other possibilities for food, the use of corn pollen, and so on.

(5) *Suicide*. In our own society, a frequent argument against suicide is consideration for the surviving family. We might therefore ask whether such a nonegoistic appeal is used in Navaho moral discourse. But first it should be noted that the act of suicide is thought to be particularly pernicious, for not only does it deprive the family of one of its members but the ghost is supposed to be even more dangerous than other ghosts.[20] Therefore, if there ever was an occasion on which appeal to the common good would be appropriate, it would be in this case.

The informant's statement of how he would argue with a person contemplating suicide follows the usual pattern of telling him that it would be for his own interest to live right. (* 159–160) The argument amounts to saying: "You'll get over your trouble and everything will be all right." There was no mention of the disasters to be anticipated by the survivors. (Perhaps my informant's type of argument would be the most effective argument in any society, but in our own, at least, a moralist is apt also to appeal to the effect on the family and friends, or to some divine or natural law.)

c. Possible difficulties

The testing of egoism is rendered difficult by the general Navaho presumption that the welfare of others is a necessary condition of one's own welfare. Hence, there are many prescriptions which might appear to be purely altruistic or societarian, but which are ultimately justified on an egoistic basis.

I think that it is quite significant that such a large proportion of the arguments given refer explicitly to the welfare of the agent, and as far as my experience goes, there are none which cite the welfare of others or of the group except when the agent is obviously included in the group.[21]

The examples given above suggest that there may be a residual non-egoistic prescription that one ought not to abandon anyone in extreme circumstances. Evidence for such a covert prescription comes not only from examples (3) and (4) above, but also from other statements, such as the statement that one ought to give money to a poor man, "because I don't like for this man to die for food" (* 69), and that one ought not to give up a man to appease an enemy tribe. (* 106)[22]

This may indeed provide a genuine difficulty for the egoistic thesis. No dogmatic solution is possible without further investigation. Nevertheless, I am inclined to think that this principle of "not abandoning someone" will eventually be shown to be egoistic. There is no doubt that Navaho moral discourse tends to emphasize the undesirable consequences of the performance or nonperformance of an act. It is therefore quite probable that we might often ignore such consequences since we tend to think of the positive rather than the negative ends of action. Furthermore, there are considerations which seem relevant to the Navaho which we might also overlook; for example, the effect of popular disfavor and the purely instrumental value of 'sticking together' when faced by imminent calamities. For, although the Navaho is egoistic in argument, he is constantly aware of his dependence on other people. Finally, the belief in ghosts must not be ignored.

XVII

Moral Goals and Moral Ideals

By the term "goals of morality" I mean those ends by which the actions in the basic prescriptions are designated, and which accordingly are applied in validating argumentation, either explicitly or by reconstruction. Such goals are not to be confused with two other distinct but related conceptions. First, the goals of morality are theoretically distinct from the moral ideal of the good man. As I shall explain presently, moral ideals belong to the order of evaluation rather than prescription. I believe that it is safe to say that the Navaho moral code does not assume 'being a good man' as the ultimate goal of moral activity, although being 'thought to be' may be a derived goal.

Second, the goals of morality should not be identified with those general goals of life which are characteristic of the Navaho culture pattern. There are many values which may be found to determine the actual behavior of Navahos and which are not included among their goals of morality; some of these are, indeed, incompatible with these goals. In addition, many ends are thought to be desirable, although they do not generate moral prescriptions. As I have already suggested, morality often runs counter to the normal tendencies of the people whose conduct it is supposed to direct. The goals of morality are those which *ought to* determine a person's behavior, even though they may not. Furthermore, as I shall argue later, for the Navahos at least, the goals of morality are not relevant to all of a person's behavior but only to a small part of it.

a. Explicit statements of these goals

It is not necessary to repeat in detail the informant's statements in which he mentions the goals of morality; so I shall only list them here.

(1) Avoidance of sickness, of trouble (for example, being hurt), of being laughed at or talked about unfavorably, not being liked, not being helped, not being poor, starving, raggy, and so on.

(2) Attainment of wealth, lots of sheep, horses, jewelry, good clothes,

a good wife and good children (good = helpful), being liked by others, being helped by others, and so on.

(3) Living a long life. (* 94, 115, 145, 163)

It is well-known that Navaho thought places much emphasis on 'living a long life,' or 'dying of old age.' Father Berard Haile has pointed out that there is a belief that if a person is one "whom old age has killed," he will go to a sort of "old age home" rather than to ghostland like others who die earlier. In other words, old people do not become ghosts when they die. "Nothing was, and still is, more desirable than this great fortune" of dying of old age.[1] This idea is reiterated in the mysterious refrain occurring in ceremonies: "saą naghai, bikeh hozhon" — "long life, happiness," although the precise meaning of this phrase is guarded as a deep esoteric secret. (* 116)

It appears that the desirability of 'living a long life' is based neither on the thought that death per se is evil, nor on the thought that per se it is good to be old. Evidence against such possible grounds is provided by my informant's reiterated remarks to the effect that he was getting too old and would like to die. (* 95, 99, 100, 102) The desirability of a long life in effect means the undesirability of dying before old age.

b. Reconstructive analysis

I should like to make two suggestions about these goals: that they are nonsubjectivistically defined; and that they are essentially negative.

All the goals listed share the characteristic of being publicly observable; that is, their attainment or nonattainment can be observed and known by other people without having to reply upon the reports of the person concerned. Anyone can see whether someone is wealthy, healthy, and has friends.

At one point during the interviews, I raised questions about happiness, which was my interpreter's translation of baa hozhon. Literally, these words mean: "general surrounding conditions are good (nice, pretty, pleasant) to him." This already suggests that happiness in this sense is not something internal or private to the person involved. It "would mean a group of people where they all are laughing, smiling." Moreover, it appears that it is not up to the person himself to decide whether he is happy, but to those around him. (* 28) In other words, the Navaho conception of "happiness" is essentially behavioristic!

There is plenty of evidence that the Navahos tend to look at things objectively, or, in a sense behavioristically, rather than subjectively as some of our Western hedonistic egoists tend to do.[2] Hence, it would not be feasible to describe the Navaho moral code as hedonistic. Although the various words for "good," "beauty," "happy," etymologically are all related to a root which has a strong hedonistic flavor,[3] I suggest that all of them refer to conditions that are publicly observable.

For these reasons, therefore, it seems to be evident that the goals of morality are objectively defined in terms of publicly observable states of the agent, and are described in concrete terms such as health, wealth, good reputation, being happy, and so on.

My second contention is that, despite the suggestion of a positive hedonic tinge just mentioned, the specific goals of the Navaho moral code, as contrasted with other culturally derived values, are negative. That is, it is my contention that not only are the negative goals paramount, but also that the positive ones are ultimately reducible to negative goals. To explain this theory, I shall try to show first the intimate logical relationship between the positive and negative ends in Navaho moral discourse.

The positivity or negativity of the goals listed reveals that they are conceived of as 'privative correlatives.' By this term, I mean a pair of opposites such that the one is identical with the absence of the other. "Light" and "darkness" are such privative correlative terms, since "darkness" means the "absence of light," and "light" means the "absence of darkness." It seems that all the items in the list of goals given above can be transformed from positive to negative, or vice versa, by adding a *not*. In other words, for each goal-term the correlative positive (or negative) term is privative. Thus, health is the absence of sickness, and prosperity is the absence of poverty. Being laughed at and not being laughed at, being helped and not being helped form similar pairs.

To bring out the peculiarity of these Navaho goals interpreted as privative correlatives, we may contrast them with pairs of positive and negative goals which are not privative correlatives in Western thought. For us, pain is not identified with the mere absence of pleasure, nor is pleasure the same as the privation of pain; ordinarily, "good" is not synonymous with the "absence of evil", nor is good considered to be just the absence of evil; again, virtue and vice are not privative correlatives.

The contention that in Navaho these pairs are privative correlatives receives some confirmation in the structure of the language. Thus, the word for "bad" is "not good," and for "wrong" is "not right." [4]

A possible exception to this interpretation is provided by the pairs, "good" and "hard" feeling, and "being liked" and "being disliked." However, I believe if the relevant passages in the field notes are consulted, it will be evident that "good feeling" is assumed to be equivalent to "no hard feeling" and "being disliked" is regarded as synonymous with "not being liked." [5]

If it be granted that all terms referring to the goals given above can be transformed into their opposite by the addition of a *not*, and that they are therefore privative correlatives, then we may ask: Which formulation is more basic — that in terms of the good to be sought or that in terms of the evil to be avoided?

The problem can be illustrated by referring to the doctrines of good and evil advanced by classical Christian theologians. Augustine and Aquinas maintained that evil is the privation of good. Therefore, they held that everything that exists is ipso facto good, although some things might also be evil by virtue of the fact that they are goods which are privations of a greater good.[6]

We may therefore speculate on whether the Navaho moralist assumes evil to be the privation of good, or good to be the privation of evil. I do not know whether an objective test of this could be devised, but I suspect that the goal of Navaho morality is negative, in the sense that all moral prescriptions require actions ultimately aimed at eliminating and preventing evil. The basic rationale of all their ethical arguments is: If you do or don't do such and such this evil might happen to you, you will get sick, starve, have to wear raggy clothes, have no friends, and so on. The main evidence for this suggestion is to be found in the preponderance of arguments in which the pernicious results of nonperformance are stressed, rather than the beneficial effects to be gained.

c. Speculations on the negativity of Navaho ethics

The thesis that the goals of morality are essentially negative by no means implies that all the goals of Navaho life are negative. Quite the contrary is probably the case. The negativity of moral goals merely shows that the sphere of morally relevant actions is restricted to a much greater extent than it is in the artificial moralities of an Aristotle, a Bentham, or a Dewey. It is a limited morality since in the ultimate analysis it restricts itself to telling a person certain specific things he ought not to do, and does not pretend to offer directives for the whole course of life.

If this negativity is distasteful to the reader, it is perfectly simple to show how the whole moral system may be interpreted as a limited morality in a positive sense. Suppose that we call the end of life for everyone "well-being," then morality is concerned only with prescribing some of the necessary conditions of well-being. In effect, it prohibits those actions which are sufficient to make the attainment of well-being impossible, and it enjoins those actions necessary to attain it. (See the paradigm of the relation of negative and positive prescriptions given in Chapter IX, section 2(d).) Every action that is not subject to one or other of these basic types of prescriptions is permitted and optional.

Therefore, the moral code is negative because its only purpose is to rule out those actions which would make life in general impossible, such as sickness, hard feeling among men, or poverty. As long as he follows the prescriptions of the code, theoretically a person is free to choose any kind of a life he wishes.

This notion of a "limited morality" is foreign to our own ethical tradition, although undoubtedly it is widely accepted in practical life. Since Plato, most philosophical moralists have sought to provide a guide for every single voluntary action of a person, although the degree of stringency attaching to the various prescriptions varies from absolute requiredness to a thin kind of desirability. The combination of an unlimited jurisdiction of morality with a wide latitude of choice was earlier stated to be characteristic of an ethics of direction, which is an ethics of positive goals. On the other hand, a limited morality with less choice was held to characterize an ethics of constraint. I suggest that the Navaho ethical system belongs in the latter category.[7]

d. Kluckhohn's conception of "harmony" [8]

These speculations are confirmed by Kluckhohn's thesis that the clue to the configuration of Navaho culture is the notion of harmony. Of course, his analysis is at a much higher level of abstraction since it is concerned with the implicit pattern of culture, and not just the pattern of the ideal aspect of overt culture. Nevertheless, it can be applied in the following suggestive way to these speculations about the moral code.

First, an analysis of the meaning of "harmony" will reveal that to some extent it is a privative term, meaning the absence of disharmony. In the moral life, those conditions which are disharmonious are the negative ends to be averted by moral action.

However, in addition to the privative aspect, "harmony" carries with it a positive connotation connected with 'beauty' and 'happiness' — or as Father Berard Haile would say, "pleasant conditions." These are the positive goals of enjoying life which are not the special concern of the Navaho moralist. So it will be seen that the conception of "harmony" includes the negative goals of morality, and goes beyond them to the positive goals of life in general.

In contrast to the "harmony" conception, one of the basic formulas for safety is "avoid excesses!" I believe that the concrete interpretation of this formula is evident in many of the moral prescriptions which I have discussed — for example, "don't become too rich or too poor." According to the Navaho theory, extremes in most situations tend to be dangerous. The principle appears to be essentially negative.

It is interesting to contrast the Navaho formula with Aristotle's golden mean: "an intermediate between excess and defect" or "that which is neither too much nor too little." [9] The Greek maxim stresses not only the avoidance of excess, but also the positive pursuit of goods so that there will be no deficiency of desires and feelings, for it is characteristic of the Greek view of life to value the fullness of self-expression. A glance at Aristotle's list of virtues will prove this positive aim of the complete life. Navaho morality, in contrast, is mainly concerned with the avoidance of hurtful actions and there is no positive demand for the realization of the various potentialities of appetite and passion which we find in Aristotle. These are no concern of the Navaho moralist — the individual is completely free to satisfy or not to satisfy any desire that he has as long as it does not conflict with the demands of the code, which in turn concerns only those actions which are *necessary* conditions of the agent's own private welfare.

In effect, the Navaho moral code says: "You may do anything you please, as long as you don't do anything stupid which will result in depriving you of the necessary conditions of life!" Aristotle's maxim, on the other hand, says: "Let your every action be guided by the golden mean." Thus it covers the whole of practical life and being an ethics of direction does not recognize an area of indifferent actions (except possibly those which are not causally significant). The differences between these two ethical systems brings out well the contrast between a negative ethics of constraint and a positive ethics of direction.

2. EGOISM AND ALTRUISM

One of the most interesting aspects of the reconstructed Navaho code of morality is the light that it throws on the relations between egoism and altruism. Western moralists have generally assumed that egoism and altruism are incompatible; and therefore, that one of them must be rejected. Sometimes the rejection of egoism has been grounded on the supposition that it conflicts with altruism, which it is thought should be retained at all costs. Conversely, Nietzsche held that altruism was fallacious because it was inconsistent with egoism.

According to the Navaho ethical system which I have outlined, it is impossible to be a good egoist without at the same time being a good altruist. Although all the moral prescriptions listed are ultimately based upon an egoistic premise, in content they are altruistic. Furthermore, as I shall presently show, the basis of Navaho evaluation of conduct is also egoistic.

a. The derivation of altruistic prescriptions

The compatibility of egoism and altruism is a consequence of two facts: that there are no egoistically based moral prescriptions of actions which could conflict with the interest of others; and that there are many egoistic prescriptions which require altruistic action.

The basic factual belief which unites egoistic premises with altruistic conclusions is that the welfare of each individual is dependent upon that of every other individual in the group. What is good for the individual is good for everyone else, and what is good for everybody is good for the individual.

I need mention only a few of these prescriptions since all of them have already been discussed in detail.

First, there is the group of prescriptions demanding altruistic actions. Among these would be the avoidance of trouble-making and the avoidance of having people 'talk about' one; also included are the injunctions to help others. All of these prescriptions which involve altruistic actions towards others, are egoistically grounded by means of the factual belief that if you treat others 'kindly,' they will treat you 'kindly' in return, and if you treat them 'roughly,' they will treat you 'roughly.' In other words, they exemplify the categorical principle of like produces like.[10]

Second, there are prescriptions which do not refer explicitly to the welfare of others but which are thought to affect it. The violation of a taboo will bring sickness not only to the violator but also will bring trouble to others; conversely, by holding a Sing one is not only doing oneself good, but benefiting others as well. Similarly, in working hard and becoming rich, advantages accrue not only to the agent but also to all those around him. These beliefs reflect the categorial principle of general effects.[11]

The most striking illustration of this form of 'altruistic egoism' is found in the Navaho economic 'theory,' which denies that there is a scarcity of goods which would lead to competition between men, and affirms positively that by becoming rich one is aiding others.[12]

b. The evaluation of actions

It will be recalled that I discussed previously at some length the notion of "evaluation" and contrasted it with that of "prescription."[13] An evaluative statement is one that is not primarily intended to influence the agent to do an action, but instead reflects the reaction of a nonagent to the action; that is, of 'judges,' 'spectators,' or 'patients.' Two other characteristics of evaluation as opposed to prescription may be repeated. First, there may be evaluation of *past* actions, whereas prescriptive statements usually apply only to future actions performable by the agent. Second, evaluative statements tend to be less definite and precise than prescriptive statements, for the very reason that the latter if accepted will tend to have practical effects, whereas the former may not. It will be recalled that this is one of the considerations which led me to adopt the approach to an ethical system through an examination of the prescriptive statements rather than the evaluative statements of informants.

The implications of the reconstructed Navaho moral code for the analysis of evaluative statements are extremely interesting, and throw a good deal of light on the relation between evaluation and egoism. I believe that it is safe to say that there is no conception of an 'impartial' moral judgment of another's actions. Every evaluation reflects the evaluator's interest in the actual past or anticipated effects of the action on him personally. Hence, evaluation can be given an egoistic analysis in much the same manner as prescription. In effect, the grounds for evaluation are something like: "That is bad, because it will bring trouble (to me)," or "that is good, because it will help (me)." [14]

Nevertheless, although the grounds of evaluation are egoistic, the contents of the evaluations are the same as those of prescriptions. An action which is positively prescribed is also positively evaluated, and one which is negatively prescribed is negatively evaluated. The obvious reason for this complete coincidence of evaluation and prescription is that moral prescriptions are altruistic by derivation, as was pointed out above.

A consequence of this distinction is the separation of the *ideal* of the good man, which is an evaluative conception, from the *goals* of the moral life, which are involved in prescription. Actually, the statement of an ideal, according to this system, is a composite of evaluation and justification for it. For instance, a "man is good because he doesn't make trouble." My interpreter suggested that whenever you said that a man was good, you had also to say *why* (* 173), and the reasons cited are the beneficial consequences of his actions for others — usually obviously including the speaker!

It follows that the 'ideal' cannot be cited as an 'end of morality,' since the only reason for doing those actions which others judge good is because they are means to one's own egoistic goals. This provides an interesting contrast with some Western ethical systems, in which the goal of morality is set forth as the fulfillment of the evaluative ideal — for example, moral perfection. Nevertheless, although the evaluative ideal of others does not establish an ultimate goal for one's own moral conduct, it is extremely relevant because one ought to do those actions which bring popular approval, and avoid those which will be disapproved — for purely prudentialist reasons.[15]

3. COMPARISON OF THE RECONSTRUCTED CODE WITH WESTERN EGOISTIC ETHICS

In lieu of a summary of the hypothetical reconstruction of the Navaho moral code, I shall compare this system briefly with the moral codes propounded by three Western philosophers who may be called "atomic egoists"; Epicurus, Hobbes, and Spinoza. The points of resemblance and of difference are illuminating. (The reader should be warned that the following comments do not pretend to be historically accurate interpretations of these authors.)

This comparison will probably raise the immediate objection that there is no sense in comparing a thinker from a non-literate society with a sophisticated Western philosopher. In the first place, it might be argued that since the Navaho system rests upon obviously false factual beliefs, such as those about the causes of sickness, we should not take it seriously. But the same objection could be raised against a philosopher like Hobbes, for surely his view of human nature is also false, and perhaps some of the important factual premises employed by Epicurus and Spinoza are false, too. Furthermore, there is no need to discuss the objection against comparing sophisticated philosophies with ideologies of ordinary men especially primitive ones. My answer is simple, namely, that the comparison is between specific moral codes, and does not involve any philosophical ethical theories which are invented to explain them.

a. Epicurus

According to Epicurus, who was an egoistic hedonist, all actions in the end should be chosen with a view to their production of happiness for the agent. This involves referring all choice and avoidance "to the health of the body and the soul's freedom from disturbance . . . for it is to obtain this end that we always act, namely, to avoid pain and fear." [16] The conditions of happiness are health and friends, and the immunity that results from retirement from the world. Old age is good, but taking public office will just make trouble for you. Possessions may be worth while because "it is easy to distribute them so as to win the gratitude of neighbours," etc.

Epicurus's attitude towards laws is interesting because he recognizes the problem of why you should obey them if you will not be caught, and he solves the dilemma just as my Navaho informant does by stating that there is always a chance that you will be caught.

These points bring out the striking similarities between the views of Epicurus and those of my Navaho informant. The differences are due to the subjectivistic orientation of Epicurus. This appears not only in his use of hedonic expressions for the goal of morality, but also in his view that the principal means to its attainment are to be found in self-restraint and self-discipline, rather than in promoting a favorable material and social environment.

b. Hobbes

The more activist approach and the objectivistic formulation of goals of the Navaho moralist suggests immediately certain similarities to Hobbes, another atomic egoist. The Navaho and Hobbes are both essentially materialists, and consequently they agree in describing their goals in objective or publicly observable terms. In fact, even the lists of goals presented by both are almost identical. Hobbes at one point says that men are motivated by the desires for gain, for safety, and for reputation, and in another place, he catalogues the powers sought as including the eminence of mind and body, and "riches, reputation, friends, and the secret working of God, which men call luck." [17] Since the Navahos lived in a state of nature before the advent of American governmental authorities, we can compare the principles of action formulated for a stateless society in the two ethical systems.

The obvious point at which the Navaho moralist and Hobbes diverge is in their view of the economy of goods. For Hobbes there is a scarcity, and men must compete for them. Hence, man in a state of nature is "solitary, poor, nasty, brutish, and short," and there is a *bellum omnium contra omnes*. The Navaho holds the opposite economic theory, namely, that there is an abundance of goods and that no man is in competition with another. Instead of fighting to attain these materialistic goals, men must help each other.

A second point of difference is the conception of the role of coercion in social life. Hobbes obviously thought that men could be made to behave themselves through the threat of punishment in civil society and through the fear of death in a state of nature. As we have seen, the Navaho believes that coercion is neither necessary nor sufficient to secure right conduct. It is not necessary because there is no scarcity of goods.

It is almost safe to say that the reconstructed moral code which I have presented is identical with Hobbes's theory except for these differences in psychological and economic 'theory.'

c. Spinoza

A third philosophical egoist, who departs from Hobbes in the respect just mentioned, is Spinoza, who writes: "Men in so far as they live in obedience to reason, necessarily live always in harmony one with another," for "Nothing is more useful to man than man". He goes on to observe that it is only because men are not reasonable that they are "troublesome one to another." [18] This statement is equivalent to one by my informant: "He knows what he is doing, so he has no hard feeling against anyone." (* 40) There are many other analogies between Spinoza's egoism and Navaho ethics (for example, the emphasis on the unreasonableness of anger), which it is not necessary to discuss here.

Nevertheless, although Spinoza's ethics is like the reconstructed Navaho code in the way in which it derives altruism from egoism, they differ radically in their 'theories of knowledge'; Spinoza is an a priori rationalist, whereas the Navaho moralist might be called a "pragmatic empiricist." In this respect, the Navaho is closer to Epicurus and Hobbes.

d. Basic dissimilarities

The foregoing brief comparisons suggest that we could rather crudely describe the reconstructed Navaho code as the Hobbesian ethical system modified by an Epicurean psychology and a Spinozistic sociology!

There is one important difference, however, between all three of these Western systems and that of the Navaho, namely, that the latter is still a limited morality and does not claim direction of all choice and action. I attributed this characterisitc to the negative quality of the goals of morality in the system. The three Westerners appear to present a fundamentally positive goal of morality, and consequently their prescriptions cover any possible action — at least in principle. (There might be some doubt about Hobbes or Epicurus.)

There is another difference of emphasis in the statements of all three Western philosophers which is not to be found in those of the Navaho moralist. This is the characteristic Western tendency to seek to derive ultimate basic prescriptions from psychological theories about the motivation of all human beings. Thus, the egoistic hedonist attempts to vindicate his principle in terms of psychological hedonism, etc. All three philosophers discussed mix psychology with their ethics not only in order to show what consequences are to be anticipated from one's actions, for the Navaho also does this, but also in order to establish the basic egoistic prescription itself. This difference of emphasis may be partially explained by the fact that in the West an egoist is on the defensive, and feels impelled to find some ground for his principles, whereas I assume that for the Navaho egoism is accepted as a matter of course. The Navaho moralist is not obliged to vindicate the basic prescription of his code, as these Western philosophers are.

These Western ethical systems thus confuse the issue (or the reader!) by not always clearly separating their doctrines of how men *actually will* behave from how they *ought* to. In the terminology I have been using, this amounts to not distinguishing between the psychological statement: "All men desire such and such an object" (for example, happiness), and the moral prescription, "Do all those actions which will promote that object." The psychological statement may indeed describe the ground-motive of the system, but it is only related to morality by means of a prescription, and should be clearly distinguished from it. The application of the basic moral prescription depends on intelligence and knowledge. In this the Navaho agrees with the three Western philosophers. Only by means of the distinction between intelligence and stupidity can the necessity for having the moralist point out what one should do be explained. A man who does not use his reason will neither fulfill the basic prescription, nor satisfy his desire for the basic goal of life (for the Western philosophers) and of morality for the Navaho. The fallacy of supposing that one can derive the basic moral principle from a general psychological principle claiming to explain all human actions is not as tempting for the Navaho with a limited morality as it is for those moralists who wish to claim all possible actions as their jurisdiction.

Nevertheless, all of these ethical egoists, Western and Navaho, ultimately stress the use of reason as necessary and generally sufficient to attain the egoistic ends of morality. In this sense, they may all be called *prudentialists*.

XVIII

Conclusion

If we wish to judge the adequacy of the foregoing account of Navaho ethics, we must ask three kinds of questions concerning it: (a) Are the data reliable and valid? (b) Do they support the hypothesis? and Has the hypothesis been sufficiently tested? (c) Is the general approach and methodology acceptable? It is obvious that any hypothesis in descriptive ethics, whether it be of Navaho, Hopi, or Bantu ethics, must satisfy these requirements.

Only if the answer to each of these questions is affirmative should one feel bound to accept the present hypothesis. With respect to these criteria, I do not wish to assume dogmatically that the hypothesis offered is completely satisfactory, or the only possible one. To repeat what was said earlier — the entire undertaking should be treated as problematic and exploratory in intent. However, I shall examine briefly the theory of Navaho ethics offered here from the point of view of each of these three questions in turn.

a. Reliability of the data

It must be admitted that there are passages in the field notes which are unreliable. These arise in part from the obvious difficulties of working with an interpreter. There is no reason to believe that the interpreter's report always accurately reflected what was said by the informant. Not only was there frequent misunderstanding by the interpreter as well as by the informant of the questions which I posed, but undoubtedly I also misinterpreted the answers as I received them. The process of translation itself is beset with hazards. It is also evident that at times the interpreter forgot what the informant had said, since the procedure we followed was to allow the informant to talk for several minutes at a time and then to translate.

Nevertheless, I am fairly well convinced that for the most part the statements recorded are a reasonably adequate rendition of the informant's views. I believe this partly because of the context of the other statements accompanying them, and partly because I find nothing in them which is incompatible with information obtained by other field workers; in fact, most of the significant statements are confirmed in other sources.

A perhaps more obvious difficulty with the present account is that it may not be valid for Navaho society in general, since it is based on the statements of very few informants. I have already commented on this subject and so it is unnecessary to repeat what I have said earlier.[1]

b. *The adequacy of the hypothesis*

If it is granted that the data are sufficiently reliable, we may ask whether they can all be explained by the hypothesis which has been offered. I have indicated that there may be doubt about what I have called "possible residual principles."

In examining the tests for the reconstructive hypothesis, we encountered two cases which appeared not to fit into the basic pattern propounded.[2] They were called the "principle of reciprocal obligation" and the "principle of not abandoning anyone in dire need." If these should be found to represent irreducible elements in the informant's discourse, they raise perplexing problems for the whole theory. I do not know what the solution is. Even if the second can be explained (for example, in terms of a concealed belief in ghosts), we still have to explain the first, which is more difficult.

If we were to suppose that no explanation of this possible residual principle in terms of factual beliefs will be found, then several possibilities lie before us. We may attribute such disconfirmation to an error in any one of several different parts of the theory:

(*a*) The analysis of the basic egoistic prescription may be unsound;
(*b*) The mode of validation may not be applicational;
(*c*) The informant's ethical opinions may be ultimately inconsistent;
(*d*) The statements involving this principle may not be statements of moral prescriptions but of some other kind of prescription; or, as I suggested earlier, they may not be prescriptive at all.

I call attention to these apparent discrepancies in order to show how any such seemingly inexplicable data affect a general hypothesis as a whole. If the theory of descriptive ethics offered in this book is accepted, we must scrupulously look for all the possible negative evidence, and explore the possible ways of modifying an hypothesis to account for it. However, any modification itself must be checked anew — for we must be careful not to resort to constructing *ad hoc* hypotheses. In other words, we should not be content to accept some one of these modifications because it sounds plausible; instead we must take pains to verify it in turn. (I did not have enough time in the field to explore any of these alternative hypotheses which might have explained the apparent discrepancies. I may also remark here that many more and varied tests of the other subhypotheses must be made before one could accept the hypothesis as satisfactorily confirmed.)

c. Other possible approaches

It should be obvious that the acceptability of the hypothesis which I have proposed depends not only on the data and adequacy of the hypotheses formulated to explain them, but on the wider question of what criterion of "ethics" is to be used, and what methods are to be followed. For those familiar with the literature on Navaho culture, it must be evident that I have included under Navaho ethics various facts which often have not previously been regarded as ethical, and that I have excluded other aspects of Navaho life which have sometimes been treated under the term "ethics."

Unfortunately, there are some experts who are not always aware of the criterion by which they categorize one aspect of Navaho life as ethical and other aspects as nonethical. The easiest way to find out what implicit criterion is being employed is to ask: *What kind of evidence is assumed by the investigator to be relevant to a determination of the informant's ethics?* The approach which I have followed stipulates that the informant's ethical discourse, that is, discourse involving moral prescriptions, is the only kind of evidence admissible. Obviously, anyone who introduces evidence other than this is employing a different criterion from mine, and his conclusions will necessarily diverge from those I have reached. To illustrate this I shall mention briefly some of the consequences of using other types of evidence.

(1) *Evidence from actual behavior.* It is easy and tempting to make inferences about a person's ethics from observing his actual conduct. Accordingly, there are many descriptions of Navaho moral principles which are based on such evidence — or at least partially so. For instance, this implicit use of a behavioral (or partially behavioral) criterion often results in the view that among the Navahos illicit sexual relations, stealing, or lying, are not considered wrong as they are in our society. On the other hand, observation of their conduct towards relatives might lead one to conclude that Navaho ethics particularly emphasizes familial obligations. The use of this behavioral criterion would have the consequence of making the traditional practices the largest part of the moral code since they are closer to actual conduct than the prescriptions I have considered to be moral.[3]

(2) *Evidence from public approval or disapproval.* Again, the use of this type of evidence will lead to somewhat different conclusions from those I have drawn. As I have argued earlier, public approval or disapproval is a very general and vague notion, and so a description of an ethical system based on them will be much more general than the one I have offered. Navaho evaluations of action do not have the quality of legitimacy which I

have stipulated as being necessary for a moral judgment. Consequently, they may reflect personal feeling towards the agent, and in general they tend to be more superficial and less rational than ethical discourse proper. Moreover, such evaluations are frequently made on the basis of expectations rather than on the basis of moral prescriptions. That is, if a person does not act as he is expected to, he incurs disapproval — even though the action in question is not morally prescribed. So again, if we use the criterion of social approval or disapproval, we should have to include many of what I have called "traditional practices," as well as all of what would normally be considered etiquette.

An even more radical difference which would emerge from the use of evaluations rather than prescriptions would be that the fundamentally egoistic interpretation of Navaho ethics would probably have to be abandoned for a more generally utilitarian interpretation, since the evaluation of actions is in general based on their beneficial social consequences.

(3) *Evidence from mythology and ceremonials.* A few writers who have mentioned Navaho ethics, have been inclined to use a theological or supernatural criterion of ethics. This type of authoritarian bias is exemplified in the adducing of evidence from the esoteric myths and ceremonials. If evidence for Navaho ethics is sought in their religious doctrines, it is obvious that a completely different description from the present one will result; for, if this criterion is used with any degree of strictness, moral prescriptions would be limited to conduct during Sings, and a very few other circumstances.[4]

(4) *The use of Western ethics as criterion.* There are quite a few otherwise valuable accounts of Navaho ethical ideas which use a classification based upon distinctions accepted in Western culture. Thus, we find lists which divide Navaho prescriptions into groups corresponding to similar prescriptions accepted or rejected by us, such as crimes, ethics, etiquette, and superstitions. The consequence is that many prescriptions are classified as mere matters of etiquette (or even superstitions) because they would be such for us, while the Navahos may regard them as moral prescriptions with the highest stringency.

A more subtle variant of this approach is the tendency to regard as 'ethical' those prescriptions which are connected with social relations and function to promote social stability. This assumption that ethics must be concerned with our conduct towards our neighbors — as it is for the most part in our culture — has the consequence of eliminating from the Navaho moral code all the prescriptions relating to animals, food, and inanimate objects. At the same time, it exaggerates the ethical importance of those familial obligations which I have classified as traditional practices.

(5) *The use of a normative criterion: one's own ethics.* Perhaps the least

ambiguous and most forthright approach is the one which denies that the Navahos have any ethics in our sense of the term. As I have indicated earlier, this is a perfectly legitimate use of the term of "ethics," for it corresponds to an analogous sense of "scientific," according to which we should deny that the Navahos have any science.[5]

The advantage of adopting this approach is that one does not delude himself into believing that the Navahos think as we do about moral problems. Accordingly, one of the foremost authorities on the Navahos is unquestionably right when he writes:

> Even today this system is not concerned with the ethics of an action, excepting if we equate ethics with transgressions of tabus and restrictions . . . Such basic concepts as conscience, duty, responsibility, right and wrong, sin and virtue, reward and punishment, morality, law, and a host of other concepts do not enter Navaho ideology.[6]

Father Berard Haile's statement should warn us against using such expressions as "ethics," or "moral standards," too glibly when talking about Navaho culture. But whether or not we use the term "ethics," I should contend that there is a code of conduct (tabus and restrictions) which does have a highly consistent and coherent character, and which partakes of the properties earlier advanced as characteristic of what I have called "ethical discourse."

In conclusion, I should like to reiterate that those criteria which have been employed by others, but which differ from those used in the present inquiry, are by no means illegitimate. They may be extremely useful for certain projects. My only point is that the present hypothesis is based on a rather narrow and constricted methodology — and it must be evaluated in those terms. (And, I should add, that on philosophical grounds I think that the criterion I have proposed is preferable to the other criteria I have examined.)

d. Comparison with Brandt's procedures

In order to bring out the significance of the theoretical questions discussed in the first two parts of this book, I shall consider briefly some of the differences between the approach which I have adopted in investigating the ethics of the Navahos and that adopted by Professor Richard Brandt, another philosopher, in his study of Hopi ethics.[7]

To begin with, it is a well established fact that the culture of the Hopi is fundamentally different from that of the Navahos. Certain obvious differences are that, in contrast to the Navahos, the Hopi belong to the pueblo group, their language belongs to a different group, their social system emphasizes status differences, and their religious ceremonials are concerned primarily with producing rainfall.[8] From the point of view of descriptive ethics it may also be important to note that it has been contended that the Hopi have a 'guilt culture' whereas the Navahos have a 'shame culture.' [9]

Nevertheless, there are a few striking similarities between some of the statements made by Brandt's informants and mine. Among these are the disapproval of aggression, the insistence on not "forcing anybody to do anything" (p. 224), the distaste for dealing with the dead (p. 232), clan exogamy, running practice, the belief in sorcery, the emphasis on the idea "to live to be old," "avoiding trouble," and so on. In all likelihood some of these similarities are the result of cultural diffusion, since they are to be found among other Southwestern Indian societies.

Granted that there are fundamental differences and similarities between the Hopi and the Navaho cultures, the interesting question is: If I had employed Brandt's procedures, would I have reached the conclusions about Navaho ethics presented in this book? I seriously doubt this, for I am convinced that in writing on the ethics of the Hopi, Brandt is describing something quite different from what I have intended to describe here. There are three main points of difference which may be mentioned.

First, Brandt selected his informants on a different basis. He was more interested in discovering the ethical conviction of the average Hopi than in the type of intensive analysis of one informant's ethical discourse which I have undertaken. In effect, he describes the views of the man of action rather than the moralist.[10] From this fact alone, we should expect that the ethical ideas which he expounds would be less systematic and rationalistic than those which I have described. It is perfectly in accord with my theory that the man of action would not be able to give detailed reasons for his ethical convictions, and this seems to be one of the conclusions which Brandt reached after interviewing his informants. Undoubtedly, the Navaho layman would be similarly hard put to give a specific justification of many moral prescriptions. It would be interesting to know whether a Hopi moralist would subscribe to a more systematic body of ethical convictions.

The second important difference between our procedures concerns the definition of "ethics." Here again Brandt was interested in investigating a much wider group of phenomena than I was; for he considers attitudes towards such things as voluntary acts, motives, traits of character, aspirations, and so on, to be part of his informant's ethics (pp. 55ff.). Thus he includes what I have called "moral evaluations," and perhaps even "traditional practices," as well as moral prescriptions under the subject matter of ethics. In fact the ethical system is studied from the point of view of evaluation rather than exclusively that of prescription. Thus the book reflects a spectator rather than the agent approach to ethics.[11] There are certain interesting logical consequences of adopting this approach; for instance, if no sharp distinction is made between the arguments for prescriptions and those for evaluations, the egoistic interpretation of each would be rendered implausible, and my distinction between ideals and goals of morality would become unintelligible.[12]

There are two other aspects of Brandt's criteria of "ethics" which differentiate his procedures from my own. The methodology which is entailed by employing the notion of attitude as a "disposition for ethical affective reaction" (p. 62), requires that the evidence which can be obtained will be only indirect, since the explicit statements of the informants can function only as indirect evidence for the existence of such ethical reactions. In contrast, I regard such ethical statements as direct evidence for my hypothesis.[13] Methodologically, Brandt's criterion also allows him to use other types of evidence, that I would not admit, as "symptoms of emotional concern," such as actual Hopi conduct, guilt feelings, punishment, and so on (pp. 159, 161). Thus, Brandt's account gives much more of the 'flesh and blood' of an ethical system, but at the expense of the type of logical rigor and objective verifiability which I have sought to obtain by restricting "ethics" to ethical discourse.

Again, by refusing to recognize an affective reaction (or attitude) as ethical "unless it has a further property — unless it is disinterested" Brandt may have excluded by definition the type of egoistic analysis which I have offered of Navaho ethics. At least the requirement of disinterestedness would eliminate many of the arguments which I have regarded as ethical. Accordingly, many of the reasons for obeying moral prescriptions given by Hopi informants, which are like those of Navahos upon which my own analysis is founded, are dismissed as "supporting beliefs." [14] Here, however, it may be the case that Hopi ethics really does include the concept of impartiality, which I found to be absent in Navaho ethics.[15]

Finally, a glance at the types of specific ethical convictions which are examined and the problems presented to the informants shows that much of Brandt's study of Hopi ethics consists of a cross-cultural investigation of the extent to which the Hopi accept principles like our own. This is an important undertaking, and it may have considerable philosophical value, but I am concerned with presenting the Navaho ethical system as it appears to the Navaho moralist informant. Consequently, Brandt uses a Western classification of moral principles to order his findings, while I attempt to reconstruct a Navaho classification. A further consequence is that Brandt pays less attention to the taboos and supporting factual, including religious, beliefs than I have.

I hope that one point will become clear from this brief discussion, namely, that there are philosophical issues to be faced by anyone attempting to investigate the ethics of a non-literate society, and that there are many different kinds of analyses which are possible. I should also like to add this warning: many of those with whom I have discussed my hypothesis that Navaho ethics is prudentialist, and in a sense egoistic, have expressed the opinion that every ethical system must be of this character; Brandt's book should prove that such a view cannot be accepted as a matter of course, since according to his analysis, the ethics of the Hopi is not egoistic. Whether or not there are other ethical systems in addition to that of the Navahos which are prudentialist is a matter for empirical investigation and cannot be decided by a priori intuition.

2. THE FUNCTION OF A MORAL CODE

It has been my contention throughout this book that a person's "ethics" or "moral code" can be *defined* independently of any function it may serve, of any of its social or psychological consequences, or of any extrinsic causal factors determining its content and structure. Hence, the investigation of the extrinsic relations and functions it may have are not a part of descriptive ethics. However, it is hoped that the methods propounded here will perhaps help in such inquiries; for by providing an independent criterion of "ethical" it will be possible to investigate such interrelations of the moral code with other aspects of social and cultural life without any danger of arguing in a circle. For instance, if a moral code does not by definition have a certain social function, then the statement that it performs one no longer is trivially true by definition but a significant addition to the store of knowledge.

We may do well to distinguish at the outset between the 'manifest' and 'latent functions' of a moral code.[16] The manifest purpose of the Navaho moral system, which a Navaho would say it is to fulfill, is to show people how to "live a long life, not to be poor," etc. Obviously, the explicit function of any moral code will be defined by what that code conceives to be the "good life." Perhaps more generally we could say that its purpose is to provide people with reasons for acting which are superior and legitimate.

The latent function of moral codes is more complicated. I shall assume with Merton that this term stands for the objective consequences of the institution in question, which in turn tend to satisfy some requirement such as social survival, social equilibrium, or satisfaction of biological needs. For our purposes, it is sufficient to consider the latent function of a moral code in terms of its objective consequences.

a. For the individual

It is evident that a moral code is supposed to have an actual effect upon the individual's conduct and discourse (including his emotional attitudes). That ethical convictions do not always have this effect is obvious. The degree to which the prescriptions of the code do determine an agent's actions or forbearances (as well as his emotional reactions) I have termed its "operational efficacy."

Here we are concerned with the operational efficacy of a moral code for the man of action, or the average person in the society. Hence, the investigation of it would be partly a matter of statistical research. I may point out some of the subtleties that must not be overlooked.

The operational efficacy of a moral code varies in several dimensions. First, there may be certain parts of the code which are accepted while others are rejected. For instance, many Navahos nowadays no longer conform to the mother-in-law taboo. This should not be taken to indicate that they have or are likely to give up the more general aspects of the code.

It would be an interesting subject for inquiries about the process of acculturation to determine which elements of the code are relinquished first, and which remain almost to the end. One might suspect from the character of the reconstructed Navaho ethical system that it would be the basic prescription and modes of justification and validation which would be the most stable. Whether or not this is true could be investigated.

Some evidence of the reluctance to give up the basic prescription of materialistic prudentialism is given by the following statement made by a Navaho informant who was interviewed about missionary activities:

But when we went further, and he [i.e. the missionary] started telling the Indians again that he didn't think it was good to have sheep, jewelry, bracelets, all of that — and some kinds of jobs too herding, and farming — they had to quit that and only go to church, and believe in Jesus. After I heard all these things I began to dislike it again. About making me forget Navaho religion, not to have sheep, farming, not to do my own work . . . so I just quit.[17]

Second, we must always bear in mind that the fact that a person does not conform in his overt conduct to certain moral prescriptions by no means can be considered to prove that he does not accept them. As I have already said many times, moral principles may be more honored in the breach than in the observance. Some objective test of the acceptance (as opposed to the fulfillment) of a prescription needs to be formulated. In this connection, the situational factors may be important determinants of the actual behavioral efficacy of moral prescriptions; for example, the presence of temptations to violate them, the behavior of others, and so on.

Third, the operational efficacy of a moral code has an additional dimension; namely, the emotional reactions which it arouses. These secondary effects have been extensively studied by psychologists, and particularly psychoanalysts. The various emotional attitudes, as well as the presence of unconscious psychoanalytic mechanisms such as guilt and shame, need to be more closely correlated with the explicit ethical convictions of the subject. It is clear that psychoanalysis itself cannot entirely ignore descrip-

tive ethics, since such phenomena as that of 'rationalization' themselves presuppose the acceptance of certain moral principles.

I have called attention to these various dimensions of operational efficacy
merely to bring out the fact that the acceptance of a moral code may manifest itself in many ways other than overt behavior. Since there is so much
possible variation in operational efficacy, it is natural to inquire, Why do
people accept certain moral standards and not others, and why do they
accept moral standards at all?

A thoroughgoing investigation of the properties of a moral code which
make it acceptable to an individual or group would be most illuminating. It
would explain, for instance, why some ethical systems spread quickly
whereas others die stillborn, and it would explain why people can be easily
converted to one system, whereas they are left untouched by the appeals of
other systems. This again would be relevant for anthropological studies of
acculturation.

Not only is it necessary to explain the peculiar characteristics of a moral
code which determine its operational efficacy, but the more general question
as to why man formulates and accepts moral codes at all may be asked here.
It may be that as a 'rational' or 'symbol-using' animal he needs to have
some general scheme to guide him in his conduct.[18]

It seems plausible to suppose that both the appeal of specific codes and
the general prevalence of moral codes may be explained in terms of their
satisfying certain basic human needs. But clearly much further empirical
analysis is required before such a statement can be construed as any more
than a verbal reformulation of the facts to be explained.

b. For society

Most functionalists are primarily concerned with the consequences of an
institution such as the moral code, for social relations, and social order in
general. If we are careful to avoid making this function a matter of definition
of a moral code, we will be forced to recognize that the effects of the acceptance of a code are subtle and complex.

To begin with, it should be obvious that a prerequisite to a moral code's
having any social consequences whatsoever is that it have a modicum of
operational efficacy among a sizable number of the members of that society.
If we grant that the reconstructed Navaho code is operationally efficacious
in this minimum sense, we can see that it is an open question to what extent
it contributes to the stability of Navaho society. That it does is indisputable,
but whether it is among the most important factors is certainly open to
question.

In this connection, I should like to point out that there are many other
factors in Navaho life which probably make a greater contribution to social

equilibrium and welfare than does the moral code as such. For instance, the practice of mutual help among relatives or of present-giving are undoubtedly potent factors which hold the society together. But these traditional practices are not the subject of moral prescriptions in my sense, although they surely have a greater effect on actual conduct than many moral prescriptions.

Furthermore, we must be ready to acknowledge that certain moral prescriptions may be dysfunctional or at least nonfunctional. Thus, for instance, it is hard to conceive of any positive function served by burying the dead with immense amounts of jewelry — as is morally prescribed. (Undoubtedly, someone will have invented an *ad hoc* function!) Certainly today many moral prescriptions are no longer functional even if they were once.

Nevertheless, even if not all the consequences of the Navaho moral code are functional, there are many which are. Among these the most effectual are unquestionably those taboos relating to incest (in the nuclear family), and those relating to witchcraft.[19]

3. DETERMINANTS OF THE CONTENT OF A MORAL CODE

In the last section we examined some of the issues involving the objective consequences of the acceptance of a moral code. Now we may review briefly some of the problems involved in the identification of causal factors which determine the content of the code. For instance, it might be eventually established that every moral code contains prescriptions of a certain sort, such as incest prohibitions, and so we might look for an explanation of this. On the other hand, we can ask for the explanation of the peculiar content of a particular code, for example, why the Navahos believe that eating fish is wrong.

The distinction made earlier between explanation and justification is relevant to these issues.[20] It will be recalled that an explanatory reason is the cause of a phenomenon attributed to it by the anthropologist, whereas the justifying reason is that given by the informant. Undoubtedly, there are many situations where the justifying reason is the best explanation of a person's acceptance of a prescription; for example, if a Navaho says that he should plant corn in a certain way to get the best harvest, his purpose and reason is perhaps the best explanation of why he accepts and fulfills the prescriptions, and past experience may account for its content. On the other hand, it is possible to give causal explanations of certain prescriptions of which the informant might be totally unaware. At present we are concerned with this latter type of explanation. Some of the explanatory theories which are available would attribute the content of a moral code to childhood training, family and kinship systems, economic and technological conditions, social functions, geographical distribution, language, and so on.

There is obviously no simple explanation of either the generic outlines of all moral codes, or of the particular content of any one of them; such as that of the Navahos. It may be advisable to divide up the content of moral codes into separate aspects which could then be accounted for differently. Accordingly, we might seek for explanations of (*a*) the prescriptions it contains, (*b*) its structure and general features, and (*c*) the particular arguments offered by it. To illustrate this procedure, I should like to offer a few suggestions.

With respect to the prescriptions contained in a moral code, we should seek an explanation of those which are to be found in every code, and of those specific to any particular code. There seems to be some plausibility to the assumption that every code contains moral prescriptions relating to such subjects as sex, family responsibilities, murder, stealing, and lying. (Whether this assumption is correct has, of course, not yet been established.) If this be granted, perhaps a functionalist account would be tenable. With respect to the particular content of the code, again, a functionalist explanation of some of its special prescriptions may be possible; for example, regulations against overeating or prohibitions of killing certain animals when they may serve some useful function. However, it is obvious that it would be difficult to account for every prescription in this manner.

When we come to explain the structure of a moral code, we must again divide the question into two parts: an explanation of the structural characteristics of codes in general, and an explanation of those characteristics peculiar to any particular code. The theory offered in Part II reduced the essential structure of a moral code to its bare skeleton and this leaves not much to be explained over and beyond the fact that there are moral prescriptions which are superior and legitimate. Granted that there are codes in every culture in this restricted sense, it may be that we shall have to account for this fact by a general theory of human nature. Perhaps psychology will also help in this venture.

The specific structure of a particular moral code may depend to a large extent on the structure of the language in which it is formulated. The intimate relationship between categories of thought and linguistic structure has received some attention, and I suspect that many of the peculiar characteristics of Navaho ethical thinking can be explained in these terms.[21] In addition, of course, the configuration of the culture, or the cultural pattern as exemplified in other aspects of the people's life may be extremely significant in this connection.

Finally, the explanation of the particular arguments offered by the moralist poses a new set of problems. Why does the argument against looking at one's mother-in-law cite going blind as a consequence? Why not some other mishap? Or why is it sickness? Why not punishment in the next life?

Certainly, part of the content of the Navaho code can be explained by certain characteristic thought-patterns; such as the general tendency to predict sickness for violating moral prescriptions. If this is the thought-pattern which the justifications of the most stringent moral prescriptions follow, we should expect a thinker who ponders other principles to link up the violation of them with sickness. Thus, some details may be accounted for by a desire for logical consistency, and the attractiveness of analogical reasoning.

Unquestionably, however, much of the particular content must be explained historically. Some of it probably comes from cultural diffusion of one kind or another, and some of it probably arose by accidental circumstances; for instance, perhaps someone who had eaten a fish actually did get sick — and so the prescription was formulated to avoid the same consequence in the future.

This hasty outline is given mainly for the purpose of calling the reader's attention to the complexity of issues involved in explaining the content of a moral code. Anthropologists are generally aware of the subtleties involved, but many philosophers are prone to accept an oversimple anthropological theory without being aware that things are not as simple as they seem.

In conclusion, I should confess that with respect to these problems I am an unregenerate pluralist. It seems obvious to me that no single all-encompassing theory would be sufficient to explain the complex content of a moral code.

4. DESCRIPTIVE RELATIVISM

Anthropologists and philosophers alike have been interested in the bearing of the study of the ethics of non-literate societies on the problem of relativism. There are so many different doctrines referred to by this label that we must make some distinctions before it is possible to examine the relevance of the present inquiry to the problems involved.

In general, the doctrine of relativism maintains that values (and moral standards) are relative to the society (and culture) in which one lives. We may begin by asking: What is it that is relative? In connection with ethics there are two possible answers: that the ethical *convictions* and accompanying beliefs are relative; and that the *rightness* or *wrongness* of particular lines of conduct are relative. Questions concerning a person's ethical convictions belong to descriptive ethics. Hence, I shall call the type of relativism involving them *descriptive relativism*. On the other hand, problems relating to the rightness and wrongness of actions are the subject matter of normative ethics. Accordingly, the view that such actual rightness and wrongness is relative will be called *normative relativism*.

It is obvious that descriptive relativism does not entail normative relativism, nor does normative relativism entail descriptive relativism, for the fact that someone thinks an action to be wrong does not make it so, nor does the fact that it is wrong make a person think it to be such. The identification of these two types of relativism presupposes the doctrine of that mad fictitious philosopher, Hamlet, who said: "There is nothing either good or bad but thinking makes it so." This principle itself, however, must be justified in some way or other, and some reason must be given for making such an identification in ethics but not in other spheres of discourse.[22] I shall return to the relevance of descriptive ethics for normative ethics presently.

Relativism, in the descriptive sense, generally consists of two separate theses: (a) that all ethical convictions are causally dependent upon certain contextual conditions which determine their character; and (b) that there is an irreducible diversity of moral standards. Although the second thesis does not logically depend upon the first, it is often thought that it is a corollary of it.

a. Causal dependence and descriptive relativism

One form of descriptive relativism identifies the relativity of ethical convictions with their causal dependence on such factors as culture, psychological conditioning, or economic modes of production. It is argued that if there is this kind of causal dependence, the character of a moral code will inevitably be determined by the conditioning factors, and will in this sense be relative to them. Examples of this view would be cultural determinism and economic determinism.

It would be absurd to assert that such factors do not act as causal determinants of the acceptance as well as of the content of a moral code. In the preceding section, I suggested what some of these factors might be. However, the thesis of the cultural determinist and other relativists of this type is stronger than this; for they are not content merely to affirm that there are causal connections, but they also wish to deny that other factors besides those they mention are operative. This one-sided form of determinism has been called *monistic determinism*. A cultural determinist in this sense would have to deny that rational considerations play any part in the determination of the character of a moral code.

Here the distinction between the man of action and the thinker must be brought into the picture. Undoubtedly, the ethical opinions of the average man are dependent to a large extent on what he has accepted without question from those around him. In this sense they may be almost completely culturally determined. The thinker, on the other hand, may inject the element of rationality as a new determinant when he interprets the same materials.

It may be countered that the thinker himself is determined to follow certain lines of thinking because he is brought up in a particular culture; here, for instance, a linguistic determinist might offer additional evidence. It must be admitted that no one can think unless he has taken over certain elements of his culture. This is a trivial truth — for even an anthropologist or physicist in our own civilization must be educated and indeed, brought up in a certain disciplinary tradition. But although such cultural conditions are necessary for thinking, they are not sufficient to account for it. Culture provides the training and materials for thinking, but cannot of itself produce that thinking or completely determine all of its products.

Many theorists are so preoccupied with the importance of some single causal factor which they have discovered, that they overlook the fact that if it were the only determinant of thinking their own theories would *ipso facto* be nullified. Thus, relativism in the sense of social or cultural determinism is self-destructive.

This by no means entails that we must reject determinism as such. Quite the contrary, for the special types of determinism are themselves indeterministic inasmuch as they deny the causal efficacy of other kinds of events! A complete determinist would have to admit that thinking itself has effects just as other events do.[23]

In short, the admission that other extraneous factors play an important part in determining a person's thoughts, always necessary and sometimes sufficient, by no means entails that human reason itself cannot at times be efficacious. Otherwise, I should think that it would be impossible to account for the rational elements in moral codes like the reconstructed Navaho code.

b. Universals

Often associated with cultural determinism is the view that every culture has its unique pattern, so that no one of its elements can be abstracted from it and compared with elements of other cultures. From this it is inferred that there are no universal categories of culture. As an a priori principle derived from an idealistic metaphysics or coherence theory of culture, this doctrine cannot be refuted by appealing to the evidence. But assuming that such apriorism has no place in our inquiry, we must look at the empirical evidence to see whether or not there are such universals. I shall confine the discussion to descriptive ethics, and shall ignore other possible universal categories such as needs, institutions, or values.[24]

It should be evident from the description of Navaho ethics that a large part of any moral code must be unique to the cultural tradition in which it is developed. In particular, the relevant factual beliefs, basic prescriptions, modes of validation and principles of justification may be expected to differ from one system to another.

Perhaps there are certain moral prescriptions derived within the code which may be found to be accepted in every culture (for example, incest). But the whole approach followed in this study has emphasized the importance of treating the moral code as a whole, since I have assumed that we cannot describe an ethical system without including the arguments as well as the specific prescriptions. This would seem to imply that there is an almost irreducible diversity of moral codes. Certainly, as a methodological principle, it is better to postulate a diversity of outlook on ethical questions in order to avoid an ethnocentric interpretation of the data.

However, the recognition of the extreme diversity of moral systems does not imply that there are no universal aspects of moral codes. The theory I have offered suggests that every system identifies moral prescriptions in a certain manner, and that they all utilize the basic logical schema of validation, and so on. Perhaps further work in descriptive ethics will uncover other universal elements.

In this sense, Kluckhohn has expressed the most plausible position when he writes: "In a certain deep sense the logic (i.e., the *manner* of interpreting relationships between phenomena) of all members of the human species is the same. It is the premises that are different. Moreover, the premises are learned as part of a cultural tradition." [25]

5. NORMATIVE RELATIVISM

This is the doctrine that the rightness or wrongness of actions is entirely relative to such circumstances as the culture or social group of the agent. Let us consider briefly the relevance of descriptive ethics to this doctrine.

a. The argumentum ex consensu and ex dissensu gentium

We may begin by examining the view that normative relativism can be deduced from descriptive relativism. It has sometimes been supposed that the universal *acceptability* of a certain ethical principle depends upon whether or not it is actually universally *accepted*. Thus, it has been argued that a certain action is right or wrong because it is always and everywhere thought to be so. On the other hand, it has been contended that no action is absolutely right or wrong because there is no universal agreement about moral principles. This assumption has begotten a furious controversy over the issue whether or not there are moral principles which are universally accepted.

This form of argument is called the *argumentum ex consensu* or *ex dissensu gentium*. In its most notorious form it has often been used to justify belief in God. Characteristically, when the facts seem to belie the universality of such a belief, they are 'fixed up' so that they will; everyone is said to implicitly believe in God even though he may not be aware of the belief. Similarly, in ethics there has been a tendency to employ the same type of *ad hoc* assumption to 'fix up' the facts to prove the universal acceptance of a moral principle which its author wishes to promote. Some proponents of the Natural Law doctrine have been especially guilty in this respect.

However, if we adhere rigorously to the definition of "ethical system" offered here, we can determine with some degree of exactitude and objectivity whether or not such universal agreement does exist.[26]

But what does universal acceptance or its absence prove? It can only be utilized in a valid argument through the postulation of the intermediate premise that an action is right (or wrong) if and only if the prescription in question is generally accepted. In addition to the arguments against Hamlet's statement cited above, there are two specific arguments against the use of the *argumentum ex consensu gentium*.

The first objection against the argument from universal acceptance is that it has the logical consequence that any critique or reform of accepted ethical systems would be either impossible or wrong since anyone who differed from the accepted view would ipso facto be in the wrong. It would therefore rule out the possibility of individualistic moralists who rebel against the immoralities of social usages. In Nietzsche's words, it would mean subscribing to the "herd morality." [27]

There is a sense in which the *argumentum ex consensu* may be derivatively self-refuting. It seems to me that it is quite likely that no society founds its moral code on the mere fact of acceptance by others. Morality, I suspect, is thought to be grounded in something more solid and less arbitrary than public opinion. Assuming that such a basis would be unanimously rejected by all societies, by universal consent the *argumentum ex consensu* would be rejected also!

In connection with the *argumentum ex consensu*, I have already suggested that it is not the number of voices adduced in support of a belief or ethical statement which count, but rather their quality. It is more reassuring to find that one wise man agrees with you, than that impressive majorities from the herd do. The only agreement which is considered relevant in thoughtful discourse (including ethical discourse) is that of the (ethically) competent.[28]

b. The recognition of relativity in normative ethics

Although the inference of normative relativism from descriptive relativism is fallacious, there is a sense in which probably every moral philosopher admits the relativity of right and wrong. There is, I believe, no philosopher who has maintained that there are hard and fast moral rules, sufficiently specific for practical application, to which everyone must unequivocally conform at every time and place. The particular situation in which the agent finds himself determines to some extent what he ought to do.

This type of relativity, which might be called *applicational relativity,* entails that a certain act which might be wrong in one set of circumstances could be right in other circumstances. Certainly everyone would admit that the conditions of social life in one non-literate society are sufficiently dissimilar from those of our own or of another group so that our specific moral obligations might sometimes be quite different. Even if we should accept as absolute the prohibition of lying, the context in which a misstatement of what is presumed to be a fact might make such an act wrong for one group and not for another. Kant illustrates this by pointing out that the ending of a letter with "your obedient servant" could hardly be considered a wrongful lie, although literally it is a lie. Thus, even the most rigoristic abstract ethics is forced in the ultimate analysis to admit some applicational relativity.

The inevitability of some sort of applicational relativity follows from my earlier analysis of prescripta, according to which I concluded that probably most if not all prescriptions must be formulated in terms of some consequence or other of a bodily movement, symbolic acts, and so on. Since the actual consequences of an act (or interpretation of it) will be determined in part by the culturally conditioned reactions of others, the formulation of any particular concrete moral prescription must take these situational factors into account.[29]

The applicational relativity of particular derived prescriptions does not entail that the basic prescription itself is relative. Basic prescriptions, as such, are regarded as, in some sense or other, universally applicable and universally binding. This follows from the legitimacy required of a moral prescription.[30] Of course, the fact that they may not be recognized and accepted universally is as irrelevant to their universal legitimacy as the fact that many people have thought the earth to be flat is to the truth, that it is round. (The further question of whether others can be persuaded to accept a basic prescription will be discussed below. Again this is irrelevant to its universal legitimacy.)

It has often been supposed that certain ethical doctrines are relativistic in their basic prescriptions as well as with respect to the derivations therefrom. For instance, conventionalism ("When in Rome, do as the Romans do") and egoism are often thought to be irretrievably relativistic. But I submit that here again we have merely other instances of applicational relativity. The conventionalistic basic prescription, "Obey the dictates of your own society!" claims to be universally binding, and it is only the application of it which is relative to the society in which one lives. Similarly, the egoistic principle, "Seek your own welfare," if it is a basic moral prescription, is held to be binding on all men, although the application of it must be different for each individual referent of the prescriptum.

There is no need to mention in more detail these varieties of ethical relativity. However, I should like to point out that the study of the ethics of other societies than our own is of immense practical importance in making us aware of the applicational relativity of moral principles, and especially of the conditions which make it necessary to modify and adapt our own specific moral rules (derived from a basic prescription accepted as universally binding) in order to make them applicable to completely different situations.

Finally, there is another important type of relativity involved in normative ethics which I shall call "relativity of disputability and persuasibility." Many sophisticates who like to call themselves "ethical relativists" employ as an argument for their position the fact that it is futile to argue with another person who is set in his mind about ethical matters. Thus, for instance, it is pointed out that it would be impossible to convince a cannibal that eating human beings was wrong. In this sense, ethical discourse would be relative to cultural conditions. But even granting the futility of arguing about ethics with people of an entirely different persuasion, it should be remembered that this is not only characteristic of ethical discourse but of many other kinds of discourse, too.

I have already discussed the problem of disputability and persuasibility under the topic of ethical competence. There is no doubt that there is a kind of cultural relativity of presumed competence as well as of actual competence, for it is clearly much more difficult to argue convincingly with a person of another culture, whose presuppositions are different from ours, than it is with those who share our general outlook. However, the fact that one cannot persuade a person to a certain view by no means implies that the view itself is not universally valid; in such a situation we still can say that he ought to accept it even though he does not and perhaps never will. (It may be noted in passing that the facts seem to belie a thoroughgoing relativism of disputability and persuadability, for in certain areas the success of missionaries proves that it is easier to persuade others than might a priori seem probable.)

Insofar as the problem of disputability and persuasibility is concerned, the study of descriptive ethics may prove invaluable, since it can help us to discover those basic presuppositions which we share in common with other peoples and so enable us to determine the potentialities as well as the limits of justifying argumentation that is possible with them. For the same reason such inquiries have important practical and political implications as well.

6. RELEVANCE OF DESCRIPTIVE ETHICS TO PHILOSOPHICAL ETHICS

a. Normative ethics

I have already rejected the notion that descriptive ethics can prove or disprove any conclusions reached in normative ethics by using the *argumentum ex consensu* or *dissensu*. However, this by no means implies that there are not many indirect benefits that may accrue from a descriptive study of the ethical systems of other peoples.

I have already pointed out the bearing of descriptive ethics on the problems of arguing with people of different cultures, and of the application of moral principles. In connection with the latter, I should like to make one suggestion. If it is assumed that a basic moral principle is universally binding then in some sense it must be universally applicable in all cultures. Consequently, for any philosopher who undertakes to formulate an ethical system, it would be an interesting exercise, if not a necessary task, to reflect on how the principles he proposes can be applied in totally different cultural situations. The mere attempt to do so might help him to a more precise and clearer formulation of the principles in question.

The acquaintance with completely alien ethical systems provides us with new points of view with which to approach our own ethical problems. The contrast with our own narrowly conceived ideas as well as the discovery of new possibilities will inevitably contribute to "the clarification and subsequent definition of aims [which] is an indispensable part of successful practical deliberation." [31]

For example, the rather neat way in which the Navaho moralist has developed a prudentialist, egoistic, and materialistic ethics might reopen the possibility of a reformulation of this ancient ethical philosophy in ways which might be acceptable to Western philosophical moralists of the present day. Moreover, the Navaho shows us how this can be done without having to resort to some form of hedonism, which may be distasteful because of advances in psychology. Navaho egoism is much more subtle than egoistic hedonism.

The Navaho moral code suggests another possibility which should be considered seriously by those concerned with normative ethics, namely, the advantages of a negative morality with limited jurisdiction. I am not sure how such an ethics could be formulated for our own complex social conditions, but the attempt to do so might open up completely new avenues of approach in normative ethics.

Again, it seems to me that the Navaho moralist (as depicted in this reconstruction) has a much more sophisticated analysis of the relationship between prescription and evaluation than I have encountered in Western philosophical writings. The irreducible difference between the point of view of the agent and that of the patient, as well as the differentation of the goals of moral conduct from the ideal of the good man, suggest a distinction which was new to me.

There are many other insights to be gained from the study of the ethical discourse of my Navaho informant, but this will suffice to illustrate its bearing on normative ethics.

b. Theoretical ethics

The study of the Navaho moral code can also make certain contributions to theoretical or analytical ethics. Contemporary philosophical analysts have talked much of the function of ethical discourse, and perhaps the examples given here may be of use in clarifying this notion.

I should like especially to call attention to one aspect of the Navaho ethical system which might require some modification of contemporary theories about 'reason in ethics.' In an essay which has acquired considerable attention in recent discussions, H. L. A. Hart has shown certain resemblances between our own ethical reasoning and certain types of legal reasoning.[32] In particular he has pointed out that the use of statements that appear to be entirely 'factual' are actually in part 'ascriptive'; for example, the statement that A trespassed on B's property includes the ascription of certain rights to B as a result of the judgment that A had trespassed. Similarly, Hart's view may be interpreted as holding that many of the reasons which are offered in ethical discourse are prima facie factual but covertly ascriptive (or prescriptive). I have already discussed this view under the selective and interpretive modes of validation. This analysis may clarify the nature of ethical reasoning in ordinary English, but I believe that there is no corresponding ascriptive or prescriptive function of factual statements adduced to support a moral prescription in Navaho ethical discourse. (We must, of course, distinguish between these functions and the ordinary requirements of relevance.)

Another contention of Hart's is that the concepts which we employ (for example, "right") are 'defeasible concepts'; that is, it is impossible to specify the necessary and sufficient conditions under which they unequivocally apply. This again is a characteristic which is not to be found in the reconstructed Navaho ethical system; my hypothesis has given in detail such necessary and sufficient conditions for an act's being considered right or wrong in Navaho ethical discourse.[33]

There are many other points emerging from this study which may have a bearing on such subjects as imperativist ethics, the authority of moral judgments, emotive meaning, and so on. Of course, the ordinary language analyst has a face-saving device if he wishes to pass off these cross-cultural facts as irrelevant on the grounds that the Navahos are a primitive people. But by doing so, he admits that his own theory is either trivial or un-empirical.

7. THE ROLE OF THE MORALIST

It may be fitting to conclude this book with some reflections on the role of the moralist as it emerges from the present study of the Navaho moral code. Perhaps we can see 'writ large', as it were, how a moral code operates even in our own society.

A moralist, it will be recalled, is any person who frequently performs the role of advising and exhorting others to moral conduct, and is accepted by the community as especially qualified to do so.[34] Here I should like to call attention to the tremendous gap which separates such men from the average man of action who is the man who is supposed to act morally. There are several ways in which this gap is evident.

First, the moralist is a thinker, for he is the one who reflects and medi-tates on human conduct, and has the knowledge, experience, and wisdom to advise others. He embodies at once the wisdom of experience and the wisdom transmitted to him through the cultural tradition. (He need not therefore be creative or original — in fact, these qualities may be incompatible with his being a true moralist.)

The man of action, on the other hand, is unreflective and takes his moral principles at second hand without knowing exactly what they are or what they are based on.

Second, for the man of action, moral prescriptions are not always the most important considerations governing his daily conduct. Thus, for in-stance, such questions as whether to build a house or get married may occupy a larger part of his attention than the fulfilling of moral injunctions. It has been my thesis that not every practical problem is a moral problem, and if this is granted, it is obvious that most of the time we are concerned with nonmoral tasks. In this sense, moral principles may be of much less significance to us than more practical matters. It is also obvious that moral principles are often disregarded in favor not only of nonmoral interests but also of immoral ones. The moralist, in contrast, teaches that moral principles are most important and of ever present interest. From his point of view, moral matters are salient, while for others they are often, as it were, on the periphery of action.

Third, the moralist is by nature an idealist, for he makes unrealistic demands which he can never expect to be fulfilled *in toto*. What he advises frequently goes against the popular trend, as well as against the normal practices of the man of action. The difference in point of view is illustrated by the Navaho moralist who always advises against 'taking chances,' while the whole cultural pattern of the Navahos encourages the layman (and the divinities!) to 'take chances.' [35]

The moralist is therefore the "voice of one crying in the wilderness." In one sense he is a social deviant, since the rules of conduct which he commends are far from the reality of the pattern of actions of the typical man of the society. Prophets, moral reformers, and all those possessed of moral wisdom are like Nietzsche's 'free spirits' who are far ahead of and above the 'herd,' although paradoxically, as moralists, they are intimately concerned with how it conducts itself.

Thus, the divergence of moral teaching and actual practice is inevitable. We are bound to make 'mistakes' or to 'sin' — and the doctrine of original sin recognizes this fact. Moreover, conceivably such errors follow from the very notion of a moral code rather than from the innate depravity of man or of some flaw in the individual's character. In other words, it is possible that man has neither fallen from a state of perfection, as the myth of the Fall of Man maintains, nor are his imperfections due to eradicable or ineradicable conditions of his environment or personality; instead, it may be the moralist with his dreams of perfection who is responsible for the disparity.

In our own culture we subscribe to the myth that every man is his own moralist. Although from the foregoing we should be able to see 'writ small' within ourselves the dual functions of moralist and man of action, in actuality the distinction between these roles has become lost; or perhaps it would be better to say that the moralist has become submerged in the man of action. There are many interesting consequences of this identification. One of these is our tendency to overlook the need for reflection and experience, which are the conditions of the moralist's wisdom; and to substitute for them a reliance upon intuition and conscience. Another consequence of this identification has been the assimilation of the moral to the practically important. All of us have a propensity to elevate every important practical issue into a moral problem, and to sanctify every significant choice with a moral quality.

Moreover, our tradition may have obscured for us the actual role which morality performs in daily life. The process of internalizing moral principles has clouded our perception of the true state of things by rationalizations and other mechanisms by which we pretend to ourselves and others that our every action is determined by moral principles. We fondly expect ourselves and others always to do what is right and not to do what is wrong, and when our expectations are not fulfilled we are surprised (and angry)! The furore caused by the publication of the Kinsey reports attests to this. Our system, whatever be its other merits, thus tends to beget hypocrisy and self-deception.

In this way the true purpose of a moral code; namely, to prescribe for conduct, has been overshadowed by various secondary functions which have perhaps more effect on us than its primary function. Thus, for instance, moral judgments are too often used to express feelings of aggression towards ourselves in the form of guilt feelings or towards others in the form of moral indignation, and the fact that they also tell us what to do or not to do is quite overlooked.

From the picture of the 'primitive moralist' given here we can once more see that morality is not the whole of life, that violations are normal, and that the chief function of moral principles is to advise us how to act rather than to punish us afterwards. As the wise old Navaho moralist, Bidaga, said:

But we always make mistakes. You're going to get mistake next few minutes or tomorrow — a little — but you don't know where mistake is. You just run into it. Or somebody puts you into it. By taking your own care you think you're good care of yourself. You don't want to lie somebody — but you get into that just the same. (* 100)

APPENDIX

Field Notes

The importance of providing a verbatim record of my interviews with Navaho informants is obvious. The only editing has been the omission of irrelevant passages and names. Otherwise, the text contains the exact words of the interpreters as they were spoken to me. But the choice of English expressions as well as the way my questions were understood or misunderstood may themselves be significant.

The following text has been divided into numbered sections for convenient reference. The material enclosed in brackets are my own comments and questions asked of the informant. The latter have sometimes been abbreviated. The words in parentheses are amplifications given by the interpreter to explain some of the informant's original statements.

There are eight day-long sessions with Bidaga, and two with another 'medicine man,' John Hawk. Finally, there are a few comments made on 'ethical expressions' by interpreter Bill Begay. An excerpt from an earlier interview with Bidaga by Kluckhohn is the only material not obtained during December and January, 1951–52. (For details on the informants, see Chapter X, section 3.)

I employed three different interpreters: Eddie Mario, Bill Begay, and Robert Baca. It should be clear from the text that their ways of translating differed somewhat. (All these names, except that of Bidaga, are standard pseudonyms used by the Comparative Values Project of the Laboratory of Social Relations, Harvard University.)

I am indebted to Professor Richard Brandt for some of the questions asked, and some of the problem situations which were used.

1936 (From Clyde Kluckhohn's field notes; later published in Kluckhohn, 1945)

1. What I tell is true. My father always told me to tell the truth. It's all wrong to lie. My father said not to lie or steal. Don't touch anybody else's rope or anything. Try not to think about stealing. Behave. Don't try to catch girls. I never did. Don't gamble or you'll forget other things. Don't drink, my father said, or you'll spend all your money. Even if I had lots of sheep, it wouldn't last long if I drank. My father said: 'Take care of yourself. Have good horses, bridle, saddle blankets so I could go anywhere to a

sing without being ashamed!' Without good clothes you couldn't go anywhere where there were lots of people. Might get ashamed where they had
good times . . . I know now my father was right.

INTERVIEWS WITH BIDAGA

December 19, 1951 (Interpreter: Eddie Mario)

2. [Tell me about the old ways of life.]
This is a whole lot different from what old people have been teaching.
Old people used to have little leather whips about 1–2′ long, and used to
carry it around all the time. Used to wake up all their children at dawn and
used to take all their clothes off — all they had on was moccasins and a pair
of shorts — and used to run for miles — 2 or 3 — every morning and even
in winter times — weather made no difference. Old people used to make
young people roll in snow and same time have to run.

Other ways — if there's a lake in winter have to break through ice and
go through ice into water. That was part of their teaching of how to make
younger men to be brave — to face anything coming to them. Himself
didn't do it. [Omission.] Reason why old people did these things was because
they used to have they used to get into fights with Pueblo Indians or
Mexicans. That's why they were teaching all their young men to be on
the alert — so they won't get scared. That's the main reason.

They only had bows and arrows, and some rifles too.

3. [What should be taught to young people now since there are not
these dangers any more?]
Said what he said before, not just to get ready to fight but contingent
[*sic*] upon working around the house or doing the farming just by themselves. That was the way they used to teach their children. This all covers
that even if they are moved separate from the family, so they could do it
by themselves. To be tough. But nowadays all these people aren't teaching
children that way or how to live. He knows that there isn't any more of
the older men he had seen or heard him talking to the people like the old
days. He said himself he still remembers some of the old things. But he
hasn't teached nobody like that but once in a while he says a few things.

[What were some of the things they said to the people?]
Said about three different things they mostly talk about to their
younger children: [1] About farming. If they farmed they could get some
food out of that and food for the horse. [2] The sheep — that if you take
care of your herd pretty good — grazing around so they could be fat so
they won't have hard time through the winter. Gets their meat out of the
sheep and the gold for the blankets and clothing out of wool. [3] The
horse — that's mostly for transportation. They were told to keep their horse
in good shape so they could get to places quicker than with a poor horse.

[What did they say about how they should treat people in their family?]

There wasn't any separate way of teaching their children. They used their own way of teaching them. There wasn't any canned food or flour, but all they had to do was to follow what their old man was teaching them take care of themselves. At that time all their clothes was a buckskin. — boys — tell them to haul wood or water, so if they got married they could Women were teached different ways to take care of the sheep and other different things so they could take corn and grind it for flour, weaving a rug, and so on. This is all what he's telling you is mostly the things the older people had done, but had touched on other things like sewing.

4. [What were some of the things they told children not to do, for example, lying, stealing, fighting?]

His grandparents taught children not to lie or not to steal and not to tell stories about what he didn't see. In old days, they don't know nothing like our whisky, wine. So people didn't talk about that until later when he was a young man that he heard they was talking about that. His father taught him not to steal, lie, buy liquor, and not to do gambling. Other thing that he was told not to do and not to talk about it. Also, that if they don't do anything about gambling — to start betting because they would lose and get nothing out of it.

[Do you think he could remember the other things?]

Another thing. Told not to fight among themselves, but if attacked by other tribes they could do fighting. [Digression on the old way of planting corn.]

5. [What did they do to people who lied, or stole?]

Even if the old people teaching these things to younger people, they still lie and steal — and if they do it and get caught they used to call this fellow back to pay for what he had stolen. He had heard even of some do get killed, the fellow has to pay some money back to family or folks. If one fellow doing a lot of lying, they used to get hold of him and take him to one of the old people where he would get instruction from old person.

[Did they ever bring such people to him for such teaching?]

Some time ago in his early days some of the people brought people to talk to him, and he did two or three different times. He said nowadays it seems no use doing that because young people do nothing but drinking and even older parents don't seem to care how their children are behaving themselves.

6. [Can he remember what he said to one of these people brought to him?]

There's almost two different thing they brought people to him. [1] drinking. He thinks he couldn't be able to talk anybody out of it because they won't listen to him what he try to tell them. [2] Like stealing, lying or being lazy — something like that — in that case he thinks he had talked some of the people. The way he had teached them was starting with the old ways of living of what his grandparents had teached him. Then if a person is lazy or doesn't give help to family he had told this fellow that he wouldn't be able to get anything — not even his clothes by sitting around — he may think he can but there is no chance. If he is out of a family that he tell them why he doesn't understand how his mother had raised him from childhood, and that now he's grown up he should help his mother backward or his father because they spent most of their time raising him when he was a baby. It would be much better even if he could build a fire for them, or hauling water and herding sheep — for them. Also said, that there's no place where he could go, there's no teaching and no one will call on him for help — so no use trying not to do anything for the family and won't get help. If he has a job and doesn't do it, the foreman will fire him. He knows all the white in different tribes go around doing work and if they lose their job — That's the way some of these other fellows are earning their living — everybody.

7. [What does he tell some one who always gets into a fight?]
No difference.

[What would they say about fellows who stole food from other Indians or Mexicans for their family and didn't get caught?]
No chance of getting away with it nowadays. Now if anyone steals they always turn you in to the officers or agency where you might be tried and you'd have to pay a fine or go in jail for it. Because nowadays the only time people steal is when they're drinking, [etc.]

[How was it in the old days?]
That time if several families living close together and one out of that family steals and didn't get caught he just keeps it (steals from people outside those families). One time that he was a leader from here one or two times some other people told him that certain family had stolen things from outside from different ranches and he went over to check up and he gets no answer, and he knows that owner won't get his property back — he just loses it.

[Why did he go? Interpreter: "Was when he was a leader."]

8. [Was this his job as a leader to see that people didn't steal like that?]
He used to get order from superintendent at Crown Point. Before that they didn't have no leaders like that. Superintendent had written a letter to white trader who had store where R—— Trading Co. is now, and this trader had sent word out among Navahos that they were going to have a meeting at the store, and to elect one of their men to be his leader — that was in the summer time. Just few came to the meeting and this white trader told people what the meeting was about. He had mentioned three different

older men he thinks good for head man around here. But all the others didn't agree with him. And later they elect him to be their leader — so they took him. So then he could order his instructions from Crown Point.

[At lunch he said he was 96 years old.]

9. [I asked him whether he was ready to go on. He said that he would go on, though if he were younger he would have a smoke first.

Some whites think smoking is as bad as lying, stealing, drinking, etc. What does he think of that?]

He thinks tobacco and liquor are very different. If you drink looks like you lose your mind and you think of things you never thought of, and you get into trouble. Same with some medicine men he knew that before bootleggers around they used to know what they are doing, and they forget their ceremonies and looks as if they are just playing. He never does that even if he is just doing Blessing Way.

About tobacco, looks like it's better than drinking, because if you smoke it makes you feel better. But its been two years since he had not liked tobacco no more.

[When people drink, don't they feel good? Interpreter: "They just lose their mind."]

10. [About being a leader, did he like being a leader?]

At the time when he was head of these people he like it to be the head of these people. He thinks that all the people minded him what he tells them. He used to go around to all different sections of the people and talked with them. And so then that he knows all his people — how they were living. And maybe it's because that there wasn't much drinking going on around. So there wasn't much trouble then at the time. After when he had moved out of that position some other took their places, quite a few had changed around then. And all these, he thinks, talk to their people the way he used to do.

[What kind of things did he tell his people?]

The main thing he used to talk was about telling his people not to get into trouble — not stealing things from neighbors, at that time there were a lot of Mexicans with lot of sheep, and said that Mexicans were pretty good to them, and if they started stealing things from them it would just make them madder and would make them enemies. So he said all he was trying to do was to make people good neighbors.

[What would he tell them to do if the Mexicans or whites stole from them?]

One time that — it must have been a white rancher that stole horses in the winter time, they didn't see themselves but all they see was the track where they had been driven off. But nobody went after it to follow to catch up with them. So that just happened — they let it go — nobody bothered about it.

[Why did they just let it go?]

At that time they were scared of them. That spring two of that horse must have got away from them and came home. But they didn't know where they drove them off to.

11. [Did he have to settle disputes between Indians themselves?]

Among his people if one of them gets into trouble, they notify him. Any kind, like stealing. That he could go there and discuss it with them at that hogan and straighten it out if he could do that. But some of them do get rough with him so he doesn't bother much with that kind of person, but reports them in to Crown Point or Fort Wingate. Over there they do have an Indian police and they usually come out and arrest the fellows that's kind of rough with him and he takes them into those places and they have their trial there. Others he just takes care of himself here.

Also ever since the government had put up the headquarters for the Navahos there was no white man sent out here to take care of this district over here. That why they were always in behind with anything they wanted to know. Even now there's no white man that could be called upon in a hurry, you still have to go a long ways to find out anything for their problems.

12. [I'm interested in the ones he settled himself. How about one where the people were quarrelling?]

Said that if there is any — things between wife and husband are quarrelling among themselves that a woman would make complaints about a husband that he doesn't treat her right — that he would fight her or get drunk. Or if man doesn't work — he'll just take a woman's things like cash or jewelry — but doesn't get it back for his wife. All these things cause the trouble between man and wife. And said that several times he was told things like this to him, so he usually goes out and call on some other older men that does do a lot of talking that he knows, and ones that leads a good life — two or three of these men get together and go out to these two people and they start discussing about their problems. They talk anything starting with the living [living for the future, long run — *iina*] and their work and it may come up that the couple will agree and they promise that they will live to better life, better living, and he had seen some of them had done it and now they're living pretty good. That was in the past time that he had done.

13. One story two years ago he still knows pretty good. Two years ago last fall one of his sons was married to a woman from A——. They have pretty good setup in own home — nice bunch of sheep, horses, nice place to live and have children. So two years ago they left their home to attend Laguna feast. Underway his son got drunk and fought with his wife and they got to Laguna and there the woman had met her father and stepmother and she told what happened on the way. So she got afraid of her husband and wants to go back with her father to A——. That's what happened. She went back to her relatives and the husband come home by himself. So the

husband come over to him and told him about what had happened. So husband wants his father to go back to the woman's place and talk things over with both families, and wants to get his wife back. So they (husband, he, and two others) four went over from here. And came to woman's family's place. He asked woman why she had left her home. And woman told him on account of her husband that she was afraid of him — that he might get drunk again and beat her up if she comes back. But he told the woman that that was just a little thing that happens. All that she got scared for was because her husband got too drunk. So he told the woman that's no reason why leaving all her sheep, horse, and children back at this other place. That he thinks it wasn't right. The woman still complaining about her husband getting drunk even before fighting going to the feast. So they called her husband what he thinks about his drinking — all were together in the hogan — he doing the talking first. So husband then said he was going to quit drinking — would drink no more. At that time, the woman's father starts telling his daughter that best thing to do was to go back to her husband, for they were making a good living and she was trying to get away from her husband just because her husband got drunk once. And they talked quite a long time there and the wife said she'd come back to her husband. So then they start coming home that same day back to their home where sheep and hogan and children were at. So he thinks that anything like that can be talked over and settled down. And now this family has moved over to A—— where woman's relatives are at. They've been gone for about a year now. Just about a month ago these two people came back to him and told him that they were living pretty good and don't have no quarreling among themselves now.

14. [If a person killed another person by mistake and promised not to do it again, should he be punished just the same?]

It all depends on what kind of person he is. If there is other people knows of this fellow's background — like he had been in trouble all the time and he had not been a good man — they probably put him in jail for that. He heard that some people have been put in jail on account of that they killed other people.

[If he is a good man, should he be let go free?]

If he was a good man and he done anything wrong that was never heard about him before. That everybody would know him that he was a good man, and what he says that most of the people will trust his word — or even if he was been in to trial and told to pay his fines. That he will have a chance of getting help from other people, his friends will help him out to pay his fines and let him out free.

15. [There was once a good old man who was put in jail by mistake and his friends came to let him out, and he didn't want to go because it was wrong (that is, Socrates). What would he do?]

[Interpreter: "Was telling story of what happened that he was told — might almost answer your question."]

Doesn't remember it very well. He said this was about his grandfather. Long time when his grandfather was living just across the railroad at Fort Wingate at that time this old man had three boys. These three boys — one had stolen a horse or mule from their neighbors (white) and this white fellow had reported to Fort Wingate that this old man had stolen his mule. So he was taken to Fort Wingate and he doesn't remember whether he said they had a trial for him or not. But does remember that they put him in jail there, locked him up, and this old man didn't say nothing — just went in there and this old man said while he was in there, these fellows watching the jail noticed that the door was open — closed but not locked (doesn't remember whether six days there) and he was wondering how it was open. So this fellow watching the jail came around to him and searched the old man thinking he might have the key. But old man said himself that he didn't bother the door or touch the door while he was in there. So they closed it up again and locked it. Then it happened three times. And they come around and asked him how he opened the door. But he said he didn't even know what a lock is — didn't use it at home either. So this old man said for the last three days when they come around the door always opened and wasn't locked. He knew it wasn't locked but didn't even go out since he was put in jail. Then old man said that maybe just for that reason they turned him lose. Just let him out. That was his story when he got home. But it was their boys that had stolen the mule from the white neighbor, but white fellow claimed it was the old man that stole it. That's about the only piece he remember the old man telling the family about it.

[Why didn't he leave?]
Didn't care about getting out. Wants to stay there since they put him in jail.

[Did he like it in jail?]
Didn't even like it there, but he stayed there.

[Could he say any more why he stayed there even though he didn't like it?]
He was a pretty good honest man. The way he said when he got home was that it would be just up to the fellows who put him in jail to see when they would let him out instead of running away. Also said that some old people thinks that way — they don't care what they do to them if it comes like that to them.

[A long irrelevant story omitted.]

16. [Tell about another case that he had settled.]
More for all the people around here. Nowadays even if they call a meeting or at any time where the people gather together — that he thinks they don't teach each other the way they used to in his days. When he was elected leader — what he used to do and used to say. Nobody has ever asked him to teach all the younger people the old ways, not even a separate

family; none have called him over and talked to him. Several meetings he had attended around here we have some maybe 4–5 men that are always called upon to be our leader but he has never heard none of them say the kind of teaching like they used to have in the old days. It seems to him that there is 2 or 3 things that should be brought out to the young people every meeting. Mostly about their drinking, stealing, and misbehaving themselves. That's mostly what is causing the trouble around this place. And he said that if there were only one white man that used to be our leader and is interested in helping us out — we could straighten up a lot of little things around here.

[Omission.]

Another thing: same thing he had mentioned about liquor, stealing, and Navaho boys making troubles in any place where there is a little meeting. If they come they always bring their bottle of wine or liquid. They don't settle down and find out what the whole meeting was supposed to be about. He doesn't go to no meetings no more on account of his sight. He thinks that all he's good for now is to stay home and eat.

December 20, 1951 (Interpreter: Eddie Mario)

17. [Does he remember another quarrel he settled?]

There's another one that's about a man named ——— when he was a young man he had a wife and three girls and two boys. Somehow that he has been getting in a fight with his wife — they always quarrelling about something. So not his father-in-law, but his step-mother-in-law (woman's step-mother) that she had tried to take this girl away from this man on account of they always get into an argument about something and this woman claim that this man doesn't take care of his wife and children — that what she was saying and she tried to separate them. So this man came over to him and told him that this woman was trying to take his wife away from him. So he (just himself) went over and talked it over with this woman's relatives. And then he spent much time trying to straighten it out for them. It was this woman's step-mother that she really wanted this man to move off — didn't want him there. But he told this lady that she really doesn't know what she's doing — told the woman that these two people had the children. So he told them that he doesn't see no reason why they had to be separated. Because he know himself that these two people living good and they had children and he told them that he knows that this man could afford to support the children and the wife and he told them that he thinks they couldn't find no other man like this fellow they're trying to move off. So he said that he talked with this woman quite a while to tell her what's going to happen if she separate these (two) couples. And finally this old woman decide that she wouldn't bother these two people any more. So this man and woman got together again and live for quite a while and then the woman died. He didn't know what caused the death. So the man is still living now and the five children still all alive.

18. [Did he get married again?]

No. He didn't get married again. Didn't even leave his children and stayed with his children all the time and living with them.

[Who took care of the children when his wife died?]

Mother died when children were all grown up to big boys — where they can do lots of work for themselves.

[How long ago did this happen?]

Doesn't remember very well when it happened — but it was when the children were young. Now they're all married and have children. About 30 years ago.

[Were these people any relation to him?]

This man's mother and he were in the same clan, and he called her his sister. [Interpreter says: "So, would be cousin? uncle?"]

[Was he especially interested because this man was his cousin?]

Yes, that's one reason and another was that this man had pretty well been behaving himself — didn't make no trouble of any kind.

[Did he talk to the wife, or just to the step-mother?]

Yes, he talked to the woman too, and also the man. He told the woman that because her husband kind of felt that it was all on account of herself that she doesn't tell her husband that she is going some — any — place. So husband thinks she might be going around with other men. So he told her to stay at home and take care of the children.

19. [Did he have any talks with people who fooled around with other people's wives?]

Yes he said he had one problem that he had talked to. That was his own son-in-law. This fellow was pretty good at home — like he does all the outside work for his wife — takes care of the home. Seems like he's pretty good man. But any time he goes to any place where there are people gets together, he used to bother other women even if they're married. So he had talked to this man that he shouldn't go around with other women while he is married and have a good wife. So he had a kind of a do away with what he's been doing. Just about then he died.

[Did he die because he was doing those wrong things?]

What caused the death was one winter that these white traders that were around here used to have a little feast on Christmas day, so one winter they came to this party and it was pretty cold — snow storm — wind blowing. At that day they said that other people had seen him that he was pretty well drunk. So from that next day he got sick. So he figures he must be caused by the liquor. He has been drinking and got a cold at the same time. He doesn't remember whether he was sick for three days and then he dies. They had a medicine man singing on him, but it didn't do any good.

20. [Is it all right for men to go around with other women if it doesn't make trouble?]

He thinks that some people are like that they're bothering other men's wife but still didn't get caught. Those kind of fellows — as long as they don't get caught — they're all right. The trouble comes any time when the woman — the wife — catches the husband bothering other women or the other woman's husband catches the wife going around with the other man that people start talking about it. Some woman and man really hates things like that [that is, philandering].

[It's all right? Interpreter: "Yes, as long as they don't get caught."]

21. [Some people say that if man and woman don't get along together they ought to stay together just the same — what does he think?]

Said that our people that some of them are doing things like that — arguing between themselves — and it's always just on one side that will be making the trouble — be the woman or the man. So sometimes they have to be told not to make any trouble — the one that's doing it. Others they just separate from each other.

[If the husband is a bad man and a bad husband, ought the wife to leave him?]

There's some things like that been happening around that I was talking about. Most time that they have to be talked over the problems of their troubles. Then some of them do get better and they live right. Some others they just separate — some of the man that doesn't — some of the others that they don't care at making a good living, those leave their wife.

22. [Should children help their father even if he's a bad man and doesn't treat them right?]

[Interpreter: "Maybe this isn't answer to your question."] That some of the man's he had known things like that — don't take care of their children. But it would be the children's grandparents that they will be watching them to help them out. So some time they do all right even if their father doesn't take care of them — if they have good grandparents. Some other children do suffer from different things — getting cold or not enough to eat.

23. [What are some of the things children ought to do for their father and mother?]

It's almost all depend on the children — on how you raise them. From time they're young children you talk them of different things or different work — or anything you make a living out of it. If they understand what you've been telling them. That those children will make a good living when they get married. He was just talking about him and his children. He was doing all the talking to his children when they were young, so now he thinks that they will be pretty good children and now that he knows that they are all helping him pretty good — clothing, food, or his transporation. He said that when he goes to different places where the children are living now, they take care of him and treat him right. All the children are not the same. Some of them they just leave their father and mother at the age where they can get around — they just leave their father and mother.

[Did he ever, while leader, have to tell (other people's) children to help their mother and father?]

Said that he used to teach them like that telling them that they ought to take care of their grandparents at that time — at that time he was telling them they would have to do that to all the older people. They usually tell all the youngsters that their mother and father had spent much time raising them when they were babies — telling them that they have been getting all the food from the mother and that had given them the milk — so when their mother and father gets old they should treat them right for all the things they need, like they should haul wood in and keep them in a warm place, if they think he's pretty low on food they should help them out.

24. He said he didn't just only talk to the people around here. One or two times when he was at a meeting at Crown Point that he was called to talk to lot of Navahos over there too, and he tells them the same thing that he tells his people around here. So now he thinks he was about the only man around here that he wasn't afraid to say anything if he was told (by the people) to do so — like teach children or make a speech at a meeting, and he said that now our leaders don't — looks like they're scared or anything that way in front of their people.

[Why does he think they're scared to talk?]

He thinks that these leaders that they probably think to themselves that they won't do much good if they tell their people not to do bad things or to make any trouble, because all their people knows that they're doing the same thing, too. It seems to him if they do say some good things in front of the people and not to do bad things, that some person will say that he's doing the same thing — why not they might as well be the way he is. They will say if the leader does a lot of drinking they might as well do the same thing, too. But he said he never did drink, and everybody knows that he was a good man, when he was a leader, that they been pretty good with him.

25. [Suppose father were a bad man, left his children and went off with another woman — got drunk and was put in jail — should his children pay his fine so he can get out?]

He thinks it all depends on how much the family — if they got enough money or something like that. If they was a poorer family and wouldn't be able to pay the fine and if when the family were pretty well off then that family if they all love their father then they can pay his fine or if they didn't they'll just let him serve in jail.

26. [If son has run away, had a fight with the family, gets drunk and gets put in jail, ought the family to pay the fine?]

He thinks that if boy of the family had done that way, if he had fought with the family and had been gone a long time, and had got into trouble and was put in jail, he doesn't think the family won't be willing to pay his fine, because he had left the family, and the same way when he got into trouble with them. If it was the first trouble he make that would be outside the family in that way the family will be kind of worried about him and pay his fine and get him out.

27. [About not lying. Can he think of any time when it would be all right to lie — for example, to help other people?]

He said it would be probably good for some person but not for others. Like if a person was pretty good and never did lie all his time and if he has to for to be good for other person — it would be kind of hard for him (complicated) to do that, because he probably won't use the direct way that he thinks he could get by with it, he'd probably get caught and get into trouble with the fellow he was trying to do good for him. So to him it looks like it would be better that other person to do the lying that had lied before and had the experience themselves.

28. [Can you ask what a *dine baa hozhon* is? Translated "happy" by the interpreter.]

Would mean a group of people where they all laughing, smiling. Said that if you get back home from here you'll probably not say that you'd not met some of the happy people.

[Why does he think I'll say that?]

It all goes for anybody that if he goes out to places when he gets home his family will ask him what kind of people he had met while he was gone. So if he had seen a lot of good people — happy people — he would tell them. [Interpreter explained that it all depended on what I think of them.]

[Does he think his people are happy?]

He said that at the time when he need to go around to his people often that they used to be pretty friendly with almost everybody, he thinks they are still the same way. They're pretty friendly and still happy. They probably won't say much the first time to strangers but when they get to know them then it will be much different.

[What kind of things make a people happy?]

If a fellow has plenty to eat — that's when they're happy. If a person is starving I don't think he'll be happy. Like now we just had a good dinner and we're willing to talk among ourselves in this room now. So seems to him when a fellow is not starving he's willing to do anything and he'll be happy to do things "when his belly's full!"

[Is the ceremony *hozhonzhi* (Blessing Way) supposed to make people happy?]

Yes, if the ceremony went through all right with no trouble or anything like that then all people will be happy about it, and he thinks the ceremony will do him a lot of good, and he'll be happy about that, too.

[Are good men always happy or can there be good men that are not always happy?]

If he's a good man and pretty well off, like if he had sheep, horses, and family, and also has a father and mother, brothers and sisters — if they all live pretty good without having any trouble with their livestock — they would be happy about it, and if he loses some of his sheep or horses, or even many of their folks — one dies or something like that — they probably be unhappy for a while — will be worrying about that. If everything goes all right he'll be happy most of the time. [Question ignored.]

It all depends what kind of person he will have been — even outside the family (relatives). If he has been a good neighbor and was known with these other folks — these folks will feel sorry if he has passed away or died. He had heard people talking that way if they lose a good friend. They usually say that it's too bad that they had lost their good friend. So even like that person if he wasn't related to him they know he was a good man — they'll be unhappy about it.

[Is the reason why people do things in order to be happy?]

It all depends on what kind of fellow he is that he would be happy all the time. If a fellow does different things at one time and does it right a fellow that studies his own problems and do it the best way he knows, and if he is going to get anything that he thinks he will make good use of it those are the fellows that can do things more easy way than those that don't think much of the things that they are getting. So it all depends on the different person — of the way he handles his problems.

If a person had thought of a problem that he wants to do himself and he works it till he finish with it and he thinks himself that it's done pretty well — then he will be happy about it.

29. [Should you try to be happy?]

He thinks that it couldn't be done. For like a person if he was kind of unhappy all his life and now he is trying to be happy — it seems to him that he had just got into the habit of doing things already so that it would be pretty hard to change it — just like people acts. If he has been a happy man all the time, and now he's trying to be unhappy — cranky — all the time it seems to him that it won't show on him like he's trying to act. Like if he's been happy and tries to be unhappy (unfriendly) it won't show on him.

[Does happiness come to a person like sickness, that is, where he has nothing to do with it?]

Guess it almost depends on your health. If you are pretty well able person that could do things of any kind you would be able to do and happy to do the work, and if a person is crippled in any part of the body and unable to do his work, he will be kind of unhappy most of the time, because he couldn't do things like other persons doing. And if a good able healthy man has a good rest every night that he will be happy to do his work the next day. Other times that people says that they didn't get a good night's sleep, or had bad dreams — lot of dreaming about some of the old people that had died a long time ago. These people they seems unhappy about their bad dreams that they don't willing to do their work the next day.

30. [Does it seem funny that I should ask so many questions about being happy?]

[Laughs.] To him that what I'm asking him seems to him a sensible question for he could give me the answer. To him it doesn't seem funny in no place what I had asked him.

[Is there anything more that he can think of about being happy?]

He thinks that this all goes for anybody — that's living — that we don't all think the same way and we don't all have the same knowledge, or something like that — for the person that thinks more that he could almost get around to anything to where he can make a better living. Those kind of a people can always improve things around his home — like for some people around here some of them are always changing their things which will last them a little longer. People thinks that way are much better off and don't have a hard time with their families. These kind of persons they don't seem to care of how much they sleep — they tend mostly to their belongings, anything that's around. But these other people that don't think much of how to get the things to be done — so that kind of people they're way behind — so he thinks it all depends how the people thinks that makes them happy. Like yourself that you had in mind to come over here to study what I have in mind — that will do a lot of good for you — so if you get the things you had wanted, you will probably be happy about it. So it all depends what different people are doing that will do them good. Maybe that's what you have in mind — that's why you came out this way to study your lesson.

31. [It's hard to be happy now when we're having all the wars. Can he tell us how to stop the wars?]

It's true. But he doesn't know much about it. He was just wondering what the other side are fighting us for. It looks to him like that if a fellow is trying to go to sleep and somebody's teasing him all the time — so he doesn't know nothing about their trouble over there.

[Some people have a new way so that everybody will have something to eat, and they want everybody to do it their way?]

If a person has an idea like that and talks about it, it seems to him that other people won't agree with him to follow his problem.

32. [What does he think about putting people in jail that don't agree with them?]

He thinks that these persons that's making the trouble and going to jail for it is about right for them to go to jail because they will be told or had known themselves that they are doing the wrong things — so he thinks putting them in jail would be the right answer for them. Of where they can find out for themselves — like there that they will be treat pretty rough.

[When bad people are running the government, like our enemies, should you try to get out of jail?]

Around here, among the people, some people they tried to do different things after their own way. Tried to tell their own people to do with them, which is not known to our government headquarters. He said they can say but it's all their own words. But if it is known to these headquarters they will have a law to cover that, like in the old days we used to live here just by ourselves and we used to do anything that we wished, we was to do — there was nothing against us, but nowadays everything is covered by laws. Like before we used to move any place, graze any place, everything was to our own. Now that's all different. So it seems to him that everything has to be right and approved before we can do anything. So he thinks that no bad man can afford to do anything that he'll be willing to do or to get because they'll be punished for it now. That it seems to him that it even goes to different countries, like now where this war is going on, there might be some mistake where the countries won't agree on. So it looks to him where no bad people will have a chance to get away.

33. [After giving him a coke: Does that make him happy?]

That's just like something he had ate, why shouldn't he be happy about it?

January 4, 1952 (Interpreter: Bill Begay)

[In the intervening days, Bidaga had had Ghost Way sung over him.]

34. [Did he settle any troubles where people did stealing?]

Used to be chief way back many years ago, but after he resigned, he is not sure whether he's a — he used to settle that kind of cases at that time. But what he remembers now he says — along the time when he was chief he only settled some small cases — like stealing. This is not heavy cases — just small things which a person steals. Now back in that time, he says, people used to be very quiet and doing their own work. Wasn't any drink among the Indians those days. People used to mind their leaders. Family used to mind their parents. Seems like pretty nice among Navahos — the way they used to live those days. But after I resigned they opened up saloon. That's what I mean they didn't open saloons right after I resigned. It's later after I resigned it happened. People start drinking. All young boys start drinking. The farther ahead they go with it they start making the trouble among themselves — among their own people. And he heard there was a lot of stealing going on. But I never pay attention of these cases, because I got too old, I'm blind and this is the way R—— people are now.

35. [What would be the best way to get people to stop drinking?]

The way he feels about it, it's this way I think about it. As long as R—— people been making trouble, and start to doing many wrong things they've been doing now. There's only one way that I think it might stop. If we have a good strong supervisor, have him live here in R—— town or out ————, and he can take care of the people, and have some Navaho leaders to help him — which I mean Chapter officers and police, and these people can hold a meeting something like once a month, and talk to the R—— people. Have a good interpreter. That might stop it. I don't think there is any other way that people could stop it. The way we are now in R—— we have no chapter officers, and we do have supervisors now in B—— but he is working for ———— and Navaho R—— people, and he only comes out here once in a great while. That doesn't help people very much. For that reason we like to have one here at R—— or at ————. If they do that for us, they can straighten out R—— people.

Like the way they're doing now — for the Navaho leaders they can get together only with the Navahos by themselves. Try to settle up these cases — which they do by drinking — the wrong things — R—— people. They cannot settle these cases — they can settle it that day but they always come back with it. In the other way, when a supervisor lives with us, I think it will be a little stronger.

36. [Why stronger with white supervisor than with Navaho leaders?]
If we had a superintendent living in the middle of us, if he start with his Navaho leaders — start working. Taking up some plans — like a jail house and have police and lock these people up who are doing wrong — or make them pay fine. That could be worked up with white man. Doing by just Navaho people I don't think they could make jail house or make pretty strong police. These plans got to be worked together with white man.

Navaho leaders — that's all they do is to just talk to these people that are doing wrong. They just use talk. Tell all these people not to get drunk, not to steal, not to do wrong things. They've been doing that for several years. Nobody minds that. People getting worser and worser every year.

[Why can't Navahos build the jails, etc.]
These people among themselves — even the leaders they don't mind each other at all. They used to listen together — but now they don't listen to each other any more. So in the other way, I say it might work the other way.

He don't even know who's president, vice-president, and secretary of the chapter now, and that's all that I know my grandson ———— we elected as delegate. ———— used to be delegate. After he resigned he went into drinking with a bunch of boys. That's what he's been doing with the boys. That's what I've been hearing about him.

[If they had a good Navaho leader, could they build a jail and do what a white supervisor would do?]
That's the way I had in mind. If we had a good strong leader among Navahos — had a good education and old enough to be delegate in R——

area. And had a good supervisor — worked together with him — I think this would be worked up all these troubles going on. They can straighten up the people then.

[What could a white supervisor do that a good strong Navaho leader couldn't do?]

White man supervisor, when he wants to take up a plan with a Navaho leader — why the Navaho leader don't think about a plan or two. The supervisor can give the plan or idea to the Navahos. White man always have a paper and pencil to write down, so he look at his paper and he remember what he's talking about. White man can take up one big plan. He might say he want to build a big building. They can do that in a short time. That's the reason I say we need a good supervisor for R—— people.

[Is it harder for a Navaho to put someone in jail than for a white man?]

White man is the man who puts a person in jail harder than Navaho man because the white man got to have a jailhouse in every state and Navaho way if a man puts a man in jail he can't hold a man in jail because we have no papers to fix it up — so we can't hold a man in jail. That's the reason I say a white man should be with us. Right now at this present time, R—— people needs some punishment. There's no one could make up any kind of punishment on these people. That's the reason we have a lot of bad people. There's no man who could stop this — even a leader or delegate.

37. Now I'm getting pretty old, when I used to be a leader, I used to have plenty help to do things. The people who think, who has a good head, and they was pretty good to talk about plans and they minded each other. All these people been died out. These leaders right now they're kind of young, and I don't think they have much idea as to get together and talk things. Because they have no man that could stand up — make speak for the R—— people. All these people they all want to go on one side — drinking and making trouble.

[If Navahos built a jail and could put people in jail, would they not do this because they're afraid of the other Navaho people?]

If Navaho people could do that, and knows how to put people into jail, I think it might work — but it wouldn't help very much.

38. [Some people think drunkards should be whipped, what does he think of that?]

[Laugh.] If only one man that does the drinking and making trouble — they could whip him. It might stop, but right now the way they are doing it, they are pretty close friends — they all get together and do the helping. If they whip one man, then they tell the others, and then they go and beat him (the whipper) up. A few days ago we been having some rain — day and night — my daughter and baby came up to my place in the night. One of my sons-in-law whipped my daughter, that's the reason she came over to my place and stayed the night. That was ——— over near ———'s store. I understand he had a friend to help him doing this — they beat her because they's been drinking too much.

[Some people think a man who steals ought to be whipped instead of jail — can you learn a lesson better by being whipped than by being put in jail?]

Whipping a man, even if you whip him pretty hard — he don't like it — it's just a short hurtness. That's [that is, jail] stronger for him.

[Laughter. Interpreter says: "Doesn't sound very good for me if I whip a grown man, he might whip me back — or next day get someone and beat me up."]

39. [What do you think about what the Mormons teach?]

Can't say very much about Mormons — think they are first located at this place here. Very few of them, and the ones that came into this place here first, don't think they're living any more. When they start living here, they used to farm and listen to each other. He thinks right now lot of young people they don't very well listen to the old ones any more. Just like our Navaho people now.

Mormons they think there's a God — they have a Bible to listen and believe.

40. [Should drinking be up to a person to decide for himself, or should everyone be forbidden to drink?]

About drinking whisky or wine, it's not very good for a man — for a woman. When a man gets too drunk he can start talking to someone or start fighting with the man or woman. That's just for put himself into trouble. When a man is drunk he can do something wrong pretty easy. He don't know what he's doing, even he's whipping his wife or his children. He don't know that he's doing that. When he's sober he can feel sorry about all those troubles that he make up. A man is not drinking or a woman is not drinking — man can go to work and make his living the best way he can — take care of his house, his home, his children, and all his livestock that he owns. He knows what he is doing. So he had no hard feeling against anyone. Now myself, and lot of the women people, want to cut it out. Don't want wine around. Lot of young boys — they just whipping their wife, brothers. So I think a man's be better off if he's not drinking.

The Indians don't know how to drink whisky or wine, and the government don't allow us drink — we Indian. Mexicans and white people they allow drink. They can get a drink any place where they want to. But lot of white people and lot of Mexicans knows how to drink. I don't see anybody at R—— or outside R—— around here — like Navahos — drinking, beating up his wife, and fighting his own neighbors. (Doesn't see any whites doing it.) But I think a lot of them white people's been drinking, but don't drink very heavy. They know how to drink it — not drink too much.

[It's all right to drink if not too much — if you know how.]

Yes it's all right to drink if not too much — just a little.

[Any reason why Indians drink so much?]

The main reason why people starts drinking, they want to drink more and more all the time. When Navaho people gets together they keep drinking all the time. They kill a bottle, and wants another one all the time. So he thinks that's the only reason why they do that. There's a lot of women people drinking now. They didn't use to do that before but lots are learning to drink.

[Some people feel good when they drink, isn't this all right?]

Some people thinks that's a good thing, and they want to feel good all the time.

[Is it bad for people to feel good?]

Myself, if I'm not drinking — lots of times boys get drunk before me and I'm not drinking, I'm watch those boys while they're drinking — talking, and I don't like the way they're acting and talking. I don't think it's any good for them.

41. [What is the right (good) way of getting to feel good (*baa hozhon*) "happy"?]

In the right way about that, when you're young just ready to settle down — get married, settle down, and live right. A man can start to making his good home — good house to live in it — and do the working — outside work, like farming, or chopping, many outside work that he could do. Or he can get a good job and earn money — get paid every pay day, and save his money. He don't care about booze, about losing money for liquor. He wants save his money for the time he is making a living. His wife can do the work inside. He can have his good dishes and take care the house [that is, she]. They can both working together. If they start having children, he can tell his children not to do anything wrong — to live right, like the way they are doing it. If he got some money ahead and plenty of food to eat, and have a good house to live in it, and have some livestock outside in good shape — then this man will feel good about it (*ei baa hozhon*). He can talk about that with his wife, and he can tell his children about that. This man will once in a while think about whisky, wine, or beer. He'll say to his wife: He will never drink that stuff, and he never has taken any yet, and he don't want to try any as long as he live. He might say to his wife: He thinks that's bad stuff to take it. In the cities, lot of people been drinking, that he's seen, and it's not a very good thing to do that. Might be two people — they're fighting together — one might have a bottle in his pocket. So that's the reason he don't want to take any of it. Where like he's making a living with his wife without drinking that makes him feel good about it.

42. [If he is a good — happy man — feels good as above, does he have to have Sings held for him?]

Don't have to have a Sing for that. In our Navaho ways we used to have father and grandfather — they used to tell us how to live right. That's where these good people, they got taught from older people. That's reason why some Navaho man don't drink. They used to say you must have a good home — don't try to spoil something or hurt anything. About drinking and stealing and other wrong things a person can do, they used to say that they mustn't do that. They used to say they should live right. They used to tell us we must tell the truth and live right.

43. [I want to ask about the Sings?]

A man if he's a good man, do right, not to steal, not to lie, not drinking, have a good home and good livestock. He go a few years, and his mind and his plan — he think his mind is not working very good, his mind is getting weak, or his talk is not very straight — that's the time he have to put up with Blessing Way Sing — with old man that knows how to sing. This Singer can bring him back where he was before. Get his mind and talking strong like he was before — so he has to have singing for that. That's Blessing Way Sing. That should be taken every two years. Wouldn't have no Sing if he's feeling good.

[What is the purpose of the Sing?]

To make the man feel happy and good.

[Could a man live his whole life until he gets old without having any Sings?]

It's for everybody, man and woman, any time he want to put up Sing, he can put up Blessing Way Sing. Anybody, man or woman, will have bad dream, they have to put up Blessing Way Sing right away. There is many other reasons they have to put up Blessing Way Sing for man or woman. For most anyone have it.

About two years — he wants to be in good way all the time. For that purpose he wants to put it two years at a time. For good hope — the main branch of Blessing Way Sing. He wants to be good man, good honest wife, have good children, and live right and have good livestock. Not to be harmed any way. So he's taking this Blessing Way every two years at a time. For bad dream there is a small branch off this Blessing Way. Only one body of Blessing Way, but can be changed around for things — bad dreams or some other reason. They who had bad dreams, they used small branches.

[All his life did he have Blessing Way every two years?]

Yes.

44. [Does it do anybody who drinks or steals any good to have a Sing?]

No this — I understand this Blessing Way was started back years ago by Holy People before the Navahos has learned it, and I heard this is for the good people. While the older people says that it wasn't for bad people — I didn't heard that. All I heard was that it was for good people. But there's nobody know that we're going to have liquor like we have today in the cities. There's a case that has been mentioned at the time — if there's one single Navaho lose his mind or acting like crazy — talks whole lot and run away from home, sometimes people ties him down so he can stay. This Blessing Way has to be used on this man, but the pray have to be changed over — another way praying and uses the smoke. Make this person smoke a pipe. (There's a man's smoke pipe and a woman's smoke pipe.) In this case liquor hasn't got anything to do with that.

45. [About punishing and spanking children — was he spanked by his parents?]

I got pretty good spanking from mother and father and my nephew (Uncle?).

[What did they spank for?]

One reason — I used to play with some other children. Different family from us. I used to whip, hit, some of the children and make them cry. I used to get whipped myself for that. Another reason, I don't mind my father and mother — they want me to chop some wood and bring it in, and I don't want to do it, and just run off. Father used to come out and catch me and bring me home and whip me for that. Lot of time I was lazy to do something. They used to whip me and make me jump up and go do things.

[Did he do same thing to his own children?]

Yes, also I hit my own children. If they found out that I was the one that make this child cry, they come after me with a whip.

[If a child fights with another child, do they always whip him?]

I always get whipped — that is, my father knows that I did it. Sometimes my parents don't know anything about it, and their parents don't. But boy reports it to their parents and they whip me.

[How old was he when he was whipped for the last time?]

Thinks he's about 10 years old, and then they don't whip him any more. Another reason he was whipped — when he's herding sheep and loses them and coyote gets them and kills them.

46. [Did he never do anything wrong after he was 10 years old?]

He hasn't done anything wrong after they stop whipping by his father and mother and other person. Right at that time he thinks his mother and father and other person learn him to do right — so I never have done anything wrong again after that. That's the way I remember it.

[How about his own children, when did he whip them last?]

I didn't whip any of my children. They don't do anything wrong badly. Whenever they do or lie or steal small things, I used to give them good talking. That's the way I teach my children.

47. [If child stole some small thing, what would he say to him?]

If a child does anything wrong like that and you give him talking telling him that it's bad, that people won't like it — father or mother won't like it.

[Did he ever say if they did it again they would be punished?]

Tells him if he did it again, he'd get a good whipping, so he won't do that again.

[Did he ever give a child who had done good things a present for that?]

A child always do some wrong things, but you have to teach him how to cut it out — them bad things. After you give him talk and after that he never tries to do that any more. When he help around — help his mother inside, or help outside — bring in a lot of wood — we buy him good shoes — good pants or hat. Then on top of that you give him a good talking again. Now you're going to wear these good shoes or good pants you must be good boy or girl — so that you can get some more after a while, if you mind your father and mother. If you don't mind you won't get any more, or you might get whipped, too. In that way he remembered that.

If boy or girl mind what you're telling them — if he listen to your talking what you're saying to him, then you can promise him something. That kind of a boy or girl, you can never whip them at all. Some other children don't listen talk. Their parents give them good talking. They never listen to their parents. Then they whip them. They try to get him not to do that any more by talking — so child don't listen, they whip him for that.

The child don't obey what the parent says we can always tell him we will whip him next. Then tell him he will be bad man or bad woman when he grows up, nobody will like him. Tell him if he minds his father and mother what he says he will be a good man when he grows up — everybody will like him. If you don't listen to this everybody will laugh about him when he is growing up. People will say he's a bad man or bad woman. He's no good. He's going to be hard up, wear poor clothes, poor shoes, he's going to be raggy.

48. [About property: What does each person own in a family, father, mother, children, etc.?]

Man and woman — when they first start married. Man have to own something — not much — 2 cows or a few sheep. And woman the same way. After they put their property together, man and woman must work together and build up their home and build up their livestock. They must work together and listen to each other, and listen how they can make a good living — as long as they live. So whole property is owned by man and woman — even they have children.

That's when man and woman work together. Woman have to listen to husband and man listen to wife. That's the only way they can build up a good home. But another side, people when they don't listen they can just break up their home. They can keep themselves broke all the time. But that's their own fault by living that way.

49. [If man and woman separate who gets the things?]

If man and woman living in the right way for years, then for some reason man wants to divorce her — that would be the man's fault. Woman wants to stay with him, but he wants to go away. Man won't get anything — he just have to go without. He just folds his arms and goes without anything. If the woman's fault to divorce, the woman have to go without. The man will keep everything right there at home.

[If woman leaves the man because he has been drinking, does she take the things with her?]

Don't know how they can handle how a man has been drinking too much, and therefore a woman can divorce him. It wouldn't be just for drinking to divorce two people — there has to be something else in the way to make two people divorce each other. On the woman's side, she know this man start to drinking and some more other wrong things a man is doing it. And she begins to think another way. She will think she can't get on with this man any more — don't listen to her any more. If a case like that comes, she can divorce man for that, and then sometimes woman wanted to pick up another man to marry and gets tired of this one, wants to divorce this one. Then still there be some more — other reason to divorce a man or woman.

[If man does the drinking and other wrong things, and woman leaves him, which get the property?]

If man starts to divorce the woman, he doesn't get no property, but woman gets it all. If woman thinks this man is drinking too much and wants divorce, she don't get anything — she can go away but gets no property [that is, it depends on who goes away, and not whose "fault" it is].

[When people get divorced, which one gets the children?]

If the children has a (maternal) grandmother they can go under the grandmother until they can able to take care of themselves.

[So they leave the father and mother?]

Yes, that's the way they used to do.

50. [When father or mother dies, who gets the property?]

Man who dies, if he had an older brother or older sister, they get the property until the children grown up. He's a good brother or good sister he can take care of the property for the children until these children can able to take care of property again like father and mother. That never work that way — it always spoil, they always — home won't be like it used to be and the livestock will lose by the time when the children grow up and everything will be spoiled them. That's the way ———— did, he used to be my son-in-law. When his wife died he turned the property over to own sister and some sheep — but we never seen the sheep back for the children — we don't have anything — nothing now. ————'s children didn't get anything.

[Did he give all he had to his sister?]

Yes, everything what they have.

[Why to the sister and not to someone else?]

————'s wife was pretty sick, she thought that she wasn't going to get well, she told her older sister to get the livestock for the children and keep the children there after she dies. But sheep was already in the herd and the children was brought there after the mother died, and ———— just go around to different homes. But ———— starts to drinking wine and got mad about the sheep and the children, got mad to this lady that's taking care of the children. ———— took the sheep away from this woman and the children, too. ———— thought he might take care of the children over there and the sheep also, but he sold all the sheep. But one of the girl got married and got a child now, and the other one (a boy) went to taken out some place working, and the third is taken care by old ————'s father's older daughter.

[Why isn't he living with ———— and his present wife?]

———— never takes care of his children since the children's mother died. He never buys clothes for the children. Lets some other people buy clothes for the children. That's the reason the younger boy stay over there with ————'s wife. He [that is, informant] wanted to have his grandchild down here so he would have somebody to take care of him — take him outside. He would buy clothes for the child. Then he would put that boy in school. But they don't want to let him have it.

51. [In the old day, when parents died did they divide up the property equally between the boys and girls — children?]

This is the way they used to handle a case like that. When mother dies and father still living. Father takes all the property and he's taking care for the children. Then the father dies again short time after woman died. If the children still small — they cannot able to take care of the property and sheep — people gets together and talk this thing over. And they have to point out a man to take care of the property again for the children until the children grew up. If one or two can able to take care of their own property, then older sister or older brother — he can take care of the whole thing — until these other kids are grown up. If everything goes in fine shape, then divide up the sheep and other property between these brothers and sisters. That's the way they used to handle it.

[The same amount each one?]

Yes. That's the way they fixed it up with ————'s children — but didn't work very well because they start to drinking and lose a lot of sheep and they only have a small amount now.

52. [What happens to the mother's jewelry?]

It goes to the oldest daughter and the oldest daughter divides it up among the other girls. Goes to the oldest daughter first, and if some boys in the bunch they always get some of the jewelry.

[Why to the oldest daughter instead of oldest son?] [The interpreter says he got it wrong — apparently he meant ————'s children.]

————'s mother had a lot of jewelry but they went into debt pretty heavy — they don't have anything now. It all went to the traders. But other question: Because sisters and brothers small yet, so have to be taken care of by oldest daughter until they grow up and can be divided among brothers and sisters.

[If oldest child is a boy?]

Same way — the jewelry goes to him (to boy if he is oldest).

When a man gets drunk it may be so, but when he has more it's like he's making up stories and telling about it. This story he's telling you is not a new story like what's going on today — like mother and father die. Different from now, when they make wills. He thinks this is the truth the way he's telling you. He's got it in his head, he thinks he can remember — most of it.

53. [If a man dies who hasn't got a wife or children, what happens to his things then?]

If a man dies, he has some property, the property goes to his close relatives. If the man has a sister the property goes to the oldest sister, if he has no sister, only a brother, the property goes to the oldest brother, if he has no oldest brother or oldest sister — then one of the relatives takes the property.

— He can give it to just a friend. They used to do that.

[Can he give it to a friend if he has children?]

No.

[Digression about people mentioned above.]

54. [Do children inherit the debts of dead parents?]

Yes if the children has money to pay with they can pay it. If a man's wife dies, the man has to pay the wife's bill. I remember my wife used to owe a big bill at the R—— Trading Store. After she died I had to pay the whole bill.

[If someone else made the bill, why does he have to pay it?]

If mother of the children died and the children are too small, and the things she gets out of the store — we all use it. That's the reason we make the payment on that.

[If no wife or children, and property goes to his brothers or sister, do they have to pay the bills too?]

Since the white people came into this country and put up store, from that time they start to owe some bills to the store, and so if man dies and he gets the property, he has to pay. In old day, they never run into debt like this. Never ran into debt in the old days.

January 6, 1952 (Interpreter: Bill Begay)

55. [What did they teach in the old days about helping people for example, working?]

About making up a hogan — get the people who live close around. Notify these people first what day they should come and work together on the hogan. And they'll be there. When they're ready to start work, the man that live there that needs the help, he kill a sheep for mutton so they can have plenty to eat while they're working.

[Interpreter asked him whether they stay till they finish or only one day?]

The big hogan they gonna build won't take one day, takes several days.

[Who would they ask to help, anyone around?]

Doesn't make any difference, get ones related to you or just pick out some people.

[Why would he ask people related to him?]

It's just the same. The ones not related to them is all right. Some times the relations live close — that's the only reason.

[Is man who build the house always supposed to have food, etc., for those helping?]

The people stays there at night, the ones that wants to, the others go home and come back in the morning. You have to tell the people before they start to work just how long you need them. If they going to stay there till the hogan is finished, then man who needed help wants to get plenty of food for these people.

[Does he promise them that he'll give them food?]

The Navaho, they don't pay these man anything, they just feed them.

56. [Suppose some man doesn't want to help, what would he say to him?]

Some of the mans when they are lazy, they don't want to come and help, sometimes they never help anybody. The man that's lazy to help anybody, they can tell them, whenever he needs the help they won't help him. That's what they used to tell him.

[Suppose he was an old man that needed help — was poor and couldn't feed them?]

If this man was poor and old, he can send some of his friend out and tell the people. He want to get some food from his people. This old man might have a lot of friends. They all pitch in and help him with some food, some meat. Then some womans might come and help to cook. Some old mans sometimes get more help than any man who has something.

[Why help the old man since he can't do them any good?]

Why they get more help — he told the people he was too old and he needed help. He might say: It's too cold to stay without a hogan. Then the people says he's too old, let's help the old man, he used to be a good man when he was young and always helped people.

[If he had been a bad man when he was young would they help him?]

Yes, if he's kind of mean to these people when he was young, people can talk about him — he never help the people. That's why people won't help him.

57. [Will his family help him?]
Just his children they help him.

[Why do his children help him?]

His children won't feel that way about him. If he's mean to his children it might work that ways.

[If such an old man came to him as Chief and said my children won't help me, what would he say?]

If man is pretty mean, then I can talk about him, tell the people that he's a bad man and he don't want to give any help to his neighbors. Even he didn't like his children much. Then I can say — let that man go — he don't want to help his neighbors — let him go. He can live by himself. There's some people already he says in the R—— area — that kind of man and they're living all by themselves now. In the nighttime when you go around you can see where he's at — you can see his fire and he stays all by himself.

[Lunch. The old man started talking with the interpreter about a poor old lady whose son doesn't visit her. She's crazy — her granddaughter just rides around — won't settle down.]

58. [If old lady came to him and complained about her granddaughter, what would he say to her?]

He says his old father when he was still living — his father used to say — they used to be young woman that didn't want to work around home. He [that is, she] wants to be out all the time. She had no husband to live with. She only go ahead and been getting different mens and been changing around. Any time when her people tries to tell her to stay home and work, she never listens to that. One time they sent a person to me, his father says, and want me to give a good talking to this woman, and make her stay at home and do her own work. And so I went down there. When I got down there, I brought her inside the hogan, and this lady wasn't related to me. That old man says he's been hearing bad news about her. Old man says they want me to talk to you about she's been running out — doing some bad things, and heard about you that you've been changing so many men. Old man says she's a good woman and young, and I didn't like to hear about you like the way the people's been talking about you. Now I going to talk to you pretty easy so you can get everything. Listen to my talk. If you listen to my talk and try to get everything what I say, I want you to come back and live right. That's what your people want you to do and I want you to do the same, too. So if you mind me what I say then people will talk about you. They will say: This is pretty good lady, doing good weaving, doing good housework. They talk nice about you. I like to hear people talk very nice about you. Now the way you're doing — go off with young boy — next day you have another different one, and you are doing that just as fast as you can. Your people tries not to do that, but you just keep going on. That's the reason I like to talk to you pretty strong.

Old man told this lady — she must get married, must pick up one of the men that she likes, and if she did that, she can settle down, and live close with me here, and I can tell you how to do the good work at home. I want you to shear sheep, and start to make blanket — how to work it, how to make up good blanket. If you're making these blankets, that's for your home. Nobody will take away that blanket from you. You can sell that rug for yourself. Besides that you gonna have some friends — that is if you start making these good blankets. People will talk about you, you are good blanket weaver. They will be a bunch of Navahos put you on the job blanket weaving, and you're living with a man — lot of people will come to your husband. They'll tell him he want to get this man to have his wife to go to work for some other people weaving, and you gonna have to learn some other work — inside the hogan — how to cook food, how to shake the blankets, keep them clean, and the people who come round your home will look better than it was before. Then I also, can listen to the people — I can ask the people how you get along now, after a few years. But what I'm going to listen for is — you are pretty good lady now — woman. You have settled down and do the good work at your home. That'll sound good to me, but I don't like to hear you're still bad woman yet.

59. [Should you help your relatives, outside family, more than others, for example, clan?]

It take just much help from the people not related to you. It looks like it's even with me . . . They help them just the same. [Interpreter explains that is makes no difference whether they are in the clan or not.]

[Every time that someone helps you, are you supposed to help him back?]

Yes. They used to exchange work. They help each other back. Sometimes who needs help, if they think it needs a lot of food for people, sometimes they kill a big horse, grown horse, for feeding the people.

60. [What did old people teach about giving presents to people?]

Anybody could do that. If you know friend, from near to ———, if he's living down there, then he'll come over here and visit him and spend two or three nights with him — that man who came will tell all his story, what's going on around out there where he is. And this man down here he tells stories, just the same, like the other. That man over there when he ready to leave, like tomorrow or today, this man down here gave a good saddle horse to the man who came. That's just gift — you don't have to pay a penny for it. If he didn't have no saddle horse, he can give pretty good sized buck — skin, deerskin. Then after that give him some sheep. Now after that give anything he can — like silver bracelet or silver belt. Now this other man might go visit this man — when he gets down there they do the same down there. The other man he give him back something when he ready to leave.

61. [If man (host) has given him all the food and lodging, why give him all the other things?]

He didn't know why they do that, but they say they used to do that. This old man said he used to do that, too [that is, informant].

[Why does he think they did it?]

They think he's got the best friends and good relatives live far away.

We feel that man came a long way to me and I want to take good care of this man while he's here spending time with me, and I can give him something before he leave. So he won't spend nothing for that trip that he made. In about a year from now, I will do the same — make a trip over there and spend time with that man.

62. [Suppose you're traveling in a distant country and come to a hogan and spend the night, and they give presents, should you do anything for them?]

If a man is coming from long ways off, and got pretty late — sundown, and he can spend the night with another family there. They only feed him there and loan him some blankets. But they don't give him anything. Just feed him and next morning he can go on again.

[Does he do anything in return for feeding him?]

The family there they just glad because they give him food, but this man there he's not thinking that he's going to get something.

[Should visitor do something for the family because they're so nice to him?]

If this visitor is a good man, he can remember about that, how he was taken good care while he was camping there. He can help the people back — some time after that.

[Would it be wrong if he didn't do anything back for them?]

These people that do the feeding won't say anything about it to them. But if he remember — If he didn't help still it's all right.

[It's all right if they didn't help back?]

Yes. That won't hurt anything — One of my sons married woman at A—— way off. They came over to me just a few days ago — man and his wife. They stopped for part of the day, and I gave them a blanket each one. I gave the woman a woman's shawl-blanket and the man a man-sized blanket. I been doing that with them for years now. When I spent a night or two with them down there. I always been take good care, with food, bedding, and they gave me something too. Now this blanket is pretty expensive — one blanket costs over $30.

[Is it all right not to give presents?]

It works both ways to your relatives and to people not related to you. Just good friends.

This is what old people did this, and I the only one that still do that. About way young people have been doing this I don't know.

No, it's not bad — even if he doesn't get anything — only a very few used to do this.

[Interpreter cleared this up: It seems that only visitors get the gifts. "The people just give the food away free. He gets everything free. That's the old way of doing that."]

63. [What are some of the other ways of helping people?]

If a man or woman is going to have a Sing like Squaw dance or 8–9 night Yeibichai dance. In first place, he doesn't have enough money, enough food — but he have to put it up anyway. Sometimes he calls his people up and they get together here, and he tell them he wants to set up Squaw dance but he hasn't got enough money or food. This man will tell these other mans — he wants all the people that lives around there to help him with some food. He wants to take a leader to make a speak for him — about this Squaw dance that he's going to put up, and people will say: We'll do the helping. After that, maybe two or three will help with the meat, sheep — the rest will help with coffee, sugar, bread, flour. They all pitch in and help that man put up Squaw dance. That's what this man got from these people, he don't have to pay for it. The people that did the helping, they don't want to get anything back. They just give it away. Let the people use up the food and things that they give.

64. [In the old days, did they use to pay people for working for them?]
They don't pay anything. They don't pay anything like a bunch of them get together and help. Back in that time, if one person wants to hire a man to get him to do some kind of a job. They used to pay him sheep or goats. Like job is pretty good size, like gonna last a week — they give him 5 sheep or 5 goats. He could pay him something else, if he didn't have any sheep.

[Who decided how many sheep — employer or employee?]
The man who works gets the sheep — after did the work. [Missed question.]

[Before work started did they talk it over?]
The job-giver will tell how much he's going to give and how long it will last, and so he can think it over.

65. [Suppose he's out on the road, and someone helps him fix a flat tire, should he do anything in return?]
For just a small thing like that they always give help to man like that on the tire — fixing — just for a little while. But they don't all do that — some don't want to help the man.

[Does he think it bad if they don't help him?] [Laughter.]
There isn't anything that's going to happen to him. The man only didn't like it because the man didn't give him any help.

[Some people think that it's wrong (*doo 'akotee da*) not to help, would he agree?]
A man or woman who thinks pretty about things pretty short, thems the ones that don't want to help anybody. Man has good mind and thinks 15 or 20 years ahead, he always help a person.

[Irrelevant gossip omitted.]

[What good will it do a fellow to have helped somebody today, twenty years from now?]
This man who thinks — has studied out already — that he might live

15 or 20 years longer and that he might need help any time. That's why he helped the people.

66. [Suppose I was a rich man and gave him 500 sheep to give to the Navahos, who would he give them to?]

I'll give them to one of my relatives — the one that knows how to handle sheep.

[Would it make any difference whether the man was poor or not?]
No. He's poor already so he won't get no sheep.

[Would he give all the sheep to the same person?]
If there's two relatives knows how to handle sheep they can split it up two ways — two people. That means how to herd them and when you put the sheep with the buck so that they can have lambs in the right month.

[Why to his relatives and not someone else?]
These people have to be known, so when they start owning the sheep they can start raising more — So the other people that's not related to him — He wouldn't know all of them. If he give the sheep to anyone, he might go ahead and lose them right away.

[If he knew a man not a relative who could take better care of the sheep would he give them to him?]
There's one way he could do that to the ones that not related. I cannot say, go ahead and take all that sheep — I give it to you. I have to talk with the person first about it. After lambing time, he could get just part of the lambs and the main bunch is still mine. Him and that other man can take care of that sheep for three or four years. That's the only way he could do with the non-relatives.

[Talk with interpreter brings out: "He cannot just give the sheep away to this man. He can't." Sounds like he gave the man the job of taking care of the sheep.]

67. [I say to you: You're the chief, and I want you to give the sheep to people, you think you ought to — would you still give them to your relatives?]

He won't give it to anybody, unless some man knows how to take care of the sheep.

[Suppose instead of sheep it was jewelry. Who would he give that to?]
I wouldn't give it to anybody else — to ones not related to me. I give it to my own children and divide it up to them.

[Why to his children instead of someone else?]
That's just because they're my children — I mean my grandchildren, too.

[Even if they were not all good people, would he still give it to them?]
I know my children and grandchildren and they will help me as long as I live, and that's the reason I give that jewelry to them.

68. [How would he advise me to give it, since I don't have any relatives among the Navahos?] [Laughs.]

He's willing for you to give it to your wife.

[My wife tells me to give it to the Navahos?]

That question sounds pretty strong to me. I don't know how —. That's up to you — who you think to give.

[Suppose some rich man from N. Y. came down here to R——, and had these things and went to him and asked him who to give it to?]

He would give it to the people that he thinks are better people than the others.

[Why?]

I rather give it to the ones that make a good living, so they don't have to waste what they get. And another thing, I have to keep it myself if I want to, that would be stingy not to give it away.

69. [If some people are starving and going to die would he still give it to those well off?]

If the man is poor, doesn't know how to make a living and starve most everyday, and had bad clothing. I will give him some money. But I'll tell the man that I'm not going to get the money back. Go ahead and use it up.

[Why would he give it to that man?]

Poor man needs something to eat and needs some clothing, so I'll help him with the money. But if I didn't give anything to this poor man, he might be hungry and die for food. I don't like for this man to die for food or have no clothes to wear — or could freeze up. So I'll help him.

[Even if this man had never helped *him?*]

Even at that, he'll do that.

[Does he think many people would do that?]

They used to be some way back. I don't think there's any now.

70. [What kind of talk would he give a young man about helping a starving man?]

Well, if I see a poor man he needed help pretty bad, I will go ahead and pick up a young man if he has something to give.

That happened to me once. In this case, it's over on the other side of —— Mountain. They call T—— C——. He came to me one time and want me to loan him $50 and he says he wants to pay it back to me later, but he sure needed the money badly for some reason. I don't know the man very well, and I afraid to loan him $50, and I tell him to try to get it from the other people in R——. So I says: I'll help you with some money. I get $15 and give it to him. I told him I don't want to get this back — just forget about it, when I give it away. There's another boy came in from the same place, and want to borrow some money from me, but I just gave $10 to him. Gave that away, too, and told the boy he didn't want to get it back.

[Returning to the question] I will tell the young man — he knows where the poor man is and who he was and how bad he needed food and clothing and had no friends. He wants him to help that man, says be good young man and help that poor person. Now someday you might get old or you might get poor. They might help you. If I had something, I'd help that old man, but I've got nothing — that's why I want you to help that old man — to do that. Way back in the old days, our Navaho people used to do that. They used to help poor people — so be kind to the poor man, I'll give him all that talk, and I think I'll get this young man to do that. I have to tell him that you won't get your money back, you just help him with it. I will sure appreciate it if you did that for that poor fellow. There will be more people will think about you the same way. I think if I gave him all this talk, I think that young boys will help poor man — if he has something to give away.

71. [If he met a man out in the woods, who was starving and going to die, and he had a little food — no one would know about it — would he give it to this man?]

When he's out there in the woods with very little food, and he met a man there starving for food — I know he's going to die — he's not going to live very long — and I'll give him some of my lunch no matter how little I have.

[Interpreter explains: "Old people used to say a man gets too hungry wherever he is, and another person gives that starving man and give him plenty — they say that after he take that food, that food will just kill him. They used to tell stories like that. I told him that if you give him the food he might died — that's why I laughed."]

[Would he give the food to the man, even if he knew that he wouldn't have enough to get home?]

[Laughs.] Yes, even if I have very little food — not enough to get home with, I give it to the man.

Another way that he could give something to the poor man. The old people the way they used to do if they haven't got anything to eat, and another fellow came along and he was more hungry than he was — most Navahos have a small sack of corn pollen in their pocket all the time — he'll put his hand in there and pick up some corn pollen and put it in his mouth and let him eat that.

If he takes that, he won't die for food. He might run into food some way. Way back many years ago 12 Navaho people run out of food. They all went hungry, but these 12 men got out in the woods and killed a chipmunk and roasted the chipmunk and divided it up for 12 people (one chipmunk for 12 people).

72. [Suppose that in the old days, before the government came, another tribe or bad white people said they would kill a lot of people if they

didn't give them 500 sheep — how would he decide who to take the sheep from?]

He says he'll give the sheep. Divide it up among the people. He give it to the people — the ones that needed help pretty bad. Then after he give these sheep away to the people, he will tell the people that they must keep their sheep and try to raise some more, and take good care of the sheep.

[It's a question of taking away the sheep — or else the bad people will kill a lot of people — how would he collect these 500 sheep?]

That seems like a pretty strong question. The one thing I could do would be to hold a pretty good sized meeting — and I explained to the people there that some other tribe wants some sheep, for me to collect 500 sheep, and I like to have you people to bring in some sheep to this place and see how many can we gather. If we didn't do this the other tribe says if they don't get the sheep they kill some people. I explained that if we got enough sheep to collect off from each man who has sheep, they might be able to make 500 — but I am afraid that's too many for R—— people. Then I know some R—— people will say — they might not like it — why they want to kill us for our own money or our sheep. That don't sound very good to us. More than half of them say that — So that's the way I feel about it.

[If all decide to give up their sheep and one decides: I won't, should they force him to?]

If there only two or three people, they're pretty stingy — they will say: No, I don't want to give my sheep away. If whole crowd says: Let's give these sheep away, we don't want to be killed out. If whole crowd says that, they might do that. But all the people who has sheep says no — they don't do that.

[Can you take the sheep away from these stingy people?]

No, he says, not. They're not going to take sheep away from man who owns the sheep.

73. [In southern Italy all the land belongs to one man who won't let anybody use it — the people just took their guns and took the land and started using it.]

In that case, it's up to the man who owns the land. He has to say yes or no. But I won't say for the man: Yes or No. Also he might have some behind him — if he thinks he have strong help he can say no — I don't give that land away. This man who owns the land, he might put up a fight for it, too — if he can able to do that. He might get mad himself and want to sell the land to the people. That question is a little bit hard for me to answer again.

[These people have all the strength on their side, and the man is a bad man — and they want to kill him, and nothing will happen. Would that be all right?]

[Laughs.] I just couldn't answer that question. If they kill this man, something might happen. He might have some other help which the people don't know. I think it wouldn't be a very good thing to kill that man.

74. [Is killing in self defense all right?]

If I get out in the wood with another fellow and we say we kill each other down there, but I like to shoot first — that if he shoot me first he might get by with it. If I shoot him first, then I don't know what happen next. In the old days, old people used to do that. Two fight together — they used a bow and arrow — take a shot at a man, and the other man shoot back before he died, so they can both be killed at the same time. They used a gun, too, an old gun.

He heard a story that happened. Two people got into a fight, and one shot the other one in back of his hip. There were just these two people — did that. There were some people there on both sides — man got shot didn't die, just fall down — laying down. The rest of the people talk about this right away, and nobody didn't get mad about it. They talked this thing over. They won't do anything to this man that shot the man. What they says that they make this man to pay the medicine man for the man he shot. And they made him do that — pay for the medicine man, and medicine man came over there and this medicine man gave some medicine to the man who got shot, and he got well. After this man got well, and started walking again, and that bullet didn't come out any place. They didn't take it out. But he got well. They named this man who got shot in the hip — he was called Hipshot after that.

[What would they have done to the man if he hadn't wanted to pay for the Sing?]

He didn't know what would happen. This man who shot the man, I heard he was my grandfather. Says he used to know the man.

75. [In the old days, did they kill the murderer?]

No. The way they did was just to make him pay something.

[Who does he pay it to?]

Yes, to the family.

[Somebody told me that if someone kills your wife or children, it's all right to kill him, what do you think?]

If he sees the man pretty close then he know he kill a person because he seen it, and then this person's parents want to kill that man. I think it all right to kill that man.

[Does it make any difference whether the man was a good or bad man?]

In the old days, if this man who killed somebody, he was bad already — but they don't kill him right away. They've got to talk it over first. They have to fix it up some way so this man won't be killed. It's on bad man's side — he has some relatives and some friends they are the ones that going to save that man.

[This is a difficult question that whites talk about. In hospital sometimes doctor has to decide whether to save the mother or the baby — which
does he think?]

My own idea — in a case like that, I say — let them both live. Don't
kill anyone, even if he lives only a short time.

[Doctor isn't killing anyone, he just has to decide which to save.]

He can't answer that question. But he says there used to be a woman
had a baby and the woman got hurt inside, and just as soon as baby born
the woman died. Baby born but they say the baby was all right. But
the woman who had the baby — the mother of the woman got hold of the
baby and killed it with a stick because she think the baby killed the
woman.

[Did they do anything to the woman who killed the baby?]

No, they didn't do anything to the woman.

[Here followed a funny story to end the day.]

January 7, 1952 (Interpreter: Robert Baca)

76. [Was he going to be involved in a Sing again?]

He did have a big Sing, he was pretty sick at that time. Since then
he feels all right — felt sore around stomach, [etc.] but he doesn't sleep at
night. He got hold of ———'s wife, she do handtrembling on him, and she
said he got to have some more singing again. He know a long time ago
he burned a rattlesnake and a water snake, too, and he eat some fish, too —
great big fish. So he had to get hold of medicine man ——— he know how
to do sandpainting on different kind of snake, and also he got to have one
more Blessing Way Sing — that's what handtrembler said. But the Blessing
Way medicine man said it have to get him from C—— way away.

[Talk about particular medicine men and sick people has been omitted.]

He [the informant] go around to the people, he sing over there and
somebody come around and say: You sing again — not to sing too many
persons a month. I sing too many person all last year. Maybe not supposed
to do that. If I sing in two places — not even get rest and get through and
go some place sing over there. If I sing four times — I have to rest first
for four days. In that way it will be all right.

77. [Is this something all Singers know about not singing too much, or
is it just because he's an old man and gets tired?]

That's really hard to say about the Blessing Way situation. Some
Blessing Way medicine man they sing three, four, five different kind, they
do. So they sing all the people — they don't care how many persons they
sing one month. It's all right. Only one kind Blessing Way he sing. I can't
change around, I can't do same way. Even if you're not old, not supposed
to sing lots of person in one month. You have to keep watching till
the day passed away and start going around Sing. He's thinking in his
mind — last night he was talking over there to his children: If you know

this Blessing Way what I got, you folks should sing on me. But you folks don't know how to sing. And another way I'm going to try to but I don't know — try to have a Blessing Way medicine man — maybe some boys around here they know how to sing Blessing Way. I will just [teach] him how to sing and all kinds of plants to get started. Maybe that will help me a little. Going to try that way. I say that way to my children and they just laughed.

[Did they laugh because they didn't want to help him or because they didn't know how to do it?]

It wasn't funny. They just can't get anybody around here to know the sing. That's why they just laugh. A long time ago, that's the way — but the story about this Blessing Way what he got. If some man, he learned from him all the Blessing Way what he gots — some man learn it — and that man he's singing Blessing Way. If the way he feel now he should get that man to come down to sing on him. But there's nobody know all my song around here. If some man learn all his medicine song from him, not even teaching how to do all Blessing Way — he just stole it — all the singing from this old man. In that way I hear about that case. If some man do that way on me, maybe that's why I'm feeling not very well. But still I don't think nobody know all my song.

78. [Why do you still keep on singing Blessing Way — for the money or for some other reason — now you're so old?]

I'm doing pretty good on going around singing. Some pay pretty good money — so I try my best to sing on them. Some people they give me very little — just enough to buy a sack of flour. Long time ago his father told him, when he start singing, and person pay pretty good, you sing pretty well on him — that's what father told him. If some people they don't pay just a little, and you sing too much. He told him if you do that way a little later on you won't be no good. Not for the people but for yourself; because not to sing too much, because some Blessing Way medicine men they don't sing too much in one month. Just four sings in a month. They don't sing five in one month. But I sing too much in one month.

[Why did you sing too much in one much?]

It's all right, because it isn't my fault. It's the people's fault, they think this Blessing Way situation — it will not hurt medicine man — that's what the people thinks. But it's really bad on him, because in winter time I sing too much in one month. Maybe 7 or 8 or 10 in one month. That's bad. Now somebody come around again and want him to sing again. I tell him right to his face, I don't care who it is — I tell him to pay a little more before I go out and do Blessing Way Sing again. The people all this R——— area — all Indians — they nice to me and also I nice to them. So I was just really hard to tell — I can't go over there. Tried to say this way, but they nice to me. Maybe they don't got too much money to give to me — so I just go over there and do the sing. But now I'm really old, and in winter it's pretty hard and nighttime is pretty hard. My voice is too old. If some-body goes around and help me sing — that's all right. If I go alone, that's too hard.

79. [In a Sing, does the Sing help everybody as well as the patient, including the Singer?]

Not even [just?] the patient to make him well. Everybody: him, the patient, the wife, all the folks living there. All the clothing, all the horses, sheep — everything what they got to make going well. Because when you start singing you got to pray a long time — to pray for what they got. So after that then they people all right. [Good for Singer, too?] Yes.

80. [Is that why he likes to sing Blessing Way?]

I always feeling happy to sing his Blessing Way. If the patient is really good man to have a Blessing Way — to tell something he always do it, and things not supposed to do while the singing is going on over the patient. When the patient is not supposed to talk bad words to his wife, children, everybody in his home, because these words pray for trying to go away — for those things not to bad on him. A patient is not supposed to sleep with his wife. He's not supposed not to hurt the sheep, the horses, dogs. It's all right to herd the sheep. If somebody will butcher the sheep outside — not supposed to get any blood on your feet or your pants. Have to keep watching himself. Because I pray for his cornfield, and all different kinds of corn, food, not to have any more bad dreams. I am doing all this kind of things when I start singing. Some patients they not very good. When I sing to them they go outside and sleep with their wife. That's bad. Not for me but for them. They going to get sick. It hurts them — not me. Some time they kick the dog, hit the sheep and horses and talk bad words to his children, and that way the patient won't do no good for sings. A little later on he's going to have another Blessing Way. If I tell them not do this, and they mind me they get well. When I finished singing on the patient I go home. I always tell before I leave, you must stay in hogan for four days, and then take a bath about four days — wash hair, water, soap, take all clothes off. But you must do it early in the morning. Do this — take a bath. From then on, you could sleep with your wife — but I don't care. You could go out and work and herd sheep. It's all right.

When I through singing, before I leave I always tell the patient: You must take care of yourself for 3–4–5 days. Don't mean to your wife, to your children — All things what you got in hogan. When I leave they always — jump on their wife and sleep with them. Just because I'm through, and I'm not there. Then after that that patient — maybe a year — maybe a month — the same man come again. Well, he said, I'm still sick again. They always say that. I say that's your fault. I tell you not to do bad things, I know he do that. I ask him what was your trouble? I had bad dream again — keep dreaming all the time — bad dream. And he told me, "You didn't sing very good on me." It's not my fault. It's your fault, I told him. I told him not to sleep with your wife or that kind of things and I pretty sure you did it — that's why the bad dreams didn't go away. I'm not going to sing on you again, you go around and find another Blessing Way singer to sing on you. That's the kind of people they say: Old man didn't sing very good — they says. But it's their fault, own fault. Some patients, they're really good — not only him but all of them — they mind me. They don't have bad dreams of their own. Some people they don't mind, they always keep bad dreams going on — they won't stop.

81. [Why is Blessing Way called *hozhonzhi*?]

This Blessing Way Sing it's not just called *hozhonzhi* — that's way make it a long time ago. We don't know. I didn't give the name. Long time ago the Holy People they called Blessing Way, *hozhonzhi*. That's why we call it that way. Even one song is kind of long. When I start singing one song, I have to name all this hogan, and the fire, and the door, and the things what all in there. When I start singing at nighttime may be Holy People they outside. They listen the singing. If I'm doing the right singing they will say: Think the singing is pretty good. So they shake their head and go back home — some place else. (Shaking head means the singing is good — going well — so they feel happy and shake their head and go.)

[If the singing isn't good, what do the Holy People do?]

If the singing is really doing well the Holy People will be sure happy. They listen to the song and they enjoy the song, and they listen outside. They stay outside all night till morning. Then they go away. The Holy People will say it's really good singing, and let's go back home — so they go back home. If the singing is not very good, he always missing the song, missing the words, the Holy People will not listen and also will not happy. Oh so too bad for the singing — if he miss the words while singing.

[Do the Holy People go back home if the singing is bad?]

The Holy People if you're missing the sing, they leave right away.

82. [What do the Holy People do for the people in the hogan?]

When the Sing is going on, the medicine man he is doing right and before he start singing — everybody come in, not supposed to go out. Then they pass around the corn pollen this way — around their backs. When they're finished this side, then pass around woman's side over there. Then they pass the corn pollen back to the Singer and he put some in his mouth and on his head. First time they have to put the patient first in his mouth. Then start singing. There's a hogan song there — about 30 hogan songs. When he finished that song — then stopped there. Then the patient will go out — going out around fire one way and back the other way. Then people if they want to go out — it's all right. Before that not supposed to go out until the person go out. So the Holy People they outside, they listen. If this singing is going pretty good, when the patient go out — they feel happy. If the Singer not doing well, the Holy People will say: It's too bad for all the people what's in there in the hogan. Not just for the patient but for all the people in there. That's what the Holy People does it.

83. [What do the Holy People do to the people in the hogan? or do for them?]

This Holy People they enjoy the people what's inside the hogan — [they enjoy] the same — they come to the Sing too, because Holy People before you go the person's home, they know your name. When someone go over here to see you to try to have a Blessing Way, he comes down and pay you for it, and wants you to go over there tomorrow evening. The next day — that evening they'll start the singing. Maybe Holy People is way out in the mountains some place. They knows that tonight there's going to be a singing and they say to each other: Let's go to the Sing — that old man's singing over there. That's the way Holy People say to each other and the same way with the Indian, too, the people around here. Maybe they get together on the road some place and they talk together and say I'm going to the Singing. The other two will say we don't know that Singing, the other two know and say let's go over there. The way people goes to the Singing. The same way people does it. When they bring lots of food inside the hogan — they put it both side — woman's side and this side. Pretty soon the food will be all gone. Nothing but the dishes left. The people don't eat all the food, because Holy People they came inside and they have eaten, too. That's why they clean all the dishes. If the Holy People don't come in, there will be some food left. That's the way it is, too.

84. [Do the Holy People ever make presents to the other people?]

The Holy People they don't give any kind of present to the people. They just listen to the songs.

[Do the Holy People get mad if things aren't done right?]

If they people not doing well with the Singing, making too much noise, laugh, not supposed to look through the keyhole — so the Holy People they feel bad. Not supposed to do that way — to look through the hogan. If you want to go in, go in right away. Don't look through the hogan.

[Do they ever punish people if they don't do things right?]

Way back, long time ago when the first time the Holy People put out this Blessing Way, the Holy People said at that time — from now on this Blessing Way will be put out going well, will be fine, they said. If they not doing well with Blessing Way singing, years and years — some day, they not going to have no more rain, no grass, not different kinds of corn, and feed, and everything. They will pretty bad on them — everybody. If they pray good — they will have some rain, corn, [etc.] all their life. Because nowadays every singing to put out — always have lots of bootleg in there, holler, fight — that's why we don't have no more rain, we can't raise no more corn now. They have to buy it at the store. Long time ago they had a lot of corn . . . The old man thinks that's the truth. I think that what Holy People say was true. The summer in the year is always changing now. If the people doing all right with their Blessing Way, about this time we still be in good shape. Now it don't look very good shape. It bad to me everywhere.

[Do Holy People ever get mad and hurt people, because people don't mind them?]

The Holy People is, they say — any person make fun of the song, make laughing at the song. The man who does it that way to Blessing Way song, that person is not going to live very long. Also make fun of the medicine man. That's the way it happens a lot around here. It seems to him that way, Indians, young people just get sick and they just dies.

[Do Holy People kill them?]

No. Holy People don't hurt people. *Hozhonzhi* — won't die — keep going.

85. [Did Holy People teach people other things besides how to hold sings?]

The Holy People they don't mind people who's not having any kind of ceremonial. They go every places where they're have a Sing. The Holy People don't go visit a person's home not having a Sing. They just go where there's a Sing [Interpreter says: They didn't teach the people anything except about the Sings.]

[Did Holy People teach about things that are *bahadzid*? Who did?]

Nobody knows this word "bahadzid." The Holy People they didn't say that word. Didn't name that word. But the people around here they always said if they saw some rattlesnake or bear, or some bad animal — they always say "*bahadzid*." The Missionary down at ——— I guess he knows who put out the *bahadzid* words.

86. [Is that all the Missionary knows about?]

[Laughs.] We Indian, we Navahos, we should stay with our religion. Long time ago, the Holy People what they done it for us. Give up this Blessing Way medicine and also some other different kinds of ceremonial. It's not just few, it's whole lots. It's all over the Reservation, here, other places, we got the same religion. The Holy People they don't want us to throw away our religion. But we should stay with it, what the Holy People done us years and years ago. They not doing just for us, they do it for Zuni, they got different kinds of ceremonials, Hopi, all different kinds of tribes — they got different kinds of ceremonial — they got. So they know who give to them. So this missionary at ——— he sure he don't like me. Every time he sees me, you have Blessing Way medicine, you got. I told him, yes, I got it, and he told me: Throw away that Blessing Way medicine; and then throw away and then come down and join in ——— church, and you will hear good story. And he told him: I won't do that. I won't throw away my medicine. I want to have it. I won't join the church. I won't have it. That isn't my religion, I told him. So that's why I want to stay with my medicine. [More on the missionary omitted.]

87. [Why did the Holy People want to help your people and teach these things?]

Long time ago, the Holy People was — they — in the first place they put out this Blessing Way or some other kind of medicine — not just Blessing Way but all kinds of singing. They put it out for us, we didn't put it out, Holy People put it out for us. If you stay with this Blessing Way medicine as long as you people got it — if you live right, you could sure have it on your hand — and also the song — you won't forget it. If you don't live right, you will forget all the song and the words of the song too. It's already lots Blessing Way medicine men — not in here but over Reservation — lots of medicine men — they die, because they don't learn it from them, so the Holy People said, if you live right and you have this ceremonial as long as you got it, and the day and night will be the same — not any fights in the world, not any war. But now everybody's going the wrong way, so we have lots of war — they destroy the mountain. The Holy People said not to destroy the mountain. So everything is bad all over nowadays. I believe what the Holy People said. If I am doing the bad medicine man, or doing the wrong way singing among the people, I won't live that way. I be dead long time ago. But I try my very best Blessing Way medicine. That's why I'm pretty old now.

88. [I lent a fellow one dollar the other day, and he said he would meet me in the store the next day and pay me back?]

You knew he needs that — Who was he? [I told him the name.]

I find it that way quite a few times around here — to some of the boys around here. They say I'm working around here, and when I get paid, I pay you back. But don't get even 5 cents. Lots around here like that. That's bad. Not long ago, maybe about a week ago, a fellow borrowed from ———— $5. Since then he got paid two times, but he never paid back. Maybe he's not going to pay me back. That day the medicine man was singing he was out there with baby, at that time he borrowed $5. [Maybe it was ———— that did the borrowing?]

[It was very little money and didn't make much difference, do you think he should have paid me back?]

It wasn't right. You should go see him pay you back. He's the one asked the money — borrowed the money. He's the one that borrowed the money. Kind of lying. Go ahead and tell pay you back.

[Why was it wrong?]

Because he thinks he's not going to pay you back. That's what he thinks. Same way with him — he's not going to lend ———— any money any more. So you shouldn't do that to that fellow. He's a liar — he said.

89. [Should you always tell the truth, is it always wrong to lie?]

That's the truth. He really big liar that boy. He didn't do it just to you, but he done it to everybody around here. If someone lend him money, and say he'll pay you back in a few days and he pays you back that's fine.

Then next time you see that man again, well said I borrow you some more money. I'm hungry, so that man said, you pay me back last time, so I lend you some more this time. If you don't pay back, you don't get any more money. That's the way that fellow is.

[Should you tell the truth, even if it's going to cause trouble?]

Even if it causes trouble, if you borrow money from somebody and if it causes trouble you should pay him back and that's all right.

I'm too old — I don't see why people ask me about money. I'm not working. I don't know why they ask me for some money. I'm old and can't see. Let them borrow from young people — they can go look for them and see them. I can't go, can't walk.

90. [Suppose a fellow goes out and sleeps with a girl — nobody else knows about it, and he comes home and his wife asks him where he was. If he tells the truth it would cause trouble — should he tell the truth?]

That man will go back to his wife and make a pretty good story, but he got into trouble. He married some girl, maybe he sleep with her over there some place. He thinks his wife, she never find him about his trouble. But when he sets close to his wife, the first time his wife will find him out. Indian woman they sure smart, if you do that way they sure find you out. May be his wife said: "What you smelling. You smelling some woman." He says: "No, I don't smell anything." "Maybe you sleep with some girl." "No." Pretty soon she finds out. That's the way they find out. Pretty easy.

91. [Suppose: one fellow chasing another with a gun to kill him. The person being chased gets there first and hides. Other comes running up and says where is the other? Should you tell the truth or tell a lie? (This is Kant on Supposed Right to Tell a Lie).]

If some Indian comes around saying a fellow with a gun, and wants to kill me and he says crawl under a box or went on. Pretty soon the fellow comes with a gun and says where's that fellow I'm going to kill him. And then I tell this man he had a gun. Yes he came in and came just a little while and he went on. I don't know which way he just run on. Then I want to tell this man: You don't want to kill this man. What's the trouble? If you kill this man, they're going to kill you, too. So just stop and put your gun down. We have officers who would straighten it out, and pretty soon he says: All right. I'm not going to kill that man and puts down his gun and goes home. When he goes home, the man comes out from under the box.

[What if he says, if you don't tell me where he is, I kill you?]

If he said that way, if he said that if you don't tell me, if he said that way. I say you no good and you's going to get into trouble. So I is taking away the gun. Until we find out what you done it to us, and until we — and see what the officers will say — That's the only thing that's good for him.

92. [Interpreter started telling Bidaga about one of his wife's relations who was in an accident and taken to hospital, etc., and now she wanted to try to get the man who was driving and was also drunk to help pay the costs.]

[Suppose he were talking over this business with the two people, what would he say to the man and what to the lady?]

If he's with the leaders that way talking about a case like that, the man who drives the truck shouldn't drink if he's hauling the people like that. He knows that liquor's not very good when a fellow gets drinking. He's old enough to know all those things. So in that way I think the lady, the woman, is right what she says — because she hurt pretty bad on the road. But her eldest daughter really hurt pretty bad — she's at Fort ———. Doctor told her to stay in bed all the time — got one broken bone in the hip down here and another place is just bent and one wrist come out of joint. She's still got a cast, and that's been quite a while now, and these people they all in one family and they way behind with their money. If it wasn't for that, that lady and children would be home working now. So he thinks it's worth to talk about that case with some people, for that family and try to get straightened up this case for both sides — so there won't be no hard feeling against one another. Looks like this man should have come back and see those family after the accidents happen, and they never came back to see family at hospital. Well, I think that woman should get paid something. Man can pay for his trouble. That's the way I feel about it. About liquor, people can get that any place — they cannot cut it out. These drinkers they don't try to listen to the people who don't use liquor. When they get hurt themselves by drinking or hurt somebody drinking, or get caught and go to jail, then they feel sorry about it, only for a short time, and I think this man who was driving could pay some of his money to these family — make the other people feel better about him then.

93. [Suppose that the people that got hurt had a lot of money and didn't need help — should the man still do something for them?]

[Laughs] If they even rich they can be needed help on that trouble. So they can get the case straightened up on both sides. Sometimes when a rich man — you think he don't need money — has lots of money, but rich man is harder than poor man. He wants to get more money all the time besides how much he got.

94. [You said the reason why you are an old man is because you held Sings properly, etc. If a man never made mistakes would he live for always?]

In the old days, the way my parents telling me, the old ones singing the Blessing Way that we used to follow — do right in your singing and do right in your own living. Then you can have long life to live. By not doing old ways, not to do right of singing or praying and not live right, you will have short life then. That's the way my parents used to tell me. I still believe the old ways. That's the way with me — I never die, I got grey hair.

95. [Is dying the worst thing that can happen to anybody?]

Holy People has a law like white man's law. If the child when it's just born, this man who make a law for people, he can say how long this child going to live, and he might say just about a year, or 10 years, or 50 years or he can get old age and die, or he can say this baby will come out dead. That have to go. But when this law says that if he says this child going to live about 50 years, this child might get sick, real sick, but he's not going to die, because law says he's going to live 50 years. That kind of case, when that comes in, he gets sick, but he gets better all the time, until his life ends just like he was told when he was born. But that law don't tell us, don't tell the people, by individual one. We just heard the story like that from our parents — several Holy People who takes care of that deadness — they decide when people going to die.

[Does that mean that you can do anything you want because you cannot die?]

It's very hard to believe, but I believe myself. Sometimes I think about it, I got too old and got sick a few times while I was living. This Holy People might give me long life — I might get too old and die. I wasn't any mean at all when I was young, and I was always good to the people, but old age is not any good to die. He thinks it's bad to him. He can't see, you don't know where you are. Start to walking — you don't know when you're going to walk in it. You might walk off a long deep cliff, even. You have to have somebody besides you to see things for you. Then many other things. It's not good things for old age.

96. [Do Holy People make laws about whether people are going to be good or bad people, as well as about when they're going to die?]

It's a hard question for me to tell about same law again. This law says when a woman is expecting a baby, for her and her husband it's going to be pretty hard for these two people when they're expecting baby like that. If they go around and look at the things — on the woman's side she can see dead coyote or a dead cow striked by lightning, or a dead snake, and many other lizard. Even they see one of those, after the baby's born baby will get sick on that, and these two people they can get a Singer — medicine man. This singing can collect [correct?], can cure the baby, and the baby can get well on that. This baby is going to get it any time, to get sick any time after he's born — right away, two years after he's born, or five years after. By seeing dead coyote these people can get corn meal, make it up dough and make up coyote figure — make up four coyote and make one dog besides that.

[Description of cure omitted.] When the medicine man learn by doing this coyote and dogs, he think they got it off from the same law, he's talking about.

97. [Did the Holy People just find out this law, or did they make it up like a plan?]

The way I heard about this, I think this law has some friends with them and talk about the plan. Take one plan at a time and they are different plan from one another. They didn't just go ahead and make up this plan by one person. The plan that they have taken up for the Navaho people that they (Navahos) are going to use it, so it means these plan was decided by these people — all these plan what was taken up at that time, it's going to do some goods to the Navaho people. I think that was the way I remember it today. I have forgotten some of it, but I still have some of it in my mind yet.

[When they talked about it did they have some good plans and some bad plans, and they chose the bad plans?]

[Lots of laughter.] He didn't think there's another law that's been taken up for bad plans. It's only for good plans that the law used to do. The way I heard about making plans in a bad way, killing a man or stealing, they didn't mention that when they was telling me about it.

[Did the Holy People tell them about lying, stealing, drinking?]

I give you another short story from way back when the beginning start. They was no mention about stealing in those days, and no lying. Right at that time, a man that called "Coyote," he did some stealing first, and he was the one that did the wrong things, starts first before anybody else starts it. So he shows that to the people. He thinks he was doing nice things from the other people. When the people sees Coyote starts like that, some people thought that might be a good thing to steal something off somebody, and they said: Coyote starts wrong thing first, that's where badness comes in. Coyote stole the two twins up and steal it.

98. [How do the Holy People know how long a man is going to live?]

Before the Navaho people start living on the earth, that's later yet, but this is way back where just the Holy People was talking together then. So one of this Holy Man must have been pretty strong, he just gives a child when baby first starts breathing inside woman yet, they used to say — nobody else is going to give this child how long he's going to live. But this man who gives the time to the people, it's just himself who gives how much time to the people. So it's that man who gives us the time — how long we're going to live. So the Navaho people didn't give anything out like that to their people. When Navaho people starts to living on the earth, they heard some stories went ahead of us already, so they just heard about that . . . The Singers, the one that are good Singers they know some of these stories. This story has all been forgotten about by young people, only the old people, just a few of them, know these story — old story. The animals and different kind of birds and many different kind of coyotes, wild cats, different kind of wild snakes, spiders, and many other things that live in the earth, this old story used to say — these things that I mentioned — they're just people then. They used to talk together like we're doing now. When the Navaho people start on the earth, they don't talk together any more. He heard that they used to understand each other, like we Navaho people understand each other.

[Question ignored.]

I don't remember all the stories like this old one we've been talking about. But I heard these Holy People used to take up a plan among themselves — but taking one at a time. I understand they used to point out one of the man, that he'll be Singer of Blessing Way, or sing Evil Way, and another ones for different chant. So these song and pray is made up way back there. So I don't really remember everything in there. My father used to ask me that he could tell a lot of story, if he wants to hear more about it that he told me he would learn me a lot. But I was waiting all the time while he was living, and he got too old and died. All the stories that I didn't know, I never heard about it. He had that story — just like he been taking it away from me. If I did learn a lot of that stories — that he would learn it four times as much as he know now. It's just my fault why I didn't learn some more from my parent. I thought he was going to live many years yet, but he died and I didn't get much story.

[Is there one among the Holy People who decides whether people are going to be good or bad?]

At the time when these Holy People was making up the plan, at same time when he's talking about the baby's going to born — that he told people that whether people is going to be boy or girl, he's going to lie about something, and he might get mad pretty easy — all the bad things that a person can do, he says, that's the way the man's going to be. He says, but they was going to be some good mans also — not lie, not steal, not do any wrong thing. Live straight.

99. [Did the Holy People say to the Navahos: Don't lie, don't steal! Or did the Navahos find that out for themselves?]

The people didn't ask for it, but the Holy People decided and give it to the people.

[Did the Holy People promise to give good things to the people if they obeyed them, or to punish them if they disobeyed?]

There's a story pretty near like that that I want to tell you about. There's four people with these good people — they're not Holy People — them four — kind of against these good people. Old Age, one of them. Second one is Poor. Third one is Starving, Hungry. Fourth one is man that wants to have no dead person — he wants to have anybody live for and years — not die, and he says — long story that he made. [Interpreter confused.]

Old Age says person must get old, he can get up where he's pretty weak — not strong any more, not to see — they can be like something's ripe —

when something's ripe you just pick it up and it tears to pieces. He's the man decides that people can get old. Those Holy People, they gave him a chance — for this Old Age to speak. So he says that. The Poor, I guess we might call him Poor people's boss, he like people to get poor. The Starving — Hungry — he's the man that says: I like to have the people get hungry once and while from he's borns out till he gets old. They might go hungry and die, some of them. We not going to have food all the time. Food's going to run out from the family lot of times.

There's another person, the man that takes care of the sleep — there are two together: one is Lice [that is, Lice and Sleep]. The Holy People was going to kill all these four people out, and they sent a man out to kill this Sleep and Lice. He was going to kill them with a stick. When he come over there to these two people, he start to hit them like that with that stick. This man who has stick, he went to sleep right now. They made him do that. So they went back to the Holy People and reported it there. They go to the next one and see what he says. They go to Poor next. This Poor says, when this man wants to kill him, he says, if you kill me you going to wear just one clothes, one color clothes all your lifetime. One color clothes — all the time — will be all raggy. He says I like to have the people wear good clothes, different kind — good blankets, good beads — if you will me — they won't have it. They went back and reported it at the place again. The Starving — he says that people will have different kind of food — better food all the time. If he's killed the people won't have that. [Interpreter confused about the story; Death comes in some place.]

About Old Age, when man gets old or woman gets old, that Old Age says: I'll be with old man or old woman and I'll put a lot of sleep upon that man or woman. So when the old man or old woman gets old he always goes to sleep pretty heavy and snores. That man's causing it. But Death — they want to kill Death — they was going to kill him. He says: Let the people die. People will be increasing all the time. If you want no death, I don't want to go with you. They say they told them they want the people to live for years and years. He says: If you want to do that, the people won't increase if they married together — they won't have no babies. There'll be the same amount for years and years. I want to see a lot of good women, good man, and lots of people. So let them die, he says, and they reported over there. And these people they was giving to them like what they want to do. That's why we have Old Age, Poor, Starve, and Death. [The interpreter said he had skipped a few sentences: namely:] These four people gave good ideas to these Holy People. Holy People kind of forgot about that. Where the clothes and jewelry has to be changed and getting old again, and people die — they think that's all right, too. By starving — that sounds like something that would be good to the people. Going to be lots of food — different kind of food. It might go scarce but it always comes back.

But now the Singers, old people like these, they just wonder why these four people talk pretty strong to the Holy People like that. They should have been killed, they say. He knows that Old Age not a very good thing to get old. There's an old man just goes back to where he was born. Can't see nothing — don't know how to think about things. He cannot able to pick up a little thing, because he can't see and weak. Looks like he have to have somebody besides him, like he was when he was a baby to take care of him. That's what the people says now. People kind of mixed up about these four men. Some think we're going to be poor all the time if we kill poor. Some people thinks it's a good thing to be poor, and lots think it's not a good thing to be poor. Lot of people don't like to get die — wants to live for years and years. Lot of people says wouldn't be very good for just a few people to live on the earth for years and years — not die. They like to be the way things is now. Let some die and let some come up.

100. [What does he think about the dying?]

[Laughs.] They both even to me he says. I think it's better to die and it's better to be dead than to live for years and years. After all this happened, there's another man want to make a speak before Holy People. That's the Sun. He says, from the morning long just the time when he's out start shining on the earth, from that time till sundown — I wanted to have something to have for my trouble — spending time between sunup and sundown. He says, there's a people, people that's talk, and besides that there's different kind of animal — then there's lot of eagles and small birds — anything that flies on the earth, and rabbits and prairie dogs — many other wild animal. Everything's on the earth. When anything dies — long in the daytime — he means whether baby, old man, lady — that's to be his payment for travel in daytime. Same way with wild animal. Same way with everything what live on earth. Anything like little worm die in daytime — that's going to be his. And then anything what's big — rich man or poor man — just take one at a time.

[Why just one?]

The story kind of mixed up. Some people says that will be his payment taking just one. But the other people says — the Sun didn't say that will be his payment. He just says people's going to have death every day, but we'll not stop that. Sun means that we will have death each day.

[Question ignored.]

In that case where I mentioned the Holy People said that the people's going to have bad action in their head — like stealing or lying or murder somebody. They say we're going to have that. So I don't — after they said that — I don't think it's going to be changed any other way. And even like you think you go around visit the people and get together the people talking about things, you might think he's pretty good man or good lady because he's speaking pretty nice. And these kind of people they might think they're good man or good woman. But we always make mistake. You're going to get mistake next few minutes or tomorrow — a little — but you don't know where mistake is. You just run into it. Or somebody puts you into it. By taking your own care you think you're good care of yourself. You don't want to lie somebody — but you get into that just the same.

[At this point Bidaga was carried off to hold a Sing. He performed three before the next interview.]

January 17, 1952 (Interpreter: Bill Begay)

[A long opening discourse about a Sing and how nice the anthropologists are has been omitted.]

101. [If a young man came to you and asked you whether he should go and fight for his country or stay at home and take care of his sick mother, what would you say (that is, Sartre's problem)?]

I can soon go to help my mother, because my mother raised me. She's the one that made me. The time when I born — start to suck on my mother — fed me good. After started eating, she takes care of me with food, until I can able to work. Then when I growed big enough to listen to what the people says, also what mother and father says, she brought up lot of nice talk to me. She says I should take care of myself — how to make my own living. That's why I want to go to my mother. Help my mother first.

[Some people think that going to war is bad, is it always so?]

There's two ways I think about that. I'd rather stay home and take care of my family. But where I don't have no family — just live by myself — I could just go to the war. He has another question — whether I go down there and get into a war — I might get killed down there. But you can never tell. I might save my life and come home.

102. [Question about volunteers for a dangerous mission in war — is that good?]

No. This answer will be where he used to be strong and brave and see pretty good. At that time he didn't afraid of anything. But I could say I go along with these people, but right now I can't able to do anything — not strong any more and blind. [Question repeated]

I pretty near become soldier one time. A lot of people of my age become soldiers — once or two times. To go out — way out south. They was looking for Apaches down there. The first bunch went down there, where they have second bunch. There's another bunch. I like to go with the people, talks to his father about that. My father didn't want me to go. He says I don't like for you to be soldier. One time the Navaho people was good friend to the Apache, before they start any kind of war. My father says I'm still friend to Apaches — that's why he don't want me to go along. Let the other people go and you stay at home. So I didn't get to go.

[If one of his grandchildren came and asked him if he should fight in Korea?]

He'd say yes. The way I feel about myself today, right now — I'm blind now and I'm too old. Very hard for me to get around. So I don't like to try to save myself any more. Might getting worse every year.

[Why say "Yes"?]

Because he's too old now. Like to be killed off!

[If he were a young man?]

When I was young, I rather live. That's the way I used to think about myself.

103. [In fighting a war, should you run away or stay and be killed and save others?]

I think it's a good thing to stay and help the rest of them. Not to run away. That is if I have a gun — something in my hand to shoot with. I be glad to shoot some of the enemies — as long as they don't shoot me.

[Why stay?]

That is when he's brave — he'll stay and help the rest of them. Rather to help his people and fight. The other soldiers think they want to win the war, so I don't like to run off. If one of us get away from there, or two of us, we make our soldiers mad. They might whip them. But the other side, when one soldier get away, just about get ready to fight, he's scared — don't like to be killed. Wants to get away from it. When his soldier win the war, then they going to laugh about him. Talking about him: he's no good at all because he ran away. They'll tell him: you just like the other side — want to run off before we stop fighting. If you want to do that again, we just might as well shoot you. So that soldier he hasn't got no good heart. He's scared. Gets scared pretty easy. Who wants to stay with the fight, he's good man, strong man, good idea.

[If all the fellows he ran away from got killed, would he feel sorry that he had run? (Informant had fallen asleep. When he awoke I repeated question!)]

They all feel pretty bad about it if the soldiers get killed off. What they sorry about is that they run off to save themselves. They save themselves but they feel sorry about it.

[Why feel sorry about having saved yourself?]

It's this way, I mean. The people that run away, they won't pay any attention for the people that got killed out, until their own people at home start to talking about it. People will say: Why did they run off? People will say: you all got away from your soldiers, that's why they got whipped. You shouldn't do that in the first place. You should fight with the others. If you stayed you might win the war. Where you fellows run off, that's what made the people sore and sorry about it. When the people tell them that much, then they might feel sorry about it — like the rest of them.

[Suppose fellow who ran away said: You ought to feel happy I'm alive — that's good?]

He don't know just how these people will get away from there, but I heard some people did it. After they do that, then they never think about it. They just don't care what the people saying about it. That's all they care — they saved. But I heard there used to be people talking about cases like that. They'll be some mans, if he has a family, children, or had a bow and arrow right here by him at the hogan. When the soldier come in, that's all he can do is run off, run away from his children and got too scared — not think about his bow and arrow. Got too scared and run off without it. That's the way they used to tell me about it. So all his children can be killed and his bow and arrow pick up by somebody.

That kind of man — the other people can make fun of him. They can tell him, he's just like a woman, because he leave his children and leave his bow and arrow. Don't remember anything, just get scared and run off.

104. [About war going on]
I don't know whether they going to quit the war soon or whether they're going to keep fighting for many years yet. I don't know whether our soldiers are strong as the other side. I just don't know what they're going to do next.

[If we knew they were stronger, ought we to give up?]
Well, if the soldier — if their power is just the same as the other, they should go ahead and fight. There'll be a lot of them killed when the war end. Then after the war passes away, the both sides can be — feel sorry about the people that's been killed at the time when the war was going on. I just look at it this way now. Nobody knows why these soldiers been fighting — what they's been fighting about is just what I don't know. There nobody tell me what's the fight all about yet. If they says they are fighting about something — but it must be something causes and that's the reason I think they've been fighting. But it seems to me they're not fighting for anything — because I can't find out about it from anybody.

105. [Another question ignored.]
When the old Navaho people was still living many years ago, there's — I put it in this way — there's a song in Ghost Way Singing. We have a song and pray for the ghosts to scare away with it. War like that when it come up, start fighting — they have — also have some songs and pray — make the soldiers stop fighting. They used to use the pray to stop the war with. That's the way the old people used to tell us about. Now on two sides, the fight that is going on now — one would like to know if Russia has anything like that to scare the war away with it.

[Did Navahos in the old days talk about going on warpath?]
Way back when the Navaho first start, I'm not sure how the war story runs. At that time, I heard some story about songs of different way singing. But people didn't mention about the war those days. I don't think, that is, Navaho people. So I couldn't answer that.

[Explained I'm interested in talk about war — not in the songs.]
He didn't know very well about that, but he'll say this much. The old people used to say, they have a song and pray for the war. Any time when the war starts, they have song ready and pray ready for them. They can sing their song and say their pray to the war. They won't be very strong. Those soldiers can't think much and their guns won't be very strong either,

just how the song and pray runs, who learn that or who taught it is what I don't know. I only heard this much, from my father.

[Did they have talks about whether to go to war?]

I don't know whether they used to talk about things like that at that time. But I don't think they ever say that we all must go and fight the war. That's all they done is to let the other war come on here first, but I don't think that Navaho people, old people, did want to fight. I heard most everybody wants to run off, get away from the war. Don't want to fight. I heard Zunis want to fight us for a long while. There was some places around here Zunis chase some Navahos. Well, they can chase them down and knock them in the head with oak stick, or catch one Navaho and take him down to the village. Feed him good there and kill the Navaho after they fed him. They do that to the womans also. These different Pueblo tribes — they want to fight the Navahos for a long while, but the Navahos didn't get mad. Whether the Navahos got together and wondered and talk about whether they're going to fight or not, they didn't do that. Not any place. I don't know what happened the Navaho people want to start fighting other tribe. That's what my father used to say.

106. [Supposing a Pueblo tribe came, said that a Navaho had murdered a Pueblo man, and that if they didn't give him up they would burn all their hogans. They knew that this man was a good man, however. What would he do?]

If it was me I won't give it up. I won't kill my man because he's the best man we got, we have — and no matter if we didn't do it, they can burn our hogans. I don't think they will burn the hogan.

107. Wants to tell another short story. Way I said old people did have songs and pray for the war. There's nobody remember here in area now. But over in Reservation there's lot of old people still living, but they keep dying out. But I'm pretty sure those songs and pray is still remember yet inside Navaho Reservation. And looks like some of the white people go around inside the Reservation and ask that question and ask if that pray or song has remembered yet by Navaho people. If they has some remember song and pray, then they can take those people close down east — or north — close the ocean and let those people use their song and pray against the soldier who's fighting us. In that way they might stop the war sooner, or whip the other side. I remember my father used to say, whenever the war start — the song and pray has to be taken against the other side. So that will make the soldier not to be brave, not strong, and their guns will be weak. All the soldiers they all get weak all at once.

108. [Told him story about South Pole explorer who sacrificed his life so that others on the expedition might have enough food to survive. Would this be right?]

If I was with the bunch and having the food that much, didn't have enough, they know they're going to run out of food soon, and they know they have to stay there for some time yet, I don't think killing the other people — that's good. I think you — they — can talk about it. They can think themselves what to do about it. I could do this. I could start and go — right away — and the other people they can go wherever they want to go. Even they got long ways to go without food — whether we'll die before we get home, or before we come to food — there's no other way that I could do — I don't think.

[Explained that one man sacrificed himself for the others.]

There's only two ways that a man could do. If he has something to kill himself with, he can kill himself. The reason that he couldn't live anyway. The other way, he can just go walking and try to go home. I don't know whether he come back home or whether he die before he gets home. I don't think there is anything else a man could do to save himself.

[He was trying to save other people by killing himself.]

Well I don't know what happened this question, pretty hard question. I hear some cases where man kill himself. Sometimes the man do wrong and after that he can feel sorry about it — keeps thinking about thing over and over and gets sick over it. No matter he has brothers and sisters and other relatives, he never think about that — only he could kill himself for that. That's happened in some places, and I seen it in some places. And that question that you ask him, I don't know how to answer that.

[Asked interpreter whether he understood the question?]

Where I can be way out and the very small food that I have, I know I can't get back with that. But I don't want to harm myself. I can just soon start direction where I could be safe, but I don't think I'll live because I'm a long way off — because that's all I can do. And for seven or five people and I will be in the bunch, and we'll be long way off — close to ocean I might say — and we have only small amount of food. If we was told we have to stay there for whole summer, and he says that's where I can't answer that very well. One man might say to me, let's go ahead and kill these other people so we have enough food to save ourselves, and I say I won't harm anybody for that. Why we want to kill these people? That food won't last long — even between the two of us — we kill the other people. We'll be dead just the same, if we kill the people because we ain't got no food. That's the way I feel about it myself. I don't know what the other people — what kind of a feeling or thinking they had about themself.

109. [Is he afraid of the ghosts of the other people?]

No — where I don't want to kill a person like that — the reason I don't want to do that — I have to do all I can for these other mans. One might die first, starve, and keep dying out like that. Then we all die for starve. Then that's all over with. But I cannot let a man go if he's still moving himself. They can starve — will have nothing else to do.

[He doesn't want to bring the ghosts in?]

[Laughs.] No. He hasn't got any feeling like that. If I kill a man and then I afraid the ghost will come back and get me. It's not for that reason. The reasons I want to help dead body to put away — so something won't want to come around and tear up and eaten by coyote. So that's why I don't want to kill a person. I heard there's some people — that's years ago — who had some kind of sickness kill a man. They used to get away from sick man before the man died. Let him die himself, and then go away from there. But I don't know why they did that.

[Maybe the ghost would be mad because they let him die alone?]

A man or woman didn't have no relatives and poor — people don't care about him — he gets sick and die. Then the time the people don't care for him, just let him die, just go away — and he dies because he has nobody to look after him. We Navaho people when Navaho people die that way — we always afraid. If we do that when this man died all by himself — his ghost might come back and hurt the people who left him. That's the way the old people used to tell us. But the other people — white, Mexican, and different kinds of tribe — they not afraid of dead body. But we do.

[One reason for not killing people at South Pole (above) is because of ghosts?]

Yes, he says, the ghost will come back on these people who kill. That's one big reason you don't kill a man or woman. [Interpreter and informant comment on terrible stories I tell.]

110. [What did the old people teach about overeating?]

This is the way the old people used to say, used to taught their children. For the man's side telling his son, he don't want to have a son eat too much. They had hardly any food those days. He wants his son to get used to food where he can eat just a little bit at a time. You cannot have food all the time, because we get food, just barely little bit to get along with. We ain't got no way to go and look for some food — where you can get some food is long ways to get it most time. But you have to walk for it down there — long ways. You might think you'll eat a lot of food if you find the food. If you find some food and eat too much of it, you'll get sick of it and it kill you. Sometimes you just go like a sheep or cow — blowed up. I don't want you to be that way. But just take a little at a time — and just take that much. That's the way they taught their children. Woman they can talk them just the same. But after the white people bring a lot of food among the Navaho people, they started eating a lot of food. Still they tell them that same thing yet. Some says when you eat too much, you'll be fat — won't look very good and if you learn how to eat food just a small amount — if you learn how to eat that much — then you will never have trouble with your stomach, and be strong.

[Did they say the same about coffee and water?]

No, they didn't use to say anything about coffee or water. But some of the young girls or boys drink lots of water and coffee. But coffee sometimes they say not to drink too much coffee — water, too. Especially from noon to sundown — The reason they say that it makes them bad sweat at night. That's for children. For the grown people they don't say anything about water drinking or coffee drinking.

111. [Could you sleep with women too much?]

[Laugh.] No they didn't say about sleeping with their woman. But in that same case — they say when you go asleep with your wife, you mustn't let woman get up first. You have to get up first because you're a man. You let the woman get up first, and that shows you're lazy. So man must get up first — long just about day break — early. Then do your work. If you get up late you can't get work done very much in a day.

[Can you work too much?]

No. They don't use to say that. But they can tell you, you can work hard.

[Omission.]

112. [Would he teach his children that it's a good thing to get rich?]

Yes. They can tell their children about getting rich.

[When you get a certain amount ought you to stop or keep on going?]

You can tell your children: you can get rich, if he listen to his parents — how to get rich. You must have a lot of sheep. But you cannot get rich unless you know sheep song, horse song, songs for soft goods (clothings) and songs for hard goods (jewelry). If you know that much then you can raise some sheep and have lot of jewelries. You must learn how to get them and how to raise sheep. If you don't know those song, you will never get rich. If you start to raising sheep and hard goods, where you get lots of sheep and lots of things besides you have sheep, then it's danger again when you start raising all these things you'll be stingy then. You can't give away hardly anything. And try to sell everything high price to the people, and you'll be raising everything — more and more all the time. You'll just die then for no sickness — that richness going to kill you. So be better to — not too rich. Not too much.

113. [Is it better to be poor than rich?]

Be poor is no good. Poor man, poor woman, he have nothing to spent for food and for clothing. And besides that lot of things. Wouldn't have good home at all, no jewelry. When a man is rich, he's better off. Have plenty money, sheep, cattle, jewelry, good home, good land, and then lot of tools to do work around home. Plenty of food for his children, family. That's a lot better than poor man. So I think it's a lot better to be rich.

[Is it better to be rich or healthy?]

Still riches is better. Healthy man is just as good as rich, but healthy man have to have something to make his living. So rich man and healthy — they like even. They both pretty good to me.

[Would he rather be a rich man who is unhealthy or a poor man healthy?]

When a man is poor and he is healthy, and how is he going to make a living. If he is healthy, but he is poor — so richer is still better to me.

114. [Better to be a rich man nobody likes, or poor man everybody likes?]

[Laughs.] A rich man never helps his people with what he has. Nobody likes him. And on the other side, when the poor people and helping with his work — all around — among his people. He thinks it's better to be on the poor man's side, because rich man has no use for his people and his people has no use for him. So he would be with the poor man — he's trying to help everybody.

[Why? Rich man can buy anything he wants?]

Poor man, he can help a family where a family needed to build a hogan. Poor man could get up and do the work for this family. And they can give him just the food, just the meal to work for, and poor man don't mind it. Poor man can haul wood for another family. If that family has a team and wagon. Everything the poor man do — what he knows — of working to help his people with, and wherever he wears out shoes and clothes — different people can buy clothing for man, and poor man won't say he work a day or two and wants to get paid for it. He tells the people he's just helping. That's why the people likes him. Rich man wouldn't do anything like that for his own people.

[Does it make any difference whether he applies this to himself or to others?]

[Laughs.] I feel this way about myself. I don't want to be real poor. I'm poor man already now. But I don't want to get real poor. And I don't want to be rich man, because I have no way to get rich right now. But I like to be at home and have few sheep, few horses, few tools, and plenty to eat. I like to be in the middle place of poor and rich. That's where I am now.

How people can talk about the poor man. You can stay at poor man's place if you're going far away and come to a poor man's home. He got nothing to feed you, and he has no good stories to tell you. He just has poor way stories, and that's not good to listen it. And that's why I don't like to be poor man.

January 18, 1952 (Interpreter: Bill Begay)

[Began questioning about weddings. Since the ceremonial details are the same as are available in other accounts they have been omitted. (See Leighton and Leighton, 1949, pp. 49–50.) The wedding dinner has just been finished.]

115. When everybody through eating, take the dishes out. These people will have a man there already. That's one kind of officer — or just a head man. One that make good speak. Starts to talking to the boy first — give

him good lesson — talking. Man will say to the couple — by having ceremonial like this for you couple, do you know what this basket and the mush
means? They can say both of them: No. That means something like marriage certificate. You must live together — and for boy's side you must mind
your wife. You will have good home. And for girl's side you must mind your
husband. If you mind each other like that, you can do your work together,
and do the work the best way you can.

The leader will say he wanted to know just how much talk he will make
— asking the boy's mother or father. The parents says we like to have you
talk to our boy — all you can. The problem like making his home very nice
and do his work right there at home, and all the others in the way he could
make a good living him and his wife. Then the leader start talking — telling
the boy: You know what your father and your mother says, and I will do
the talking and you will listen to me just what I want to tell you about.
Your marriage tonight — I want you to start to build up your home. Build
up nice hogan. And start to buying some dishes and food for your home,
and then you will be working outside — and outside work will be farming.
We all want to have something to raise in summer time. Want you to build
good fence around your crop. It will be lots of work for you to do around
home. Besides that work what you do, you can also help your father-in-law
and your mother-in-law. They need some work—got to be done, and they
need help. You must listen to your father-in-law and mother-in-law whatever he want you to do, you must do it for them. Anything what you don't
know how to do, you go ahead and ask your father-in-law what to do next
and how to do it, if you don't know how. Now if you listen all this — you
will have some children and then you start having children. And then you'll
have some more work to do for your children. You must think hard and try
hard of the work that you're doing. This all what I mean is for you do the
good work and be honest.

Try to get on with your people. Not to get mad to your people or to
your wife. You must do right. Be honest. Your mother-in-law and father-in-
law don't like you to tell a story, tell a lie. They won't like it, your doing
that. After you have settled down good, building up your home — where
you can have all these works, can think you can do by yourself — you can
separate your home off from your mother-in-law and father-in-law. After
that you can building up your sheep or wagon, farm tools. You can start that
yourself. You and your wife — and start to take care of your own property.
You must not go around to Sings too much. Go once and a while, but not too
close together.

Man will say: I will have this in mind from now on — after I go home
from here in a month time or two I will ask about young people: How
you're getting along. I will ask about you people all the time. If you tend
to your own business and help all your people — make up yourself good
man — then I will be happy about it. That's all the leader have to say to the
boy.

And he says the same thing to the girl, telling the girl that she must mind the man doing the housework, cleaning the house inside, cleaning up the dishes. Tell her that he [that is, she] must think about herself — that's she's going to live many years ahead, and that she's young and she have to do her work right and tell the truth about everything what's going on — from the time his [that is, her] marriage until his life end. Some years ahead you might have a boy or girl — son or daughter — they can be married, too — like the way we just did, and you will ask the leader — your son or your daughter — have to be taught just like this way we doing. So you must do right to your own people — no matter whether a man or woman is not related to you. Be kind to them. Not to be mean to the people. Not to be mean to your livestock. In that way you can make your people get along with you. Now if you do that you're going to live a long time.

116. [I asked whether word for living a long time was *saą naghai*. They said it was related.]

Saa naghai — that's the word that every song that ends with it. But that's something like one of the Holy People have a word. That's a name. But all the Singers they's kind of afraid to talk about Blessing Way song. They kind of feel bad about it if they talk about. They won't talk about it for nothing. Only time they can talk about it is when Singer is talking song to young man — then he can tell that story there.

Bikeh hozhon — goes with that. They hang together. Only the Singer who sings Blessing Way and the other Singers — all different ways they're singing. They only know this word. But they don't tell it out to the people what it is. They are afraid to talk about those two words. Only time when Singer is learning the Song to another man. When a man is through learning, then that comes in behind all these song. Then this man will ask that he wants to learn what's meaning by that two word. Then Singer he has a right to tell that little story to man who learned the Song. He didn't have to tell about it if the man learned just a little bit of the Song. That's only time when man sing the whole Blessing Way. They can talk about good living and living a long life anytime.

117. About being afraid of your mother-in-law. In the old strong way, anytime when the wedding's happened, they used to tell on the boy's side he shouldn't see his mother-in-law. [Interpreter adds, "that's *bahadzid*."] Seeing your mother-in-law that means you're young and you will spoil your eye. You go blind in the future, and you will not be very strong and your body will be weak all the time. That's for two reasons you mustn't look at your mother-in-law.

118. [Why did the leader tell the boy not to go to too many Sings?]

The reason the leader says that — every place where they have Sing there will be young boys there, and these young boys they can get together and start talking to each other. They can do some things which they shouldn't do. Or start steal something from somebody. Or they can go and start talking to the girls. They can get together with them. So this young boy where he married, he must do right after that. By telling that boy, they want him to build up a good home — more than what he was doing before — he wasn't attending to his business before he married. These young boys always get together at the Sings. That's why they don't want him to go around small ceremony. This leader will know if this boy starts going around these Singing, he will never build up his home.

119. [What did the old people teach about boys and girls sleeping together before marriage?]

When anything happened like that — boy and girl like that before married. If the girl's mother or father find that out what's going on — they make the boy pay something for it. And they report it to the boy's mother and father. The girl's mother she wants to get paid for it. And make the boy stop doing that. No punishment. Boy's father and mother, and girl's parents they can get together about it, and have the girl and boy there with them. Girl's mother might say she don't like that boy. The reason that she'll say that is that she think she'll never get along with that boy. She'll say she knows that that boy is telling lie and don't do much work. She might say she go ahead and said that she make the boy pay. They talk over that case and they'll say they'll pay for it. And tell the girl and the boy not to do that any more. That's the only way they can do. Some places they have to call the leader talk to this two people. They could marry them afterward — if the parents wants to do that on both sides. Leaders could fix it up that way most places. Boy just pays the girl's mother — they might come back together again. If they couldn't fix that up, the best way to do about that is — bring in the leader for it and let him — he will tell the parents on both sides — let them marry together. After they married together your leader could give them good instruction after they're married. That's the only way they can do about it.

[Suppose it's the girl who has been bothering the boy, what do they say to her?]

That's pretty hard to stop it. Boy's family, father and mother, brothers and sisters, they can talk that over about it. They can say that girl — she's running too much with different boys. They think that's hard to stop that girl doing that. They might say they just pay the mother of the girl. That payment will make the father and mother feel good about it. Boy's mother and father can go ahead and look for girl that they wanted for the boy. They can have that girl and boy — marry them right away. So the boy can never go back to the other girl. And for the other party, if they don't like the boy, they can do the same to the girl.

120. [While he was leader, did he ever have to talk to such a girl who runs around? What did he say?]

If the girl is doing too much of that with the boys or mans, it's pretty hard to stop the girl doing that. Girl's father and the mother — they can take the girl inside and tell the girl in there they just didn't like for her doing that with the boys. If you keep on doing like that, some of these boys or mans — they have bad disease — you might run into one. Now if you get one kind of disease, you'll have that disease right away — wouldn't take long. Like you sleep with a boy or man, you might have it next day. Now you can't get by with that. You will find out just how much hurt you will get. First you can have just a little pain, where you make water. You can't make water good — it just hurts like anything. It will grow worse and worse every day, and where you piss the water will be bloody, and what come next is all bloody, pus, yellow, nasty. You can't hide it at all. You just have to get a good medicine man to cure that right away.

This looks like pretty bad story I'm tell you about — so you must listen to this talk. You can never get well on that. Nobody can cure you. You just get worse every day — more and more. A good medicine man could cure it right away, but it's worth pretty good sized money to pay for it. To get cured. But I know they'll stop it — they'll stop it right now if you get medicine from him. [Interpreter adds: "So that's *bahadzid*."]

[After lunch the informant continued:]

I want to go back where my story ends — that isn't all. Where this sickness comes pretty strong, then it's going to be pretty hard to cure for medicine man. One way that disease will do will make a lot of sore in here [points], then that sore goes inside of you, and begins to eat up in here. So you can't able to walk. Then next here in this place all eaten up by sore. You'll be laying down with your legs open, and it'll have some kind of worms — inside down in there. Those worms can stick their head out of there. These worms will have a black head. Long that time, you won't live any more. It will kill you. Now I am telling the girl that way did he [she] understand all about this. It isn't only that kind of disease, different kind of disease will show some other way. Way you going to get this — man will have it. Yes, girl says, she understand it. Then girl gets scared about it. She don't believe she can go and ask some *older people* about it, see what he says about it. Well, after that lot of girls stop after they hear story about that.

[I asked the interpreter to explain phrase about 'older people.' He replied: "She can go and ask one of the good Singer. He can tell her the same thing about it." The informant continued describing venereal diseases. This has been omitted.]

121. [What did they tell the girls before they knew about this disease?]

This story was already known way back where Navaho people start living on the earth. So they start to telling for the boys' side and girls' side — where Navaho people start. There's a lizard about that long [6"] had four legs — little bigger around than my thumb — long tail. He's one of this disease and flies help him this lizard. When sickness cause any person like that, he going just before he takes medicine, swallowing medicine, this lizard and others can be watching him — whether he's going to swallow or not. They can say word — nobody will hear them. They can say: Patient must vomit the medicine out. If the patient vomits it out, then these lizards say that patient not going to live now because he didn't swallow the medicine.

[Did they have the disease in those days?]
They only had the story at that time. They didn't have it (disease) at that time. But where the people start to get into that disease — until the time Mexican people, white people, different tribes — they start to meet together in places — then they start to getting it. A man or woman, can have it by just having a little pain in here. Don't get any worse — just have little pain — all the time. But that kind of disease will go inside. They'll pain all the time in here — but he'll have it inside. Then they can give it to another person — pass it on to different one. That kind of disease could be passed to different ones.

122. [Would going around like that be all right if you didn't get the disease?]
You can never tell whether you're going to get into this. That's for boys, mans, women. Sometimes woman have that disease in her already, and looks good outside — skin is good [etc.] — looks like he's healthy. Same way with man's side. Young man might have it inside, and looks good outside. Woman can't tell whether he's sick or not. Man is just the same, and I seen where old people had one sickness of that kind. And they made some of this medicine. Let him take some and he was a little late about it — got all skinny. Medicine man has to work pretty hard — make this man well. Mr. ——— had same disease, too. And got where he was all skinny — hardly any meat on his body — all bone. But they make him well, too. He got well, too, and lived a long time after that.

123. [Why does boy's family have to pay girl's family for boy's sleeping with girl?]
That payment what they make these for boy's side. That payments has to be made always. The girl's mother don't want to let her daughter do it for free. Wants to get something all the time — that's on the woman's side. Mans they can say just the same — what the woman says. So we have to pay for our boy all the time, when anything happen like that. He says for white people's side, they don't do that. They don't pay any money for anything. So I think it seems like funny to you.

[If girl likes it just as much as boy, why should boy pay instead of girl?]
They don't go by the boy and girl. They go by girl's mother and father. Mother and father says they want to be paid for that. If boy's side, says all right — we'll pay that — we'll pay something, and never pay for many years, the girl's mother will be old and blind. She might come around when this man who goes with this lady's daughter. Lady will ask whether this man right man — got her daughter one time and didn't pay yet. And that lady

will come to man. That old lady will have stick like this. That lady can put her stick on him and won't let him go — though she's blind.

[Is that like paying somebody for hurting them, or killing somebody in the family?]

That's just something like a rule, that persons should go by that rule and do it. It's paying for that girl. So lot of people says: I pay for that girl and she's mine now. Parents got nothing to do with it. Lot of Navaho people says that now.

124. [What happens if the girl has a baby?]

Way back they didn't use to say anything about baby. Even the girl has a baby. If the father goes away, they can just let him go away. Baby can take care by mother, and grandmother and grandfather. That's the way they did before white people came in. Until after white people came in — where baby born like that — father gets away — they make the woman to track this man up where he is living or not — or give them his names so they can track him up, who he is. If he says he don't want to live with that woman — pay his baby so much every month. That's the way they're doing it now. But man have to say: Yes, he'll do that. Sometimes the man says: The baby's not his and don't want to pay anything to the baby. And they turn around to the woman and ask whether he's telling the truth about the baby — belongs to the man. She says: Yes, she's telling the truth — the baby's his — then they take him to Fort Defiance and lock him up down there in jail. He stays in jail for few days, and sometimes the boy comes back and tells the truth and says the baby's his all right — and they make him pay his baby each month. Sometimes judge might give him 30 days in jail before he go out.

125. [Does he think it better the way they did it in old days or now?]

He likes it the way they handle the people now — likes the white people's way. The white peoples are handling cases like that — they talk about it — by law — so they know already in the law — what way should be taken. Way back there, the Navaho people didn't have any kind of law. They used to just talking about it together, and get the things straightened up by talking together — maybe three or four people talking together. But still we have law and white people's way now. There's some people getting by with it yet. Some of the boys just giving the babies to the woman and run off, and they can say it's not their baby. ———, he's doing that. They doing that cause we have no judge, no police — we have supervisor at B—— but he don't come around very often among R—— Navaho people. That's why I mention all about these officers the other day. R—— peoples need it — chapter officers, president, vice president, secretary and delegate and good supervisors who could live here at R—— town or ———, and police. If we had all these officers, people might do right then. Make the young boys behave themselves, and mans and womans. They might make them stop drinking wine also. Since we don't have any kind of officers among R——

people, they're not afraid of anybody. So these young boys and young womans, whose doing wrong among the people — they should be punished like white people's way.

126. [Some people think white people's way is wrong, why does he like it?]

Right now what I'm talking about is where young man and young woman doing wrong. And they could be punished for those things that they're doing. I do not want to harm the young Navahos and young women. What I like for them is to take care of themself — take care of their wife and children. About our wife and children — that's more important to think about it and talk about it. Instead of their going on with their stealing and changing wifes and giving the babies to woman, and go off and get away from it. That's not right for young boys to do that, and woman. In this case, that's where I like to be handle it by white people's law. In that way, these people might mind how to do right things.

Right now where the leaders could make pretty strong talk to these young people — mans and womans, they won't mind at all. They have one hand holding bottle in it, and one to get smart — to be smart to their people. They think they know a whole lot, and they think they can do things. So by just talking to these people they can never stop it.

127. [In the old days, who decided who was going to marry whom?]

The boy's parents — father and mother — will bring this up before the whole family there. About the age of the boy will be 20 or 21 years old. Mother and father wants to have his son to marry a girl — put them together — so they can live together. He says to his people there's some girls around here close — telling the people what girl they want to pick up for the boy. They can talk about the girls around there. They can say about different family. They might say there's a girl we know and we seen it, and she belongs in that family what we know already. Sometimes they say: We don't want to take poor people. This is where they want to do — so the boy can stay there a long time. He can make his home there. If all the family likes to have that girl, they can ask the boy whether he likes that girl, whether he seen it already. Boy might say: I like that girl but I don't think she want me. But they tell the boy they're going to ask the other party about that. After that, then they want tell the other party just how much they're going to give for the girl — whether it'll be money, or jewelry, or sheep, or cow, or horses. Then they have to tell the father of the boy or the mother — one of them could go down there where the girl is living. So one of them goes out there. When he comes to that place and tell them there *Ya'at'eeh* [that is, "Hello"] and everything else — after that, that what he want to come down here for is to let the boy married here to girl that's there. We talked about it, and we all decided and picked out this girl and we liked the family that's living here. I think the boy will do right when he married this girl here, and boy, too, to pay for the girl. He can say: We give you a cow. If they didn't have any cow, give them so much money. And they can ask the girl there whether she like the boy or not. Sometimes girl says: Yes, I will marry that boy. Then they set the date — what day the boy's people will come up and the boy will come along. If they think four days is all right — there will be one of the woman or mans will say — just give them a little more time. On the girl's side some of the family might be working out. They have to notify the people that's working outside so they can be there that day. Then they can say: Make it seven days. In that way, they says: Boy says yes, girl says yes, families on both sides says yes. Sometimes the girl's mother not satisfied by that payment. She has to say she wants a little more. So the other side, has to do it, just like the girl's mother says. And this man goes home and he brings his message back to the other people. While he's out there talking to the other people, the other people's waiting for him to see what kind of luck he has when he come back. When he gets back he tells the people. Everybody says Yes. We put boy and girl — marry them seven days from today. Everybody will be happy about that. They can be working till that day. If they had no money — if they say horses — they can take horses down — ride them over that day, and corral them there that night. Next morning the horses will be — them horses — father gets one, mother gets one, nephew gets one [etc.]. While they last. For money they can divide it up in small amounts to parents of girl, and brothers and sisters. Girl won't get anything.

128. [If boy or girl says No, will they go through with it just the same?]

For girl's side, it will be one reason she could be afraid of boy. That is there isn't boy who has touched her yet. But most places, most every girl says: Yes. If the girl says No, if she says No pretty strong they just let her go. The leaders says they can't force a girl like that if she says No. For the boy's side, it's the same way. If he didn't want to marry the girl, if he says No — they can just let him go. And there is a boy over here. ———'s brother now — about twenty years old now. His brother ——— told him he wants him to get married and live with a woman, and that boy says: No, I don't want no woman. I want to stay single all the time. There is some more people in his family want him to do that, but he don't want to do that. Where the girl don't want to marry that boy. Boy's family can go and look for another girl, They might get that girl then, second time. Sometimes when this girl says No, they might give him [her] talk pretty nice about marriage to this girl — parents will do this to the girl. They like for her to marry boy. They like the family. It's good thing to married, and have a home of your own and your people where your people and the other side will married you together — where Navaho chief or leader could make very nice talk to you and the boy. In that way they can get the girl says: Yes, she could be married. They don't want to punish boy or girl for that. They just want to give them a nice talk, why they want them to get married — make a nice home, then build up his home. In that way they can get them back where they could be married.

129. [How about having more than one wife?]
That's one of the reasons young boy's and girl's parents have to get them married in the right way, so they won't have too many wives for boy's side. Girl's side same way. That have to be taught out from the leaders to the couple at the wedding. That's nobody's fault only a man who got married in the right way, and got all the understanding from the leader what he said to him. But he don't listen that very close and he might start to doing that. This man and another girl, they can like each other, and he can go ahead and take that girl also. So he can have two. Still this boy he can pick up another one yet. That other girl still likes him. They can live together between all three of them — for just a short time. Then this other girl, the one he married might get mad about it and tell her father and mother. They stop it lot of times, but it's pretty hard to stop those people. Man can go back with the other two yet after the other people stopped. Some times they stop it right then — don't do it any more, and then come right back to his first wife. That's the way they used to do.

130. [Do they have a wedding ceremony for second and third wife?]
Interpreter answered: No, they just live together informally. Head man has nothing to say. They may tell their family.

[Sometimes they marry two sisters?]
Yes, they used to do that pretty often. But where they make — marry this couple, they can tell them not to bother this girl's sister. They tell him that he just married one girl, and so he's not to bother the sister. So they don't do that much like before they was doing it.

[Did family never tell them to take a second wife?]
Way back in the old days they used to do that. When they make this girl and boy marry together, and boy's doing just like the way he was told and being nice to the people, and work hard for the people, something like a year or two years, after that that man wants to go ahead, if it's all right with the family, go ahead and marry the sister of that wife. The girl's father and mother — they have to OK that. They might say Yes, it's all right with us because the boy's been very nice to us and he's working hard for us. Then they ask the man's wife — see if it's all right with her. There won't be no leaders there to do the talking, and there will be no one from the boy's family. It's all by himself with the girl's family. If the woman says Yes, then that goes, and he can marry the other girl, too. And they'll be living one place. That's the way they do in the old days before the white people came in here. But there's some cases going on right now like that. There's is some mans — they're getting by with that. When they report it to the leaders, they can bring it up and make the man quit and make the man have one.

[Told him that a Mormon had had fifty wives.]

[Laughed.] No he says he didn't hear about big man have fifty wives. But he heard about the man did have six wives (a Navaho). Doesn't believe about fifty wives!

This man who had six wives, this was Navaho woman who was related to me was telling me about it — man who have six wives. That's all he said about it. Didn't know how long he stayed and lived with the six womans. When these Mormons first located this place, they start to living — I found out some of the people have three wives, four wives, so on. But I think they stopped them to having too many wives. So they quit the others and took just one. Those mans and womans — they not living any more. They got old and died.

131. [What does he think about crying (weeping)?]
There will be a family, will have father and mother, brothers and sisters living all together, and one will get hurt badly. The family of this person that's hurt — shouldn't cry for that person because he got hurt badly. He's going to get well. That's the way the old people used to say. But what they have to do right away is to get medicine man for that person. Old people now, old ladies, they cry for their grandchildren, if grandchild gets hurt badly. They say that means bad luck. Cry about live person. So they think it's better not to cry for the sick man.

[Is it bad luck for the person who's sick or for the person crying?]
Crying for sick person like that — they didn't say that was bad luck for either side. But it's bad luck when old people cry for nothing. Like he has a home like this, and had lot of relatives around him, and grandchildren — he's not supposed to cry in that family. It's bad luck then — bad luck for the family.

[What will happen to the family?]
First this old lady he thinks he's [she] crying about something he knew in the middle of this family. Sometimes he can tell the family what he's crying for. But she might say she did have mother and father, sisters and older brothers, which she knows — they's all gone. That's what she's crying about. It's all right if you cry about that, but not in the middle of the family like that. That means one of the family will get sick of that and die in short time after that. It might be all right when she can cry by herself — not in the middle of the family like that. But the people says there's no use to cry for the older people that's been died already — she cannot make these people come back again and live with her. These people are already taken places where they are now.

132. [If mother knows her baby is going to die, is it all right for her to cry about it?]
Where the woman's baby got real sick or hurt real bad, and baby's mother think baby couldn't able to live any more, and she cries for it. They say it's not bad luck. It's all right for her to cry for the baby because baby is not going to live. No matter how sick that baby is, how much hurt he

has, more than three people thinks that the baby's going to die, but baby gets well — even at that. Of that crying, that's not bad luck.

[If baby dies and she keeps on crying?]

She keeps on crying and the other people can make her stop. That's all right to cry after baby's died. In everything what live on the earth — or people of each tribe — horses and wild animals — and what could fly — birds of different kinds and sizes, I think they can cry for their youngsters.

[Suppose it's the woman's husband who is going to die?]

He thinks that's all right if woman's husband is so sick, and she think the man is not going to live, and cry for that man. He didn't think that's bad luck for anybody.

[You can't cry too much?]

No. You can't cry too much.

[If this woman's husband dies, and she keeps on crying, should she stop?]

It's all right for woman to cry — a little but not too much. The other people can tell her that — some of her family people — the relatives of this lady: That man's not dead yet, why should you cry — you mustn't cry like that for a live man. They tell her that much and she won't cry a whole lot.

[Why not cry like that so much?]

If you cried like that too much, then that man won't get well — they can tell that lady she's just helping the sickness put upon this sick man. So if you cry too much you won't get well.

133. [If man dies, should she stop crying or keep on crying?]

She can cry more if the man die, but she's a grown woman already — she have to know she don't have to cry too much — all at one time. She can cry just a little at a time. Wherever she remembers the man she can cry a little — but most places they get over it right away.

[What happens if she cries too much?]

There won't be anything happen. Where most people can stop crying for that reason for short time after a person die.

The way the woman will feel about it after man died, if the woman was taken care of by the husband very well and she has nobody to do that for her any more, and she's all by herself from then on. Man did good work for her and taking good care of children and her, and get lot of work outside — what's she's crying about. Lady will feel she's poor now. Can't do much for herself. And there's some people — no matter whether a man or woman — they can start crying pretty easy. And some other people don't hardly cry — even man or woman died right there same family. So it's that way — some people cry pretty easy — and other people don't hardly cry. People who don't hardly cry — he has a strong heart and strong mind. That's the reason he don't cry much. If people cries a lot, his heart won't be very strong. That's why he cries more than the others.

134. [Are the people who don't cry afraid to cry?]

That's just like I say man who have a strong heart and strong wind — them is the ones not to cry — but they not afraid to cry.

[Do they think it's bad luck?]

No, it isn't bad luck. These Mormon people who living around here, Mr. ——— [a white man] used to have father-in-law called ———. He got behind a horse with a gun and killed his own self one morning, and there's a bunch of people around him. They all started crying about him. Then Mr. ——— crying with the people a lot. So most any people cry when a person cry. He didn't know how that man start and killed himself. He had café — people been eating there. Had two or three sons and daughters, and people didn't know why he done that.

135. [What did the old people say about gossiping ('aseezį)?]

That's a man or woman can start to telling about the man or woman. That they are living away from his home. He can talk about that man over there. He can say that man he says that — he's telling his own people here. Where he made it up himself, he wants to blame it to the other man. These people start to talking about that. Sometimes these people will tell that man over there — they'll tell him what this man says. That man over there, he gets mad about it, because he didn't say that, and that's called 'aseezi.

Woman can start to say that, too, as well as the man. Just bringing the lie among the people. But this man who's talking that way, nobody help him — he's just bringing up himself.

For that man over there and one of the men here. They're been getting along pretty good. This man who tells the story didn't like these two men to get along together. Try to get these two mans to get mad each other — not to get along together. I think that's why this man been telling stories that way.

Two ladies where they work together, and helping together, and they are pretty strong to do things, and this woman can get between of these two women and she can make up a story and tell one side, and that's the way the woman tries to get these two women mad at each other.

136. [Does it make any difference whether stories are true or not?]

These people they can get together about that and talk it over. Each side will know this man is lying about the other man. They bring that man in there and ask him: Why did he say that about that man? He can say that he didn't say anything like that about that man. He turn right around and tell the other people they're lying about him. They can tell him he's the one that's bringing all the lies among the people and making trouble among the people and that's not right. Tell them not to tell anything like that among the people. Tell him to leave him alone, not to talk about him. So that don't look very much to us — people can just give that man or woman good talking. They behave themself — but they still talk about the people yet, but not too much.

137. [Is it all right to talk about people if you don't tell lies?]

Best way is to talk about people, tell the truth. Not to lie about the other man. Says ———— seems to be that way. Tells too much lie, and I talked to him about that two times already. But he won't stop. He keeps going on with it. He's been that way ever since he was a boy, and now he's getting tough where nobody will stop him talking like that. He tell too much lies.

[Is it bad to tell bad things about a person, even though they're true?]

If he's a good honest man and wants to be good to everybody — if I start to telling about some other people [that is, to him] that those people are lying or stealing — he'll say I don't want all that stuff — I don't want to listen it. So I don't think I'll tell anything like that before the good honest man.

138. [Some people think that better than being rich, good, healthy is getting to be a leader — what does he think?]

For a man wants to be a leader, wants to get ahead of everybody — about a man that think about himself that way — I don't think the man himself will tell the people that he'll be more leader. But where the people gets together and talks about this man, he can make better leader if he had good head and good brain to think with. Where lot of people wants him to be leader — so that's lot of people puts him in there. By thinking by his own self — wants to get ahead of everybody — I don't think he could do that.

[Is it good to try to be a leader?]

This is about the chief. That's in the old days — way back. When the baby's born — just born — a boy — they used to have a song to wash that baby and to erect up something to keep him warm. Had songs to do that with. Then go on to pinion tree (pine tree) and cut out for the baby cradle and have songs for that baby cradle to make up till it's finished. And these people there, they can say — this will be honest man when he grows up and we'll make him our Navaho chief-leader. Where the people will like him, they'll all mind him — what he says. In that way, this baby boy can be leader or Navaho chief. That's the way I heard about it way back.

When he begins to be leader, some of these people can say about him — they can put the Blessing Way singing over him early in the spring. He can get along with that till fall after everything is frozen the way. Then along there they can put up another Blessing Way singing again. They do that for a man every year. His people should do that for him, for their leader.

This Blessing Way singing for to make the leader's word worth something to the people. That his word will be strong. Make the people listen to him. Where this leader makes the speak at the meeting he can talk to the mans first. When he get through with the men people he goes on with the women people. That's for the man will listen to the leaders and how to do the taking up different kind of plans. They have to work hard for their children and do right — not to do any stealing or lying between the people. They should build up their home — as they go on living for years. For the womans side the same way. They can also mind each other and mind their leaders and take care of their livestock and work the best way they can. Learn how to weave. Learn from the mothers — and try and learn how to weaving, and combing the wool, and spinning the wool. There's some more other works that women could do. He thinks that was the way they used to make their leaders. Where he makes a Blessing Way singing, makes the leader stronger and all his people can listen to him and mind him.

139. [Would some people feel sorry they weren't leaders? Is that good or bad?]

In that case a man won't feel sorry about that. By one individual man he can't go ahead and say he's going to be leader. They kind of afraid of being leader.

[Why?]

When a man makes pretty good talk to all his people, and his people begins to listen to him, then most of these people got along fine. Most of them have a good home, better livestock, and jewelries. They can think this leader is doing that by his talk. Some of the witch people begin try to kill this leader out.

They're afraid of these witch people and the cases where they have two wives and stealing — you can straighten up for the people. They can also hate you for that. In that way they don't want to be leader. To be leader causes too much trouble. He wants to do right, and other people wants to do wrong. So he just as soon not be a leader.

INTERVIEWS WITH JOHN HAWK

January 13, 1952 (Interpreter: Bill Begay)

[Started by questioning him about which ceremonies he could sing. His answers are omitted.]

140. [How long did it take to learn all of these?]

Take a lot of time to learn. When he first started was 15 years old, and kept on learning it along up till he was 40 years old, and then got to know it pretty well. All this different way singing — some of the places too hard for him and he didn't learn some of it — each one. Just like white man got to know Navaho language pretty well — that's the way I am with my song. [That is, just as whites, can't speak Navaho very well!]

When your tongue is young yet it's easy. But when it gets tough — hard for you to learn. When he learn all these songs, you have it in your head and in your mouth. Then you might lose one of your tooth, and the song runs out of where your tooth is — it run away and you lose your song again. [Laughs.] Pretty hard to learn it all these songs. Just like young children that's been to school that his teacher might say the word for "plane" — so he can say that until he says that very plain. Now learning a song from a Singer is just the same. You have to say it just right. You have to start singing by yourself before the Singer. Then Singer says that's all right and then you go on with the next one. That's hard work.

141. [How much would he have to pay a Singer to learn one of these Songs?]

This is the way they work it. When he learn a song from the Singer, somebody might come after him to sing for them [that is, for John Hawk], and he go down there and sing for that patient. Whatever they paid him there — he had to give that to man who taught sing to him. He'll have to done that four times — he don't get anything — that go to the Singer. Then after that he still taking care of the Singer. Sometimes he makes moccasins like this for Singer and buys clothes for the man. You have to look after that Singer until he gets old and die. When he learned some good songs on top of that you will get good talking from the medicine man who taught him. Don't like for him to do some lies while he is doing the medicine and bad words and hurt — and he told he has to do his medicine in right way. People will want him all the time. People like his song — they will come after him. From all these people when he live — even from long ways or from home. That he must do medicine in right way for the people. That he mustn't start to fight with somebody or try to beat up someone. He mustn't hurt a person. That he was told that any time when he hurt a man or woman — that's not fair thing to do. He might go ahead and sing for that person. Cure that person. That's the way I remember what my Singer used to tell me. This is for everybody — from a baby when he's just born — if baby sick.

[Do Singers have to be better people than others just because they're Singers?]

He thinks they're all the same. But the Singers, most people likes the Singers. Singer is always used at the people where's sick. They are pretty good people — Singers all — but there's lot of good people, too, even if they're not Singers. But any place where the Singers can cure the sick people — then he makes the people happy. Sometimes a man or woman got sick and had pretty strong headache, and tried different kind of medicine, won't cure him. Lot of times Singer used some of his medicine for that man or woman and he cures it. When he cures it and he goes back and does his own work and feel good about it.

142. [Here followed a long disquisition comparing Navaho medicine men with white doctors. He included a description of how to set a broken bone. He continued:]

Want to go back where these Singers start where the Navahos start way back. All these different ways of singing was know by old medicine people. They start and go ahead with it. Most of these medicine people died out — hardly anybody learn it — like the way it was known by old people. For that reason we lose most our medicine and singing. Where the young people don't pay any attention to it — like the way they are now — we won't have much of this singing left in a few years.

Way back where the old people used to doing this — that's where the young people should learn from these old people and go along with the medicine people. We should have lot of these songs left — pray too. We would remember a lot today.

[What will happen when everyone forgets this medicine?]

I can't say very much about it. But they'll just lose that much. Only white doctors — looks like their learning and teaching out younger ones. White people will have theirs and we won't have any left.

White doctors they always put something over a broken bone. I don't know how long before they take that off again. Navahos — they put the medicine and four sticks over that for 30 days, and they take it off. That looks pretty near the same as white doctor.

143. [Question.]

The Navaho Singer sometimes people talks about him, he's bad and wants to kill a man. This might be happen way back and that Singer didn't try to learn it off from a good Singer — a good medicine man. He might just go ahead and learn whatever he can off from a Singer. Uses that on the patient, Navaho, that's for himself — wants to make something. But nobody teach him how to do all these things. He says he never did learn off from medicine man, and those kind of people they act bad to the people sometimes. But a man who learns off from this medicine man, he have to do right because give the medicine to the patient. And medicine man can also not to do anything wrong to his people after he becomes a medicine man, he must treat his people right. That's the only way his people can get along with him.

[Are these bad people witches?]

Yes. They hated people and uses their medicine where they shouldn't be used for the people. When the bad Singer make up the medicine for a patient, patient can go and be sick and sick all the time and be a little worse. When he uses that medicine, this patient will become weaker and weaker all the time until he is all skinny. The way the others, good Singers, will be too late — too late for them to use that. The patient can just die. Sometimes that could be found out by handtrembling. That have to be a good honest man, or honest woman — handtrembling way using.

144. [Why should a Singer behave better than others?]

A good Singer ain't supposed to lie. But I think we can lie to the people, just the same as the other. That's one way that we are lying to the people — we can lie to anybody. Suppose one fellow can come over to me this afternoon and wants me to go over and sing tomorrow. And I'll tell this man that I come down tomorrow — have everything ready by tomorrow when I get there. I put up my promise like that. And he goes home — and late that evening or night — and somebody might come along again — and he has somebody pretty sick at his place and want him to go over there right now. And he tell this man that he promised the man already. This man will say that he needed the medicine man more worse than the other. Some of his own family will say: Why don't you go with this man, this man need the medicine more bad than the other fellow? So he can make up his mind, and he go over to the second man. He might stay two days or three nights with this other fellow down there, and there's where he lied. That happened lots of times. Lot of people will say that when they talk about me, that I was a big liar, but I don't lie only such cases come like that. But they don't all get together where they can say that I was big liar all together. They pretty near all know that's not lying the people. That's only two sickness come up the same time — that causes it. We can talk together with the other Singers about that. The other Singer says: Lot of times, that happened with them too. They can go where there's the man is pretty sick — I think he need help more than the other. Where the Singer could be needed real bad, then the man come along when you're sleeping, towards daylight, and you can get up and go and work for him. They know that the other patient will get along without the singing. In cases like that it always come up before the singing.

145. He want to go back where I learned my song. When I got learned it, these songs from my Singer. That my Singer says I did very good job learning all these songs. He must keep his song like that for all the time — for his lifetime. Try to remember the best way he can. He used to say: I shouldn't add anything to it, but forgetting these songs — it would have to be forgotten — some of it. Keep it all together is hard. I know there's some people, they know some of the songs, and they just picked the songs up themselves from the Singers. Song has never taught to him. If they want to go ahead and use that's not right to do that. They won't live very long. They do a lot of mistakes on those songs. By making all those mistakes, they'll get sick on it — nobody will get the songs straightened up for him. By learning like you did — that's the way to do and you will live a long time.

By using bad medicine, I don't know what kind of medicine would be bad — They mean that a plant medicine some times it will be bad poison weeds. I understand that's what they use. In that way they are doing bad to their own people. Sometimes he kill his patient. If that goes he can get sick about that and go die just the same in a short time [that is, the Singer will die also].

146. [What makes him die?]
The patient will get sick first and then he will die kind of slowly. Then

this Singer he'll get sick, and people won't know why he get sick. But where way back where the Navaho songs start and one holy man whoever taught songs to Navaho people, he'll put sick upon this bad man because he's doing wrong with all these songs. So Holy People is the one that make this bad man sick and die.

[Can they find that out by handtrembling?]

Yes, they can. Old people used to say they's lot of medicine different kind — that should be take up different ways. The medicine is too many — it's like this rug — you can see all these different spots. Same way there is lots of medicine. White doctor has lots of medicine different kinds — like one is cough medicine — another is for sore — another one to rub on where it's pain. And these medicines have to be used where it's good for pain, good for sore, and it's pretty hard to remember all of that. In that way some of these Singers have to be pretty careful about that. They just have to use the right kind. It have to be learned pretty close. Just picking out the medicine from the plant you have to know just how tall the plant is — what kind of stem it has, what kind of leaves, and what color flower it has, and what does it smell like, and what it tastes like. And it has a name for each one of these plants. That's the way the medicine man taught his new medicine man.

In different ways sickness that the people — if one way sickness comes in the person, the medicine man thinks he has medicine for it. Medicine man don't give too much one kind. He starts with a little piece. Let the patient take it. He used that medicine — if the patient feels better after that — he let him take it — just very little. Each plant has a name for it — no matter there's whole lot of plants — they've got a name for it.

147. [Why do you have to be paid by your own son?]

Yes, that's right. You always have to be paid. And it's just like I says before, even if you get paid for one time you might get paid for it again after a while. That will be person — man or woman — that you cured him when he was very sick. That will be up to the person who you cure. If he thinks he able to do that he can do that. But for myself — I don't like to say that I want something else. Because I got paid already. That's all I feel good about where I cured the patient.

148. [If somebody was so poor that they couldn't pay, would you still sing for him?]

I have short story for that. When a man or woman or child is very sick, and the family is poor and himself is poor — real poor — have no live-stock, no animals, don't have anything — but you look at him, he's very sick and you can tell it. And before they tell you that they haven't got anything to pay you — but he wants to help this patient. If he gets well — This patient's folks — one of the women can grind between two grinding stones, and mix it up with water. Make dough out of that, and make up four pieces of a like corn bread. Roast it in the ashes, and when he — this is done in the ashes, just take it out of the ashes, let it cool off, just rub the ashes off the bread — not to get too clean — have some ashes on the bread, and give it to this medicine man. And this medicine man will eat some of these bread. Medicine man thank for that — that will be the payment of the man who's sick or woman. If the patient didn't have any corn to make up that bread, medicine man can take just one stone of arrowhead. If he didn't have no arrowhead, he can give one kind of shellblue shell, black shell, or abalone shell. This is learned way back where the Navaho people just started.

If the patient is real poor — doesn't got anything like that, the patient will say that I just need help awful bad, but I don't have anything to give you. He can tell the medicine man he can just help him. Medicine man can say: No, or Yes — I want to help you — though you can't pay anything. But if you cure this patient this patient give something to this medicine man who cured him. He can say to the medicine man: You sure helped me one time, and you cured me one time. If wasn't for that I might be dead long time ago. But I still remember that so I give you something now. He can get something for that. That medicine man he just leave it up for patient who he cures.

149. [Medicine and singing would be just as good even if man didn't pay?]
Yes, it's still good. In that same case, where the man is pretty sick and didn't have anything — he can just soon help the man there. That's all he have in mind. After he cured the patient he can get a pack of cigarettes — that's all that's good for him. There's no other way this poor man can help himself and pay him. I feel sorry for each one that gets sick.

This is the way when a good man gets pretty sick [that is, a rich man] and he needs treatment from medicine man, but this man will pay for it — either sheep or money [etc.]. But this Singer he do the singing for this man. He might use some medicine. And then after he is through with him he don't pay this medicine man like he says. This sickness will take a long time to get well. He goes to the bad man who is very sick, and this poor man is sick and needed help and will pay the medicine man right there. If the medicine man cures him right away, he get well quick. He thinks that just for that reason sometime the patient lie to a medicine man — he don't get well very quick. So they both the same, they can get well pretty quick if they pay right off.

150. [A man who steals sheep, is he harder to cure than an honest man?]
They not hard both of them if they pay for it. If something else comes in — about the man that do the stealing — something he might give you something — bracelet or sheep and you take the sheep or money or bracelet from that man, and that man will get well right away. But then just a

few days after that man or woman will come along — that the thing that you got from that patient — it's stolen by that man who you cured. He says that bracelet is mine that he steals off from me, and sometimes he might take away that bracelet.

[Does anything happen to the man who gave him the bracelet?]

This man who claims the bracelet will take this medicine man over to the other person who did the stealing. Man will say: This is my bracelet and say: You stole it off from me and give it to medicine man. Man might say: I want you to pay the medicine man, something that really belong to you, and I want you to pay medicine man right now. Man that did the stealing — he think that he stole the bracelet from that fellow, so he have to pay medicine man right there before the other. The other man can just walk off with that bracelet.

Wants him to pay the medicine man more now than he paid him before. This man got his bracelet back, was good bracelet. That man he can pay the medicine man just a little to make the medicine man feel good about it (*baa hozhon*).

151. [Can you cure people for things that are *bahadzid*?]

The mother-in-law — he ain't supposed to see mother-in-law, and this mother-in-law is very sick, and she wants to be treated by son-in-law. He could go and do the medicine for the mother-in-law. And mother-in-law got well and went pretty well and got strong again. This Singer who's her son-in-law, then she have to go and talk with her son-in-law and work together and not afraid again after that. From that time you can call her "my mother" and she can say, "my son." That's the only way that you can get the mother-in-law to see her and to work together like your mother.

You can talk quite a while with your mother-in-law after that if she get well. You can shake hands with your mother-in-law, and she can shake hands with you. Now we mustn't afraid again from now on as long as we live, and talk together and work together. I can say "shima" [my mother] and she can say "shiazh" [my son]. I done that myself to my mother-in-law.

152. Now the other cases where boy and girl they can get together with close relatives — like sister and brother. And they get sick a short time after that, there's a plant medicine for that if that's really happen — that could be cured pretty easy — he says. But knowing the plant and where to find this plant — that's a big job where to find it and where it grows. The plant is about that tall [2′] and the top of this plant flower — one like that red color and another flower has white like that and one color like that dark red. There is lot of flowers on one plant — all the kind of colors, and butterflies and bees will jump on that flower and they can be just stick to it. Even humming bird or small different kind of birds it will kill all these birds. There will be some dead birds laying under this kind of flower and all kinds of bees. And the medicine man have to know this flower —

and how to use it. Get these two people together and use this kind of medicine. Take some of it and boil it real hard. Then clean the water like that. Let the two people drink as much as they can. Sometimes they make them vomit out, what water is left they can bathe with it.

You can tell a person or woman if he has that kind of sickness. His lips will go that way, his eyes will move that way, and his face, and his hand is trembling like this. If he had that thing strong he can make his head shake once and a while. If they had no medicine for those kind of sickness, they can die right away. And I see — don't see many people that way, but I see some white people that act that way. They might did that. I think they might have that kind of sickness, and might be some other kind of sickness causing that, too.

153. [What happens to people that see their mother-in-law?]

About seeing your mother-in-law — you're not supposed to do that — that what old people say. If you see your mother-in-law — that's bad they used to say. You go blind while you're young, and have a lot of pains in your arms and head — all over. Then your heart won't be very strong. That's the way we used to believe — old people. But since the government starts the school, young people Navaho in the schools, white teachers says they think it's wrong to be afraid of their mother-in-law. In vacation time, the children come home, tell their parents about it. In talking all over about it, and lot of these young Navaho people got good education — they believe white people what they say about mother-in-law. They think it's foolish to be afraid of their mother-in-law or son-in-law. And white people was telling young people they must talk to their mother-in-law and look at it, and work together with them, and not to be afraid. That's why the young people they not afraid of their mother-in-law any more.

[Any kind of cure for this blindness?]

No medicine or there isn't anything that could be done for that.

154. [What happens if you cross a coyote's trail?]

That's all right if you cross, but sometimes it can follow a Navaho man or woman and is crying. That's bad.

Or if cross right in front of you or gets smell off from you. That means you'll get sick soon, or some of your pretty close relatives — they will die soon. That's bad luck. Right at time if you know what to do about that — you go near his track and talk a lot of pray with it — that helps it sometimes. Sometimes that may help. A few medicine man if you go over to somebody, wanted to do some medicine down there. If coyote come around that way — that's no good going over there — just to turn around and not to go over there. Coyote can change that around. In the summertime in the morning when first day break, you can hear coyote howling. He means that it's going to rain soon. Brings rain that day. Do that in winter time, too. Where he howls in the evening just a little after dark — that brings snow. He thinks that's the truth. There's lot of Navaho people heard that the white people wants to kill off all the coyote. And talked about it two years ago. Lot of older Navaho people feel sorry about it. That might be one of the reasons why they didn't have no rain for two years. We all miss coyote for two years. We didn't hear coyote in the morning or evening for two years. Just last fall along in November sometime, once in a while we hear coyote howling again. And after we heard coyote howling again we see snow and rain right now — for a while.

155. [Suppose you were in the forest with very little food left and met a starving man. Would you give him some of the food?]

If I was a long way from home, way off a long way, in the woods, had little food, and I met a man who was starving, and I know this won't help me to get back home. But then I have to give some to this poor man. I can give him this much a piece [1"] — after he swallows that I can get my corn pollen out of my pocket, let him take some — and put some in the middle of his top head — and tell him to go home on that, and I take some myself, too. And we'll feel like just had too much food. We feel like we had a lunch a while ago — just about like that. And we can go back home on that — no matter how long it is — even if it is a long way from home.

There is one kind of cactus — round kind of big. If he didn't have no food or corn pollen use that cactus, burn a fire, and then burn all that needles away from cactus, and clean it off with your hand. And eat that cactus. That will help you, too. And then there is one more other kind of medicine — they are round like potato — it's in the ground, but we can tell the plant, we can dig around there for brown medicine. Can eat some of that and it will help you a whole lot. That used to be food for Navaho people way back.

[Suppose there were no cactus, no corn pollen, etc.]

I don't [think] there will be no food there. There will be lots that we can pick up Navaho way. There will be some chipmunk, rat, and porcupine. There's one kind of sticky mud, kind of white — you can pick that up and mix it up. That's good — good as peanut butter. Still there's some other medicine that tastes like salt, that's good too. Lot of people don't know about that — if they don't know they can get hungry and die right there.

[Suppose that they didn't know about these things?]

For himself, he might do that — keep it for himself. Just let the other fellow go. Where man gets real thirsty, might be out long ways from home, no water — he can peel some of the bark off the cedar tree. Use that bark and the body of the tree. There's something like the paper between the bark and the tree — that's pretty wet. They used to eat that when they get thirsty. And they used to get along that way.

January 14, 1952 (Interpreter: Bill Begay)

156. [After the cure is it all right for brother and sister to live together?]

No it isn't all right for them to live together. They just have to separate, and not do that any more.

That's why you cure the two parties, tell them not to bother each other again like they did, because they are related together. If they didn't use that medicine, they won't live. They'll both die right away.

[Any singing as well as medicine?]

If they use this plant medicine, there's one way of singing that's got to be used over these two people — but that singing is all forgotten. Don't think there is any of it left now. About this plant medicine, very few people know about it. Using the medicine without singing — doing the singing, they can use this medicine at singing. [Moth Way?] Yes, that's right.

[Did he ever have to perform this? or find out by handtrembling?]

This is really nowhere where it happened. Where there is a man and woman have a family, and this same family two of them might get together like that. If parents will find that out by — might be one or two of the people that know what is going on. The farther ahead they go with it, they can get sick on that. They can both act like they are drunk. When a man gets drink pretty heavy, he likes to get near the fire all the time. When these two people get sick like that, they want to get near the fire all the time. They can roll their sack in the fire, let the other people take them out of the fire, roll them away. That's the way they can find this out. Then sometimes they can find that out by handtrembling — handtrembling way they can find that out. This is what they been telling me. No, hasn't done it himself.

About this plant medicine, it could be used for that sickness of that kind, and also could be used where a person has broken bones. And that's the reason that I know that plant. Where the people put up a singing for that kind of sickness, I never have seen it.

There is another medicine that could be used for that sickness, they all have white flowers flat and white. In the night when you're travelling you can see that flower even if it is dark and we used to call that medicine Nightwhite [in Navaho language] but they don't use that medicine any more — it's all forgotten.

I have another sort of story about singing over these two people. Where these two people medicine man will use fire before morning, when they get their clothes off inside, they always use a rag (breechcloth) it has to be coyote skin for man side, and badger skin for woman. They both sit here [west side], facing each way — their back have to be together. While they bumping and drinking this medicine, and vomiting as they are sitting. Right there while the sing is going on, each day and each night, medicine man will tell out story about these two patients telling the rest of the young people not to do like these two people did. Not to go ahead and bother your own sister or nephew or close relative. They must all listen to this story — that's the way the Singer tells out to the relatives. That's a good instruction for young people to listen to.

Now since this school starts all these young Navahos — boys and girls, there's a whole lot of them go together with their relatives. Some places they have children, boy or girl, are not very stout, kind of weak, because they are going together with relatives. So I don't think it is a very good thing to go ahead and bother your relative like that. We all want to raise good children. There used to be a lady down there little ways west and she went around with her relatives, and had a boy baby. That boy was pretty weak a long time — that boy lived 14 years and then got up and died.

[How about father and daughter?]

That's the same bad as the brother.

[Same cure?]

Yes.

157. [How can the Holy People get away with it? Interpreter says that informant didn't get the question.]

In first place, the Coyote he's the one that did this first. He's the man that married his own sister first. Somebody know this medicine and singing five nights, they both got the medicine and it cured them. After that Coyote went to Badger's home, and Badger wasn't home with his wife, and Coyote went to sleep with this woman, Badger's wife, while Badger was away hunting. And they didn't get sick of that, because they are not relatives. And the old lady still living down here, and she went to pick one of her relatives and start to live with this man, they both get sick on that, and use up this way of singing — they did the singing for him — they was cured for few years. Man died, lady pretty old and blind now. But I say lady — sickness she had at that time — the way the children was acting at the time, that was all cured away but she got it back again short time ago. The moths came out from between the eyes while the Sing was going on. After that worm came out, then the woman got well. Man was called Tsii-coza — was the man that knows this medicine, and he was the man that cured these two people. That man got too old and died many years ago.

[First Man and First Woman?]

First Woman and First Man they didn't get together with their own relatives. They both says people shouldn't do that. But right at that time Coyote did it. First Man and First Woman they know the medicine, and they both cured Coyote and his sister.

158. [Are all people who get old good people?]

That question there is hard all right. It isn't old age — it isn't just for man he's honest and good man — even just for that to get old. When two young people can get married together what they do is they can do a job and make up for boy baby or girl baby — that's making up person inside mother. As the months goes by, until baby ready to be born, just at the time the baby come out — born — even if baby came out, and don't move for a minute or two — something like three minutes, and then baby start moving and cried. He says Holy Man says there is someone waiting for that baby right at that time. Just as soon as baby comes out, this person who waiting there — get into this baby. That will be the baby's life. But before he gets into the body he makes a speech, that he will say just how long this baby can live. He might say the baby will live, but he can say he will live something like fifty years. Then when the time comes, he will just get out, and that person's life is gone. That person says he will stay in the life until old age has come. So our life comes into us when we just baby. Somebody keeps time for us when we should die. But our life is small wind — moves limbs, talking, thinking — that's our life. So he's the one that keeps our time when we should die.

Just up to that wind when he will get out of the body, and then die. But this wind himself he knows just what year and what month and what time the person will die, and when the time comes he just jumps out of it. In that case, when the wind gets out of the body the place where he was, the body is dead — and everything spoils there. Wind is also spoiled. After that he can be ghost. From that time where the Holy Man for this man to go to another place — there's another place for him to go. I never did hear anything like that. Right after the man or woman died inside the hogan, we begin to afraid of that home. They used to say that ghost hangs around there, inside the hogan where the person die. When a person dies inside the hogan, we burn the hogan up and move to another place. They say when you get sickness of Ghost Way, we begin to call that bad wind, ghost wind. That's why we sing Ghost Way — to scare this ghost away from this patient. They told us he is afraid of eagle feather. They use that eagle feather most of the time for that singing.

159. [If a man is very sick, or nobody likes him, is it all right for him to kill himself?]

Where a man start to get mean among his people wants to fight with somebody, mad all around. Then he goes to stealing too among his people, stealing horses or sheep. And the people has been missing lot of things. Might be several people that find him out who's doing it. And they point to one man who's doing the stealing whole lot from the people. He can hear the people saying that he's doing it. First for a while he can say he's not doing it. Some of the people already seen him doing it. Where he had done lots mistakes he can feel bad about it, and people have been talking about him — bad man. But most all the people hate him, where he got too much of it and worried about it in daytime and the night, then he can kill himself. That's one way a person can kill himself. That's a little branch off of where the wind gets out of the body. But this is man kill himself, not die for the sickness. That's the only way a man can kill himself.

160. [Suppose a man came to him and said I'm going to kill myself, what would he say?]

If this bad man came into my place, he telling me he wants to kill himself. Tell me all about why he wants to kill himself. I'll tell the man he shouldn't kill himself. That's a wrong idea to thinking that way about himself. I know you are worrying too much about what you did and what you still doing. Stealing and all the mistakes that you made. But you must quit all that stealing, and cut it out and forget about it. I think it's better for you to live right. That's all you have to do is to work for your own self, work with your relatives, be honest to them, and forget about stealing. Treat the people right. If you quit all that just like I telling you now, I think you come back to your own people where you could live like the rest of them. So if you mind me what I'm saying to you — if your father is living and mother, or your brothers or sisters, you can go over there and tell them the same thing what you told me. I'm pretty sure they'll tell you same thing just what I said. If they tell you the same thing like I said, they'll say we like to have you tell the truth, if you are going to live like a good man, and forget about making mistakes among your own people. If you come back and start to living right with us, we going to put up Blessing Way singing for you, and man who knows he can do it for you. If you telling lie, if you keep on doing wrong thing after this, we're not going to help you. So we like to have you choose two ways, whether you want to do right, we're going to help you if you do right. If you want to keep yourself like the way you are now, we won't be with you. So that's up to him. If he says Yes, I'll do right from now on, I want to do right, stay with you people as long as I live — then they can put up a Sing for that man. Then the Singer will tell him: give him some more talk. Tell him he have to behave after that. Be honest and mind the people. That's the only way he can get along with his people, if he did that if people won't hate him. These people will come back to him. They'll like him again.

For man, the thing he should do is to mind the people that gave him talking like that. Farther on the people will find out that he is good man again. People will come back to him — like him. He don't mind this — the worry will come on him more heavy. Then he gets sick about it — even he didn't kill himself — he gets headache for it, and pain all over his body. And his arms and legs will become swelling up. He gets too much of the swelling until he die.

161. I want to come back to where I says that is one of the branch where the wind gets out of the body. There is four people wind — at one time want to get into the body. If good wind gets into the body, he'll be good man. If bad wind — does the stealing too much — he'll be bad person. If wind is bad and makes lots of mistakes — don't know how to think good, that man will be just the same.

[What are the four winds?]

[1] Good; [2] steal; [3] makes mistakes; [4] one wind is pretty happy — happy all the time. We can see when a man happy all the time. One is called Mad Wind — he gets mad pretty easy — mad to his children, to

his wife, to people all around. Happy man — you can't make him mad at all. He laugh all the time. The one that steals. Good wind — he's just a good man — have good idea all the time and honest all the time. Bad wind when he gets into the body, when he go to work he breaks tool pretty easy, break wagon pretty easy.

Before you get old you mean to get mean to the people, but that mean nobody will take it out of your mind. You will have it in your mind for always. Even you get old — you being mean to your grandchildren. That's the way it goes.

Thinks it's pretty hard when you get old, we can see and watch old people. One gets pretty old and he stretch himself all over — that's all we can see he stretch his body up. And we can see all wrinkle on the body. And another one has little spotty all over his body — skin.

[The interpreter explains that the four winds are: Mean, Happy, Good, Bad. Mean is worse than bad.]

162. [Is happy better than good?]
Means happy all the time.

[Can man who is happy make mistakes?]
He don't make bad mistakes. He just makes little mistakes — but he's more good. He doesn't do anything badly wrong.

[Which makes more mistakes a good or happy man?]
Bad man makes more mistakes. They both even (good-happy). Even one is good and the other is good just like the other.

[Is happy man a good man and happy in addition?]
That means he is happy all the time and doesn't do anything wrong.

163. [If he were choosing his winds, which would he choose?]
When I was young, Bidaga's father, they went after that man — my parents did, and brought that man down here where we were living. And this man came down here. They take me inside where this old man was. This man told me that he was bad to his people [that John Hawk was bad] — that's why they got me the old man. Says they want me to give you a good talking. Old man says: Anything what they want you to do you don't mind it, and you always talking back to your own parents. So old man gave him good talking to. He says he mustn't do that. He must behave, and mind what his father says. Anything what they want you to do you must do it. And you must take care of the horses, and sheep, and learn how to handle it. And take care of your mother and father. He says that I was young and I have to live for a long time. Told me if I was to live right way, I'll be living for years and years, even I get old and die — you will still remember my talk. And you are my grandson, that's the reason I am talking to you pretty strong about all these things. I like to hear people talking about you — you are good honest boy — and behave. I don't like to hear people talk about you: You bad man or boy. After he gave me all this talk, he sure talked plenty to me, and he says he going to give me four pieces of corn

pollen. He says he sing a song. He gave me these pieces of corn pollen one at a time while he was singing. That corn pollen is mixed up with good medicine. That's something like my talk. He said, this medicine will make you do right and behave — mind. When he got through with me, I told him I'll remember his talk. I says I will do like you tell me. I want to do right from now on. From then I behave myself. That's the way I kept myself till today.

[Did this talk make him happy too?]

Yes, that's right. That's why he's happy all the time. That's why I don't hit my children and my grandchildren. Also I never hurt my wife. Try to be kindly to everybody.

164. [Which wind would he choose — Happy or Good?]

They both good, one is happy and the other is good. They both seem the same to me — so I like both.

[Doesn't he want to choose?]

Don't want to choose.

[What is the difference between happy man and good man?]

It's this way to me — happy man is happy all the time. That's why lot of people happy. So I can't rub that off — say No. So I am saying now — happy is all right and I like to be happy. Good man is honest, and tell the truth to the people, and have lot of money and lot of livestock. And he's helping some people — poor people — so he's good man. That's just as good as happy — that's the reason I can't choose one — they both the same.

[Can a good man be unhappy?]

If good man is unhappy — he is still for the two of them — I mean this way — here's a dollar bill here and one silver dollar here. I'd just as soon take the two of them — these two men.

[Does he know a man who is good and unhappy?]

Yes, there's is some people that we know.

165. [Which is worse, Mean or Bad?]

Mean and bad — bad is just bad for small things. I think that mean is more stronger than the other one. Sometimes you met a man in the city or outside the city, and you don't know him much — the kind of man he is. But he talk very nice to you — kind to you, and go around with him. And you start to drinking with him. First you didn't like to go with him, but he says: Go with him. But he puts you in trouble. But another way, he can get after you and hit you all over with a hand or stick — and I think that's a mean man that do that.

[First bad, second mean?] Yes, the first is bad and the second is mean. Mean man can't do anything for you, he can do any kind of bad thing. That means he can steal some money off from you. Also he can make you spend lot of money, and he don't spend anything. He wants you to do the paying all the time while you are with him. Then he keeps on going ahead with it, until he puts you something bad. Can put you in jail for the bad mistake. That's why he is causing all that. After that you can pay the fine — for him and for your own. That's a mean man will do that.

[Interpreter explained that both mean and bad man make mistakes.]

I don't think a person can go very far with that. People will find out right away. Then they can stop him right away — stop him from doing that.

[Would a good man and one who never hurts anybody be the same? — In terms of the paper and silver dollar above — Some difficulty with this question.]

He choose the man that don't hurt anybody — the good man. The silver dollar is less longer, but they still the same for me. I like the two. I cannot choose the one. For this reason I say that a man who couldn't hurt anybody or hurt himself, I might say — that's only way I might say he's good — that's the only reason I might say this man is good. But still it's good to me — both of them.

166. [Some people think a man ought to be punished even if he promises not to do it again — what does he think?]

Yes, if anybody do the wrong — he can be punished. But first we can tell him he mustn't do that again. He didn't want to be punished that's why he say that. We can tell him that he mustn't do that again, so we just let him go. So they won't punish him. They just take his word. If he didn't tell the truth, like he say he was going to be, and start to doing all that again — then we won't take his word again, he have to be punished, and by punish he might stop doing that. But he don't listen to that he can go to the big jail or penitentiary — that's as far as I know about that.

167. [Return to suicide — If a man is mean — can't do anything but mean things — is unhappy — is it all right for him to commit suicide?]

Whatever wind gets into his body, if he wants to kill himself. This wind might help him to get rid of himself — because his time is just about then. Of killing himself besides that he has no other way to make himself die. Then that wind can just send him to where he can kill himself. That's because his lifetime is just about finished.

[Is it good or bad for him to kill himself?]

That's not very good. That's bad to kill himself.

[Why is it bad?]

Nobody will like him. He is bad before. He's stealing, and acting mean among his people. They don't like him to be with the people. That's why he's bad. That's why he killed himself.

[Maybe they will like him because he did kill himself?]

It would be a little better if somebody else killed him — but when he killed himself that's another bad he did.

[Why is it more bad — he killed himself — he's dead?]

That's the way he said he did lots of wrong things first, and got worried about it — got to thinking too much about that and got sick of it. From that time he should have gone on and think about himself — think about some good things that he might studied out. By thinking that way he might become good man again. Instead of thinking that way he had another bad thought in his mind. So he just thought that out and wanted to kill himself — and killed himself. So there's nobody else's fault but his own fault. So I think that's a bad way of doing that. To go the other way, and try to straighten up himself — I think he is a better man that way. Well, I understand that kind of man — when his life is end like that. He's bad ghost then from then on. I understand they hurt people. They'll be bad against his people. Says ghost will get after his people and get sick upon his people.

168. [Told him following story: He was out hunting with a man who had a lot of money along with him. The man started to die, and made him promise to take his money and when he returned to have a monument erected for him. The man died. Upon his return he found that some poor starving people needed the money badly. What would he do?]

Didn't get the question very plain. He says going out hunting trip like that. There's no hunter could carry a whole lot of money with him when he was out hunting. And back many years ago the Navaho people used to make trip on horseback hunting, and they don't carry much money with them. When white people came in and had automobiles, and make a trip with automobiles out hunting, and still I think they don't carry much money with them. So I don't know how to answer this question. But I might think it out how to answer it while you [the interpreter] telling this much.

[Tell him that this is a white man who is very foolish and doesn't know about carrying money.]

That question is pretty hard for me to answer. If it was for somebody else to take this money back, that man who died says he wants to have this money used for the thing that he wants. But this man who got the money, he might just keep the money. Not to spend it for somebody else. Nobody else besides him when this man was talking to him about this money. Even he found some more people needed help pretty bad, but he won't say a thing — a word about money. If he thinks he can get by with it, if he did that he'll be very bad way. That's a great mistake that he will make. But it was for myself, the money is turned over to me, and I will take it back. I will use that money for give that man who could make up a thing for that man, and explain to him where that money come from — and I will give him all the money. Before I let the money go, I found some poor people that need that money worse than — even at that I can't give it to them. I have to keep the dead man's word, because he was with me and I was with him out in the woods — and he listened to me and I listened to him. If I used this money like he said, then I'll do it for him. I feel good after that, because I used the money just like he wanted to use. I feel good about it afterwards. And I think that's the right way to do. I do that for myself if it was me.

[Any difference if man was a friend or stranger?]

If this man was strange to me and I just met him way out in the woods long way from home, I'll do it just the same for a strange man, because I like to be honest all I can to the people, even to the strange people. Still for strange man, out on the way where he is taking the money, there's some very poor man needing help — I had the money here but I can't use that money for something else. I want to let this money go — where to take it — just like that dead man says in the woods. So I have nothing to worry about afterwards.

[Is he afraid of the ghost of this man?]

Yes, that's the reason, he says. The life of this man who died, jumped out of the body, and he's around, and he's kind of watching me. If I spent this money, not take it over there, I might get punished some way. And then I got to be honest with the people. So there's two ways I am kind of afraid about: being liar and be worried about it. There is lot of worries that this dead man put upon him — maybe put him to sleep. I look at it this way, this money belonged to this dead man, and where it's robbing the money off him this dead man, that looks pretty bad to me — so just like he says — take this money over there and use like he wants to. That's the way I heard about it, that's the way they (witches) rob the dead people.

[Later the interpreter volunteered the information that it is more dangerous to break a promise to a dead man than to a living man.]

TALK WITH BILL BEGAY ABOUT ETHICAL WORDS

January 19, 1954

Some random notes taken during a discussion with Bill Begay about the use of certain key 'ethical words.'

169. *doo 'akotee da* — "wrong, that's wrong" — *bahadzid* — "means dangerous, and wrong."

The following are *bahadzid:* sleeping with sister, seeing mother-in-law, in ceremonials — going out of hogan at wrong time, sleeping with wife while ceremony is going on. Making a mistake in the singing is *doo 'akotee da,* not *bahadzid.* Also: not burying someone properly, coyote passing in front of you, sleeping with prostitutes because of venereal disease. Sleeping with a girl otherwise is merely *doo 'akotee da. Bahadzid* — "hurts you — something is going to hurt you."

170. [Does *doo 'akotee da* mean that it's going to hurt you?]

"It's more the other way, you're going to try something and you try it, and you don't do it right. Anything that you want to try out. Try out something, that's where it's used mostly: [for example] shooting a gun, trying to lift up a man — that's not right."

"Sometimes they put *doo 'akotee da* in front of *bahadzid. Ei bahadzid* — that's bad, dangerous."

The following are also *bahadzid:* driving a car dangerously, bad sickness, war ("can't use *doo 'akotee da* here"), lightning, bear, snakes, bad water, fire — that's *bahadzid;* feces, etc., witch is bad, crossing water in front of road (dangerous for car). The Navaho would put *bahadzid* on signs where we put DANGER.

"Lot of people clean their ears with a stick — that's all right with a (stick) but not with a match, because match might go off in ear. If you put a stick in your ear, that's dangerous because some child might push against it and injure the ear." Children are told that about lollipops.

"A child would understand that word. Children say to each other *yii yaah bahadzid* when playing with knives. *Yii yaah* is main word for a child."

171. "Child wouldn't understand *doo 'akotee da*."

Things that are *doo 'akotee da* but not *bahadzid:* when singing ceremonial songs with teacher — "Songs — that's wrong all right but that's not going to hurt you." Therefore, *doo 'akotee da* means that's wrong but it's not going to hurt anybody. "Man teaching song would say to pupil that's wrong." "Mother teaching child how to cook — *doo 'akotee da.* One of children might start cooking, mother would say *doo 'akotee da* — go ahead and do it the way you want to, it's not going to hurt anybody. Mother might say: But you will find it out after a while. But one of the children might say: What does that mean *doo 'akotee da* — we don't understand that."

"You can use *doo 'akotee da* for child who is lazy. It's not very hard word. You have to tell them more about it before they understand it. *Doo 'akotee da* for herding sheep in wrong place. You'd have to tell them why."

More things that are *doo 'akotee da:* telling lies (not *bahadzid*); stealing — some people use *bahadzid* for that because you might be caught and put in prison; sleeping with another man's wife is *bahadzid.* "That's where it is really used — because man might shoot you." Sleeping with a girl that isn't married, that's *bahadzid* too. The mother and father will tell the leader and can made you pay something. Make the price heavy for you. Right now they can just report it to white people and they can lock you up for that. Lots of people don't think it's *bahadzid* — that's right. Inside Reservation they can't do that now, it sure is *bahadzid* there."

Gossiping: "They can use *bahadzid* there — man might get mad about it and can do anything to that man. He might get mad because that fellow's making up stories about him."

172. "When your wife menstruates, and you beat your wife right then, that's *bahadzid.* That'll make your backbone hurt. Sometimes they say you might put menstrual blood in your hand or your mouth — that's bad *bahadzid.* Pretty near all Navaho woman tells the man when they have that. The womans that run around with the boys too much, they never tell — just hide it away. Navaho boys in sweat bath discuss how they went with a woman, not intending to marry her, and when they got off their pants they got all bloody. Some says too bad, then lot of people says about that when a man do that [that is, sex] when she is menstruating that she will get a baby

right off — that blood brings the baby right off. Older people said that if you wanted a baby you should sleep with your wife while she is menstruating. Nothing wrong with that, only — try not to do that when she is menstruating, that is *bahadzid* — might break your backbone. Then all crippled up in here. In that part, all the Navaho still afraid of that yet. They are more afraid of doing that than if they are going to make a baby or not. They don't want to sleep while menstruating. Some of the women they won't let you do that — they've been talking about that."

[Beating your wife when she's not menstruating?]

"No that's not *bahadzid*. That's *doo 'akotee da*. *Doo 'akotee da* to beat your wife up."

Breaking a promise is *doo 'akotee da* but not *bahadzid*. "Where the man dies [that is, promisee], that's *doo 'akotee da,* also *bahadzid*."

Getting drunk is *bahadzid*. "If it's winter time you might freeze." [A drunken Indian had recently frozen to death.]

Death: " *'azee bahadzid* — death is bad, because he's dead."

Killing somebody is *doo 'akotee da*, but not *bahadzid*. "You kill him and then he's dead on the ground, then *bahadzid* then. Dead body is *bahadzid*. They say *doo 'akotee da* where he kill it. Then use *bahadzid* where he's dead on the ground. A man is a witch that's *bahadzid*. *Ei hastiin, 'antị bahadzid*." [Only applied to a witch.]

173. [About *ya'at'eeh* — good.]

"If you say, *'ashkii ya'at'eeh* [a good boy] — you have to say why — because he is happy all the time. They are good workers, that's why they are good."

"Good man — why he's good: If man comes up to me and says that man is good. I can ask: Why, what's he good about. Because I work for him and he don't want to be hard on me — pays me right off."

Man could be good because he pays you, but bad because he beats his wife. "I will say, *hastiin doo ya'at'eeh da* [a bad man], he is lying, he is mean to his wife. He is good one way, and bad another way."

"He's good but he's no good for one way."

"This man is good but he is also bad. But I won't say in front of man, he might get me. I think you're right, it's hard to find anybody like that. But I did find some people around here, they do that. The traders, sometimes they very nice to you. They can be honest with you one way, and then another way he can rob you. So he's good for both ways; one is good for himself, and one is good for me." [Laughs.]

References

This list contains only those books which have been cited in the text. In the footnotes the titles have been referred to by date of publication, and in cases where the author has published more than one item in a year, the separate titles have been designated by letters (for example, 1949a, 1949b).

For classical works of philosophy I have employed the original title, since there are usually several editions available. These titles have generally been abbreviated. The numbers in parentheses throughout the text refer to sections in the Appendix.

Special abbreviations have been adopted for the following: *SH* for Sellars and Hospers, 1952; *OMH* for Dyk, 1938.

ABEL, T.
   1948.   The Operation Called *Verstehen*. *American Journal of Sociology*, vol. 54. Included in Feigl and Brodbeck, 1953.
ACH, N.
   1951.   Determining Tendencies. Translated and edited in D. Rapaport, *Organization and Pathology of Thought: Selected Sources.* New York.
AIKEN, H. D.
   1945.   Review of Stevenson's Ethics and Language. *Journal of Philosophy*, vol. 42, no. 17.
   1952a. The Authority of Moral Judgments. *Philosophy and Phenomenological Research*, vol. 12, no. 4.
   1952b. Definitions, Factual Premises and Ethical Conclusions. *Philosophical Review*, vol. 61, no. 3.
   1955.   Moral philosophy and Education. *The Harvard Educational Review*, vol. XXV, no. 1.
AQUINAS, St. Thomas.
   Summa Theologica.
ARISTOTLE
   Nicomachean Ethics. Translated by W. D. Ross. Oxford, 1915.
   Posterior Analytics. Translated by G. R. G. Mure. Oxford, 1925.
   Rhetoric. Translated by W. Rhys Roberts. Oxford, 1924.
AUSTIN, J.
   1873.   *Lectures on Jurisprudence*. London.
AYER, A. J.
   1936.   *Language, Truth and Logic*. London. Partly included in Sellars and Hospers, 1952.
BAILEY, F.
   1952.   Navaho Motor Habits. *American Anthropologist*, vol. XLIX, no. 2.

1950. Some Sex Beliefs and Practices in a Navaho Community. *Peabody Museum of Harvard University, Papers,* vol. XL, no. 2.

BECK, L. W.

1949. (Translator and editor) *Kant's Critique of Practical Reason and Other Writings in Moral Philosophy.* Chicago.

BENEDICT, R.

1934. *Patterns of Culture.* New York.

BENTHAM, J.

Principles of Morals and Legislation. Included in Burtt, 1939.

BRANDT, R.

1954. *Hopi Ethics.* Chicago.

1955a. The Definition of an "Ideal Observer" Theory in Ethics. *Philosophy and Phenomenological Research,* vol. XV, no. 3.

1955b. Some Comments on Professor Firth's Reply. *Philosophy and Phenomenological Research,* vol. XV, no. 3.

BURTT, E. A.

1939. (Editor) *English Philosophers from Bacon to Mill.* New York.

BUTLER, J.

1726. *Sermons.*

CARNAP, R.

1935. *Philosophy and Logical Syntax.* London.

1946. *Introduction to Semantics.* Cambridge, Mass.

CARRITT, E. F.

1947. *Ethical and Political Thinking.* Oxford.

CARROLL, J. B.

1953. *The Study of Language.* Cambridge, Mass.

CHISHOLM, R. M.

1952. Intentionality and the Theory of Signs. *Philosophical Studies,* vol. 3, no. 4.

COHEN, M. R. and NAGEL, E.

1934. *An Introduction to Logic and Scientific Method.* New York.

CORNFORD, F. M.

1935. *Plato's Theory of Knowledge: The Theaetetus and the Sophist Translated with a Running Commentary.* London.

DEWEY, J.

1922. *Human Nature and Conduct.* New York.

DUCASSE, C. J.

1940. Nature and Function of Theory in Ethics. *International Journal of Ethics,* vol. LI, no. I.

1949. *Nature, Mind, and Death.* La Salle, Illinois.

1953. *Scrutiny of Religion.* New York.

DUNCAN-JONES, A. E.

1952a. *Butler's Moral Philosophy.* London.

1952b. Assertions and Commands. *Proceedings of the Aristotelian Society,* new series, vol. 52.

DURKHEIM, E.
  1953. *Sociology and Philosophy*. Translated by D. F. Pocock. Glencoe, Illinois.
DYK, W.
  1938. *Son of Old Man Hat*. New York.
  1947. *A Navaho Autobiography*. Viking Fund Publications in Anthropology, no. 8.
  1951. Notes and Illustrations of Navaho Sex Behavior. In G. B. Wilbur, and W. E. Muensterberger, *Psycho-analysis and Culture*. New York.
EPICURUS
  Letter to Menoeceus. Included in Oakes, 1940.
FALK, W. D.
  1953. Goading and Guiding. *Mind,* vol. LXII, no. 246.
FEIGL, H.
  1950. De Principiis Non Est Disputandis. In Max Black, editor, *Philosophical Analysis*. Ithaca, New York.
  1952. Validation and Vindication. In Sellars and Hospers. 1952.
FEIGL, H. and BRODBECK, M.
  1953. *Readings in the Philosophy of Science*. New York.
FEIGL, H. and SELLARS, W.
  1949. *Readings in Philosophical Analysis*. New York.
FIRTH, Raymond.
  1951. *Elements of Social Organization*. London.
FIRTH, Roderick.
  1952. Ethical Absolutism and the Ideal Observer. *Philosophy and Phenomenological Research,* vol. XII, no. 3.
  1955. Reply to Professor Brandt. *Philosophy and Phenomenological Research,* vol. XV, no. 3.
FLUGEL, J. C.
  1949. *Man, Morals and Society*. London.
FRANCISCAN FATHERS
  1910. *An Ethnologic Dictionary of the Navaho Language*. St. Michaels, Arizona.
FRANKENA, W. K.
  1950. Obligation and Ability. In Max Black, editor, *Philosophical Analysis*. Ithaca, New York.
  1951. Moral Philosophy at Mid-Century. *Philosophical Review,* vol. LX, no. 1.
  1952. The Concept of Universal Human Rights. In *Science, Language and Human Rights,* American Philosophical Association Papers, vol. 1. Philadelphia.
FROMM, E.
  1947. *Man for Himself*. New York.

HAILE, B.

1933. Navaho Games of Chance and Taboo. *Primitive Man,* vol. VI. Washington.

1943a. Soul Concepts of the Navaho. *Annali Lateranensi,* vol. VII. Rome.

1943b. *Origin Legend of the Navaho Flintway.* Chicago.

1947. *Starlore among the Navaho.* Santa Fe.

1950a. *A Stem Vocabulary of the Navaho Language.* St. Michaels, Arizona.

1950b. *Legend of the Ghostway Ritual in the Male Branch of Shootingway.* St. Michaels, Arizona.

1950c. Aspects of Navaho Life. *The Americas,* vol. VII, no. 1.

HALL, E.

1952. *What is Value?* London.

HAMPSHIRE, S.

1949. Fallacies in Moral Philosophy. *Mind,* vol. LVIII.

HARE, R. M.

1952. *The Language of Morals.* Oxford.

HARRIS, Z.

1952. Discourse Analysis. *Language,* 28.

HART, H. L. A.

1952. The Ascription of Responsibility and Rights. In A. Flew, editor, *Logic and Language.* Oxford.

HEGEL, G. W. F.

Philosophy of Right. Translated by T. M. Knox. Oxford, 1942.

HEMPEL, C. G.

1952. Fundamentals of Concept Formation in Empirical Science. *Encyclopedia of Unified Science,* vol. II, no. 7.

HEMPEL, C. G. and OPPENHEIM, P.

1948. Studies in the Logic of Explanation. *Philosophy of Science,* 15. Included in Feigl and Brodbeck, 1953.

HERSKOVITS, M. B.

1948. *Man and his Works.* New York.

HILL, W. W.

1938. The Agricultural and Hunting Methods of the Navaho Indians. *Yale University Publications in Anthropology,* no. 18. New Haven.

1943. Navaho Humor. *General Series in Anthropology,* no. 9.

HOBBES, T.

1651. *Leviathan.*

HOBSON, R.

1954. Navaho Acquisitive Values. *Peabody Museum of Harvard University, Papers,* vol. XLII, no. 3.

HOGBIN, H. I.

1934. *Law and Order in Polynesia.* New York.

HOIJER, H.

1951. Cultural Implication of Some Navaho Linguistic Categories. *Language,* 27.

1954. *Language in Culture*. Chicago.

HUME, D.

Enquiries Concerning the Human Understanding and Concerning the Principles of Morals. Edited by L. A. Selby-Bigge. Oxford, 1902.

JAMES, W.

1890. *Psychology*. New York.

JOHNSON, W. E.

1921. *Logic*. Cambridge, England.

KANT, I.

Foundations of Ethics. Included in Beck, 1949.

Perpetual Peace. Included in Beck, 1949.

KAUFMANN, F.

1944. *Methodology of the Social Sciences*. New York.

KELSEN, H.

1945. *General Theory of Law and State*. Cambridge.

KLUCKHOHN, C.

1952. Patterning as Exemplified in Navaho Culture. In Leslie Spier, A. I. Hallowell, and Stanley S. Newman, editors, *Language, Culture, and Personality*. Menasha, Wisconsin.

1942. Myths and Rituals. *Harvard Theological Review*, vol. 35, pp. 45–79.

1944. Navaho Witchcraft. *Peabody Museum of Harvard University, Papers*, vol. XXII, no. 2.

1945. A Navaho Personal Document with a Brief Paretian Analysis. *Southwestern Journal of Anthropology*, vol. 1, no. 2, pp. 260–283.

1948. As an Anthropologist Views It. In Albert Deutseh, editor, *Sex Habits of American Men, a Symposium on the Kinsey Report*. New York.

1949. The Philosophy of the Navaho Indians. In F. S. C. Northrup, editor, *Ideological Differences and World Order*. New Haven.

1951. Values and Value-Orientation: An Exploration in Definition and Classification. In T. Parsons and E. Shils, editors, *Toward a General Theory of Action*. Cambridge, Mass.

1953. Universal Categories of Culture. In A. L. Kroeber, editor, *Anthropology Today*. Chicago.

KLUCKHOHN, C. and LEIGHTON, D.

1946. *The Navaho*. Cambridge.

KLUCKHOHN, C. and VOGT, E. Z.

1955. The Son of Many Beads: 1866–1954. *American Anthropologist*, vol. 57, no. 5.

KLUCKHOHN, C. and WYMAN, L. C.

1940. An Introduction to Navaho Chant Practice. *American Anthropological Association Memoirs*, no. 53.

KNEALE, W.

  1950. Objectivity in Morals. *Philosophy,* vol. 25. Included in Sellars and Hospers, 1952.

KROEBER, A. L.

  1947. A Southwestern Personality Type. *Southwestern Journal of Anthropology,* vol. 3.

LADD, J.

  1951. White on 'Desirability' and 'Normativeness' in Dewey. *Philosophical Review,* vol. LX, no. 1.

  1952a. Ethics and Explanation. *Journal of Philosophy,* vol. XLIX, no. 15.

  1952b. Free Will and Voluntary Action. *Philosophy and Phenomenological Research,* vol. XII, no. 3.

  1952c. Review of A. MacBeath's *Experiments in Living. Journal of Philosophy,* vol. 49, no. 19.

  1953. Reason and Practice. In John Wild, editor, *The Return to Reason.* Chicago.

LANGER, S. K.

  1942. *Philosophy in a New Key.* Cambridge, Mass.

LAZARUS, M.

  1900–01 *Ethics of Judaism.* Philadelphia.

LEIGHTON, A. H. and LEIGHTON, D. C.

  1949. Gregorio, the Hand-Trembler. *Peabody Museum of Harvard University, Papers,* vol. XL, no. 1.

LEIGHTON, D. and KLUCKHOHN, C.

  1947. *Children of the People.* Cambridge.

LLEWELLYN, K. N. and HOEBEL, E. A.

  1941. *The Cheyenne Way.* Norman, Oklahoma.

LOCKE, J.

  1689. *Essay on the Human Understanding.*

MacBEATH, A.

  1952. *Experiments in Living.* New York.

MacDONALD, M.

  1950. Ethics and the Ceremonial Use of Language. In Max Black, editor, *Philosophical Analysis.* Ithaca, New York.

MacQUORDALE, K. and MEEHL, P. E.

  1948. On a Distinction Between Hypothetical Constructs and Intervening Variables. *Psychological Review,* vol. 55. Included in Feigl and Brodbeck, 1953.

MALINOWSKI, B.

  1926. *Crime and Custom in Savage Society.* London.

MATTHEWS, W.

  1899. The Study of Ethics among the Lower Races. *Journal of American Folk-Lore,* vol. 12, pp. 1–9.

MEAD, M.

  1937. (Editor) *Cooperation and Competition among Primitive Peoples.* New York.

MELDEN, A. I.
    1952. The Concept of Universal Human Rights. In *Science, Language, and Human Rights*. American Philosophical Association Papers, vol. 1. Philadelphia.
MERTON, R.
    1949. *Social Theory and Social Structure*. Glencoe, Illinois.
MILL, J. S. *A System of Logic*.
        Utilitarianism. Included in Burtt, 1939.
MOORE, G. E.
    1911. *Ethics*. Partly included in Sellars and Hospers, 1952. London.
MURDOCK, G. P.
    1949. *Social Structure*. New York.
NEWCOMB, F. J.
    1940. *Navajo Omens and Taboos*. Santa Fe.
NOWELL-SMITH, P. H.
    1954. *Ethics*. London.
OAKES, W. J.
    1940. *The Stoic and Epicurean Philosophers*. New York.
OPLER, M. E.
    1949. Reply to Voegelin. *Word*, vol. 5, no. 1.
PARSONS, T.
    1937. *The Structure of Social Action*. Glencoe, Illinois.
PARSONS, T. and SHILS, E. A.
    1951. *Toward a General Theory of Action*. Cambridge, Mass.
PATON, H. J.
    1946. *The Categorical Imperative: A Study in Kant's Moral Philosophy*. London.
PEIRCE, C. S.
    1923. The Fixation of Belief. In Morris Cohen, editor, *Chance, Love, and Logic*. New York.
    1931. *Collected Papers*. Edited by Charles Hartshorne and Paul Weiss. Cambridge, Mass.
PERRY, R. B.
    1926. *General Theory of Value*. Cambridge, Mass.
    1954. *Realms of Value*. Cambridge, Mass.
PIERS, G. and SINGER, M. B.
    1953. *Shame and Guilt*. Springfield, Illinois.
PLATO. *Theaetetus*. In Cornford, 1935.
        The Republic. Translated by F. M. Cornford. New York.
POPPER, K.
    1935. *Logik der Erfahrung*. Vienna.
PRICE, H. H.
    1953. *Thinking and Experience*. London.
PRICE, R. H.
    1948. *Review of the Principal Questions of Morals* (1787). Edited by D. D. Raphael. Oxford.

434   REFERENCES

PRICHARD, H. A.

   1912. Does Moral Philosophy Rest Upon a Mistake? *Mind,* vol. 21. Included in Sellars and Hospers, 1952.

   1950. *Moral Obligation.* New York.

QUINE, W. van O.

   1940. *Mathematical Logic.* New York.

RADCLIFFE-BROWN, A. R.

   1934. Social Sanctions. *Encyclopaedia of the Social Sciences,* vol. xiii, pp. 531–534.

   1939. *Taboo.* Cambridge.

RADIN, P.

   1927. *Primitive Man as Philosopher.* New York.

   1953. *The World of Primitive Man.* New York.

RAPOPORT, R. N.

   1954. Changing Navaho Religious Values. *Peabody Museum of Harvard University, Papers,* vol. XLI, no. 2. Cambridge, Mass.

REICHARD, G. A.

   1928. Social Life of the Navaho Indians. *Columbia University Contributions to Anthropology,* vol. 7.

   1936. Attitudes toward Avoidance: a Suggestion. In *Essays in Anthropology Presented to A. L. Kroeber.* Berkeley, California.

   1944. Prayer the Compulsive Word. *Monographs of the American Ethnological Society,* vol. 7.

   1950. *Navaho Religion.* New York.

RICE, P. B.

   1955. *On the Knowledge of Good and Evil.* New York.

ROSS, W. D.

   1930. *The Right and the Good.* Oxford. Partly included in Sellars and Hospers, 1952.

   1939. *Foundations of Ethics.* London.

ROTHACKER, E.

   1947. *Logik und Systematik der Geisteswissenschaften.* Bonn.

RYLE, G.

   1949. *The Concept of Mind.* London.

SAPIR, E. and HOIJER, H.

   1942. *Navaho Texts.* Linguistic Society of America, Iowa City.

SCHOPENHAUER, A.

      Preisschrift über die Grundlage der Moral. Translated by A. B. Bullock: *The Basis of Morality.* London, 1903.

SELBY-BIGGE, L. A.

   1897. *British Moralists.* Oxford.

SELLARS, W. and HOSPERS, J.

   1952. *Readings in Ethical Theory.* New York.

SIMMONS, D. C.

   1950. The Alamo Navaho Kinship and Sib Systems. Unpublished MA thesis, Yale University.

SMITH, W. and ROBERTS, J. M.
  1954. Zuni Law, a Field of Values. *Peabody Museum of Harvard University, Papers,* vol. XLIII, no. 1. Cambridge, Mass.
SPENCER, K.
  Mythology and Values: An Analysis of Navaho Chantway Myths. *Journal of American Folklore Memoirs.* In preparation.
SPINOZA
  Ethics.
STEVENSON, C. L.
  1944. *Ethics and Language.* New Haven.
  1950. Reply to Brandt. *Philosophical Review,* vol. LIX, no. 4.
SUMNER, W. G.
  1906. *Folkways.* Boston.
TOMAS, V. A.
  1951. Ethical Disagreements and the Emotive Theory of Values. *Mind,* vol. 60, pp. 205–222.
TOULMIN, S.
  1950. *An Examination of the Place of Reason in Ethics.* Cambridge, England.
TSCHOPIK, H. Jr.
  1938. Taboo as a Possible Factor in the Obsolescence of Navaho Pottery and Basketry. *American Anthropologist,* vol. 40. pp. 257–262.
VAN VALKENBURGH, R.
  1938. Navaho Common Law. *Museum Notes,* Museum of Northern Arizona, vol. X.
VOEGELIN, C. F.
  1949. Linguistics without Meaning and Culture without Words. *Word,* vol. 5, no. 1.
  1951. Culture, Language and the Human Organism. *Southwestern Journal of Anthropology,* vol. 7.
VOGT, E. Z.
  1951. Navaho Veterans, a Study of Changing Values. *Peabody Museum of Harvard University, Papers,* vol. XLI, no. 1. Cambridge, Mass.
VON WRIGHT, G. H.
  1951a. Deontic Logic. *Mind,* vol. LX, no. 237.
  1951b. *An Essay in Moral Logic.* Amsterdam.
WESTERMARCK, E.
  1932. *Ethical Relativity.* New York.
WHITE, M. G.
  1950. Toward an Analytic Philosophy of History. In M. Farber, editor, *Philosophic Thought in France and the United States.* Buffalo.
WHORF, B.
  1941. The Relation of Habitual Thought and Behavior to Language. In Leslie Spier, A. I. Hallowell, and Stanley S. Newman, editors, *Language, Culture, and Personality.* Menasha, Wisconsin.

WILD, J.
  1948. *Introduction to Realistic Philosophy.* New York.
WISDOM, J.
  1952. Gods. In A. Flew, editor, *Logic and Language.* Oxford.
WYMAN, L. C. and BAILEY, F.
  1943. Navaho Girl's Puberty Rite. *New Mexico Anthropologist,* vols. 6 and 7.
WYMAN, L. C. and HILL, W. W. and OSANAI, I.
  1942. Navaho Eschatology. *University of New Mexico Bulletin,* 377.
WYMAN, L. C. and KLUCKHOHN, C.
  1938. Navaho Classification of Their Song Ceremonials. *American Anthrological Association Memoirs,* no. 50.
WYMAN, L. C. and THORNE, B.
  1945. Notes on Navaho Suicide. *American Anthropologist,* vol. 47, pp. 278–288.
YOUNG, R. W.
  1949. (Editor and translator) The Ramah Navahos by the Son of Former Many Beads. *Navaho Historical Series,* no. 1. Indian Service, Department of the Interior. Phoenix, Arizona.
YOUNG, R. W. and MORGAN, W.
  1943. *The Navaho Language.* Education Division, U. S. Indian Service.

Notes

1. Firth, 1951, pp. 190ff.

2. For further discussion of this type of definition, see Chapter IV, section 3(b).

3. In accounts of this type there is quite frequently an implicit argument of the following type: if people of every society (or culture) tend to act in the same way in similar situations, or if there are regularities of behavior observable in every society, then we may conclude that these actions reflect universal categories which give us a foundation for ethics. Such an inference, however is actually a part of normative rather than of descriptive ethics; and even granted that it is valid (which it is not!), we should not confuse it with the describing of a certain moral code; see Chapter XVIII, sections 4 and 5.

4. For further discussion of these questions, see Chapter XVIII, sections 2 and 3.

5. I am indebted for this example to my colleague, R. M. Chisholm; see his article, 1952.

6. This category of inferred beliefs cannot be adequately analyzed here. It might be maintained that there is no belief until it has been formulated, and that we are only inferring that the person in question would have the belief in question if and when it is formulated. On the other hand, we encounter beliefs that cannot be formulated in terms that communicate them to others, although they are in some sense formulated in that person's mind; a special case of this would be a foreigner who has difficulty in expressing his beliefs in English although not in his native tongue. But for our purpose, further exploration of these problems is not necessary. See H. H. Price, 1953, pp. 306ff. On p. 307, Price distinguishes between "rehearsed and unrehearsed thinking. It is only rehearsed thinking which ever has a full dress and fully formulated character".

7. See Kluckhohn's definition of value (1951, p. 395): "A value is a conception, explicit or implicit, distinctive of an individual or characteristic of a group, of the desirable which influences the selection from available modes, means, and ends of action."

8. See Langer, 1942.

9. H. H. Price, 1953, p. 159 (the first italics are mine). See also Ryle, 1949, especially p. 296.

10. C. S. Peirce, 1931, vol. IV, par. 537. The distinction is roughly the same as the analogous distinction in linguistics between "allophone" and "phoneme," except that it is applied to sentences rather than to sounds.

11. For further details on the distinction between prescriptions and propositions, see Chapter V, section 2(b). Although the distinction between a prescription and a prescriptive statement is important in some contexts, in later discussions where there is no danger of misunderstanding I shall sometimes use the less cumbersome expression "prescription" with the meaning of "prescriptive statement."

12. Radin, 1953, chapter III.

13. See Chapter X, section 2.

14. I am indebted to Dr. May Edel for pointing out this possible objection to my procedures.

15. See Kluckhohn, 1941. For a controversy concerning this subject, see also Voegelin, 1949, and Opler's reply (1949) to that article.

16. Voegelin (1951, p. 364) writes of the relation of linguistics to anthropology: "operationally, linguistic study belongs to mathematics; substantively, to anthropology

or, if one prefers, to cultural anthropology." Perhaps descriptive ethics bears somewhat the same relation to cultural anthropology (if we substitute 'philosophical ethics' for 'mathematics').

17. I have drawn heavily in this section on John B. Carroll, 1953. The points which I make are so general that they can be found in many of the more technical writings in this field.

18. Carroll, 1953, p. 12.

19. See Harris, 1952.

20. The problem of differentiating ethical from other types of discourse will be discussed in Chapters III–V.

21. Carroll, 1953, p. 12.

22. Carroll, 1953, p. 29.

23. It was once suggested to me by a distinguished linguist that we might invent a pair of terms, "allo-eth" and "eth-eme," to correspond to the allophone and phoneme distinction. Thus 'allo-eth' actions distinguishable by the anthropologist might not be differentiated as 'eth-emes' in some ethical systems.

24. See particularly Hoijer, 1951 and 1954. I shall return to this topic later in the discussion of the Navaho moral code. See Chapters XII, section 2(b), and XVIII, section 3.

CHAPTER II   THE METHOD OF HYPOTHETICAL RECONSTRUCTION

1. The distinctions mentioned here may be found in most books on symbolic logic. Perhaps the clearest exposition appears in Carnap, 1946, chapter 1.

2. I have also adopted the practice of omitting double quotation marks when the expression mentioned is written in italics. Single quotation marks are used to indicate that the word is being used in a special or unusual sense.

3. The distinction between prescriptive and descriptive discourse proposed here is very crudely drawn since it is not essential for my general theory. It corresponds roughly to Carnap's distinction (1946) between pure and descriptive semantics and syntax. Prescriptive discourse will be discussed later in Chapter V, section 2.

4. Quine, 1940, p. 89. For another type of prescriptive meta-inquiry, see Morton White's conception of "meta-history" in "Toward an Analytic Philosophy of History," 1950.

5. Frankena, 1952, p. 189, see also Frankena, 1951.

6. Stevenson, 1950, p. 528.

7. For a more complete discussion see Ladd, 1952a. I have called the latter version of meta-ethics "ethical theory."

8. See Hempel and Oppenheim, 1948. The present discussion follows the general lines of this article, and the description of the scientific method to be found in Cohen and Nagel, 1934.

9. See Popper, 1935; see also Kaufmann, 1944, p. 86.

10. The theory proposed here for descriptive ethics resembles very closely Ducasse's conception of "ethical theory" (1940) according to which "theorizing has in ethics the same nature, functions and criteria of validity as anywhere else and that (aside from degree of development) the only essential difference between ethical theorizing and, e.g., physical theorizing is one of subject matter . . . The facts primitive . . . for ethics . . . consist of some of the judgments that would be expressed by such statements as 'This act is wrong,' 'This man is evil,' 'This ought to be done,' 'This state of affairs is good.' "

11. Among revisionists I should include Plato, Hobbes, Locke, Bentham, Mill, Dewey, Perry, etc.; and among conservatives, Aristotle, Butler, Hume, Adam Smith, Kant, contemporary British intuitionists, and the emotivists. For the conservatives, ethical inquiry is a "matter of philosophical curiosity."

12. MacQuordale and Meehl, 1948, in Feigl and Brodbeck, 1953, p. 605.

13. It should be noted that this reduction is valid only for descriptive ethics but not for normative ethics — for reasons which need not be given here.

14. Although there were earlier proponents of the method of *Verstehen,* the first detailed use of it was developed by William Dilthey; see his *Ideen ueber eine beschreibende und zergliedende Psychologie.* The term *Geisteswissenschaften* was originally intended to be a translation of of J. S. Mill's "moral sciences," and so I have chosen this expression to translate it back into English.

15. See, for example, Rothacker, 1947, p. 45.

16. Dilthey, however, distinguishes *Verstehen* from *Sympathie.*

17. This distinction is set forth most clearly in Rothacker, 1947, pp. 124ff.

18. See Parsons, 1937, p. 589, and *passim.* A critical analysis of the concept of *Verstehen* is to be found in Abel, 1948.

CHAPTER III   SCRUTINY OF DEFINITIONS OF "ETHICS," I

1. Durkheim, 1953.

2. These might be called "hypothetical obligations" to distinguish them from moral obligations which are categorical (in Kantian terms).

3. Hempel, 1952, p. 11.

4. Ibid.

5. Aristotle illustrates this point neatly in the case of defining an "eclipse" as "privation of light from the sun through intervention of the moon," and shows that such a definition presupposes knowledge of the interrelation of the sun and moon; see *Posterior Analytics,* book ii, chapter 8.

6. William James, 1890, vol. I, pp. 196–197 (I have omitted James's italics).

7. It should be noted that Durkheim (1953) is careful to distinguish between moral facts and his explanation of them; for the first, see pp. 40–49, and for the second, pp. 49–62. Although I am in sympathy with his analysis of "moral facts," I am inclined to reject his explanation of them.

8. For an *explanation* of the various taboos such as mother-in-law avoidance and incest, see Murdock, 1949, p. 279.

9. See Chapter I, section 1.

10. I find this weakness particularly obvious in many of the writings of Malinowski and his school. Although their writings are of inestimable value to general anthropology, they may entirely mislead those engaged in descriptive ethics. See Ladd, 1952c.

11. In philosophical ethics this transition from explanation to justification without any intermediary explication has been variously called the *naturalistic fallacy* (G. E. Moore) or *persuasive definition* (C. L. Stevenson).

12. Durkheim, 1953, pp. 35–62. The page references in parentheses are to this book.

13. For certain reasons to be given later, I prefer the term "moral prescriptions" to "rules of conduct," but I am in essential agreement on this point. See Chapter V, section 2(b).

14. For a more detailed analysis of command ethics, see the later discussion in Chapter V, section 1(f).

15. See section 2(c).

16. For a philosophical critique of authoritarianism, see Perry, 1954, pp. 88–89. Authoritarian ethical systems will be discussed in Chapter IX, section 4(d).

17. Radcliffe-Brown, 1934, p. 531.

18. Herskovitz, 1948, p. 222.

19. Bentham, *Principles of Morals and Legislation,* chapter iii; also in Burtt, 1939, p. 800.

20. Such a semantical 'stretching' is a commonplace in jurisprudence where words like "right" and "duty" are used nonethically but appear to retain their original normative character.

21. "In any 'persuasive definition' the term defined is a familiar one, whose meaning is both descriptive and strongly emotive. The purport of the definition is to alter the descriptive meaning of the term, usually by giving it greater precision within the boundaries of its customary vagueness; but the definition does *not* make any substantial

change in the term's emotive meaning. And the definition is used, consciously or unconsciously, in an effort to secure, by this interplay between emotive and descriptive meaning, a redirection of people's attitudes." Stevenson, 1943, p. 210.

22. These two types of obligation have been called by Kelsen (1945, pp. 6off.) secondary and primary norms respectively.

23. I am indebted for this suggestion to Professor Kurt B. Mayer.

24. For an excellent discussion, see MacBeath, 1952, pp. 149ff.

25. Herskovitz, for example (1948, p. 222) appears to recognize this sense when he adds to the definition cited in section 4(a) that "sanctions, viewed from another point of view, are those validations of custom that people tend to rationalize, when they express them at all."

26. Mead, 1937, p. 493.

27. See Piers and Singer, 1953, especially pp. 48ff.

28. See Piers and Singer, 1953, for a critique of this interpretation of "internal sanction."

29. See Bentham, *Principles of Morals and Legislation,* chapter III, and Mill, *Utilitarianism,* chapter III.

30. This type of distinction between internal and external sanction may be what Mead (1937, p. 439) had in mind when she described internal sanctions as follows: "The individual child may be so educated that he internalizes the standards of his society and obeys them in the absence of force exerted upon him from the outside, as in obeying a tabu for fear of death of disease, or in abstaining from illicit sex activities for fear of punishment by ghosts."

31. Chapter XIII, section 3(b)(6).

32. We noted above that this distinction was recognized by Durkheim.

33. Shame and guilt have been distinguished psychoanalytically on the grounds that shame represents a tension between Ego and Ego-Ideal, whereas guilt represents the tension between Ego and Super-Ego; see Piers and Singer, 1953, part I.

34. See section 2.

35. The common criticisms of the so-called "Conscience Theory" apply to this conception, and I need not repeat them here. They may be found in any elementary textbook in ethics.

36. Flugel, 1945, p. 255.

37. See Malinowski, 1926, *passim,* especially p. 26; see also Malinowski's introduction in Hogbin, 1934. It should be noted that Malinowski himself does not use this principle to identify morality, but rather 'law.' Others have used it for this purpose, however.

CHAPTER IV   SCRUTINY OF DEFINITIONS OF "ETHICS," II

1. See Perry, 1926, chapter 12.

2. From this broad point of view, we can employ Kluckhohn's definition of "value," which was quoted above in Chapter 1, note 7. For some of the problems involved in defining the "desirable," see Ladd, 1951.

3. The best recent exponents of this view are H. A. Prichard and W. D. Ross. The moral goodness of an action is held to depend on the motives of the agent and the circumstances under which he acted as well as, or perhaps irrespective of, the rightness of the act.

4. See Firth, 1951, chapter VI, *passim.* Similar examples could be found in many other anthropological writings on the ethics of non-literate societies.

5. See Westermarck, 1932.

6. Westermarck, 1932, pp. 90, 93. For Brandt's version, see Brandt, 1954, p. 64. His approach is discussed later in Chapter XVIII, section 1(d).

7. Some of these difficulties are discussed in detail in the controversy between Firth (1952 and 1955) and Brandt (1955a and 1955b) over the definition of the "ideal observer."

8. See MacBeath, 1952, pp. 161–162. My Navaho informant did not always think that public opinion was inviolable. This seems a matter of common sense!

9. Even Westermarck (1932, p. 112) is careful to point out that his theory does not entail this absurdity.

10. This identification, however, is accepted by some writers. It is suggested by Hume in *Enquiry Concerning Morals,* Appendix I, 1902, p. 291. It also seems to be the core of Santayana's ethical theory, and is the ground for what his critics call his "amoralism."

11. This point has been thoroughly discussed by Prichard, 1950, and Ross, 1930; their discussion may also be found in SH, pp. 149–162 and 163–174.

12. See MacBeath, 1952, p. 161, where examples are cited from other cultures.

13. Hampshire, 1949.

14. See Richard Price, *Review* (1787), 1948, pp. 79ff. I assume that the phrase, "ought to be praised," means that "everyone ought to praise it."

15. Modern writers in jurisprudence do not subscribe to the rather naive picture of legal justice just given. However, at present I am interested merely in giving the picture which may have influenced the development of moral notions.

16. The difference between Western notions of the qualifications and functions of a judge and those of other societies is brought out in the studies of Zuni law and Cheyenne law. In Zuni law, for instance, judges are not disqualified on the grounds of being interested, although they are supposed to be "fair" and not "lose their tempers." The aim of judicial procedure is to have the parties "reconcile their differences" and to restore "harmony." There seems to be no conception of the need for disinterestedness as such, nor that the aim of law is to 'protect the rights of the individual' as such. See Smith and Roberts, 1954, pp. 104ff; see also Llewellyn and Hoebel, 1941.

17. I have not mentioned the influence of the Judaic conception of God as the all-wise and all-knowing Judge. He might be considered to be the impartial spectator par excellence!

18. See Chapter XVII, section 2(b).

19. This approach was used by Brandt (1954) in his study of Hopi ethics. In consequence he has probably omitted many convictions which would be included under their "ethics" as I shall define it; see Chapter XVIII, section 1(d).

20. This type of anthropological interpretation of the data obtained in field work, in my opinion, has led at least one eminent philosopher to misconstrue the nature of the ethical systems of non-literate peoples; see MacBeath, 1952, and my review (1952c) of this book.

21. Duncan-Jones, 1952, pp. 167ff.

22. Kneale, 1950; also in SH, pp. 681–697.

23. SH, p. 688.

CHAPTER V   THE DEFINITION IN TERMS OF MORAL PRESCRIPTIONS

1. Although some philosophers distinguish between "oughtness" and "obligation," in order to simplify the exposition I shall regard these terms as synonymous. There are two grounds on which such a distinction has been based. First, "obligation" is sometimes taken to refer to the fact of an agent's being bound to a certain act or forbearance, while "ought" is used in statements about the acts or forbearance themselves. This is a distinction which is frequently employed by eighteenth-century British moralists, and involves the problem of the relation of motivation to moral judgment. (This problem will be discussed in section 2.) The second type of distinction is quite a different one; namely, it is one which is used to differentiate among different kinds of 'oughts.' Here "obligation" refers to a species of right acts arising out of special relationships to the obligee; for example, an obligation arising from having made a promise. This is a distinction which can be made only within a certain type of ethical system such as intuitionism, and hence is too narrow for our purposes and can be ignored here.

2. This approach to ethical discourse is similar in some respects to those of S. Toul-

min, 1950, and R. M. Hare, 1952. These books have provided me with many useful suggestions in the present analysis, although I should disagree with them on important points. The theory presented in this chapter bears marked resemblance to that proposed by Nowell-Smith, 1954, although the technical terms used are quite different. Unfortunately, this book appeared after the present chapter was written, and I was unable to draw on it.

3. See Chapter III, section 3.

4. Butler, *Sermons,* preface (the italics are mine except for the last one).

5. See MacDonald, 1950, and Aiken, 1952a. I have profited immensely from numerous informal discussions with Aiken on the subject of this chapter. He has made many points clear to me, which otherwise I should have left obscure. However, he should not be held responsible for my views.

6. I am sure that neither MacDonald nor Aiken had such an authoritarian interpretation in mind when they used the term "authority." But I think that Durkheim and Butler clearly did.

7. See Chapter I, section 5.

8. For a thorough-going analysis of the problems of the relation of fact and value, see Hall, 1952; see also Chapter IV, section 1.

9. Ross, 1930, p. 105; for further discussion, see Ladd, 1951.

10. These functions of ends-in-view and the other elements mentioned here, are excellently portrayed in Dewey, 1922. I have coined the term "action-in-view" to designate those actions which are contemplated 'in the imagination' as possibilities.

11. Aristotle (*Nicomachean Ethics,* 1111a 24) defines "voluntary action" as "that of which the moving principle is in the agent himself, he being aware of the particular circumstances of the action." This is, of course, a quite different notion from the one I am explicating here, although I find it quite acceptable; for more on voluntary action, see Ladd, 952b.

12. This question involves the problem of the ontological status of propositions, and the more general problem of universals. I do not wish to enter into these controversies, but I might point out in passing that some of the same problems that arise in connection with propositions also confront us in connection with prescriptions; for instance, the explanation of how the same prescription (or proposition) can be accepted by different persons at different times. It is possible that prescriptions may have to be given a Platonic kind of being to solve this problem. On the other hand, prescriptions perhaps could be analyzed, as propositions have been, in terms of classes of statements (sentences).

13. If one accepts a pragmatist version of judgments in general as being practical, all propositions would have to be considered as prescriptions, rather than the other way around. This might raise problems in connection with the analysis of "propositions," but it does recognize the practical character of prescriptions — which is all that we want here.

14. This point will require some emendation if we consider so-called "reconstructed prescriptions." At present, I am only concerned with those prescriptions of which the informant is cognizant — those which are included in his ethical discourse.

15. This is probably what Aristotle meant by his term *proairesis* (often translated as "choice"), which is a kind of policy decision which is the outcome of deliberation. Thus, an incontinent man (that is, one succumbing to temptation) "pursues the excesses of things pleasant — not by choice but contrary to choice and his judgment"; that is, contrary to the prescriptions he has accepted. See *Nicomachean Ethics,* 1148a 9, and book iii, chapters 2 and 3.

16. The view proposed here seems to accord with some of Nowell-Smith's statements (1954, p. 195 and chapter 13, *passim*). For instance, "'Smith ought to do Y' when spoken by Smith expresses a decision, but when spoken by Jones expresses an injunction."

17. It should be noted that a prescriptive disposition is a special kind of habit which is learned not by repeated performance but through verbal instruction. The best psy-

chological description of the phenomenon with which I am acquainted is to be found in Narziss Ach's conception (1951) of "determining tendency."

18. We may further distinguish between *executing* and *performing* a prescribed act, in order to distinguish between prescriptions that can be entirely fulfilled in the sense of being completed and satisfied, and those prescriptions that can be fulfilled without completing and satisfying the prescription. Take for example the following two prescriptions: "You ought to tell the truth," and "You ought to erect an altar here to God." The first prescription can never be executed because your telling the truth once does not satisfy the prescription forever. You can only perform such a prescription, not execute it. On the other hand, the second prescription can be executed — when the altar is completed the prescription is fulfilled once and forever.

19. The view proposed here raises the Socratic problem of whether one does what one ought not to do intentionally rather than through ignorance. Since we are concerned with a general analysis which will account for ethical systems in which this Socratic doctrine is denied as well as those in which it is accepted, we need not decide on the merits of the case here. I might point out that some libertarians would include an act of free will as a necessary antecedent condition of fulfillment. Also, it is interesting to note that the process sometimes called "rationalization" often takes the form of excusing oneself by maintaining that the antecedent invoking circumstances did not exist or were not recognized to exist by the agent; for example, a person excusing himself for breaking a promise might try to make himself or others believe that he had not made the promise; or, children sometimes think that by crossing their fingers an intended falsehood is not really a lie!

20. This is the principal thesis of Hare, 1952; see also Hall, 1952, chapter 6. For earlier versions, see Carnap, 1935, pp. 23ff., and Mill, *Logic,* book vi, chapter 11.

21. This is one of the many illuminating remarks made to me in private conversation with Father Berard.

22. Ayer, 1936, p. 108; also in SH, p. 397.

23. This point has been clearly argued by my colleague, Tomas (1951). The same point of triviality applies to the persuasive use of judgments in general.

24. Falk, 1953.

25. The most noted exponent of this view is Stevenson (1944); see also the review of this book by Aiken (1945) whose interpretation is followed for the most part in the present analysis.

26. It should be noted that my view departs from other types of 'attitude theories,' because it emphasizes the disposition to act as against the disposition to react affectively. The exaggeration of emotional responses as such, seems to me to distort the essentially practical character of moral convictions. I do not deny that they exist, but they are of secondary importance in ethics (and, incidentally, reflect the spectator approach).

27. For the most recent and sophisticated analysis of ethical discourse in terms of the use of language, see Nowell-Smith, 1954.

28. *De Cive,* chapter XIV. A somewhat similar definition is given by John Austin in *Jurisprudence,* lecture I: "A command is the expression of a will" and "the party to whom it is directed is liable to evil from the other, in case he comply not with the desire." However, I should like to point out that "command" can be defined without reference to sanctions. For a critique, see Kelsen, 1945, pp. 30ff. I am indebted to Kelsen for some of the remarks made here.

29. In this connection it may be contended that prescriptions are 'impersonal commands' but this seems to me to be a contradiction in terms.

30. I shall return to a consideration of 'command ethics' under the topic of authoritarian ethics; see Chapter IX, section 3(d).

31. There is another possibility, namely, that historical references may be used to teach moral precepts by example. In such cases, the references to the past can be treated as auxiliaries to direct prescriptive discourse. But as every historian knows, moral judgments about past events are likely to be dangerous and misleading.

32. A similar analysis is presented by Locke in his *Essay on Human Understanding,*

book ii, chapter 28, pars. 4ff., where he calls "morality the conformity, or disagreement, men's voluntary actions have to a rule to which they are referred, and by which they are judged of." This view is also worked out in greater detail by Kneale, 1950.

33. It is interesting to note in this connection that when we say that Napoleon ought to have done something, or that Eisenhower ought to do such and such, we also are implying that he did not or will not do what we say he ought to. This connotation of ought-statements in which they seem to be about unfulfilled states of affairs, accounts for the fact that such statements serve an informative function which is often more important than their prescriptive function.

34. See Chapter IV, section 2.

35. Strictly speaking it is incorrect to say that a person ought or ought not to desire an object, since as I contended above, "ought" applies only to actions. The analysis of the type of sentence given in the text will be given later; see Chapter VII, section 1(b).

36. The Kantian nature of this account should be obvious. I am convinced that Kant would agree on the last two points, and the failure to recognize this has resulted in much misunderstanding of his ethics. The first point, the need for invoking occasions, is taken care of in his conception of the 'maxim' of conduct. (Incidentally, this is almost identical with my conception of prescription.) The second point, the possibility of moral actions with respect to an end, is fully covered in his *Metaphysical Principles of Virtue* (for excerpts, see Beck, 1949, pp. 352ff.). It should also be noted that the two characteristics of sufficiency and ultimacy are to be found in Aristotle, *Nicomachean Ethics,* book i, chapter 7.

37. See Chapter IV, section 2.

38. See comments on Duncan-Jones, Chapter IV, section 3(d).

CHAPTER VI COMPONENTS OF A PRESCRIPTION: PRESCRIPTIVE QUALITIES

1. I shall use the terms "to enjoin" and "injunction" always to stand for prescribing positively and positive prescriptions. In other words, they stand for the opposites of "to prohibit" and "prohibition."

2. See Chapter V, section 2(d).

3. See Hall, 1952, chapter 6 for references; see also Hare, 1952, Duncan-Jones, 1952, and von Wright, 1951a and 1951b.

4. Or "is," or "will be," depending upon the time designation which should be included in the propositional part. Perhaps the recognition that tense expressions referring to the time of action belong in the propositional part will help us to understand how a prescription may refer to the past — thus "Brutus's *having* killed Caesar *is* wrong." See comments made earlier in Chapter V, section 2(g). This interpretation does not sound as plausible for imperatives, because it does seem somewhat anomalous to *command* Brutus not to have killed Caesar. Such considerations suggest that the logic of imperatives suffers from an inadequate analysis of imperative qualities.

5. For further explanation of squares of opposition, see any elementary logic textbook.

6. See section 4.

7. We can see this from Ross's discussion of the implications of the obligation to return a book. It does not matter *how* the situation of putting the book in the owner's hands is achieved; for example, I can post it or take it to him myself (always with the proviso that the means employed do not conflict with other moral principles). Ross, 1930, p. 42; also in SH, p. 193.

8. It is always necessary to compare prescriptions referring to the same act (prescriptum), to bring out the different implications of the positive and negative versions of them. These differences probably can be formulated in logical symbols, but such an undertaking is unnecessary here.

9. The difference is also evident in the translations of the following prescriptions:

"Shooting the tyrant is obligatory," and "Shooting the tyrant is wrong." The first might be equivalent to: "Someone ought to shoot the tyrant," while the second would be: "No one ought to shoot the tyrant."

10. Further elaboration of this principle has interesting consequences for the similar analysis of other practical principles. Thus it can be applied to the pair of commands: "Stay here" and "Do not leave", because staying and leaving are mutually exclusive categories which exhaust the possibilities in the context. But if the context is changed by one's not being 'here,' then one could avoid violating the prohibition without fulfilling the injunction. Again, by employing this analysis we can elucidate the ambiguities in such pairs as "be brave" and "don't be cowardly"; or "keep your promises" and "don't break your promises"; it is clear that sometimes these pairs are equivalent and sometimes not. This analysis is also extremely illuminating when applied to attitudinal opposites such as "love" and "hate", or "respect" and "disrespect"; see Chapter IX, section 2(d).

11. See Chapter VII.

12. It should be noted that the term "stringency" is not used here as it is by certain intuitionist writers, such as Ross, merely to refer to the comparative degrees of stringency of various prima facie duties. "Stringency" is defined here in terms of the obligatoriness or wrongness of the act without reference to acts which may conflict with it, although perhaps it would include this use when conflicts are involved.

13. *Catholic Encyclopaedia*, vol. iv, p. 436; see also Aquinas, *Summa Theologica*, Second Part of the Second Part, question 184ff.

14. Matt. 19: 16–22.

15. See Henry Home, Lord Kames, *The Principles of Morals;* also in Selby-Bigge, 1897, vol. ii, p. 308. Aristotle also appears to distinguish justice from the other virtues, although how he does this is not quite clear.

16. Kant, *Foundations of Morals,* in Beck, 1949, p. 80n; see also Paton, 1946, pp. 147ff.

17. Hall, 1952, p. 128. Hall states that this corresponds to the law of the excluded middle in ordinary logic.

18. See section 2(b).

19. Another example: "It is right to pay your debts by check" means "There are other possible ways of paying, for example, by check, in cash, etc., and one or other of these ways is obligatory but it is not obligatory to pay by check, etc."

20. In answer to other moral philosophers (for example, Kames), Richard Price explicates at some length this method of avoiding the irreducible distinction between duties of justice and those of benevolence; Price, *Review* (1787), 1948, pp. 119–124; also partly in Selby-Bigge, 1897, vol. ii, pp. 166ff.

21. Price recognizes this objection, and attempts to answer in terms of a distinction corresponding to that proposed earlier between prescription and evaluation. A morally desirable act would be one which is rated as "more amiable," that is, as having greater moral value or praiseworthiness. This way of saving the law of exhaustiveness may be a feasible solution of a difficult problem, but I suspect that the law itself must be given up because it fails to generate a prescription; see Price, *Review* (1787), 1948, p. 123.

22. Dewey, 1922, p. 278.

23. Moore, 1911, pp. 67ff.; also in SH, p. 56.

24. See section 2(a).

CHAPTER VII COMPONENTS OF A PRESCRIPTION: PRESCRIPTA

1. See Ladd, 1952b.

2. The conception of "ethical competence" and its relation to authoritarian ethics will be discussed in more detail in Chapter IX, section 4. See earlier discussion of the generalizability of agents in Chapter IV, section 3(d).

3. Ross, 1930, p. 42; also in SH, p. 193.

4. Prichard, 1950, pp. 34–35.

5. Prichard, 1950, chapter 2; Ross, 1939, chapter vii. For a subtle discussion of the principle that "ought" implies "can," as it occurs in this type of argument, see Frankena, 1950.

6. It is true, of course, that we can say that a person ought to accept a certain prescription, and this ought can be fulfilled without the prescription itself being fulfilled. The curious thing about such statements is that the reasons for accepting a prescription are identical with the reasons for performing the prescribed act itself. The situation is similar to the intimate relationship between an injunction to try to do something and the injunction to do it (in many cases, although not all). The relationship appears to be as follows: If one ought to do A, then it follows that one ought to accept the prescription to do A and one ought to try to do A. In other words, the prescription to do A seems to be the basic prescription from which the other two are derived.

7. Matt. 5: 48.

8. In answer to Prichard, I should point out that I agree with him that where the agent is unable to perform the act prescribed, the prescription is canceled for that particular situation. However, I differ from him, in denying that it is always necessary that the agent *know* whether he has the duty or not. In practice we usually assume that we know about the consequences of a proposed act, even though some error is possible. This seems to be sufficient for many moral systems. For instance, the Navaho code, as represented by my informant, presupposes that we do know that certain consequences will follow from certain acts. Compare the injunction against stealing based on the belief that one will always be caught: "No chance of getting away with it nowadays." (* 7)

9. This distinction was pointed out long ago by Aristotle, when he said that we can only choose the means, but we can *wish* for an end, even if it is entirely outside our power; *Nicomachean Ethics,* book iii, chapters 2–4.

10. See Parsons, 1937, p. 319. However, it should be remembered that Durkheim's analysis is primarily sociological rather than ethical.

11. For example, Hoijer writes (1954, p. 102) that "the Navaho speaks of 'actors' and 'goals' . . . not as performers of actions or ones upon whom actions are performed, as in English, but as entities linked to actions already defined in part as pertaining especially to classes of beings."

12. See Kant, "On a supposed right to lie from altruistic motives" (Beck, 1949, pp. 346ff). The question propounded by Kant was used in questioning my Navaho informant. His answer (* 91) is interesting and enlightening.

13. Prichard, 1950, p. 21 (the italics are mine). Prichard later qualifies this formulation to conform to a 'subjective' interpretation of the situation. The quotation given here is involved, but it is clear that the whole formulation is in 'situational terms.'

14. Prichard, 1950, p. 7; also in SH, p. 154.

15. A suggestion made by E. F. Carritt, who is a follower of Prichard in this respect; see Carritt, 1947, p. 11.

CHAPTER VIII   THE LOGIC OF ETHICAL DISCOURSE: VALIDATION

1. "If, e.g., we refer to the act of repaying X by a present merely as giving X a present, it appears, and indeed is, necessary to give a reason. In other words, wherever a moral act is regarded in this incomplete way the question *'Why* should I do it?' is perfectly legitimate." Prichard, 1950, p. 8; also in SH, p. 155.

2. The distinction between validation and justification (or between logic and rhetoric) in W. E. Johnson's terms (1921, vol. I, pp. 2–3) might be said to be that between the "constitutive" and the "epistemic" requirements of ethical argumentation.

3. For references, see Chapter VI, section 1(a).

4. *Modus ponens* states: If p, then q, and p, therefore q. *Modus tollens* states: If p, then q, but not q, therefore not p.

5. In practice, prescriptions about means and ends are usually more complicated because they allow for a choice of means. The example given above is of a *necessary*

means. A less stringent form of the argument might be as follows: If you do *p*, then you must do either *q* or *r* or *t*, etc.; you ought to do *p*, therefore do either *q* or *r* or *t*, etc. For example: If you are to support your wife, then you must either have inherited money or get a job or marry someone with money, etc. You ought to support your wife. Therefore either inherit money or get a job or marry someone with money, etc. It is evident that numerous combinations of these basic formulae are possible.

6. For further examples and rules see von Wright, *1951a,* and Duncan-Jones, *1952b.* *Modus ponens (A)* is called the "law of commitment" by von Wright.

7. I shall henceforth use the term "factual premise" to stand for a nonprescriptive statement used in ethical argument. I do not intend thereby to prejudice the question whether or not there are prescriptive (for example, moral) facts. Social scientists following Max Weber, have generally used the term "existential judgment" — but it seems inadvisable to use it here, because of other philosophical connotations.

8. Not, however, that of Aristotle (*De Motu Animalium,* 700b), which is discussed in Ladd, 1953.

9. Mill, *Logic,* book vi, chapter 11, par. 1. Mill's only mistake is that he is not quite clear whether the major premise is a prescription or an end. The ambiguity is resolved if we recognize that to prescribe an end (that is, to choose an end) is equivalent to prescribing the means to the end. The scheme which I have suggested here is more inclusive than Mill's since it is intended to apply to all ethical systems, utilitarian and formalistic.

10. See Hart, 1952; see also Wisdom, 1952.

11. "We do not originally approve or condemn particular actions; because, upon examination, they appear agreeable or inconsistent with a certain general rule. The general rule, on the contrary, is formed, by finding from experience, that all actions of a certain kind, or circumstanced in a certain manner, are approved or disapproved of." Adam Smith, *Theory of Moral Sentiments,* also in Selby-Bigge, 1897, vol. i, p. 304. Possibly Smith belongs not under particularism, but under the interpretive mode discussed in (e).

12. This is a view which I find in Ross, 1930, chapter ii; also in SH, pp. 174–197. It is clear, however, that if he ever held it, it was abandoned in his later book (1939, pp. 169ff).

13. Ross, 1930, p. 31; also in SH, p. 185.

14. Kelsen, 1945, pp. 132ff. The page references in parentheses are to this book.

15. This mode of validation under the epithet "deductivism" was repudiated by me in my article of 1953, on the ground that it seemed to be an artificial logical construction not corresponding to any 'natural' ethics. Since then my study of the Navaho ethical code has convinced me that it is a perfectly genuine mode of validation. This is a good example of the influence of anthropological knowledge on philosophical inquiry!

16. This mode of validation is discussed in more detail in my article of 1953.

17. Aristotle, *Nicomachean Ethics,* 1107a 3.

18. Dewey uses different terms in his various writings to describe this ultimate basic prescription and the principle of interpretation.

19. Kelsen, 1945, p. 129.

20. See, for example, Wild, 1948, p. 66, and Aquinas, *Summa Theologica,* First Part, question 83, article 1.

21. The distinctions mentioned in connection with the mode of interpretation are well illustrated by the doctrine of natural law advanced by St. Thomas Aquinas. According to this theory, built upon Aristotelian foundations, there is a universal and general natural law, common to all men and nations. Upon the natural law particular sovereigns create specifications appropriate for the situation of their own country, and this is called positive law. In the outline given above, natural law corresponds to the ultimate basic schematic prescription, and the positive law to the interpretations of it. Positive law can only be created by a public authority, "someone who has care of the common good." It derives its bindingness from the natural law. Finally, any ordinance which

conflicts with the natural law is "no law at all"; that is, it is invalid. See Aquinas, *Summa Theologica,* First Part of the Second Part, questions 90ff.

CHAPTER IX   THE RHETORIC OF ETHICAL DISCOURSE: JUSTIFICATION

1. Schopenhauer (*Foundations of Ethics*) makes a similar distinction between what he calls *Grundsätze* (basic prescriptions) and *Grundtriebfedern* (ground-motives). Schopenhauer clearly sees the problem of linking morality with motivation, but he fails to see that the ground-motive must not only be a motive, but an especially authoritative one. In other words, he fails to account for the priority, ultimacy, and legitimacy of moral judgments, although he perhaps does try to answer the requirement of sufficiency. Schopenhauer's own *Grundsatz* is, "neminem laede, imo omnes, quantum potes, juva," and his moral *Triebfeder* is the motive of sympathy.

2. I shall use the word "existential" to refer to those rather general views about the world which are elements in the ground. The more particular nonprescriptive beliefs that enter into ethical argument have been called "factual beliefs". Thus, my use of the term "existential" is more restricted than that of Max Weber, and perhaps more in accord with philosophical usage (for example in "existentialism"!).

3. I have not included any ground-motive for the ethics involving "impersonal" ends. It is difficult to discover any adequate motivation for such basic prescriptions. Perhaps this is one reason why a system like that of Bentham is felt to be so inadequate. Sometimes benevolence or sympathy are cited as motives for this type of system, but they could not be ground-motives in my sense because they are not 'preeminent.'

4. Fromm, 1947; Perry, 1926, pp. 645ff.; Aristotle, *Nicomachean Ethics,* book ii, chapter 6, and *passim.*

5. The logic involved here was discussed earlier in Chapter VI, section 4.

6. This appears to be the case with the Navahos. The application of these distinctions will be considered in more detail later.

7. Quoted from the *Samyutta Nikaya* by Ducasse, 1953, p. 50.

8. Additional confirmation of this surmise is offered by the Aristotelian-Thomistic doctrine that evil is the privation of good, a necessary adjunct of the belief that God created the world and it was good. For a comparison of Aristotle's doctrine of the mean with similiar Navaho tenets, see Chapter XVII, section 1(d).

9. A system founded on the attitude of respect may be exemplified by Kant's ethics. For example, "Duty is the necessity of an action done from respect for the law," "Respect is properly the conception of a worth which thwarts my self-love" (Beck, 1949, pp. 61, 62n.). The problems involved, including the problem of an objective instead of a subjective formulation, are revealed in all their complexity in Kant's philosophy.

10. Note that such a simple equivalence does not obtain for teleological prescriptions. For example, "Act so as to promote the greatest happiness" is not equivalent to "Avoid doing those actions which will not promote the greatest happiness," for there might be indifferent acts, which do not conform to the positive injunction, but are not therefore forbidden.

11. The admission of this equivalence reduces this type of injunction to what I have earlier called "disguised prohibitions," which appear as positive prescriptions restricted to a specific context. Within that context every act is either enjoined or forbidden because it is assumed that the nonperformance of one is equivalent to the performance of the other. For instance, if when talking, one does not tell the truth he is lying. Similarly, if one does not treat his fellows with respect, he treats them with disrespect; or if he does not love his neighbor, he has some negative attitude towards him. In other words, the present view is founded on the assumption that the absence of a positive attitude (in the context) is identical with the presence of a negative attitude. This, of course, entails the law of the excluded middle — but only within the context in question. See Chapter VI, section 2(b).

12. I owe the above distinction between validation and vindication to Feigl's illuminating essays on the subject. As an example of vindication of theoretical knowledge, Feigl cites the pragmatic justification of the principle of induction. He also suggests the possibility of a similar 'pragmatic' justification of basic moral principles. At this point, I depart from Feigl's view that in ethics 'pragmatic' argument is a vindication rather than a teleological validation, employing a basic teleological prescription. I suggest that even teleological (including pragmatic) prescriptions need to be vindicated. Hence, I shall use the term "vindication" more broadly than Feigl does. See Feigl, 1950; see also Feigl, 1952, in SH, pp. 667–680.

13. Mill, *Utilitarianism,* Chapter 1; also in Burtt, 1939, p. 898.

14. See Chapter VIII, section 2(b).

15. Peirce, "The Fixation of Belief."

16. I have already commented on the use of such arguments in validation. See Introduction, and a more detailed discussion of this use in Chapter XVIII, section 5(b).

17. See Toulmin, 1950, pp. 13ff. See also Nowell-Smith, 1954, pp. 51ff.

18. The notion of "competence" will be examined in the next section.

19. A possible interpretation of the *argumentum ex consensu gentium* might be that it is a way of convincing a hearer that he must already accept the principle in question 'implicitly' because it is accepted by all men and so must be accepted by him since he is a man. However, I doubt whether the argument is generally used for this particular purpose.

20. See Chapter V, section 4.

21. This notion of competence may approximate part of what Melden (1952, pp. 173ff.) calls "significance conditions." Such 'significance conditions' are the conditions of 'meaningful use' of moral utterances. Similarly, my competence conditions are the conditions of meaningful use of reasonable discourse in any particular sphere.

22. This requirement seems to be agreed upon by most of the eighteenth-century British moralists; for example, Butler, Hutcheson, Price, Hume, and so on. See Selby-Bigge, 1897, vol. i, pp. 206, 215, 413, 417, and vol. ii, p. 187.

23. ". . . for wickedness perverts us and causes us to be deceived about the starting-points of actions [that is, basic prescriptions]. Therefore it is evident that it is impossible to be practically wise without being good" (*Nicomachean Ethics,* 1144a 35).

24. All this follows from the earlier analysis of "sanction." See Chapter IV, section 4(a).

25. Authority in the sense used here probably implies a 'charismatic' element, and the discussions of Max Weber have thrown a good deal further light on the notion. However, I should like to warn the reader that my discussion relates only to the conception of *ethical* authority, and therefore sociological considerations which might be relevant to other types of authority are not relevant here. See Parsons, 1937, pp. 658ff.

26. See Psalm 19: 7–11.

27. Judaic ethics has been interpreted in many different ways. Several different ethical systems have been developed to serve as a philosophical basis for the many prescriptions it contains. In the Old Testament, the doctrine as developed by the prophets and priests was probably authoritarian in the sense just mentioned. Later rabbis have tended towards an interpretation of the prescriptions in the Torah as *symbols* of obedience to God, rather than as commands given by God for the best interest of the people, and to be obeyed because of his special competence. There are other interpretations; see Lazarus, 1900, vol. I, pp. 111ff.

CHAPTER X   THE APPLICATION OF THE GENERAL THEORY

1. Radin, 1953, pp. 43, 45. Radin's illustrations refer to other categories of thought than ethics, and perhaps I have interpreted his position more generally than he has stated it.

2. See Chapter V, sections 4 and 5.

3. Mr. Moustache, as he is called in the literature on the Navahos, has frequently served as an informant. Consequently, there are numerous references to him by anthropologists. Most important of these are: a short autobiography recorded by Kluckhohn, 1945, and some autobiographical accounts in Young, 1949. He died on July 30, 1954. An obituary which gives a brief sketch of his life and an appreciative account of his personality was written by Kluckhohn and Vogt, 1955.

4. Kroeber, 1947, pp. 109, 110.

CHAPTER XI   NAVAHO ETHICS IN GENERAL

1. For a reader who knows little about the Navahos and wishes to learn more about their life and culture, there is no better way of beginning than by reading Kluckhohn and Leighton, 1946.

2. See Chapter I, section 4.

3. See Reichard, 1944. See also OMH, p. 23, where the bears are spoken to, and pp. 215–216 for snakes and lightning. This might be called magic, but perhaps rationalism, itself, could equally be considered a form of magical belief, that is a belief in the 'magic of reason.'

4. Kluckhohn, 1949, p. 362.

5. OMH, p. 20. All quotations from this book are by permission of the publishers, Harcourt, Brace and Company.

6. "He was going crazy the way he acted" (Dyk, 1947, p. 83).

7. The severity of going crazy is indicated by the fact that this is the supposed effect of violating the incest taboos, which are perhaps the strongest taboos in Navaho society. The fear of losing one's mind induced one girl to commit suicide — a quite extreme act considering the Navaho fear of death (see Wyman and Thorne, 1945).

8. A Singer, or medicine man, is the chief officiant at the elaborate religious curing ceremonies. There is a great variety and number of these ceremonies and each Singer usually knows only a few of them. After he has gone through the strenuous discipline of learning the rites, the teacher then will tell his student the *myth* which gives the origin of the rites with the Holy People. "There is a lot more story, but I ain't supposed to tell you people if you not learning," is what a Singer tells his friends if asked about them (Leighton and Leighton, 1949, p. 71). See also (* 116). Actually, much of this 'secret knowledge' has been recorded and published. For details and bibliography, see Spencer.

9. See Chapter XIV.

10. For a general account, see Kluckhohn and Leighton, 1946, especially chapter 9; see also Kluckhohn, 1949.

11. See Kluckhohn, 1945.

12. Kluckhohn estimates that in 1936–37 about 20 per cent of their income was spent on ceremonies. He tells me that it is probably less now. In a way, therefore, it might be said that 20 per cent of the income goes to paying for doctors, medicines, and hospital bills. This is, of course, only true for the manifest function of these ceremonies. There are many latent functions which they serve which are fulfilled by other activities in other societies. See Kluckhohn and Leighton, 1946, Chapter 7.

13. See Malinowski, 1926, *passim*. See also Kluckhohn, 1941, pp. 116–117, where the distinction is made between ideals and modes of behavior in the overt cultural pattern. Whether my explanation is valid could be tested by comparing the moral code of one of the pueblos with that of the Navahos.

14. For a more detailed description and analysis of the various factors leading to security and insecurity in one individual, see Leighton and Leighton, 1949.

15. See, for example, Dyk, 1947, p. 216, n.53: "The good man was the one who always had plenty to eat." See also Leighton and Leighton, 1949, and Kluckhohn, 1945.

16. See Dyk, 1947, p. 169, n.1. For a general account of Navaho ideas about property, see Hobson, 1954.

17. "I could get no response except astonishment about the ownership of house and farm adjoining . . . Everyone owns it who uses it" (Reichard, 1928, p. 92). This

statement must be modified if we include "ownership" in a wider sense than it is being used here. Thus: "Farm and range land 'belongs' to a family. The dominant Navaho idea of ownership of such land has been well called 'inherited use-ownership'; that is, the man who 'owns' farm or range land can only control it for a limited period, and no 'owner' can give away or otherwise alienate land from his family" (Kluckhohn and Leighton, 1946, p. 59).

18. Dyk, 1947, p. 186, n.33. It may also be significant that my aged informant made gifts instead of loans when he was approached for a loan (* 70). See also (* 55).

19. "The right of property is an individual's right against all other individuals that they shall behave in a certain way relative to the former, namely, that all the other individuals shall refrain from any interference with the former's disposition of a certain thing" (Kelsen, 1945, p. 86).

20. OMH, p. 31.

21. Hobson, 1954, p. 27.

22. "If a woman wishes to make a proposal, honorable or otherwise, she may do so by taking away a man's property" (Dyk, 1947, p. 147, n.45; also p. 196, n.7). For examples of the three situations in which a woman is paid, is the seducer, and is seduced, see OMH, pp. 288 and 344, pp. 329 and 359, and p. 160 and *passim*. See also Dyk, 1947, pp. 174, n.45, and p. 196, n.5.

23. Hobson, 1954, p. 27. For further discussion of this topic, see Chapter XII, section 2(e) and Chapter X, section 1(b).

24. See Chapter III, section 3; Chapter V, section 2(f); Chapter IX, section 4(d).

25. See Chapter IV, section 3(a) and 3(b).

26. For further discussion of the consequences following from the use of different definitions of "ethics", see Chapter XVIII, section 1(c).

27. See Chapter XV, section 2.

28. See the discussion of traditional practices, Chapter XIV, section 4.

29. See Chapter XVI, section 3. Egoism and altruism are compatible in the reconstructed code. See Chapter XVII, section 2.

30. OMH, p. 254.

31. OMH, pp. 8–9. See also (* 2).

32. OMH, p. 76.

33. See also OMH, p. 254.

34. See also (* 48), and Leighton and Leighton, 1949, p. 50 (note that the speaker, Mr. Moustache, is the same person as my informant). See also, Dyk, 1947, pp. 109–110, and OMH, pp. 305–306.

35. OMH, p. 301.

CHAPTER XII   BELIEFS ABOUT MAN AND THE WORLD

1. See Chapter X, section 4.

2. Reichard (1950, p. 53) distinguishes the deities in the Navaho pantheon according to the following groups: "Persuadable deities, undependable deities, helpers of deity and man, intermediaries, unpersuadable deities, dangers conceived as deities, beings between good and evil." I propose that we consider these as differentiating characteristics not only of the 'deities' but of all beings in the world, including human beings.

3. For their relevance to Navaho ethics, see Chapter XIV. A good account of these kinds of beings may be found in Kluckhohn and Leighton, 1946, pp. 122–132. For a definition of "holy," see Haile, 1950a, vol. II, p. 155.

4. Father Berard Haile (1950a, vol. II, p. 68) has discussed at length this conception of 'inner form.' "Sun, moon, perhaps constellations, the dawn, horizontal blue, evening twilight, darkness, mountains of the cardinal points, trees, water or springs, animals and plants, all are provided with — an inner form which animates them." The inner form is not destroyed when its carriers (that is, particular manifestations) are.

5. See Wyman, Hill, and Osanai, 1942, for a full discussion of Navaho beliefs

about ghosts. See also Haile, 1950b, p. ix, and Kluckhohn and Leighton, 1946, p. 127.

6. For more about this doctrine of the wind soul, see Chapter XV, section 3(c).

7. See Reichard, 1950, p. 433; see also Haile, 1950a, vol. II, p. 122.

8. See the extensive study of Navaho beliefs about witchcraft by Kluckhohn (1944).

9. See Dyk, 1947, p. 112.

10. For a general discussion of these beliefs, see Kluckhohn and Leighton, 1946, Chapter 5. For more detailed information about the divinities, see Reichard, 1950, especially chapters 4 and 5.

11. Kluckhohn (1949) has already expounded some of these categories. My speculations are based upon his conclusions, but are developed in more detail with the specific purpose of elucidating the categories employed in ethical thinking.

12. For an account of the importance of the conception of time and its relation to linguistic categories, see Whorf, 1941, pp. 75–93.

13. See OMH, p. 252. Old Man Hat says, "The Enemy Rite and Feather Rite are bothering me . . . [because] years ago" he has killed a Mexican, and also a deer.

14. A possible exception to this principle may be found in beliefs about "Frenzy Witchcraft" where a young man is supposed to lure his female victim by playing a flute. However, sound has the obvious characteristic of travelling through space quickly and at great distances — in this case, there is clearly a belief that the sound (even if unheard) acts upon the victim. Perhaps the power of sound (talk, thunder) may be linked with its spatial characteristics (see below). For "Frenzy Witchcraft," see Kluckhohn, 1944, pp. 118ff. Witchcraft practices all appear to involve some physical accoutrement, although there may be exceptions.

15. Kluckhohn, 1944, p. 15.

16. Kluckhohn and Leighton, 1946, p. 142. Perhaps the only way something can 'stand for' another thing is to have been in physical contact with it, or to resemble it. The latter exemplifies the principle of "like produces like." For the moral prescriptions regarding witchcraft and lightning, see Chapter XIII, section 2(b), (5) and (8).

17. Where "verbs predicate references to conditions in space and time, to fit and unfit conditions of health and life, the xo-prefix must be substituted." Haile, 1950b, p. viii. The important ceremonial, called *hozhonji,* is translated "Blessing Way"; Kluckhohn (1949, p. 363) has pointed out the importance to understanding Navaho culture of the ideas associated with the word, *hozhon,* which may variously be translated "beauty," "happiness," "harmony," "pleasantness," etc.; see also Kluckhohn, 1941, p. 128. *Hochonji,* translated "Ghost Way" or "Evil Way," is directed at the exorcising of ghosts, and the place where someone has died or is buried is called *hochon.*

18. Kluckhohn has pointed out to me that not only are the chant-legends filled with place names, but that the average Navaho demands complete precision about places in ordinary conversation; see also Kluckhohn, 1944, p. 97n.

19. Hoijer, 1951, p. 117. For illustration of the use of motion-words in 'prayers,' see Reichard, 1944, p. 31.

20. For another example of explanation of diseases by a plurality of causes, see OMH, p. 252, where an illness is attributed to having killed a deer, and to having murdered a Mexican. See also, Leighton and Leighton, 1949, p. 73.

21. This is discussed below in Chapter XIII, section 2(c).

22. "In most cases one factor is thought of as being able to cause a variety of maladies, with one or two outstanding. Likewise, the same disease may result from one of various factors." Wyman and Kluckhohn, 1938, p. 15.

23. See Kluckhohn and Leighton, 1946, pp. 142ff. For an account of diagnoses of sickness, see Reichard, 1950, p. 91.

24. OMH, p. 81, see also p. 77.

25. For further remarks on property conceptions, see Chapter XI, section 3(b); and Chapter XIV, section 1(b).

26. For the use of this economic principle in ethical discourse, see Chapter XIV, section 2(b) (2); Chapter XVII, section 2.

27. For a discussion of this point and its relation to the theory of the 'wind-soul,' see Chapter XV, section 4(c).

CHAPTER XIII THE DATA: NEGATIVE PRESCRIPTIONS

1. Throughout this book, except when quoting from other sources, I have adopted the orthography of Young and Morgan, 1943. For simplicity, I have also omitted the accents which indicate that the vowel is to be pronounced with high tonal quality. Anyone desiring more exact knowledge about these linguistic expressions and about the various linguistic forms should consult the works of Father Berard Haile, Sapir, Hoijer, Young, and others.

2. For further discussion of this point, see Chapter XVII, section 1(c). For other words occurring in Navaho ethical discourse, see Chapter XIII, section 2(b). It should be noted that the English words offered as translations are only roughly equivalent grammatically, because there is no adjectival form in Navaho.

3. See Chapter V, sections 2(e) and 5.

4. Kluckhohn, 1941, p. 110.

5. I have selected this word to refer to prescriptions that cite "what people will say," because it is etymologically derived from the Latin *dicere,* to say (although, of course, the word "interdiction" is ordinarily used in a quite different sense).

6. I do not pretend that "taboo" as so defined corresponds to other ordinary or technical uses of the term. It should be noted that I have omitted any explicit mention of ritual status, which is essential to Radcliffe-Brown's definition of "taboo." Since my intent is to give only an ethical analysis of these prohibitions, wider anthropological and sociological ramifications are unnecesary and irrelevant at this point; see Radcliffe-Brown, 1939.

7. It is quite characteristic of Navaho mentality that if one diagnosis or cure fails they will try another. They can never be sure that the diagnosis and cure given by their 'doctors' has been correct until the patient is well again. To a layman there seem to be a remarkably large number of successful cures — although these can certainly be attributed to other causes than are supposed by the Navaho medical theories. For a list of incurable diseases, see Haile, 1950b, p. xv. For the Navaho theory of disease, see Reichard, 1950, chapters 6 and 7; see also Kluckhohn and Leighton, 1946, pp. 132–133 and 153–156, and Wyman and Kluckhohn, 1938.

8. Haile, 1933, pp. 35–38. Quoted by Kluckhohn, 1944, p. 35.

9. For illustrations, see Vogt, 1951. For interesting comments on this taboo, see Reichard, 1936.

10. See Murdock, 1949, p. 279.

11. See Dyk, 1947, pp. 172–173. There are quite a number of other exceptions allowed.

12. The Navaho word meaning "one not looked at" is translated "mother-in-law" or "son-in-law"; Haile, 1950a, vol. I, p. 92.

13. In conversation with Bill Begay; see also Reichard, 1938, p. 72. Even if this belief is not widespread, it illustrates the tendency to ascribe to the divinities the same motives as are found among mortals.

14. See Haile, 1950a, vol. I, p. 47. For a general account of clan exogamy, see Sapir-Hoijer, 1942, p. 307. The chant, Coyote Way, may also be used to cure incest-sickness; see Kluckhohn, 1944, p. 22.

15. See OMH, p. 26.

16. Leighton and Kluckhohn, 1947, p. 101.

17. See OMH, p. 13, where the mother scolds her child for playing with menstrual pads.

18. See OMH, *ibid.*; see also Bailey, 1950, p. 10, for similar statements and references.

19. Bailey, 1950, p. 118.

20. Bailey, 1950, chapter 7; see also Haile, 1938, p. 85. For a description of female

puberty rites, see Leighton and Kluckhohn, 1947, p. 76, and Wyman and Bailey, 1943.

21. Newcomb, 1940, p. 57; see also chapter viii, for a list of food taboos, and the consequences following from their violation.

22. See Newcomb, 1940, for details. Most of these were mentioned by a Navaho informant to Kluckhohn and recorded in his field notes of June 1940.

23. OMH, pp. 6, 64. The taboos mentioned here are to be found in Newcomb, 1940, chapter xii; see also pp. 35, 47. Unfortunately, I did not have time to investigate these taboos during my visit to the Navahos. They are all well-attested in the literature.

24. Newcomb, 1940, p. 35.

25. Newcomb, 1940, p. 47.

26. Haile, 1943b, pp. 5, 52.

27. Newcomb, 1940, p. 57, and *passim*.

28. Field notes of Tschopik, 1938, VII 33–36.

29. Newcomb, 1940, p. 53.

30. Kluckhohn tells me that this taboo is related to what the Holy People did.

31. OMH, pp. 213–214.

32. See Hill, 1938.

33. Sapir-Hoijer, 1942, p. 433.

34. For an account of an actual death and the succeeding events, see OMH, pp. 275–278. Other descriptions are to be found in Sapir-Hoijer, 1942, pp. 431–433; Dyk, 1947, p. 60 and p. 185 n.21; Franciscan Fathers, 1910, pp. 453–456. For a discussion of ghosts in general, see Wyman, Hill, and Osanai, 1942.

35. Field notes of Clyde Kluckhohn, May 1940. This informant, Gregorio, volunteered: "Bad child sometimes called 'ghost.' " See Wyman, Hill, and Osanai, 1942.

36. (* 131–134). See also OMH, p. 224, for advice against crying too much.

37. Newcomb, 1940, p. 33; see also Dyk, 1947, p. 148.

38. Kluckhohn, 1944, Appendix I, p. 79; see also pp. 31–32.

39. Leighton and Kluckhohn, 1947, pp. 88 and 101 respectively. For illustrations of the effect of these taboos on actual conduct, see Dyk, 1951. "Before entering the sweathouse it is customary for the men to tie the prepuce over the glans penis with a piece of string. It is believed that unless this is done blindness will ensue" (Hill, 1943, p. 14).

40. Leighton and Kluckhohn, 1947, p. 54.

41. See Bailey, 1950, pp. 32–37. For other taboos of this general group, see Newcomb, 1940.

42. "There are so many things that I can't do when I make baskets, that I don't know what I can do and what I cannot do any more" (informant's statement in Tshopik, 1938, p. 261). For further bibliography on these restrictions, see Reichard, 1950, pp. 589–590.

43. There are many more of these taboos. They are fully treated in the extensive literature on Navaho ceremonial practice. See Kluckhohn and Wyman, 1940, pp. 18ff.

44. See Chapter XIV, section 2(d).

45. See earlier remarks on property in Chapter XI, section 3(c). On sex jealousy, see Chapter XII, section 2(d).

46. This theme of harmony and order has been pointed out by Kluckhohn, 1949. "Straightening out" will be discussed in the next chapter.

47. OMH, p. 378.

48. "You must not lie, you must not steal, you must not try to cheat anybody, and you must not talk about women in a crowd" (OMH, p. 254).

49. See Chapter IV, section 2.

50. For a general list of these prohibitions, see Van Valkenburgh, 1938.

51. Remarks on the evils of drinking can be found in the Appendix. See, for example (* 6, 9, 34–5, 40–42, 92, 125).

52. In Vogt, 1951, p. 54, Mr. Moustache (Bidaga) includes as reasons for his grand-

son having an Enemy Way that he had "seen lots of dead Germans . . . And he might also have killed them" (see also pp. 125, 147, 165).

53. Punishment for murder will be discussed later. In practical life, the presence of white law-enforcing authorities is a sufficient reason for not committing murder. The problem only appears in situations in which no such authorities are present — as in situations proposed in my field notes, and in the days before the advent of white law enforcing agencies.

54. OMH, p. 31.

55. For use of names in 'cussing,' see Dyk, 1947, p. 216 n.55. Names are used before the owner only to insult him or to show unusual respect. The use of names will be mentioned later.

56. OMH, p. 377. Although the hero sleeps with other men's wives many times, he is always afraid of being caught (for example, pp. 160–162, 310, 344, 373). See also Chapter XIV, section 1(b) (6).

57. OMH, p. 331. In the old days it is supposed to have been the practice to mutilate an adulterous wife.

58. Dyk, 1947, p. 93.

59. OMH, p. 267.

60. OMH, p. 331.

61. See Dyk, 1947, p. 179 n.5, for a general description of actual practice relating to adultery.

62. Haile, 1950a, vol. II, p. 4. In addition, Kluckhohn tells me that sickness is supposed to be a consequence of adultery, and that there is a chant ceremony to cure this sickness.

63. Kluckhohn and Leighton, 1946, pp. 218–219. See also Leighton and Kluckhohn, 1947, pp. 170, 207; Reichard, 1950, p. 131; Matthews, 1899, pp. 3, 5. An account showing the complete 'innocence' with which peaches are stolen is to be found in OMH, pp. 336–337.

64. Van Valkenburgh, 1938, III, p. 42.

65. See Kant, "On a supposed right to lie from altruistic motives" (Beck, 1949, pp. 346ff). See also Chapter XVI, section 2(b)(1).

66. See Leighton and Kluckhohn, 1947, p. 106, for the feeling of shame: "I would feel very uncomfortable if anyone saw me deviating from accepted norms."

67. OMH, p. 376 (italics mine).

68. Matthews, 1899, pp. 6–7.

69. "Technically a couple that has had sexual relations are married," (Dyk, 1947, p. 174 n.47). Although such "common-law" marriages are frequent, there are also formal weddings; see (* 115). For separation, see Dyk, p. 169 n.4, and (* 21–22). However, my impression is that getting married means settling down with one particular person.

70. See OMH, p. 244. There appears to be considerable reticence in talking about these escapades except years afterwards. See also Dyk, 1947, p. 181 n.12. This fear of being embarrassed probably explains the remarkable reticence of the son of Old Man Hat to admit to his sexual exploits even when others knew about them.

71. See Bailey, 1950, pp. 99–101.

72. For an account of the actual sex habits of the Navahos, see Kluckhohn, 1948.

73. Bailey, 1942, p. 233. See also Kluckhohn, 1944, p. 32. There have been murders of supposed witches in recent years; see Kluckhohn and Leighton, 1946, p. 175.

74. Sapir-Hoijer, 1942, p. 295; that is, they are suspicious of 'evil ones.' See Newcomb, 1946, p. 34; "One Navajo should never address another by his ceremonial name." See Kluckhohn, 1944, p. 18, where sorcerers are said to employ names in their spells. See Reichard, 1950, pp. 96ff.

75. See Dyk, 1947, p. 216 n.55 for an extended discussion of the use of names. Kluckhohn and Leighton, 1946, p. 67.

76. OMH, p. 357; see also Hobson, 1954, p. 19.

77. In this passage quoted there is no mention of witches, probably because my informant was reluctant to discuss them, but 'dying for no sickness' is attributed to witch attacks, and another informant (Robert Baca) explicitly mentioned the susceptibility of rich people to such attacks. This is confirmed extensively in the literature. See Hobson, 1954, p. 20.

78. Kluckhohn, 1944, p. 31.

79. See OMH, p. 357. Kluckhohn tells me that it is thought that Singers 'go dry' without witchcraft.

80. This is frequently called a "social sanction," but I have indicated earlier that I prefer not to use this expression because of the variety of senses in which it has been employed; see Chapter III, section 4.

81. The following is a partial list of passages in the Field Notes where this kind of reason is given: (* 20, 47, 56, 58, 103, 115, 136, 160, 163).

82. This is clearly pointed out by Leighton and Kluckhohn, 1947, pp. 104–106.

83. OMH, pp. 245–246, and p. 323. For other examples of this practice of joking relationships, see Hill, 1943, p. 21.

84. Leighton and Kluckhohn, 1947, pp. 32, 87. See also earlier discussion, section 2(b) (9).

85. See OMH, pp. 248–249, for an account of the embarrassment caused by a woman's dress accidentally falling off.

86. See OMH, pp. 308–309, for the use of nicknames in ridicule.

87. See Kluckhohn and Leighton, 1946, pp. 66–68.

88. Mr. Moustache (Bidaga) in Kluckhohn, 1945, p. 272. See also Leighton and Leighton, 1949, p. 64: "They told me I ain't got very good clothes to go to the Sing. They says people would just laugh about me when I got to the Sing."

89. See section 3(b) (8).

CHAPTER XIV   THE DATA: POSITIVE PRESCRIPTIONS

1. Although the purpose of Blessing Way is prophylactic rather than curative, this is a theme underlying the Sings in general. See Kluckhohn and Leighton, 1946, p. 149. For a general account of the "theory of curing," see also Reichard, 1950, chapter 7; see Haile, 1943b, p. 8: "The ultimate aim of every chantway and rite, regardless of its ritual, is restoration, meaning that the patient is to be rendered diɣin [holy], immune to further attack from the supernatural which has bothered him."

2. Haile, ibid.; see also Wyman and Kluckhohn, 1938, pp. 13ff.

3. See Van Valkenburgh, 1938, pp. 43–45 for a table of crimes and how they are handled by the primitive society, the 'semi-primitive' and the Indian courts.

4. See OMH, pp. 161–162 for an account of such a peace-making speech.

5. See OMH, p. 239, where a stick kills a horse, but the father consoles his boy, the owner, by giving him another one: "There he paid me for the stick. The stick killed my horse, but the stick didn't pay me; he paid me for the stick."

6. See Chapter XI, section 3(d), for other references.

7. Dyk, 1947, p. 206 n.12.

8. See OMH pp. 143ff., for a case of fighting where the older brother mediates successfully. See also Dyk, 1947, which is an almost continuous account of the difficulties a man has with his wives, but he keeps returning to them. The first quarrel over some beads occurs on p. 26, and, typically, the wife's clan-uncle attempts to mediate.

9. See Dyk, 1947, pp. 87ff., for a description of a husband who remains with his adulterous wives. This passage also provides an example of a 'talk' given to the unfaithful wives.

10. See also OMH, pp. 162–163. Since relatives are always ready to adopt children, such separations do not affect their welfare as seriously as in our own society. For disposition of property after separation, see (* 49). Although this seems to differ from accounts in OMH (pp. 144, 162), neither account prescribes that any property com-

pensation be given as 'alimony' — and the conception of the party at *fault* plays no role in it. The deprivation of property, if any, applies to the one who leaves. (* 49)

11. Simmons, 1950, pp. 22–23; see also Van Valkenburgh, 1938, pp. 40–41.

12. See OMH, pp. 224, 237, 240, 278.

13. See Dyk, 1947, p. 19.

14. See Chapter XI, section 5.

15. OMH, p. 236.

16. OMH, p. 240; see also Hobson, 1954, pp. 17ff.

17. See Chapter XII, section 2(e), and Chapter XVII, section 2.

18. See Dyk, 1947, p. 177 n.30 for references; see also Hobson, 1954, pp. 12–16.

19. See section 1(b) (6).

20. See Dyk, 1947, p. 186 n.33. See also (* 62, 63).

21. Instead of saying: "Thanks, I hope to do the same for you some day," a Navaho once said to me: "Thanks, you can do it again some day."

22. One informant told Kluckhohn that she disapproved of the way her son neglects his children and wastes their property. "Says he'll sure have some bad luck coming to him" (Kluckhohn, Field Notes, September 11, 1942).

23. For another example see Dyk, 1947, p. 88, where a mediator points out to the unfaithful wives that they had been well treated by their husband. Perhaps, by implication, he was suggesting that if they reformed they would receive more of the same.

24. See Kluckhohn, 1944, pp. 31, 59–60, 134. Possibly dead parents will also 'ghost' you.

25. See Kluckhohn, 1941, where he points out that in the ideal pattern "anyone can help" with a Sing, although in the behavioral pattern it is the patient's own family or clan which helps.

26. For the distinction between counsels and injunctions, see Chapter VI, section 3(a). It should be noted that this distinction is not identical with that between moral prescriptions and traditional practices (see below). A counsel is a moral ideal, whereas a practice is merely a stylized mode of conforming to the ideal. This distinction should become clear in the discussion which follows.

27. See Chapter VI, sections 2(b) and 2(c).

28. See Kluckhohn, 1941, p. 117. The analysis which I am presenting owes much to the many suggestive conceptions advanced in this essay.

29. See Bailey, 1942.

30. See OMH, pp. 317, 319. The hero might be suspected of having made the visits merely in order to collect the gifts.

31. See Kluckhohn, 1941, pp. 119–120; see also OMH, p. 326.

32. See Dyk, 1947, p. 185 n.16, n.24; p. 194 n.48.

33. See Dyk, 1947, p. 185 n.23, and Reichard, 1928, chapter 8.

34. For details, see Hill, 1943.

35. See Kluckhohn, 1941, p. 122. For other references, see earlier discussion in Chapter XI, section 3(d). The practice of "prowling" might also be included under this category. See Dyk, 1951, and Kluckhohn, 1948.

36. OMH, p. 278.

37. See Chapter XV, section 1.

38. See Chapter V, sections 3 and 4. The consequences of using other criteria will be examined in Chapter XVIII, section 1(c).

CHAPTER XV   THE STRUCTURE OF THE RECONSTRUCTED CODE

1. See Chapter XVIII, section 1(c).

2. See Chapter XIII, section 2(c).

3. See Chapter XII, sections 2(c) and 2(d).

4. This procedure was attempted several times unsuccessfully; see, for example (* 7, 168).

5. See my earlier discussion of "authoritarianism" in Chapter IX, section 4(d).

6. See MacBeath, 1952, for references and a criticism of this general approach.

7. See remarks made earlier on the content of moral prescriptions, Chapter XI, section 4(a). Here the 'sociological' bias is applied to the justification of the prescriptions rather than to their content. Any account of Navaho ethics which uses as *direct* evidence materials drawn from mythology or social life is open to the suspicion of employing one of these criteria. See Chapter XVIII, section 1(c) (3).

8. Chapter III, section 2(b) and 2(c).

9. In contrast, some Christian theologians writing on Creation might be said to be concerned with showing that the evils of the world are disguised goods which fulfill God's purpose in Creation. In doing so they are 'justifying' evil.

10. Bidaga, in my first and unrecorded interview with him.

11. See, for example, Haile, 1950b: "Monster slayer instructed them, his mind directed them. 'Now then my grandchildren, let this direct you for all times to come, be careful not to make a change!' he said" (p. 190). "So you see at present people only imitate these" (p. 174). Note that they "imitate" rather than "obey."

12. On the other hand, Bidaga said: "Holy People don't hurt people" (* 84). The obscurity may possibly be accounted for in terms of the name "Holy People," which Reichard (1950, p. 51) points out may not refer to specific individual deities, but rather to those who happen to be in a friendly mood or attitude. (However, there is probably no unequivocal meaning for this term.) Wyman and Kluckhohn (1938, p. 14) suggest that ceremonial sicknesses are caused by the Holy People involved.

13. Kluckhohn, 1944, p. 76.

14. See Spencer.

15. Haile, 1950c, p. 70.

16. Sumner, 1906, p. 28.

17. See, for example, OMH, pp. 8–9, 76, 254, and *passim*. The full text of Bidaga's statements quoted here is to be found in Kluckhohn, 1945. The autobiographies in which the father's teaching is hardly mentioned are Dyk, 1947, and Leighton and Leighton, 1949.

18. See MacBeath, 1952, pp. 162, 215, 239ff., and *passim,* for evidence that other 'primitive' societies do not ground their moral rules on customs.

19. I do not think that the 'nonauthoritarianism' of Navaho ethics is a matter of controversy among those who know most about Navaho culture; see Kluckhohn and Leighton, 1946, pp. 218–219.

20. See Chapter IX, section 4(b) and 4(c).

21. See Chapter XI, section 1.

22. For illustrations, see the early chapters of OMH.

23. This two-stage conception was suggested by an informal interview with a Navaho youth, which was not recorded. It may explain why in OMH (pp. 15–16) the child is not reprimanded for lying. Quite likely there is no sharp separation of the stages, and they may exist for some time side by side.

24. For further details on the conditions of ethical competence, see Chapter IX, sections 4(c) and 4(d). Brandt reports that he encountered such arguments among the Hopi; see below, Chapter XVIII, footnote 15.

25. For example, see Dyk, 1947, p. 83: "Your boy hasn't any sense at all." See also OMH, p. 20 and p. 328. For other relevant comments, see Chapter XI, section 1.

26. See (* 28, 37, 65, 115, 133).

27. "The first cause of sin is in the will, which commands all voluntary acts, in which alone sin is to be found." Aquinas, *Summa Theologica*, First Part of the Second Part, question 71, article 6.

28. The denial of the necessity of coercion is, of course, an ideal.

29. Haile, 1943a, p. 93; see also 1950a, vol. II, p. 169.

30. "What I think about this woman is, there is no way of straightening her out. That's the kind of woman she is" (Dyk, 1947, p. 97).

31. Dyk, 1947, pp. 93, 193.

32. Haile, 1943a, p. 87.

33. Kluckhohn, 1949, p. 360.

34. See Chapter VIII, section 2.

35. For examples of arguments, see (* 6, 12, 13, 17, 23, 47, 56, 58, 70, 91, 108, 110, 115, 120, 160, 163).

36. "It's up to you, mother. You like them very well, so go ahead and pay for them" (OMH, p. 236). See Chapter XI, section 3(c).

37. I believe that the conclusions of this chapter are confirmed in general terms by what Kluckhohn (1949) says about Navaho ethics; see also Kluckhohn and Leighton, 1946, pp. 218ff.

CHAPTER XVI   THE CONTENT OF THE RECONSTRUCTED CODE

1. See Chapter IX, section 2(d).

2. It is unnecessary to discuss Personal Prescriptions because they so obviously follow from the basic egoistic prescription hypothesized.

3. From a rigorous philosophical point of view, perhaps the distinction between a teleological and a formalistic ethics cannot be as sharply drawn as is here suggested. This is because many formalists might deny that they use any but purely prospective references to past facts; for example, the 'guilt' of a criminal may be conceived of as a present or future condition caused by a past act of his, and consequently punishment may be thought of as a means of remedying the present or future state of 'guilt' which one knows will be there from his knowledge of the past. Such refinements are not necessary here, because the final definition of the "teleological thesis" could be deferred until the complete hypothesis has been proven. The separation of the hypothesis into these theses is in this sense perhaps artificial, although useful.

4. See Chapter XIII.

5. It would be interesting to know if any Navaho has ever obeyed the prohibition against lying in such situations. This is one place where the ideal surely departs radically from the practice.

6. Sapir-Hoijer, 1942, p. 433; Brandt, 1954, p. 225. Brandt's Hopi informants seemed to think quite differently from mine on this question.

7. See Haile, 1943a, p. 86. For many examples of behavior where chances are taken, see OMH, *passim*.

8. Aristotle, *Nicomachean Ethics,* book v, chapters 2–4.

9. "The injury (the penalty) which falls on the criminal is not merely *implicitly* just . . . it is also a right established within the criminal himself . . ." (Hegel, *Philosophy of Right,* 1942, p. 70).

10. See Chapter XIV, section 1.

11. See OMH, pp. 180ff. and p. 200, for an example of how people would not give up a murderer to the white man, despite their belief that they would be killed for their failure to do so. My surmise could have been tested by proposing to the informant a similar situation involving a 'guilty' or 'bad' man.

12. Matt. 26: 29.

13. This term was introduced by Malinowski, 1926, but it is not quite clear whether it refers to a 'moral' concept. In any case, Malinowski as a 'functionalist' would probably regard it as a utilitarian principle. For a critical examination of this notion, see MacBeath, 1952, pp. 129–134.

14. See also (* 6, 56, 101), and Chapter XIV, section 3(b).

15. It may be significant that in OMH (p. 253) the dying father does not ask his son to take care of his mother, but tells him instead that after his mother is gone, he will have to take care of himself.

16. Chapter XIV, section 3(b) (6).

17. See OMH, *passim,* for an example of the complete unwavering devotion of son to mother, even when she wants him to marry women that he does not like.

18. I do not wish to assert that these theories have anything more in common than their being societarian. For convenience, we may include Bentham's utilitarianism under societarian theories.

19. The relation between evaluation and prescription in the Navaho code will be discussed in Chapter XVII, section 2.

20. See Wyman and Thorne, 1945.

21. I believe that this is also true of all the relevant passages in OMH and Dyk, 1947.

22. These cases were quoted earlier in section 2(d), under the topics of distributive and corrective justice respectively.

CHAPTER XVII MORAL GOALS AND MORAL IDEALS

1. See Haile, 1943a, p. 89; see also Haile, 1947, pp. 17ff.

2. See Kluckhohn and Leighton, 1946, pp. 228, 231. The mind-body dualism does not, of course, exist in the sense in which it is accepted in Western thought. See also Kluckhohn, 1949, p. 365.

3. See Haile, 1950a, vol. 1, p. 282. All these words contain the stem "zhon," from which the interesting word "hozhon" is compounded. The latter is translated "pleasant conditions" by Haile (1947, p. 24), and as "beautiful," "harmonious," "good," "blessed," "pleasant," and "satisfying" by Kluckhohn (1949, p. 369). See earlier comments in Chapter XII, section 2(b).

4. See Chapter XIII, section 1(a).

5. Note that the question is not whether these terms in English are privative correlatives, but rather whether they operate as such in Navaho discourse. To investigate this fully would require a specialist's knowledge of the Navaho language.

6. See, for example, Aquinas, *Summa Theologica,* First Part, question 14, article 10. This doctrine was clearly motivated by the desire to explain the compatibility of the existence of evil with the goodness of God and of his creation.

7. See Chapter VI, section 2(c).

8. See Kluckhohn, 1949, and 1941, pp. 109ff.

9. Aristotle, *Nicomachean Ethics,* 1106a 30.

10. See Chapter XII, section 2(e).

11. See Chapter XII, section 2(c).

12. See Chapter XIV, section 2(b) (2).

13. See Chapter IV, section 2(b).

14. See earlier discussion of the ideal of the "good man," Chapter XI, section 5(c).

15. See "Social Interdictions," Chapter XIII, section 4.

16. Epicurus, "Letter to Menoeceus," in Oakes, 1940, p. 31. All the statements from the writings of Epicurus which appear here can be found in Oakes.

17. See Hobbes, *Leviathan,* part I, chapters x and xiii.

18. These statements are all quoted from the *Ethics,* part IV, prop. xxxv and corollaries.

CHAPTER XVIII CONCLUSION

1. See Chapter X, section 4; see also section 2(a) of this chapter.

2. See Chapter XVI, section 3(d).

3. For considerations against accepting the traditional practices as moral prescriptions, see Chapter XIV, section 5(c).

4. I find that the writings of even such a distinguished authority as Washington Matthews (1899) suffer from this preconception of the nature of "ethics." The relation

between religion and ethics was discussed in Chapter XV, section 2(a). It should be noted that here I am concerned with the use of religious doctrines as a defining criterion of ethical connections, whereas earlier a substantive issue was involved.

5. See Chapter IV, section 3(a).

6. Haile, 1943a, pp. 84, 94.

7. Brandt, 1954. The page references in parentheses are to this book.

8. Brandt gives some of the details mentioned here in chapters II and III. These may be contrasted with the account of Navaho culture in Kluckhohn and Leighton, 1946.

9. See Piers and Singer, 1953, pp. 59ff., and the accompanying bibliographical references.

10. See Chapter X, section 2.

11. See Chapter IV, section 2.

12. See Chapter XVII, section 1.

13. It will be recalled that the technical terms employed in my hypothetical reconstruction have the logical status of intervening variables and can be eliminated by logical reductions. See Chapter II, section 4(b). The relationship between the evidence and ethical affective reactions is indirect, somewhat in the sense in which it is construed by the mentalist or in the use of inferred beliefs other than reconstructed beliefs. See Chapter I, sections 3 and 4.

14. See, for example, such statements as "The old Hopi . . . just didn't want to have trouble" or "Bad behavior is likely to make you sick," etc. (Brandt, 1954, pp. 181, 182). My arguments for regarding such statements as within the ethical system are to be found in Chapter XV, section 2; the philosophical basis of my view is stated in Chapter V, section 3(a).

15. Thus, Brandt writes that some officials in New Oraibi were sensitive to such appeals as "You wouldn't want to be treated in such-and-such a way, if you were in my shoes" (p. 101). According to my analysis, it would be perfectly possible for some ethical systems to contain as a constituent the requirement of disinterestedness, as a condition of ethical competence. See Chapter IX, section 4(c). However, I have also argued against the notion of "disinterestedness" as a differentia of the ethical. See Chapter IV, section 2(a).

16. See Merton, 1949. Merton's distinction between 'manifest' and 'latent' function, and his general analysis of "function" seems to me to be a most illuminating elucidation of this hazy notion. I have relied heavily upon it in the present section.

17. Rapoport, 1954, p. 33. This study provides many other illustrations of the tenacity of the basic goals of the Navaho moral code, while it also shows the willingness of some Navahos to give up certain detailed prescriptions contained in it.

18. "Man, as a symbol-using animal, appears to feel the need not only to act but almost equally to give verbal or other symbolic 'reasons' for his acts" (Kluckhohn, 1942, p. 56).

19. The latent functions of the latter have been set forth in detail by Kluckhohn, 1944.

20. See Chapter III, section 2(b).

21. See Whorf, 1941, and Hoijer, 1951. See also Chapter XII, section 2.

22. Of course, if such a principle be made a matter of definition, we might not require a justification. But on the other hand, such a definition would be unsatisfactory because circular; for, if we ask for a definition of "x is thought to be right" we should have to say "x is thought to be thought to be right," etc. This fact indicates that the meaning of "rightness" and "wrongness" cannot be given exhaustively in terms of what is thought to be so.

23. See Ladd, 1952b. The problem of whether determinism in this general form is tenable cannot be discussed here.

24. For a more general discussion, see Kluckhohn, 1953.

25. Kluckhohn, 1949, p. 358.

26. It should be noted that I am only concerned with the acceptance of *moral principles* as such (either explicit or reconstructed). The problem of the ethical relevance of a universality of needs, implicit and explicit values, etc., will not be discussed here since it arises only after certain ethical commitments have been made.

27. The same kind of argument was given earlier against the use of general approval as a *definition* of "ethics"; see Chapter IV, section 2(a).

28. See Chapter IX, section 4.

29. See Chapter VII, section 1.

30. Some sceptics might maintain that although we all think that moral prescriptions have universal legitimacy, in fact, there are none which do. This view, which I call "ethical scepticism," is not a type of relativism but must be handled completely differently. I shall not discuss it here, but I may point out that its adherents, if they wish to be consistent, must abstain from ethical discourse (as defined here) entirely.

31. Aiken, 1952b, p. 343.

32. Hart, 1952. See also Wisdom, 1952.

33. As I have already mentioned, I, at one time, held a view close to that of Hart, but the study of Navaho ethics convinced me that it was untenable; see Ladd, 1953, and Chapter VIII, section 2(d).

34. See Chapter X, section 2.

35. See Chapter XVI, section 3(c). I do not think this contention entails a kind of Platonic view of morals, for it may be perfectly compatible with Dewey's conception of "ends-in-view."

Index

Subjects listed in the table of contents are not included.

152; use does not imply authoritarianism, 189

Impersonality of moral statements: and disinterestedness, 70–72, 80; and imperatives, 95; and legitimacy, 105–106; and anonymity of agents, 134. *See also* Authority of morality; Moralist, role of

Incest: taboos, 230–231, 412–413, 423; and notion of bothering, 236; syllogistic argument against, 264; sickness and cure, 412–413, 414–416, 453 n14. *See also* Holy People; Witches

Incompatibility of objectives: concept of, 117–118; and immediate inferences, 131; and the derivation of prescriptions, 171–176 *passim*

Indifference, moral: defined, 115

Inference, rules of ethical, 148–149, 152, 153

Injunction: defined, 88, 111, 444 n1

Injury. *See* Payment

Inner form: defined, 218 and 451 n4

Interpreters, 200, 201, 227, 310, 335

Intersubjective validity: and legitimacy, 105–106; and universality of agents, 134

Intervening variables, 38–39

Jail: escaping from, 285–286, 341–342; Bidaga stresses need for, 351–352. *See also* Punishment

James, W.: on the psychologist's fallacy, 46

Jesus, 124, 125, 136

Johnson, W. E., 446 n2

Joking relations, 246, 258

Judaism: a codification of natural ethics, 37, 38; development from negative to positive morality, 124; degrees of stringency in, 125–126, 175; categorization of acts, 139; conception of neighbor, 140–141; factual premises in, 159; existential beliefs, 166; classified, 167, 170, 449 n27; Navaho ethics contrasted with, 266, 268. *See also* Theistic ethics

Judgment: use of term, 23

Judicial ethics, 71

Jurisprudence. *See* Law, philosophy of

Justice: Navaho conception of, 286–290

Kant, I.: on the nature of morality, 7, 51, 444 n36; and command ethics, 50–51, 99; on hypothetical imperatives, 64; the categorical imperative, 103, 160; on perfect and imperfect duties, 126; on respect, 139, 175, 448 n9; neglects special

obligations, 141; on lying, 142; vs. Navahos on lying, 242, 285, 378; anti-egoistic, 293; recognizes relativity of duties, 327

Kelsen, H.: quoted, 157–158, 160, 443 n28, 451 n19; cited, 443 n28

Killing. *See* Animals; Homicide

Kluckhohn, C.: on desirability, 62 and 440 n2; on the part standing for the whole, 221; on interpreters' cliches, 227; on ideals and modalities of behavior, 257; on adultery, 258 and 457 n35; on harmony, 302–303, 452 n17; on man as symbol-using animal, 319 and 461 n18; on universality of logic, 325; definition of value, 437 n7; mentioned, 335, 450–461 *passim*

Kneale, W., 80, 443–444 n32

Kroeber, A. L.: on Bidaga, 199–200

Langer, S. K., 18

Language. *See* Linguistics; Navaho language; Philosophy

Laughing. *See* Ridicule

Laziness, 252, 253, 255, 338

Law of excluded middle in ethics, 129

Law of exhaustiveness in ethics, 127, 129

Law, philosophy of: judicial analogies implied in impartial spectator theory, 71–72, 441 nn15, 16; ethical and legal reasoning, 156–158, 160, 330; mechanical jurisprudence, 157; Western and primitive law, 441 n16

Leaders: talks at weddings, 214, 392–394; liable to attacks by witches, 245, 406; Bidaga as a leader, and criticisms of, 338–352 *passim;* undesirability of being, 405–406; Blessing Way Sing for, 406

Legalistic ethics, 139

Leighton, D. C. and A. H., 450–456 *passim,* 458, 460

Lightning. *See* Thunder

Limited morality. *See* Constraint, ethics of

Linguistics: descriptive ethics compared to, 25–27; and classification of actions, 27, 139; and content of moral codes, 321; and determinism, 324; and anthropology, 437 n16. *See also* Navaho language

Living a long life: conception explained, 229; a moral goal, 214, 299; mentioned, 379–380, 394, 409

Loans, 242, 367, 377–378

Locke, J., 51, 287, 443 n32

Love, ethics of: categorization of acts, 139; uses interpretive mode, 160, 161; basic prescription of, 167, 169; degrees of